Introduction to Paralegalism

Perspectives, Problems, and Skills
Volume II, PCDI Version

Fourth Edition

William P. Statsky

WEST PUBLISHING

an International Thomson Publishing company I(T)P®

Albany • Bonn • Boston • Cincinnati • Detroit • London • Madrid
Melbourne • Mexico City • Minneapolis/St. Paul • New York • Pacific Grove
Paris • San Francisco • Singapore • Tokyo • Toronto • Washington

NOTICE TO THE READER

Publisher does not warrant or guarantee any of the products described herein or perform any independent analysis in connection with any of the product information contained herein. Publisher does not assume, and expressly disclaims, any obligation to obtain and include information other than that provided to it by the manufacturer.

The reader is notified that this text is an educational tool, not a practice book. Since the law is in constant change, no rule or statement of law in this book should be relied upon for any service to any client. The reader should always refer to standard legal sources for the current rule or law. If legal advice or other expert assistance is required, the services of the appropriate professional should be sought.

The publisher makes no representation or warranties of any kind, including but not limited to, the warranties of fitness for particular purpose or merchantability, nor any such representations implied with respect to the material set forth herein, and the publisher takes no responsibility with respect to such material. The publisher shall not be liable for any special, consequential, or exemplary damages resulting, in whole or part, from the readers' use of, or reliance upon, this material.

■ Contents

■ 15   Informal and Formal Administrative Advocacy   719

I

The Paralegal
in the Legal System

Contents

The Emergence and Development of a New Career in Law

■ Outline

■ Section A. Questions, Frustration, and Challenge

Welcome to the field! You probably fall into one or more of the following categories:

■ You have never worked in a law office and have many questions about the career of a paralegal.

■ You are employed or were once employed in a law office and now want to upgrade your skills.

■ You have not made up your mind about whether to become an attorney and see the paralegal career as a way to learn more about the legal profession.

As Chief Justice Burger points out in the quote at the beginning of this book, the paralegal career is still in a state of development. By definition, therefore, a number of important questions still exist. The task of the first part of this book is to address these questions:

■ What is a paralegal?

■ Where do paralegals work?

"Paralegals: a novelty in the sixties, an asset in the seventies, a necessity in the eighties."
Hon. Richard A. Powers III, Magistrate, United States District Court for the Eastern District of Pennsylvania, 1986.

"Our profession is still growing and evolving. Be part of this evolution!"
Bobbi J. McFadden, President, Cincinnati Paralegal Association, 1991.

- What are the functions of a paralegal?
- How do I obtain a job?
- What is the difference between an attorney and a paralegal?
- What is the difference between a paralegal and the clerical staff of a law office?
- What problems do paralegals encounter on the job and how can these problems be resolved?
- How is the paralegal field regulated? Who does the regulating and for what purposes?
- What are the ethical guidelines that govern paralegal conduct?
- What is the future of the paralegal field?

Unfortunately *and* fortunately, definitive answers to these questions do not yet exist. As we shall see, considerable controversy surrounds many of them. It would be foolhardy for anyone to enter the field without having a comprehensive understanding of what the controversies are. According to Deanna Shimko-Herman, a paralegal in Milwaukee, "It is incumbent upon paralegals to be fully informed of the issues, and to operate from that informed base."[1] At times, however, the controversy seems to breed more confusion than constructive dialogue. This confusion can be frustrating to someone new to the field. From another point of view, however, this state of affairs presents you with the ultimate challenge of shaping your own answers to these questions. If Chief Justice Burger is correct that "we have only scratched the surface," the creative opportunities that exist for you are boundless. You will not simply be performing a job—you will be *helping to create a new profession*. This challenge would not exist if all the answers to the fundamental questions were already written in stone.

Section B. Major Players: The Big Five

During our examination of this challenge, we will meet many organizations. Five in particular have had a dramatic influence on the development of paralegalism. These five (not necessarily listed in order of influence) are as follows:

- National Federation of Paralegal Associations *(NFPA)*
- National Association of Legal Assistants *(NALA)*
- American Bar Association *(ABA)*
- Your state's bar association
- Your local paralegal association

While these organizations will be covered in some detail throughout the remaining chapters of the book, a brief word about each will be helpful at this point.

National Federation of Paralegal Associations (NFPA)

NFPA is an association of local associations. There are local paralegal associations throughout the country. Over sixty of them have affiliated with

---

[1]Shimko-Herman, *Should Paralegals Be Regulated with Limited Licensing?*, 17 On Point 10 (National Capital Area Paralegal Ass'n, February 1991).

NFPA. (See Appendix B). From its national headquarters in Kansas City, Missouri, NFPA promotes paralegalism through education and political action.

National Association of Legal Assistants (NALA)

NALA is primarily an association of individuals, although there are also a number of local paralegal associations that are affiliated with NALA. (See Appendix B.) From its national headquarters in Tulsa, Oklahoma, NALA is equally active in the educational and political arenas. One of the major differences between NALA and NFPA concerns the issue of certification. NALA has instituted a voluntary program of certifying paralegals through a series of examinations. For reasons we will explore in Chapter 4, NFPA strongly opposes this certification program.

American Bar Association (ABA)

The ABA is a voluntary association of attorneys; no attorney must be a member. Yet it is a powerful entity because of its resources, prestige, and the large number of attorneys who have joined. The ABA has a Standing Committee on Legal Assistants that has had a significant impact on the growth of the field. Recently, paralegals have been allowed to become Associate Members of the ABA, a development not everyone initially welcomed.

State Bar Association of Your State

Every state has at least one bar association that plays a major role in regulating attorneys under the supervision of the state's highest court. (See Appendix C.) Most of the state bar associations have taken formal positions (in guidelines or ethical opinions) on the use of paralegals by attorneys. A few have followed the lead of the ABA and have allowed paralegals to become associate members. Whenever a paralegal issue arises, you will inevitably hear people ask, "What has the bar said about the issue?"

Your Local Paralegal Association

There are three main kinds of local paralegal associations: statewide, county or regionwide, and citywide.[2] In Appendix B, you will find a list of every local association in the country with an indication of whether it is affiliated with NFPA, affiliated with NALA, or unaffiliated. For a great many paralegals in the country, major career support and inspiration have come through active participation in their local paralegal association.

· · · · · · · · · · · · · ·

While these five organizations will dominate our discussion of paralegalism, we will also be referring to other important groups, such as *LAMA,* the Legal Assistants Management Association (an association of people who supervise other paralegals in large law offices); and *ALA,* the Association of Legal Administrators (an association of people who manage law offices).

---

[2]In addition, there are associations of paralegals connected with particular schools.

■ ASSIGNMENT 1.1

It is not too early in your education to make contact with paralegal associations. In the back of this book, after the index, you will find several forms: "Paralegal Associations: National" and "Paralegal Associations: Local." By filling out and mailing the forms now, you can begin this contact.

 Section C. Job Titles

For convenience, this book uses the job title *paralegal*. An equally common and synonymous term is *legal assistant*. Not everyone uses one of these titles. In fact, there is considerable diversity in the job titles that are used. There is also controversy (for example, a recent lawsuit was brought to prevent certain people from calling themselves paralegals or legal assistants); and confusion (for example, there are some licensed attorneys who work under the title of legal assistant, particularly in the government).

To begin sorting through the maze, we examine three categories of people: employees of attorneys (the dominant category), self-employed individuals who work for attorneys (a growing but much smaller category), and self-employed individuals who provide their services directly to the public without attorney supervision (the smallest but most controversial category). In none of these categories is there universal agreement on what job title should be used. Some titles (paralegal, legal technician) are used in more than one category, but not always on a consistent basis.

1. Employees of Attorneys

The vast majority (over 95%) are employees of attorneys. They may be called:

paralegal	legal service assistant
legal assistant	paralegal specialist
certified legal assistant	junior legal assistant
senior legal assistant	legal technician
lawyer's assistant	legal paraprofessional
attorney assistant	case clerk
project assistant	legal assistant clerk
lay assistant	document clerk
lawyer's aide	depo summarizer

The most commonly used titles are paralegal and legal assistant. As indicated, these titles are synonymous.[3] They are as interchangeable as the words lawyer and attorney.

---

[3]Someone once proposed that the word *paralegal* be used primarily as an adjective and the phrase *legal assistant* primarily as a noun. Under this proposal, a legal assistant would perform paralegal tasks. The proposal has never been considered seriously.

All of the titles listed thus far are generic in the sense that they do not tell you what area of law the person works in. Other employee job titles are more specific:

litigation assistant	conflict-of-interest coordinator
corporate paralegal	family law paralegal
probate specialist	welfare paralegal
personal injury paralegal	international trade paralegal
real estate paralegal	worker's compensation paralegal
bankruptcy paralegal	claims negotiator
water law paralegal	

Occasionally, when the office wants its paralegal to perform more than one job, *hybrid titles* are used. For example, an office might call an employee a *paralegal/investigator,* a *paralegal/librarian,* or a *paralegal/legal secretary.*

When a paralegal becomes part of management in an office with a large number of paralegals, titles reflecting this new status are often used—such as paralegal supervisor, legal assistant manager, or case manager.

2. Self-Employed Individuals Working for Attorneys

All of the above titles cover people who are employees of attorneys in one law office. A much smaller number are *independent contractors* who have formed their own businesses that provide services for attorneys from more than one office. (Independent contractors are self-employed persons who control the methods of performing tasks; the objectives or end products of the tasks are controlled by those who buy their services.) They move from office to office for relatively short-term projects and periods, or they work in their own office on projects mailed to them (or transmitted by "fax" machine or by modem) from different attorneys around town. Such self-employed individuals have different titles such as:

freelance paralegal

independent paralegal

contract paralegal

3. Self-Employed Individuals Serving the Public

Finally, there is a controversial category of people who do not work for (and who are not supervised by) attorneys. They sell their services directly to the public. Among the titles used by such practitioners are:

legal technician	legal typist
limited practice officer	independent paralegal
certified closing officer	freelance paralegal
public paralegal	scrivener
forms practitioner	

Bar associations have often tried to prosecute these individuals for unauthorized practice of law. Yet there is a movement, in the form of limited licensing, toward legitimizing some of their activities. We will examine this in Chapter 4.

· · · · · · · · · · · · · · ·

Established paralegals are not always happy with the diversity of titles. For example, a number of paralegal associations object to anyone in the third category (self-employed individuals serving the public) using the word *paralegal* in his or her title. To avoid confusion in the mind of the public, such associations want to limit these words to those who work under the supervision of an attorney. They prefer the title *legal technician,* for example, to *independent paralegal.* One paralegal association refers to everyone in the third category as "nonparalegals"! For similar reasons, the National Association of Legal Assistants recently asked a court to prevent inmates from using the title of paralegal or legal assistant. They had completed a course in legal research to allow them to work on their own legal problems and those of fellow inmates.[4] Since they would not always be working under the supervision of attorneys, NALA wanted them to use a title other than paralegal or legal assistant.

There may come a time when a legislature or court will establish definitive titles for certain categories of individuals in this area. As the present time, however, official titles do not exist. There is no requirement, for example, that individuals be licensed by the state in order to work in any of the three categories listed above. Hence there are no rules on who can use titles such as paralegal or legal assistant. If a form of licensing is instituted, this may change. Again we will discuss this possibility in Chapter 4.

Section D. Job Definitions

What comes to mind when people think of a paralegal? Perhaps the most common definition is: a nonattorney who helps an attorney. While essentially correct, there are problems with this definition—as we will see. In this book, the following definition is used:

> A paralegal is a person with legal skills who works under the supervision of an attorney or who is otherwise authorized to use those skills; this person performs tasks that do not require all the skills of an attorney and that most secretaries are not trained to perform.

Definitions have been formulated by the American Bar Association, the National Association of Legal Assistants, and the National Federation of Paralegal Associations. American Bar Association:

> A legal assistant is a person, qualified through education, training, or work experience, who is employed or retained by a lawyer, law office, governmental agency, or other entity in a capacity or function which involves the performance, under the ultimate direction and supervision of an attorney, of specifically delegated substantive legal work, which work, for the most part, requires a sufficient knowledge of legal concepts that, absent such assistant, the attorney would perform the task.

National Association of Legal Assistants:

> Legal Assistants [also known as paralegals] are a distinguishable group of persons who assist attorneys in the delivery of legal services. Through formal education, training, and experience, legal assistants have knowledge and expertise

---

[4]*Alan Gluth et al vs. Arizona Department of Corrections* (CB-84-1626 PHX CAM) (United States Court of Appeals for the Ninth Circuit). See 17 Facts & Findings 6 (NALA, Fall 1990).

regarding the legal system and substantive and procedural law which qualify them to do work of a legal nature under the supervision of an attorney.

National Federation of Paralegal Associations:

A paralegal/legal assistant is a person qualified through education, training, or work experience to perform substantive legal work that requires knowledge of legal concepts and is customarily, but not exclusively, performed by a lawyer. This person may be retained or employed by a lawyer, law office, governmental agency, or other entity, or may be authorized by administrative, statutory or court authority to perform this work.

■ ASSIGNMENT 1.2

Assume that John Jones is authorized by law to represent clients in social security hearings for a fee. He works alone in his own office. Is John a legal assistant or paralegal under the ABA definition? Under the NALA definition? Under the NFPA definition?

In Chapter 3, we will discuss the issue of career ladders within the paralegal field. Unless a law office employs a relatively large number of paralegals, career ladders usually do not exist. Yet career ladders are becoming increasingly common if there are three or more paralegals in the office. This requires more than one definition of a paralegal to reflect the different steps on the ladder—from the entry-level paralegal to the paralegal manager. In Figure 1.1 you will find an example of the definitions proposed by the Legal Assistants Management Association (LAMA), an organization of over 500 legal assistant managers. Of course, not all large offices use these titles or definitions, but their use is increasing.[5]

A number of points need to be made about the definition of a paralegal—or the absence of a definition about which everyone can agree:

1. *To date, there is no official terminology imposed by law.*

There are three ways that a person becomes a paralegal—by experience, by training, and by fiat.[6] See Figure 1.2. Twenty years ago, the first route was the most common way to become a paralegal. Today, the second route is the most common. While the third route still exists, those who enter the field this way are sometimes resented by paralegals who entered the field by experience or training.

Why do these three methods of becoming a paralegal exist? Primarily because there are no licensing or other laws on who can be a paralegal, at least at the present time. Consequently, there is nothing to prevent a law office from calling its messenger a paralegal! Bar associations, paralegal associations, and educators have attempted to formulate definitions, as we have seen, but nothing has emerged as universally acceptable. To some, this state of affairs is healthy since the absence of official terminology encourages diversity. To others, it is frustrating:

---

[5]For example, the legal assistant manager might be called a paralegal supervisor in some offices. For a more complete list, see Figure 2.2 in Chapter 2.

[6]Malone, *Let Your Staff Shine as "Paralegals,"* The Compleat Lawyer 4 (Winter 1990).

Unfortunately, some law firms seem to be using the phrases "legal assistant" and "paralegal" with alarming regularity without regard to the tasks being performed. And firms are hiring these people at a lower pay scale, thus lowering the salary of the average paralegal.[7]

2. *Definitions are often phrased in the negative.*

Some definitions do a better job of telling us what a paralegal is *not* than what one *is*. A paralegal is *not* an attorney, *not* a secretary, *not* a *law clerk* (someone studying to be an attorney), etc. This can be frustrating, as evidenced by the following statement of Karen Dodge, an Oregon paralegal: "I am, along with thousands of other legal assistants, more than a non-lawyer!" [8]

3. *Many definitions have four main components.*

- The paralegal is not an attorney.
- The paralegal has legal knowledge and skills.

FIGURE 1.1

Sample Job Descriptions of Paralegals in a Large Law Office

Legal Assistant Clerk

A person who, under the supervision of a legal assistant, performs clerical tasks such as document numbering, alphabetizing documents, labeling folders, filing, and any other project that does not require substantive knowledge of the transaction or litigation.

Legal Assistant [also called a Paralegal]

A person who assists an attorney in the practice of law. His or her duties can include factual research, document analysis, cite checking and shepardizing, drafting certificates and corporate transactional documentation, drafting pleadings, coordinating document productions, administering trusts and estates, assisting with pension plan administration, assisting with real estate transactions, and handling substantive functions in practice areas that do not require a law degree.

Senior Legal Assistant

An experienced legal assistant with the ability to supervise or train other legal assistants. He or she may have developed a specialty in a certain practice area.

Supervising Legal Assistant

Someone who spends about 50% of his or her time supervising other legal assistants, and about 50% on client cases as a legal assistant.

Case Manager

An experienced legal assistant who can coordinate or direct legal assistant activities on a major case or transaction.

Legal Assistant Manager [also called Paralegal Administrator, Paralegal Coordinator, Director of Legal Assistant Services, and Supervisor]

A person responsible for recruiting, interviewing, and hiring legal assistants. May also be responsible for training legal assistants, monitoring work assignments, and handling personnel and administrative matters that relate to legal assistants. May have budget responsibility for the legal assistant program, and play a role in salary and billing rate administration. The Legal Assistant Manager works few or no billable hours.

Source: Ernst & Young, *Legal Assistant Managers and Legal Assistants,* 388 (3rd ed. 1989), Legal Assistants Management Association.

---

[7]6 *Ka L'eo O* (Hawaii Ass'n of Legal Assistants, February 1983).
[8]Karen Dodge, Paragram (Oregon Legal Assistants Ass'n, September 1984).

By experience:	A secretary, office clerk, or other member of the clerical staff starts to perform paralegal responsibilities. Eventually, he or she is given the title of paralegal.
By training:	A graduate of a paralegal training program who has never worked in a law office is hired as a paralegal.
By fiat:	An office hires an individual with the title of paralegal even though he or she has never had any law office experience or paralegal training.

FIGURE 1.2

Three Ways to Become a Paralegal

■ The paralegal works under the supervision of an attorney.

■ The paralegal does not practice law.

4. *There are problems with each of these four components.*

First, there *are* some attorneys who are classified as paralegals. There are attorneys working in America, for example, who are licensed in a foreign country. Some states consider such attorneys to be paralegals. The same may be true of attorneys working in one state but licensed to practice in another state. Occasionally a suspended or disbarred attorney will try to continue work in the law as a paralegal. Under certain circumstances, as we will see in Chapter 5, such work is ethical and legal. Finally, there is nothing to prevent an attorney from applying for and receiving a paralegal job. This is not uncommon in a tight market where there are many unemployed attorneys looking for work.

Second, we learn very little when we are told that a paralegal has legal knowledge and skills. So do attorneys, law clerks, legal secretaries, investigators, many real estate brokers, bankers, etc.

Third, not all paralegals work under the supervision of an attorney. As we will see later, many paralegals working for the government are not supervised by attorneys. There are also special laws that permit nonattorneys to engage in legal work independent of attorneys. To be sure, most paralegals work in private law offices under the supervision of an attorney. Yet there are some who are otherwise situated.

Fourth, it is inaccurate to say that paralegals cannot practice law. The more correct statement of the principle is that paralegals cannot engage in the *unauthorized* practice of law. The existence of rules on the *un*authorized practice of law governing paralegals presupposes the existence of an *authorized practice of law* by paralegals. It is true that the spectrum of authorized practice for paralegals is quite narrow—but it does exist. In our society, the practice of law is not the exclusive domain of the attorney. This will be explored in greater detail in Chapters 4 and 5.

5. *The definitions that we have require further definitions.*

In law, the presence of a definition usually prompts a search for a definition of the definition! Paralegal definitions sometimes contain words and phrases such as *supervision, substantive legal work, practice of law, assistance,* etc. We must be concerned about what these words and phrases mean—they must be defined. These definitions will then probably require clarifications that are, in effect, further definitions. This phenomenon is not peculiar to paralegalism. The process of legal analysis itself calls for an extended series of definitions and sub-definitions, as we will demonstrate in Part II of this book.

Other disciplines face the same difficulty. In the medical profession, for example, a close counterpart to the paralegal is the *physician assistant*. The following is a proposed definition of this career:

> Physician assistant means an individual who is qualified by academic and clinical training to provide patient care services under the supervision and responsibility of a doctor of medicine or osteopathy.[9]

Among the major phrases in this definition that require further defining are: "qualified," "patient care services," and "supervision."

6. *A title and definition should serve three main functions.*

In the quest for an acceptable title and definition, there is a danger of losing sight of the reasons that should govern the search. A title and definition should:

- Convey enough information about the field to a prospective student.
- Convey enough information about the field to a prospective employer.
- Convey enough information about the field to the public, as prospective clients.

7. *Unanimity may be unnecessary, undesirable, and impossible to achieve.*

The above three purposes can arguably be served without ever achieving total agreement on terminology. We bang our heads against a stone wall when we insist on terminology that:

- Precisely and definitively distinguishes this career from that of other law office personnel.
- Includes everyone who should be included.
- Excludes everyone who should be excluded.

This is simply too much to ask because of the great diversity in the field. We do not yet know all the boundary lines. The wiser course at this stage of development is *not* to insist on trying to achieve unanimity.

8. *Terminology and credentialization.*

It does not seem to disturb anyone that we do not have a definitive definition of an attorney. An attorney is someone with a license to practice law. Attorneys are defined primarily by the *credential* that they hold. Any attempt to provide a descriptive definition poses substantial difficulties. There has been endless litigation, for example, on trying to define the *practice of law*. The same is true of terms such as *legal advice* and *professional judgment*. We will explore some of this controversy in Chapters 4 and 5. The point, however, is that a precise definition of an attorney (in terms of what an attorney does) is no more easy to identify than a precise definition of a paralegal. We should not ask of paralegalism that it achieve a level of definitional precision that the legal profession has never been able to achieve.

When a career is having difficulty defining itself, it sometimes tries to use credentialization as a way out of the difficulty. The paralegal career may also

---

[9]44 Federal Register 36,177 (No. 121, 6/21/79).

move in this direction. A paralegal may someday be defined primarily as someone with a license or a certificate to be a paralegal. If this happens, the debate on role will not end. Shifting the question from "What is a paralegal?" to "What credentials should a paralegal have?" will not stop the controversy.

9. Functional Definition

While many organizations and individuals are engaged in a theoretical debate over the definition of a paralegal, the marketplace may be forcing a practical definition on us. As we will see in a moment, there are several kinds of cases in which the winning party can force the losing party to pay the attorney fees *and the paralegal fees* of the winning party. (When this occurs, the paralegal fees, of course, go to the supervising attorney of the paralegal; they do not go directly to the paralegal.) But everything a paralegal does on a case does *not* qualify for an award of paralegal fees. Consequently, if attorneys want to increase the chance of obtaining an award of paralegal fees, they must make sure that the tasks of the paralegal fit within the criteria for such an award. The main criterion is that the paralegal is performing tasks that are not purely secretarial or clerical. This reality may lead to a practical or functional definition of a paralegal: a person who performs tasks that qualify for an award of paralegal fees.

■ ASSIGNMENT 1.3

In this assignment, we explore what the world thinks a paralegal or legal assistant is. So much will depend on what the public has heard about this field. It is not as well known as other new occupations such as *paramedic*. In many parts of the country, the word *paramedic* is printed in large bold print on ambulances racing throughout the city. This visibility has increased the public's understanding of what a paramedic is. Media attention is also important. Many paralegals were disappointed, for example, when a prime-time attorney soap opera, *L.A. Law,* failed to include a paralegal for a role in the law firm that was the center of this very popular television program. Some wrote to the program producer to protest this glaring omission, but to no avail. This does not mean, however, that any kind of media attention would be welcomed. Shelly Widoff, a paralegal consultant in Boston, has her fingers crossed: "I just hope we all don't cringe when the media get hold of us on a TV sitcom." [10] Recently, many paralegals not only cringed but also vigorously protested when *Quincy,* a medical television program, portrayed a paralegal as an arch villain. Thankfully this occurred in only one of its episodes!

Douglas Parker, a litigation paralegal, believes that the public has "as many different perceptions of our occupational status as there are craters on the moon." [11] To gauge whether this is true in your community, contact the following individuals in your area. Ask each of them the question: "What is a paralegal or legal assistant?"

(a) A neighbor or friend who does not work in a law office and who has probably never been in a law office.
(b) A neighbor or friend who does not work in a law office but who has hired an attorney at least once in his or her life.
(c) A legal secretary.
(d) An attorney who has never hired a paralegal.
(e) An attorney who has hired a paralegal.
(f) A working paralegal who is not now in school.

---

[10]S. Widoff, *On the Docket,* 4 Legal Assistant Today 10 (January/February 1987).
[11]Parker, *Legal Assistants: A Case of Uncertain Identity,* 7 Legal Professional 10 (September/October 1989).

(g) A high school student.

(h) A student in a law school studying to be an attorney.

(i) A police officer.

(j) A person who runs a small business.

(k) A local judge.

(l) A clerk in a local court.

Take careful notes on their answers to the question. Compare the answers.

- What common ideas or themes did you find in the definitions?
- What two definitions were the most different? List the differences.
- Do you think that your survey raises any problems about the perception of paralegals in your area? If so, what are these problems, and how can they be solved?

 ## Section E. Salaries

How much do paralegals make? While some data is available to answer this question, there is no definitive answer because of the great variety of employment settings. According to a 1991 study of over 2,600 paralegals by the National Association of Legal Assistants, the national average annual salary of paralegals was $27,082, with an average annual bonus of $1,793.[12] A 1991 study of 587 paralegals reported that the national average annual salary was $27,772.[13] It is important to note that none of these are entry-level salaries; most of the paralegals surveyed had been on the job for one or more years.[14] The Legal Assistants Management Association conducted one of the most comprehensive surveys of paralegal salaries in 1989. Over 6,000 paralegal salaries were examined. The results are reported in Figures 1.3 and 1.4. Note that a paralegal's salary will tend to increase in direct proportion to his or her experience (Figure 1.3) and level of responsibility (Figure 1.4). A number of other generalizations can be made about salaries across the country:

- Paralegals who work in the law departments of corporations (banks, insurance companies, other businesses) tend to make more than those who work in private law firms. In a 1989 survey of just under a thousand corporate law departments, the average salary for a paralegal was $29,973. About 150 of them reported receiving an average bonus of $2,243 (Altman & Weil).

- Paralegals who work in large private law firms tend to make more than those who work in smaller private law firms.

- Paralegals who work in large metropolitan areas (over a million in population) tend to make more than those who work in rural areas.

- Paralegals who work for the government in civil service positions tend to make less than those who work for large private law firms or corporations.

- Paralegals who work in legal aid or legal service offices that are funded by government grants and charitable contributions tend to make less than all other paralegals.

---

[12]NALA, *The Legal Assistant Profession: National Utilization and Compensation Survey Report,* 35 (1991).

[13]Milano, *Salary Survey Results,* 8 Legal Assistant Today 27 (May/June 1991).

[14]One study of a relatively small number of law offices in Colorado showed that the average salary for entry-level paralegals was $17,900. Acree, *The CBA Economic Survey,* 20 The Colorado Lawyer 451 (March 1991).

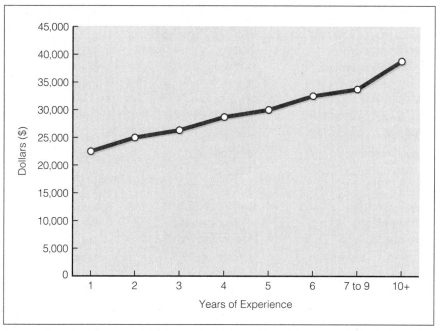

FIGURE 1.3

1989 Total Compensation (Median) by Years of Experience

Source: Ernst & Young, *Legal Assistant Managers and Legal Assistants,* ix (3rd ed. 1989).

FIGURE 1.4

1989 Average Compensation by Level of Responsibility

Position	NON-BONUS RECEIVERS Total Compensation*	BONUS RECEIVERS Base Salary*	Bonus	Total Compensation**
Legal Assistant Manager	$37,180	$43,112	$4,131	$47,243
Supervising Legal Assistant	$37,847	$39,819	$3,050	$42,868
Senior Legal Assistant	$34,925	$35,063	$3,091	$38,154
Case Manager	$29,636	$32,170	$4,787	$36,957
Legal Assistant	$25,636	$26,697	$1,781	$28,477
Legal Assistant Clerk	$17,888	$18,958	$850	$19,808

*1989 base salary
**1989 base salary plus 1988 bonus (does not include overtime where paid)

Source: Ernst & Young, *Legal Assistant Managers and Legal Assistants,* p. 16 (3rd ed. 1989).

■ Paralegals working for attorneys who understand the value of paralegals tend to make more than those working for attorneys who have a poor or weak understanding of what paralegals can do.

■ Paralegals who work in an office where there is a career ladder for paralegals, plus periodic evaluations and salary reviews, tend to make more than those who work in offices without these options.

■ Paralegals who are career-oriented tend to make more than those less interested in a long-term commitment to paralegal work.

■ Salary projections to the year 2,000 are found in Figure 1.5.

FIGURE 1.5

Salary Projections in the "Hot Careers"

JOB	CURRENT SALARY	PROJECTED SALARY
	1989	2000
Accountant	$26,000	$41,600
Computer Programmer	$30,600	$48,960
Dental Hygienist	$24,850	$39,800
Dentist	$75,300	$120,480
Electrical Engineer	$40,000	$64,000
Employment Interviewer	$16,000–$30,000	$25,600–$48,000
Legal Assistant	**$24,900**	**$39,840**
Management Consultant	$36,300–$44,000	$58,100–$70,400
Nurse	$26,800	$42,900
Nurse-Anesthetist	$34,000–$49,000	$54,400–$78,400
Photographer	$19,800–$40,500	$31,700–$64,800
Physical Therapist	$28,500–$60,000	$45,600–$96,000
Publicist	$29,000	$46,400
Real-Estate Agent	$20,550	$32,880
Real-Estate Broker	$39,800	$63,700
Retail Salesperson	$12,500–$16,800	$20,000–$26,800
Travel Agent	$18,200	$29,120
Source: Gates, *Hot Careers for the '90s,* Working Mother 68 (May 1989).		

There are a few paralegals in the country—*very few*—who command salaries of over $100,000. Lee Henderson, for example, is such a paralegal; she works for a large Dallas law firm. "Lee Henderson, a paralegal with 25 years' experience in the mortgage banking business, supervises a staff of 38. Her department manages closings for residential mortgage loans. She has also helped develop computer programs to assist other departments." [15] Again, such salaries, while possible, are rare.

In addition to the payment of bonuses, other fringe benefits must also be considered, e.g., vacation time, health insurance, parking facilities. A comprehensive list of such benefits will be presented in Chapter 2. (See Figure 2.12.)

One final point to keep in mind about salaries. Once a person has gained training *and experience* as a paralegal, there are possibilities of using this background to go into other positions that are law-related. For example, a corporate paralegal in a law firm might leave the firm to take a higher-paying position for a corporation as a securities analyst, or an estates paralegal at a law firm might leave for a more lucrative position as a trust administrator at a bank. A more extensive list of these law-related jobs will be given at the end of Chapter 2.

 ## Section F. Historical Perspective

In the late 1960s, most attorneys would draw a blank if you mentioned the words *paralegal* or *legal assistant*. According to Webster's *Ninth New Collegiate Dictionary,* the earliest recorded use of the word *paralegal* in English occurred in 1971. Today, the situation has changed radically. There are few offices that do not employ paralegals or that are not seriously thinking about

---

[15]Marcotte, *$100,000 a Year for Paralegals?*, 73 American Bar Association Journal 19 (October 1987).

hiring them. A recent survey reports that there is one paralegal for every four attorneys in law firms and one paralegal for every two attorneys in the law departments of corporations.[16] It has been estimated that the number of paralegals may eventually exceed the number of attorneys in the practice of law. The United States Bureau of Labor Statistics has projected that paralegals will constitute one of the fastest growing fields in the country, with a growth of over 75% between the years 1988 and 2000 (see Figure 1.6).

What has caused this dramatic change? The following factors have been instrumental in bringing paralegalism to its present state of prominence:

1. The pressure of economics.
2. The call for efficiency and delegation.
3. Promotion by the bar associations.
4. The organization of paralegals.
5. The restructuring of professions generally.

1. The Pressure of Economics

Perhaps the greatest incentive to the development of paralegals has been arithmetic. Law firms simply add up what they earn without paralegals, add up

OCCUPATION	EMPLOYMENT		CHANGE IN EMPLOYMENT
	1988	Projected, 2000	1988–2000
Paralegals	83,000	145,000	+75.3%
Medical assistants	149,000	253,000	+70.0%
Home health aides	236,000	397,000	+67.9%
Radiologic technologies and technicians	132,000	218,000	+66.0%
Data processing equipment repairers	71,000	115,000	+61.2%
Medical record technicians	47,000	75,000	+59.9%
Medical secretaries	207,000	327,000	+58.0%
Physical therapists	68,000	107,000	+57.0%
Surgical technologies	35,000	55,000	+56.4%
Operations research analysts	55,000	85,000	+55.4%
Securities and financial services sales workers	200,000	309,000	+54.8%
Travel agents	142,000	219,000	+54.1%
Computer systems analysts	403,000	617,000	+53.3%
Physical and corrective therapy assistants	39,000	60,000	+52.5%
Social welfare service aides	91,000	138,000	+51.5%
Occupational therapists	33,000	48,000	+48.8%
Computer programmers	519,000	769,000	+48.1%
Human services workers	118,000	171,000	+44.9%
Respiratory therapists	56,000	79,000	+41.3%
Correction officers and jailers	186,000	262,000	+40.8%

Source: U.S. Department of Labor, Bureau of Labor Statistics, *Occupational Outlook Quarterly*, 6 (Spring 1990).

FIGURE 1.6

The Fastest Growing Occupations, 1988–2000

---

[16]Ernst & Young, *Legal Assistant Managers and Legal Assistants*, xi (3rd ed. 1989).

what they could earn with paralegals, compare the two figures, and conclude that the employment of paralegals is profitable. There "can be little doubt that the principal motivation prompting law firms to hire legal assistants is the economic benefit enjoyed by the firm." [17] The key to increased profits is *leveraging.* Leverage, often expressed as a ratio, is the ability to make a profit from the income-gathering work of others. The higher the ratio of paralegals to partners in the firm, the more profit to the partners (assuming everyone is generating income from billable time).[18]

In the best of all worlds, some of this increased profit will result in lower fees to the client. For example, Chief Justice Warren Burger feels that some attorneys charge "excessive fees for closing real-estate transactions for the purchase of a home. A greater part of that work can be handled by trained paralegals, and, in fact, many responsible law firms are doing just that to reduce costs for their clients." [19]

Figure 1.7 provides an example of the economic impact of using a paralegal. In the example, a client comes to a lawyer to form a corporation.[20] We will compare (a) the economics of an attorney and secretary working on the case, assuming a fee of $2,000, and (b) the economics of an attorney, secretary, *and* paralegal working on the same case, assuming a fee of $1,600. As you can see, with a paralegal added to the team, the firm's profit is increased almost 25% in spite of the lower fee, and the attorney has more billable time to spend elsewhere. Some studies have claimed an even higher profit increase because of the use of paralegals.

The example assumes that the attorney's fee is $200 per hour and that the attorney billed the client $40 per hour for the paralegal's time. According to a 1988 study of relatively large law firms, the billing rate that firms charged clients for paralegal work ranged from $41 to $60 an hour, and the average number of chargeable billable hours each paralegal reported in these firms was 1,350 per year.[21] A more recent study showed that the average paralegal fee allowed by the courts was $48.10 per hour.[22] (See also Figure 14.4 in Chapter 14.)

When a law firm bills clients for paralegal time, the paralegal becomes a *profit center* in the firm. In such cases, paralegals are not simply part of the cost of doing business reflected in the firm's *overhead;* [23] they generate revenue (and therefore, profit) for the firm. To calculate the amount of profit, the *rule of three* is often used as a general guideline. To be profitable, a paralegal must bill three times his or her salary. Of the total revenue brought in through paralegal bill-

---

[17]*The Expanding Role of Legal Assistants in New York State,* 7 (N.Y. State Bar Association, Subcommittee on Legal Assistants).

[18]The same, of course, is true of associates in the firm. The higher the ratio of associates to partners, the greater the profit to the partners.

[19]U.S. News & World Rep., Feb. 22, 1982 at 32.

[20]Adapted from Jespersen, *Paralegals: Help or Hindrance?* The Houston Lawyer 111, 114–16 (March/April 1977).

[21]Ernst & Young, *Legal Assistant Managers and Legal Assistants,* xii (3rd ed. 1989).

[22]Carla Teague, *Case Law Trends Affecting the Paralegal Profession,* 16 National Paralegal Reporter 18 (NFPA, Fall 1991). A 1991 survey of all members of NALA concluded that the average billing rate for NALA members was $55.00 per hour. NALA, *The Legal Assistant Profession,* see footnote 12 at p. 29.

[23]Overhead includes the cost of office space, furniture, equipment, and insurance, plus the cost of secretarial or other clerical staff whose time is usually not billed separately to clients.

TASK: TO FORM A CORPORATION

a. Attorney and Secretary

	Time	
Function	Attorney	Secretary
1. Interviewing	1.0	0.0
2. Advising	1.0	0.0
3. Gathering information	1.0	0.0
4. Preparing papers	2.0	4.0
5. Executing and filing papers	1.0	1.0
	6.0	5.0

Assume that the attorney's hourly rate is $200 per hour. Assume that the overhead cost of maintaining a secretary is $20 per hour.

Attorney (6 × $200)	$1,200
Secretary (5 × $20)	100
Total cost	$1,300
Fee	$2,000
Less cost	1,300
Gross profit	$ 700

b. Attorney, Secretary, and Paralegal

	Time		
Function	Attorney	Paralegal	Secretary
1. Interviewing	0.5	0.5	0.0
2. Advising	1.0	0.0	0.0
3. Gathering information	0.0	1.0	0.0
4. Preparing papers	0.5	1.5	4.0
5. Executing and filing papers	0.5	0.5	1.0
	2.5	3.5	5.0

In addition, assume a paralegal hourly rate of $40 per hour.

Attorney (2.5 × $200)	$500
Paralegal (3.5 × $40)	140
Secretary (5 × $20)	100
Total cost	$740
Fee	$1,600
Less cost	740
Gross profit	$ 860

COMPARISON

Fee: a. Attorney and Secretary $2,000
       b. Attorney, Secretary, and Paralegal $1,600
Saving to client $400
Increased profitability to lawyer ($860 vs. $700) $160

By using a paralegal on the case, the attorney's profit increases almost 25% over the profit realized without the paralegal. Furthermore, the attorney has 3.5 hours that are suddenly available to work on other cases, bringing in additional revenue of $700 (3.5 × the attorney's hourly rate of $200).

FIGURE 1.7

The Profitability of Using Paralegals

ing, one-third is allocated to salary, one-third to overhead, and one-third to profit. Phrased another way, when the gross revenue generated through paralegal billing equals three times the paralegal's salary, the firm has achieved its minimum profit expectations.

For example:

Paralegal's salary:	$30,000
Paralegal rate:	$35 per hour

Billings the firm hopes this para-
legal will generate: $90,000

Rule-of-three allocation:
—paralegal salary: $30,000
—overhead for this paralegal: $30,000
—profit to the law firm: $30,000[24]

■ ASSIGNMENT 1.4

(a) In the example just given, how many billable hours per year would this paralegal have to produce in order to generate $30,000 per year in profits for the firm? Is this number realistic? If not, what must be done?

(b) Assume that a paralegal seeks a salary of $25,000 a year and that the law firm would like to be able to pay this salary. Using the "rule of three," if this person is able to generate 1,400 billable hours per year, how much must this paralegal's time be billed at in order for the attorney and the paralegal to be happy?

Paralegals can be even more profitable to the firm in cases where clients pay a fixed fee or a contingency fee. A *fixed fee* (e.g., $20,000) is paid regardless of the number of hours it takes the firm to complete the case—and regardless of the outcome of the case. A *contingency fee* is usually a percentage (e.g., 33%) that is paid only if the client wins, regardless of the number of hours it takes the firm to complete the case. In most cases where a client pays a fixed fee or a contingency fee, there is no hourly billing. Greater use of paralegals on such cases can lead to greater profits. The "more the attorney uses legal assistant services as opposed to attorney services," the less cost is incurred, "thereby maintaining more of the fee as a profit."[25]

Not every law firm agrees, however, that hiring paralegals inevitably leads to greater profits for the firm. A number of factors complicate the attempt to determine the economic effect of hiring paralegals. For example:

■ At some firms, there is a relatively high turnover of paralegals. This means increased in-house training costs for newly hired paralegals and, therefore, higher overhead.

■ Many attorneys are looking for work, particularly recent law school graduates. Some are working part-time for law firms,[26] or are accepting comparatively low-paying *staff attorney*[27] positions at the firms. These attorneys have no hope of ever becoming partners in the firm—unlike the traditional associates at the firm. In fee-generating cases, some firms may be more likely to delegate work to a part-time attorney or to a staff attorney than to paralegals, since the firm can bill an attorney's time at a higher rate. This tendency is even greater if the salary of this attorney is not significantly different from the salary of the paralegals in the firm. When low-salaried attorneys are available, some firms are not as convinced that it's economical to hire paralegals.

---

[24]Adapted from State Bar of Texas, *Attorneys' Guide to Practicing with Legal Assistants*, VI(3) (1986).

[25]L. Hangley, "The Role of the Legal Assistant" in *The Team Approach to Practice Development*, 5 (Professional Education Systems, 1989).

[26]Part-time attorneys are sometimes called "contract attorneys" or "project attorneys."

[27]Also referred to as second-tier attorneys.

■ An experienced legal secretary can sometimes earn more than a new paralegal. Where this is so, a firm might be tempted to assign some secretarial tasks
to the paralegal. When this occurs, the profitability of paralegals may diminish, since a firm cannot bill paralegal rates for secretarial tasks.

Yet such factors have not diminished the movement toward hiring increased
numbers of paralegals. Furthermore, the cost-effectiveness of a paralegal should
not be judged solely by the amount of revenue directly generated by his or her
efforts. Paralegals often perform valuable but *nonbillable* tasks, such as recruiting new employees, managing other paralegals, updating and organizing pleadings files, and doing most of the work on cases that the attorney would normally
do for free (e.g., probating the estate of the attorney's brother-in-law). This, of
course, enables attorneys to direct more of their efforts to fee-generating matters. Furthermore, if a paralegal is not as profitable as an employer had hoped,
the problem may be the lack of an effective strategy to incorporate paralegals
into the office and to manage them effectively. "In fact, if the hiring, allocation
and utilization of paralegals is not actively planned and managed by the law
firm, productivity and profitability will not be improved." [28] We will examine
this theme in greater depth later.

■ ASSIGNMENT 1.5

The following historical overview provides two theories to explain the development of paralegals. Why do you think the author feels that the "second has held
the profession back"?

"Historically, the legal assistant's role evolved from efficient use of legal secretaries. There
are two theories as to how this happened. One theory suggests that the attorney, seeing
the benefit to his clients in providing increased services through the use of his legal
secretary, provided his secretary with further education and training and she then performed substantive legal services. The other theory is that the attorney, looking for areas
where he might bill his client for the secretary's service, determined that if he called his
secretary a legal assistant, he could more easily charge for the secretarial services. Both
of these approaches contributed to the evolution. While the first concept has elevated the
paralegal profession, the second has held the profession back." [29]

Thus far the focus of our discussion has been law firm profit when the revenue generated by the law firm comes from the firm's own clients—through
hourly fees, a fixed fee, or a contingent fee. Earlier we briefly mentioned another
kind of case where the paralegal can play a significant role in the firm's profit
picture. There are a number of special cases (for example, employment discrimination and antitrust violations), where *the losing side pays the attorney fees of
the winning side.* Most courts agree that in addition to recovering attorney fees,
the winning side can recover for its paralegal time spent in litigation. But in
what amount? Two possibilities exist:

(a) Prevailing Market Rate for Paralegals.   This is the amount a law firm
charges its clients for paralegal time, e.g., $50 an hour.

---

[28] A. Olson, *Law Firms, Paralegals and Profitability* 4 Journal of Paralegal Education and Practice
31, 32 (October 1987).
[29] L. Hangley, "The Role of the Legal Assistant" in *The Team Approach to Practice Development,*
3 (Professional Education Systems, 1989).

(b) Actual Cost to the Law Firm.   This is the amount that the law firm pays to keep its paralegal, e.g., $20 an hour, to cover the paralegal's salary, fringe benefits, and other overhead items related to the paralegal.

There can be a dramatic difference between market rate and actual cost, since the former includes the profit that the firm makes through the paralegal. When a losing party must may for the paralegal time of the winning party, how much is paid? Market rate or actual cost? Different states answer this question in different ways when the litigation involves a state matter.

For certain kinds of *federal* cases, however, the United States Supreme Court settled the question in the very important 1989 opinion of *Missouri v. Jenkins* when it ruled that the prevailing market rate was to be the standard of recovery. The relevant portions of this opinion are reprinted below.

The case involved a Kansas City suit in which a claim was made under § 1988 of the Civil Rights Act. The lower court awarded the winning party $40 an hour for paralegal time, which was the prevailing rate in Kansas City at the time. On appeal, the losing party argued that it should pay no more than $15 an hour, which represented the actual cost to the law firm of employing the paralegal. The United States Supreme Court did not accept this position.

Many consider this opinion to be a great victory for the paralegal movement. "Waves from the ripple effect" of the opinion "will wash the doorsteps

---

Missouri v. Jenkins

United States Supreme Court
491 U.S. 274,
109 S.Ct. 2463, 105 L.Ed.2d 229 (1989)

Justice Brennan delivered the opinion of the Court. . . . [T]o bill paralegal work at market rates . . . makes economic sense. By encouraging the use of lower-cost paralegals rather than attorneys wherever possible, permitting market-rate billing of paralegal hours "encourages cost-effective delivery of legal services and, by reducing the spiraling cost of civil rights litigation, furthers the policies underlying civil rights statutes." *Cameo Convalescent Center, Inc. v. Senn*, 738 F.2d 836, 846 (CA7 1984), cert. denied, 469 U.S. 1106, 105 S.Ct. 780, 83 L.Ed.2d 775 (1985).*

Such separate billing appears to be the practice in most communities today.** In the present case, Missouri concedes that "the local market typically bills separately for paralegal services," Transcript of Oral Argument 14, and the District Court found that the requested hourly rates of $35 for law clerks, $40 for paralegals, and $50 for recent law graduates were the prevailing rates for such services in the Kansas City area. . . . Under these circumstances, the court's decision to award separate compensation at these rates was fully in accord with § 1988. . . .

---

* It has frequently been recognized in the lower courts that paralegals are capable of carrying out many tasks, under the supervision of an attorney, that might otherwise be performed by a lawyer and billed at a higher rate. Such work might include, for example, factual investigation, including locating and interviewing witnesses; assistance with depositions, interrogatories, and document production; compilation of statistical and financial data; checking legal citations; and drafting correspondence. Much such work lies in a gray area of tasks that might appropriately be performed either by an attorney or a paralegal. To the extent that fee applicants under § 1988 are not permitted to bill for the work of paralegals at market rates, it would not be surprising to see a greater amount of such work performed by attorneys themselves, thus increasing the overall cost of litigation.

Of course, purely clerical or secretarial tasks should not be billed at a paralegal rate, regardless of who performs

them. What the court in *Johnson v. Georgia Highway Express, Inc.*, 488 F.2d 714, 717 (CA5 1974), said in regard to the work of attorneys is applicable by analogy to paralegals: "It is appropriate to distinguish between legal work, in the strict sense, and investigation, clerical work, compilation of facts and statistics and other work which can often be accomplished by non-lawyers but which a lawyer may do because he has no other help available. Such non-legal work may command a lesser rate. Its dollar value is not enhanced just because a lawyer does it."

** *Amicus* National Association of Legal Assistants reports that 77 percent of 1,800 legal assistants responding to a survey of the association's membership stated that their law firms charged clients for paralegal work on an hourly billing basis. Brief for National Association of Legal Assistants as *Amicus Curiae* 11.

of virtually every law office which employs or which is contemplating utilizing legal assistants in its delivery of legal services." [30] The highest Court in the land not only acknowledged the value of paralegals, but also provided a clear demonstration of how profitable paralegals can be in these kinds of cases. Equally important is the admonition of the Court's footnote that "purely clerical or secretarial tasks [performed by a paralegal] should not be billed at a paralegal rate." If a law firm wants to recover paralegal fees at market rates from the opposing side, the firm must be able to show that it gave the paralegal substantial, nonsecretarial tasks to perform in the case. As we shall see later, a major complaint of some paralegals is that they are not delegated enough challenging tasks. *Missouri v. Jenkins* should help combat this problem. Attorneys will be more inclined to use paralegals properly when they see that their economic livelihood is enhanced by doing so. [31]

It must be noted, however, that some courts do *not* adopt the approach of the United States Supreme Court in *Missouri v. Jenkins*. This opinion involved the interpretation of the Civil Rights Act. If another court is interpreting a different statute, it might reach a different conclusion on how to handle paralegal time. There are a few courts that refuse to allow any separate compensation for paralegal time. In such courts, paralegal fees are simply not recoverable. Yet the trend is definitely in the direction of following the approach of *Missouri v. Jenkins*.

■ ASSIGNMENT 1.6

(a) Earlier in this chapter, you were given sample job descriptions of paralegals in a large law office: legal assistant clerk, legal assistant, senior legal assistant, supervising legal assistant, case manager, and legal assistant manager. (See Figure 1.1). Assume that the law firm of Smith & Smith is large enough to have employees under all of these categories and that employees within each of them work on a major case for which an award of paralegal fees can be made. How would a court make a determination of paralegal fees in this case?

(b) What has been the impact of *Missouri v. Jenkins* in your state?

---

2. The Call for Efficiency and Delegation

Attorneys are overtrained for a substantial portion of the tasks that they perform in a law office. This is one of the major reasons that traditional law offices are charged with inefficiency. Paralegals have been seen as a major step toward reform. The results have been quite satisfactory as evidenced by the following comments from attorneys who have hired paralegals:[32]

> A competent legal assistant for several years has been effectively doing 25% to 35% of the actual work that I have been doing for many years prior to that time.

---

[30]*The Paralegal Factor,* 9 The California Lawyer 47 (June 1989).

[31]There is another dimension to these fee-award cases that should be considered. Suppose that an attorney seeks an award of *attorney* fees to cover time spent on tasks that the attorney should have delegated to a paralegal. In such a case, a court might refuse to award the attorney his or her normal hourly fee. One court phrased the problem this way: "Routine tasks, if performed by senior partners in large firms, should not be billed at their usual rates. A Michelangelo should not charge Sistine Chapel rates for painting a farmer's barn." *Ursic v. Bethlehem Mines,* 719 F.2d 670, 677 (3rd Cir. 1983).

[32]Oregon State Bar, Legal Assistants Committee, *Legal Assistant Survey* (1977).

> The results of our 3 attorney—3 paralegal system have been excellent. Our office's efficiency has been improved and our clients are receiving better service.
>
> It has been our experience that clients now ask for the legal assistant. Client calls to the attorneys have been reduced an estimated 75%.

It has taken a *very* long time for attorneys to realize that something was wrong with the way they practiced law. The following historical perspective presents an overview of how attorneys came to this realization.[33]

During the American Colonial period, the general populace distrusted attorneys because many of them sided with King George III against the emerging independent nation. Some colonies tolerated the existence of attorneys, but established roadblocks to their practice. In 1641, for example, the Massachusetts Bay Colony prohibited freemen for hiring attorneys for a fee:

> "Every man that findeth himself unfit to plead his own cause in any court shall have libertie to employ any man against whom the court doth not except, to help him, Provided he gave him noe fee or reward for his pains." [34]

Furthermore, almost anyone could become an attorney without having to meet rigorous admission requirements.

Up until the nineteenth century, the attorney did not have assistants other than an occasional apprentice studying to be an attorney himself. The attorney basically worked alone. He carried "his office in his hat." [35] A very personal attachment to and devotion to detail were considered to be part of the process of becoming an attorney and of operating a practice. In the early nineteenth century, George Wythe commented that:

> It is only by drudgery that the exactness, accuracy and closeness of thought so necessary for a good lawyer are engendered.[36]

The same theme came from Abraham Lincoln in his famous "Notes for a Law Lecture":

> If anyone . . . shall claim an exemption from the drudgery of the law, his case is a failure in advance.[37]

Attorneys would be somewhat reluctant to delegate such "drudgery" to someone working for them, according to this theory of legal education.

During this period, attorneys often placed a high premium on the personal relationship between attorney and client. As late as 1875, for example, Seward and his partners "would have none of the newfangled typewriters" because clients would "resent the lack of personal attention implied in typed letters." [38] The coming of the Industrial Revolution, however, brought the practice of law closer to industry and finance. Some law offices began to specialize. As attor-

---

[33]The research for part of the section on the historical background of paralegals was conducted by the author and subsequently used with his permission in the following article: Brickman, *Expansion of the Lawyering Process through a New Delivery System: The Emergence and State of Legal Paraprofessionalism* 71 Columbia Law Review 1153, 1169ff (1971).

[34]"Body of Liberties," cited in R. Warner, *Independent Paralegal's Handbook,* 8 (Nolo Press, 1986).

[35]Lee, *Large Law Offices,* 57 American Law Review 788 (1923).

[36]Lewis, ed., "George Wythe," in Great American Lawyers: A History of the Legal Profession in America, vol 1, 55 (1907).

[37]Nicolay & Hay, eds., "Notes for a Law Lecture," in Complete Works of Abraham Lincoln, 142 (1894). See also Frank, Lincoln as a Lawyer, 3 in (1961).

[38]Swaine, *The Cravath Firm and Its Predecessors: 1819–1947,* vol 1, 365, 449.

neys assumed new responsibilities, the concern for organization and efficiency grew. To be sure, large numbers of attorneys continued to carry their law offices "in their hats" and to provide an essentially one-to-one service. Many law offices in the 1850s, however, took a different direction.

Machines created new jobs. The typewriter introduced the typist. Librarians, investigators, bookkeepers, office managers, accountants, tax and fiduciary specialists, and research assistants soon found their way into the large law office. Although nonattorneys were primarily hired to undertake clerical or administrative responsibilities, they soon were delegated more challenging roles. As one study of a law firm noted with respect to several female employees who had been with the firm a number of years:

> In addition, these women were given considerable responsibility in connection with their positions as secretary or head bookkeeper. The head bookkeeper acted as assistant secretary to the partner-secretary of certain charitable corporations the firm represented. In this capacity, she recorded minutes of director's meetings, issued proxy statements, supervised the filing of tax returns for the organization and attended to other significant administrative matters.[39]

In this fashion, attorneys began delegating more and more nonclerical duties to their clerical staff. This was not always done in a planned manner. An employee might suddenly be performing dramatically new duties as emergencies arose on current cases and as new clients arrived in an already busy office. In such an environment, an attorney may not know what the employee is capable of doing until the employee does it. Despite its haphazard nature, the needs of the moment and *OJT* (on-the-job training) worked wonders for staff development.

By the 1960s, attorneys started to ask whether a new category of employee should be created. Instead of expanding the duties of a secretary, why not give the new duties to a new category of employee—the paralegal? A number of studies were conducted to determine how receptive attorneys would be to this idea on a broad scale. The results were very encouraging. The conclusion soon became inevitable that attorneys can delegate many tasks to paralegals without sacrificing quality of service. Today this theme has become a dominant principle of law office management. Most attorneys no longer ask, "Can I delegate?" Rather they ask, "Why *can't* this be delegated?" Or, "How can the delegation be effectively managed?" It is a given that substantial delegation is a necessity.

This is not to say, however, that all attorneys immediately endorse the paralegal concept with enthusiasm. Many are initially hesitant, as demonstrated by the following report on the hiring of legal assistants within the California Department of Health, Education, and Welfare (HEW):

> When the legal assistant program began in early 1977 in HEW, it was met with some skepticism, especially in offices in cities other than Sacramento. There was concern that the quality of the work might be diminished by legal assistants. However, team leaders and deputies are not only no longer skeptical, they are now enthusiastic supporters of the legal assistant program. The attorneys feel that the work product is at least as good, and more thorough, than that provided by attorneys, mainly because the legal assistants have developed an expertise in a narrow area of the law and the work is more stimulating to the legal assistants than it was to the attorneys.
>
> The legal assistants processed 152 cases in fiscal year 1977/78 and 175 cases in 1978/79. It was estimated that legal assistants are as efficient as attorneys in processing the preliminary phase of these cases. As a result, a legal

---

[39]Dodge, *Evolution of a City Law Office,* 1955 Wisconsin Law Review 180, 187.

assistant in this instance produces as many pleadings as a deputy attorney general would have produced in the same amount of time. For this reason the section has been able to provide a faster turnaround time for the client agencies.[40]

Proponents of greater use of paralegals in government argue that, in addition to efficiency, considerable savings can result from such use. For example, in order to save money and increase efficiency, a bill was introduced into the California Assembly:

"to require each state agency and department that employs attorneys to begin to utilize a combination of hiring practices and attrition which will result in a ratio of one paralegal . . . to every 5 attorneys employed by the state by January 1, 1990."[41]

Unfortunately, this bill was not enacted into law—largely because of opposition from government attorneys.

Another call for more cost-effective methods of practicing law by the government came from the Council for Citizens Against Government Waste (the "Grace Commission") which recommended that the United States Department of Justice increase the ratio of paralegals to attorneys in order to achieve a savings of $13.4 million over three years. Soon thereafter, legislation was proposed in Congress to establish an Office of Paralegal Coordination and Activities in the Department of Justice to work toward the increased use of paralegals in the department.[42] While this proposal was not passed by Congress, the effort is typical of the momentum toward paralegal use throughout the practice of law.

3. Promotion by the Bar Associations

The bar associations assumed a large role in the development of paralegals. This has given great visibility to the field. In 1968, the House of Delegates of the American Bar Association established a Special Committee on Lay Assistants for Lawyers (subsequently renamed the Standing Committee on Legal Assistants), and resolved:

(1) That the legal profession recognize that there are many tasks in serving client's needs which can be performed by a trained, non-lawyer assistant working under the direction and supervision of a lawyer;
    (2) That the profession encourage the training and employment of such assistants. . . .[43]

Most of the state bar associations now have committees that cover the area of paralegal utilization. As we will see in Chapter 5, some of these committees have established guidelines for the use of paralegals in a law office. The real impact on the growth of paralegalism, however, has come from those bar association committees that deal with legal economics and law office management. Such committees have sponsored numerous conferences for practicing attorneys. These conferences, plus articles in bar association journals, have extensively promoted paralegals.

---

[40]*Study of Paralegal Utilization in the California Attorney General's Office*, 23, Management Analysis Section. California Department of Justice, (December 1980).

[41]Assembly Bill No. 2729 (January 21, 1986).

[42]H.R. 5107, 99th Cong., 2d Sess.

[43]Proceedings of the House of Delegates of the American Bar Association, 54 American Bar Association Journal 1017, 1021 (1968).

4. The Organization of Paralegals

Paralegals have been organizing. There are approximately 200 paralegal organizations throughout the country. (See list in Appendix B.) This has greatly helped raise everyone's consciousness about the potential of paralegalism. As indicated earlier, there are two major national associations, the National Federation of Paralegal Associations (NFPA) and the National Association of Legal Assistants (NALA). We will examine the work and the impact of these associations in the chapter on regulation. It is no longer true that attorneys are the sole organized voice speaking for paralegals and shaping the development of the field.

5. Restructuring of Professions and Occupations Generally

The creation of new careers within an established profession or occupation is not unique to the law.

Doctors

There are approximately eleven paramedical personnel for every doctor in the United States. The hospital patient confronts a substantial number of nondoctor personnel: registered nurse, practical nurse, inhalation therapist, laboratory technician, occupational therapist, physical therapist, medical record librarian, medical technologist, cytotechnologist, radiologic technologist, radiation therapy technologist, nuclear medical technician, dietician, etc. It has been estimated that in the field of nursing alone, there are hundreds of different programs. The most recent stratification has been the licensing of the *physician assistant,* whose ranks were initially filled by many veterans who were medics or medical corpsmen while members of the armed services.

Dentists

There are approximately 250 dental assistant training programs, 175 dental hygiene training programs, and 30 dental laboratory technician training programs. The demand for "dental auxiliary personnel" has been steadily increasing.

A more radical development is denturism. A *denturist* is a nondentist who produces and dispenses removable dentures directly to the public. As might be expected, denturists are vigorously opposed by organizations such as the American Dental Association.

Teachers

Studies have shown that teachers spend from 20% to 70% of their time on nonteaching responsibilities. Teacher aides were initially created to relieve teachers of some of their clerical tasks so that they could spend more time on education. A growing number of aides, however, have been participating directly in the instructional process. It has been estimated that we may reach a ratio of one aide for every two teachers in the various departments of a large school.

Architects

The American Institute of Architecture reports that the 30,000 American architects need 127,000 supportive personnel in areas such as drafting, estimation, information and data processing, and graphic arts. More than 250 architecture technician programs are currently offered at colleges and institutes.

Law Enforcement

Auxiliary police, probation aides, and parole aides are becoming a standard part of law enforcement and correctional administration. In police science, for example, numerous programs have been developed to free the police officer from community relations responsibilities through the hiring of police aides so that the police officer can devote more energies to criminal work. The employment of ex-felons as probation and parole aides has been heralded as one of the most significant innovations in the field of corrections.

. . . .

The development of a new occupation is due to several different but related factors. One of these factors is *technological,* as we have seen. Just as there would be no such thing as an airline pilot without the development of the manned flight, there probably would never be the secretary in the modern sense without the development of the typewriter, telephone, etc.

Another basic factor is *economic.* As occupations become more and more complex (or more and more lucrative), the people who perform them begin to delegate their so-called routine tasks to other people who work for them. Nurses "paraprofessionalized" the field of medicine in this way. New specialists and subspecialists then emerged. Occupations not only "routinized down," but "specialized out." One example of the latter is the bank trust manager who is doing work that attorneys previously did. The ability of trust managers to specialize in one small area of the law allowed them to take away a share of the trust and estate market from attorneys. This was substantially due to economic forces; the generalist attorney simply could not compete with the services offered by this particular kind of banker. The public demand for the services of the latter is too acute for the legal profession to regain its full monopoly. The attorney, of course, saves face by agreeing to refrain from labeling the banker's activities "the practice of law." Underlying such a concession, however, are some elemental forces of economics.

The third major factor influencing the development of occupations is *social.* Society's insistence on universal education, for example, has led to the growth of a large civil-service teacher occupation. Urbanization has launched a variety of occupations, for example, social workers, criminologists, environmentalists, highway patrol officers, etc.

As occupations proliferate, competition among the occupations develops. This competition has led to some artificial results, the most prominent of which is a tendency to draw rigid jurisdictional lines among workers. Social workers are not psychologists; teachers are not social workers; attorneys are not accountants. We know, however, that such categorizations are misleading. Any one job often requires the individual to function within a variety of disciplines. Public school teachers, for example, would be quite surprised if told that they need have no skills in psychology, social work, or "police work" to perform in the urban classroom.

There is, however, security in the outward appearance of definitive boundary lines. Thirty years ago, researchers asked the following question at random: "Who are you?" Most often, they received a geographical answer ("I am a New Yorker"), then an ethnic answer ("I am a Canadian"), and finally an occupational answer ("I am a dentist"). The same question asked today produces an entirely different frequency of responses. An overwhelming majority of the respondents will base their answer on their occupation. We are what we *do*. Hence the increased tendency to insist on sharp career boundaries.

Within particular occupational categories, however, there is considerable turmoil over who should do what. As indicated, delegation within an occupation has created innumerable suboccupations or co-occupations. The best example of this is, again, the nurse. Doctors defined a series of functions that they were overtrained to perform. They then created the role of the nurse to undertake them. Nurses, in turn, defined a similar set of functions within their own sphere and delegated them to a new entity, the licensed practical nurse.

The legal profession is undergoing a comparable phenomenon. Typical of the progression in the law is the experience of the Paraprofessional Law Clinic at a state prison in Graterford, Pennsylvania. A group of inmates were authorized to set up a paralegal "law firm" to serve the needs of fellow inmates who need help processing their legal papers to challenge the validity of their incarceration. No attorneys are involved in the program, except for occasional outside attorneys who lend assistance to the paralegals on particular problems encountered in the firm's caseload. The most frustrating aspect of the program to the paralegals is its success. They have been able to win a large number of cases involving a miscalculation of sentence-time by prison administrators who have the responsibility of counting the day-to-day time owed by the inmates. Apparently the bureaucratic process of identifying the exact release date after deducting time served before trial, time earned for good behavior, etc., is complex. The prison staff often makes mistakes. During the first six months of the firm's existence, the paralegals claim to have had 15,924 days credited to the sentences of 103 inmates. Given the scope of the problem, the paralegals have been deluged with sentence computation cases; they have little time for anything else. While their success rate is a source of satisfaction to them, they are not happy with their caseload because they would prefer to work on cases that involve constitutional law, the so-called test cases. Their plan is to systematize computation cases and train other inmates to undertake them so that they can devote their energies to the more difficult cases. *In effect, these paralegals want to create a class of para-paralegals, or assistant paralegals, through delegation.* And so the process continues, leading potentially to an occupational structure of considerable stratification.

Note on the Delivery of Legal Services in Other Countries

England

The English legal profession has two main branches consisting of solicitors and barristers. The *solicitor* handles the day-to-day legal problems of the public with only limited rights to represent clients in certain lower courts. The bulk of litigation in the higher courts is provided by the *barrister*. When representation in such courts is needed, the solicitor arranges for the barrister to enter the case. Solicitors often employ one or more *Legal Executives,* who are the equivalent of the American paralegal. Legal Executives are delegated many responsibilities under the supervision of the solicitor. They undergo extensive training programs and take rigorous examinations at the Institute of Legal Executives. Once qualified, the Legal Executive obtains Fellowship in the Institute and is entitled to use the letters "F.Inst.L.Ex." after his or her name.

Canada

The Institute of Law Clerks of Ontario defines a *law clerk* as "a trained professional doing independent legal work, which may include managerial duties, under the direction and guidance of a lawyer and whose function is to relieve a lawyer of routine legal and administrative matters and assist him in the more complex ones." The title of legal assistant is more common outside Ontario. The number of legal assistants throughout Canada is estimated to be 4,000. One of the important organizations of legal assistants is the Canadian Association of Legal Assistants.

Japan

Attorneys are not the only providers of legal services in Japan. A separate category of workers called judicial scriveners has special authority to assist the public in preparation of legal documents such as contracts and deeds. The granting of this authority is conditioned on the successful completion of an examination.

Cuba

In Cuba, legal assistants work with attorneys in law offices or collectives called *bufetes*. The assistants draft legal documents, interview clients, conduct legal research, file papers in court, negotiate for trial dates, etc.

Soviet Union

Attorneys-at-law in the Soviet Union are organized in lawyers' colleges. Membership in the colleges is granted to three kinds of individuals: first, graduates from university law schools; second, individuals with legal training of six months or more, with experience in judicial work, or at least one year as a judge, governmental attorney, investigator, or legal counsel; and third, persons without legal training but with at least three years' experience. Also, there are nonlawyer notaries who prepare contracts and wills for the public.

Finland

In Finland, only members of the Finnish Bar Association can use the title of advocate. Advocates, however, do not enjoy an exclusive right of audience in the courts. Litigants can plead their own case or retain a representative who does not have to be an advocate.

Germany

In Germany, as in many European countries, the *notary* has a major role in legal matters. As a skilled impartial advisor, the notary (who is not necessarily an attorney) oversees the contents of documents to insure that legal transactions will withstand court challenges. Notaries often advise parties on the legal implications of commercial affairs.

■ Section G. Stages in the Development of Paralegalism

Paralegalism became a self-conscious movement in the late 1960s. The following stages, or eras, of development summarize the progress of the field since

I.	1967–1971	The era of **discovery**
II.	1972–1976	The era of **education**
III.	1977–1981	The era of **politics**
IV.	1982–1986	The era of **management**
V.	1987 and on	The era of **credentialization**

FIGURE 1.8

Paralegal Development

then. A single theme characterizes each era, but there is overlap. The five themes have been discussed throughout the history of paralegalism. Yet, one theme dominates in each era.

1. The Era of Discovery

During this time, we were finding out what paralegals are and can do. It was a time of discovery. Attorneys experimented with new roles for nonattorneys in the delivery of legal services. Surveys and studies were undertaken. The results were reported at national conferences and within the literature. Since the results were impressive, the news spread quickly. Attorneys were told that there was a new way to practice law. The discovery of paralegals generated considerable enthusiasm, debate, and controversy. There is little doubt that paralegals are now a fixture in the vast majority of settings where law is practiced. The one possible exception is in some rural areas of the country where it is taking a little longer for attorneys to integrate paralegals into the practice of law. To this extent, the discovery of paralegals is still going on.

This is not to say that most attorneys hire paralegals or use them effectively. The expansion and development of paralegalism has by no means reached its peak. The point, however, is that the day has long passed when it was common within the legal profession to ask, "What's a paralegal?"

2. The Era of Education

In the early 1970s, there was an explosion in the creation of paralegal training programs. The American Bar Association introduced a controversial plan to approve paralegal schools, as we will see in Chapter 4. Texts for paralegals began to emerge from the law publishers. At times, it appeared that few schools were *not* considering the creation of a paralegal program. Today the growth in programs has leveled off; new programs are not as common as they were in the early 1970s.

A more recent development in the field has been the creation of programs for *continuing* education for employed paralegals. Almost every newsletter of paralegal associations throughout the country announces an upcoming seminar on substantive law topics (such as, securities fraud or condominium conversions), or on paralegalism issues (such as, overtime compensation or networking). These seminars may last several days or part of an afternoon in conjunction with the association's regularly scheduled monthly or annual meeting.

3. The Era of Politics

Politics, of course, has always been part of paralegal history. For example, during the era of education, paralegals began to organize into local and national associations to protect their own interests as well as to pursue their professional development. Between 1977 and 1981, however, a period of intense political debate began both among paralegals and between paralegals and attorneys. While the debate continues today, it is no longer the dominant theme, as it was in those years. For example,

■ The lines were sharply drawn between the National Federation of Paralegal Associations and the National Association of Legal Assistants on the issue of whether the certification of paralegals was premature.

■ There were intensive lobbying drives by paralegal associations to slow down regulatory efforts of some bar associations, and to insure that paralegals would be close participants with attorneys in this regulation. Strategies were planned within most paralegal associations on how to combat problems common to paralegals.

■ New local paralegal associations were formed with the active encouragement of the older associations. Considerable debate existed within some of these new associations over whether to affiliate with the National Federation of Paralegal Associations, with the National Association of Legal Assistants, or to remain unaffiliated.

4. The Era of Management

Earlier in this chapter, factors such as economics and efficiency were listed as major reasons for the rapid expansion of paralegal use. While this enthusiasm has not died down, it became clear that the field needed a period of consolidation. Many law offices hired proportionately large numbers of paralegals within a short time. They were encouraged to expand by the promotional literature of the bar associations and by the increased income that the employment of the first paralegal generated. Some studies, however, have shown that a law office's increase in income tends to level off when larger numbers of paralegals are hired.[44]

Furthermore, not all offices are equipped to deal with the administrative problems that are found in an office with diverse personnel. Attorneys, for example, "who endorse the paralegal concept and hire recent graduates are often those whose workload is already too heavy. They have little time to provide individualized on-the-job training. The result is that paralegals feel frustrated with their lack of adequate preparation, and employers are disillusioned with their new employees."[45]

Attorneys are not trained as managers, yet management skills are fundamental to the effective use of paralegals. Hiring law office managers has helped, as has development of the relatively new career of legal administrator, but they have not eliminated the need for attorneys to educate themselves in the principles of management and systemization.

The mentality of the attorney is to work alone. Attorneys are trained to view each case as unique—every case can eventually be fought to the Supreme Court. This mentality and approach do not always encourage the attorney to delegate responsibility effectively. It certainly does not necessarily prepare the attorney to run an office in a businesslike and efficient manner. The skills required to have a law declared unconstitutional are radically different from the skills required to manage people. Unfortunately, paralegals can be one of the victims of this defect in attorney training. It is not enough that paralegals are

---

[44]Bower, *Can Paralegals Be Profitable?* Michigan Bar Journal 173 (March 1980).

[45]American Bar Association, *NFPA/NALA Focus: Two Perspectives,* 3 Legal Assistant Update 90 (1983).

competent; they must also be *used* competently. Paralegals must be challenged and be secure in their relationship with attorneys and with other law office personnel. This is easier said than done, as we will see in Chapter 3 on employment dynamics.

There are, however, visible signs of change. Greater attention is given by many law schools to the problems of law office administration. The bar associations are also intensifying their efforts in this direction. Slowly, attorneys have come to the realization that the incorporation of paralegals into an office requires careful planning and an understanding of human nature. Management assistance is becoming available. There is now a vast body of experience on which to draw.

An important sign that change is on the way is the relatively recent creation of a new position in the larger law office—the legal assistant manager or paralegal administrator. Many firms with four or more paralegals have added a paralegal administrator to oversee the recruitment, training, assignment, and management of the office paralegals. The paralegal administrator (see Figure 2.2 in Chapter 2 for the different titles used for this position) often reports to an individual with broader management responsibility in the office, such as a legal administrator, office manager, managing partner, or chairperson of the management committee. Almost always, the paralegal administrator is someone with several years of experience as a paralegal who is intrigued by the invitation to move into management. Depending on the size of the office, some still perform paralegal duties on client cases in addition to their management duties. The number of paralegal administrators is growing every day. As indicated earlier, they recently formed a national organization—the Legal Assistants Management Association (LAMA).

Attorneys now realize that they need this kind of specialized help to incorporate paralegals into the practice of law. In the old days, many attorneys had the mistaken notion that they could immediately make a lot of money simply by hiring paralegals. Thankfully, we are moving out of this era.

5. The Era of Credentialization

The dust has not yet settled from all the controversies surrounding paralegalism. By the early 1980s none of the credentialing issues had been settled. Most people agreed that it was premature to launch extensive programs of licensing or certification. While some efforts in this direction were taken, as we will see in Chapter 4, the consensus was that more time was needed to sort out all the factors involved in a program of credentialization.

It is anticipated, however, that this will change. Momentum is building toward developing some form of official credentialization, such as limited licensing. According to Kay Field, former president of the National Association of Legal Assistants:

> Those of us who have worked hard to become qualified legal assistants resent the law firm who hires a high school girl to do the filing, [and] calls her a legal assistant, . . . We all agree that there needs to be some specific standards, but unfortunately we cannot all agree first of all who is to prepare them, secondly how stringent they will be, and lastly, who will enforce them. I say to you, however, that these matters must be addressed by us before they are done for us.[46]

---

[46]K. Field, *Legal Assistants: Where Do We Go from Here?* 10 Facts and Findings 17, 18 (National Association of Legal Assistants, May/June 1984).

President Field and her organization do not advocate licensing, but they do advocate action before it is too late. Intense debate rages among paralegals over the issue of credentialization, which we will examine in Chapter 4. There is a very real danger that while paralegals continue to fight among themselves over the issue, attorneys and legislatures might suddenly step in to impose a scheme of regulation and control that will satisfy no one. Unless paralegals resolve the issue, it will be resolved for them. How could this happen? One possible scenario is as follows: The legislature imposes a license requirement after widespread publicity is given to an incident of negligence committed by an untrained and unqualified paralegal. To prevent such precipitate action by the legislature, it is critical that paralegals collectively decide what they want and how it should be achieved. The next four chapters are designed to provide you with the data you need to participate in this still-emerging aspect of paralegalism.

☐ Chapter Summary

A *paralegal* is a person with legal skills who works under the supervision of an attorney or who is otherwise authorized to use those skills; this person performs tasks that do not require all the skills of an attorney and that most secretaries are not trained to perform. It is an exciting time to become a paralegal, even though many questions about the field remain to be resolved. There are three main categories of paralegals: those who are employed by attorneys (the largest), self-employed people working for attorneys, and self-employed people providing their services directly to the public. Within these categories, there is great diversity over the titles that are used. Nor is there universal agreement over the definition of a paralegal, or of the different kinds of paralegals. This diversity and lack of agreement are primarily caused by the fact that at present there are no licensing requirements to be a paralegal. People continue to enter the field by one of three routes: experience, training, or fiat. They do not enter through the vehicle of a unifying licensing system.

Paralegal salaries are influenced by a number of factors: experience, level of responsibility, kind of employer, geographic area, the employer's understanding of the paralegal's role, and the extent to which the paralegal is committed to the field as a career.

Bar associations and paralegal associations have promoted the value of paralegals extensively. The economic impact they have had on the practice of law is the major reason paralegals have flourished and grown so rapidly. In a properly leveraged firm, paralegals can be a "profit center" without any sacrifice in the quality of the service delivered by the firm. In most states, attorneys can charge their clients paralegal fees in addition to traditional attorney fees. Furthermore, under *Missouri v. Jenkins,* there are some cases in which a firm can obtain an award of paralegal fees at market rates from losing parties in litigation. Also, a paralegal can help attorneys redirect some of their energies from nonbillable to billable tasks. A firm operates more efficiently and profitably when it consistently and systematically delegates tasks to competent people with lower billing rates, so that other people with higher billing rates will be available to perform tasks at higher rates. This is not to say, however, that paralegals are always profitable to a firm. Proper use and supervision of paralegals are key components of profitability.

Since the late 1960s, paralegalism has gone through a number of stages. During the era of discovery, people were finding out what paralegals were capable of. This knowledge encouraged hundreds of institutions throughout the country to open paralegal schools during the era of education. The era of politics gave us a proliferation of paralegal associations at the national and local levels to address the emerging issues of this new field. In the era of management, greater attention was given to the ingredients of a successful paralegal-attorney relationship. Recognizing that attorneys have never been famous for their management skills, specialists emerged—for example, legal assistant managers—to help attorneys better integrate paralegals into an office. Today we are in the era of credentialization, during which we are likely to see limited licensing or other forms of official regulation.

Key Terms

NFPA
NALA
ABA
bar association
LAMA
ALA
paralegal
legal assistant
hybrid titles
independent contractor
freelance paralegal
independent paralegal
contract paralegal
nonparalegal
legal assistant clerk

senior legal assistant
supervising legal assistant
case manager
legal assistant manager
law clerk (America)
authorized practice of law
physician assistant
credentialization
paralegal fees
leveraging
delegation
apprentice
OJT
Standing Committee on Legal
    Assistants
denturist
solicitor

barrister
legal executive
law clerk (Ontario)
notary
profit center
overhead
rule of three
fixed fee
contingency fee
staff attorney
contract attorney
project attorney
associate
nonbillable tasks
fee generating
market rate
Missouri v. Jenkins

4

The Regulation of Paralegals

■ Chapter Outline

■ Section A. Kinds of Regulation

The activities of paralegals could be regulated in seven important ways:

- Laws on the unauthorized practice of law and on the *authorized* practice of law by nonattorneys
- State licensing
- Regulation of education
- Self-regulation
- Fair Labor Standards Act
- Tort Law (e.g., the negligence of paralegals and of attorneys who employ them)
- Ethical rules

The first six of these methods of regulation are covered in this chapter. Ethics will be examined in the next chapter. As we explore these methods, you should keep in mind the terminology of regulation outlined in Figure 4.1.

FIGURE 4.1

The Terminology of Regulation

Accreditation is the process by which an organization evaluates and recognizes a program of study (or an institution) as meeting specified qualifications or standards.

Approval means the recognition that comes from accreditation, certification, licensure, or registration. As we will see, the American Bar Association uses the word "approval" as a substitute for "accreditation" of paralegal education programs.

Certification is the process by which a nongovernmental organization grants recognition to an individual who has met qualifications specified by that organization. Three of the most common qualifications are:

- Graduating from a school or training program, or
- Passing a standard examination, or
- Completing a designated period of work experience.

Once certification has been bestowed by one or a combination of these methods, the individual is said to have been *certified*. If the certification comes from a school or training program, some prefer to say that the person has been *certificated*. (Occasionally a government agency will have what it calls a certification program. This program may be similar to those described above, or it may in fact be a license program.)

Code is any set of rules that regulates conduct.

Ethics are rules that embody standards of behavior to which members of an organization are expected to conform.

Guideline is suggested conduct that will help an applicant obtain accreditation, certification, licensure, registration, or approval.

Licensure is the process by which an agency of government grants permission to persons meeting specified qualifications to engage in an occupation and/or to use a particular title.

Limited Licensure (also called *specialty licensure*) is the process by which an agency of government grants permission to persons meeting specified qualifications to engage in designated activities that are customarily (but not always exclusively) performed by another license holder. (If in the future paralegals are granted a limited license in a particular state, they will be authorized to sell designated services—now part of the attorney monopoly—directly to the public in that state.)

Registration or *enrollment* is the process by which individuals or institutions list their names on a roster kept by an agency of government or by a nongovernmental organization. There may or may not be qualifications that must be met before one can go on the list.

Regulation is any governmental or nongovernmental method of controlling conduct.

■ Section B. Unauthorized and Authorized Practice of Law

(a) Defining the Practice of Law

Every state has laws on who can be an attorney and on the *unauthorized practice of law*. In many states it is a *crime* to practice law illegally. It is not a crime to represent yourself, but you risk going to jail if you practice law on behalf of someone else. Why such a harsh penalty? Legal problems often involve complicated, serious issues. A great deal can be lost if citizens do not receive competent legal assistance. To protect the public, the state has established a system of licensing attorneys to provide this assistance and to punish anyone who tries to provide it without the license.

The *practice of law* involves three major kinds of activities:

- Representing someone in court or in an agency proceeding
- Preparing and drafting legal documents for someone
- Providing legal advice on someone's rights and obligations

The essence of legal advice is to relate the law to an individual's specific legal problem.

Suppose that you write a self-help book on how to sue your landlord. The book lists all the laws, provides all the forms, and gives precise guidelines on how to use the laws and the forms. Are you practicing law? No, since you are not addressing the *specific* legal problem of a *specific* person. It is not the practice of law to sell legal books or similar materials to the general public even if a member of the public uses them for his or her specific legal problem. Now suppose that you open an office in which you sell the book and even type the forms for customers. Practice of law? No, *unless you provide individual help in filling out the forms.* You can type the forms so long as the customer does all the thinking about what goes in the forms! So too:

- It is proper for a nonattorney to charge citizens a fee to type legal forms in order to obtain a divorce. But it is the unauthorized practice of law to provide personal assistance on how to fill out the forms.

- It is proper for a nonattorney to charge citizens a fee to type their will or trust. But it is the unauthorized practice of law to provide personal assistance on what should go in the will or trust.

For years, attorneys have complained that large numbers of individuals were crossing the line by providing this kind of personal assistance. Bar associations often asked the state to prosecute many of them. Yet some charged that the attorneys were less interested in protecting the public than in preserving their own monopoly over the practice of law. Perhaps the most famous recent case involving this controversy was that of Rosemary Furman and the Florida Bar.

Rosemary Furman: Folk Hero?

Rosemary Furman, a former legal secretary, believes that you should be able to solve simple legal problems without hiring an attorney. Hence she established the Northside Secretarial Service in Jacksonville, Florida. She compiled and sold packets of legal forms (for $50) on divorce, name changes, and adoptions. The price *included her personal assistance in filling out and filing the forms.* The Florida Bar Association and the Florida courts moved against her with a vengeance for practicing law illegally. She was convicted and sentenced to 30 days in jail.

Widespread support for Ms. Furman developed. Her case soon became a cause célèbre for those seeking increased access to the legal system for the poor and the middle class.[1] Many were outraged at the legal profession and the judiciary for their treatment of Ms. Furman.

The CBS program *60 Minutes* did a story that was favorable to her cause. Other national media, including *Newsweek,* covered the case. Warner Brothers considered doing a docudrama on the story. Rosemary Furman struck a responsive cord when she claimed that for every $50 she earned, an attorney lost $500. An editorial in the *Gainesville Sun* said, "Throw Rosemary Furman in jail? Surely not after the woman forced the Florida bar and the judiciary to confront its responsibility to the poor. Anything less than a 'thank you' note would indeed show genuine vindictiveness on the part of the legal profession" (Nov. 4, 1984). There were, however, other views. An editorial in *USA Today* said, "If she can give legal advice, so can charlatans, frauds, and rip-off artists" February 2, 1984).

The events in the Rosemary Furman story are as follows:

- 1978 & 1979: The Florida Bar Association takes Rosemary Furman to court, alleging that she is practicing law without a license.

- 1979: The Florida Supreme Court rules against her. She is enjoined from engaging in the unauthorized practice of law.

---

[1] Peoples & Wertz, *Update: Unauthorized Practice of Law,* 9 Nat'l Paralegal Reporter 1 (Nat'l Federation of Paralegal Associations, February 1985).

- 1982: The Florida Bar Association again brings a complaint against her business, alleging that she was continuing the unauthorized practice of law.
- 1983: Duval County Circuit Judge A. C. Soud, Jr. finds her in contempt of court for violating the 1979 order. The judge makes this decision in a nonjury hearing. She is then ordered to serve 30 days in jail.
- 1984: The United States Supreme Court refuses to hear the case. This has the effect of allowing the state jail sentence to stand. The Court is not persuaded by her argument that she should have been granted a jury trial of her peers rather than have been judged solely by members of a profession (attorneys and judges) that was biased against her.
- Her attorneys ask the Florida Supreme Court to vacate the jail sentence if she agrees to close her business.
- The Florida Bar Association tells the Florida Supreme Court that the jail term is a fitting punishment and should be served.
- November 13, 1984: The Florida Supreme Court orders her to serve the jail sentence for practicing law without a license. (451 So.2d 808)
- November 27, 1984: Rosemary Furman is granted clemency from the 30-day jail term by Florida Governor Bob Graham and his Clemency Board. She does not have to go to jail.
- Furman and her attorneys announce that they will work on a constitutional amendment defining the practice of law to make it easier for citizens to avoid dependency on attorneys in civil cases. Says Ms. Furman, "I have only begun to fight."

This case has had an impact in Florida and elsewhere in the country. Recently, for example, Florida has been considering a dramatic change in the definition of unauthorized practice of law. Under this proposal, it "shall not constitute the unauthorized practice of law for nonlawyers to engage in limited oral communications to assist a person in a completion of a legal form approved by the Supreme Court of Florida. Oral communications by nonlawyers are restricted to those communications reasonably necessary to elicit factual information to complete the form and inform the person how to file the form."[2] Later in this chapter, we will discuss the even more dramatic concept of *limited licensing* for paralegals, which is being considered in a number of states. Some have referred to these developments as "the long shadow of Rosemary Furman."

---

[2] Florida Bar News 12 (August 1, 1989).

■ ASSIGNMENT 4.1

(a) Define the practice of law in your state. Quote from your state code, court rules, or other official authority that is available.

(b) Would Rosemary Furman have been prosecuted for the unauthorized practice of law in your state today?

Legal Assistant regulation is on the horizon in one form or another, [and possibly in many forms]. It is imperative that we approach the regulation "can of worms" from an informed and knowledgeable vantage point, and that we participate in the formative process.

Gail White Nicholson, Vice-President, Greenville Association of Legal Assistants, 1991

The Furman case involved direct competition with attorneys. More indirect competition comes from people engaged in law-related activities, such as accountants, claims adjusters, real estate agents, life insurance agents, and officers of trust departments of banks. For years, bar associations complained about such activities. In many instances, they challenged the activities in court as the unauthorized practice of law. The problem was so pervasive that some bar associations negotiated a "statement of principles" (sometimes called a treaty) with these occupations in an attempt to identify boundary lines and methods of resolving difficulties. Most of these treaties, however, have been ineffective in defining the kinds of law-related activities that can and cannot be performed by nonattorneys. A tremendous amount of effort and money is needed to negotiate, monitor, and enforce the treaties. The resources are simply not available. Furthermore, there is a concern that such efforts by attorneys to restrain competition might violate the antitrust laws, as we will see later in the chapter.

Some practitioners of law-related occupations have gone directly to the legislature to seek enactment of statutes that authorize what would otherwise be the unauthorized practice of law. In many instances, they have been successful. For example:

Ga.Code Ann. § 9-401 (Supp. 1970). § 9-401. . . . Provided that, a title insurance company may prepare such papers as it thinks proper, or necessary, in connection with a title which it proposes to insure, in order, in its opinion, for it to be willing to insure such title, where no charge is made by it for such papers.

Utah Code Ann. 1968, 61-2-20. § 61-2-20. Rights and privileges of real estate salesmen—brokers.—It is expressly provided that a real estate salesman shall have the right to fill out and complete forms of legal documents necessary to any real estate transaction to which the said broker is a party as principal or agent, and which forms have been approved by the commission and the attorney general of the state of Utah. Such forms shall include a closing real estate contract, a short-form lease, and a bill of sale of personal property.

Tenn. Code Ann. § 62-1325 (1955). § 62-1325. Licensed Real Estate Brokers may draw contracts to option, buy, sell, or lease real property.

The effect of such statutes is to allow members of designated occupations to perform certain legal tasks that are intimately related to their work without having to hire attorneys or without forcing their clients to hire them.

(b) Authorized Practice of Law

Examine the following phrase closely: unauthorized practice of law by nonattorneys. If there is such a thing as the *un*authorized practice of law, then, by implication, there must be an *authorized* practice of law. And indeed there is. The treaties and statutes discussed above are examples of this. There are also other areas where nonattorneys are given a special authorization to practice law. Occasionally attempts are made to call what they do something other than the *practice of law*, but as we will see, these attempts conflict with reality since the nonattorneys are doing what attorneys do within the sphere of the special authorization. These special authorizations have been vigorously opposed by attorneys on the ground that the authorizations conflict with the privileged domain of attorneys. The latter are not always this blunt in stating their opposition. The objection is usually couched in terms of "protection of the public," but in large measure, the opposition has its roots in turf protection. Attorneys are not above engaging in battles for economic self-preservation.

Some members of the public view attorneys as fighters, people who will pursue an issue to the bitter end. While this trait may place attorneys in a favorable light in the eyes of clients for whom they are doing battle, many feel that the aggressive inclination of the attorney can be counterproductive. Administrative agencies, for example, are often suspicious of the involvement of attorneys. They are viewed as combatants who want to turn every agency decision into an adversarial proceeding. Agencies often see courtroom gymnastics and gimmicks as the attorney's primary mode of operation. The attorney is argumentative to a fault.

This image of the attorney as someone who complicates matters is best summed up by an old accountant's joke that taxation becomes more and more complex in direct proportion to attempts by attorneys to *simplify* the tax law. Whether or not this view of the attorney is correct, it has accounted for some erosion of the legal profession's monopoly over the practice of law.

The unavailability of attorneys has also helped produce this result. A vast segment of our population has legal complaints that are never touched by lawyers. This is due, in part, to the fact that most of these complaints do not involve enough money to attract attorneys.

We now turn to a fuller exploration of these themes under the following headings:

1. Court "representation" by nonattorneys
2. Attempted restrictions on the activities of the "jailhouse lawyer" and the broader policy considerations raised by such restrictions
3. Agency representation by nonattorneys

(1) Court Representation

In the vast majority of courts in this country, only attorneys can represent someone in a judicial proceeding. There are, however, some limited—but dramatic—exceptions.

In Maryland, a nonattorney employee of a nonprofit legal service office can represent tenants in a summary ejectment proceeding in the District Court of Maryland! A special Lay Advocacy Program oversees this form of court advocacy by nonattorneys.[3] Another extraordinary example exists in North Dakota where lay advocates assist women who are petitioners seeking protective orders in domestic violence cases. Some judges "encourage and allow" the lay advocate "to conduct direct and cross-examination of witnesses and make statements to the court." A proposal has been made to formalize this activity by creating a new position called a Certified Domestic Violence Advocate. Under this proposal, the following activities of this nonattorney would *not* be considered the unauthorized practice of law: helping a petitioner fill out printed forms, sitting with the petitioner during court proceedings, and making written or oral statements to the court.[4]

There are some lower courts in the country, particularly in the West, where parties can have nonattorneys represent them. Examples include Justice of the Peace Courts, Magistrates Courts, and Small Claims Courts. It is relatively rare, however, for parties to have any representation in such courts.

---

[3]*Lay Advocacy Program Defends Indigent Tenants*, 6 Bar Bulletin 3 (Maryland Bar Ass'n, January 1991). Annotated Code of Maryland § 10–101 (1991 Supp).
[4]*Role of Lay Advocates in Domestic Violence Proceedings*, 15 Note Pad 1 (State Bar Ass'n of North Dakota, April 5, 1991).

As we learned in Chapter 2, Tribal Courts on Indian reservations have jurisdiction over designated civil and criminal matters involving Native Americans. In many of these courts, both parties are represented by nonattorney advocates.

Government employees occasionally act in a representative or semi-representative capacity in court proceedings, even though they are not attorneys. In North Carolina cases involving the termination of parental rights, for example, the United States Supreme Court has noted the role of nonattorneys:

> In fact, . . . the North Carolina Departments of Social Services are themselves sometimes represented at termination hearings by social workers instead of by lawyers.[5]

It is well known that attorneys waste a good deal of pretrial time traveling to court and waiting around simply to give documents to the judge and to set dates for the various stages of pretrial and trial proceedings. Another problem is that an attorney may have to be in two different courtrooms at the same time. For example, the time spent at an early morning hearing may be unexpectedly extended so that the attorney cannot appear at a previously scheduled mid-morning proceeding in another courtroom on a different case. In such situations, wouldn't it be helpful if the attorney's paralegal could "appear" in court for the limited purpose of delivering papers to the judge, asking for a new date, or presenting some other message? *In most states, such activity is strictly prohibited.*

On August 16, 1982, a Kentucky paralegal learned about this prohibition in a dramatic way. Her attorney was involved in a trial at the Jefferson Circuit Court. He asked the paralegal to go to another courtroom during "Motion Hour," where attorneys make motions or schedule future proceedings on a case. He told her to ask for a hearing date on another case that he had pending. She did so. When the case was called during "Motion Hour," she rose, identified herself as the attorney's paralegal, and gave the message to the judge, asking for the hearing date. Opposing counsel was outraged. He verbally assaulted the paralegal in the courtroom and filed a motion to hold the paralegal and her attorney in contempt of court for the unauthorized practice of law. When a hearing was later held on this motion, members of a local paralegal association packed the courtroom. Tensions were high. When the judge eventually denied the motion, after a hearing on the matter, the audience broke out into loud applause. "Apparently the judge concluded that [the paralegal] had rendered no service involving legal knowledge or advice, but had merely transmitted to the court [the attorney's] message regarding disposition of the motion, that is, she had been performing a function that was administrative, not legal in nature."[6]

About twenty years earlier, a celebrated Illinois opinion, *People v. Alexander,*[7] took a position similar to this Kentucky court. In this opinion, the defendant was an unlicensed law clerk who appeared before the court to state that his employing attorney could not be present in court at the moment because he was trying a case elsewhere. On behalf of his employer, the law clerk requested a continuance. The defendant's actions were challenged. It was argued that any

[5]*Lassiter v. Dept. of Social Services,* 452 U.S. 18, 29, 101 S.Ct. 2153, 2161, 68 L.Ed.2d 640, 651 (1981).
[6]Winter, *No Contempt in Kentucky,* 7 Nat'l Paralegal Reporter 8 (Nat'l Federation of Paralegal Associations, Winter 1982).
[7]53 Ill.App.2d 299, 202 N.E.2d 841 (1964).

People v. Alexander

Appellate Court of Illinois, First District
53 Ill.App. 299, 202 N.E.2d 841 (1964)

. . .

In the case of People ex rel. Illinois State Bar Ass'n v. People's Stock Yards State Bank, 344 Ill. 462, at page 476, 176 N.E. 901, at page 907, wherein a bank was prosecuted for the unauthorized practice of law, the following quotation is relied upon:

"According to the generally understood definition of the practice of law in this country, it embraces the preparation of pleadings, and other papers incident to actions and special proceedings, and the management of such actions and proceedings on behalf of clients before judges and courts * * *."

Since this statement relates to the appearance and management of proceedings in court on behalf of a client, we do not believe it can be applied to a situation where a clerk hired by a law firm presents information to the court on behalf of his employer.

We agree with the trial judge that clerks should not be permitted to make motions or participate in other proceedings which can be considered as "managing" the litigation. However, if apprising the court of an employer's engagement or inability to be present constitutes the making of a motion, we must hold that clerks may make such motions for continuances without being guilty of the unauthorized practice of law. Certainly with the large volume of cases appearing on the trial calls these days, it is imperative that this practice be followed.

In Toth v. Samuel Phillipson & Co., 250 Ill.App. 247 (1928) the court said at page 250:

"It is well known in this county where numerous trial courts are sitting at the same time the exigencies of such a situation require that trial attorneys be represented by their clerical force to respond to some of the calls, and that the court acts upon their response the same as if the attorneys of record themselves appeared in person."

After that opinion was handed down, the number of judges was substantially increased in the former Circuit and Superior Courts and the problem of answering court calls has at least doubled. We cannot add to the heavy burden of lawyers who in addition to responding to trial calls must answer pre-trial calls and motion calls—all held in the morning—by insisting that a lawyer must personally appear to present to a court a motion for a continuance on grounds of engagement or inability to appear because of illness or other unexpected circumstances. To reduce the backlog, trial lawyers should be kept busy actually trying lawsuits and not answering court calls.

appearance by nonattorneys before a court in which they give information as to the availability of counsel or the status of litigation constitutes the unauthorized practice of law. The Illinois court took the unique position that this was not the practice of law. The reasoning of the court is presented in the excerpt from the opinion printed above.

It must be emphasized that most states would *not* agree with Kentucky and Illinois. Most states would prohibit nonattorneys from doing what was authorized in these two states. Fortunately, however, there are at least a few additional states that have begun to move in the direction of the minority view.

The Allen County Bar Association of Indiana has taken the bold move of permitting paralegals to perform what hitherto had been considered attorney functions in court. A paralegal is authorized:

- To "take" default judgments
- To "set" pretrial conferences, uncontested divorces, and all other hearing dates
- To "file" stipulations or motions for dismissal
- Etc.

The paralegal, however, must perform these tasks with court personnel other than judges; nonattorneys cannot communicate directly with judges.

The vast majority of attorneys in the country would be amazed to learn what is going on in Allen County. Once the shock subsides, however, these attorneys will probably see the wisdom and common sense of what Allen County has done and begin to think of ways to try it themselves.

The rules of the Allen County program are as follows:

Paralegal Rules of Practice
Allen County Bar Association (Indiana)

1. Generally, a legal assistant employee shall be limited to the performance of tasks which do not require the exercising of legal discretion or judgment that affects the legal right of any person.

2. All persons employed as legal assistants shall be registered [see Figure 4.2] by their employer law firm with the Allen County Circuit and Superior Court Administrator and the Clerk of the Allen Superior and Circuit Courts. Said law firm shall, by affidavit, state that it shall be bound and liable for the actions of its legal assistant employee, and that any and all actions or statements made by such personnel shall be strictly and completely supervised by his employer member of the Bar. All documents the legal assistant presents or files must contain the attorney's signature, either as an attorney for the petitioning party, or a statement affixed indicating that the documents were prepared by said attorney. Each law firm shall certify in writing that the legal assistant employee is qualified in each field in which they will act with the Courts (probate, dissolution of marriage, collection, etc.). A copy of such statement and certification shall be given to such legal assistant and shall be carried by such person whenever activity with the Court is pursued by such person. There shall be one legal assistant certified by each law office desiring same, but [an] alternate shall be allowed in case of illness, vacation or unavailability. However, in those instances where a single law firm has more than one full time legal assistant, each of whom operate in separate specialized areas, a certification can be had by more than one person, showing that such person's specialization on a full time basis is limited to one specific area. Otherwise, there should be a limit of one person certified as a legal assistant per law firm.

3. Such employee shall be limited to the following acts:

   (a) Such employee may take default judgments upon the filing of an affidavit in each case stating the amount of damages and that proper service was obtained sworn to by affidavit.

   (b) Such employee shall have authority to set Pre-Trial Conferences, Uncontested Divorces, and all other hearing dates.

   (c) Such employee shall have authority to obtain trust account deposits at the Allen County Clerk's Office but only in the name of his employer firm.

   (d) Such employee shall have authority to file stipulations or motions for dismissal.

   (e) Such an employee shall have the authority to do all filing of documents and papers with the Clerk of the Allen Superior Courts and Circuit Court where such documents and papers are not to be given to anyone authorized to affix a judge's signature or issue Court orders.

   (f) Notwithstanding the limitations of subparagraph (e) above, such employee shall have the authority to obtain from the law clerk the signature stamp of the judge on non-discretionary standard orders and notices, such as notice of hearing, and orders to appear and to answer interrogatories on the filing of a Verified Motion for Proceedings Supplemental. Note: Standard orders which depart from the usual format, restraining orders, suit and support orders, bench warrants, and body attachments must be secured by an attorney.

   (g) Such employee is not to negotiate with opposing litigants within the Courthouse nor confer with a judge on legal matters. Matters requiring communications with a judge, require an attorney.

   (h) Where circumstances permit, attorneys shall take precedence over such employees in dealings with courts and clerks.

Note again that the above program does not allow the paralegal to talk directly with a judge in performing the authorized tasks. ("Matters requiring communications with a judge, require an attorney.") Why such a restriction? Wouldn't it make sense to allow paralegal-judge communication on some procedural matters that are of a routine nature? *No,* would be the response of most bar associations.

Yes, however, is the refreshing response of several county bar associations in the state of Washington. Under the sponsorship of the Seattle-King County

FIGURE 4.2

Allen County
Circuit and
Superior Court
Certification of
Legal Assistants

STATEMENT OF CERTIFICATION

This is to certify that _____
is employed by the law firm of _____.
Said law firm binds itself and takes full responsibility and liability for the actions of its legal
assistant employee above-named and that any and all actions or statements made by such
personnel shall be strictly and completely supervised by a member of the Bar of the State
of Indiana. This is to certify that the above-mentioned legal assistant is qualified to assist
an attorney in the _____ area of law.

LAW FIRM OF: _____

BY: _____

STATE OF INDIANA, COUNTY OF ALLEN, SS:

Subscribed and sworn to before me, a Notary Public in and for said County and State, this
_____ day _____ , 19_____ .

_____
Notary Public

Bar Association and the Tacoma-Pierce County Bar Association, paralegals are allowed to "present" certain orders to judges. The orders must be those that the parties have already agreed on, or must be ex parte (which means involving one party only). In presenting such orders to a judge, the paralegal must obviously deal directly with—and perhaps even communicate with—an almighty judge! The prohibition in Allen County, Indiana on communicating with a judge does not exist in these two counties of Washington state.

(2) The Jailhouse Lawyer

A *jailhouse lawyer* is a nonattorney who helps fellow prisoners with their legal problems. Some prisons attempted to prevent the jailhouse lawyer from providing this legal assistance even though no meaningful alternatives for such assistance were provided by the prisons. This prohibition was struck down, however, by the United States Supreme Court in *Johnson v. Avery* in 1969. The basis of the opinion was that without the jailhouse lawyer, prisoners may not have access to the courts. The concurring opinion of Justice Douglas has become one of the most widely quoted and influential statements in the field of paralegalism.

Johnson v. Avery
Supreme Court of the United States, 1969.
393 U.S. 483, 89 S.Ct. 747, 21 L.Ed.2d 718

. . .

Mr. Justice DOUGLAS, concurring.

While I join the opinion of the Court [in striking down the prohibition on the activities of jailhouse lawyers] I add a few words in emphasis of the important thesis of the case.

The increasing complexities of our governmental apparatus at both the local and the federal levels have made it difficult for a person to process a claim or even to make a complaint. Social security is a virtual maze; the hierarchy that governs urban housing is often so intricate that it takes an expert to know what agency has jurisdiction over a particular complaint; the office to call or official to see for noise abatement, for a broken sewer line, or a fallen tree is a mystery to many in our metropolitan areas.

A person who has a claim assertable in faraway Washington, D.C., is even more helpless, as evidenced by the increasing tendency of constituents to rely on their congressional delegation to identify, press, and process their claims.

We think of claims as grist for the mill of the lawyers. But it is becoming abundantly clear that more and more of the effort in ferreting out the basis of claims and the agencies responsible for them and in preparing the almost endless paperwork for their prosecution is work for laymen. There are not enough lawyers to manage or supervise all of these affairs; and much of the basic work done requires no special legal talent. *Yet there is a closed-shop philosophy in the legal profession that cuts down drastically active roles for laymen. . . . That traditional, closed-shop attitude is utterly out of place in the modern world where claims pile high and much of the work of tracing and pursuing them requires the patience and wisdom of a layman rather than the legal skills of a member of the bar.* [Emphasis added.]

"If poverty lawyers are overwhelmed, some of the work can be delegated to sub-professionals. New York law permits senior law students to practice law under certain supervised conditions. Approval must first be granted by the appellate division. A rung or two lower on the legal profession's ladder are laymen legal technicians, comparable to nurses and lab assistants in the medical profession. Large law firms employ them, and there seems to be no reason why they cannot be used in legal services programs to relieve attorneys for more professional tasks." Samore, Legal Services for the Poor, 32 Albany L.Rev. 509, 515–516 (1968).

The plight of a man in prison may in these respects be even more acute than the plight of a person on the outside. He may need collateral proceedings to test the legality of his detention or relief against management of the parole system or against defective detainers lodged against him which create burdens in the nature of his incarcerated status. He may have grievances of a civil nature against those outside the prison. His imprisonment may give his wife grounds for divorce and be a factor in determining the custody of his children; and he may have pressing social security, workmen's compensation, or veterans' claims.

While the demand for legal counsel in prison is heavy, the supply is light. For private matters of a civil nature, legal counsel for the indigent in prison is almost nonexistent. Even for criminal proceedings, it is sparse. While a few States have post-conviction statutes providing such counsel, most States do not. Some States like California do appoint counsel to represent the indigent prisoner in his collateral hearings, once he succeeds in making out a prima facie case. But as a result, counsel is not on hand for preparation of the papers or for the initial decision that the prisoner's claim has substance.

Notes

1. "Jailhouse lawyers, or *writ writers,* as they are sometimes called, have always been part of prison society. But in recent years their numbers as well as the amount of litigation they generate, his increased substantially. In 1985, prisoners filed 33,400 petitions in federal and state courts, . . ." One

Jailhouse lawyer,
Fernando Jackson,
Soledad Prison, California

jailhouse lawyer at Soledad prison "devotes 16 hours a day to his legal work, subscribes to dozens of legal publications (at a cost of $1,800 a year), and files a steady stream of lawsuits." Suing "has become almost a national pastime. Prisoners act no differently from other citizens in a litigious society." Kroll, *Counsel Behind Bars: Jailhouse Lawyers . . .* , 7 California Lawyer 34 (June 1987).

2. The *Johnson* opinion stressed that the prison provided *no* alternative to the jailhouse lawyer. If alternatives had been available, the inmate would not be allowed to practice law. In *Williams v. U.S. Dept of Justice,* 433 F.2d 958 (5th Cir. 1970), the court held that the presence of law students in the prison could be an alternative, but only if it is demonstrated that the students are meeting the need for inmate legal services. If the inmates had to wait a considerable period of time, for example, before they could be interviewed by the law students, then no alternative existed and the jailhouse lawyer could not be prevented from helping other inmates.

3. In *Gilmore v. Lynch,* 319 F. Supp. 105 (N.D. Cal. 1970), affirmed by the United States Supreme Court in *Younger v. Gilmore,* 404 U.S. 15 (1971), the court held that California either had to satisfy the legal needs of its prisoners or expand the prison law library to include a more comprehensive collection of law books. See also *Bounds v. Smith,* p. 221.

4. Finally, the right of an inmate to assist a fellow inmate in legal matters does *not* extend to representing the inmate in court. *Guajardo v. Luna,* 432 F.2d 1324 (5th Cir. 1970). Nor can a nonattorney represent an inmate in court even if this nonattorney is not an inmate himself or herself. This latter point was decided by the United States Supreme Court in *Hackin v. Arizona,* 389 U.S. 143 (1967).

5. How far can the rationale of *Johnson* be extended? Suppose, for example, it is demonstrated that many claimants before state administrative agencies are not receiving legal services because attorneys cannot be afforded. Would the *Johnson* opinion permit paralegal representation before such agencies even if the latter prohibited it? What is the difference between an inmate's right to have access to the courts and *anyone's* right to complain to an agency? How do you think Justice Douglas would handle the case if it came before him?

"Although the *Johnson* case is admittedly narrow in scope, it does nevertheless, give aid and comfort to the view that whenever lawyers are unavailable for whatever reason, society will sanction alternative systems for the delivery of legal services. The paramount consideration will not be ethics nor the exclusivity of the right to practice law, but rather it will be the facilitation of access routes to the grievance machinery set up for the resolution of claims. If lawyers are not available to assist the citizenry with these claims, then the question arises as to whether skilled nonlawyers represent a viable alternative. The inevitability of this question becomes clear when we listen to the statistics on the demand for the services of a lawyer. Estimates have been made to the effect that if every lawyer devoted full time to the legal needs of the poor, there would still be a significant shortage of lawyers for the poor. If the legal needs of the middle class are added, the legal service manpower shortage becomes overwhelming." Statsky, W. and Lang, P., *The Legal Paraprofessional as Advocate and Assistant: Roles, Training Concepts and Materials,* 49–50 (1971).

See also Statsky, W., *Inmate Involvement in Prison Legal Services: Roles and Training Options for the Inmate as Paralegal* (American Bar

Procunier v. Martinez

Supreme Court of the United States, 1974.
416 U.S. 396, 94 S.Ct. 1800, 40 L.Ed.2d 244

. . .

The District Court also enjoined continued enforcement of Administrative Rule MV-IV-02, which provides in pertinent part:

"Investigators for an attorney-of-record will be confined to not more than two. Such investigators must be licensed by the State or must be members of the State Bar. Designation must be made in writing by the Attorney."

By restricting access to prisoners to members of the bar and licensed private investigators, this regulation imposed an absolute ban on the use by attorneys of law students and legal paraprofessionals to interview inmate clients. In fact attorneys could not even delegate to such persons the task of obtaining prisoners' signatures on legal documents. The District Court reasoned that this rule constituted an unjustifiable restriction on the right of access to the courts. We agree.

The constitutional guarantee of due process of law has as a corollary the requirement that prisoners be afforded access to the courts in order to challenge unlawful convictions and to seek redress for violations of their constitutional rights. This means that inmates must have a reasonable opportunity to seek and receive the assistance of attorneys. Regulations and practices that unjustifiably obstruct the availability of professional representation or other aspects of the right of access to the courts are invalid. Ex parte Hull, 312 U.S. 546, 61 S.Ct. 640, 85 L.Ed. 1034 (1941).

The District Court found that the rule restricting attorney-client interviews to members of the bar and licensed private investigators inhibited adequate professional representation of indigent inmates. The remoteness of many California penal institutions makes a personal visit [by attorneys] to an inmate client a time-consuming undertaking. The court reasoned that the ban against the use of law students or other paraprofessionals for attorney-client interviews would deter some lawyers from representing prisoners who could not afford to pay for their traveling time or that of licensed private investigators. And those lawyers who agreed to do so would waste time that might be employed more efficaciously in working on the inmates' legal problems. Allowing law students and paraprofessionals to interview inmates might well reduce the cost of legal representation for prisoners. The District Court therefore concluded that the regulation imposed a substantial burden on the right of access to the courts.

Bounds v. Smith

Supreme Court of the United States, 1977
430 U.S. 817, 97 S.Ct. 1491, 52 L.Ed.2d 72

[In this opinion the Supreme Court is again concerned with the need of prisoners to have access to the courts and the use of nonlawyers in helping to obtain that access. The Court held that prisons must assist inmates in the preparation and filing of meaningful legal papers by providing the inmates with adequate law libraries or adequate assistance from persons trained in the law. The Court rejected the claim that nonlawyer inmates were ill-equipped to use the "tools of the trade of the legal profession." In the Court's experience, nonlawyer petitioners are capable of using law books to file cases raising claims that are "serious and legitimate" whether or not such petitioners win the cases. In outlining the options available to a prison, the Court specifically referred to paralegals:]

It should be noted that while adequate law libraries are one constitutionally acceptable method to assure meaningful access to the courts, our decision here, . . ., does not foreclose alternative means to achieve that goal. Nearly half the States and the District of Columbia provide some degree of professional or quasi-professional legal assistance to prisoners. . . . Such programs take many imaginative forms and may have a number of advantages over libraries alone. Among the alternatives are the training of inmates as para-legal assistants to work under lawyers' supervision, the use of paraprofessionals and law students, either as volunteers or in formal clinical programs, the organization of volunteer attorneys through bar associations or other groups, the hiring of lawyers on a part-time consultant basis, and the use of full-time staff attorneys, working either in new prison legal assistance organizations or as part of public defender or legal services offices.

Association, Commission on Correctional Facilities and Services, Resource Center on Correctional Law and Legal Services, 1974).

• • • • • • • • • • • • • •

Two other important Supreme Court cases involving nonattorneys in prison need to be considered: The *Procunier* case and the *Bounds* case. See page 221.

■ ASSIGNMENT 4.2

Jim Mookely is an attorney who represents fifty inmates on a consolidated case in the state court. The inmates are in fourteen different institutions throughout the state. Jim asks the director of the state prison system to allow his paralegal, Mary Smith, to interview all fifty inmates at a central location. The director responds as follows:

- He refuses to transport the inmates to one location. The inmates would have to be interviewed at the institutions where they are currently living.
- He refuses to let anyone in any institution unless the individual has either a law degree *or* has been through the prison's two-week orientation program totaling twenty hours in the evening at the state capital.

Mary Smith has not taken the orientation program, and it would be very inconvenient for her to do so since she lives 150 miles from the capital. How would *Johnson, Procunier,* or *Bounds* apply to this problem?

---

(3) *Agency Representation*

A considerable number of administrative agencies will permit a paralegal or other nonattorney to represent clients at the agency. These individuals are usually called agents, practitioners, or representatives. They engage in informal advocacy for their clients at the agency or formal advocacy, including representation at an adversarial administrative hearing. (A proceeding is adversarial if another side appears in the controversy, whether or not the other side is represented. If there is no other side present in the matter before the agency, the proceeding is considered nonadversarial.) Often the issues before the agency are economic, statistical, or scientific, but legal issues are also involved. It is clear that in conducting an adversarial hearing before an agency, the nonattorney can be practicing law in a manner that is remarkably similar to an attorney's representation of a client in court. Our study of this phenomenon will begin with federal administrative agencies, and then we will cover state agencies.

Nonattorney Practice before Federal Administrative Agencies.   For federal agencies, Congress has passed a statute, the Administrative Procedure Act, that gives each federal agency the power to decide for itself whether only attorneys can represent clients before it:

Administrative Procedure Act 5 U.S.C.A. § 555 (1967). (b) A person compelled to appear in person before an agency is entitled to be accompanied, represented, and advised by counsel or, if permitted by the agency, by other qualified representative. . . .

See Appendix E on the extent of nonattorney representation in federal agencies.

When an agency decides to use this power to permit nonattorney representation, it can simply allow anyone to act as the agent or representative of another before the agency, or it can establish elaborate qualifications or standards of admission to practice before it. If the agency takes the latter course, its qualifications or standards could include a specialized test to demonstrate competency in the subject matter regulated by the agency, minimum educational or experience requirements, registration or enrollment on the agency's approved roster of representatives, and an agreement to abide by designated ethical rules of practice—a violation of which could result in suspension and "disbarment."

The United States Patent Office has established criteria for individuals to practice (as *registered agents*) before this agency by drafting and filing applications for patents, searching legal opinions on patentability, etc.[8] In 1982, there were approximately 12,000 registered agents who had met this criteria at the agency. Of this number, about 1,900 (or 15.8%) were nonattorneys. At the Interstate Commerce Commission, close to 10,000 nonattorney "practitioners" have been authorized to represent clients at ICC proceedings that often involve issues such as rate increases and service extensions for railroads and other transportation carriers.[9] Perhaps the largest use of nonattorneys in federal agencies is at the Internal Revenue Service within the Treasury Department.[10] Any certified public accountant is authorized to practice before the IRS. There are over 190,000 members of the American Institute of Certified Public Accountants, most of whom are not attorneys.[11] In addition, the IRS has enrolled, i.e., registered, thousands of nonattorneys to represent taxpayers at all administrative proceedings within the IRS. These individuals, called *enrolled agents,* charge clients fees for their services. (Once a dispute goes to court, however, an attorney must take over.) To become an enrolled agent, an individual must either pass a written IRS examination or prove that he or she once worked at the IRS for five years interpreting and applying tax laws. In most states there are organizations of enrolled agents; the major national organization is the National Association of Enrolled Agents.

While many federal agencies allow nonattorney representation, it is not true that extensive numbers of nonattorneys actually use the authority they have. A recent study by the American Bar Association of thirty-three federal administrative agencies reached the following conclusion: "We found that the overwhelming majority of agencies studied permit nonlawyer representation in both adversarial and nonadversarial proceedings. However, most of them seem to encounter lay practice very infrequently (in less than 5% of adjudications), while only a few encounter lay practice as often as lawyer practice. Thus, although universally permitted, lay practice before federal agencies rarely occurs."[12]

One agency where nonattorney representation is fairly high (about 15%) is the Social Security Administration. Paralegals are frequently appointed by clients (see Figure 4.3) to represent them before the agency. In 1983, a study compared the success of clients at hearings based upon the kind of representation they received. The results were as follows:

- 59% of clients were successful when they were represented by attorneys.

- 54.5% of clients were successful when they were represented by nonattorneys.

[8]37 C.F.R. 1.341–1.348 (1983).

[9]49 C.F.R. 1103.1–1103.5 (1983).

[10]31 C.F.R. 10.3–10.75 (1983); 20 U.S.C. 1242 (1975).

[11]Rose, *Representation by Non-Lawyers in Federal Administrative Agency Proceedings* (Administrative Conference of the United States, 1984); Vom Baur, *The Practice of Non-Lawyers before Administrative Agencies,* 15 Federal Bar Journal 99 (1955).

[12]ABA Standing Committee on Lawyers' Responsibility for Client Protection, *Report of 1984 Survey of Nonlawyer Practice before Federal Administrative Agencies* (October 19, 1984).

FIGURE 4.3

Appointment of
Representative

DEPARTMENT OF
HEALTH AND HUMAN SERVICES
SOCIAL SECURITY ADMINISTRATION

NAME (Claimant) (Print or Type)   SOCIAL SECURITY NUMBER

WAGE EARNER (if different)   SOCIAL SECURITY NUMBER

Section I   APPOINTMENT OF REPRESENTATIVE

I appoint this individual _____
(Name and Address)

to act as my representative in connection with my claim or asserted right under:

☐ Title II (RSDI)   ☐ Title XVI (SSI)   ☐ Title IV FMSHA (Black Lung)   ☐ Title XVIII (Medicare Coverage)

I authorize this individual to make or give any request or notice; to present or elicit evidence; to obtain information; and to receive any notice in connection with my pending claim or asserted right wholly in my stead.

SIGNATURE (Claimant)   ADDRESS

TELEPHONE NUMBER   DATE

(Area Code)

Section II   ACCEPTANCE OF APPOINTMENT

I, _____, hereby accept the above appointment. I certify that I have not been suspended or prohibited from practice before the Social Security Administration; that I am not, as a current or former officer or employee of the United States, disqualified from acting as the claimant's representative; and that I will not charge or receive any fee for the representation unless it has been authorized in accordance with the laws and regulations referred to on the reverse side hereof. In the event that I decide not to charge or collect a fee for the representation, I will notify the Social Security Administration. (Completion of Section III satisfies this requirement.)

I am a / an _____
(Attorney, union representative, relative, law student, etc.)

SIGNATURE (Representative)   ADDRESS

TELEPHONE NUMBER   DATE

(Area code)

Section III (Optional)   WAIVER OF FEE

I waive my right to charge and collect a fee under Section 206 of the Social Security Act, and I release my client (the claimant) from any obligations, contractual or otherwise, which may be owed to me for services I have performed in connection with my client's claim or asserted right.

SIGNATURE (Representative)   DATE

WAIVER OF DIRECT PAYMENT

I ONLY waive my right to direct certification of a fee from the withheld past-due benefits of my client (the claimant). I do NOT, however, waive my right to petition for and be authorized to charge and collect a fee directly from my client.

SIGNATURE (Representative)   DATE

Form SSA-1696-U4 (3-88)   (See Important Information on Reverse)
Destroy prior editions   FILE COPY

- 43.7% of clients were successful when they represented themselves.[13]

Fees can be charged by attorneys or paralegals for these services, but the agency must specifically approve the fee. This is not to say, however, that attorneys and paralegals are treated alike. If an attorney successfully represents a claimant, the agency will deduct up to 25% of the claimant's award, which will be paid directly to the attorney to cover fees. On the other hand, if a paralegal successfully represents a claimant, the paralegal must collect the fee directly from the client, since the Social Security Administration will not deduct anything from the award in such cases.[14]

Nonattorney Practice before State Administrative Agencies. At the *state* level, there is often a similar system for authorizing nonattorneys to provide represen-

---

[13]DSS/OHA *Participant Involvement in Request for Hearing Cases for Fiscal 1983*, Table 6, (May, 1984).
[14]42 U.S.C. 406 (1975).

tation at many, but by no means all, state administrative agencies. Many states have their own version of the federal Administrative Procedure Act quoted above.

Of course, the organized bar has never been happy with this special authorization given to nonattorneys within federal or state administrative agencies. Since there are state statutes on who can practice law (and often criminal penalties for nonattorneys who practice law in violation of these statutes), how can an administrative agency allow a nonattorney to engage in activity that is clearly the practice of law? The answer to this question is somewhat different for federal and state agencies.

If the agency permitting nonattorney representation is a *federal* agency (for example, the United States Patent Office, the Interstate Commerce Commission, the Internal Revenue Service, and the Social Security Administration), its authorization takes precedence over any *state* laws on the practice of law that would prohibit it. This principle was established in the United States Supreme Court case of *Sperry v. State of Florida ex rel the Florida Bar.*[15] The case involved a nonattorney who was authorized to represent clients before the United States Patent Office. The Florida Bar claimed that the nonattorney was violating the state practice-of-law statute. The Supreme Court ruled that the *Supremacy Clause* of the United States Constitution gave federal laws supremacy over conflicting state laws. The Court also said:

> Examination of the development of practice before the Patent Office and its governmental regulation reveals that: (1) nonlawyers have practiced before the Office from its inception, with the express approval of the Patent Office and to the knowledge of Congress; (2) during prolonged congressional study of unethical practices before the Patent Office, the right of nonlawyer agents to practice before the Office went unquestioned, and there was no suggestion that abuses might be curbed by state regulation; (3) despite protests of the bar, Congress in enacting the Administrative Procedure Act refused to limit the right to practice before the administrative agencies to lawyers; and (4) the Patent Office has defended the value of nonlawyer practitioners while taking steps to protect the interests which a State has in prohibiting unauthorized practice of law. We find implicit in this history congressional (and administrative) recognition that registration in the Patent Office confers a right to practice before the Office without regard to whether the State within which the practice is conducted would otherwise prohibit such conduct.
>
> Moreover, the extent to which specialized lay practitioners should be allowed to practice before some 40-odd federal administrative agencies, including the Patent Office, received continuing attention both in and out of Congress during the period prior to 1952. The Attorney General's Committee on Administrative Procedure which, in 1941, studied the need for procedural reform in the administrative agencies, reported that "[e]specially among lawyers' organizations there has been manifest a sentiment in recent years that only members of the bar should be admitted to practice before administrative agencies. The Committee doubts that a sweeping interdiction of nonlawyer practitioners would be wise. . . ."

. . . .

Suppose, however, that a *state* agency permits nonattorney representation. Can this be challenged by the bar? The issue may depend on who has the *power* to regulate the practice of law in a particular state. If the state legislature has this power, then the agency authorization of nonattorney representation is valid, since the agency is under the jurisdiction and control of the legislature. So

15373 U.S. 379, 83 S.Ct. 1322, 10 L.Ed.2d 428 (1963).

long as the nonattorney representation is based on a statute of the legislature, it is valid. If, however, the state judiciary has the power to control the practice of law in a state, then the courts may be able to invalidate any nonattorney representation that is authorized by the agency.

Nonattorneys who have the authority to provide representation at an administrative agency may do so as independent paralegals, or as full-time employees of attorneys. The following ethical opinion from California involves the latter—a paralegal employee of a law firm. The opinion discusses some of the issues that are involved when the law firm wants its paralegal to use the special authorization for nonattorney representation at a particular administrative agency—the Worker's Compensation Appeals Board. Later in Chapter 5 we will examine the ethical issues involved in this opinion in greater depth.

Formal Opinion 1988–103
State Bar Committee on
Professional Responsibility and Conduct
California

Issue

May a law firm, having advised its clients of its intention to do so, delegate authority to a paralegal employee to make appearances at Workers' Compensation Appeals Board hearings and to file petitions, motions or other material?

Digest

A law firm may delegate such authority, provided that the paralegal employee is adequately supervised.

Authorities Interpreted

Rules 3-101, 3-103 and 6-101 of the Rules of Professional Conduct of the State Bar of California.

* * *

Issue

A client has contracted for the services of a law firm for representation in a matter pending before the Workers' Compensation Appeals Board (hereinafter "WCAB"). The law firm employs and intends to utilize the services of the paralegal in connection with the proceedings pending before the WCAB to make appearances, file petitions and present motions.

The client has consented to the law firm utilizing the services of the paralegal, after being informed as to the potential consequences of representation by a person of presumably lesser qualification and skill than may be reasonably expected of an attorney. In addition, the status of the employee as a paralegal rather than an attorney will be fully disclosed at all proceedings at which the paralegal appears and on all documents which the paralegal prepares.

Discussion

It is unlawful for any person to practice law in this state without active membership in the State Bar of California. (Bus. & Prof. Code, ¶6125) The practice of law includes the performing of services in any matter pending in a court or administrative proceeding throughout its various stages, as well as the rendering of legal advice and counsel in the preparation of legal instruments and contracts by which legal rights are secured. (cf. *Smallberg v. State bar* (1931) 212 Cal. 113.)

It has been held that the representation of claimants before the Industrial Accident Commission (predecessor to the WCAB) constitutes the performance of legal services. (*Bland v. Reed* (1968) 261 Cal.App.2d 445, 448.) However, the representation by a nonattorney of an applicant before the WCAB is expressly authorized by Labor Code 5501 and 5700 as follows:

> The application may be filed with the appeals board by any party in interest, his attorney, or other representative authorized in writing . . .,
> . . . Either party may be present at any hearing, in person, by attorney, or by any other agent, and may present testimony pertinent under the pleading.

Thus, the principal issue is whether an attorney may hire a nonattorney to engage in conduct on behalf of the attorney's client which the employee is authorized to perform independently, but which, if performed by the attorney, would constitute the practice of law.

It is the opinion of the Committee that because the client has been informed about, and has consented to the involvement of the paralegal, no violation occurs with respect to dishonesty or deceit. (See Bus. & Prof. Code, ¶6106, 6128, subd.(a).) In addition, if the status of the employee as a paralegal rather than attorney is fully disclosed at all proceedings at which the paralegal appears and on all documents which the paralegal prepares, no violation of the prohibition on an attorney lending his or her name to be used as an attorney by a person not licensed to practice law will occur. (See Bus. & Prof. Code, ¶6105.)

In addition, because Labor Code sections 5501 and 5570 expressly authorize nonattorneys to represent applicants before the WCAB, the proposed arrangements would not constitute a violation of Rule of Professional Conduct 3-101(A), which provides as follows:

> A member of the State Bar shall not aid any person, association, or corporation in the *unauthorized* practice of law. (Emphasis added.)

Further, there is no indication that the facts presented that the relationship between the paralegal and the law firm would constitute a partnership in violation of Rule of Professional Conduct 3-103, which provides as follows:

> A member of the State Bar shall not form a partnership with a person not licensed to practice law if any of the activities of the partnership consist of the practice of law.

The pivotal consideration is that the client contracted for the services of the law firm, rather than a paralegal, for representation. However, since the safeguards mentioned above have been taken to avoid misleading or deceiving the client or any one else regarding the status of the paralegal, the Committee finds no ethical insufficiency inherent in the participation of paralegals.

A lawyer or law firm contemplating entering into such an arrangement should remember that an attorney stands in a fiduciary relationship with the client. (*Krusesky v. Baugh* (1982) 138 Cal.App.3d 562, 567.) When acting as a fiduciary, the law imposes upon a member the strictest duty of prudent conduct as well as an obligation to perform his or her duties to the best of the attorney's ability. (*Clark v. State Bar* (1952) 39 Cal.2d 161, 167; and cf. Bus. & Prof. Code, ¶6067; Rule of Professional Conduct 6-101(A). However, an attorney does not have to bear the entire burden of attending to every detail of the practice, but may be justified in relying to some extent on nonattorney employees. (*Moore v. State Bar* (1964) 62 Cal.2d 74, 80; *Vaughn v. State Bar* (1972) 6 Cal.3d 847, 857.)

The attorney who delegates responsibilities to his or her employees must keep in mind that he or she, as the attorney, has the duty to adequately supervise the employee. In fact, the attorney will be subject to discipline if the lawyer fails to adequately supervise the employee. (*Chefsky v. State Bar* (1984) 36 Cal.3d 116, 123; *Palomo v. State bar* (1984) 36 Cal.3d 785; *Gassman v. State Bar* (1976) 18 Cal.3d 125.)

What constitutes adequate supervision will, of course, depend on a number of factors, including, but not limited to, the complexity of the client matter, the level of experience of the paralegal and the facts of the particular case.

It is the opinion of the Committee that, even though the paralegal will be providing substantive legal services to the client, adequate supervision under these unique facts does not require the attorney to ensure that the paralegal performs the services in accordance with the level of competence that would be expected of the attorney under rule 6-101.

So long as the paralegal is adequately supervised and the law firm does not mislead the client that the services will be performed in accordance with the attorney level of competence or that an attorney will be handling the matter, the Committee does not believe the attorney would be in violation of the Rules of Professional Conduct.

This opinion is issued by the Standing Committee on Professional Responsibility and Conduct of the State Bar of California. It is advisory only. It is not binding upon the courts, the State Bar of California, its Board of Governors, or any persons or tribunals charged with regulatory responsibility or any member of the State Bar.

■ ASSIGNMENT 4.3

Make a list of every state and local administrative agency in your state. Have a class discussion in which students identify as many state and local agencies as they can. Then divide the total number of agencies by the number of students in the class so that each student will be assigned the same number of agencies. For your agencies, find out whether nonattorneys can represent citizens. What are the requirements, if any, to provide this representation informally (e.g., calling or writing the agency on behalf of someone else) or formally (e.g., representing someone else at an agency hearing)? Check your state statutes. Check the regulations of the agency. If possible, call the agency to ask what its policy is and whether it can refer you to any statutes or regulations on the policy.

■ **ASSIGNMENT 4.4**

Paul is a nonattorney who works at the Quaker Draft Counseling Center. One of the clients of the center is Dan Diamond. Paul says the following to Mr. Diamond:

> You don't have anything to worry about. The law says that you cannot be drafted until you have had an administrative hearing on your case. I will represent you at that hearing. If you are drafted before that hearing, I will immediately draft a habeas corpus petition that can be filed at the United States District Court.

Any problems with Paul's conduct?

 Section C. Licensing of Paralegals

Many occupations (electricians, brokers, nurses, etc.) are licensed by the government. To date, *no* federal, state, or local government has imposed a licensing requirement on traditional paralegals. Proposals for licensing have been made in some legislatures, but none has been enacted into law. For paralegals who work under the supervision of attorneys, licensing is arguably unnecessary, since the public is protected by this supervision. But what about the relatively small number of independent paralegals who work directly with the public without attorney supervision? Many have argued that there *is* a need to license them in order to protect the public. The phrase *limited licensing* refers to a government authorization to perform a designated number of activities that are now part of the attorney monopoly. While no limited licensing proposal has yet been enacted into law, the likelihood of passage is very real in spite of substantial attorney opposition. Before covering limited licensing, let's examine efforts to enact broad-based licensing schemes covering all activities of all paralegals.

Broad-Based Licensing

A number of states have proposed legislation to license all paralegals. Many of these proposals confuse the word *certification* with *licensure*. Certification is usually a statement by a *non*governmental organization that a person has met certain qualifications. Licensure, on the other hand, is a permission or authorization *by a government* to engage in a certain activity.

In 1977, for example, the Michigan legislature gave serious consideration to passing the Legal Assistant Act to "regulate the practice of legal assistants." Under this proposal, a nine-member commission would be created to establish the requirements for the "certification" of legal assistants. Even though the proposal uses the word certification, it was a licensure program, since it would establish the qualifications to engage in a particular occupation. If this legislation had been enacted, a person could not be a legal assistant in Michigan without passing a statewide examination and having the educational credentials identified by the commission.

This plan was *not* adopted in Michigan. Such licensing schemes are usually vigorously opposed by paralegal associations as being premature, unnecessary, and unduly restrictive. A commonly voiced fear is that the license might limit what paralegals are now authorized to do without a license, and that some competent paralegals who now work in law offices might not fit within rigid eligibility criteria that might be established for the license. The organized bar is also opposed to broad-based licensing. The following excerpts from bar association reports give some of the reasons why:

North Carolina Bar, *Report of Special Committee on Paralegals* 3 (1980)

Several states have considered the possibility of adopting a licensing statute for paralegals, but none has done so. Licensing itself is subject to great public and legislative concern at present. So long as the work accomplished by non-lawyers for lawyers is properly supervised and reviewed by a licensed and responsible attorney, there would seem to be no need for a further echelon of licensing for the public's protection. Furthermore, licensing might be more dangerous than helpful to the public. The apparent stamp of approval of a license possibly could give the impression to the public that a person having such a license is qualified to deal directly with and give legal advice to the public. Although the Committee would not attempt to close the door on licensing of paralegals in the future if circumstances change and if, for example, the use of independent, non-lawyer employee paralegals were to become widespread, present conditions, at least, do not call for any program of licensing for paralegals.

Illinois State Bar Association, *Report on the Joint Study Committee on Attorney Assistants* 6 (6/21/77)

Our Joint Committee arose because there was a suggestion that attorney assistants be licensed. After due consideration we recommend no program of licensure or certification of attorney assistants or other lay personnel.

We are opposed to licensure because the standards on which licensure are to be based are difficult or impossible to formulate. Furthermore, we have started with a premise that precedes this conclusion; to wit: no delegation of any task to an attorney assistant shall diminish the responsibility of the attorney for the services rendered. We believe that any program which purports to say who is "licensed" and who is "not licensed" creates a standard which will diminish the attorney's responsibility. It furthermore may exclude from useful and desirable employment people who, under the supervision and control of an attorney, may perform useful tasks but who may not meet the standards of licensure involved.

We are further opposed to licensure because of the danger that it poses to the public. If a group of persons appears to be authorized to perform tasks directly for the public, without the intervening control of an attorney, it would be humanly inevitable that many of the licensed persons would try to deal directly with the public. We think these risks would be substantially increased by licensure.

■ ASSIGNMENT 4.5

How would you characterize the opposition to licensure expressed in the above excerpts from the bar reports? Do you think there is a conflict of interest in attorneys making these judgments about paralegal control? Explain.

Limited Licensing

As we saw earlier, some independent, or freelance, paralegals have their own businesses, through which they sell their services to attorneys. A smaller number work directly for the public without attorney supervision. For example, a paralegal might sell divorce forms and type them for clients. This is not the illegal practice of law, so long as no legal advice is given in the process. One of the reasons Rosemary Furman got into trouble was that she gave such advice along with the forms she typed, and hence was charged with the unauthorized practice of law by the Florida bar.

Some have argued that the law that led to the prosecution of people like Rosemary Furman should be changed. Why not grant them a limited license (sometimes called a specialty license) to practice law? Remarkably, a suggestion to this effect was actually made by a Commission of the American Bar Association! The ABA does not favor broad-based licensing of all paralegals. In a 1986 report, however, an ABA Commission on Professionalism cautiously suggested—on page 52 of the report—that there be "limited licensing of paralegals" and "paraprofessionals" to perform certain functions such as handling some real estate closings, drafting simple wills, and performing certain tax work. The report argued that such a proposal could help reduce the cost of legal services:

> No doubt, many wills and real estate closings require the services of a lawyer. However, it can no longer be claimed that lawyers have the exclusive possession of the esoteric knowledge required and are therefore the only ones able to advise clients on any matter concerning the law.[16]

This remarkable proposal caused quite a stir. Many refer to the controversy it created as the "page 52 debate." For years, many attorneys were suspicious of paralegalism because of a fear that paralegals might eventually be licensed and compete with attorneys. Then along comes a report of an ABA Commission that recommends licensing! Yet it must be remembered that neither the report nor the Commission speaks for the entire ABA. In fact, the proposal in the report "drew the ire" of other ABA members *and is unlikely to be given serious consideration by the ABA as a whole any time soon.* This will not, however, prevent continued suggestions in favor of some form of licensing—even from within segments of the ABA itself.

Before paralegals had time to recover from the drama of the "page 52 debate," another shock wave arrived. In 1989, the State Bar of California stated that there was "an overwhelming unmet need" for better access to legal services, and created a *Commission on Legal Technicians* to study whether independent paralegals can help meet this need. Its answer was *yes!* The Commission recommended that the California Supreme Court adopt a Rule of Court authorizing nonattorneys to engage in the practice of law in the following three areas: bankruptcy law, family law, and landlord-tenant law. (Other areas might be added later.) As "licensed independent paralegals," they would not be required to have attorney supervision. They could open an office and sell their services directly to the public. In effect, the state's rules on the unauthorized practice of law would be abolished for those services. Court representation, however, would not be included. If a client needed to go to court, an attorney would have to be hired. This "limited license" program would be administered by the California State Department of Consumer Affairs with help from an Advisory Committee consisting of two independent paralegals, one attorney, and four members of the public who are not independent paralegals or attorneys.

Here are some of the other features of the proposal:

- Applicants for the license must be at least 18 years of age.
- Applicants must submit fingerprints.

---

[16]*In the Spirit of Public Service: A Blueprint for Rekindling of Lawyer Professionalism* , 52 (ABA, Comm'n on Professionalism, 1986).

- All applicants must take and pass a two-part written examination: (1) a general knowledge examination, including an ethics section, and (2) a specialty exam in an area of practice. In order to be licensed, an applicant must take and pass both the general and specialty examinations within a two-year period.

- Applicants must meet minimum levels of education and/or experience, as recommended by the Advisory Committee. However, as of the date of implementation of the enabling legislation, persons who have practiced in the field for two years should have the right to take the examination without additional entry requirements. (The last sentence constitutes the grandfathering provision of the proposal.)

- For license renewal, licensees must fulfill annual continuing education requirements.

- Complaints and investigations would be handled by the Department of Consumer Affairs' centralized services.

- A client security fund would be established to provide compensation to victims of independent paralegal thefts. The initial annual fee would be $25.00 per licensee and the Advisory Committee would develop recommended guidelines for disbursement, including an appropriate cap to be placed on each claim paid by the fund.

- Standards for denial of licensure and for discipline would be established.

- The Supreme Court would approve a code of professional conduct for licensed independent paralegals.

The reaction among paralegals to this proposal has been surprisingly mixed. The two national paralegal associations—the National Association of Legal Assistants (NALA) and the National Federation of Paralegal Associations (NFPA)—have taken very different positions. As we will see later, this is not the first time that these two giants have clashed over the issue of regulating paralegals.

The National Association of Legal Assistants is *against* the California proposal for a number of reasons. First, the proposal does not provide guidelines to determine the kinds of bankruptcy, family law, or landlord-tenant cases an independent paralegal is competent to handle. Many of these cases are complex at the outset or become complex as they unfold. Such cases require the attention of an attorney. Independent paralegals are not in the best position to determine when a case is beyond their skills. Second, the licensing of independent paralegals could eventually lead to a climate in which traditional paralegals and legal assistants who work for attorneys would have to become licensed. Third, the licensing of independent paralegals will lead to open warfare with attorneys and to public disillusionment with the legal system. "For all practical purposes, . . ." the independent paralegals covered by the California proposal, ". . . will become direct and fierce competitors of . . . lawyers who will not look kindly upon these untrained 'mini-lawyers.' It is only a matter of time . . . [until] the inevitable will occur; the public will have a bad experience working with one of these untrained, inadequately educated non-lawyers and it will become further disillusioned with the legal system. Thus the results will further blacken the public's image of lawyers and the law profession."[17] Finally, NALA objects to the use

---

[17]National Ass'n of Legal Assistants, *Statement to . . . State Bar of California* (1991).

Demonstration in front of
the California State Bar
Association on the issue
of limited licensing

of the word *paralegal* for anyone who does not work under the supervision of an attorney.

The National Federation of Paralegal Associations, on the other hand, has taken a different approach. While not directly endorsing or opposing the California proposal, the NFPA has laid out the conditions under which it will support "regulation of paralegals who deliver legal services directly to the public." The conditions are as follows:

- the regulation expands the utilization of paralegals to deliver cost-efficient legal services,

- there is a demonstrated public need,

- the regulation includes minimum criteria for performing independent paralegal services such as experience under the supervision of an attorney or of a licensed paralegal,

- the paralegals pass a performance-based proficiency examination.

Applying these conditions to the California proposal, the NFPA would probably favor the proposal, although, as indicated, no formal position has been taken on it.

As revolutionary as this proposal is, there is another proposal in California from *HALT (Help Abolish Legal Tyranny)* that is even more radical. HALT is a national legal consumer group. It has proposed that nonattorneys be allowed to practice law in fourteen specialty areas.[18] A Board of Legal Technicians in the Department of Consumer Affairs would decide which of these specialty areas require registration (involving little more than providing information about yourself), and which require licensing (involving passing an examination).

---

[18]The areas are: Immigration law, family law, housing law, public benefits law, litigation support law, conservatorship and guardianship law, real estate law, liability law, estate administration law, consumer law, corporate/business law, intellectual property law, estate planning law, bankruptcy law. (Under the HALT proposal, other specialty areas might be added later.)

Other states are also considering proposals for limited licensing. In Illinois, for example, an Independent Paralegal Licensing Act was introduced in the legislature. The origin of this plan is quite interesting. A paralegal student designed a regulation plan as part of a class assignment. When this student went to work for an Illinois state legislator, the plan eventually became the basis of the licensing plan that was actually introduced in the legislature!

As you might expect, many attorneys have been intensely opposed to any form of limited licensing. A former president of the State Bar of California said, "It's like letting nurses do brain surgery." Here are some other comments from attorneys: "This is the worst thing since the plague!" They think "just about everybody should be able to practice law. I guess they think everybody should be able to slice open a belly and remove an appendix." "I cannot think of anything that would be more injurious to the public." This is an idea "whose time has not yet come." And "this is potentially the most fractious and controversial issue ever confronted" by the bar association. So far, such opposition has been successful since none of the limited license proposals have been enacted into law.

A much more modest form of limited licensing, however, has in fact been enacted into law in the state of Washington. A totally new category of worker has been created in the real estate industry, the *Limited Practice Officer* (LPO), also referred to as a Closing Certified Officer. This individual is a nonattorney with the authority "to select, prepare and complete legal documents incident to the closing of real estate and personal property transactions." [19] The State Supreme Court has created a Limited Practice Board to which applicants apply for "admission" to become an LPO. (See Figure 4.4.) The Board approves the form of the documents that the LPO can "select, prepare, and complete" in a closing, e.g., deeds, promissory notes, guaranties, deeds of trust, reconveyances, mortgages, satisfactions, security agreements, releases, Uniform Commercial Code documents, assignments, contracts, real estate excise tax affidavits, and bills of sale. Like the system for regulating attorneys, an LPO applicant must demonstrate "good moral character" and pass a combined essay and multiple-choice examination on the law. Once certified, LPOs can be disciplined for violating their authority. At present, there are no educational requirements to become an LPO, although such requirements are anticipated. LPOs must provide proof of financial responsibility by such means as purchasing a liability insurance policy ("errors and omissions insurance coverage") or showing that coverage exists under a bond taken out by their employer.

■ ASSIGNMENT 4.6

(a) Compare the LPO program in Washington with the two proposals for limited licensing in California.

(b) Do you agree with NALA's position on limited licensing, or that of NFPA? Why?

What are the chances of a licensing requirement becoming law? Even though proposals for broad-based licensing continue to appear, passage is unlikely in view of widespread opposition from attorneys and paralegals. Limited licensing, on the other hand, may eventually become a reality, in spite of the

---

[19]Washington Supreme Court Rule 12(a).

FIGURE 4.4

Application for
Admission to
Limited Practice as
a Limited Practice
Officer in the State
of Washington
under the
Admission to
Practice Rule 12

To the Washington State Limited Practice Board:

I hereby apply for a limited license to practice law in the State of Washington as a limited practice officer under the Admission to Practice Rule 12.

Applicant's Name in Full _____

                                    Last   First   Middle

Applicant's Date of Birth _____

                                    Month   .   Day   Year

Applicant's Business Address _____

                                              Address

                                  City   State   Zip Code

Applicant's Business Phone   (   )_____

                                  Area Code   Number

Applicant's Home Address _____

                                              Address

                                  City   State   Zip Code

Applicant's Home Tel. No.   (   )_____

                                  Area Code   Number

Applicant's Social Security Number _____

Please list:

Employers/Supervisors	**From**	**To**	**Telephone Number**
(Past five years) Attach separate sheet if needed.			

---

position of NALA. The LPO program in Washington represents a small crack in the door. Will current proposals, such as those under serious consideration in California and Illinois, eventually kick the door through?

It is becoming increasingly difficult for attorneys to oppose limited licensing on the basis of the need to protect the public. A system now exists for identifying and punishing unscrupulous and incompetent attorneys; a similar system could be designed to regulate independent paralegals. And, of course, no one is proposing the equivalent of allowing nondoctors to perform brain surgery. The proposals for limited licensing simply try to identify services that do not require all of the skills of an attorney.

Perhaps the most compelling argument for limited licensing is the fact that attorneys have priced themselves out of the market. Recent studies continue to document a vast unmet need for legal services in our society. Attorneys, however, point to the reforms that have made legal services more accessible at a lower cost. See Figure 4.5. Yet, in spite of these reforms and in spite of the dramatic increase in the number of attorneys coming out of our law schools, the unmet need for legal services among the poor and middle class continues to grow. Here, for example, are some of the conclusions of legal-needs studies covering two large states:

> Each year in Illinois, by conservative estimates, 300,000 low-income families face approximately 1,000,000 civil legal problems for which they do not receive legal help.[20]

---

[20] Illinois State Bar Association and Chicago Bar Association, *Illinois Legal Needs Study* 5 (1989).

FIGURE 4.5

Reforms in the
Practice of Law

- *Pro bono work*. Many law firms and corporations give their attorneys time off to provide free legal services to the poor.
- *Simplified forms*. Bar associations have helped create legal forms that are relatively easy for the public to use without the assistance of an attorney.
- *Prepaid legal services*. Some companies and unions have developed programs of legal insurance under which participants pay a set amount each month for designated legal services that might be needed while the participant is in the program.
- *Attorney advertising*. Advertising has arguably made the public more aware of legal services and more inclined to use such services.
- *Publicly funded legal services*. The bar associations have consistently supported increased funding by the government for organizations that provide free legal services to the poor.
- *Traditional paralegals*. The increased use of paralegals by attorneys can lead to lower client costs since the billing rate for paralegal time is considerably lower than the billing rate for most attorneys.

> The poor in New York face nearly 3,000,000 civil legal problems per year without legal help. Not more than 14% of their overall need for legal assistance is being met.[21]

The statistics are even more alarming if the legal needs of the middle class are included. In the light of these numbers, critics are calling for drastic reform.

In areas such as divorce and bankruptcy, an increasingly large underground network of nonattorneys are providing low-cost legal services to citizens. Why not bring these nonattorneys out into the open? Subject them to testing and other license requirements to help ensure competence and honesty. While many attorneys see this cure as worse than the disease, others are more receptive to the idea.

Each state must make its own determination of whether limited licensing should be adopted. It is quite possible that one or two states will take the plunge in the near future and enact limited licensing. Will your state do so? Keep in mind that even if it does, it will probably affect very *few* paralegals in your state. The likelihood is that the requirement will apply only to those paralegals who do not work for attorneys. This means that the vast majority of paralegals in the state who work for attorneys would continue as they are—with no license requirement. It is true that some paralegals favor limited licensing for traditional paralegals who work under the supervision of attorneys in order to expand what they are allowed to do for attorneys. But any movement toward such expansion is considerably weaker than the current momentum toward licensing independents.

. . . .

When a licensing proposal—or a proposal for any kind of paralegal regulation—comes before the legislature, here are some of the steps that should be taken immediately:

What to Do When the Legislature Proposes Legislation to Regulate Paralegals

(In general, see also *How to Monitor Proposed Legislation,* p. 599.)

1. Obtain a copy of the proposed legislation or bill as soon as possible. If you know the name of the legislator sponsoring the bill, write or call him or her

---

[21]New York State Bar Association, *New York Legal Needs Study: Draft Final Report,* 196 (1989).

directly. Otherwise contact the office of the Speaker of the House, Speaker of the Assembly, President of the Senate, etc. Ask how you can locate the proposed bill.

2. Find out the exact technical status of the bill. Has it been formally introduced? Has it been assigned to a committee? What is the next scheduled formal event on the bill?

3. Immediately inform the sponsoring legislator(s) and the relevant committee(s) that you want an opportunity to comment on the bill. Find out if hearings are going to be scheduled on the bill. Make known your interest in participating in such hearings. Your goal is to slow the process down so that the bill is not rushed into enactment. Be particularly alert to the possibility that the paralegal bill may be buried in proposed legislation on a large number of related or unrelated topics. Again, there is a real danger that the bill will get through relatively unnoticed.

4. Determine why the paralegal bill is being proposed. What is the *public* reason given for the proposal of the bill? More important, what is the underlying *real* reason for the proposal? Perhaps some special interest or small group, real estate agents, for instance, is seeking a special privilege in a law-related field. Yet the language of the bill they are proposing may be so broad that paralegals will be adversely affected.

5. Alert your local paralegal association. It needs to be mobilized in order to express an organized position on the bill. Contact the major national paralegal associations: NFPA and NALA (see Appendix B). Do they know about the proposed legislation? Have they taken a position? They need to be activated.

6. If your local bar association has a paralegal committee, seek its support.

7. Launch a letter-writing campaign. Make sure that large numbers of paralegals in the area know about the bill and know how to express their opinion to the legislature.

8. Ask local paralegal schools to take a position.

. . . .

Keep in mind that we are talking about mandatory *licensing* by the state, not voluntary *certification* by entities such as paralegal associations. The certification debate will be covered later in the chapter.

■ ASSIGNMENT 4.7

(a) Do you favor broad-based licensing for every paralegal? Limited licensing? Will licensing advance or restrict the development of paralegalism?

(b) If all attorneys in the country drastically cut their fees, would there be a need for paralegal licensing?

(c) There are some tasks that even paralegals who work for attorneys cannot perform, such as taking the deposition of a witness. Should there be limited licensing to authorize such tasks?

■ ASSIGNMENT 4.8

Evaluate the following observation: "The emerging professions and the more established professions have frequently sought greater regulation of their occupational group. They are often motivated, despite the obligatory language on protection of the public interest, to do so in efforts to establish their 'territorial imperative' or to establish barriers to entry into the profession and thereby enhance their economic self-interest." Sapadin, *A Comparison of the Growth and Development of the Physician Assistant and the Legal Assistant,* in Journal of the American Association for Paralegal Education: Retrospective 1983, 142 (1983).

Section D. Bar Association Control of Paralegal Education

Since the early 1970s, the American Bar Association has been "approving" paralegal training programs after a recommendation is made by its standing Committee on Legal Assistants, all of whose members are attorneys. There is no requirement that a school be ABA-approved in order to train paralegals. In fact, most training programs are not so approved. The approval process is voluntary, and the majority of programs have decided *not* to apply for approval. A program must meet state government accreditation standards, but it does not have to seek the approval of the ABA or of any other bar association.

The ABA approval process has been controversial from its inception. Those who oppose total attorney control of paralegalism feel that the bar associations are inappropriate mechanisms to regulate training institutions. Since a major objective of attorneys is to increase their profits by employing paralegals, critics argue that it is a conflict of interest for attorneys to control the field totally. When regulatory decisions must be made on matters such as the approval of schools, whose interest would the attorneys be protecting in making these decisions? The interest of the paralegals? The interest of the public? Or the profit interest of the attorney-regulators?

The ABA has been somewhat sensitive to this criticism, and, as we will see, at one time considered withdrawing from the approval process. In recent years, challenges have been made to the monopoly that bar associations exercise over the practice of law. In 1975, the United States Supreme Court sent shock waves throughout the legal profession when the Court ruled that attorneys were no longer exempt from the *antitrust* laws, and that some minimum fee schedules are a violation of these laws.[22] In 1979, an antitrust charge was brought against the ABA on the ground that its paralegal-school approval process was designed to eliminate competition from, and restrict entry into, the market for recruitment, training, and placement of paralegals. The ABA won this case.[23] Despite the victory, the ABA remains vulnerable to future challenge.

Note that the ABA uses the word "approval" rather than accreditation in describing its process of exercising control over educational institutions. Yet the process meets the accepted definition of accreditation presented in Figure 4.1 at the beginning of this chapter. The use of the more euphemistic word "approval" may be an indication that the ABA is itself not sure whether it should be in the business of regulating paralegal education. Indeed, in 1981, the House of Delegates of the ABA instructed its Committee on Legal Assistants to terminate ABA involvement in the approval process. However, some schools that had al-

---

[22]Goldfarb v. Virginia State Bar, 421 U.S. 773 (1975).
[23]*Paralegal Institute, Inc. v. American Bar Association,* 475 F. Supp. 1123 (E.D.N.Y. 1979).

ready received approval objected. As a result, the Committee proposed and the House of Delegates accepted an alternative system of approving schools.

The alternative was the creation of an ABA Approval Commission to implement the approval process. The final decision on approval of individual schools is still left in the hands of the ABA. The Commission makes its recommendations on approval to the Committee on Legal Assistants, which in turn makes it recommendations to the House of Delegates of the ABA. The major difference between the Committee and the Commission is that the latter must contain nonattorney members. There are eleven members of the Commission, all of whom are appointed by the president of the ABA on advice from the Committee:

- Three attorneys (one of whom has taught in a paralegal program)
- One attorney who represents the ABA Committee on Legal Assistants
- One paralegal nominated by the National Federation of Paralegal Associations (NFPA)
- One paralegal nominated by the National Association of Legal Assistants (NALA)
- Two representatives nominated by the American Association for Paralegal Education (AAfPE)
- One representative nominated by the Association of Legal Administrators (ALA)
- One nonlegal educator
- One representative of the general public

The ABA does not view the Commission as a permanent institution. The plan is to phase it out over a period of years and to replace it with an *independent* accrediting body that is equally broad based. It is unclear, however, whether this replacement is feasible. It depends on the willingness of paralegal schools to submit themselves to this still-voluntary approval process. Furthermore, an independent body would be very expensive to run. Its revenues would come from fees paid by the schools that apply for approval and for renewals of approval. If large numbers of schools continue to bypass a national accrediting or approval entity, the process will lose both the political and financial support it needs. Since there is no realistic hope that an independent accrediting body will be formed, the ABA will probably continue its approval program indefinitely.

■ ASSIGNMENT 4.9

Who should control accreditation? Are there too many attorneys on the ABA Approval Commission? Too few paralegals? Could there be too many paralegals on such a body? Do you favor an independent accrediting entity? Who should run it? Should it be voluntary?

Only one thing is sure: change is on the horizon. The legal profession can no longer feel secure in its privileged position, as the following speech demonstrates.

The Legal Profession:
A Bow to the Past—a Glimpse of the Future
by J. Sims

[Mr. Sims was the Deputy Assistant Attorney General in the Antitrust Division of the United States Department of Justice. The following are excerpts from a speech he delivered on February 11, 1977, before a conference of the Federation of Insurance Counsel in Arizona.]

Today, in Los Angeles, legal services are being advertised on television. That fact alone gives us some idea of how much change has come to the legal profession in the last few years.

That change has not always come easy, but the fact that it has come so far, so fast, tells us quite a bit about what will happen in the future. We lawyers as a group have grumbled and argued, fought and yelled, struggled and been confused—but there are now lawyers advertising on television. Even a casual observer cannot fail to appreciate the significance of this change.

Competition, slowly but surely, is coming to the legal profession. This opening of traditional doors, the breaking of traditional barriers is the result of many forces—the number of new lawyers, the awakening of consumerism, the growing realization that the complexity of our society requires legal assistance in more and more areas. But one contributing factor has been antitrust litigation and the Department of Justice. . . .

[T]he Supreme Court fired the shot heard 'round the bar [o]n June 16, 1975. [I]n a unanimous decision [Goldfarb v. Virginia State Bar, 421 U.S. 773 (1975)], the Court held that the minimum fee schedule challenged by the Goldfarbs violated Section 1 of the Sherman Act. This decision broke the dam and released the flood of change that we see engulfing the profession today. For better or worse, the Goldfarbs had set in motion a series of events that were to change the character of the legal profession forever.

The Court decided several things in Goldfarb, but the most important was that the legal profession was subject to the antitrust laws—there was no "professional exemption." The response to Goldfarb was fascinating. A large number of private suits were filed challenging various aspects of bar regulation. . . .

[An] area sure to be controversial in the future is unauthorized practice. There is already at least one antitrust challenge, against the Virginia State Bar, seeking to prohibit the bar from promulgating unauthorized practice opinions. This case, which involves title insurance, is a direct challenge to the extraordinary power that the legal profession now has—in most states—to define the limits of its own monopoly. It would be strange indeed for a state to hand over to, say its steel industry, not only the power to regulate entry into the industry and the conduct of those within it, but also the power to define what the industry was. In many states, that is exactly the power the organized bar now has, and that power is being challenged as inconsistent with the antitrust laws.

The heart of this challenge is that lawyers shouldn't be deciding what is the practice of law—defining the scope of the legal monopoly. The papers filed in that case . . . indicate that the objection is not to such a decision being made; the objection is to the State's delegation of that power to the profession.

In fact, of course, the principle behind this lawsuit could be expanded not only to other subject matter areas, but also to arrangements between the organized bar and other professions which have as their basic result the division of commercial responsibilities.

For example, the American Bar Association has entered into "statements of principles" with respect to the practice of law with a variety of other professions and occupations ranging from accountants to claim adjusters, publishers, social workers, and even professional engineers [page 212]. These documents generally set forth the joint views of the professions as to which activities fall within the practice of law and which activities are proper for members of the other profession. They nearly all provide that each profession will advise its clients to seek out members of the other profession in appropriate circumstances.

As a general rule, two competitors may not agree with each other to allocate markets, or bids, or even functions; if they do, they violate the antitrust laws. At the least, this traditional antitrust principle raises some questions about the legal effect of such "statements of principles." . . .

[T]he efforts of the bar to limit the scope of paralegal responsibilities and, in some jurisdictions, to seek a certification requirement for paralegals are seen by many as simply another effort to preserve and protect the legal services monopoly. Many believe that non-lawyers could perform many tasks reserved today for people with law degrees. . . .

■ **ASSIGNMENT 4.10**

What are the implications of Mr. Sims' remarks on the role of bar associations in regulating paralegal education?

■ Section E. Should Paralegals Become Part of Bar Associations?

At present, no paralegals are full members of any bar associations. In 1981, however, the State Bar of Texas created a Legal Assistant Division of the bar. Its unique aspect is that all of its regular members *must* be paralegals. Hence, while paralegals cannot become members of the bar association, they can become members of a *Division* of the bar association. The Division is not a mere advisory committee of the bar; it is part of the bar association itself, which means that it is under the ultimate control of the Board of Directors of the State Bar of Texas.

The qualifications for membership in the Division are as follows:

■ The applicant must *not* be a Texas attorney.

■ The applicant must perform "substantial paralegal services in rendering direct assistance to an attorney." (Someone who does occasional paralegal work would not qualify.)

■ The applicant's supervising attorney must certify that the applicant performs substantial paralegal services for that attorney.

Members pay annual dues of $25.

The bylaws of the Division state its purpose as follows: "to enhance legal assistants' participation in the administration of justice, professional responsibility and public service in cooperation with the State Bar of Texas." All the officers of the Division are paralegals elected by the membership. The budget of the Division, however, must be approved by the State Bar of Texas.

The Division has been very popular among paralegals in Texas; by the middle of 1990, almost 2,000 paralegals had joined. The State Bar of Michigan recently adopted a similar program by creating a Legal Assistant Section of the bar consisting of legal assistants who are *affiliate members* of the bar. Other bar associations have also created special membership categories. There are, for example, *associate members* of the Columbus Bar Association (Ohio), associate members of the Bar Association of San Francisco, paralegal affiliate members of the Association of Trial Lawyers of America, and associate members of the American Immigration Lawyers Association.[24] Not all bar associations, however, have moved in this direction. The Louisiana State Bar Association, for example, voted in 1989 *not* to offer associate membership to paralegals because "the occupation of paralegals has not been sufficiently defined so as to provide guidance as to who is a trained and qualified paralegal, and who is not."[25]

---

[24]As of 1991, associate membership status existed or was under serious consideration in the following states either in the bar itself or in one of its committees or sections: Alaska, Arizona, Colorado, Connecticut (pending), District of Columbia, Florida, Illinois, Massachusetts, Michigan, Missouri (St. Louis County Bar only), New Jersey, New Mexico, North Dakota, Ohio (pending), Pennsylvania (pending), Texas, Wisconsin (pending), and West Virginia. Maze, *Bar Associate Membership Status for Legal Assistants,* 17 Facts & Findings 6 (NALA, March 1991).

[25]Landers, *Louisiana State Bar Association Decides Against Associate Membership for Paralegals,* 4 The Advocate (Louisiana State Paralegal Ass'n, August 1989).

■ ASSIGNMENT 4.11

Does the state, city, or county bar association where you live have a membership category for paralegals? If so, what are the eligibility requirements for membership and what are the benefits of membership?

What about the major national bar association—the American Bar Association (ABA)? For a long time, many argued that paralegals should become affiliated with the ABA in some way. In 1982 the ABA Committee on Legal Assistants proposed that the ABA create a new category of membership for paralegals. The National Association of Legal Assistants (NALA) warmly endorsed the proposal, while the National Federation of Paralegal Associations (NFPA) opposed it. Initially the House of Delegates of the ABA rejected the proposal of the Committee on the ground that the addition of this nonattorney membership category would further "dilute" the primary attorney category. Eventually, however, this objection was overcome. The House of Delegates agreed to accept a *legal assistant associate* category of membership. (For an application form, see Figure 4.6.) An ABA member who supervises the legal assistant must sign the latter's application for associate membership. As of 1991, there were 1200 Legal Assistant Associates in the ABA.

As indicated, not all paralegals endorsed the concept of associate or affiliate membership in bar associations when the idea was first proposed. Here are some typical comments in opposition:

> I haven't been able to understand why paralegals would want to become second class members of an organization that represents the interests of another profession. [Some paralegals view associate membership] as a positive development, while the very idea is enough to raise the blood pressure of other paralegals.[26]

> [It is] in the public interest that the allied legal professions remain autonomous. [It is] necessary and advisable that paralegals retain primary control in the development of the paralegal profession.[27]

> It is a recognized and uncontested fact that the purpose of any bar association is to promote and protect attorneys and their practice of law, rather than legal assistants. Further, associate members do not participate in the administrative and substantial legal decisions which are made by the Bar Association, e.g., no vote on dues, by-laws, budget or substantive issues of membership requirements. [A separate identity may] eliminate possible conflicts of interest on issues where attorneys and legal assistants hold differing perspectives and opinion regarding the future of legal practice.[28]

Those who viewed paralegals as an autonomous, self-directed profession tended to disagree with the effort to join bar associations in any form. Yet this point of view is *not* shared by the majority of paralegals today. The momentum is toward more and more bar associations creating membership categories for paralegals. The reasons are best summed up by the following comment made

---

[26]Whelen, *An Opinion: Bar Association's Paralegal Non-Voting Membership,* 15 At Issue 9 (San Francisco Ass'n of Legal Assistants, May 1987).

[27]*NFPA Findings,* 8 The Journal 3 (Sacramento Ass'n of Legal Assistants, January 1986).

[28]Heller, *Legal Assistant Associate Membership in the ABA,* 14 On Point 1, 14 (Nat'l Capital Area Paralegal Ass'n, August 1988).

FIGURE 4.6
ABA Associate Membership Application

Legal Assistant Associate** Persons who, although not members of the legal profession, are qualified through education, training, or work experience, are employed or retained by a lawyer, law office, governmental agency, or other entity in a capacity or function which involves the performance, under the direction and supervision of an attorney, of specifically-delegated substantive legal work, which work, for the most part, requires a sufficient knowledge of legal concepts such that, absent that legal assistant, the attorney would perform the task.

**An ABA member who supervises you MUST sign your application under Annual Associate Dues on page 3.

ABA ASSOCIATE APPLICATION
(Valid through August 31, 1991)

Membership Department • American Bar Association • 750 North Lake Shore Drive, Chicago, Illinois 60611, (312) 988-5522 FAX: (312) 988-6281

ADDRESS

Please print the way you wish your name and address to appear in the ABA records and on your Associate card and certificate. All materials will be sent to this address.

Name ______

Firm/Agency/Organization ______

Address ______

______

City ______ State ______ Zip Code ______

Country ______

This address is my ☐ Home ☐ Business ☐ Both

Home Phone ( )______ Business Phone ( )______

Birth Date ____/____/____ Gender ☐ Male ☐ Female

EMPLOYMENT

Employer ______

Your Title ______

Number of Years in this position ______

For Judicial Associate applicants only, please indicate:
☐ Judge ☐ Court administrator ☐ Federal court executive

Employment Setting (Check one):
1 Law Firm 2 Corporate Law Dept. 3 Gov't. 4 Judiciary
5 Law School 6 Legal Service/Public Defense Agency 7 Military
9 Other ______

Number of attorneys at this office:
A Solo B 2-5 C 6-9 D 10-19 E 20-99 F 100+

EDUCATION

Institution ______

Type of Degree or Certificate ______

ANNUAL ASSOCIATE DUES ARE $75

The ABA year runs from Sept. 1 to Aug. 31. Associates who join after October 1st receive a pro-rated credit toward next year's dues. Section dues are not pro-rated. *Some Associate categories REQUIRE you to join an ABA section. They are indicated by an* *. These required section dues are reflected in the total annual dues.

Check your selection(s): **Total Annual Dues**

☐ Administrative Law Associate
Administrative Law and Regulatory Practice Section* ($25.00) $100.00
☐ Bar Executive Associate .... $ 75.00
☐ Criminal Justice Associate
Criminal Justice Section* ($25.00) $100.00
☐ Educational Associate
Legal Education and Admissions to the Bar Section* ($25.00) $100.00
☐ Governmental Business Associate .... $ 75.00
☐ Industrial Organization Economist Associate .... $ 75.00
☐ International Associate .... $ 75.00
Jurisdiction(s) in which admitted to practice ______
______ Admission year(s): ______
Bar associations or legal organizations of which applicant is a member, and any offices held in them ______
☐ Judicial Associate
Judicial Administrative Division* ($25.00) $100.00
☐ Law Librarian Associate .... $ 75.00
☐ Law Office Administrative Associate
Law Practice Management Section* ($27.50) $102.50
☐ Legal Assistant Associate .... $ 75.00
Supervising Attorney Verification: I, ______, ABA Membership I.D. Number: ______, a member of the Bar of the State of ______ verify that the above applicant for Legal Assistant Associate does or has performed for me in a capacity which meets the requirements described on page 2.
Attorney Signature (required) ______

Subtotal (from above) $ ______

Subtotal for additional sections (from page 4) $ ______

Total $ ______

REQUIRED CERTIFICATION

I certify that I meet the criteria for the category of Associate affiliation I have selected (as defined on page 2).

If elected an Associate of the American Bar Association, I will abide by its Constitution and Bylaws, and the authority of the Board of Governors with respect to Associates.

Signature (required) ______

FULL PAYMENT (Must be enclosed)

☐ Check enclosed (payable to ABA)
☐ VISA ☐ MasterCard

Card Number | Exp. Date

Signature

International Associates:
Please make payment in U.S. funds drawn on a U.S. bank, or a wire transfer through the First National Bank of Chicago, Account Number 50-03997 (include your name, address and "New Applicant" on the transfer for reference). **Your application CANNOT otherwise be processed.**

Associate Dues for the American Bar Association and ABA sections, divisions and forum committees are not deductible as charitable contributions for federal income tax purposes. However, such dues may be deductible as business expense.

Associate dues include a basic subscription to the *ABA Journal*, and Section dues include basic subscriptions to the section publications as shown on page 4.

AMERICAN BAR ASSOCIATION ASSOCIATE AFFILIATION

Article Three of the ABA Constitution and Bylaws provides for the establishment of classes of Associates, composed of non-members with whom affiliation is considered to be in the interest of the Association. Associates are not members of the Association and do not, as a group, constitute a membership classification. Associates of the American Bar Association, except for International Associates, are non-lawyers who are not eligible for membership within the Association, but serve within the legal profession. Pursuant to Article 21.12 of the Association Bylaws, persons who are ineligible to be members of the Association may qualify for election by the Board of Governors as Associates if they are in one of the classifications listed above, and satisfy such further eligibility requirements as may be approved by the Board.

PRIVILEGES OF ASSOCIATES

1. To attend meetings of the Association, including sessions of the House of Delegates and the Assembly, and to enjoy any floor privileges extended to non-members.
2. To receive Association publications that are regularly provided to all members of the Association.
3. To be appointed to any Committee or Commission of the Association for which non-members are eligible for appointment.
4. To participate in the economic benefit programs available to ABA members, with the exception of the insurance programs of the American Bar Endowment.
5. To affiliate with one or more of the sections of their choice, upon application and payment of the annual section dues then in effect. All Associates under the age of 36 shall automatically become Associates of the Young Lawyers Division (see page 4).

before the ABA created the associate membership category:

> It is time our profession stopped being paranoid about ABA Associate Membership and open our eyes to opportunities presented to us. [We should not be spending time] dreaming up reasons to reject a chance for growth and improved relations within the established legal community. No guarantees have been given to assure us that associate membership would be beneficial, but why close *any* doors opened to us? If just a few paralegals would like to take advantage of this opportunity, why slam the door in their faces? The spirit of cooperation and teamwork within the legal community are the key reasons to encourage associate membership.[29]

■ ASSIGNMENT 4.12

(a) Should paralegals become a formal part of bar associations? What effect do you think associate membership would have on existing paralegal associations? Strengthen them? Destroy them? Is it healthy or unhealthy for paralegals to organize themselves as independent entities? Is it healthy or unhealthy for them to be able to challenge the organized bar? What is the conflict-of-interest argument against associate membership? Do you agree with this argument?

(b) Should a paralegal association allow *attorneys* to become associate members of the *paralegal* association? Why or why not?

(c) Under the ABA associate membership category, what kinds of paralegals are excluded from membership? Is such exclusion a good idea?

(d) To become an associate or affiliate member of a bar association, the applicant usually must obtain the signed statement of an attorney-employer asserting or attesting certain facts about the applicant—for instance, that he or she is a paralegal who works for the attorney. The statement is called an attorney attestation. For example, to obtain affiliate membership in the State Bar of Michigan, the attorney must "hereby attest" that the applicant "is employed by me and is recognized as a legal assistant (paralegal) and that he/she, under the supervision and direction of a lawyer, performs the services" specified elsewhere on the application. Some *paralegal* associations require the same kind of attorney attestation as a condition of allowing paralegals to join the paralegal association. Do you think attorney attestation is a good idea for associate/affiliate membership in a bar association? For full membership in a paralegal association?

(e) As indicated elsewhere in this book, there are a fairly large number of paralegals who have moved on to management positions as paralegal coordinators or legal assistant managers. Should these individuals become members of traditional paralegal associations?

■ Section F. Self-Regulation by Paralegals: The Certification Debate

As we have seen, there are two major national associations of paralegals:

■ National Federation of Paralegal Associations (NFPA): An association of associations; its membership consists of state and local paralegal associations

■ National Association of Legal Assistants (NALA): an association of individuals, plus a number of state and local paralegal associations, and several student paralegal associations

---

[29]Anderson, *ABA Associate Membership: A Different Perspective,* 3 Findings and Conclusions 7 (Washington Ass'n of Legal Assistants, August 1987).

In Appendix B, there is a list of state and local paralegal associations, with a notation of whether they are part of NFPA, part of NALA, or unaffiliated.

NALA is *not* a member of NFPA, and vice versa. In fact, the two groups take very different positions on a number of issues, two of the most important of which are limited licensing of independent paralegals and certification of all paralegals. Earlier in this chapter we examined the clash of views on limited licensing. We turn now to the older and perhaps more bitter debate over certification. NALA has created two major certification programs for paralegals—the Certified Legal Assistant (CLA) program and the Certified Legal Assistant Specialist (CLAS) program. The major opponent of the very existence of these programs has been NFPA. The following two excerpts present a detailed description of the position of both associations on certification. At the end of the descriptions, you will be asked which side is correct.

The Case for Certification[30]

by Jane H. Terhune

[Jane H. Terhune is a past president of the National Association of Legal Assistants. She is employed as a legal assistant for the firm of Hall, Estill, Hardwick, Gable, Collingsworth & Nelson, Tulsa, Oklahoma.]

Professional competence of an *individual* can be assessed by two recognized mechanisms: licensing or certification. Accreditation or approval, on the other hand, examines educational *programs* to determine whether they meet established standards of quality. Although the ABA has an institutional approval process, this paper is concerned only with the assessment of *individual* competence and therefore will not deal with the issue of institutional accreditation or approval.

Since the early 1970s legal assistants have obtained employment by means of formal training, in-house training, or other law office experience. While each method of training has certain advantages, no one method has proven superior to the others. Thus the dilemma: how can prospective employers or clients assess or legal assistants demonstrate paralegal skills and knowledge when there is no standard for performance?

Is licensing the appropriate mechanism to assure professional competence of legal assistants at this time? Several states have recently considered it, but none has yet adopted it. It is generally agreed that requirements for licensing would either severely limit the growth and development of the still new paralegal field or be so weak as to be meaningless. Licensing,

by definition, is a mandatory requirement and is usually administered and controlled by government entities or well-established and strong professional associations. It is doubtful that state legislatures can define the legal assistant profession well enough to regulate it effectively at this time. Therefore, licensing appears to be impractical as well as premature.

Certification, on the other hand, is a voluntary professional commitment that appears to be a practical alternative, and the National Association of Legal Assistants believes that one national certification program is preferable to a multitude of possible state programs. Certification is not new or unique. Many professions and paraprofessions have developed and supported certification as an alternative to licensing or other forms of regulation. Certification recognizes expertise and proven ability without limiting entrance into or employment in the field, and the same standards are applied regardless of the individual's background or training. Furthermore, a certification program can help guide educational institutions in developing and evaluating their legal assistant curricula. It is argued that certification would limit the development of the paralegal field, but the PLS (Professional Legal Secretary) certification of legal secretaries has in no way interfered with their employment. To the contrary, secretaries with the Certified PLS title are regarded as professionals in their respective fields.

In 1974, as part of an effort to set high professional standards for legal assistants while the field was in its early development, the NALA Certifying Board for Legal Assistants was created. It was composed of nine members—five legal assistants (working in different areas of the law), two paralegal educators, and two attorneys. The composition of the Board has remained the same to date, and in number is similar to many certification boards or committees in other fields. During the first year of its existence the Certifying Board

---

[30] American Bar Association, Standing Committee on Legal Assistants, *Legal Assistant Update '80* 5–16 (1980). This article has been updated to reflect current positions of NALA and NFPA.

acted mainly as a feasibility study group. All known national professional associations with certification programs were contacted for advice and guidance. Paralegal educators were contacted for information about their programs as well as entrance and graduation requirements. Legal assistant duties and responsibilities in various areas of the law were surveyed, and correspondence with the Institute of Legal Executives in England began. Our English counterparts were anxious to share their ten years of experience with NALA. After several months of gathering information, replies were tabulated and summarized and the NALA Certifying Board for Legal Assistants was ready to embark on its task. Its first task was to create an examination. Passing this examination would enable a legal assistant to become a CLA—Certified Legal Assistant.

Although many legal assistants work in special areas of law rather than as generalists, there are general skills and knowledge which apply to all legal fields and, for this reason, general subjects or topics were selected for inclusion in the examination.

The CLA Examination—Outline

The two-day CLA examination contains objective questions, such as multiple choice, true/false, and matching. There are also essay questions and short answer questions. The examination covers the follow areas:

Communications. This section of the CLA examination contains questions on:

word usage	capitalization	grammar
number usage	vocabulary	correspondence
punctuation	word division	nonverbal communication
sentence structure	concise writing	

Ethics. This section deals with ethics in the legal assistant's contacts with employers, clients, co-workers, and the general public. Unauthorized practice, ethical rules, practice rules, and confidentiality are among the topics tested by this section. Knowledge of the American Bar Association Rules of Professional Conduct and the National Association of Legal Assistants, Inc., Code of Ethics and Professional Responsibility is required for this examination.

Human Relations and Interviewing Techniques. The Human Relations portion encompasses professional and social contacts with the employer, clients, and other office visitors, co-workers, including subordinates, and the public outside of the law office. For this reason, the legal assistant should be familiar with: authorized practice, ethical rules, practice rules, delegation of authority, consequences of delegation, and confidentiality.

Interviewing techniques covers basic principles, as agreed upon by most authors on the subject, definitions of terms of basic principles, and handling of specialized interviews. Subject areas included in this section of the examination are:

General considerations for the interviewing situation: courtesy, empathy, and physical setting	Manner of questions
	Use of checklists for specific matters
Initial Roadblocks—lapse of time, prejudice, etc.	Special-handling situations: the elderly, the very young

The test covers initial and subsequent interviews as well as both client and witness interviews.

Judgment and Analytical Ability.   The sections of this part deal with (1) analyzing and categorizing facts and evidence; (2) the legal assistant's relationship with the lawyer, the legal secretary, the client, the courts, and other law firms; (3) the legal assistant's reactions to specific situations; (4) handling telephone situations; and (5) reading comprehension and data interpretation.

Legal Research.   It is extremely important for the legal assistant to be able to use the most important "tool" of the legal profession—the law library. The purpose of the legal research section of the CLA Examination is to test your knowledge of the use of state and federal codes; the statutes; the digests; case reports, various legal encyclopedias, court reports, shepardizing, and research procedure.

Legal Terminology.   The sections of this part deal with (1) Latin phrases; (2) legal phrases or terms in general; and (3) utilization and understanding of common legal terms. The questions involve legal terminology and procedures used in general practice.

Substantive Law.   The substantive law section of the CLA examination is divided into nine parts: (1) general (which includes American Legal System); (2) bankruptcy; (3) corporate; (4) estate planning and probate; (5) contract; (6) litigation; (7) real estate; (8) criminal; and (9) administrative law. Each examinee will be required to take the first part and must select four out of the remaining eight parts.

After passing the examination, a legal assistant may use the *CLA (Certified Legal Assistant)* designation, which signifies certification by the National Association of Legal Assistants, Inc. CLA is a service mark duly registered with the U.S. Patent and Trademark Office (No. 1131999). Any unauthorized use is strictly forbidden.

Based on the premise that education, a commitment of all professionals, is a never ending process, Certified Legal Assistants are required periodically to submit evidence of continuing education in order to maintain certified status. The CLA designation is for a period of five years, and if the CLA submits proof of continuing education in accordance with the stated requirements, the certificate is renewed for another five years. Lifetime certification is not permitted.

Continuing education units are awarded for attending seminars, workshops or conferences in areas of substantive law or a closely related area. The seminars, etc., do not have to be sponsored by NALA, although all NALA seminars and workshops qualify.

The development of the specific test items was a time-consuming and difficult project. Rather than employ professional testing companies unfamiliar with the legal assistant field, it was decided that the Certifying Board, composed of legal assistants, attorneys, and educators from the legal assistant field, was best qualified to prepare the exams. Then followed a series of meetings to review, refine, and evaluate the proposed exams. The exams were pilot-tested, testing times were noted, results were systematically analyzed, and problems were identified. Every question in each section was carefully scrutinized for "national scope," and questions which did not apply to all states were removed from the exam.

Eligibility Requirements for CLA Examination

Applicants for the Certified Legal Assistant examination must meet one of the following three requirements at the time of filing the application.

1. Graduation from a legal assistant program that is:

   a) Approved by the American Bar Association; or

   b) An associate degree program; or

   c) A post-baccalaureate certificate program in legal assistant studies; or

   d) A bachelor's degree program in legal assistant studies; or

   e) A legal assistant program which consists of a minimum of 60 semester hours (or equivalent quarter hours) of which at least 15 semester hours (or equivalent quarter hours) are substantive legal courses.

2. A bachelor's degree in any field plus one (1) year's experience as a legal assistant.

3. A high school diploma or equivalent plus seven (7) years' experience as a legal assistant under the supervision of a member of the Bar plus evidence of a minimum of twenty (20) hours of continuing legal education credit to have been completed within a two (2) year period prior to the application date.

Applicants meeting any one of these criteria may take the exam. They need not be members of the National Association of Legal Assistants to apply for or receive the CLA (Certified Legal Assistant) certification.

The CLA examination was first offered in November, 1976, at regional testing centers. Approximately 50 percent of the first group of applicants passed the entire exam, and the board was particularly pleased that the passing percentage was uniform throughout the country, a fact which seemed to indicate that the test was free of state or regional bias. Although the passing rate has fluctuated slightly in subsequent testing, the uniformity has been maintained. In the March 1990 exam, there was a 51.5% pass rate, as 504 of 977 legal assistants passed the test. As of April 1991, there were 4,265 CLAs in the country. The following states have the most CLAs:

Florida:	1120	Colorado:	122
Texas:	967	Kansas:	106
Arizona:	316	Iowa:	77
Oklahoma:	202	Louisiana	73
California:	157	New Mexico:	63

Certification is an ambitious and expensive project for a young professional association. Over $20,000 and thousands of hours were initially invested in the CLA program, but the National Association of Legal Assistants believes it has been a wise investment. Traditionally, where new professions do not set their own standards, related professions or governments have done so for them. NALA felt a responsibility to develop a quality national certification program for legal assistants desiring professional recognition. The CLA exam has been in use for a number of years, but work on the project continues. The question bank is continually expanded so that an indefinite number of exam versions can be created, and questions are being reviewed and updated constantly.

Specialty Certification

Recently NALA launched a major new component of its CLA program. It is now possible for someone who has already achieved CLA status to take additional examinations in order to receive *Specialty Certification* in one or more of the following areas:

■ **Civil Litigation** covers Federal Rules of Civil Procedure, Federal Rules of Evidence, and Federal Rules of Appellate Procedure; document control; drafting pleadings; abstracting information; and general litigation procedures.

■ **Probate and Estate Planning** covers general probate and trust law, federal estate tax, fiduciary income tax, drafting wills and trusts, and estate planning concepts.

■ **Corporate and Business Law** covers the knowledge and applications of those principles of contract, tort, property, agency, employment, administrative, corporate, and partnership law which commonly constitute the subject matter known as business law. Examinees must be thoroughly familiar with the Uniform Commercial Code, Uniform Partnership Act, Uniform Limited Partnership Act, Model Business Corporate Act, as well as with the regulatory authority of those federal agencies which affect the business relationship such as the SEC, FTC, OSHA, and EPA.

■ **Criminal Law and Procedure** covers an applicant's knowledge in the area of criminal procedure and law from arrest through trial. The examination covers components of substantive criminal law, procedural matters, and constitutional rights guaranteed to defendants. Applicants must be thoroughly familiar with the Federal Rules of Criminal Procedure, Federal Rules of Evidence, the Model Penal Code, and major United States Supreme Court cases.

■ **Real Estate** covers the applicant's knowledge in the area of real estate purchases, sales, terminology, actions affecting title, landlord-tenant relations, oil and gas, easements, abstracts, title insurance, liens, cluster developments, types of conveyances, methods of passing title included in conveyances, legal remedies associated with real estate, and legal descriptions of real estate.

Each of these specialty examinations takes four hours to complete. Upon passing one of them, the legal assistant becomes a *CLAS—a Certified Legal Assistant Specialist.* The CLA examination tests broad *general* skills required of *all* legal assistants. Specialty certification, on the other hand, recognizes significant competence in a *particular* field. Yet both the CLA exam and the CLAS exam are similar in that they do not test the law of any particular state. They are national in scope, since NALA believes that standard national examinations will ensure uniformity of professional standards as well as permit legal assistants to move from one state to another without loss of certified status.

From the inception of the CLAS program in 1982 to 1990, 298 legal assistants have achieved CLAS status in the country.

The Case Against Certification
by Judith Current

[Judith Current is a past president of the National Federation of Paralegal Associations. She is employed as a legal assistant in the firm of Holme, Roberts & Owen, Denver, Colorado.]

The National Federation of Paralegal Associations (NFPA) is a professional organization composed of fifty-two state and local paralegal associations representing over 17,000 paralegals across the country. NFPA was founded in 1974 and adopted the following purposes in 1975:

■ to constitute a unified national voice of the paralegal profession

■ to advance, foster, and promote the paralegal concept

■ to monitor and participate in developments in the paralegal profession

■ to maintain a nationwide communications network among paralegal associations and other members of the legal community

NFPA has continued to foster these goals through its established policies and activities. In 1977 NFPA adopted its Affirmation of Responsibility (p. 313).

NFPA recognizes that certification of paralegals is of national concern, but it feels that there has been insufficient study as to the impact of certification and the means by which certification should be administered. NFPA will only support a certification program which is coordinated by a national, broadly based, autonomous body in which paralegals have at least equal participation with attorneys and other members.

The topic of certification of legal assistants has been of concern to NFPA since its inception. It has found every certificate proposal advanced to date to be seriously lacking in the understanding of the true nature of the profession, particularly its diversity, and the proposals have offered a structure that provides little or no representation to the persons most affected, the legal assistants themselves.

Specifically, its reservations fall within the following areas:

Need/Prematurity

Since there is tremendous diversity in the functions and classifications of paralegals, it is extremely difficult to create generalized standards that can be fairly applied. This problem may eventually find an acceptable solution; but it will require much study and considerable input from all affected sectors.

No studies have been conducted that have demonstrated a need for certification. A study conducted by the American Bar Association in 1975 concluded that certification was premature. The California State Bar in 1978 rejected a proposal for certification and accreditation after nearly two years of study. Other states have similarly rejected certification. Until a need for certification is clearly demonstrated, certification will be premature.

Premature regulation runs a risk of foreclosing yet unseen avenues of development, as well as creating yet another layer of costly bureaucracy when, in fact, none may be needed. NFPA sees nothing to prevent, and everything to encourage, an extremely cautious approach to the enactment of any program of certification. Meanwhile, the normal mechanisms of the marketplace, the existing unauthorized practice laws and ethical guidelines, the increasing numbers of legal assistants with demonstrable experience, and the ever-growing reputations of various training programs can serve as guidelines for those who seek the sorts of yardsticks that certification might provide.

Impact of Certification

No studies have been conducted that satisfactorily assess the potential impact of certification on the delivery of legal services. Some of the possible negative effects include:

1. *The growth, development, and diversity of the paralegal profession could be diminished by certification.* The paralegal profession has been developing steadily without a demonstrated need for such regulation. Regulating the profession could curtail development into new areas, stifling the potential growth of the field and unnecessarily limiting the role of the paralegals in the delivery of legal services.

2. *Certification could result in a decrease of the availability of legal services to the poor.* Legal aid offices [page 83] are economically dependent upon paralegals who represent clients at various administrative hearings. Most of these paralegals are in-house trained specialists who are paid lower salaries than private sector paralegals. If certification is implemented, it is conceivable that administrative agencies may initiate a system in which only certified paralegals, or attorneys, would be allowed to represent clients at the hearings. Many paralegals successfully working in this area might not meet the educational or testing requirements imposed by certification, and the legal aid offices would not be able to meet the salary demands that would be made by certified paralegals.

3. *Innovation in paralegal education programs could diminish as a result of certification.* Schools would be forced by necessity to gear their courses to a certification examination rather than to the needs of the legal community and the marketplace. While some standardization of training programs might be desirable in the future, it would be premature at this time because the training programs have not been in existence long enough to determine which types of programs are most effective and because the paralegal profession is still in a dynamic stage of development. Experimentation and variety are currently essential to the field of paralegal education.

4. *Entry into the profession could be curtailed by certification.* At the present time, a paralegal can enter the profession in a variety of ways, including formal education, in-house training, promotion from legal secretary, or a combination thereof. Certification could limit these entry paths by establishing prescribed educational requirements.

No Acceptable Model for Certification

In the opinion of NFPA, no acceptable model or program of certification has yet been devised. Oregon is the only state to have adopted a certification program, but it was discontinued shortly after it began because of a lack of interest from paralegals and attorneys in the state. NFPA questions the propriety of the Oregon State Bar controlling the certification of paralegals, and deplores the fact that the paralegals were denied equal representation on the certifying board. The Oregon program failed adequately to recognize specialization and failed to make any distinctions between the tasks which may be performed by a certified paralegal and those which may be performed by an uncertified paralegal. Thus, certification did not enhance the position of paralegals in Oregon.

NFPA feels that the certification program conducted by the National Association of Legal Assistants (NALA) is unacceptable. The criteria for eligibility to take the certification examination is not based on objective data. The examination, in the Federation's opinion, contains questions irrelevant to a practicing paralegal and is not an effective measure of a person's ability to work successfully as a paralegal. The NALA certification program is not officially recognized by a governmental body, and a person certified under this program is not allowed to perform any tasks other than those which may also be performed by uncertified paralegals.

Control and Representation

No certification program will be acceptable to NFPA unless it is developed, implemented, and controlled by an autonomous group which is composed of an equal number of attorneys, paralegals, paralegal educators, and members of the public. Self-regulation is unacceptable to NFPA since self-regulation can become self-interest, and self-interest can conflict with the public interest. NFPA strongly believes that bar control of paralegals is inappropriate in that such regulation may meet the interests of the organized bar and lawyers but not necessarily the interests of the public or the paralegal profession. NFPA also questions the propriety of the organized bar attempting to regulate another profession.

National Coordination

NFPA believes that any program of certification will be most efficient and equitable if it is developed as a national program rather than on a state-by-state basis. A national program would eliminate duplication of effort on the part of each individual state. It would allow for mobility and would avoid a conflict of standards between states.

NFPA recommends that the need for and possible methods of certification be studied in much greater depth, and that this study be conducted by an autonomous group which provides equal representation to paralegals, attorneys, paralegal educators, and members of the public. NPFA also recommends that bar associations work with paralegals and educators to educate lawyers in the proper and effective utilization of paralegals and that paralegals work to promote the growth and the development of the profession through support of and participation in the local and national paralegal associations.

■ ASSIGNMENT 4.13

(a) Which side is correct? Conduct a debate in your class on the advantages and disadvantages of certification.

(b) Do you agree with NFPA that self-regulation is unacceptable?

Certification in Florida

Florida Legal Assistants (FLA) is a statewide paralegal association that is affiliated with the National Association of Legal Assistants. Florida is a big NALA state; over 25% of all CLAs in the country live in Florida. Several years ago, FLA began its own exam on Florida law for those legal assistants who had passed the CLA exam of NALA. In 1984, FLA launched the Certified Florida Legal Assistant Examination. A person who is a CLA and passes this exam on Florida law can become a *CFLA—a Certified Florida Legal Assistant.* Like the CLA exam, the CFLA exam is voluntary; no one is required to take it. The program is not endorsed by any of the bar associations in Florida. It is run exclusively by FLA. "Some legal assistants view the CFLA designation as a step up from NALA's CLA designation."[31]

Certification in Texas?

The Florida certification program was inaugurated with relative calm. The exact opposite occurred when certification proposals emerged in Texas. As we saw earlier, there is a *Legal Assistant Division* within the State Bar of Texas. A survey of the members of the Division revealed very high interest in adopting a voluntary certification program specifically for Texas. Over 76% of the members indicated that they would take a certification exam if it were offered. Consequently, the Division drafted two certification proposals and conducted a series of hearings on them in 1986. The proposals were as follows:

Proposal 1. The Division would develop and administer its own two-day exam on generic topics (such as legal analysis and communications) and on Texas law. Only legal assistants with at least two years working experience as a legal assistant would be eligible to take the exam.

Proposal 2. The Division would join forces with NALA and give two exams. NALA would administer its two-day Certified Legal Assistant (CLA) exam. Then the Division would administer its half-day exam designed with a focus on Texas law. Anyone who had previously passed the CLA exam would be required to have worked as a legal assistant in Texas for one year before taking the Division's Texas exam.

---

[31]Morris, *State Certifying Test for Legal Assistants in Florida: Is Arizona Next?*, The Digest, p. 1 (Arizona Paralegal Ass'n, October 1989).

These two proposals stirred great controversy in Texas and throughout the country. The National Federation of Paralegal Associations (NFPA) vigorously opposed both proposals, raising many of the same arguments against certification discussed earlier. But the Dallas Association of Legal Assistants (which is a member of NFPA) criticized NFPA for its opposition. The National Association of Legal Assistants (NALA) endorsed the Texas move toward certification. Of course, this is not surprising in view of NALA's history of supporting certification. And NALA would play a major role if the second proposal were adopted.

The debate was not limited to NFPA and NALA. Eight public hearings were held throughout Texas, and 187 persons submitted written comments. *But no clear consensus emerged from the hearings on the two proposals.* There was considerable confusion about the nature, purpose, and scope of the two proposals, and indeed, about the value of certification itself.

In spite of these difficulties, there is continued interest in developing a state-specific certification program in Texas within the structure of the state bar association. The most recent proposal under consideration is the establishment of a series of voluntary specialty examinations on Texas law to recognize "advanced professional competency" within a particular specialty. The likelihood of enacting such a proposal is very high. The Legal Assistants Committee has appointed a Certification Committee to study it.

Position of the American Bar Association on Certification

The ABA has taken the following positions on paralegal certification:

1. Certification of *minimal,* or *entry-level,* paralegal competence is *not* appropriate.
2. Voluntary certification of *advanced* paralegal competence or proficiency in specialty areas of the law *might* be appropriate *if* it were administered by the appropriate body.
3. The ABA is *not* the appropriate body to undertake a program of certifying paralegals in advanced competence or proficiency in specialty areas of the law.
4. A voluntary program of certifying advanced paralegal competence or proficiency in specialty areas of the law, if undertaken at all, should be undertaken on a national basis by a board that includes attorneys, paralegals, educators, and members of the general public.
5. Since such a board does not presently exist, there should not be any certification at this time.

According to the ABA, certification of minimal competence does not have the benefits that would justify the time, expense, and effort to implement it. Furthermore, any of the benefits would be outweighed by potential detriment from it. A major danger the ABA sees is that such certification could evolve into licensure, which the ABA opposes.

But the ABA does see benefit in certifying paralegals in areas of specialization *after* they have been on the job. This kind of advanced certification would be a way of recognizing professional advancement. "Such certification would be a measure of quality of work and experience. Its function would be to demonstrate to employers or prospective employers a high degree of legal assistant competence in a particular area of practice that has already been obtained, rather than just the potential for such competence." [32]

The ABA feels, however, that advanced certification must be administered by the appropriate body. This body should be broad based, including attorneys, paralegals, educators, and members of the public. The ABA recognizes that it is *not* such a body. Neither is the National Association of Legal Assistants nor the National Federation of Paralegal Associations. In fact, such a body simply does not exist. It would take a great deal of money, energy, and political skill to create one. Beyond a lot of rhetoric, no one is even trying.

Hence, as a practical consequence, it can be said that the ABA is opposed to *any* certification at this time.

■ ASSIGNMENT 4.14

When a new local paralegal association is formed, it is often lobbied by NALA and by NFPA to become a part of one of these national organizations. The local association will usually make one of three decisions: affiliate with NALA, affiliate with NFPA, or remain unaffiliated. If you were a member of a local association faced with the decision of whether to join NALA, NFPA, or stay unaffiliated, what would your vote be? Why?

■ ASSIGNMENT 4.15

Is it a good idea to have two national associations? Why or why not?

Throughout this book the importance of paralegal associations has been stressed. They have had a major impact on the development of paralegalism. Many state and local bar associations as well as the ABA have felt the effect of organized paralegal advocacy through the associations.

As soon as possible, you should join a paralegal association. Find out if the association allows students to become members. (See the form at the end of this book after the index.) If an association does not exist in your area, you should form one and decide whether you want to become part of the National Federation of Paralegal Associations or the National Association of Legal Assistants. The paralegal association is your main voice in the continued development of the field. Join one now and become an active member. In addition to the educational benefits of membership and the job placement services that many associations provide, you will experience the satisfaction of helping shape your career in the years to come. Attorneys and the bar associations should not be the sole mechanism for controlling paralegals.

 G. Fair Labor Standards Act

Yes, I am paid overtime. I am paid at time and a half rate. I agree with being paid overtime. If the attorney asks me to work additional long hours and weekends, then yes I do believe I should be compensated for yielding my free time

---

[32]ABA Standing Committee on Legal Assistants, *Position Paper on the Question of Legal Assistant Licensure or Certification,* 5 Legal Assistant Today 167 (1986).

for work. This does not make me any less of a professional. My professionalism will show through my work product.[33]

My firm doesn't pay paralegals overtime, and I don't want to be classified as a person eligible for overtime. For one thing, people paid overtime are non-professionals, and I don't think of myself as a non-professional. I feel that my salary, salary increases, and bonuses reflect a degree of compensation for the extra hours I work.[34]

One of the "hot topics" in the field is GOD: the Great Overtime Debate. "The mere mention of the subject of overtime in any group of working legal assistants is guaranteed to spark a prolonged session of horror-story telling." [35] The topic is so controversial that one paralegal association recently established a hotline to answer questions confidentially. Some paralegals have filed—and won—lawsuits against their employers for failure to pay *overtime compensation* for hours worked beyond forty hours in a week.

There is a definite body of law that determines whether overtime compensation must be paid; the issue is not dependent on the preferences of individual paralegals. The governing law is the federal *Fair Labor Standards Act,*[36] which is enforced by the Wage and Hour Division of the U.S. Department of Labor. Under the Act, overtime compensation must be paid to employees unless they fall within one of the three "white collar" exemptions. Exempt employees are those who work in a professional, administrative, or executive capacity.[37] The vast majority of traditional paralegals do *not* fit within any of these exemptions. Since they are nonexempt, they *are* entitled to the protection of the Act. Phrased another way, they are not considered professionals, administrators, or executives under the Act and must therefore be paid overtime compensation. If, however, the paralegal is a supervisor with extensive management responsibilities over other employees, an exemption may apply. But this would cover only a small segment of the paralegal population. The following opinion letter explains the position of the government on this issue. As you will see, the criteria

---

[33]*The Member Connection,* 14 Facts & Findings 7 (NALA, June 1988).

[34]*The Membership Responds,* 9 The ParaGraph (Georgia Ass'n of Legal Assistants, September/ October 1987).

[35]Acosta, *Let's Talk About Overtime!,* 10 Ka Leo O' H.A.L.A. 6 (Hawaii Ass'n of Legal Assistants, August/September 1987).

[36]29 U.S.C.A. §§ 201 *et seq.* (1976).

[37]The Professional Employee Exemption:

■ Primary duty consists of work requiring knowledge of an advanced type in a field customarily acquired by a prolonged course of specialized intellectual instruction and study. (Such course of study means at least a baccalaureate degree or equivalent.)

■ Work requires the consistent exercise of judgment and discretion.

■ Work is predominantly intellectual and varied in character, as opposed to routine, mental or physical work.

The Administrative Employee Exemption:

■ The employee's primary duty consists of work related to management policies or general business operations.

■ The employee regularly exercises discretion and independent judgment.

The Executive Employee Exemption:

■ The employee's primary duty consists of work related to management policies or general business operations.

■ The employee regularly supervises two or more other employees. 29 C.F.R. part 541 (1983).

used to distinguish exempt from nonexempt employees are the actual job responsibilities of the employee, not the job title or compensation policy of the office.

■ ASSIGNMENT 4.16

(a) If you had a choice, would you want to receive overtime compensation as an entry-level paralegal?

(b) Surveys have shown that between twenty and forty percent of nonexempt paralegals today do *not* receive overtime compensation. Can you explain this startling fact?

Wage and Hour Division
United States Department of Labor
September 27, 1979

This is in further reply to your letter of July 12, 1979, . . . concerning the exempt status under section 13(a)(1) of the Fair Labor Standards Act of paralegal employees employed by your organization, . . .

The specific duties of the paralegal employees (all of which occur under an attorney's supervision) are interviewing clients; identifying and refining problems; opening, maintaining, and closing case files; acting as the liaison person between client and attorney; drafting pleadings and petitions, and answering petition, and interrogatories; filing pleadings and petitions; acting as general litigation assistant during court proceedings; digesting depositions, and preparing file profiles; conducting formal and informal hearings and negotiations; preparing and editing newsletters and leaflets for community development and public relations purposes; performing outreach services; coordinating general activities with relevant local, State, and Federal agencies; assisting in establishing and implementing community legal education programs; and working as a team with other employees to deliver quality legal services. You state that the job requires at least two years of college and/or equivalent experience.

[The Fair Labor Standards] Act provides a complete minimum wage and overtime pay exemption for any employee employed in a bona fide executive, administrative, or professional capacity . . . . An employee will qualify for exemption if all the pertinent tests relating to duties, responsibilities and salary . . . are met. In response to your first question, the paralegal employees you have in mind would not qualify for exemption as bona fide professional employees as discussed in section 541.3 of the regulations, since it is clear that their primary duty does not consist of work requiring knowledge of an advanced type in a field of science or learning customarily acquired by a prolonged course of specialized intellectual instruction and study, as distinguished from a general academic education and from an apprenticeship and from training in the performance of routine mental, manual, or physical processes.

With regard to the status of the paralegal employees as bona fide administrative employees, it is our opinion that their duties do not involve the exercise of discretion and independent judgment of the type required by section 541.2(b) of the regulations. The outline of their duties which you submit actually describes the use of skills rather than discretion and independent judgment. Under section 541.207 of the regulations, this requirement is interpreted as involving the comparison and evaluation of possible courses of conduct and acting or making a decision after the various possibilities have been considered. Furthermore, the term is interpreted to mean that the person has the authority or power to make an independent choice, free from immediate direction or supervision with respect to matters of significance.

The general facts presented about the employees here tend to indicate that they do not meet these criteria. Rather, as indicated above, they would appear to fit more appropriately into that category of employees who apply particular skills and knowledge in preparing assignments. Employees who merely apply knowledge in following prescribed procedures or determining whether specified standards have been met are not deemed to be exercising independent judgment, even if they have some leeway in reaching a conclusion. In addition, it should be noted that most jurisdictions have strict prohibitions against the unauthorized practice of law by lay persons. Under the American Bar Association's Code of Professional Responsibility, a delegation of legal tasks to a lay person is proper only if the lawyer maintains a direct relationship with the client, supervises the delegated work and has complete professional responsibility for the work produced. The implication of such strictures is that the paralegal employees you describe would probably not have the amount of authority to exercise independent judgment with regard to legal matters necessary to bring them within the administrative exemption. . . .

With regard to your [other] questions, all non-exempt employees, regardless of the amount of their wages, must be paid overtime premium pay of not less than one and one-half times their regular rates of pay for all hours worked in excess of 40 in a workweek. The fact that an employee did not obtain advanced approval to work the overtime does not relieve

the employer from complying with the overtime provisions of the Act.

We hope this satisfactorily responds to your inquiry. However, if you have any further questions concerning the application of the Fair Labor Standards Act to the situation you have in mind please do not hesitate to let us know.

Sincerely,

C. Lamar Johnson
Deputy Administrator

Section H. Tort Liability of Paralegals

Thus far we have discussed a number of ways that paralegal activities are or could be regulated:

- Criminal liability for violating the statutes on the unauthorized practice of law
- Special authorization rules on practice before administrative agencies and other tribunals
- Licensing
- Bar rules on paralegal education
- Self-regulation
- Labor laws

Finally, we come to *tort liability,* which is another method by which society defines what is and is not permissible. A tort is a private wrong or injury other than a breach of contract or the commission of a crime, although some breaches of contract and crimes can also constitute torts.

Two questions need to be kept in mind. First, when are paralegal employees *personally liable* for their torts? Second, when are employers *vicariously liable* for the torts of their paralegal employees? (As we will see, vicarious liability simply means being liable because of what someone else has done or failed to do.) The short answer to the first question is: *always*. The short answer to the second question is: *when the wrongdoing by the paralegal was within the scope of employment*. After covering both questions, we will then examine the separate question of when malpractice insurance will pay for such liability.

Several different kinds of wrongdoing are possible. The paralegal might commit:

- The tort of negligence
- An intentional tort, such as battery.
- An act which is both a crime (such as embezzlement) *and* an intentional tort (such as conversion).

A client who is injured by any of these torts can sue the paralegal in the same manner that a patient in a hospital can sue a nurse. Paralegals are not relieved of liability simply because they work for, and function under the supervision of, an attorney. Every citizen is *personally* liable for the torts he or she commits. The same is true of criminal liability.

Next we turn to the employers of paralegals. Are they *also* liable for wrong-doing committed by their paralegals? Assume that the supervising attorneys did nothing wrong themselves. For example, the attorney did not commit the tort or crime as an active participant with the paralegal, or the attorney was not careless in selecting and training the paralegal. Our question is: Can an attorney be liable to a client solely because of the wrongdoing of a paralegal? When such liability applies, it is called *vicarious liability,* which exists when one person is liable solely because of what someone else has done or failed to do. The answer to our question is found in the doctrine of *respondeat superior,* which makes employers responsible for the torts of their employees or agents when the wrongdoing occurs within the scope of employment.[38]

Hence, if a tort is committed by a paralegal within the scope of employ-ment, the client can sue the paralegal or the attorney, or both. This does not mean that the client recovers twice; there can be only one recovery for a tort. The client is simply given a choice in bringing the suit. In most cases, the pri-mary target of the client will be the employer, who is the so-called *deep pocket,* meaning the one who has resources from which a judgment can be satisfied.

Finally we need to examine what is meant by "scope of employment." Not every wrongdoing of a paralegal is within the scope of employment simply be-cause it is employment related. The test is as follows: Paralegals act within the scope of employment when they are furthering the business of their employer, which for our purposes is the practice of law. Slandering a client for failure to pay a law firm bill certainly furthers the business of the law firm. But the op-posite is probably true when a paralegal has an argument with a client over a football game and punches the client during their accidental evening meeting at a bar. In the latter example, the client could not sue the paralegal's employer for the intentional tort of battery under the doctrine of *respondeat supe-rior,* because the battery was not committed while furthering the business of the employer. Only the paralegal would be liable for the tort under such circumstances.

The most common tort committed by attorneys is negligence. This tort oc-curs when a client is injured because of a failure to use the ordinary skill, knowl-edge, and diligence normally possessed and used, under similar circumstances, by a member of the profession in good standing. In short, the tort is committed by failure to exercise the reasonable care expected of an attorney. An attorney is not, however, an insurer. Every mistake will not lead to negligence liability even if it causes harm to the client. The harm must be due to an unreasonable mistake, such as forgetting to file an action in court before the statute of limi-tations runs out.

When a paralegal commits negligence for which the attorney becomes liable under *respondeat superior,* the same standard applies. Since the work product of the paralegal blends into the work product of the supervising attorney, the attorney becomes as fully responsible for what the paralegal did as if the attor-ney had committed the negligence. Unreasonableness is measured by what a

---

[38]We are talking here of vicarious *civil* liability, or more specifically, the tort liability of employers because of the torts committed by their employees. Employers are not subject to vicarious *criminal* liability. If a paralegal commits a crime on the job, only the paralegal goes to jail (unless the em-ployer actually participated in the crime).

reasonable attorney would have done, not what a reasonable paralegal would have done.

There have not been many tort cases in which paralegals have been sued for wrongdoing in a law office. Yet as paralegals become more prominent in the practice of law, more are expected to be named as defendants. The most common kinds of cases involving paralegals have occurred when the paralegal was a notary and improperly notarized signatures under pressure from the supervising attorney.

■ ASSIGNMENT 4.17

Mary Smith is a paralegal at the XYZ law firm. One of her tasks is to file a document in court. She negligently forgets to do so. As a result, the client has a default judgment entered against her. What options are available to the client?

■ ASSIGNMENT 4.18

Go to the *American Digest System*. For information on this digest and its use, see pages 498 and 557. Give citations to and brief summaries of court cases on the topics listed in (a) and (b) below. Start with the Descriptive Word Index volumes of the most recent Decennial. After you check the appropriate key numbers (page 555) in that Decennial, check those key numbers in all the General Digest volumes that follow the most recent Decennial. Then check for case law in at least three other recent Decennials. Once you obtain citations to case law in the digest paragraphs, you do not have to go to the reporters to read the full text of the opinions. Simply give the citations you find and brief summaries of the cases as they are printed in the digest paragraphs.

(a) Cases, if any, dealing with the negligence of attorneys in the hiring and supervision of legal secretaries, law clerks, investigators, and paralegals. (If there are many, select any five cases.)

(b) Cases, if any, dealing with the negligence of doctors and/or hospitals in the hiring and supervision of nurses, paramedics, and other medical technicians. (If there are many, select any five cases.)

■ Section I. Malpractice Insurance

Legal *malpractice* generally refers to wrongful conduct by an attorney for which an injured party (the attorney's client) can receive damages. Just as doctors purchase malpractice insurance against suits by their patients, so too attorneys can buy such insurance to cover suits against them by their clients for alleged errors and omissions. We need to examine how paralegals fit into this picture.

Until the 1940s, not many attorneys bought malpractice insurance because suits by clients were relatively rare. Today, the picture has changed radically; cautious attorneys do not practice law without such insurance against their own malpractice. "Statistically, the new attorney will be subjected to three claims before finishing a legal career." [39] Hence, very few attorneys are willing to *go bare,*—that is, practice without insurance. This change has been due to a num-

---

[39] R. Mallen & J. Smith, *Legal Malpractice*, 3rd ed., 2 (1989).

FIGURE 4.7

Malpractice
Liability Claims
Against Attorneys

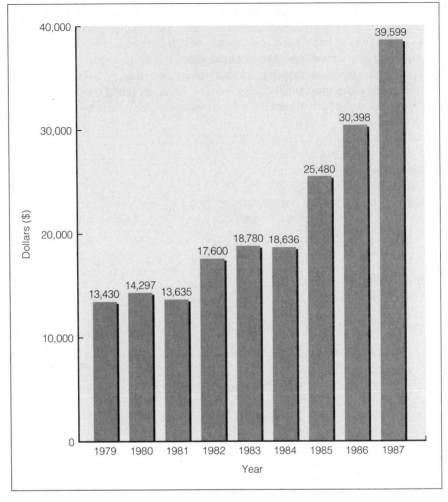

In 1979 the average claim paid, including all expenses, was $13,430. By 1987 this amount rose 295% to a new average of $39,599.

Source: St. Paul Fire & Marine Insurance Company

ber of factors. As the practice of law becomes more complex, the likelihood of error increases. Furthermore, the public is becoming more aware of its right to sue. In spite of disclaimers by attorneys that they are not guaranteeing any results, client expectations tend to be high, and hence clients are more likely to blame their attorney for an unfavorable result. And attorneys are increasingly willing to sue each other. In fact, some attorneys have developed a legal malpractice specialty in which they take clients who want to sue other attorneys. As malpractice awards against attorneys continue to rise (see Figure 4.7), the market for malpractice insurance has dramatically increased. And so has the cost. In some cities, the premium for insurance is over $6,000 per year per attorney.

There are two kinds of professional liability insurance policies covering attorney malpractice: occurrence policies and claims-made policies. An *occurrence policy* covers all occurrences (such as negligent error or omission) during the period the policy is in effect, even if the claim on such an occurrence is not actually filed until after the policy expires. Insurance companies are reluctant to write such policies because of the length of time it sometimes takes to uncover the existence of the negligent error or omission. Here's an example: An attorney makes a careless mistake in drafting a will that is not discovered until the person who hired the attorney dies many years later. Under an occurrence policy, the attorney is protected if the mistake occurred while the policy was in effect, even if the actual claim was not filed in court until after the policy terminated. The most common kind of policy sold by insurance companies today is the *claims-made policy* under which coverage is limited to claims actually filed (made) during the period in which the policy is in effect.[40]

Malpractice policies usually cover all the attorneys *and* the nonattorney employees of the law office. One policy, for example, defines the individuals covered—"the insured"—as follows:

> The insured includes the firm, all lawyers within the firm, and all non-lawyer employees, as well as former partners, officers, directors and employees solely while they acted on behalf of the insured firm.[41]

Such inclusion of employees is not always automatic, however. The policies of some insurance companies do not include paralegals or secretaries unless the law firm specifically requests coverage for them and pays an additional premium for their inclusion. Paralegals should therefore ask their employers if their malpractice policy explicitly covers paralegals.

What about freelance or independent paralegals who sell their services to attorneys? Although they may not be considered employees of the firm, they will usually be covered under the firm's policy in the same manner as full-time, in-house paralegal employees. So long as the employing attorney supervises and is responsible for the conduct of the paralegal, the malpractice policy usually provides coverage. In the language of one widely used policy, coverage is provided for "any other person for whose acts, errors or omissions the insured is legally responsible,"[42] which would include freelance paralegals.

Nevertheless, some freelance paralegals have explored the possibility of obtaining their own malpractice insurance policies. To date, most traditional insurance companies have not made such policies available, although there are exceptions. Complete Equity Markets, Inc., for example, offers "Paralegals Professional Indemnity Insurance" as a claims-made policy. For approximately $1,800 a year, a paralegal can purchase $250,000 worth of malpractice insurance. Since most paralegals work for an attorney and are already covered under the attorney's policy, few paralegals have purchased their own policy. Yet if paralegals are eventually granted a form of limited license that authorizes them to sell their services directly to the public, separate paralegal malpractice policies will become common and may even be mandated as a condition of receiving the license.[43]

---

[40]It is possible for a claims-made policy to cover a negligent error or omission that took place *before* the effective date of the policy, but most companies exclude coverage for prepolicy claims that the attorney knows about or could have reasonably foreseen at the time the policy is applied for.

[41]Home Insurance Companies, Professional Liability Insurance.

[42]American Home Assurance Company, Lawyers Professional Liability Policy.

[43]As we saw earlier, most Enrolled Agents are nonlawyers who are authorized to provide certain tax services to the public. The National Association of Enrolled Agents offers a "Professional Liability Insurance Plan" through the St. Paul Fire and Marine Insurance Company. The Association's brochure says, "You can now secure protection against an unexpected lawsuit or penalty for damages arising from services you provide as an Enrolled Agent." Attorneys are not eligible to purchase this insurance.

☐ Chapter Summary

Criminal prosecution may result from violating statutes on the unauthorized practice of law. In general, they prohibit nonattorneys from appearing for another in a representative capacity, drafting legal documents, and giving legal advice. Nonattorneys can sell forms and other legal materials but cannot give individual help in using them.

There are some major exceptions to the prohibitions on nonattorney conduct. In a limited number of circumstances, nonattorneys are authorized to do what would otherwise constitute the unauthorized practice of law. For example:

- In most states, a real estate broker can draft sales contracts.

- Several specialized courts allow nonattorneys to represent clients in court, although this is rare.

- A few states allow paralegals to "appear" in court to request a continuance or a new date for the next hearing in a case.

- An inmate can "practice law" in prison—for example, he or she can draft court documents for and give legal advice to another inmate if the prison does not offer adequate alternative methods of providing legal services.

- Many administrative agencies, particularly at the federal level, allow nonattorneys to represent clients before the agencies.

A number of states have considered broad-based licensing (which would cover all activities of all paralegals), and limited licensing (which would cover specified activities of those paralegals, often called legal technicians, who are not supervised by attorneys). To date, neither kind of licensing has been enacted. Relatively soon, however, a limited-license requirement will probably be enacted in one or two states. While this would be a dramatic event, it would affect very few paralegals, since limited licensing would not apply to paralegals who work for attorneys.

All paralegal schools in the country must be licensed by their state. There is no requirement that they be accredited by the bar association. The American Bar Association, however, has an "approval" process whereby a school can be approved by the ABA.

A number of bar associations allow paralegals to become associate or affiliate members. For example, the American Bar Association has a membership category called Legal Assistant Associate.

Certification has been a major point of disagreement between the National Association of Legal Assistants (NALA) and the National Federation of Paralegal Associations (NFPA). NALA has instituted a national test that leads to certification as a Certified Legal Assistant (CLA). Even though this is a voluntary program, NFPA opposes its very existence.

The Fair Labor Standards Act requires employers to pay overtime compensation to employees unless they function in an executive, administrative, or professional capacity. Paralegal managers with major responsibility for the supervision of other paralegals would fall within one of the exceptions, and hence would not be entitled to overtime compensation. All other paralegals, however, do not fall within an exception and therefore must be paid overtime compensation.

If a paralegal commits a tort, such as negligence, he or she is personally liable to the defendant. Under the theory of *respondeat superior*, the supervising attorney is also liable for the wrong committed by the paralegal if it occurred within the scope of employment. Most attorneys have a claims-made malpractice insurance policy that covers their employees.

Key Terms

accreditation	limited licensure	treaties
approval	specialty licensure	certified domestic violence
certification	registration	advocate
certified	regulation	ex parte order
certificated	practice of law	jailhouse lawyer
ethics	unauthorized practice of law	writ writer
guideline	authorized practice of law	*Johnson v. Avery*
licensure	statement of principles	Administrative Procedure Act

registered agent
agency practitioner
enrolled agent
supremacy clause
page 52 debate
legal technician
licensed independent
     paralegal
HALT
limited practice officer
pro bono
prepaid legal services
legal insurance
approval commission

antitrust
monopoly
associate members
affiliate members
attorney attestation
CLA
CLAS
CFLA
specialty certification
legal assistant division
entry-level certification
advanced certification
GOD
Fair Labor Standards Act

overtime compensation
Wage and Hour Division
exempt paralegal
nonexempt paralegal
tort liability
personal liability
vicarious liability
respondeat superior
deep pocket
malpractice
go bare
occurrence policy
claims-made policy

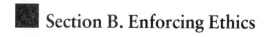

5

Attorney Ethics and Paralegal Ethics

■ Chapter Outline

■ Section A. The Ten Commandments of an Ethical Conservative

When it comes to ethics, *a paralegal must be conservative.* To an ethical conservative, the question is not, "What can I get away with?" but rather, "What is the right thing to do?" With this guideline in mind, we will examine many ethical principles in this chapter. Some of the most important are presented in Figure 5.1.

■ Section B. Enforcing Ethics

1. Ethics and Sanctions

Ethics are rules that embody standards of behavior to which members of an organization must conform. The organization is often an association of individuals in the same occupation—for example, attorneys, paralegals, stockbrokers, or accountants. The ethical rules of some organizations are enforced by *sanctions.* A sanction is any penalty or punishment imposed for unaccepta-

FIGURE 5.1

Paralegal Ethics:
The Ten
Commandments of
a Conservative

---

1. Know the ethical rules governing attorneys. If you understand when attorneys are vulnerable to charges of unprofessional conduct, you will be better able to help them avoid such charges.

2. Know the ethical rules governing paralegals. At the start of your paralegal career, promise yourself that you will adhere to rigorous standards of professional ethics, even if these standards are higher than those followed by people around you.

3. Never tell anyone who is not working on a case anything about that case. This includes your best friend, your spouse, and your relative.

4. Assume that people outside your office do not have a clear understanding of what a paralegal or legal assistant is. Make sure that everyone with whom you come in contact (clients, attorneys, court officials, agency officials, the public) understand that you are not an attorney.

5. Know what legal advice is and refuse to be coaxed into giving it, no matter how innocent the question asked of you appears to be.

6. Never make contact with an opposing party in a legal dispute, or with anyone closely associated with that party, unless you have the permission of your supervising attorney and of the attorney for the opposing party, if the latter has one.

7. Don't sign your name to anything if you are not certain that what you are signing is 100% accurate and that the law allows a paralegal to sign it.

8. Never pad your time sheets. Insist that what you submit is 100% accurate.

9. Know the common rationalizations for misrepresentation and other unethical conduct:

   ■ it's always done

   ■ the other side does it

   ■ the cause of our client is just

   ■ if I don't do it, I will jeopardize my job.

   Promise yourself that you will not allow any of these rationalizations to entice you to participate in misrepresentation or other unethical conduct.

10. If what you are asked to do doesn't feel right, don't proceed until it does.

---

ble conduct.[1] Other organizations, however, have ethical rules that are not tied to any system of enforcement.

All of the major national paralegal associations have adopted ethical rules, as we shall see later in the chapter. But none are enforced by sanctions. No paralegal, for example, has ever been thrown out of a paralegal association for unethical conduct. It could happen, but it is unlikely since it is very expensive to establish and operate an enforcement system. Paralegal associations simply do not have the resources that would be required.

Attorneys, on the other hand, *are* subject to enforceable ethical rules. These rules attempt to govern everything an attorney does in the practice of law. Of course, one of the things an attorney does is employ paralegals. Hence, as we will see, there are rules on how an attorney can use paralegals ethically. Unethical use of paralegals can subject the attorney to sanctions.

2. Paralegals and Attorney Ethics

Can a paralegal *also* be sanctioned for violating these ethical rules? No. The rules govern attorney conduct only.[2] Since paralegals cannot join a bar associ-

---

[1]Another meaning of the word sanction is to authorize or to give formal approval. Example: the court *sanctioned* the payment of attorney fees.

[2]Remarkably, there is one jurisdiction—the District of Columbia—that allows a nonattorney to become a full owner/partner of a law firm! This individual must agree to abide by the ethical code that governs attorneys. In D.C., therefore, the ethical rules governing attorneys *do* apply to nonattorneys. (The first nonattorney to become a partner of a law firm was an accountant.)

ation as full members, they cannot be sanctioned by a bar association or by any other agency set up to monitor attorney conduct. Serious wrongdoing by paralegals may result in their being fired and might subject them to negligence suits or to criminal prosecution (as we saw in Chapter 4,) but they cannot be punished for unethical conduct by the entity that regulates attorneys.

This does not mean, however, that paralegals can ignore the ethical rules governing attorneys. Quite the contrary. *One of the paralegal's primary responsibilities is to help an attorney avoid being charged with unethical conduct.* (A recent seminar conducted by the Los Angeles Paralegal Association was entitled "Law Firm Ethics: How to Keep Your Attorneys off '60 Minutes'!") Hence, the paralegal must be intimately familiar with ethical rules. Our goal in this chapter is to provide you with that familiarity.

3. Courts, Legislatures, and Bar Associations

In most states, the regulation of attorneys is primarily under the control of the highest court in the state (often called the Supreme Court), which determines when an attorney can be granted a license to practice law and under what conditions the license will be taken away or suspended because of unethical conduct. Since the state legislature may also exert some regulatory authority over attorneys, a dispute occasionally arises over which branch of government can control a particular aspect of the practice of law. The judiciary often wins this dispute and becomes the final authority. In practice, however, the judicial branch and the legislative branch usually share regulatory jurisdiction over the practice of law, with the dominant branch being the judiciary. The day-to-day functions of regulation are delegated to an entity such as a state bar association and a disciplinary board or grievance commission.

There are three kinds of bar associations:

- National (for example, American Bar Association, Association of Trial Lawyers of America, Hispanic National Bar Association)
- State (for example, Illinois State Bar Association, State Bar of Montana) and
- Local (for example, Boston Bar Association, San Diego County Bar Association).

All national and local bar associations are voluntary; no attorney is required to be a member. The majority of state bar associations in the country are *integrated,* which simply means that membership is required as a condition of practicing law in the state. (Integrated bar associations are also referred to as *mandatory* or *unified* bar associations. See Figure 5.2.) There is a state bar association in every state. Most, but not all, are mandatory.

Under the general supervision of the state's highest court, the state bar association has a large role in regulating most aspects of the practice of law. For example, dues charged by integrated bar associations are used to fund the state's system of enforcing ethical rules. States that do not have integrated bar associations often have a *registration* requirement. Each attorney in the state registers to practice law and pays a registration fee that is used to fund that state's system of enforcing the ethical rules. Even in these states, the state bar association has a great influence over the regulation of attorneys. Given this dominant role of bar associations, the method of regulating attorneys in America is essentially that of self-regulation: attorneys regulating attorneys.[3]

---

[3]This is so even in states that allow nonattorneys to serve on boards or commissions that regulate an aspect of the legal profession.

FIGURE 5.2

States with Unified
Bar Associations
(1991)

Alabama	Idaho	Montana	North Dakota	Utah
Alaska	Kentucky	Nebraska	Oklahoma	Virginia
Arizona	Louisiana	Nevada	Oregon	Washington
California	Michigan	New Hampshire	South Carolina	West Virginia
Florida	Mississippi	New Mexico	South Dakota	Wisconsin
Georgia	Missouri	North Carolina	Texas	Wyoming

There is no national set of ethical rules that applies to every state. Each state can adopt its own rules to regulate the attorneys licensed in that state. The rules are found in documents with various names, such as code of ethics, canons of ethics, code of professional responsibility, model rules. In fact, however, there is considerable similarity in the rules that the states have adopted. The reason for this similarity is the influence of the American Bar Association.

As indicated, the American Bar Association is a voluntary national bar association; no attorney must belong to it. Yet approximately 55% of the attorneys in America do belong to the ABA. It publishes ethical rules but does *not* discipline attorneys for unethical conduct. The role of the ABA in this area is to write ethical rules and to *propose* to the individual states that they be accepted. A state is free to adopt, modify, or reject them. The current recommendation of the ABA is found in a document called the *Model Rules of Professional Conduct*.[4] This document has been very influential throughout the country. Many states adopted it with relatively minor changes.

4. Accusation of Unethical Conduct

When an attorney is charged with unethical conduct, the case is investigated by a disciplinary body appointed by the state's highest court. The name

---

[4]The *Model Rules of Professional Conduct* is a 1983 revision of the ABA's *Model Code of Professional Responsibility*. The latter document consists of three main parts. First, there are nine *canons*, which are general statements of norms that express the standards of professional conduct expected of attorneys. Second, and more important, there are *disciplinary rules* (abbreviated DR), which are mandatory statements of the minimum conduct below which no attorney can fall without being subject to disciplinary action. Third, there are *ethical considerations* (abbreviated EC) which represent the objectives toward which each member of the profession should strive.

for this body differs from state to state, e.g., the Grievance Commission, the Attorney Registration and Disciplinary Commission, the Committee on Professional Conduct, the Board of Professional Responsibility.

A hearing is held to determine whether unethical conduct was committed by the accused attorney. The commission, committee, or board then makes its recommendation to the state's highest court which makes the final determination of whether to accept this recommendation. A number of sanctions can be imposed by the Court. See Figure 5.3.

Section C. The Ethical Rules

We turn now to an overview of specific ethical rules that apply to attorneys. Where appropriate, a paralegal perspective on the rules will be presented. At the end of the overview, there will be a more concentrated focus on paralegals, particularly on ethical issues not covered earlier in the chapter. The overview is based on the ABA *Model Rules of Professional Conduct.* The rule numbers used in the discussion (such as Model Rule 1.5) refer to these *Model Rules,* which will either be quoted or summarized.

1. Competence

An attorney shall provide competent representation to a client. Model Rule 1.1

A *competent* attorney uses the *knowledge* and *skill* that are reasonably necessary to represent a particular client. What is reasonably necessary depends on the complexity of the case. A great deal of knowledge and skill, for example, may be needed when representing a corporate client accused of complicated antitrust violations.

How do attorneys obtain this knowledge and skill? They draw on the general principles of legal analysis and legal research learned in law school. But more importantly, they take the time needed to *prepare* themselves. They spend time in the law library. They talk with their colleagues. In some instances, they formally associate themselves with more experienced attorneys in the area. Attorneys who fail to take these steps are acting unethically if their failure means that they do not have the knowledge and skill reasonably necessary to represent a particular client.

Some attorneys have so many clients that they could not possibly give proper attention to each. Always looking for more lucrative work, they run the risk of neglecting the clients they already have. As a consequence, they might miss court dates or other filing deadlines, lose documents, fail to determine what law governs a client's case, etc. Such an attorney is practicing law "from the hip"—incompetently and unethically.

> Example: Mary Henderson, Esq. has a large criminal law practice. She agrees to probate the estate of a client's deceased son. She has never handled such a case before. Five years go by. No progress is made in determining who is entitled to receive the estate. If some minimal legal research had been done, Henderson would have been able to close the case within six months of taking it.

Henderson has probably acted unethically. The failure to do basic research on a case is a sign of incompetence. The need for such research is clear in view

FIGURE 5.3

Attorney Sanctions
for Unethical
Conduct

DISBARMENT:	The termination of the right to practice law. The disbarment can be permanent or temporary. If it's temporary, the attorney will be allowed to apply for readmission after a designated period.
SUSPENSION:	The removal of an attorney from the practice of law for a specified minimum period, after which the attorney can apply for reinstatement. An *interim suspension* is a temporary suspension pending the imposition of final discipline.
REPRIMAND:	A public declaration that the attorney's conduct was improper. This does not affect his or her right to practice. Reprimand is also called *censure* or *public censure*.
ADMONITION:	A nonpublic declaration that the attorney's conduct was improper. The mildest form of punishment that can be imposed, it does not affect his or her right to practice. An admonition is also known as a *private reprimand*.
PROBATION:	Allowing the attorney to continue to practice but under specified conditions, such as submitting to periodic audits of client funds controlled by the attorney or making restitution to a client whose funds were wrongly taken by the attorney.

of the fact that she has never handled a probate case before. Either she must take the time to find out how to probate the estate, or she must contact another attorney with probate experience and arrange to work with this attorney on the case. Not doing either is unethical.

The vast majority of graduates of law schools need a good deal of on-the-job study and guidance before they are ready to handle cases of any complexity. A law school education does little more than help ensure that the attorney is equipped to go out and *continue* learning through experience and legal research. A good attorney is always learning the law—long after law school is over. The first day on the job for new attorneys is often a very nervous event because they are acutely aware of how much they do *not* know.

In addition to sanctions for unethical conduct, an attorney's incompetence may have other consequences as well. The client might try to sue the attorney for negligence in a legal malpractice case. (Such suits were discussed in Chapter 4.) If the client is a criminal defendant who was convicted, he or she may try to appeal the conviction on the ground that the attorney's incompetence amounted to a denial of the effective "Assistance of Counsel" guaranteed by the 6th Amendment of the U.S. Constitution.

Paralegal Perspective:

- "An attorney who utilizes a legal assistant's services is responsible for determining that the legal assistant is competent to perform the tasks assigned, based on the legal assistant's education, training, and experience . . . ."[5] While the attorney has this supervisory responsibility, paralegals also have a responsibility to maintain their own competence.

- If you are given assignments that are beyond your knowledge and skill, let your supervisor know. Either you must be given training with close supervision, or you must be given other assignments. A "lawyer should explain to

---

[5]ABA Standing Committee on Legal Assistants, *Model Guidelines for the Utilization of Legal Assistant Services,* Draft, Comment to Guideline 1 (March 1991). (Hereinafter cited as ABA *Model Guidelines.*)

the legal assistant that the legal assistant has a duty to inform the lawyer of any assignment which the assistant regards as beyond his capability." [6]

■ After you complete an assignment, look for an opportunity to ask your supervisor how you could have improved your performance on the assignment. Do not wait for a year-end evaluation to learn what you can do to become a more competent paralegal.

■ Find out which attorneys, administrators, paralegals, and secretaries in the office have a reputation for explaining things well. Spend time with such individuals even if you do not work with them on a daily basis. Take them to lunch. Find time to sit with them on a coffee break. Ask lots of questions. Let them know you respect high-quality work and appreciate anything they can tell you to help you increase your competence.

■ Take the initiative in continuing your formal paralegal education after you are employed. Do not wait for someone to suggest further training. Find out what seminars and conferences are being conducted by paralegal associations and bar associations in your area. Attend those that are relevant to your job even if you must pay for them yourself.

2. Diligence/Unwarranted Delay

An attorney shall act with reasonable diligence and promptness in representing a client. Model Rule 1.3

An attorney must make reasonable efforts to expedite litigation. Model Rule 3.2

Angry clients often complain that attorneys take forever to complete a case, and keep clients in the dark about what is happening. "He never answers my calls." "It took months to file the case in court." "He keeps telling me that everything is fine, but nothing ever gets done." Such complaints do not necessarily indicate unethical behavior by the attorney. Events may be beyond the control of the attorney. For example, the court calendar is crowded, the other side is not responding. Yet this does not excuse a lack of regular communication with clients to keep them reasonably informed about the status of their case.

Other explanations for a lack of diligence and promptness, however, are more serious:

■ The attorney is disorganized. The law office has not developed adequate systems to process cases. The delays are due to careless mistakes and a lack of skill.

■ The attorney is taking many more cases than the office can handle. Additional personnel should be hired to do the needed work, or new cases should not be accepted.

Often, the failure to use reasonable diligence and promptness causes harm to the client. For example, the attorney neglects to file a suit before the statute of limitations has run against the client. Unreasonable procrastination, however, can be unethical even if such harm does not result.

Another problem is the attorney who intentionally seeks numerous delays in an effort to try to wear the other side down. It is unethical to engage in such

---

[6]Section 20–110, Committee Commentary, *New Mexico Rules Governing the Practice of Law* (Judicial Pamphlet 16).

dilatory practices. Attorneys must use reasonable efforts to expedite litigation, consistent with protecting the interests of their clients.

Paralegal Perspective:

- An overloaded attorney probably works with an overloaded paralegal. Successful paralegals often take the initiative by asking for additional work. But reason must prevail. If you have more work than you can handle, you must let your supervisor know. Otherwise, you might be contributing to the problem of undue procrastination.

- Learn everything you can about office systems. Find out how they are created. (See Chapter 3.) After you have gained some experience in the office, you should start designing systems on your own initiative.

- When a busy attorney is in court or cannot be disturbed because of pressing work on another case, someone in the office should be available to communicate with clients who want to know the status of their case. In many offices, the paralegal is in a position to provide this information. The role is delicate, however, since in addition to asking about the status of their case, clients often asks questions that call for legal advice. Giving such advice may constitute the unauthorized practice of law. Later we will examine in greater depth the temptations and pressures on a paralegal to give legal advice.

3. Fees

An attorney's fee shall be reasonable. Model Rule 1.5(a)

There is no absolute standard to determine when a fee is excessive and therefore unreasonable. A number of factors must be considered: the amount of time and labor involved, the complexity of the case, the experience and reputation of the attorney, the customary fee in the locality for the same kind of case, etc.

> Examples: In 1979, a court ruled that $500 an hour was excessive in a simple battery case involving a guilty plea and no unusual issues. In 1984, a court ruled that a fee of $22,500 was excessive in an uncomplicated real estate case involving very little time. The case was settled through the efforts of someone other than the attorney.

The basis of the fee should be communicated to the client before or soon after the attorney starts to work on the case. This is often done in the contract of employment called a *retainer.*[7]

At one time, bar associations published a list of "recommended fees" that should be charged for designated kinds of services. These *minimum-fee schedules* have now been prohibited by the United States Supreme Court. They constitute illegal price fixing by the bar in violation of the antitrust laws.

Contingent fees can sometimes present ethical problems. A contingent fee is a fee that is dependent on the outcome of the case. (Other kinds of fees will be examined in Chapter 14.)

---

[7]Another meaning of the word *retainer* is the amount of money or other assets that will serve as an advance payment for services. Depending on the agreement reached, the retainer may or may not be refundable in the event that the attorney-client relationship ends before all the legal services are performed.

> Example: An attorney signs a retainer to represent a client in an automobile negligence case. If the jury awards the client damages, the attorney will receive 30% of the award. If the client loses the case, the attorney receives no fee.

This is a contingent fee since it is dependent on the outcome of the negligence case.

The benefit of a contingent fee is that it provides an incentive for an attorney to take the case of a client who does not have funds to pay an attorney while the case is pending. But contingent fees are not ethical in every case, even if the amount to be received by the successful attorney is otherwise reasonable. A contingent fee in a criminal case, and in most divorce cases, for example, is unethical.

> Example: Gabe Farrell is a client of Sam Grondon, Esq. in a criminal case where Gabe is charged with murder. Gabe agrees to pay Grondon $100,000 if he is found innocent. Grondon will receive nothing if Gabe is convicted of any crime.

This fee agreement is unethical. Contingent fees are not allowed in criminal cases. Note the pressures on Grondon. He arguably has no incentive to try to negotiate a guilty plea to a lesser charge, since such a plea would mean a conviction and, hence, no fee. In such a situation, the attorney's own personal interest (obtaining the $100,000) could conflict with the interest of the client (receiving a lesser penalty through a negotiated plea). Similar pressures can arise in family-law cases.

> Example: To obtain a divorce from his wife, a client hires an attorney. The fee is $25,000 if the divorce is granted.

As the case develops, suppose there is a glimmer of hope that the husband and wife might reconcile. Hence, the attorney's interest (obtaining the $25,000) could conflict with the interest of the client (reconciling). This might lead the attorney to discourage the reconciliation or to set up roadblocks to it. Reconciliation obviously removes the possibility of the contingency—obtaining the divorce—from occurring. In family law cases, therefore, contingent fees are unethical if the fee is dependent on securing a divorce, on the amount of alimony obtained, on the amount of support obtained, or on the amount of a property settlement in lieu of alimony or support. Model Rule 1.5(d). This is so even if the terms of the contingent fee are otherwise reasonable.

One final theme should be covered: *fee splitting*. The splitting or division of a fee refers to a single client bill covering the fee of two or more attorneys who are not in the same firm.

> Example: John Jones, Esq. is hired by a singer who is charging her record company with copyright infringement and breach of contract. Jones calls in Randy Smith, Esq., a specialist in copyright law from another firm. Both work on the case. The singer receives one bill for the work of both attorneys even though they work for different law firms.

The attorneys are splitting or dividing the fee between them.[8] This arrangement is proper under certain conditions. For example, the total fee must be reasonable, and the client must be told about the participation of all the attorneys and not object.

Suppose, however, that the attorney splits the fee with a nonattorney.

---

[8]The attorney who refers a case to another attorney receives what is called a *referral fee* or *forwarding fee* from the latter.

> Example: Frank Martin is a freelance investigator. He refers accident victims to a law firm. For every client he refers to the firm, he receives 25% of the fee collected by the firm.

> Example: Helen Gregson is a chiropractor. She refers medical malpractice cases to a law firm which compensates her for each referral.

These are improper divisions of fees with nonattorneys—even if the amount of the division is reasonable and the clients brought in by Martin or Gregson consent to their receiving a part of the fee. An attorney cannot share with a nonattorney a portion of a fee paid by particular clients. The rationale behind this prohibition is that the nonattorney might exercise some control over the attorney and thereby jeopardize the attorney's independent judgment.

For the same reason, an attorney cannot form a partnership with a nonattorney if any of the activities of the partnership consist of the practice of law. If the office practices law as a corporation, a nonattorney cannot own any interest in the company or be a director or officer.[9]

Paralegal Perspective:

- An attorney or law firm may include paralegals and other nonattorney employees in a compensation or retirement plan, even though the plan is based in whole or in part on a profit-sharing arrangement. Model Rule 5.4(a)(3).

  > Example: Frank is a paralegal at a law firm. The firm has a retirement plan under which the firm contributes a portion of its profits into the plan. Frank is a member of this retirement plan.

  The firm is not acting unethically. In most states, paralegals can receive compensation and retirement benefits that are based on the fees received by the firm so long as they are not receiving all or part of *particular* legal fees. "The linchpin of the prohibition [against splitting fees with a legal assistant] seems to be the advance agreement of the lawyer to 'split' a fee based on a pre-existing contingent arrangement. There is no general prohibition against a lawyer who enjoys a particularly profitable period recognizing the contribution of the legal assistant to that profitability with a discretionary bonus. Likewise, a lawyer engaged in a particularly profitable specialty of legal practice is not prohibited from compensating the legal assistant who aids materially in that practice more handsomely than the compensation generally awarded to legal assistants in that geographic area who work in law practices that are less lucrative. Indeed, any effort to fix a compensation level for legal assistants and prohibit greater compensation would appear to violate the federal antitrust laws."[10]

- A related restriction in many states is that an attorney cannot give a paralegal any compensation for referring business to the attorney. "It appears clear that a legal assistant may not be compensated on a contingent basis for a particular case or paid for 'signing up' clients for a legal practice."[11]

---

[9]Wolfram, C., *Modern Legal Ethics,* § 9.2.4 (1986). In the District of Columbia, however, where nonattorneys are allowed to be owner-partners in law firms, nonattorneys can obviously share legal fees with attorneys. See footnote 2.

[10]ABA *Model Guidelines,* Comment to Guideline 9, see footnote 5.

[11]Ibid.

- Attorneys must not allow their paralegals to accept cases, to reject cases, or to "set fees." The responsibility "for establishing the amount of a fee to be charged for a legal service" may not be delegated to a paralegal.[12]

- "A lawyer may include a charge for the work performed by a legal assistant in setting a charge for legal services." [13] As we saw in Chapter 1, most attorneys bill clients for paralegal time. Paralegals record their time on time sheets that become the basis of bills sent to clients. The amount that an attorney bills for paralegal time must be reasonable. Reasonableness is determined by a number of factors, such as the experience of the paralegal, the nature of the tasks the paralegal undertakes, and the market rate for paralegals in the area.

- *Double billing* must be avoided. The paralegal's time should not have already been figured into the attorney's hourly rate. Some states ask the attorney to submit an affidavit to support the amount claimed for the paralegal's time. The affidavit must give a detailed statement of the time spent and services rendered by the paralegal, a summary of the paralegal's qualifications, etc. In New Mexico, the attorney must disclose to the client the amount to be charged for the services of the paralegals in the office.

- As a paralegal, your time records should be contemporaneous, that is, made at approximately the same time as the events you are recording. Try to avoid recording time long after you perform tasks that require time records.

- Time sheets must also be accurate; padding is clearly unethical. Padding occurs when someone records time that was not in fact spent. When a client is billed on the basis of time sheets that have been padded, fraud has been committed. Padding is a serious problem in the practice of law:

  > [It] occurs most typically when attorneys are under the gun to bill a large number of hours. Everyone knows of lawyers who begin work at 8:00, leave the office at 6:00 and yet bill 10 hours a day—a feat that utterly amazes me. Whether it be eating lunch, talking to a spouse, working with support staff, reading advance sheets or just taking a break, some portion of every day is spent on non-billable matters. [A young Midwestern associate at a medium-sized firm says] padding or fabrication of entries is encouraged, or at the very least tolerated, at his firm, and many others, to judge from his friends' experiences. The pressure to pad is intense.[14]

  Unfortunately, paralegals can find themselves under a similar pressure, which, of course, should be resisted.

  > One of the most common temptations that can corrupt a paralegal's ethics is to inflate billable hours, since there is often immense pressure in law firms to bill high hours for job security and upward mobility. Such "creative billing" is not humorous; it's both morally wrong and illegal. It's also fraudulent and a plain and simple case of theft.[15]

---

[12]ABA *Model Guidelines,* Guideline 3(b), see footnote 5.

[13]ABA *Model Guidelines,* Guideline 8, see footnote 5.

[14]Doe, *Billing: Is "Padding" Widespread?,* 76 American Bar Ass'n Journal 42 (December 1990).

[15]Smith, *AAfPE National Conference Highlights,* 8 Legal Assistant Today 103 (January/February 1991).

4. Crime or Fraud by an Attorney

An attorney must not engage in criminal or fraudulent conduct. Model Rule 8.4

Sadly, it is not uncommon for an attorney to be charged with criminal conduct, such as theft of client funds, *insider trading* and securities fraud, falsifying official documents, or tax fraud. Since such conduct obviously affects the attorney's fitness to practice law, sanctions for unethical conduct can be imposed in addition to prosecution in a criminal court. Once an attorney is convicted of a serious crime in court, a separate disciplinary proceeding is often instituted to suspend or disbar the attorney for unethical conduct growing out of the same incident.

Paralegal Perspective:

- Value your integrity above all else. A paralegal in Oklahoma offers the following advice: "Insist on the highest standards for yourself and for your employer. One small ethical breach can lead to a series of compromises with enormous" disciplinary and "legal malpractice consequences." [16]

- If your supervisor is charged with criminal conduct, the chances are good that you will be questioned by prosecutors, and you might become a suspect yourself.

- In the highly charged, competitive environment of a law office, there are attorneys who are willing to violate the law in the interest of winning. Be sensitive to the overt and subtle pressures on you to participate in such violations. Talk with other paralegals who have encountered this problem. Don't sit in silence. If there is no one in the office with whom you can frankly discuss the elimination of these pressures, you must consider quitting. (See Section F of this chapter.)

- Paralegals who are also notaries are sometimes asked by their supervisors to notarize documents that should *not* be notarized. In fact, paralegals "are most often named as defendants for false notarization of a signature." [17] Such acts may not be covered in malpractice liability insurance policies since they are intentional acts. Be extremely cautious of what you are asked to sign.

- At some law firms, employees have succumbed to the temptation of using a "hot tip" that crosses their path in a corporate takeover case.[18] Assume that Company X is planning to merge with Company Y. The news is not yet public. When it does become public, the value of the stock in Company X is expected to rise dramatically. You work at a law firm that represents Company X and you find out about the planned merger while at work. If you buy stock in Company X before the announcement of the merger, you would benefit from the increased value of the stock that would result after the announcement. This might be an illegal use of inside information. In a dramatic recent case, a paralegal who worked at a securities law firm in Boston was charged with insider trading by the Securities and Exchange Com-

---

[16]Tulsa Ass'n of Legal Assistants, *Hints for Helping Your Attorney Avoid Legal Malpractice,* TALA Times (August 1989).

[17]Race, *Malpractice Maladies,* Paradigm 12 (Baltimore Ass'n of Legal Assistants, July/August 1989).

[18]Milford, *Law Firms Expected to Take Steps to Avert Insider Trading Scandals,* The News Journal D3 (October 16, 1989).

mission (SEC). While working on a case involving a proposed merger, she learned certain information which she gave to outside investors who used it to make illegal profits in the stock market. The story made national news. One headline read, "SEC Says Boston Paralegal Gave Tip Worth $823,471." Soon after the incident, she was fired. All employees of law firms must be extremely careful. Innocently buying stock as a personal investment could turn into a nightmare. One attorney "recommends that any paralegal who would like to buy or sell securities should check first with a corporate attorney in the firm to see if the firm represents the issuer or a company negotiating with the issuer. If it does, an accusation of 'insider trading' might later be made." [19] The same caution applies when a member of the paralegal's immediate family buys or sells such securities.

- Another problem area is the use of so-called *pirated software*. Many businesses buy one copy of computer software and then copy it so that other employees in the office can use it on other terminals. This is illegal, and can subject violators to fines and other criminal penalties.

- In all aspects of your career as a paralegal, adopt the motto, "If it doesn't feel right, it probably isn't."

5. Crime or Fraud by a Client

An attorney shall not counsel a client to engage in conduct the attorney knows is criminal or fraudulent. Model Rule 1.2(d)

The client hires the attorney and controls the purpose of the attorney-client relationship. Furthermore, the client is entitled to know the legal consequences of any action he or she is contemplating. This does not mean, however, that the attorney must do whatever the client wants.

Example: The president of a corporation hires Leo Richards, Esq. to advise the company on how to dump toxic waste into a local river.

Note that the president has not asked Richards *if* the dumping is legal. It would be perfectly ethical for Richards to answer such a question. In the example, the president asks *how* to dump. If Richards feels that the dumping can legally take place, he can so advise the president. Suppose, however, that it is clear to Richards that the dumping would violate the federal or state criminal code. Under such circumstances, it would be unethical for Richards to advise the president on how to proceed with the dumping. The same would be true if the president wanted help in filing an environmental statement that misrepresented the intentions of the company. Such an application would be fraudulent, and an attorney must not help someone commit what the attorney knows is fraudulent conduct.

When attorneys are later charged with unethical conduct in such cases, their defense is often that they did not know the conduct proposed by the client was criminal or fraudulent. If the law applicable to the client's case is unclear, an attorney can make a good faith effort to find a legal way for the client to achieve his or her objective. The point at which the attorney crosses the ethical line is when he or she *knows* the client is trying to accomplish something illegal or fraudulent.

---

[19]Shays, *Ethics for the Paralegal*, Postscript 15 (Manhattan Paralegal Ass'n, August/September 1989).

Paralegal Perspective:

■ An attorney will rarely tell paralegals or other staff members that he or she knows the office is helping a client do something criminal or fraudulent. But you might learn that this is so, particularly if there is a close, trusting relationship between you and your supervising attorney. You must let this attorney or some other authority in the office know you do not feel comfortable working on such a case.

6. Frivolous Legal Positions

An attorney must not bring a frivolous claim or assert a frivolous defense. Model Rule 3.1

A client has a right to an attorney who is a vigorous advocate. But there are limits on what this can entail. It is unethical, for example, for an attorney to assert *frivolous positions* as claims or defenses. There are two major tests for determining when a legal position is frivolous: the good-faith test and the intentional-injury test. First, a position is frivolous if the attorney is unable to make a good-faith argument that existing law supports the position, or the attorney is unable to make a good-faith argument that existing law should be changed or reversed to support the position. A position is not necessarily frivolous simply because the attorney happens to think that the client will ultimately lose. The key is whether there is a good-faith argument to support the position. If the attorney can think of absolutely no rational support for the position, it is frivolous. Since the law is often unclear, it is difficult to establish that an attorney is acting unethically under the test of good faith.

Second, a position is frivolous if the client's primary purpose in having the position asserted is to harass or maliciously injure someone.

Paralegal Perspective:

■ In the heat of controversy, tempers can run high. Attorneys do not always exhibit the detachment expected of professionals. They may so thoroughly identify with the interests of their clients that they lose perspective. Paralegals working for such attorneys may get caught up in the same fever, particularly if there is a close attorney-paralegal working relationship on a high-stakes case that has lasted a considerable time. The momentum is to do whatever it takes to win. While this atmosphere can be exhilarating, it can also create an environment where less and less attention is paid to the niceties of ethics.

7. Safekeeping Property

An attorney shall hold client property separate from the attorney's own property. Model Rule 1.15

A law office often receives client funds or funds of others connected with the client's case—for example, attorneys receive money as trustees of a will or trust, as escrow agents in closing a business deal, or as settlement of a case. Such funds should be held in separate accounts, with complete records kept on each. The attorney should not *commingle* (i.e., mix) law firm funds with client funds. It is unethical to place everything in one account. This is so even if the firm maintains accurate records on what amounts in the single account belong to which clients and what amounts belong to the firm. In a commingled account, the danger is too great that client funds will be used for nonclient purposes.

Paralegal Perspective:

■ Use great care whenever your responsibility involves client funds, such as receiving funds from clients, opening bank accounts, depositing funds in the proper account at a bank, and making entries in law firm records on such funds. It should be fairly obvious to you whether an attorney is violating the rule on commingling funds. It may be less clear whether the attorney is improperly using client funds for unauthorized purposes. Attorneys have been known to "borrow" money from client accounts and then return the money before anyone discovers what was done. They may even arrange to pay the account interest while using the money. Elaborate bookkeeping and accounting gimmicks might be used to disguise what is going on. Such conduct is unethical even if the attorney pays interest and eventually returns all the funds. In addition, the attorney may eventually be charged with theft or criminal fraud. Of course, anyone who knowingly assists the attorney could be subject to the same consequences.

8. False Statements and Failure to Disclose

An attorney shall not knowingly:
(1) make a false statement of material fact or law to a tribunal,
(2) fail to disclose a material fact to a tribunal when disclosure is necessary to avoid assisting a client commit a criminal or fraudulent act,
(3) fail to tell a tribunal about laws or other authority directly against the position of the attorney's client if this law or authority is not disclosed by opposing counsel, or
(4) offer evidence that the attorney knows is false. Model Rule 3.3(a)

One of the reasons the general public holds the legal profession in low esteem is their perception that attorneys seldom comply with Model Rule 3.3(a). Our legal system is *adversarial,* which means that legal disputes are resolved by neutral judges after listening to fiercely partisan opponents. In effect, the parties do battle through their attorneys. This environment does not always encourage the participants to cooperate in court proceedings. In fact, quite the opposite is often true. In extreme cases, attorneys have been known to lie to the court, to offer knowingly false evidence, etc. Under Model Rule 3.3(a), such conduct is unethical.

Subsection (3) of Model Rule 3.3(a) is particularly startling.

Example: Karen Singer and Bill Carew are attorneys who are opposing each other in a bitter case involving a large sum of money. Singer is smarter than Carew. Singer knows about a very damaging but obscure case that goes against her client. But because of sloppy research, Carew does not know about it. Singer never mentions the case and it never comes up during the litigation.

Singer must pay a price for her silence. She is subject to sanctions for a violation of her ethical obligation of disclosure under Model Rule 3.3(a)(3).

Another controversial part of Model Rule 3.3(a) is subsection (2) requiring disclosures that involve criminal or fraudulent acts. Since this raises issues of confidentiality, we will discuss such disclosures later when we cover confidentiality.

Paralegal Perspective:

■ Be aware that an attorney who justifies the use of deception in one case will probably repeat such deceptions in the future on other cases. To excuse the deception, the attorney will often refer to the necessity of protecting the client or to the alleged evilness of the other side. Deceptions are unethical despite such justifications.

- Chances are also good that employees of such an attorney will be pressured into participating in deception—for example, give a false date to a court clerk, help a client lie (commit perjury) on the witness stand, help an attorney alter a document to be introduced into evidence, or improperly notarize a document.

- Do not compromise your integrity no matter how much you believe in the cause of the client, no matter how much you detest the tactics of the opposing side, no matter how much you like the attorney for whom you work, and no matter how important this job is to you.

9. Withdrawal

An attorney must withdraw from a case: if continuing would result in a violation of ethical rules or other laws; if the client discharges the attorney, or if the attorney's physical or mental condition materially impairs his or her ability to represent the client. Model Rule 1.16(a)

Attorneys are not required to take every case. Furthermore, once they begin a case, they are not obligated to stay with the client until the case is over. If, however, the case has already begun in court after the attorney has filed a notice of appearance, *withdrawal* is usually improper without the permission of the court.

There are circumstances in which an attorney *must* withdraw from a case that has begun:

- Representation of the client would violate ethical rules—for example, the attorney discovers that he or she has a conflict of interest with the client which cannot be cured (i.e., corrected or overcome) by the consent of the client.

- Representation of the client would violate the law—for example, the client insists that the attorney provide advice on how to defraud the Internal Revenue Service.

- The client fires the attorney. (An attorney is an agent of the client. Clients are always free to dismiss their agents.)

- The attorney's physical or mental condition has deteriorated (through problems with alcohol, depression due to marital problems, etc.) to the point where the attorney's ability to represent the client has been materially impaired.

An attorney has the option of withdrawing if the client insists on an objective that the attorney considers repugnant (such as pursuing litigation solely to harass someone), or imprudent (such as refiling a motion the attorney feels is an obvious waste of time and likely to incur the anger of the court). Model Rule 1.16(b)(3).

Paralegal Perspective:

- When you have a close working relationship with an attorney, you become aware of his or her professional strengths and personal weaknesses, particularly in a small law office. Bar associations around the country are becoming increasingly concerned about the *impaired attorney,* someone who's not functioning up to speed due to alcohol, drugs, or related problems. A paralegal with such an attorney for a supervisor is obviously in a predicament. Seemingly small problems have the potential of turning into a crisis. If it is not practical to discuss the situation directly with the attorney involved, you need to seek the advice of others in the firm.

10. Confidentiality of Information

An attorney must not reveal information relating to the representation of a client unless (a) the client consents to the disclosure or (b) the attorney reasonably believes the disclosure is necessary to prevent a client from committing a criminal act that is likely to result in imminent death or substantial bodily harm. Model Rule 1.6

Information is confidential if others do not have a right to receive it. When access to information is restricted in this way, the information is considered *privileged.* While our primary focus in this section is on the ethical dimensions of confidentiality, we also need to examine confidentiality in the related contexts of attorney-client privilege and the attorney work-product rule.

Ethics and Confidentiality

The ethical obligation to maintain *confidentiality* applies to *all* information that relates to the representation of a client, whatever its source. Note that the obligation is broader than so-called secrets or matters explicitly communicated in confidence. Confidentiality has been breached in each of the following examples:

At a party, an attorney tells an acquaintance from another town that the law firm is representing Jacob Anderson, whose employer is trying to force him to retire.

At a bar association conference, an attorney tells an old law school classmate that a client named Brenda Steck is considering a suit against her brother over the ownership of property left by their deceased mother.

A legal secretary carelessly leaves a client's file open on his desk where a stranger (e.g., another client) can and does read parts of it.

The rule on confidentiality is designed to encourage clients to discuss their case fully and frankly with their attorney, including embarrassing and legally damaging information. Arguably, a client would be reluctant to be open with an attorney if he or she had to worry about whether the attorney might reveal the information to others. The rule on confidentiality makes it unethical for attorneys to do so.

Of course, a client can always consent to an attorney's disclosure about the client—*if* the client is properly consulted about the proposed disclosure in advance. Furthermore, sometimes the client implicitly authorizes disclosures because of the nature of his or her case. In a dispute over alimony, for example, the attorney would obviously have to disclose certain financial information about the client to a court or to opposing counsel during the settlement negotiations.

Disclosure can also be ethically permissible in cases involving future criminal conduct.

Example: An attorney represents a husband in a bitter divorce action against his wife. During a meeting at the law firm, the husband shows the attorney a gun which he says he is going to use to kill his wife later the same day.

Can the attorney tell the police what the husband said? Yes. It is not unethical for an attorney to reveal information about a crime if the attorney reasonably believes that disclosure is necessary to prevent the client from committing a criminal act that could lead to someone's imminent death or substantial bodily harm.

Finally, some disclosures can be proper in suits between attorney and client. Suppose, for example, that the attorney later sues the client for nonpayment of a fee, or the client sues the attorney for malpractice. In such proceedings, an attorney can reveal information about the client if the attorney reasonably believes disclosure is necessary to present a claim against the client or to defend against the client's claim.

Attorney-Client Privilege

The *attorney-client privilege* serves a similar function as the ethical rule on confidentiality. The two doctrines overlap. The attorney-client privilege is an *evidentiary* rule that applies to judicial and other proceedings in which an attorney may be called as a witness or otherwise required to produce evidence concerning a client. Under the attorney-client privilege, the attorney can refuse to disclose communications with his or her client whose purpose was to facilitate the provision of legal services for the client. The privilege also applies to employees of an attorney with respect to the same kind of communication—those whose purpose was to facilitate legal services.

Who May Not Testify Without Consent
Colorado Revised Statutes (1984 Cum. Supp.)
13-90-107 (1)(b)

An attorney shall not be examined without the consent of his client as to any communication made by the client to him or his advice given thereon in the course of professional employment; nor shall an attorney's secretary, paralegal, legal assistant, stenographer, or clerk be examined without the consent of his employer concerning any fact, the knowledge of which he has acquired in such capacity.

The *ethical* rule on confidentiality tells us when sanctions can be imposed on attorneys for disclosing confidential client information to anyone outside the law office. The *attorney-client privilege* tells us when attorneys (and their employees) can refuse to answers questions pertaining to confidential client information.

Attorney Work-Product Rule

Suppose that, while working on a client's case, an attorney prepares a memorandum or other in-house document that does *not* contain any confidential communications. The memorandum or document, therefore, is *not* protected by the attorney-client privilege. Can the other side force the attorney to provide a copy of the memorandum or document? Are they *discoverable,* meaning that an opposing party can obtain information about it during discovery? This question leads us to the work-product rule.

Under this rule, the *work product* of an attorney is considered confidential. Work product consists of any notes, working papers, memoranda, or similar documents and tangible things prepared by the attorney in anticipation of litigation. An example is a memorandum the attorney writes to the file indicating his or her strategy in litigating a case. Attorneys do not have to disclose their work product to the other side. It is not discoverable.[20] To the extent that such documents are not discoverable, they are privileged. (The work-product rule is sometimes referred to as the work-product privilege.)

Inadvertent Disclosure of Confidential Material

The great fear of law office personnel is that the wrong person will obtain material that should be protected by ethics, by the attorney-client privilege, or by the work-product rule. This can have devastating consequences. For example, if a stranger overhears a confidential communication by a client to the attorney or to the attorney's paralegal, a court might rule that the attorney-client privilege has been waived. At a recent paralegal conference, a speaker told a stunned audience that a paralegal in her firm accidentally "faxed" a strategy memo on a current case to the opposing attorney! The paralegal punched in the wrong phone number on the fax machine!

Paralegal Perspective:

- Attorneys must instruct their paralegals and other nonattorney assistants on the obligation not to disclose information relating to the representation of a client. "It is the responsibility of a lawyer to take reasonable measures to ensure that all client confidences are preserved by a legal assistant."[21]
- As we shall see later, the two major national paralegal associations also stress the ethical obligation of confidentiality in their own ethical codes:
  - "A legal assistant must protect the confidences of a client, and it shall be unethical for a legal assistant to violate any statute . . . controlling privileged communications." Canon 7. National Association of Legal Assistants, Code of Ethics and Professional Responsibility (page 314).
  - "A paralegal shall preserve client confidences and privileged communications. Confidential information and privileged communications are a vital part of the attorney, paralegal, and client relationship. The importance of preserving confidential and privileged information is understood to be an uncompromising obligation of every paralegal." IV. National Federation of Paralegal Associations, Affirmation of Professional Responsibility (page 314).
- There are *many* temptations on paralegals to violate confidentiality. For example, a paralegal inadvertently reveals confidential information:
  - while networking with other paralegals at a paralegal-association meeting;
  - during animated conversation with another paralegal at a restaurant or on an elevator;

---

[20]An exception exists if the "party seeking discovery has substantial need of the materials in the preparation of his case" and is unable to obtain them without undue hardship by other means. This test is rarely met. Federal Rule of Civil Procedure 26(b)(3).

[21]ABA *Model Guidelines,* Guideline 6, see footnote 5.

- after returning home from work during casual discussions with a relative, spouse, or roommate about interesting cases at the office.

Recall the scope of the rule: *all* information relating to the representation of a client must not be revealed. Some paralegals make the mistake of thinking that the rule applies only to damaging or embarrassing information or that the rule simply means you should not reveal things to the other side in the dispute. Not so. The rule is much broader. *All* information relating to the representation of a client must not be revealed to *anyone* who is not working on the case in the office.

- In Missouri, the obligation of silence is even broader. The paralegal must not disclose information—"confidential or otherwise"—relating to the representation of the client.[22] In Texas, confidential information includes both privileged information and unprivileged client information. An attorney must "instruct the legal assistant that all information concerning representation of a client (indeed even the fact of representation, if not a matter of public record) must be kept strictly confidential."[23] In Philadelphia, paralegals are warned that it is "not always easy to recognize what information about your firm's clients or office is confidential. Moreover, a client of your office might be offended to learn that a . . . firm employee has discussed the client's business in public, even if the information mentioned is public knowledge. The easiest rule is to consider *all* work of the office to be confidential: do not discuss the business of your office or your firm's clients with any outsider, no matter how close a friend, at any time, unless you are specifically authorized by a lawyer to do so."[24] Under guidelines such as these, there is very little that paralegals can tell someone about their work!

- During the war, sailors were told that "loose lips sink ships." The same applies to law firms. One law firm makes the following statement to all its paralegals, "Throughout your employment, you will have access to information that must at all times be held in strictest confidence. Even the seemingly insignificant fact that the firm is involved in a particular matter falls within the orbit of confidential information. Unless you have attorney permission, do not disclose documents or contents of documents to anyone, including firm employees who do not need this information to do their work."[25]

- If you attend a meeting on a case outside the law office, ask you supervisor whether you should take notes or prepare a follow-up memorandum on the meeting. Let the supervisor decide whether your notes or the memo might be discoverable.[26]

- Be *very* careful when you talk with clients in the presence of third persons. Overheard conservations might constitute a waiver of the attorney-client privilege.

- Use a stamp marked *privileged* on protected documents.

---

[22]*Guidelines for Practicing with Paralegals,* Missouri Bar Ass'n (1987).

[23]State Bar of Texas, *General Guidelines for the Utilization of the Services of Legal Assistants by Attorneys* (1981). Rule 1.01, Texas Disciplinary Rules of Professional Conduct (1990).

[24]*Professional Responsibility for Nonlawyers,* Professional Responsibility Committee of the Philadelphia Bar Ass'n (1989) (emphasis added).

[25]*Orientation Handbook for Paralegals* 2 (Lane, Powell, Moses & Miller, 1984).

[26]Daniels, *Privileged Information for Paralegals,* 17 At Issue 15 (San Francisco Ass'n of Legal Assistants, November 1990).

■ During a job interview, be very careful about submitting writing samples that contain confidential information, such as privileged communications or the identity of clients at law offices where you may have worked or volunteered in the past.[27] Your lack of professionalism in carelessly referring to confidential information during an interview will probably destroy your chances of getting the job.

11. Conflict of Interest

An attorney should avoid a conflict of interest with his or her client.

"Like obscenity, *conflicts of interest* are difficult to define, but easy to recognize."[28] A conflict of interest is divided loyalty that actually or potentially places one of the participants to whom undivided loyalty is owed at a disadvantage. Such conflicts can exist in many settings.

> Example: Bill Davenport is a salesman who does part-time work selling the same type of product manufactured by two competing companies.

Davenport has a conflict of interest. How can he serve two masters with the same loyalty? Normally, a company expects the undivided loyalty of people who work for it. How can Davenport apportion his customers between the two companies? There is an obvious danger that he will favor one over the other. The fact that he may try to be fair in his treatment of both companies does not eliminate the conflict of interest. A *potential* certainly exists that one of the companies will be disadvantaged. It may be that the two companies are aware of the problem and are not worried. This does not mean that there is no conflict of interest; it simply means that the affected parties have consented to take the risks involved in the conflict.

The same kind of conflict can exist in other settings.

> Example: Frank Jones is the head of the personnel department of a large company. Ten people apply for a job, one of whom is Frank's cousin.

Frank has a conflict of interest. He has loyalty to his company (pressuring him to hire the best person for the job) and a loyalty to his cousin (pressuring him to help a relative). There is a potential that the company will be disadvantaged, since Frank's cousin may not be the best qualified for the job.

The conflict exists even if the cousin *is* the best qualified, and even if Frank does *not* hire his cousin for the job, and even if the company *knows* about the relationship but still wants Frank to make the hiring decision. For conflict of interest to exist, all you need is the potential for disadvantage due to *divided loyalties;* you do not have to show that disadvantage actually resulted.

In a law office, a number of conflict-of-interest issues can arise:

(a) Business transactions with a client

(b) Loans to a client

(c) Gifts from a client

---

[27]As we will see later, you may have to disclose the names of cases and clients in order to help the office decide whether you are "tainted" with a conflict of interest and hence could cause the disqualification of the office if you are hired. But this disclosure should occur only when the employment discussions are getting serious *and* with the knowledge of your former employers.

[28]Holtzman, *Conflicts of Interest,* 14 Legal Economics 55 (October 1988).

(d) Multiple representation

(e) Former client/present adversary

(f) Law firm disqualification

(g) Switching jobs and "the Chinese wall"

As we examine each of these topics, our central concern is whether the independence of the attorneys' professional judgment is compromised in any way because of conflicting interests.

(a) Business Transactions with a Client

Attorneys sell professional legal advice and representation. When they go beyond such services and enter a business transaction with the client, a conflict of interest can arise.

> Example: Janet Bruno, Esq. is Len Oliver's attorney in a real estate case. Oliver owns an auto repair business for which Bruno has done legal work. Oliver sells Bruno a 30% interest in the repair business. Bruno continues as Oliver's attorney.

Serious conflict-of-interest problems may exist here. Assume that the business runs into difficulties and Oliver considers bankruptcy. He goes to Bruno for legal advice on bankruptcy law. Bruno has dual concerns: to give Oliver competent legal advice and to protect *her own* 30% interest in the business. Bankruptcy may be good for Oliver but disastrous for Bruno's investment. How can an attorney give a client independent professional advice when the advice may go against the attorney's own interest? Bruno's concern for her investment creates the potential that Oliver will be placed at a disadvantage. Divided loyalties exist.

This is not to say, however, that it is always unethical for an attorney to enter a business transaction with a client. If certain strict conditions are met, it can be proper.

> *An attorney shall not enter a business transaction with a client, unless*
> *(i) the terms of the business transaction are fair and reasonable to the client and are fully disclosed to the client in understandable language in writing, and*
> *(ii) the client is given reasonable opportunity to seek advice on the transaction from another attorney who is not involved with the transaction or the parties, and*
> *(iii) the client consents to the business transaction in writing.* Model Rule 1.8(a)

In our example, Oliver must be given the chance to consult with an attorney other than Bruno on letting Bruno buy a 30% interest in the business. Bruno would have to give Oliver a clear, written explanation of their business relationship. And the relationship must be fair and reasonable to Oliver.

(b) Loans to a Client

An attorney, like all service providers, wants to be paid. Often a client does not have the resources to pay until *after* the case is over.

> Example: Harry Maxell, Esq. is Bob Stock's attorney in a negligence action in which Stock is seeking damages for serious injuries caused by the defendant. Since the accident, Stock has been out of work and on welfare. While the case is pending, Maxell agrees to lend Stock living expenses and court-filing fees.

The loan covering *living expenses* creates a conflict-of-interest problem. Suppose that the defendant in the negligence case makes an offer to settle the case with Stock. Should he accept the offer? There is a danger that Maxell's advice on this will be colored by the fact that he has a financial interest in Stone—he wants to have his loan repaid. The amount of the offer to settle may not be enough to cover the loan. Should he advise Stock to accept the offer? It may be in Stock's interest to accept the offer but not in Maxell's own interest. Such divided loyalty is an unethical conflict of interest. Model Rule 1.8(e).

The loan covering *litigation expenses,* such as filing fees and other court costs, is treated differently. The amount of such a loan is usually relatively small, and hence unlikely to interfere with the independence of the attorney's judgment. In our example, Maxell's loan to cover the cost of the filing fees is proper.

(c) Gifts from a Client

Clients sometimes make gifts to their attorneys or to the spouse or relative of their attorneys. Such gifts rarely create ethical problems except when a document must be prepared to complete the gift.

> Example: William Stanton, Esq. has been the family attorney of the Tarkinton family for years. At Christmas, Mrs. Tarkinton gives Stanton a television set and tells him to change her will so that Stanton's ten-year-old daughter would receive funds for a free college education.

If a document is needed to carry out the gift, it is unethical for the attorney to prepare that document. Its preparation would create a conflict of interest. In our example, the gift of money for college involves a document—Mrs. Tarkinton's will. Note the conflict. It would be in Mrs. Tarkinton's interest to have the will written so that she, and the executor of her will, retained considerable flexibility when questions arise on how much to pay for the college education. (For example, is there to be a maximum amount? Is room and board included?) And they need flexibility on the effect of contingencies, such as a delay or an interruption in going to college. (What happens if the daughter does not go to college until after she marries and raises her own children?) Other questions could arise as well. Stanton, of course, would want the will drafted so that his daughter received the most money possible; he does not want any contingencies in the will that might threaten receipt of the funds. It is in his interest to prepare the will so that Mrs. Tarkinton and her executor have very little flexibility.

Because of this conflict, an attorney cannot prepare a document such as a will, trust, or contract that results in any substantial gift from a client to the attorney or to the attorney's children, spouse, parents, or siblings. If a client wants to make such a gift, *another* attorney must prepare the document.[29] There is, however, one exception. If the client is *related* to the person receiving the gift, the attorney can prepare the document. Model Rule 1.8(c).

There does not appear to be any ethical problem in taking the gift of the television set from Mrs. Tarkinton. No documents are involved.

(d) Multiple Representation

A client is entitled to the independent professional judgment and vigorous representation of an attorney. Rarely can this occur in a case of *multiple repre-*

---

[29]This other attorney should not be a member of the same law firm. See the related discussion (later) on imputed disqualification.

sentation (also referred to as *common representation*), where the same attorney represents both sides in a legal dispute.

> Example: Tom and Henry have an automobile accident. Tom wants to sue Henry for negligence. Both Tom and Henry ask Mary Franklin, Esq. to represent them in the dispute.

Franklin has a conflict of interest. How can she give her undivided loyalty to both sides? Tom needs to prove that Henry was negligent; Henry needs to prove that he was not negligent, and perhaps that Tom was negligent himself. How can Franklin vigorously argue that Henry was negligent and at the same time vigorously argue that Henry was not negligent? How can she act independently for two different people who are at odds with each other? Since Tom and Henry have *adverse interests*, she cannot give each her independent professional judgment. (Adverse interests are simply opposing purposes or claims.) The difficulty is not solved by Franklin's commitment to be fair and objective in giving her advice to the parties. Her role as attorney is to be a *partisan advocate* for the client. It is impossible for Franklin to play this role for two clients engaged in a dispute where they have adverse interests. An obvious conflict of interest would exist. In every state, it would be unethical for Franklin to represent Tom and Henry in this case.

Furthermore, this is a case in which consent is *not* a defense. Even if Tom and Henry agree to allow Franklin to represent both of them, it would be unethical for her to do so. The presence of adverse interests between the parties makes it unethical for an attorney to represent both sides.

Suppose, however, that the two sides do not have adverse interests. There are cases that must go before a court even though the parties are in agreement about everything.

> Example: Jim and Mary Smith are separated, and both want a divorce. They have been married only a few months. There are no children and no marital assets to divide. George Davidson, Esq. is an attorney that Jim and Mary know and trust. They decide to ask Davidson to represent both of them in the divorce.

Can Davidson ethically represent both sides here? There are some states that *will* allow him to do so, on the theory that there is not much of a conflict between the parties. Jim and Mary want the divorce, there is no custody battle, and there is no property to fight over. All they need is a court to decree that their marriage is legally over. Hence the potential for harm caused by multiple representation in such a case is almost nonexistent. Other states, however, disagree. They frown on multiple representation in so-called "friendly divorces" of this kind.

There is no absolute ban on all multiple representation in the Model Rules, although such representation is certainly discouraged.

> *An attorney shall not represent a client if the representation of that client will be directly adverse to another client, unless*
> *(i) the attorney reasonably believes the representation will not adversely affect the relationship with the other client, and*
> *(ii) both clients consent after consultation about the risks of the multiple representation.* Model Rule 1.7

In the Smith example, both conditions can probably be met. Such a divorce is little more than a paper procedure since there is no real dispute between the parties. Hence Davidson would be reasonable in believing that his representation of Jim would not adversely affect Mary, and vice versa. Davidson can represent both sides so long as Jim and Mary consent to the multiple representation after Davidson explains whatever risks might be involved.

Nevertheless, attorneys are urged *not* to engage in multiple representation even if it is ethically proper to do so under the standards listed above. The case may have been "friendly" at the outset, but years later when everything turns sour, one of the parties inevitably attacks the attorney for having had a conflict of interest. Cautious attorneys always avoid multiple representation.

(e) Former Client/Present Adversary

As indicated earlier, clients are encouraged to be very open with their attorney since the latter needs to know favorable and unfavorable information about the client in order to evaluate the legal implications of the case. The more trust that exists between them, the more frank the client will usually be. Assume that such a relationship exists and that the case is eventually resolved. Months later, another legal dispute arises between the same parties, but this time the attorney represents the other side!

> Example: Helen Kline, Esq. represented Paul Andrews in his breach-of-contract suit against Richard Morelli, a truck distributor. Andrews claimed that Morelli failed to deliver five trucks that Andrews ordered. A court ruled in favor of Morelli. Now, a year later, Andrews wants to sue Morelli for slander. After accidentally meeting at a conference, they started discussing the truck suit. Morelli allegedly called Andrews a liar and a thief. In the slander suit, Andrews hires Michael Manna, Esq. to represent him. Morelli hires Helen Kline, Esq.

A former client is now an adversary. Kline once represented Andrews; she is now representing a client (Morelli) who is an adversary of Andrews. Without the consent of the former client (Andrews), it is unethical for Kline to *switch sides* and represent Morelli against him. Model Rule 1.9(a). Consent is needed *when the second case is the same as the first one or when the two are substantially related*. The slander suit is substantially related to the breach-of-contract suit, since they both grew out of the original truck incident.

If the cases are the same or are substantially related, the likelihood is strong that the attorney will use information learned in the first case to the detriment of the former client in the second case. Kline undoubtedly found out a good deal about Andrews when she represented him in the breach-of-contract case. She would now be in a position to use that information *against* him while representing Morelli in the slander case.

Kline had a duty of loyalty when she represented Andrews. This duty does not end once the case is over and the attorney fees are paid. The duty continues if the same case arises again or if a substantially related case arises later—even if the attorney no longer represents the client. A conflict of interest exists when Kline subsequently acquires a new client who goes against Andrews in the same case or in a substantially related case. This, of course, is what happened in our example. Her duty of undivided loyalty to the second client would clash with her *continuing* duty of undivided loyalty to the former client in the original case.

Suppose, however, that an attorney *can* take the second case against a former client because the second case is totally unrelated to the first. There is still an ethical obligation to refrain from using any information relating to the representation in the first case to the disadvantage of the former client in the second case. There is no ethical ban on taking the case, but if there is any information in the office relating to the first case, that information cannot be used against the former client in the second case.[30]

(f) Law Firm Disqualification

If an attorney is disqualified from representing a client because of a conflict of interest, every attorney in the *same law firm* is also disqualified unless the client being protected by this rule consents to the representation.

> Example: Two years ago, John Farrell, Esq. of the law firm of Smith & Smith represented the stepfather in a custody dispute with the child's grandmother. The stepfather won the case, but the grandmother was awarded limited visitation rights. The grandmother now wants to sue the stepfather for failure to abide by the visitation order. John Farrell no longer represents the stepfather. The grandmother asks John Farrell to represent her. He declines because of a conflict of interest, but sends her to his law partner, Diane Williams, Esq., down the corridor at Smith & Smith.

The *stepfather* would have to consent to the representation of the grandmother by Williams. There would certainly be a conflict of interest if John Farrell tried to represent the grandmother against the stepfather. The custody dispute and the visitation dispute are substantially related. Once one attorney in a firm is disqualified because of a conflict of interest, every other attorney in that firm is also disqualified. (This is known as *imputed disqualification* or *vicarious disqualification*.) The entire firm is treated as one attorney. The disqualification of any one "tainted" attorney in the firm contaminates the entire firm. In our example, Farrell's partner (Williams) is disqualified because Farrell would be disqualified. Model Rule 1.10.

(g) Switching Jobs and "the Chinese Wall"

Finally we need to consider the conflict-of-interest problems that can arise from changing jobs. We just saw that there can be an imputed disqualification of an entire law firm because one of the attorneys in the firm has a conflict of interest with a client. If that attorney now goes to work for a *new* firm, can there be an imputed disqualification of the new firm because of the same conflict of interest?

> Example: Kevin Carlson, Esq. works at Darby & Darby. He represents Ajax, Inc. in its contract suit against World Systems, Inc. The latter is represented by Polk, Young & West. Carlson quits his job at Darby & Darby and takes a job at Polk, Young & West.

While Carlson was at Darby and Darby, he obviously acquired confidential information about Ajax. Clearly, he cannot now represent World Systems in the contract litigation against Ajax. Blatant side-switching of this kind is highly unethical. But what about other attorneys at Polk, Young & West? Is the *entire* firm contaminated and hence disqualified from continuing to represent World Systems because of the hiring of Carlson? If other attorneys at Polk, Young & West are allowed to continue representing World Systems against Ajax, there would be pressures on Carlson to tell these attorneys what he knows about Ajax. Must Polk, Young & West therefore withdraw from the case? The states do not all answer this question in the same way.

---

[30]While this duty might exist, it is not easy to enforce. Think of how difficult it might be to prove that the attorney in the second case used information obtained in the first case.

In many states, the answer is *yes,* because the tainted attorney[31]—Carlson—possesses confidential information about Ajax, and the case at the new firm involves the same or substantially the same matter as at the prior firm. The confidential information learned at the prior firm would be material to the matter being handled by the new firm. In these states, the only way to avoid disqualification is if Ajax waives its right to object. Ajax must be told that Carlson now works at Polk, Young & West, which represents World Systems, and must consent to allowing an attorney at Polk, Young & West (other than Carlson) to continue to represent World Systems in the case. It is unlikely, however, that Ajax will give this consent. Why would it want to take the chance that Carlson will reveal confidential communications to his new colleagues at Polk, Young & West?

To avoid the drastic penalty of imputed disqualification, law firms often promise to build a *Chinese wall* (sometimes called an *ethical wall* or *cone of silence*) around the attorney who created the conflict of interest—the *tainted* or *contaminated* attorney. The goal of the wall is to screen the tainted attorney from any contact with a case where earlier confidentiality could be compromised. In many states, however, this promise is *ineffective* to avoid the disqualification. Yet there are states that are more sympathetic to a firm that wants to avoid the disqualification, depending on how involved the tainted attorney was in the case while at the previous firm and on the quality of the wall at the new firm.

The screening of the Chinese Wall should take several forms. For example:

- The tainted attorney promises not to discuss what he or she knows with anyone in the new firm.

- Those working on the case in the new firm promise not to discuss it with the tainted attorney.

- The tainted attorney works in an area that is physically segregated from work on the case in the new firm.

- The files in the case are locked so that the tainted attorney will have no access to the files. In addition, colored labels or "restricted flags" are placed on each of these files to indicate that they are off limits to the tainted attorney.

- All employees in the new firm are formally told that if they learn anything about the case, they must not discuss it with the tainted attorney.[32]

A tainted employee around whom a Chinese Wall is built is called a *quarantined* employee.

As indicated, there are states where a Chinese Wall will *not* be successful in preventing the imputed disqualification of the new firm.[33] There is skepticism that the tainted attorney will be able to resist the pressure to disclose what he or she knows in spite of these screening mechanisms. "Whether the screen is breached will be virtually impossible to ascertain from outside the firm."[34]

Yet again, not all states take this position. There are states that will not order a disqualification if the court can be convinced that harm to the former

---

[31]Also called the *contaminated* attorney or *infected* attorney.

[32]Another dimension of the Chinese Wall is to forbid the tainted attorney from earning any profit or financial gain from the case in question.

[33]The Model Rules explicitly recognize a Chinese Wall to prevent imputed disqualification only where the attorney has moved from a government position to private employment. Model Rule 1.11.

[34]C. Wolfram, *Modern Legal Ethics* § 7.6.4 (1986).

FIGURE 5.4

Computer Software
Used for Conflicts
Checks

```
┌─────────────────────────────────────────────────────────┐
│          LEGALMASTER Conflicts Found                    │
│ Conflicts checked for case: SAMUE—(10 matches on 3 names)│
│ Rubin (2 matches)                                       │
│     CSP-          CLNT Rubin Phillip                    │
│     FFIC-5        JUDGE Rubin Laurie                    │
│ Samuel* (6 matches)                                     │
│     GREGS-1       OPATT Samuels Fritz                   │
│     SCOTT-1       EXPRT Samuels Phillip J.              │
│     SMITH-PI      JUDGE Samuels Norman I.               │
│     IBM-          OPATT Samuels Jacob                   │
│     CSP-          OPATT Samuels Jacob                   │
│     ISIS-2        EXPRT Samuelson Juan                  │
│ Savag* (2 matches)                                      │
│     IBM-          CLNT Savage Norm                      │
│     GRUPE-7       CLNT Savage Emily                     │
│             Press any key to exit.                      │
└─────────────────────────────────────────────────────────┘
```

Legalmaster's Conflicts Module. Computer Software for Professionals, Inc.

client can be avoided. This is most likely to happen if the Wall was in place at the new firm at the outset of the employment transfer, if the new firm built the Wall before the other side raised the conflict-of-interest issue, and, most important, if the tainted attorney's involvement in the case at the old firm was relatively minor. This, of course, was not true for Kevin Carlson, Esq. in our example, since he actually represented Ajax while at Darby & Darby.

Imputed disqualification is a drastic consequence of job switching. In the Carlson example, somebody at Polk, Young & West made a major blunder in hiring Carlson. Before hiring him, a *conflicts check* should have been performed in order to determine whether he might taint the new firm and, if so, whether a Chinese Wall could prevent disqualification. This is done by obtaining the names of the clients Carlson and his old law firm (Darby & Darby) worked for and by determining whether the new firm (Polk, Young & West) ever worked *against* any of them.[35] Unfortunately, law firms often perform such conflicts checks carelessly or not at all.

Some large firms assign paralegals to perform the check under the supervision of an attorney. This paralegal will enter data on parties into a "conflicts index system" and compare it with data already in the system to identify potential conflicts. Computer programs (such as the one shown in Figure 5.4.) have been developed to assist in the task.

Insurance companies that issue malpractice policies to attorneys are very concerned about conflicts of interests that can arise from a *lateral hire,* in which a law firm hires an attorney from another law firm. The same concerns exist when one law firm buys or merges with another law firm. In Figure 5.5, you will find a series of questions one insurance company asks of all law firms applying for malpractice insurance.

Paralegal Perspective:

■ "A lawyer should take reasonable measures to prevent conflicts of interest resulting from a legal assistant's other employment or interests insofar as

---

[35]For each client that is a corporation, the firm should also cross-check the names of the parent corporation, all subsidiary corporations, and the names of chief executive officers. If the client is a partnership, the same kind of check is needed for the names of all general partners.

FIGURE 5.5

Questions on Malpractice Insurance Application about Conflict-of-Interest Avoidance

ADMINISTRATIVE SYSTEMS AND PROCEDURES—CONFLICT OF INTEREST	YES	NO
22. Do you have a written internal control system for maintaining client lists and identifying actual or potential conflicts of interest?	☐	☐
23. How does the firm maintain its conflict of interest avoidance system? ☐ Oral/Memory ☐ SIngle Index Files ☐ Multiple Index Files ☐ Computer		
24. Have the firm members disclosed in writing, all actual conflicts of interest and conflicts they reasonably believe may exist as a result of their role as director, officer, partner, employee or fiduciary of an entity or individual other than the applicant firm?	☐	☐
25. Do firm members disclose to their clients, in writing, all actual conflicts of interest and conflicts they reasonably believe may exist?	☐	☐
26. Upon disclosure of actual or potential conflicts, do firm members always obtain written consent to perform ongoing legal services?	☐	☐
27. Has the firm acquired, merged with or terminated a formal business relationship with another firm within the last three years?	☐	☐
28. Does the firm's conflict of interest avoidance system include attorney-client relationships established by predecessor firms, merged firms and acquired firms?	☐	☐
Source: The St. Paul Companies, Professional Liability Application for Lawyers.		

such other employment or interests would present a conflict of interest if it were that of the lawyer." [36] Many paralegals change jobs one or more times in the course of their careers. Such changes can create the same kind of conflicts problems that result when attorneys change jobs:

> Example: Paul Benton is a paralegal who works for Sands, Leonard & Wiley. One of the cases Paul works on is Mary Richardson v. Jane Quigly. Sands, Leonard & Wiley represents Richardson. The law firm of Neeley & Neeley represents Quigly. Before the case is resolved, Paul quits in order to take a job as a paralegal with Neeley & Neeley.

Neeley & Neeley is now in a position to determine what Paul found out about Richardson while he worked for Sands, Leonard & Wiley. The latter firm will probably ask a court to force Neeley & Neeley to withdraw from the case because it hired a tainted paralegal—Paul. The courts in some states will do just that. In these courts, imputed disqualification can result from tainted paralegals as well as from tainted attorneys. Yet other states say that paralegals should not be treated the same as attorneys. Under this view, a court is more likely to accept a Chinese Wall built around a tainted paralegal (who becomes a quarantined paralegal) as an alternative to disqualifying the law firm this paralegal recently joined. This view is represented in the ethics opinion of the American Bar Association (Informal Opinion 88-1526) printed below. It must be emphasized, however, that not all states follow this opinion.

■ In a recent, dramatic case, a San Francisco law firm was disqualified from representing nine clients in asbestos litigation involving millions of dollars.

---

[36] ABA *Model Guidelines*, Guideline 7, see footnote 5.

The sole reason for the disqualification was that the firm hired a paralegal who had once worked for a law firm that represented the opponents in the asbestos litigation. Soon after the controversy arose, the disqualified firm laid off the tainted paralegal who brought this conflict to the firm. He was devastated when he found out that he was being let go. "I was flabbergasted, totally flabbergasted." He has not been able to find work since.[37] The case was widely reported throughout the legal community. A front-page story in the *Los Angeles Daily Journal* said that it "could force firms to conduct lengthy investigations of paralegals and other staffers before hiring them." [38]

■ One law firm makes the following statement to all its paralegals, "If you or a temporary legal assistant working under your supervision were formerly employed by opposing counsel, this could be the basis for a motion to disqualify" this law firm. "So also could personal relationships such as kinship with the opposing party or attorney or dating an attorney from another firm. Make your attorney aware of such connections." [39]

■ If you have worked (or volunteered) for an attorney in the past in *any* capacity (as a paralegal, as an investigator, as a secretary, etc.), you should make a list of all the clients and cases with which you were involved. When you apply for a new job, your list may be relevant to whether the law firm will be subject to disqualification if you are hired. You must be careful, however, with the list. Do not attach it to your resume and randomly send it around town! Until employment discussions have become serious, do not show it to the prospective employer. Furthermore, try to notify prior attorneys with whom you have worked that you are applying for a position at a law firm where its "conflicts check" on you must include knowing what cases you worked on with previous attorneys. Giving them this notice is not always practical, and may not be required. Yet it is a safe procedure to follow whenever possible.

■ Freelance paralegals who work for more than one attorney on a part-time basis are particularly vulnerable to conflict-of-interest charges. For example, in a large litigation involving many parties, two opposing attorneys might unknowingly use the same freelance paralegal to work on different aspects of the same case, or might use two different employees of this freelance paralegal. Another example is the freelance paralegal who worked on an earlier case for a client and now works on a different but similar case in which that client is the opponent. The California Association of Freelance Paralegals has attempted to address this problem in Article 11 of its proposed Code of Ethics: "A freelance paralegal shall avoid conflicts of interest relating to client matters. The freelance paralegal shall not accept any case adverse to the client of [an attorney who hires the paralegal] if the latter case bears a substantial connection to the earlier one or if there is a possibility that the two cases are substantially related, regardless of whether confidences were in fact imparted to the freelance paralegal by the attorney or the attorney's client in the earlier case." [40] There are practical problems with such rules. It is not always easy

---

[37]Motamedi, *Landmark Ethics Case Takes Toll on Paralegal's Career, Family,* 7 Legal Assistant Today 39 (May/June 1990). *In re Complex Asbestos Litigation,* ___Cal.App.3d ___, 283 Cal.Rptr. 732 (Cal.Ct.App. 1991).

[38]M. Hall, *S.F. Decision on Paralegal Conflict May Plague Firms,* 102 Los Angeles Daily Journal 1, col. 2 (September 25, 1989).

[39]Orientation Handbook for Paralegals 3 (Lane, Powell, Moses & Miller, 1984).

[40]California Ass'n of Freelance Paralegals, "CAFP's Proposed Code of Ethics," Article 11, *Freelancer* 9 (July/August 1991).

to determine whether two cases are "adverse" or bear a "substantial connection" with each other. If there is doubt, it is in the economic self-interest of the freelance paralegal *not* to tell the attorney since he or she will most likely refuse to hire the paralegal rather than take the risk of later disqualification because of contamination injected into the case by this paralegal. Finally, conducting a conflicts check could be somewhat difficult for a busy, experienced freelance paralegal who has worked for scores of attorneys and hundreds of clients over the years.

Standing Committee on Ethics and Professional Responsibility of the American Bar Association
Informal Opinion 88-1526

A law firm that employs a nonlawyer who formerly was employed by another firm may continue representing clients whose interests conflict with the interests of clients of the former employer on whose matters the nonlawyer has worked, as long as the employing firm screens the nonlawyer from information about or participating in matters involving those clients and strictly adheres to the screening process described in this opinion and as long as no information relating to the representation of the clients of the former employer is revealed by the nonlawyer to any person in the employing firm. In addition, the nonlawyer's former employer must admonish the nonlawyer against revelation of information relating to the representation of clients of the former employer.

The Committee is asked whether, under the ABA Model Rules of Professional Conduct (1983, amended 1987), a law firm that hires a paralegal formerly employed by another lawyer must withdraw from representation of a client under the following circumstances. The paralegal has worked for more than a year with a sole practitioner on litigation matters. One of those matters is a lawsuit which the sole practitioner instituted against a client of the law firm that is about to hire the paralegal and wishes to continue to defend the client. The paralegal has gained substantial information relating to the representation of the sole practitioner's client, the plaintiff in the lawsuit. The employing firm will screen the paralegal from receiving information about or working on the lawsuit and will direct the paralegal not to reveal any information relating to the representation of the sole practitioner's client gained by the paralegal during the former employment. The Committee also is asked whether the paralegal's former employer must take any actions in order to comply with the Model Rules.

Responsibilities of Employing Firm

The Committee concludes that the law firm employing the paralegal should not be disqualified from continuing to defend its client in the lawsuit, as long

as the law firm and the paralegal strictly adhere to the screening process described in this Opinion, and as long as no information relating to the representation of the sole practitioner's client is revealed by the paralegal to any person in the employing firm.

The Model Rules require that a lawyer make reasonable efforts to ensure that each of the lawyer's nonlawyer employees maintains conduct compatible with the professional obligations of the lawyer, including the nondisclosure of information relating to the representation of clients. This requires maintaining procedures designed to protect client information from disclosure by the lawyer's employees and agents. . . .

It is important that nonlawyer employees have as much mobility in employment opportunity as possible consistent with the protection of clients' interests. To so limit employment opportunities that some nonlawyers trained to work with law firms might be required to leave the careers for which they are trained would disserve clients as well as the legal profession. Accordingly, any restrictions on the nonlawyer's employment should be held to the minimum necessary to protect confidentiality of client information.

Model Rule 5.3 imposes general supervisory obligations on lawyers with respect to nonlawyer employees and agents. The obligations include the obligation to make reasonable efforts to ensure there are measures in effect to assure that the nonlawyer's conduct is compatible with the professional obligations of the lawyer. With respect to new employees who formerly worked for other lawyers, these measures should involve admonitions to be alert to all legal matters, including lawsuits, in which any client of the former employer has an interest. The nonlawyer should be cautioned: (1) not to disclose any information relating to the representation of a client of the former employer; and (2) that the employee should not work on any matter on which the employee worked for the prior employer or respecting which the employee has information relating to the representation of the client of the former employer. When the new firm becomes aware of such matters, the employing firm must also take reasonable steps to ensure that the employee takes no action and does no work in relation to matters on which the nonlawyer worked in the prior employment, absent client consent after consultation.

Circumstances sometimes require that a firm be disqualified or withdraw from representing a client when the firm employs a nonlawyer who formerly was employed by another firm. These circumstances are present either: (1) where information relating to the representation of an adverse party gained by the nonlawyer while employed in another firm has been revealed to lawyers or other personnel in the new firm . . .; or (2) where screening would be ineffective or the nonlawyer necessarily would be required to work on the other side of the same or a substantially related matter on which the nonlawyer worked or respecting which the nonlawyer has gained information relating to the representation of the opponent while in the former employment. If the employing firm employs the nonlawyer under those circumstances, the firm must withdraw from representing the client, unless the client of the former employer consents to the continued representation of the person with conflicting interests after being apprised of all the relevant factors.

Responsibilities of Former Employer

Under Model Rule 5.3, lawyers have a duty to make reasonable efforts to ensure that nonlawyers do not disclose information relating to the representation of the lawyers' clients while in the lawyer's employ and afterwards. On the facts presented to the Committee here, once the lawyer learns that the paralegal has joined the opposing law firm, the lawyer should consider advising the employing firm that the paralegal must be isolated from participating in the matter and from revealing any information relating to the representation of the lawyer's client. If not satisfied that the employing firm has taken adequate measures to prevent participation and disclosures, the lawyer should consider filing a motion in the lawsuit to disqualify the employing law firm from continuing to represent the opponent. . . .

Therefore, the lawyer who hires the paralegal, under the circumstances before the Committee, must screen the paralegal from participating in the lawsuit with the employing law firm. Both the employing firm and the sole practitioner should admonish the paralegal not to disclose information relating to the representation of the plaintiff in the lawsuit and also of any other client of the sole practitioner for whom the paralegal formerly worked while with the former employer.

The standards expressed in this Opinion apply to all matters where the interests of the clients are in conflict and not solely to matters in litigation. The Committee also notes that these standards apply equally to all nonlawyer personnel in a law firm who have access to material information relating to the representation of clients and extends also to agents who technically may be independent contractors, such as investigators.

---

12. Communication with the Other Side

In representing a client, an attorney shall not communicate with a party on the other side about the subject of the case if the attorney knows that the party is represented by another attorney. The latter attorney must consent to such a communication. Model Rule 4.2

If the other side is not represented, an attorney must not give him or her the impression that the attorney is uninvolved. The attorney should not give this person advice other than the advice to obtain his or her own attorney. Model Rule 4.3

The ethical concern here is that an attorney will take an unfair advantage of the other side.

Example: Dan and Theresa Kline have just separated and are thinking about a divorce. Each claims the marital home. Theresa hires Thomas Farlington, Esq. to represent her. Farlington calls Dan to ask him if he is interested in settling the case.

It is unethical for Farlington to contact Dan about the case if Farlington knows that Dan has his own attorney. Farlington must talk with Dan's attorney. Only the latter can give Farlington permission to communicate with Dan. If Dan does not have an attorney, Farlington can talk with Dan, but he must not allow Dan to be misled about Farlington's role. Farlington works for the other side; he is not disinterested. Dan must be made to understand this fact. The only advice Farlington can give Dan in such a situation is to seek his own attorney.

Paralegal Perspective:

■ The ethical restrictions on communicating with the other side apply to the employees of an attorney as well as to the attorney. "The lawyer's obligation is to ensure that the legal assistants do not communicate directly with parties known to be represented by an attorney, without that attorney's consent, on the subject of such representation."[41] You must avoid improper communication with the other side. If the other side is a business or some other large organization, do not talk with anyone there unless your supervisor tells you that it is ethical to do so. Never call the other side and pretend you are someone else in order to obtain information.

■ If your office allows you to interview someone who is not represented by an attorney, you cannot give this person any advice other than the advice to secure his or her own attorney.

13. Solicitation

> *In person, an attorney may not solicit employment from a prospective client with whom the attorney has no family or prior professional relationship when a significant motive for doing so is the attorney's monetary gain.*[42] Model Rule 7.3

People in distress are sometimes so distraught that they are not in a position to evaluate their need for legal services. They should not be subjected to pressures from an attorney who shows up wanting to be hired, particularly if the attorney is not a relative or has never represented them in the past.[43] Such in-person solicitation is unethical.

> Example: Rachael Winters, Esq. stands outside the police station and gives a business card to any individual being arrested. The card says that Winters is an attorney specializing in criminal cases.

Winters is obviously looking for prospective clients. Doing so in this manner is referred to as *ambulance chasing,* which is a pejorative term for aggressively tracking down anyone who probably has a legal problem in order to drum up business. There is no indication either that Winters is related to any of the people going into the police station or that she has any prior professional relationship with them (for example, they are *not* former clients). Winters appears to have one goal: finding a source of fees. Hence her conduct is unethical. Such direct, in-person, one-on-one solicitation of clients in this way is not allowed. The concern is that an attorney who approaches strangers in trouble

---

[41]Section 20-104, Committee Commentary, *New Mexico Rules Governing the Practice of Law* (Judicial Pamphlet 16).

[42]This prohibition also applies to *live* telephone conversations in which the attorney seeks to be hired.

[43]Furthermore, the improper solicitation of clients and promotion of litigation constitutes the crime of *barratry* in some states. For example, in 1990 three attorneys and an employee of a law firm were indicted in Texas on charges that they illegally sought clients at hospitals and funeral homes after twenty-one students were killed and sixty-nine were injured in a school bus accident. *4 Said to Have Used Bus Crash to Get Business for Law Firm,* New York Times 8, col. 5 (April 7, 1990).

may exert undue influence on them. This is less likely to occur if the solicitation comes in the mail, even if it is sent to individuals known to need legal services.

> Example: An attorney obtains the names of homeowners facing foreclosure and sends them the following letter: "It has come to my attention that your home is being foreclosed on. Federal law may allow you to stop your creditors and give you more time to pay. Call my office for legal help."

While critics claim that such solicitation constitutes "ambulance chasing by mail," the technique is ethical in most states so long as it is truthful and not misleading.[44] *In-person* solicitation, however, is treated differently because of the obvious pressure that it imposes. It is "easier to throw out unwanted mail than an uninvited guest." [45]

Paralegal Perspective:

- An unscrupulous attorney may try to use a paralegal to solicit clients for the office.

  > Example: Bill Hill is a senior citizen who lives at a home for senior citizens. Andrew Vickers, Esq. hires Bill as his "paralegal." His sole job is to contact other seniors with legal problems and to refer them to Vickers.

  Andrew Vickers is engaging in unethical solicitation through Bill Hill. Attorneys cannot hire a paralegal to try to accomplish what they cannot do themselves. Nor can they use a *runner*[46]—an employee or independent contractor who contacts personal-injury victims or other potential clients in order to solicit business for an attorney.

- See also the related discussion above on splitting fees with nonattorneys.

14. Advertising

An attorney may advertise services on radio, on TV, in the newspaper, or through other public media so long as the ad is neither false nor misleading and does not constitute improper in-person solicitation. Model Rule 7.2

There was a time when almost all forms of advertising by attorneys were prohibited. Traditional attorneys considered advertising to be highly offensive to the dignity of the profession. In 1977, however, the United States Supreme Court stunned the legal profession by holding that truthful advertising cannot be completely banned.[47] The First Amendment protects such advertising. Furthermore, advertising does not pose the same danger as in-person solicitation by an attorney. A recipient of advertising is generally under very little pressure to buy the advertised product—in this case, an attorney's services. Hence, attorneys can ethically use truthful, nonmisleading advertising to the general public in order to generate business.

Studies have shown that over one third of all attorneys in the country engage in some form of advertising. Most of it consists of listings in the Yellow

---

[44]*Shapero v. Kentucky Bar Ass'n,* 486 U.S. 466, 108 S.Ct. 1916, 100 L.Ed.2d 475 (1988). Some states impose additional requirements on mail solicitations—for example, the phrase "Advertising Material" must be printed on the outside of the envelope, and the word "advertisement" must be printed at the top of each page of the letter.

[45]Metzner, *Strategies That Break the Rules,* National Law Journal, 16 (July 15, 1991).

[46]Also called a *capper* if the person uses fraud or deception in the solicitation.

[47]*Bates v. State Bar of Arizona,* 433 U.S. 350, 97 S.Ct. 2691, 53 L.Ed.2d 810 (1977).

Pages. The use of other marketing tools is also on the rise. Revenue for television advertising, for example, was more than $89 million in 1989.[48] Former Chief Justice Warren Burger commented that some attorney ads "would make a used-car dealer blush with shame." Proponents of attorney advertising, however, claim that it has made legal services more accessible to the public and has provided the public with a better basis for choosing among available attorneys.

15. Reporting Professional Misconduct

Attorneys with knowledge that another attorney has committed a serious violation of the ethical rules must report this attorney to the appropriate disciplinary body. Model Rule 8.3

Attorneys may pay a price for remaining silent when they become aware of unethical conduct. The failure of an attorney to report another attorney may mean that both attorneys can be disciplined for unethical behavior. Not every ethical violation, however, must be reported. The ethical violation must raise a substantial question of the attorney's honesty, trustworthiness, or fitness to practice law.

Paralegal Perspective:

- If a paralegal is aware of unethical conduct of his or her own attorney supervisor, is it unethical for the paralegal to fail to report the attorney to the bar association? No. As indicated earlier, the ethical rules under consideration here apply only to attorneys. Yet the paralegal is still in a predicament. If there is no one to talk to at the firm, he or she must decide whether to remain at this job. Sooner or later, unethical attorneys will probably ask or pressure their paralegal to participate in unethical conduct.

16. Appearance of Impropriety

How would you feel if you were told that, even though you have not violated any rule, you are still going to be punished because what you did *appeared* to be improper? That would be the effect of an obligation to avoid even the appearance of impropriety. In some states, however, it *is* unethical for attorneys to engage in such appearances.[49] The ABA Model Rules, however, does not list appearance of impropriety as an independent basis of determining unethical conduct. To be disciplined in states that have adopted the Model Rules, an attorney must violate one of the specific ethical rules. Yet even in these states, there are conservative attorneys who are as worried about apparent impropriety as they are about specific, actual impropriety.

17. Unauthorized Practice of Law

An attorney shall not assist a nonattorney in the unauthorized practice of law. Rule 5.5(b)

In Chapter 4, we saw that it is a crime in many states for a nonattorney to engage in the *unauthorized practice of law*. Our main focus in Chapter 4 was

---

[48]Hornsby, *The Complex Evolution of Attorney Ad Regs*, Nat'l Law Journal S4 (August 6, 1990).
[49]See Canon 9 of the *ABA Code of Professional Responsibility* (1981). "A lawyer should avoid even the appearance of professional impropriety."

the nonattorney who works for an office other than a traditional law office. An example would be a do-it-yourself divorce office that sells kits and typing services. Now our focus is the nonattorney who works under the supervision of an attorney in a law office. We want to explore the ways in which attorneys might be charged with unethically assisting *their own paralegals* engage in the unauthorized practice of law. For example, an attorney might allow a paralegal to give legal advice, to conduct depositions, or to sign court documents. These areas will be discussed below along with an overview of other major ethical issues involving paralegals.

18. Paralegals

We turn now to a more direct treatment of when attorneys can be disciplined for the unethical use of paralegals. We will cover the following topics:

(a) Paralegals, the ABA Model Code, and the ABA Model Rules

(b) Misrepresentation of paralegal identity or status

(c) Doing what only attorneys can do

(d) Absentee, shoulder, and environmental supervision

(a) Paralegals, the ABA Model Code, and the Model Rules

The first major statement by the American Bar Association on the ethical use of paralegals by attorneys came in its *Model Code of Professional Responsibility:*

> DR 3-101(A): A lawyer shall not aid a nonlawyer in the unauthorized practice of law.

> EC 3-6: A lawyer often delegates tasks to clerks, secretaries, and other lay persons. Such delegation is proper if the lawyer maintains a direct relationship with his client, supervises the delegated work, and has complete professional responsibility for the work product. This delegation enables a lawyer to render legal services more economically and efficiently.[50]

A 1967 opinion elaborated on these standards:

American Bar Association

Formal Opinion 316 (1967)

A lawyer can employ lay secretaries, lay investigators, lay detectives, lay researchers, accountants, lay scriveners, non-lawyer draftsmen or non-lawyer researchers. In fact, he may employ non-lawyers to do any task for him except counsel clients about law matters, engage directly in the practice of law, appear in court or appear in formal proceedings as part of the judicial process, so long as it is he who takes the work and vouches for it to the client and becomes responsible for it to the client. In other words, we do not limit the kind of assistance that a lawyer can acquire in any way. to persons who are admitted to the Bar, so long as the non-lawyers do not do things that lawyers may not do or do the things that lawyers only may do.

From these documents we learn that an attorney can hire a paralegal and is responsible for what the paralegal does. There are two levels of this responsibility: civil liability for malpractice and ethical liability for violation of ethical rules.

---

[50]See footnote 4 on the meaning of DR and EC in the ABA Model Code.

> Example: The law firm of Adams & Adams represents Harold Thompson in his negligence suit against Parker Co. At the firm, Elaine Stanton, Esq. works on the case with Peter Vons, a paralegal whom she supervises. Peter neglects to file an important pleading in court, and carelessly gives confidential information about Thompson to the attorney representing Parker. All of this causes Thompson great damage.

Stanton is fully responsible to the client, Thompson, who might decide to bring a malpractice suit in court against her. She cannot hide behind the fact that her paralegal was at fault. (See the discussion of malpractice liability and respondeat superior in Chapter 4.)

What about ethics? Can Stanton be reprimanded, suspended, or disbarred because of what her paralegal did? None of the materials quoted above answer this question. Responsibility to a client for malpractice often raises separate issues from responsibility to a bar association (or other disciplinary body) for unethical conduct. The two kinds of responsibility can be closely interrelated because the same alleged wrongdoing can be involved in the malpractice suit and in the disciplinary case. Yet the two proceedings are separate and should be examined separately.

In 1983, the ABA replaced the *Model Code of Professional Responsibility* with its *Model Rules of Professional Conduct.* The Model Rules, which have been our main focus in this chapter, are more helpful in telling us when attorneys are subject to ethical sanctions because of their paralegals. This is done in *Model Rule 5.3,* covering paralegals. All attorneys in the law firm are not treated the same in Rule 5.3. As you read this rule, note that different standards of ethical responsibility are imposed on the following three categories of attorneys:

- Any attorney in the firm
- A partner in the firm
- An attorney in the firm with direct supervisory authority over the paralegal

---

Model Rules of Professional Conduct
Rule 5.3. Responsibilities
Regarding Nonlawyer Assistants

With respect to a nonlawyer employed or retained by or associated with a lawyer:

(a) a partner in a law firm shall make reasonable efforts to ensure that the firm has in effect measures giving reasonable assurance that the person's conduct is compatible with the professional obligations of the lawyer;

(b) a lawyer having direct supervisory authority over the nonlawyer shall make reasonable efforts to ensure that the person's conduct is compatible with the professional obligations of the lawyer; and

(c) A lawyer shall be responsible for conduct of such a person that would be a violation of the Rules of Professional Conduct if engaged in by a lawyer if:

(1) the lawyer orders or ratifies the conduct involved; or

(2) the lawyer is a partner in the law firm in which the person is employed, or has direct supervisory authority over the person, and knows of the conduct at a time when its consequences can be avoided or mitigated but fails to take reasonable remedial action.

Comment:

Lawyers generally employ assistants in their practice, including secretaries, investigators, law student interns, and paraprofessionals. Such assistants, whether employees or independent contractors, act for the lawyer in rendition of the lawyer's professional services. A lawyer should give such assistants appropriate instruction and supervision concerning the ethical aspects of their employment, particularly regarding the obligation not to disclose information relating to representation of the client, and should be responsible for their work product. The measures employed in supervising nonlawyers should take account of the fact that they do not have legal training and are not subject to professional discipline.

Let us analyze Rule 5.3 by applying it to Elaine Stanton, Esq. in our example. First of all, under 5.3(c)(1), *any* attorney in the firm who "orders" the paralegal to commit the wrongdoing in question is ethically responsible for that conduct. The same is true if the attorney "ratifies" (that is, approves or endorses) the wrongdoing after the paralegal commits it. There is no indication in the example that Stanton or any other attorney in the firm told Peter not to file the pleading in court, or told him to give confidential information about Thompson to the other side. Nor is there any indication that an attorney approved of Peter's conduct after it occurred.[51] Therefore, Rule 5.3(c)(1) does not apply.

We need to know whether Stanton is a partner in the firm. If so, she has an ethical obligation under 5.3(a) to "make reasonable efforts to ensure that the firm has in effect measures giving reasonable assurance" that the paralegal's conduct "is compatible with the professional obligations of the lawyer." Hence a partner cannot completely ignore office paralegals in the hope that someone else in the firm is monitoring them. Reasonable steps must be taken by every partner to establish a system of safeguards. Here are some examples:

- Make sure that all paralegals in the firm are made aware of the ethical rules governing attorneys in the state.
- Make sure that all paralegals in the firm are made aware of the importance of deadlines in the practice of law and of the necessity of using date-reminder (tickler) techniques.

In the example, Peter Vons is supervised by Elaine Stanton, Esq. Hence she is an attorney with "direct supervisory authority" over Peter. Rule 5.3(b) governs the conduct of such attorneys. This section requires her to "make reasonable efforts to ensure" that the paralegal's conduct "is compatible with the professional obligations of the lawyer."

Assume that Stanton is charged with a violation of Rule 5.3(b) because her paralegal, Peter, failed to file an important pleading in court and disclosed confidential information about a client. At Stanton's disciplinary hearing, she would be asked a large number of questions about how she supervised Peter. For example:

- How do you assign tasks to Peter?
- How do you know if he is capable of handling an assignment?
- How often do you meet with him after you give him an assignment?
- How do you know if he is having difficulty completing an assignment?
- Has he made mistakes in the past? If so, how have you handled them?

Peter might be called as a witness in her disciplinary hearing and be interrogated extensively. For example:

- How were you trained as a paralegal?
- What kinds of assignments have you handled in your paralegal career?
- How long have you worked for Elaine Stanton?
- How does she evaluate your work?
- What do you do if you have a question on an assignment but she is not available in the office?

---

[51]By Peter's conduct, we mean both what he did (disclose confidential information) and what he failed to do (file the papers in court).

- Why didn't you file the court document on time?
- Describe the circumstances under which you revealed confidential information to the opponent in the Thompson case.

All of these questions of Stanton and of Peter would be designed to find out if Stanton made "reasonable efforts" to ensure that Peter did not violate ethical standards. Note that attorney supervisors do not have to guarantee that a paralegal will act ethically. They simply have to "make reasonable efforts" that this will occur. The above questions are relevant to whether Stanton exerted such efforts with respect to Peter.

Another basis of ethical liability under the Model Rules is Rule 5.3(c)(2). Both a partner and a supervisory attorney can be subject to discipline if they knew about the paralegal's misconduct yet failed to take reasonable corrective steps at a time when such steps would have avoided or minimized ("mitigated") the damage. At their disciplinary hearing, a partner and/or a supervising attorney would be asked questions such as:

- When did you first find out that Peter did not file the court document?
- What did you do at that time? Why didn't you act sooner?
- When did you first find out that Peter spoke to opposing counsel?
- What did you do at that time? Why didn't you act sooner?

So, too, Peter might be asked questions at the hearing relevant to when his supervising attorney (Stanton) or any partner in the firm found out about what he had done—and what they did when they found out.

(b) Misrepresentation of Paralegal Identity or Status

"It is the lawyer's responsibility to take reasonable measures to ensure that clients, courts, and other lawyers are aware that a legal assistant, whose services are utilized by the lawyer in performing legal services, is not licensed to practice law." [52] People who come into contact with paralegals must not think that they are attorneys. Paralegals should not misrepresent their status intentionally or accidentally. The following status issues need to be covered:

- Titles
- Disclosure of status
- Business cards
- Letterhead
- Signature on correspondence
- Advertisements, announcement cards, signs, lists, and directories
- Name on court documents

What Title Can Be Used?   There are no ethical problems with the titles *paralegal* or *legal assistant*. No one is likely to think that persons with such titles are attorneys. There are some bar associations that prefer titles that are even more explicit in communicating nonattorney status—for example, *lawyer's assistant* and *nonattorney assistant*. Yet, they are seldom used because of the widespread acceptance and clarity of the titles *paralegal* and *legal assistant*. Some years ago,

---

[52]ABA *Model Guidelines*, Guideline 4, see footnote 5.

the Philadelphia Bar Association[53] said that the latter titles should be given only to employees that possessed "the requisite training and education." No state, however, is this explicit in stating who can use the titles.

It is unethical to call a paralegal an "associate" or to refer to a paralegal as being "associated" with a law firm. The title, "paralegal associate," for example, should not be used. The common understanding is that an associate is an attorney. In Iowa, similar problems exist with the title, "Certified Legal Assistant," as we shall see shortly. (See Figure 5.7).

Note on Disbarred or Suspended Attorney as Paralegal.   When attorneys have been disbarred or suspended from the practice of law for ethical improprieties, they may try to continue to work in the law as a paralegal for an attorney willing to hire them. Some states will not allow this because it shows disrespect for the court that disciplined the attorney and because of the high likelihood that the individual will engage in the unauthorized practice of law by going beyond paralegal duties. Other states are more lenient but impose other restrictions, such as not allowing a disbarred or suspended attorney to have any client contact while working as a paralegal.

Should Paralegals Disclose Their Nonattorney Status to Clients, Attorneys, Government Officials, and the General Public?   Yes, this disclosure is necessary. The more troublesome questions are: What kind of disclosure should you make and when must you make it? Compare the following communications by a paralegal:

- "I work with attorney Ward Brown at Brown & Tams."
- "I am a paralegal."
- "I am a legal assistant."
- "I am not an attorney."

The fourth statement is the clearest expression of nonattorney status. The first is totally unacceptable since you have said nothing about your status. For most contacts, the second and third statements will be ethically sufficient to overcome any misunderstanding about your nonattorney status. Yet there are still members of the public who are confused about what a paralegal or legal assistant is. Hence, the only foolproof communication in all circumstances is the fourth.

In some states, the disclosure of nonattorney status is necessary only if a client, an attorney, a government official, or a member of the public is unaware of this status. Other states say that the paralegal should always disclose his or her nonattorney status at the outset of the contact. "Common sense suggests a routine disclosure at the outset of the conversation." Furthermore, the failure to provide an oral clarification of status is *not* cured simply by handing over a business card that says you are a paralegal or a legal assistant.

Do not assume that a person with whom you come in contact knows you are not an attorney; the safest course is to assume the opposite!

May a Paralegal Have a Business Card?   Every state allows paralegals to have their own *business cards* as long as their nonattorney status is clear. (See Figure 5.6.) At one time, some states wanted the word "nonlawyer" used along

---

[53]Throughout this discussion, there will be references to the opinions of specific bar associations. For a summary of these opinions and their citations, see Appendix F.

FIGURE 5.6

Paralegal
Business Card

Ethically proper in every state.

FIGURE 5.7

Paralegal
Business Card

John Simpson, CLA
PARALEGAL

PHONE
(319) 456-9103

JONES, DAY, OVERTON & DAVIS, P.C.
8262 PRESTWICK DR.
WATERLOO, IA 50702

Ethically proper in every state *except* in Iowa.

with the paralegal's office title. This is rarely required today. Since paralegals are not allowed to solicit business for their employer, the card may not be used for this purpose. The primary focus of the card must be to identify the paralegal rather than the attorney for whom the paralegal works. Finally, there must be nothing false or misleading printed on the card. In most states, a paralegal who is a *Certified Legal Assistant (CLA)* can include this fact on their card. In Iowa, however, this is not permitted, as we will see when we discuss signatures on correspondence. (See Figure 5.7.)

May the Letterhead of Law Firm Stationery Print the Name of a Paralegal?   States differ in their answer to this question, although most now agree that nonattorneys' names can be printed on *law-firm letterhead* if their title is also printed so that their nonattorney status is clear. (See Figure 5.8.) Before 1977, almost all states did *not* allow attorney stationery to print the names of nonattorney employees. The concern was that the letterhead would be used as a form of advertising by packing it with names and titles in order to make the office look impressive. This concern, however, evaporated in 1977 when the Supreme Court held that all forms of attorney advertising could not be banned.[54] After this date, most states withdrew their objection to the printing

---

[54]See footnote 47 above.

FIGURE 5.8

Attorney
Letterhead that
Prints Paralegal
Names

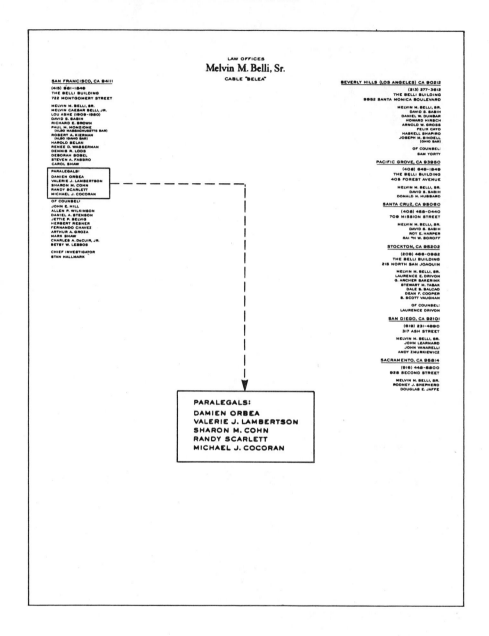

of paralegal names on attorney letterhead as long as no one would be misled into thinking that the paralegals were attorneys. In Michigan, it was recommended, but not required, that attorneys and nonattorneys be printed on different sides of the stationery to "enhance the clarification that the paraprofessional is not licensed to practice law." A few states adhere to the old view that only attorney names can be printed on law-firm letterhead. Yet, to the extent that it is still based on a prohibition of attorney advertising, this view is subject to challenge.

May a Paralegal Write and Sign Letters on Attorney Stationery? There is never an ethical problem with a paralegal writing a letter that will be reviewed and signed by an attorney. Suppose, however, that the attorney wants the paralegal to sign his or her own name to the letter. Most states will permit this if certain conditions are met. For example, a title must be used that indicates the signer's nonattorney status, and the letter must not give legal advice.

The following formats are proper:

Sincerely,	Sincerely,	Sincerely,
Leonard Smith Paralegal	Pauline Jones Legal Assistant	Jill Strauss Legal Assistant for the Firm

The following formats, however, pose difficulties:

Sincerely,	Sincerely,	Sincerely,
William Davis	John Simpson, CLA	Mary Page Certified Legal Assistant

The first format is ethically improper. The lack of a title could mislead the reader into thinking that William Davis is an attorney. In most states, using the designations "CLA" or "Certified Legal Assistant" is also proper. (See Chapter 4 for a discussion of the CLA program.) In Iowa, however, they cannot be used. "A reader might think that CLA was a legal degree;" and if "Certified Legal Assistant" is used, "the public might be misled about his or her nonlawyer status." Hence, the second and third formats just shown cannot be used in Iowa. Presumably this also applies to a business card with the CLA designation. (See Figure 5.7.) This is an extreme view and is unlikely to be followed elsewhere.

In most states, there are no limitations on the persons to whom a paralegal can send letters. Yet there are a few states (such as New Jersey) where only an attorney can sign a letter to a client, to an opposing attorney, or to a court. A very minor exception to this rule would be "a purely routine request to a court clerk for a docket sheet." A paralegal can sign such a letter. This also is an extreme position. So long as the paralegal's nonattorney status is clear, and so long as an attorney is supervising the paralegal, restrictions on who can be the recipient of a paralegal-signed letter make little sense.

May an Attorney Print the Name of a Paralegal in an Advertisement, an Announcement Card, a Door Sign, an Outdoor Sign, a Law Directory or Law List, an Office Directory, or a Telephone Directory?   Attorneys communicate to the public and to each other through advertisements, law directories or lists (that print the names of practicing attorneys), office directories, general telephone directories, door signs, outdoor signs, and announcement cards (that announce that the firm has moved, opened a new branch, merged with another firm, taken on a new partner, etc.). It is relatively rare that an attorney will want to print the name of his or her paralegal in one of these vehicles of communication. In a small city or town, however, a solo practitioner or small law firm might want to do so. While several states will not allow attorneys to do this, most states that have addressed the issue say it is ethically permissible if nothing false or misleading is said about the paralegal and the latter's nonattorney status is clear.

May an Attorney Print the Name of a Paralegal on a Court Document?
Formal documents that are required in litigation, such as appellate briefs, memoranda supporting a motion, complaints, or other pleadings, must be signed by an attorney representing a party in the dispute. With rare exceptions, the document cannot be signed by a nonattorney, no matter how minor the formal document may be. In most states, a paralegal can sign a letter on a routine

matter to a clerk or other nonjudge, but formal litigation documents require an attorney's signature.

Suppose, however, that the attorney wishes to print on a document the name of a paralegal who worked on the document *in addition to* the attorney's name and signature. The attorney may simply want to give a measure of recognition to the efforts of this paralegal. Most states permit this as long as there is no misunderstanding as to the paralegal's nonattorney status, and no attempt is made to substitute a nonattorney's signature for an attorney's signature.

Occasionally, a court opinion will recognize the contribution of a paralegal. Before the opinion begins, the court lists the names of the attorneys who represented the parties. The name of a paralegal might be included with these attorneys. Here, for example, is the list of attorneys that includes the name of a paralegal (Becky Strickland) in the case of *United States v. Cooke,* 625 F.2d 19 (4th Cir. 1980):

> Thomas J. Keith, Winston-Salem, N.C., for appellant.
> David B. Smith, Asst. U.S. Atty. (H. M. Michaux, Jr., U.S. Atty., Durham, N.C., Becky M. Strickland, Paralegal Specialist on brief), for appellee.
> Before HALL and PHILLIPS, Circuit Judges, and HOFFMAN, Senior District Judge.

(c) Doing What Only Attorneys Can Do

There are limitations on what attorneys can ask their paralegals to do. We just examined one such limitation: paralegals should never be asked to sign court documents. The failure to abide by these limits might subject the attorney to a charge of unethically assisting a nonattorney to engage in the unauthorized practice of law. The areas we need to examine are as follows:

- Legal advice
- Nonlegal advice
- Drafting documents
- Real estate closings
- Depositions
- Executions of wills
- Settlement negotiations
- Court appearances
- Counsel's table
- Administrative hearings

May a Paralegal Give Legal Advice?   Unfortunately, it is not easy to define legal advice or the practice of law. According to the American Bar Association:

> It is neither necessary nor desirable to attempt the formulation of a single, specific definition of what constitutes the practice of law. Functionally, the practice of law relates to the rendition of services for others that call for the professional judgment of a lawyer. The essence of the professional judgment of the lawyer is his educated ability to relate the general body and philosophy of law to a specific legal problem of a client. . . . Where this professional judgment is not involved, non-lawyers, such as court clerks, police officers, abstracters, and

many governmental employees, may engage in occupations that require a special knowledge of law in certain areas. But the services of a lawyer are essential
in the public interest whenever the exercise of *professional judgment* is
required.[55]

The major way that an attorney communicates this professional judgment is
through *legal advice*. According to the ABA, it occurs when "the general body
and philosophy of law" is related or applied "to a specific legal problem." You
are giving legal advice when you tell a particular person how the law might
affect a particular legal problem or how to achieve a particular legal result that
solves or avoids such a problem. Giving such advice is the unauthorized practice
of law, whether or not you charge for the advice, and whether or not your
advice is correct.

Compare the following sets of statements:

General Information about the Law	Information about the Law as Applied to a Specific Person
"The Superior Court is located at 1223 Via Barranca."	"Your case must be heard in the Superior Court which is located at 1223 Via Barranca."
"There are several different kinds of bankruptcy."	"There are several different kinds of bankruptcy, but you should file under Chapter 13."
"The failure to pay child support will lead to prosecution."	"Your failure to pay child support will lead to prosecution."

Arguably, the statements in the second column constitute legal advice; general
information about the law has been related or applied to a particular legal problem of a particular person. The legal questions or problems addressed are: What
court can hear (has jurisdiction over) *your* case? What kind of bankruptcy
should *you* file? Can *you* be prosecuted for not paying child support?

The statements in the first column do not appear to focus on any particular
person's legal problem. Hence such statements do not constitute legal advice, at
least not explicitly. But we need to examine some of these statements more
closely. When you tell someone that there are "several different kinds of bankruptcy," are you, by implication, telling that person that he or she should consider, and may qualify for, at least one of the kinds of bankruptcy? When you
tell someone that the "failure to pay child support will lead to prosecution," are
you, by implication, telling that person that his or her failure to pay child support will lead to his or her prosecution? The moment there is a focus on a particular person's legal problem, you are in the realm of legal advice. This
focus can be express or implied. Hence, whenever *any* statement about the law
is made, you must ask yourself two questions:

- Am I trying to relate legal information to any particular person's legal problem? (If so, I am giving express legal advice.)
- Could a person reasonably interpret what I am saying as relating legal information to a particular person's legal problem even if this is not my intent? (If
  so, I am giving implied legal advice.)

Great care is sometimes needed to avoid giving legal advice.

---

[55]EC 3–5, *ABA Model Code of Professional Responsibility* (1981).

There are a number of circumstances that increase the likelihood that statements can reasonably be interpreted as giving implied legal advice. For example:

■ The statement is made by someone who works in the law, such as an attorney, paralegal, or legal secretary.

■ The statement is made by someone who has helped the person with his or her legal problems in the past.

■ The statement is made by someone who knows that the person has a current legal problem.

■ The person is distressed about his or her current legal problem.

Under such circumstances, the person is likely to interpret *any* statement about the law as being relevant to his or her particular legal problem.

A number of paralegals have pointed out how easy it is to fall into the trap of giving legal advice:

> Legal assistants should be alert to all casual questions [since your answers] might be interpreted as legal advice.[56]

> Most of us are aware of the obvious, but we need to keep in mind that sometimes the most innocent comment could be construed as legal advice.[57]

> A . . . typical scenario, particularly in a small law office where legal assistants have a great deal of direct client contact, is that the clients themselves will coax you to answer questions about the procedures involved in their cases, and lead you into areas where you would be giving them legal advice. Sometimes this is done innocently—because the attorney is unavailable and they are genuinely unaware of the difference between what you can do for them and what their legal counsel is authorized to do. . . . They will press you for projections, strategy, applicable precedents—in short, legal advice. Sometimes you are placed in situations where you are not adequately supervised and your own expertise may be such that you know more about the specialized area of law than the attorney does anyway. . . . We have all walked the thin line between assisting in the provision of legal services and actually practicing law.[58]

When a paralegal gives legal advice in these circumstances, he or she is engaged in the unauthorized practice of law. An attorney who permits this to occur, or who fails to take the preventive steps required by Model Rule 5.3, is aiding the paralegal in the unauthorized practice of law—and hence is acting unethically.

There are a number of situations, however, in which a paralegal *can* give legal advice. First, a paralegal can tell a client precisely what the attorney tells the paralegal to say, even if the message constitutes legal advice. The paralegal, however, cannot elaborate on or explain this kind of message from the attorney. Paralegals "may be authorized to communicate legal advice so long as they do not interpret or expand on that advice." [59] Second, the paralegal may be working in an area of the law where nonattorneys are authorized to represent clients, such as social security hearings. (See Chapter 4.) In such areas, the authorization includes the right to give legal advice.

---

[56]King, *Ethics and the Legal Assistant*, 10 ParaGram 2 (Oregon Legal Assistants Ass'n, August 1987).

[57]DALA Newsletter 2 (Dallas Ass'n of Legal Assistants, December 1990).

[58]Spiegel, *How to Avoid the Unauthorized Practice of Law*, 8 The Journal 8–10 (Sacramento Ass'n of Legal Assistants, February 1986).

[59]ABA *Model Guidelines*, Comment to Guideline 3, see footnote 5.

May a Paralegal Give a Client Nonlegal Advice?   Yes. An attorney may allow a paralegal to render specialized advice on scientific or technical topics. For example, a qualified paralegal can give accounting advice or financial advice. The danger is that the nonlegal advice might also contain legal advice or that the client might reasonably interpret the nonlegal advice as legal advice.

May a Paralegal Draft Legal Documents?   Yes. A paralegal can draft any legal document as long as an attorney supervises and reviews the work of the paralegal. Some ethical opinions say that the document must lose its separate identity as the work of a paralegal and must leave the office as the work product of an attorney. In West Virginia, for example, "anything delegated to a nonattorney must lose its separate identity and be merged in the service of the lawyer." The key point is that an attorney must stand behind and be responsible for the document.

May a Paralegal Attend a Real Estate Closing?   The sale of property is finalized at an event called a real estate closing. Many of the events at the closing are formalities, such as signing and exchanging papers. Occasionally, however, some of these events turn into more substantive matters where negotiation, legal interpretation, and legal advice are involved.

In most states, paralegals can attend closings in order to assist their attorney-supervisor. The real question is whether they can attend alone and conduct the closing themselves. Chicago has one of the most liberal rules. There, paralegals can conduct the closing without the attorney-supervisor being present if no legal advice is given, if all the documents have been prepared in advance, if the attorney-supervisor is available by telephone to provide help, and if the other attorney consents. In some states, additional conditions must be met before allowing paralegals to act on their own. For example, the closing must take place in the attorney's law office with the attorney readily accessible to answer legal questions. It must be noted, however, that this is a minority position. Most states would say that it is unethical for an attorney to allow a paralegal to conduct a real estate closing alone.

May a Paralegal Conduct a Deposition?   No. Paralegals can schedule depositions, can assist in preparing a witness who will be deposed (called the deponent), can take notes at the deposition, and can summarize deposition transcripts, but they cannot conduct the deposition. Asking and objecting to questions are attorney-only functions.

May a Paralegal Supervise the Execution of a Will?   In Connecticut, the execution of a will must be supervised by an attorney. A paralegal can act as a witness to the execution, but an attorney must direct the procedure. Most other states would probably agree, although few have addressed this question.

May a Paralegal Negotiate a Settlement?   Some states allow a paralegal to negotiate with a nonattorney employee of an insurance company, such as a claims adjuster, as long as the paralegal is supervised by an attorney. Most states, however, limit the paralegal's role to exchanging messages from the supervising attorney, and do not allow any actual give-and-take negotiating by the paralegal.

May a Paralegal Make a Court Appearance?   In the vast majority of courts, a paralegal cannot perform even minor functions in a courtroom, such as asking a judge for a hearing date. As we saw in Chapter 4, very few exceptions to this rule exist. Only attorneys can act in a representative capacity before a judge. There are, however, a small number of specialized courts, like the small claims court of some states, where you do not have to be an attorney to represent parties. This exception, however, is rare. And, as mentioned earlier, a paralegal should not sign a formal court document that is filed in litigation.

May a Paralegal Sit at Counsel's Table During a Trial?   In many courts, only attorneys can sit at counsel's table during a trial. Yet, in some courts a paralegal is allowed to sit with the attorneys if permission of the presiding judge is obtained. When allowed, it is sometimes referred to as sitting *second chair* in the courtroom.

May a Paralegal Represent Clients at Administrative Hearings?   Yes, when this is authorized at the particular state or federal administrative agency. (See Chapter 4 and Appendix E.)

(d) Absentee Supervision, Shoulder Supervision, and Environmental Supervision

It is difficult to overestimate the importance of attorney supervision in the arena of ethics. Almost every ethical opinion involving paralegals (and almost every attorney malpractice opinion involving paralegals) stresses the need for effective supervision. The justification for the very existence of perhaps 95% of paralegal activity is this supervision. Indeed, one of the main reasons many argue that paralegal licensing is not necessary is the protective cover of attorney supervision.

What is meant by supervision? The extremes are easy to identify. Figure 5.9 provides this spectrum of extremes. *Absentee supervision* refers to the attorney who is either never around or never available. Once tasks are assigned, paralegals are on their own. At the other extreme is *shoulder supervision,* practiced by attorneys who are afraid to delegate. When they do get up enough courage to delegate something, they constantly look over the shoulder of the paralegal, who is rarely left alone for more than two-minute intervals. Such attorneys suffer from *delegatitis,* the inordinate fear of letting anyone do anything for them.

Both kinds of supervision are misguided. If you work for an attorney who practices absentee supervision, disaster is just around the corner. You may feel flattered by the confidence placed in you; you may enjoy the challenge of independence; you may be highly compensated because of your success. But you are working in an office that is traveling 130 miles per hour in a 50 miles per hour zone. Any feeling of safety in such an office is illusory. Shoulder supervision, on the other hand, provides safety at the expense of practicality. Perpetual step-by-step surveillance will ultimately defeat the economy and efficiency motives that originally led the office to hire paralegals.

Perhaps the most effective kind of supervision is *"environmental supervision,"* or what might be called *holistic supervision.* It is far broader in its reach than the immediate task delegated to a paralegal. It addresses the essential question: What kind of environment will lead to a high-quality paralegal work product without sacrificing economy? The components of this kind of supervision

FIGURE 5.9

Levels of Supervision: The Spectrum of Extremes

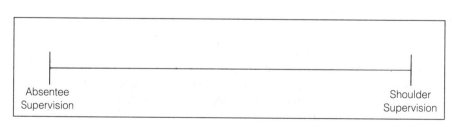

are outlined in Figure 5.10. Environmental supervision requires *hiring* the right people, *training* those people, *assigning* appropriate tasks, *providing* the needed resources, *monitoring* the progress, *reviewing* the end product, and *rewarding* competence.

FIGURE 5.10

"Environmental Supervision": The Ethical Ideal

1. Before paralegals are hired, the office undertakes a study of its practice in order to identify what tasks paralegals will perform and what levels of ability will be required to perform those tasks.

2. As part of the interview process, the office conducts background checks on applicants for paralegal jobs in order to ensure that competent people are hired who already have the needed skills or who are trainable so that they can acquire these skills on the job.

3. A program of orientation and training is created to introduce paralegals to the office and to prepare them for the tasks ahead.

4. Paralegals are given a copy of the ethical rules governing attorneys in the state. In addition to reading these rules, they are given training on the meaning of the rules.

5. Paralegals are told what to do if they feel that an ethical problem exists. Lines of authority are identified if the paralegal needs to discuss the matter with someone other than, or in addition to, his or her immediate supervisor.

6. The office does not assume that every attorney knows how to supervise paralegals. Paralegals are assigned to attorneys who have the required supervisory sensitivity and skill. Furthermore, the office is always looking for ways to increase this sensitivity and skill.

7. An attorney reviews all paralegal work. While paralegals may be given discretion and asked to exercise judgment in the tasks assigned, this discretion and judgment is always subjected to attorney review.

8. No task is assigned that is beyond the capacity of the paralegal. Specialized instruction always accompanies tasks the paralegal has not performed before.

9. Once a task is assigned, the paralegal is told where to receive assistance if the immediate supervisor is not available. This lack of availability, however, is relatively rare.

10. For tasks that the office performs on a recurring basis, manuals, office procedures, checklists, or other written material are available to the paralegal to explain how the tasks are performed and where samples or models can be found. If such *systems* material does not currently exist, the office has realistic plans to create them.

11. To cut down on misunderstanding, every paralegal assignment includes the following information:

    ■ A *specific due date.* ("Get to this when you can" is unacceptable and unfair.)

    ■ A *priority assessment.* ("Should everything else be dropped while I do this assignment?")

    ■ A *context.* ("How does this assignment fit into the broader picture of the case?") and

    ■ A *financial perspective.* ("Is this billable time?")

12. At reasonable times before the due date of selected assignments, the supervisor monitors the progress of the paralegal to ensure that the work is being done professionally and accurately.

13. A team atmosphere exists at the office among the attorneys, paralegals, secretaries, and other employees. Everyone knows each other's functions, pressures, and potential as resources. A paralegal never feels isolated.

14. Evaluations of paralegal performance are constructive. Both the supervisor and paralegal feel that they are opportunities for further learning.

15. The office sends the paralegal to training seminars conducted by paralegal associations and bar associations to maintain and to increase the paralegal's skills.

16. The office knows that an unhappy employee is prone to error. Hence the office ensures that the work setting of the paralegal encourages personal growth and productivity. This includes matters of compensation, benefits, work space, equipment, and advancement.

Unfortunately, most law offices do *not* practice environmental supervision as outlined in Figure 5.10. The chart represents the ideal. Yet you need to know what the ideal is so that you can advocate for the conditions that will bring it about.

Thus far, our discussion on supervision has focused on the traditional paralegal who works full time in the office of an attorney. We also need to consider the freelance paralegal who works part-time for one or more attorneys. Very often this freelance or independent paralegal works in his or her own office. (See Chapters 1 and 4, and Appendix I.) How can attorneys fulfill their ethical obligation to supervise such paralegals?

> Example: Gail Patterson has her own freelance business. She offers paralegal services to attorneys who hire her for short-term projects which she performs in her own office.

Arguably, attorneys who hire Gail often do not provide the same kind of supervision that they can provide to a full-time paralegal who works in their office. We saw earlier that Model Rule 5.3(c)(2) says that an attorney has the responsibility to take steps to avoid the consequences of an ethical violation by a paralegal or to mitigate the consequences of such a violation. Suppose that Gail commits an ethical impropriety—for example, she reveals confidential communications. Since she works in her own office, the attorney who hired her may not learn about this impropriety in time to avoid or mitigate its consequences. Conflict of interest is another potential problem. Gail works for many different attorneys and hence many different clients of those attorneys. It is possible that she could accept work from two attorneys who are engaged in litigation against each other without either attorney knowing that the other has hired Gail on the same case. (See the earlier discussion of this problem on page 292.)

A few bar associations have declared that it is ethically improper for an attorney to hire a freelance paralegal because of the difficulties of providing meaningful supervision. It is not enough that the attorney vouches for, and takes responsibility for, the final product submitted by the freelance paralegal. Ongoing supervision is also needed under Model Rule 5.3. Not many states, however, have addressed this area of ethics. In the future, we will probably see the creation of new standards to govern this kind of paralegal.

▉ Section D. Doing Research on an Ethical Issue

1. At a law library, ask where the following two items are kept:
   - The code or rules of ethics governing the attorneys in your state
   - The ethical opinions that interpret the code or rules

2. Contact your state bar association. Ask what committee or other body has jurisdiction over ethics. Contact it to find out if it has published any opinions, guidelines, or other materials on paralegals. Also ask if there is a special committee on paralegals. If so, find out what it has said about paralegals.

3. Do the same for any other bar associations in your area, such as city or county bar associations.

4. At a law library, ask where the following two items are kept:
   - The ABA's Model Rules of Professional Responsibility
   - The ethical opinions that interpret these Model Rules as well as the earlier Model Code of Professional Responsibility of the ABA

5. Examine the *ABA/BNA Lawyers' Manual on Professional Conduct.* This is a loose-leaf book containing current information on ABA ethics and the ethical rules of every state.

6. Other material to check in the library:

   - C. Wolfram, *Modern Legal Ethics* (1986) (treatise)
   - *The Georgetown Journal of Legal Ethics* (periodical)
   - *Lawyers' Liability Review* (newsletter)

7. Computer research in either WESTLAW or LEXIS will enable you to do legal research on the law of ethics in your state. (See Chapters 11 and 13.) Here, for example, is a query (question) you could use to ask WESTLAW to find cases in your state in which a paralegal was charged with the unauthorized practice of law:

   paralegal "legal assistant" /p "unauthorized practice"

   After you instructed WESTLAW to turn to the database containing the court opinions of your state, you would type this query at the keyboard in order to find out if any such cases exist.

8. Another way to find court opinions on ethics in your state is to go to the digest covering the courts in your state. Use its index to find cases on ethical issues.

■ Section E. Ethical Codes of the Paralegal Associations

As indicated at the beginning of this chapter, there are no binding ethical rules published by paralegal associations. Yet the two major national associations—the National Federation of Paralegal Associations (NFPA) and the National Association of Legal Assistants (NALA)—have written ethical codes. These important documents of NFPA and of NALA are presented below, followed by a broader document of NALA, its Model Standards and Guidelines.

Affirmation of Professional Responsibility
of the National Federation of Paralegal Associations

Preamble

The National Federation of Paralegal Associations recognizes and accepts its commitment to the realization of the most basic right of a free society, equal justice under the law.

In examining contemporary legal institutions and systems, the members of the paralegal profession recognize that a redefinition of the traditional delivery of legal services is essential in order to meet the needs of the general public. The paralegal profession is committed to increasing the availability and quality of legal services.

The National Federation of Paralegal Associations has adopted this *Affirmation of Professional Responsibility* to delineate the principles of purpose and conduct toward which paralegals should aspire. Through

this Affirmation, the National Federation of Paralegal Associations places upon each paralegal the responsibility to adhere to these standards and encourages dedication to the development of the profession.

I. Professional Responsibility

A paralegal shall demonstrate initiative in performing and expanding the paralegal role in the delivery of legal services within the parameters of the unauthorized practice of law statutes.

Discussion: Recognizing the professional and legal responsibility to abide by the unauthorized practice of law statutes, the Federation supports and encourages new interpretations as to what constitutes the practice of law.

II. Professional Conduct

A paralegal shall maintain the highest standards of ethical conduct.

Discussion: It is the responsibility of a paralegal to avoid conduct which is unethical or appears to be unethical. Ethical principles are aspirational in character and embody the fundamental rules of conduct by which every paralegal should abide. Observance of these standards is essential to uphold respect for the legal system.

III. Competence and Integrity

A paralegal shall maintain a high level of competence and shall contribute to the integrity of the paralegal profession.

Discussion: The integrity of the paralegal profession is predicated upon individual competence. Professional competence is each paralegal's responsibility and is achieved through continuing education, awareness of developments in the field of law and aspiring to the highest standards of personal performance.

IV. Client Confidences

A paralegal shall preserve client confidences and privileged communications.

Discussion: Confidential information and privileged communications are a vital part of the attorney, paralegal and client relationship. The importance of preserving confidential and privileged information is understood to be an uncompromising obligation of every paralegal.

V. Support of Public Interests

A paralegal shall serve the public interests by contributing to the availability and delivery of quality legal services.

Discussion: It is the responsibility of each paralegal to promote the development and implementation of programs that address the legal needs of the public. A paralegal shall strive to maintain a sensitivity to public needs and to educate the public as to the services that paralegals may render.

VI. Professional Development

A paralegal shall promote the development of the paralegal profession.

Discussion: This Affirmation of Professional Responsibility promulgates a positive attitude through which a paralegal may recognize the importance, responsibility and potential of the paralegal contribution to the delivery of legal services. Participation in professional associations enhances the ability of the individual paralegal to contribute to the quality and growth of the paralegal profession.

Code of Ethics and Professional Responsibility
of the National Association of Legal Assistants

Preamble

It is the responsibility of every legal assistant to adhere strictly to the accepted standards of legal ethics and to live by general principles of proper conduct. The performance of the duties of the legal assistant shall be governed by specific canons as defined herein in order that justice will be served and the goals of the profession attained.

The canons of ethics set forth hereinafter are adopted by the National Association of Legal Assistants, Inc., as a general guide, and the enumeration of these rules does not mean there are not others of equal importance although not specifically mentioned.

Canon 1

A legal assistant shall not perform any of the duties that lawyers only may perform nor do things that lawyers themselves may not do.

Canon 2

A legal assistant may perform any task delegated and supervised by a lawyer so long as the lawyer is responsible to the client, maintains a direct relationship with the client, and assumes full professional responsibility for the work product.

Canon 3

A legal assistant shall not engage in the practice of law by accepting cases, setting fees, giving legal advice or appearing in court (unless otherwise authorized by court or agency rules).

Canon 4

A legal assistant shall not act in matters involving professional legal judgment as the services of a lawyer are essential in the public interest whenever the exercise of such judgment is required.

Canon 5

A legal assistant must act prudently in determining the extent to which a client may be assisted without the presence of a lawyer.

Canon 6

A legal assistant shall not engage in the unauthorized practice of law and shall assist in preventing the unauthorized practice of law.

Canon 7

A legal assistant must protect the confidences of a client, and it shall be unethical for a legal assistant to violate any statute now in effect or hereafter to be enacted controlling privileged communications.

Canon 8

It is the obligation of the legal assistant to avoid conduct which would cause the lawyer to be unethical or even appear to be unethical, and loyalty to the employer is incumbent upon the legal assistant.

Canon 9

A legal assistant shall work continually to maintain integrity and a high degree of competency throughout the legal profession.

Canon 10

A legal assistant shall strive for perfection through education in order to better assist the legal profession

in fulfilling its duty of making legal services available to clients and the public.

Canon 11

A legal assistant shall do all other things incidental, necessary, or expedient for the attainment of the ethics or responsibilities imposed by statute or rule of court.

Canon 12

A legal assistant is governed by the *American Bar Association Model Code of Professional Responsibility* and the *American Bar Association Model Rules of Professional Conduct.*

Model Standards and Guidelines for Utilization of Legal Assistants

of the National Association of Legal Assistants

Preamble

Proper utilization of the services of legal assistants affects the efficient delivery of legal services. Legal assistants and the legal profession should be assured that some measures exist for identifying legal assistants and their role in assisting attorneys in the delivery of legal services. Therefore, the National Association of Legal Assistants, Inc., hereby adopts these Model Standards and Guidelines as an educational document for the benefit of legal assistants and the legal profession.

Definition

Legal assistants* are a distinguishable group of persons who assist attorneys in the delivery of legal services. Through formal education, training, and experience, legal assistants have knowledge and expertise regarding the legal system and substantive and procedural law which qualify them to do work of a legal nature under the supervision of an attorney.

Standards

A legal assistant should meet certain minimum qualifications. The following standards may be used to determine an individual's qualifications as a legal assistant:

1. Successful completion of the Certified Legal Assistant (CLA) examination of the National Associ-

---

*Within this occupational category some individuals are known as paralegals.

ation of Legal Assistants, Inc.;

2. Graduation from an ABA approved program of study for legal assistants;

3. Graduation from a course of study for legal assistants which is institutionally accredited but not ABA approved, and which requires not less than the equivalent of 60 semester hours of classroom study;

4. Graduation from a course of study for legal assistants, other than those set forth in (2) and (3) above, plus not less than six months of in-house training as a legal assistant;

5. A baccalaureate degree in any field, plus not less than six months in-house training as a legal assistant;

6. A minimum of three years of law-related experience under the supervision of an attorney, including at least six months of in-house training as a legal assistant; or

7. Two years of in-house training as a legal assistant.

For purposes of these standards, "in-house training as a legal assistant" means attorney education of the employee concerning legal assistant duties and these Guidelines. In addition to review and analysis of assignments, the legal assistant should receive a reasonable amount of instruction directly related to the duties and obligations of the legal assistant.

Guidelines

These guidelines relating to standards of performance and professional responsibility are intended to aid legal assistants and attorneys. The responsibility rests with an attorney who employs legal assistants to educate them with respect to the duties they are assigned and to supervise the manner in which such duties are accomplished.

Legal assistants should:

1. Disclose their status as legal assistants at the outset of any professional relationship with a client, other attorneys, a court or administrative agency or personnel thereof, or members of the general public.
2. Preserve the confidences and secrets of all clients; and
3. Understand the attorney's Code of Professional Responsibility and these Guidelines in order to avoid any action which would involve the attorney in a violation of that Code, or give the appearance of professional impropriety.

Legal assistants should not:

1. Establish attorney-client relationships; set legal fees; give legal opinions or advice; or represent a client before a court; nor
2. Engage in, encourage, or contribute to any act which could constitute the unauthorized practice of law.

Legal assistants may perform services for an attorney in the representation of a client, provided:

1. The services performed by the legal assistant do not require the exercise of independent professional legal judgment;
2. The attorney maintains a direct relationship with the client and maintains control of all client matters;
3. The attorney supervises the legal assistant;
4. The attorney remains professionally responsible for all work on behalf of the client, including any actions taken or not taken by the legal assistant in connection therewith; and
5. The services performed supplement, merge with and become the attorney's work product.

In the supervision of a legal assistant, consideration should be given to:

1. Designating work assignments that correspond to the legal assistants' abilities, knowledge, training and experience;

2. Educating and training the legal assistant with respect to professional responsibility, local rules and practices, and firm policies;
3. Monitoring the work and professional conduct of the legal assistant to ensure that the work is substantively correct and timely performed;
4. Providing continuing education for the legal assistant in substantive matters through courses, institutes, workshops, seminars and in-house training; and
5. Encouraging and supporting membership and active participation in professional organizations.

Except as otherwise provided by statute, court rule or decision, administrative rule or regulation, or the attorney's Code of Professional Responsibility; and within the preceding parameters and proscriptions, a legal assistant may perform any function delegated by an attorney, including, but not limited to the following:

1. Conduct client interviews and maintain general contact with the client after the establishment of the attorney-client relationship, so long as the client is aware of the status and function of the legal assistant, and the client contact is under the supervision of the attorney.
2. Locate and interview witnesses, so long as the witnesses are aware of the status and function of the legal assistant.
3. Conduct investigations and statistical and documentary research for review by the attorney.
4. Conduct legal research for review by the attorney.
5. Draft legal documents for review by the attorney.
6. Draft correspondence and pleadings for review by and signature of the attorney.
7. Summarize depositions, interrogatories, and testimony for review by the attorney.
8. Attend executions of wills, real estate closings, depositions, court or administrative hearings and trials with the attorney.
9. Author and sign letters, provided the legal assistant's status is clearly indicated and the correspondence does not contain independent legal opinions or legal advice.

■ Section F. An Ethical Dilemma: Your Ethics or Your Job!

Throughout this chapter we have stressed the importance of maintaining your integrity through knowledge of and compliance with ethical rules. There may be times, however, when this is much easier said than done. Consider the following situations:

- You are not sure whether an ethical violation is being committed. Nor is anyone else in the office sure. Like so many areas of the law, ethical issues can be complex.

- You are sure that an ethical violation exists, and the violator is your supervisor!

- You are sure that an ethical violation exists, and the violators are everyone else in the office!

You face a potential dilemma (1) if no one seems to care about the ethical problem or, worse, (2) if your supervising attorney is the one committing the ethical impropriety or (3) if the entire office appears to be participating in the impropriety. People do not like to be told that they are unethical. Rather than acknowledge the fault and mend their ways, they may turn on the accuser, the one raising the fuss about ethics. Once the issue is raised, it may be very difficult to continue working in the office.

You need someone to talk to. In the best of all worlds, it will be someone in the same office. If this is not practical, consider contacting a teacher whom you trust. Paralegal associations are also an excellent source of information and support. A leader in one paralegal association offers the following advice:

> I would suggest that if the canons, discipline rules, affirmations, and codes of ethics do not supply you with a clear-cut answer to any ethical question you may have, you should draw upon the network that you have in being a member of this association. Getting the personal input of other paralegals who may have been faced with similar situations, or who have a greater knowledge through experience of our professional responsibilities, may greatly assist you in working your way through a difficult ethical situation.[60]

Of course, you must be careful not to violate client confidentiality during discussions with someone outside the office. Never mention actual client names or any specific information pertaining to a case. You can talk in hypothetical terms. For example, "an attorney working on a bankruptcy case asks a paralegal to. . . ." Once you present data in this sterilized fashion, you can then ask for guidance on the ethical implications of the data.

If handled delicately, most ethical problems that bother you can be resolved without compromising anyone's integrity or job. Yet the practice of law is not substantially different from other fields of endeavor. There will be times when the clash between principle and the dollar cannot be resolved to everyone's satisfaction. You may indeed have to make a choice between your ethics and your job.

■ ASSIGNMENT 5.1

(a) What is the name of the code of ethics that governs attorneys in your state?

(b) To what body or agency does a client initially make a charge of unethical conduct against his or her attorney in your state?

(c) List the steps required to discipline an attorney for unethical conduct in your state. Begin with the complaint stage and conclude with the court that makes the final decision. Draw a flow chart that lists these steps.

---

[60]Harper, *Ethical Considerations for Legal Assistants,* Compendium (Orange County Paralegal Ass'n, April 1987).

■ ASSIGNMENT 5.2

Paul Emerson is an attorney who works at the firm of Rayburn & Rayburn. One of the firm's clients is Designs Unlimited, Inc. (DU), a clothing manufacturer. Emerson provides corporate advice to DU. Recently Emerson made a mistake in interpreting a new securities law. As a consequence, DU had to postpone for six months the issuance of a stock option. Has Paul acted unethically?

■ ASSIGNMENT 5.3

(a) Three individuals in Connecticut hire a large New York law firm to represent them in a proxy fight in which they sought control of a Connecticut bank. They lose the proxy fight. The firm then sends these individuals a $358,827 bill for 895 hours of work over a one month period. Is this bill unethical? What further facts would you like to have to help you answer this question?

(b) Victor Adams and Len Patterson are full partners in the law firm of Adams, Patterson & Kelly. A client contacts Patterson to represent him on a negligence case. Patterson refers the case to Victor Adams who does most of the work. (Under an agreement between them, Patterson will receive 40% and Adams will receive 60% of any fee paid by this client.) Patterson does not tell the client about the involvement of Adams in the case. Any ethical problems?

(c) An attorney establishes a bonus plan for her paralegals. A bonus will be given to those paralegals who bill a specified number of hours in excess of a stated minimum. The amount of the bonus will depend on the amount billed and collected. Any ethical problems?

■ ASSIGNMENT 5.4

Mary works in a law firm that charges clients $125 an hour for attorney time and $55 an hour for paralegal time. She and another paralegal, Fred, are working with an attorney on a large case. She sees all of the time sheets that the three of them submit to the firm's accounting office. She suspects that the attorney is padding his time sheets by overstating the number of hours he works on the case. For example, he lists thirty hours for a four-day period when he was in court every day on another case. Furthermore, Fred's time is being billed at the full $55-an-hour rate even though he spends about 80% of his time typing correspondence, filing, and other clerical duties. Mary also suspects that her attorney is billing out Mary's time at the attorney rate rather than the paralegal rate normally charged clients for her time. Any ethical problems? What should Mary do?

■ ASSIGNMENT 5.5

Smith is an attorney who works at the firm of Johnson & Johnson. He represents Ralph Grant, who is seeking a divorce from his wife, Amy Grant. In their first meeting, Smith learns that Ralph is an experienced carpenter but is out of work and has very little money. Smith's fee is $150 an hour. Since Ralph has no money and has been having trouble finding work, Smith tells Ralph that he won't have to pay the fee if the court does not grant him the divorce. One day while Smith is working on another case involving Helen Oberlin, he learns that Helen is looking for a carpenter. Smith recommends Ralph to Helen, and she hires him for a small job. Six months pass. The divorce case is dropped when the Grants reconcile. In the meantime, Helen Oberlin is very dissatisfied with Ralph's carpentry work for her; she claims he didn't do the work he contracted to do. She wants to know what she can do about it. She tries to call Smith at Johnson & Johnson but is told that Smith does not work there anymore. Another attorney, Georgia Quinton, Esq. helps Helen. Any ethical problems?

■ ASSIGNMENT 5.6

John Jones is a paralegal working at the XYZ law firm. The firm is handling a large class action involving potentially thousands of plaintiffs. John has been instructed to screen the potential plaintiffs in the class. John tells those he screens out (using criteria provided by the firm) in writing or verbally that "unfortunately, our firm will not be able to represent you." Any ethical problems?

■ ASSIGNMENT 5.7

A paralegal quits the firm of Smith & Smith. When she leaves, she takes client documents she prepared while at the firm. The documents contain confidential client information. The paralegal is showing these documents to potential employers as writing samples.

(a) What is the ethical liability of attorneys at Smith & Smith under Model Rule 5.3?

(b) What is the ethical liability of attorneys at law firms where she is seeking employment under 5.3?

(c) What is the paralegal's liability?

■ ASSIGNMENT 5.8

(a) Mary Smith is a paralegal at the ABC law firm. She has been working on the case of Jessica Randolph, a client of the office. Mary talks with Ms. Randolph often. Mary receives a subpoena from the attorney of the party that is suing Ms. Randolph. On the witness stand, Mary is asked by this attorney what Ms. Randolph told her at the ABC law office about a particular business transaction related to the suit. Randolph's attorney (Mary's boss) objects to the question. What result?

(b) Before Helen became a paralegal for the firm of Harris & Derkson, she was a chemist for a large corporation. Harris & Derkson is a patent law firm where Helen's technical expertise in chemistry is invaluable. Helen's next-door neighbor is an inventor. On a number of occasions he discussed the chemical makeup of his inventions with Helen. Regarding one of these inventions, the neighbor is being charged by the government with stealing official secrets to prepare the invention. Harris & Derkson represent the neighbor on this case. Helen also works directly on the case for the firm. In a prosecution of the neighbor, Helen is called as a witness and is asked to reveal the substance of all her conversations with the neighbor concerning the invention in question. Does Helen have to answer?

■ ASSIGNMENT 5.9

Bob and Patricia Fannan are separated, and they both want a divorce. They would like to have a joint-custody arrangement in which their son would spend time with each parent during the year. The only marital property is a house, which they agree should be sold, with each to get one half of the proceeds. Mary Franklin, Esq. is an attorney whom Jim and Mary know and trust. They decide to ask Franklin to represent both of them in the divorce. Any ethical problems?

■ ASSIGNMENT 5.10

Alice is a freelance paralegal with a specialty in probate law. One of the firms she has worked for is Davis, Ritter & Boggs. Her most recent assignment for this firm has been to identify the assets of Mary Steck, who died six months ago. One of Mary's assets is a 75% ownership share in the Domain Corporation. Alice learns a great deal about this company, including the fact that four months ago it had difficulty meeting its payroll and expects to have similar difficulties in the coming year.

Alice's freelance business has continued to grow because of her excellent reputation. She decides to hire an employee with a different specialty so that her office can begin to take different kinds of cases from attorneys. She hires Bob, a paralegal with four years of litigation experience. The firm of Jackson & Jackson hires Alice to digest a series of long deposition documents in the case of Glendale Bank v. Ajax Tire Co. Jackson & Jackson represents Glendale Bank. Peterson, Zuckerman & Morgan represents Ajax Tire Co. Alice assigns Bob to this case. Ajax Tire Co. is a wholly owned subsidiary of the Domain Corporation. Glendale Bank is suing Ajax Tire Co. for fraud in misrepresenting its financial worth when Ajax Tire Co. applied for and obtained a loan from Glendale Bank.

Any ethical problems?

■ ASSIGNMENT 5.11

Assume that you owned a successful freelance business in which you provided paralegal services to over 150 attorneys all over the state. How should your files be organized in order to avoid a conflict of interest?

■ ASSIGNMENT 5.12

Joan is a paralegal who works for the XYZ law firm, which is representing Goff in a suit against Barnard, who is represented by the ABC law firm. Joan calls Barnard and says, "Is this the first time that you have ever been sued?" Barnard answers, "Yes it is. Is there anything else that you would like to know?" Joan says *no* and the conversation ends. Any ethical problems?

■ ASSIGNMENT 5.13

Mary is a paralegal who is a senior citizen. She works at the XYZ legal service office. One day she goes to a senior citizens center and says the following:

> All of you should know about and take advantage of the XYZ legal service office where I work. Let me give you just one example why. Down at the office there is an attorney named Armanda Morris. She is an expert on insurance company cases. Some of you may have had trouble with insurance companies that say one thing and do another. Our office is available to serve you.

Any ethical problems?

■ ASSIGNMENT 5.14

(a) What restrictions exist on advertising by attorneys in your state? Give an example of an ad on TV or in the newspaper that would be unethical. On researching an ethical issue, see page 312.

(b) In *Bates v. State Bar of Arizona,* 433 U.S. 350 (1970), the United States Supreme Court held that a state could not prohibit all forms of lawyer advertising. Has *Bates* been cited by state courts in your state on the advertising issue? If so, what impact has the case had in your state? To find out, shepardize *Bates.* The specific techniques of shepardizing a case are found in Checklist 4a, page 569.

■ ASSIGNMENT 5.15

Mary Jackson is a paralegal at Rollins & Rollins. She is supervised by Ian Gregory. Mary is stealing money from the funds of one of the firm's clients. The only attorney who knows about this is Dan Roberts, Esq., who is not a partner at the firm and who does not supervise Mary. Dan says and does nothing about Mary's actions. What ethical obligations does Dan have under Model Rule 5.3?

■ ASSIGNMENT 5.16

John Smith is a paralegal who works for the firm of Beard, Butler, and Clark. John's immediate supervisor is Viola Butler, Esq. With the full knowledge and blessing of Viola Butler, John Smith sends a letter to a client of the firm (Mary Anders). Has Viola Butler acted unethically in permitting John to send out this letter? The letter is as follows:

Law Offices of
Beard, Butler, and Clark
310 High St.
Maincity, Ohio 45238
512-663-9410

Attorneys at Law   *Paralegal*

Ronald Beard   **John Smith**
Viola Butler
Wilma Clark

May 14, 1991

Mary Anders
621 S. Randolph Ave.
Maincity, Ohio 45238

Dear Ms. Anders:

   Viola Butler, the attorney in charge of your case, has asked me to let you know that next month's hearing has been postponed. We will let you know the new date as soon as possible. If you have any questions don't hesitate to call me.

Sincerely,

John Smith
Legal Intern

JS:wps

■ ASSIGNMENT 5.17

Under what circumstances, if any, would it be appropriate for you to refer to a client of the office where you work as "my client"?

■ ASSIGNMENT 5.18

John Jones is a paralegal who works for an attorney named Linda Sunders. Linda is away from the office one day and telephones John, who is at the office. She dictates a one-line letter to a client of the office. The letter reads, "I advise you to sue." Linda asks John to sign the letter for her. The bottom of the letter reads as follows:

Linda Sunders
by John Jones

Any ethical problems?

■ ASSIGNMENT 5.19

Mary is a paralegal who works at the XYZ law firm. She specializes in real estate matters at the firm. Mary attends a real estate closing in which her role consists of exchanging documents and acknowledging the receipt of documents. Analyze this problem on the basis of the following variations:

(a) The closing takes place at the XYZ law firm.

(b) The closing takes place at a bank.

(c) Mary's supervising attorney is not present at the closing.

(d) Mary's supervising attorney is present at the closing.

(e) Mary's supervising attorney is present at the closing except for thirty minutes, during which time Mary continued to exchange documents and acknowledge the receipt of documents.

(f) During the closing, the attorney for the other party says to Mary, "I don't know why my client should have to pay that charge." Mary responds: "In this state that charge is always paid in this way."

■ ASSIGNMENT 5.20

John is a paralegal who works for the XYZ law firm, which is representing a client against the Today Insurance Company. The Company also employs paralegals who work under the Company's general counsel. One of these paralegals is Mary. In an effort to settle the case, Mary calls John and says, "We offer you $200.00." John says, "We'll let you know." Any ethical problems?

■ ASSIGNMENT 5.21

John Smith is a paralegal who works for Beard, Butler, and Clark. He sends out the following letter. Any ethical problems?

John Smith
Paralegal
310 High St.
Maincity, Ohio 45238
512-663-9410

June 1, 1991

State Unemployment Board
1216 Southern Ave.
Maincity, Ohio 45238

Dear Gentlepeople:

   I work for Beard, Butler, and Clark, which represents Mary Anders, who has a claim before your agency. A hearing originally scheduled for June 8, 1991 has been postponed. We request that the hearing be held at the earliest time possible after the 8th.

Sincerely,

John Smith

JS:wps

■ **ASSIGNMENT 5.22**

   In Section C of Chapter 2, there is a long list of tasks that paralegals have performed, and comments by paralegals working in the specialties covered. Identify any three tasks or paralegal comments that *might* pose ethical problems or problems of unauthorized practice. Explain why.

■ **ASSIGNMENT 5.23**

   Compare the Affirmation of Professional Responsibility of NFPA with the Code of Ethics and Professional Responsibility of NALA, page 313. Make a list of the topics or themes covered in one of the documents but not in the other. Is there a difference in emphasis between the two documents?

■ **ASSIGNMENT 5.24**

   Draft your own paralegal code as a class project. First, have a meeting in which you make a list of all the issues that you think should be covered in the code. Divide up the issues by the number of students in the class so that every student has roughly the same number of issues. Each student should draft a proposed rule on each of the issues to which he or she is assigned. Accompany each rule with a brief commentary on why you think the rule should be as stated. Draft alternative versions of the proposed rule if different versions are possible and you want to give the class the chance to examine all of them. The class then meets to vote on each of the proposed rules. Students will make presentations on the proposed rules they have drafted. If the class is not happy with the way in which a particular proposed rule was drafted by a student, the latter will redraft the rule for later consideration by the class. One member of the class should be designated the "code reporter," who records the rules accepted by the class by majority vote.

After you have completed the code, you should consider inviting attorneys from the local bar association to your class in order to discuss your proposed code. Do the same with officials of the closest paralegal association in your area.

☐ Chapter Summary

Attorneys are regulated by the highest court in the state, often with the extensive involvement of the state bar association. Since paralegals cannot practice law and cannot become full members of a bar association, they cannot be punished for a violation of the ethical rules governing attorneys. The American Bar Association is a voluntary association; no attorney must be a member. The ABA publishes ethical rules which the states are free to adopt, modify, or reject.

The current rules of the ABA are found in its *Model Rules of Professional Conduct*. These ethical rules require attorneys to be competent, to act with reasonable diligence and promptness, to charge fees that are reasonable, to avoid conduct that is criminal and fraudulent, to avoid asserting claims and defenses that are frivolous, to safeguard the property of clients, to avoid making false statements of law and fact to a tribunal, to withdraw from a case for appropriate reasons, to maintain the confidentiality of client information, to avoid conflicts of interest, to avoid improper communications with an opponent, to avoid improper solicitation of clients, to avoid improper advertising, to report serious professional misconduct of other attorneys, to avoid assisting nonattorneys engage in the unauthorized practice of law, and to supervise paralegal employees appropriately.

Ethical opinions and guidelines exist in almost every state on the proper use of a paralegal by an attorney. All states agree that the title used for this employee must not mislead anyone about his or her nonattorney status, and that the employee must disclose his or her nonattorney status when necessary to avoid misunderstanding. Rules also exist on other aspects of the attorney-paralegal relationship, but not all states agree on what these rules should be. The following apply in most states:

Under attorney approval and supervision, paralegals in most states:

- can have their own business card
- can have their name printed on the law firm letterhead
- can sign law firm correspondence
- can give nonlegal advice
- can draft legal documents
- can attend a real estate closing
- can represent clients at agency hearings if authorized by the agency

With few exceptions, paralegals in most states:

- cannot give legal advice
- cannot conduct a deposition
- cannot sign formal court documents
- cannot supervise the execution of a will
- cannot make an appearance in court

Separate ethical rules and guidelines have been adopted by the National Association of Legal Assistants and by the National Federation of Paralegal Associations.

Key Terms

ethics	integrated bar association	Model Rules of Professional Conduct
sanctions	mandatory bar association	
national bar association	unified bar association	Model Code of Professional Responsibility
state bar association	registration	
local bar association	self-regulation	DR

EC
disbarment
suspension
interim suspension
reprimand
private reprimand
censure
public censure
admonition
probation
competence
malpractice
6th amendment
reasonable diligence
reasonable fee
retainer
minimum fee schedule
antitrust law
contingent fee
fee splitting
referral fee
forwarding fee
double billing
padding time sheets
insider trading
pirated software
frivolous positions
commingle funds
adversarial system

withdrawal
cured
impaired attorney
privileged
confidentiality
attorney-client privilege
work-product rule
discoverable
waiver
conflict of interest
divided loyalty
multiple representation
common representation
adverse interests
friendly divorce
switching sides
imputed disqualification
vicarious disqualification
Chinese wall
ethical wall
cone of silence
tainted/contaminated
    employee
quarantined paralegal
conflicts check
lateral hire
disinterested
in-person solicitation
barratry

ambulance chasing
attorney advertising
runner/capper
unauthorized practice of law
model rule 5.3
tickler
associate/associated
business card
CLA
law-firm letterhead
law directory
legal advice
professional judgment
separate identity of document
real estate closing
deposition/deponent
supervision
delegatitis
second chair
freelance paralegal
Affirmation of Professional
    Responsibility (NFPA)
Code of Ethics and
    Professional
    Responsibility (NALA)
Model Standards and
    Guidelines for Utilization
    of Legal Assistants
    (NALA)

11

Legal Research

■ Chapter Outline

■ Section A. A Strategy for Studying Legal Research

This chapter does not cover every aspect of legal research, nor does it treat every conceivable law book that could be found in a law library. Rather, the chapter examines the major components of legal research with the objective of identifying effective starting points.

FIGURE 11.1

A Strategy for
Studying Legal
Research

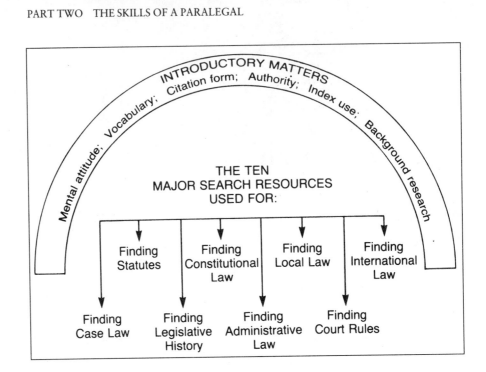

A great deal of information is provided in the pages that follow. You should first read the chapter through quickly to obtain an overview and to begin seeing where some concepts are covered in more than one place. The second time you read the chapter, you should begin collecting the terminology called for in Assignment 11.1. The best way to avoid becoming overwhelmed is to start feeling comfortable with terminology as soon as possible.

When you walk into a law library, your first impression is likely to be one of awe. You are confronted with row upon row of books, most of which seem unapproachable; they do not invite browsing. To be able to use the law library, your first responsibility as a legal researcher is to break down any psychological barrier that you may have with respect to the books in it. This is done not only by learning the techniques of research but also by understanding the limitations of the law library.

A major misunderstanding about the law library is that it contains the answer to every legal question. In many instances, legal problems have no definitive answers. The researcher often operates on the basis of "educated guesses" of what the answer is. To be sure, your guess is supported by what you uncover through legal research in the law library. The end product, however, is only the researcher's opinion of what the law is, rather than the absolute answer. No one will know for sure what the "right" or final answer is until the matter is litigated in court. If the problem is never litigated, then the "right" answer will be whatever the parties accept among themselves through negotiation or settlement. The researcher will not know what answer carries the day for the client until the negotiation process is over.

Many simple problems, however, can be answered by basic (easy) legal research. If someone wants to know, for example, the name of the government agency in charge of incorporating a business or the maximum number of weeks one can receive unemployment compensation, finding the answer is not difficult if the researcher knows what books to go to and how to use their indexes. Most legal research problems, however, are not this simple.

Perhaps the most healthy way to approach the law library is to view it not as a repository of answers but as a storehouse of ambiguities that are waiting to be identified, clarified, manipulated, and applied to the facts of a client's case. You may have heard the story of a client who walked into a law office and asked to see a one-armed attorney. When asked why he required an attorney meeting such specifications, he replied that he was tired of presenting problems to attorneys and having them constantly tell him that "on the one hand" he should do this but "on the other hand" he should do that; he hungered for an attorney who would give him an answer. This concern is well taken. A client is entitled to an answer, to clear guidance. At the same time (or, on the other hand), part of the attorney's job is to identify alternatives or options and to weigh benefits and liabilities of any one particular course of action. Good attorneys are so inclined because they understand that our legal system is infested with unknowns and ambiguities. Good legal researchers also have this understanding. They are not frightened by ambiguities; they thrive on them.

Section B. The Importance of Legal Research

You will eventually forget most of the law that you learn in school. If you do not forget most of it, you should! No one can know all of the law at any given time, even in a specialty. Furthermore, the law is always changing. Nothing is more dangerous than someone with out-of-date "knowledge" of the law. Law cannot be practiced on the basis of the rules learned in school, since those rules may no longer be valid by the time you try to use them in actual cases. Thousands of courts, legislatures, and administrative agencies spend considerable time writing new laws and changing or adapting old ones.

The law library and the techniques of legal research are the indispensable tickets of admission to current law. School teaches you to think. *You teach yourself the law through the skill of legal research.* Every time you walk into a law library, you are your own professor. You must accept nothing less than to become an expert on the topic of your research, no matter how narrow the topic. The purpose of the law library is to enable you to become an expert on the current law of your topic. Do not fall into the trap of thinking that you must be an expert in an area of the law to research it properly. The reverse is true. A major way for you to become an expert in an area is through what you discover in the law library on your own.

Never be reluctant to undertake legal research on a topic simply because you know very little about the topic. Knowing very little is often the most healthy starting point for the researcher! Preconceptions about the law can sometimes lead you away from avenues in the library that you should be traveling.

To become an expert through comprehensive legal research does not necessarily mean that you will know everything. Experts are not simply people who know the answers; they also know how to *formulate the questions that remain unanswered even after comprehensive legal research*. An expert is someone who can say:

> This is what the current law says, and these are the questions that the law has not yet resolved.

Of course, you cannot know what is unresolved until you know what is resolved. The law library will help tell you both.

◼ Section C. Frustration and Legal Research

You are in the position of the king who sadly had to be told that there is no royal road to geometry. If he wanted to learn geometry, he had to struggle through it like everyone else. Legal research is a struggle and will remain so for the rest of your career. The struggle will eventually become manageable and even enjoyable and exciting—but there is no way out of the struggle no matter how many short cuts you learn. The amount of material in a law library is simply too massive for it to be otherwise, and the material is growing every day with new laws, new formats for law books, and new law publishers offering different services that must be mastered.

Unfortunately, many cannot handle the pressure that the law library sometimes seems to donate in abundance. Too many attorneys, for example, stay away from the library, and consequently practice law "from the hip." Such attorneys need to be sure that they have extensive malpractice insurance!

Legal research will be difficult for you at the beginning, but with experience in the law library, the difficulties will become manageable. The most important advice you can receive is *stick with it*. Spend a lot of time in the library. Be inquisitive. Ask a lot of questions of fellow students, teachers, librarians, lawyers, paralegals, legal secretaries, etc. Be constantly on the alert for tips and techniques. Take strange books from the shelf and try to figure out what they contain, what they try to do, how they are used, and how they duplicate or complement other law books that are not strange to you. Do not wait to be taught how to use sets of books that are new to you. Strike out on your own.

The coming of computer technology to legal research is of some help, but computers cannot eliminate your need to learn the basics. The struggle does not disappear if you are lucky enough to study or work where computers are available. Intelligent use of computers requires an understanding of the fundamental techniques of legal research.

At this stage of your career, most of the frustration will center on the question of how to *begin* your legal research of a topic. Once you overcome this frustration, the concern will then become how to *end* your legal research. After having located a great deal of material, you will worry about when to stop. In this chapter, our major focus will be the techniques of beginning. Techniques of stopping are more troublesome for the conscientious researcher. It is not always easy to determine whether you have found everything that you should find. Although guidelines do exist and will be examined, a great deal of experience with legal research is required before you can make the judgment that you have found everything available on a given topic. Don't be too hard on yourself. The techniques will come with time and practice. You will not learn everything now; you can only begin the learning that must continue throughout your career.

Keep the following "laws" of legal research in mind:

1. *The only books that will be missing from a shelf are those that you need to use immediately.*

2. *A vast amount of information on law books and research techniques exists, most of which you will forget soon after learning.*

3. *Each time you forget something, relearning it will take half the time it previously took.*

4. *When you have relearned something for the fourth time, you own it.*

At times you will walk away from a set of law books that you have used and wonder what you have just done—even if you obtained an answer from the books. At times you will go back to a set of books that you have used before and draw a blank on what the books are and how to use them again. These occurrences are natural. You will forget and you will forget again. Stay with it. Be willing to relearn. You cannot master a set of books after using them only a few times. Learning legal research is a little like learning to play a musical instrument: a seat is waiting for you in the orchestra, but you must practice. A royal road does not exist.

Section D. Flexibility in Legal Research

Researchers have reached an enviable plateau when they understand the following paradox: You sometimes do not know what you are looking for until you find it. Since simple answers are rare, researchers are constantly confronted with frustration and ambiguity. As they pursue avenues and leads, they invariably come upon new avenues and thoughts that never occurred to them initially. An entirely new approach to the problem may be uncovered that radically changes their initial perceptions. They reached this stage not because they consciously sought it out but because they were flexible and open-minded enough to be receptive to new approaches and perceptions. This phenomenon is by no means peculiar to legal research. Take the situation of the woman in need of transportation. She sets herself to the task of determining the most economical way to *buy* a good car. In her search, she stumbles upon the practice of leasing cars. After studying this option, she concludes that leasing is the most sensible resolution of her transportation problem. She did not know what she was looking for—a car *leasing* deal—until she found it. Compare this situation with that of a client who comes into a law office for advice on how to write a will so that a certain amount of money will pass to designated individuals upon death. The attorney asks you to do some legal research in the area of wills. While in the law library studying the law of wills, you see reference to life insurance policies as a substitute for wills in passing cash to beneficiaries at death. You bring this to the attention of the attorney, who decides that this option is indeed worth pursuing. You did not know what you were looking for—a will substitute— until you found it.

■ Section E. The Vocabulary of Legal Research: A Checklist

This section includes a list of 175 words and phrases, most of which are examined in the remainder of the chapter. The page number in parentheses indicates where the item is covered in the text. The list is the vocabulary of legal research. Before you are finished with this text, one of your goals should be to know the meaning or function of everything on the list. You must learn to speak the language of legal research, as well as to do legal research. See Figure 11.2.

■ ASSIGNMENT 11.1

For each of the words and phrases in Figure 11.2, prepare a three-by-five-inch index card on which you include the following information:

- The word or phrase
- The pages in this text where the word or phrase is discussed (begin with the page number given in parentheses, then add other page numbers as the word or phrase is discussed elsewhere in the text)
- The definition of the word or phrase, or the function of the word or phrase
- Other information about the word or phrase that you obtain as you use the law library
- Comments by your instructor in class about any of the words and phrases

Some words and phrases will call for more than one card. You should strive, however, to keep the information on the cards brief. Place the cards in alphabetical order. The cards will become your own file system on legal research that you can use as a study guide for the course and as a reference tool when you do legal research in the library. Be sure to add cards for words and phrases as you come across new ones in class and in the library.

See also Assignment 11.7 for other data that you can add to your cards.

■ Section F. Finding Law Libraries

The availability of law libraries depends to a large degree on the area in which you live, study, or work. Rural areas have fewer possibilities than larger cities or capitals.

Twelve different law library possibilities are listed below. Find out which ones exist in your area. You may need permission to use some of them. (This is certainly true of a private law firm's library.) If a law school or university library is a *depository library,* you must be allowed to use it, or at least those sections of the library that contain the law books that the library receives free of charge from the federal government.

- Law school library
- General university library (may have a law section)
- Law library of a bar association
- State law library (in the state capital and perhaps in branch offices in counties throughout the state)
- Local public library (may have a small law section)
- Law library of a court

1. Act (486)	56. Constitution (329)
2. Administrative code (486)	57. Corpus Juris Secundum (C.J.S.) (496)
3. Administrative decision (329)	58. Cumulative (497)
4. Administrative regulation (329)	59. Current Law Index (579)
5. Advance Sheet (for reporters) (486)	60. Decennial Digest (499)
6. Advance Sheet (for Shepard's) (487)	61. Descriptive Word Index (DWI) (556)
7. A.L.R. Blue Book of Supplemental Decisions (560)	62. DIALOG (587)
8. A.L.R. Digest to 3d, 4th, Federal (559)	63. Dicta, dictum (357)
9. A.L.R. First, A.L.R.2d, A.L.R.3d, A.L.R.4th, A.L.R. Fed (487)	64. Digests (for reporters) (497)
10. A.L.R. First Series Quick Index (559)	65. Digests (for A.L.R. annotations) (559)
11. A.L.R.2d Digest (559)	66. Docket Number (355)
12. A.L.R.2d Later Case Service (560)	67. Et. Seq. (573)
13. American Digest System (498)	68. Executive Order (329)
14. American Law Institute (508)	69. Federal Digest (498)
15. Am. Jur. 2d (487)	70. Federal Practice Digest 2d (499)
16. Amicus curiae brief (491)	71. Federal Practice Digest 3d (499)
17. Annotated reporter (487)	72. Federal Practice Digest 4th (499)
18. Annotation (487)	73. Federal Supplement (F. Supp.) (492)
19. Annotation History Table (A.L.R.) (561)	74. Federal Register (502)
20. Appellant (448)	75. Federal Reporter 2d (F.2d) (492)
21. Appellate brief (491)	76. Federal Rules Decisions (F.R.D.) (502)
22. Appellate court (331)	77. General Digest (499)
23. Appellee (448)	78. Headnote (503)
24. Atlantic Digest (499)	79. Hornbook (504)
25. Atlantic 2d (A.2d) (494)	80. Index Medicus (581)
26. Authority, mandatory (517)	81. Index to Legal Periodicals (578)
27. Authority, persuasive (517)	82. Index to Annotations (A.L.R.) (559)
28. Authority, primary (517)	83. Insta-Cite (657, 659)
29. Authority, secondary (517)	84. Key topic and number (497)
30. Auto-Cite (586)	85. Law review (505)
31. Bill (490)	86. Lawyer's Edition (L. Ed.) (491)
32. Bluebook (citations) (490)	87. Legal dictionary (504)
33. Blue and White Book (490)	88. Legal encyclopedia (504)
34. Brief of a case (353)	89. Legal newspaper (505)
35. California Reporter (Cal. Rptr.) (491)	90. Legal periodical (578)
36. CALR (585)	91. Legal Resource Index (581)
37. Case (491)	92. Legal thesaurus (505)
38. Casebook (495)	93. LegalTrac (581)
39. Case on point (518)	94. Legislative history (337)
40. CCH U.S. Supreme Court Bulletin (492)	95. LEXIS (585)
41. CD ROM (495)	96. Loose-leaf service (506)
42. Century Digest (498)	97. Majority opinion (357)
43. Certiorari (Cert.) (449)	98. Maroon Book (539)
44. Charter (329)	99. Martindale-Hubbell (506)
45. CARTWHEEL (544)	100. Memorandum opinion (355)
46. Citation (496)	101. Military Justice Reporter (492)
47. Citator (496)	102. Modern Federal Practice Digest (499)
48. Cite checking (539)	103. National Reporter System (493)
49. Cited material (Shepard's) (510)	104. National Reporter Blue Book (490)
50. Citing material (Shepard's) (510)	105. New York Supplement (N.Y.S.) (507)
51. Code, codify (496)	106. NEXIS (587)
52. Code of Federal Regulations (C.F.R.) (496)	107. Nominative reporter (531)
53. Common law (358)	108. North Eastern 2d (N.E.2d) (494)
54. Concurring opinion (357)	109. North Western Digest (499)
55. Congressional Record (496)	110. North Western 2d (N.W.2d) (494)
	111. Notes of decisions (591)
	112. Official citation (491)
	113. Opinion (court) (329)

FIGURE 11.2

The Vocabulary of Legal Research: A Checklist*

*The numbers in parentheses refer to pages in this book.

Continued

FIGURE 11.2

The Vocabulary of
Legal Research:
A Checklist
—Continued

114. Opinion of the Attorney General (329)
115. Ordinance (329)
116. Pacific 2d (P.2d) (494)
117. Pacific Digest (499)
118. Parallel Cite (526)
119. Parallel Table of Authorities and
     Rules (in C.F.R.) (596)
120. Per Curiam (355)
121. Permanent A.L.R. Digest (559)
122. Pocket part (508)
123. Popular Name Table (595)
124. Public Law (PL) (329)
125. Record (508)
126. Remand (449)
127. Regional digest (499)
128. Reporter (491)
129. Respondent (448)
130. Restatements (508)
131. Rules of court (329)
132. Scope Note (556)
133. Series (509)
134. Session Law (571)
135. Shepardize (510)
136. Slip law (510)
137. Slip opinion (513)
138. South Eastern Digest (499)
139. South Eastern 2d (S.E.2d) (494)
140. Southern 2d (So.2d) (494)
141. South Western 2d (S.W.2d) (494)
142. Squib (497)
143. Star paging (491)
144. Statute, private (329)
145. Statute, public (329)
146. Statutes at Large (513)
147. Statutory code (513)
148. Superseded annotation (A.L.R.) (561)
149. Supplemented Annotation
     (A.L.R.) (561)
150. Supreme Court Reporter (S. Ct.) (491)
151. Syllabus (355) (567)
152. Table of Authorities (628)
153. Table of Courts and Circuits
     (A.L.R.) (560)
154. Table of Jurisdictions Represented
     (A.L.R.) (560)
155. Table of Laws, Rules, and
     Regulations (A.L.R.) (559)
156. Total Client-Service Library (514)
157. Treatise (515)
158. Treaty (329)
159. A Uniform System of Citation (490)
160. Unofficial citation (491)
161. U.S. Code (U.S.C.) (514)
162. U.S. Code Annotated (U.S.C.A.) (514)
163. U.S. Code Service (U.S.C.S.) (514)
164. U.S. Code Congressional and
     Administrative News (USCCAN) (515)
165. U.S. Court of Appeals (332)
166. U.S. District Court (332)
167. U.S. Law Week (U.S.L.W.) (516)
168. U.S. Reports (U.S.) (491)
169. U.S. Statutes at Large (516)
170. U.S. Supreme Court Digest
     (L. Ed.) (500)
171. U.S. Supreme Court Digest
     (West) (500)
172. VERALEX (586)
173. WESTLAW (585)
174. WILSONLINE (587)
175. Words and Phrases (504)

- Law library of the legislature or city council
- Law library of the city solicitor or corporation counsel
- Law library of a private law firm
- Law library of the district attorney or local prosecutor
- Law library of the public defender
- Law library of a federal, state, or local administrative agency (particularly in the general counsel's office of the agency)

You may need some ingenuity to locate these libraries and to gain access to them. Try more than one avenue of entry. Do not become discouraged when the first person you contact tells you that the library is for members or private use only. Some students adopt the strategy of walking into a library—particularly a library supported by public funds—and acting as if they belong. Rather than asking for permission, they wait for someone to stop them or to question their right to be there. Other students take the wiser course of seeking permission in advance. Yet, even here, some creativity is needed in the way that you ask for permission. The bold question, "Can I use your library?" may be less effective than an approach such as, "Would it be possible for me to use a few of your law books for a short period of time for some important research that I must do?''

There is one other law library that you need to consider: your own. It is not too soon for you to start collecting your own law books, beginning with your course books on law. But never buy a practice book or manual without checking with at least two attorneys or paralegals on the *practical* value of the book. Ask them how often they consult the book. It is not necessarily wise to purchase a book simply because it treats an area of the law you need to know something about. Also, be prepared for sticker shock when you find out what many of these books cost.

Once you gain access to a law library, you may face another problem. There are library employees who resent spending a great deal of time answering the questions of students. At a recent conference of the American Association of Law Libraries, an entire session was devoted to the theme of student paralegal requests for assistance which ''can take a tremendous amount of the law librarian's time and energy.'' Even if an employee at the desk is willing to give you all the time you need, the supervisor of that employee may be opposed to the attention you are getting. Use your common sense in such situations. Keep your requests to a minimum, particularly if there are other students seeking the same kind of help. Before you ask a question, reread the textbook. Many questions can be answered on your own.

■ Section G. A Glossary of Law and Law Books: Introduction

There are ten major categories of law. The purpose of legal research is to find these laws, to check their current validity, and to apply them to the facts of the research problem. Step one is to know the definitions of the categories.

Categories of Law

Opinions	Ordinances
Statutes	Rules of court
Constitutions	Executive orders
Administrative regulations	Treaties
Administrative decisions	Opinion of attorney general
Charters	

These categories of law (plus opinions of the attorney general) were defined in Chapter 6. See page 329. You should review these definitions now.

A word of caution on the vocabulary of law and legal research: The same word or phrase can often have a different meaning depending on the context in which it is used. *Supreme Court,* for example, refers to the *highest* court in our federal judicial system as well as to the *trial* court in New York State; and the word *opinion* can refer to the judicial decisions of courts and to the administrative decisions of agencies. Although standard definitions are generally used, you should be prepared to find variations.

We now begin examining the sets of books in the library that are relevant to these categories of laws. For each category, four types of books should be kept in mind:

- Sets of books that contain the full text of a certain kind of law
- Sets of books that can be used to locate that kind of law
- Sets of books that can be used to help explain that kind of law
- Sets of books that can be used to help determine the current validity of that kind of law

Some sets of books cover more than one category of law and serve more than one of these four functions. The chart in Figure 11.3 presents a catalog of research materials according to their functions.

The following is a glossary of some of the major legal research books and terms, including many used in Figure 11.3.

Act; Acts and Resolves

An *act* is the official document that contains the statute passed by the legislature. *Acts and Resolves* is the set of books that contain all the acts of the legislature. They are also sometimes called Session Laws, Statutes, Statutes at Large, Laws, etc. A major characteristic of all of these books is that the statutes in them are printed chronologically as they are passed. They are not classified or organized by subject matter. (See *Code.*)

Administrative Code

An *administrative code* is a collection of the regulations of one or more agency. The regulations in a code are organized by subject matter. Generally, the regulations of state and local administrative agencies are poorly organized and difficult to obtain. Not so for the federal agencies.

Advance Sheet

An *advance sheet* is a pamphlet printed before (in advance of) a bound volume, or a thicker pamphlet, that will consolidate the material in several of the earlier advance sheets. When the bound volume or thicker pamphlet comes out, the advance sheet is thrown away. There are two kinds of advance sheets in the law library: an advance sheet for reporters and one for Shepard's.

Example of a pamphlet containing session laws

Advance sheet for a reporter (here the *Supreme Court Reporter*). The advance sheet contains the full text of court opinions that will later be printed in a bound *Supreme Court Reporter* volume.

Advance sheet for Shepard's (here *United States Citations* covering cases of the U.S. Supreme Court). The advance sheet contains the "shepardizing" data that will later be printed in thicker pamphlets and eventually in a bound Shepard's volume.

A.L.R., A.L.R.2d, A.L.R.3d, A.L.R.4th, A.L.R. Fed.

- A.L.R.: *American Law Reports*, First Series
- A.L.R.2d: *American Law Reports*, Second Series
- A.L.R.3d: *American Law Reports*, Third Series
- A.L.R.4th: *American Law Reports*, Fourth Series
- A.L.R. Fed.: *American Law Reports*, Federal Series.

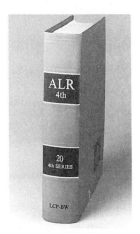

These sets of books contain the complete text of *selected* court opinions followed by extensive commentary or research papers on issues within the opinions selected. These research papers are called annotations. The sets of books are therefore called annotated reports. They are published by Lawyers Cooperative Publishing Company (Lawyers Co-op.). As we shall see later, annotations are excellent case finders. Recently, all of the annotations (except for those in A.L.R. First Series) were placed "online" so that they can now be found and read on a computer screen. The two computer systems that provide this service are LEXIS and VERALEX. (Although the abbreviation A.L.R. refers primarily to the First Series, it sometimes refers to all of the sets collectively.)

American Law Reports, Fourth Series

American Digest System

A multivolume set of digests. *See* Digests (p. 497, p. 553).

American Jurisprudence 2d (Am. Jur. 2d)

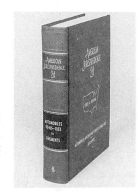

Am. Jur. 2d is a national legal encyclopedia (published by Lawyers Co-op.) that summarizes almost every area of the law. It is particularly useful (a) as background reading before beginning legal research on a topic, and (b) as a case finder because of the extensive footnotes. (Am. Jur. 2d is the second edition of Am. Jur. First.) The main competitor of Am. Jur. 2d is *Corpus Juris Secundum*.

Annotation

To *annotate* means to provide notes or commentary. An annotated bibliography, for example, is a list of references (citations) plus brief summaries or comments on each entry in the list. (See p. 608.) An annotated reporter is a volume containing the full text of court opinions plus notes or commentary on the opinions in it. The word *annotation* mainly refers to the notes and commentary that follow the opinions found in A.L.R., A.L.R.2d, A.L.R.3d, A.L.R.4th,

FIGURE 11.3

A Catalog of Research Materials

Kind of Law	Materials That Contain the Full Text of This Kind of Law	Materials That Can Be Used to Locate This Kind of Law	Materials That Can Be Used to Help Explain This Kind of Law	Materials That Can Be Used to Help Determine the Current Validity of This Kind of Law

(a) Opinions	Reports
	Reporters
	A.L.R., A.L.R.2d,
	  A.L.R.3d,
	  A.L.R.4th,
	  A.L.R. Fed.
	Legal newspapers
	Loose-leaf services
	Slip opinion
	Advance sheets
	WESTLAW
	LEXIS
		Digests
		Annotations in
		  A.L.R., A.L.R.2d,
		  A.L.R.3d,
		  A.L.R.4th,
		  A.L.R. Fed.
		Shepard's
		Legal periodicals
		Legal encyclopedias
		Legal treatises
		Loose-leaf services
		Words and Phrases
			Legal periodicals
			Legal encyclopedias
			Legal treatises
			Annotations in
			  A.L.R., A.L.R.2d,
			  A.L.R.3d,
			  A.L.R.4th,
			  A.L.R. Fed.
			Loose-leaf services
				Shepard's
				Insta-Cite
				Auto-Cite

(b) Statutes	Statutory Code
	Statutes at Large
	Session Laws
	Laws
	Compilations
	Consolidated Laws
	Slip Laws
	Acts & Resolves
	WESTLAW
	LEXIS
		Index volumes of
		  statutory code
		Loose-leaf services
		Footnote references
		  in legal
		  encyclopedias,
		  legal periodicals,
		  etc.
			Legal periodicals
			Legal encyclopedias
			Legal treatises
			Annotations in
			  A.L.R., A.L.R.2d,
			  A.L.R.3d,
			  A.L.R.4th,
			  A.L.R. Fed.
			Loose-leaf services
				Shepard's

(c) Constitutions	Statutory Code
	Separate volumes
	  containing the
	  constitution
	WESTLAW
	LEXIS
		Index volumes of
		  statutory code
		Loose-leaf services
		Footnote references
		  in legal
		  encyclopedias,
		  legal periodicals,
		  etc.
			Legal periodicals
			Legal encyclopedias
			Legal treatises
			Annotations in
			  A.L.R., A.L.R.2d,
			  A.L.R.3d,
			  A.L.R.4th,
			  A.L.R. Fed.
			Loose-leaf services
				Shepard's

(d) Administrative Regulations	Administrative Codes
	Separate volumes
	  containing the
	  regulations of
	  certain agencies
	Loose-leaf services
	WESTLAW
	LEXIS
		Index volumes of the
		  administrative
		  code
		Loose-leaf services
		Footnote references
		  in legal
		  encyclopedias,
		  legal periodicals,
		  etc.
			Legal periodicals
			Legal treatises
			Annotations in
			  A.L.R., A.L.R.2d,
			  A.L.R.3d,
			  A.L.R.4th,
			  A.L.R. Fed.
			Loose-leaf services
				Shepard's (for some
				  agencies only)
				List of Sections
				  Affected

(e) Administrative Decisions	Separate volumes of
	  decisions of some
	  agencies
	Loose-leaf services
	WESTLAW
	LEXIS
		Loose-leaf services
		Index or digest
		  volumes to the
		  decisions
		Footnote references
		  in other materials
			Legal periodicals
			Legal treatises
			Annotations in
			  A.L.R., A.L.R.2d,
			  A.L.R.3d,
			  A.L.R.4th,
			  A.L.R. Fed.
			Loose-leaf services
				Shepard's (for some
				  agencies only)

Continued

FIGURE 11.3
A Catalog of Research Materials —*Continued*

Kind of Law	Materials That Contain the Full Text of This Kind of Law	Materials That Can Be Used to Locate This Kind of Law	Materials That Can Be Used to Help Explain This Kind of Law	Materials That Can Be Used to Help Determine the Current Validity of This Kind of Law
(f) Charters	Separate volumes containing the charter Municipal Code State session laws Official journal Legal newspaper	Index volumes to the charter or municipal code Footnote references in other materials	Legal periodicals Legal treatises Annotations in A.L.R., A.L.R.2d, A.L.R.3d, A.L.R.4th, A.L.R. Fed.	Shepard's
(g) Ordinances	Municipal Code Official journal Legal newspaper	Index volumes of municipal code Footnote references in other materials	Legal periodicals Legal treatises Annotations in A.L.R., A.L.R.2d, A.L.R.3d, A.L.R.4th, A.L.R. Fed.	Shepard's
(h) Rules of Court	Separate rules volumes Statutory code Practice manuals	Index to separate rules volumes Index to statutory code Index to practice manuals Footnote references in other materials	Practice manuals Legal treatises Annotations in A.L.R., A.L.R.2d, A.L.R.3d, A.L.R.4th, A.L.R. Fed. Legal encyclopedias Loose-leaf services	Shepard's
(i) Executive Orders	Federal Register Code of Federal Regulations U.S. Code Congressional and Administrative News U.S.C./U.S.C.A./ U.S.C.S. WESTLAW LEXIS	Index volumes to the sets of books listed in the second column Footnote references in other materials	Legal periodicals Legal treatises Annotations in A.L.R., A.L.R.2d, A.L.R.3d, A.L.R.4th, A.L.R. Fed.	Shepard's Code of Federal Regulations Citations
(j) Treaties	Statutes at Large (up to 1949) United States Treaties and Other International Agreements Department of State Bulletin International Legal Materials United Nations Treaty Series	Index within the volumes listed in second column World Treaty Index Current Treaty Index Footnote references in other materials	Legal periodicals Legal treatises Annotations in A.L.R., A.L.R.2d, A.L.R.3d, A.L.R.4th, A.L.R. Fed.	Shepard's U.S. Code Service (Notes to Uncodified Laws and Treaties)
(k) Opinions of the Attorney General	Separate volumes containing these opinions WESTLAW LEXIS	Digests Index in separate volumes of the opinions Footnote references in other materials		

and A.L.R. Fed. You are being directed to these sets of books when someone asks you to "find out if there are any annotations on this issue." The phrase *annotated code* or *annotated statutes* is also sometimes used (e.g., United States Code Annotated). Annotated codes or statutes are sets of statutes that contain the full text of the statutes organized by subject matter, plus research references such as summaries of opinions interpreting the statutes. The abbreviation for annotated is "Ann." (e.g., Del. Code Ann. for Delaware Code Annotated) or "A" (e.g., U.S.C.A. for United States Code Annotated).

Atlantic Digest

A digest that summarizes cases in the *Atlantic Reporter*. *See* Digests (page 497).

Atlantic Reporter 2d (A.2d)

A regional reporter. *See* Cases (page 493).

Ballentine's Law Dictionary

See Legal Dictionary (page 504).

Bill

A *bill* is a proposed statute (one that has not yet been enacted into law). A bill is printed in a small booklet or pamphlet called a slip law. (Federal bills are also printed in the *Congressional Record*.)

Black's Law Dictionary

See Legal dictionary (page 504).

Blue Book

The phrase *blue book* will usually refer to one of the three following books or sets of books:

- *A Uniform System of Citation* (the Bluebook)
- *National Reporter Blue Book*
- *A.L.R. Blue Book of Supplemental Decisions*

A Uniform System of Citation. A small blue pamphlet published by the law reviews of several law schools. The pamphlet covers the "rules" of citation form. It is considered by many to be the bible of citation form.

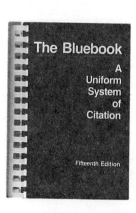

National Reporter Blue Book. A set of books published by West Publishing Company that will enable you to find a parallel cite to a court opinion. The *National Reporter Blue Book* covers every state. Some states have a *Blue and White Book*, which provides parallel cites for one state only.

The *A.L.R. Blue Book of Supplemental Decisions* will enable you to update the annotations found in *A.L.R. First Series.*

Brief, Appellate

An *appellate brief* is a written document prepared by a party for submission to an appellate court in which arguments are presented on the correctness or incorrectness of what a trial court or lower court of appeals did or failed to do.

Amicus curiae means friend of the court. An *amicus curiae brief* is also an appellate brief, but it is prepared and submitted by a nonparty. A court must give permission for the nonparty to submit such a brief.

It is often possible to locate appellate briefs written on recent cases. The briefs are found in the clerk's office of the court where they were submitted, in large law school libraries, in court libraries, and in state law libraries. They can provide excellent research leads for cases with similar issues.

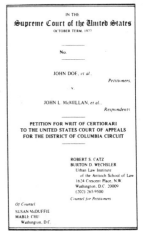

Front cover of an appellate brief submitted to the U.S. Supreme Court

Bulletin

A bulletin is a publication issued on an ongoing or periodic basis (such as *Internal Revenue Bulletin*).

California Reporter (Cal. Rptr.)

A court reporter containing selected California cases. *See* Cases (page 493).

Cases

A *case* is a dispute that has been litigated in court or that is now in litigation. The word is sometimes used interchangeably with the word *opinion,* although the latter word is more often used to mean the court's written explanation for reaching a particular result. The full text of cases is found in volumes called reports or reporters. An *official reporter* is published under the authority of the government and is often printed by the government itself. An *unofficial reporter* is printed by a private or commercial publishing company (such as West) without special authority from the government. We will now examine the reporters containing opinions of the federal courts. Then we look at the reporters for state courts.

Federal Court Opinions.   The opinions of the United States Supreme Court are printed in an official report, *United States Reports* (abbreviated "U.S."), and in several unofficial reporters: the *Supreme Court Reporter* published by West (abbreviated "S. Ct.") and *United States Supreme Court Reports,* Lawyers' Edition, published by Lawyers Co-op. (abbreviated "L. Ed.").

When an opinion is printed in the *United States Reports,* it will also be printed word-for-word in S. Ct. and in L. Ed., the unofficial reporters—but not necessarily on the same page numbers. Suppose that you are reading an opinion in an unofficial reporter and you want to quote from it. The standard practice is to give the reference or citation to the quote as it appears in the *official* reporter. Suppose, however, that the latter is simply not available in your library, but one of the unofficial reporters is. How do you quote a page number in an official reporter when all you have available is an unofficial reporter? You use a technique called "star-paging." While you are reading a page in an unofficial reporter, you will find a notation of some kind provided by the printer (an asterisk, a star, or a special indentation) plus a page number, usually in black bold

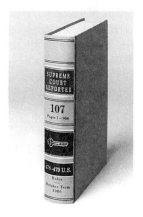

The three major reporters containing opinions of the United States Supreme Court

print. The latter is a reference to a page number of the same case in the official reporter. *Star paging* therefore enables you to determine on what pages the same court language can be found in official and unofficial reporters.

Two loose-leaf services (page 506) also print the text of all U.S. Supreme Court opinions:

- *United States Law Week* (U.S.L.W.) published by Bureau of National Affairs (BNA).

- *United States Supreme Court Bulletin* (S.Ct.Bull.) published by Commerce Clearing House. S. Ct. Bull. (CCH).

· · · · · · · · · · · · · · · ·

We turn now to reporters for the *lower* federal courts. Two major reporters contain the full text of opinions from lower federal courts:

Federal Reporter, Second Series (F.2d). Currently contains the full text of the opinions written by the United States Courts of Appeals.

- Federal Reporter (abbreviated "F.")
  Federal Reporter, Second Series (abbreviated "F.2d")
- Federal Supplement (abbreviated "F. Supp.")

These are all unofficial reporters published by West. They do *not* print every opinion written by the courts that they cover. The courts decide which opinions are sufficiently important to submit to West for publication.

In addition to F., F.2d, and F. Supp., West publishes several specialty or topical reporters that also cover federal courts. For example:

Federal Rules Decisions (F.R.D.)
- Contains opinions of the U.S. District Courts on the Federal Rules of Civil and Criminal Procedure, and also
- Contains articles, speeches, and conference reports on procedural issues

Military Justice Reporter (M.J.)
- Contains opinions of the United States Court of Military Appeals and the Courts of Military Review for the army, navy-marines, air force, and coast guard

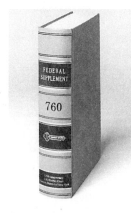

Federal Supplement (F. Supp.) Currently contains the full text of the opinions written by the United States District Courts and the United States Court of International Trade.

Bankruptcy Reporter (B.R.)
- Contains opinions of the United States Bankruptcy Courts and selected bankruptcy opinions of other federal courts

Education Law Reporter

Social Security Reporting Service

United States Claims Court Reporter

FIGURE 11.4
National Reporter
System Map

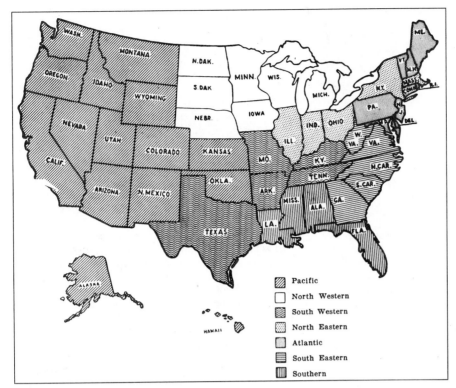

Pacific
North Western
South Western
North Eastern
Atlantic
South Eastern
Southern

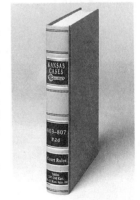

Example of an official
state reports volume

State Court Opinions.   At one time, all states had official reports containing the opinions of their highest state courts. A large number of states, however, have discontinued their official reports. For such states, the unofficial reporters are the main or only source where you can find the opinions of their state courts.

The major publisher of unofficial state reports is West Publishing Company through its *National Reporter System.* There are seven *regional reporters* in the System. For a photo of each reporter, see page 494.

The seven regional reporters and the states they cover can be seen on the map in Figure 11.4.

If a law office subscribes to a regional reporter covering its own state, the office is also receiving opinions of other states in the same region. These other opinions may be of little practical value to the office. West therefore publishes special state editions for many of the states. These special edition state reporters contain only the opinions of an individual state that are also printed in the regional reporter. For example, you saw that the opinions of the highest court in Kansas are printed in the *Pacific Reporter.* A Kansas attorney who does not want to subscribe to the *Pacific Reporter* can subscribe to the special edition Kansas reporter, called *Kansas Cases.*

Finally, West publishes three separate reporters for New York, California, and Illinois:

■ New York Supplement (N.Y.S.)

■ California Reporter (Cal. Rptr.)

■ Illinois Decisions (Ill. Dec.)

Each contains the opinions of the highest court in the state as well as selected opinions of its lower courts.

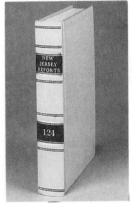

A volume of **Kansas
Cases** (a special edition
state reporter) containing
all the Kansas opinions
printed in *Pacific
Reporter, 2d*

The Seven Regional Reporters in the National Reporter System

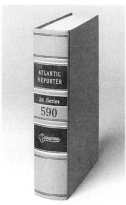

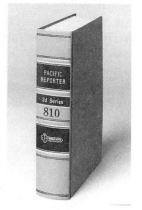

Atlantic Reporter (A.), Atlantic Reporter, Second Series (A.2d). The opinions of the highest state court and some intermediate appellate courts in the following states: Conn., Del., D.C., Me., Md., N.H., N.J., Pa., R.I., Vt.

North Eastern Reporter (N.E.), North Eastern Reporter, Second Series (N.E.2d). The opinions of the highest state court and some intermediate appellate courts in the following states: Ill., Ind., Mass., N.Y., Ohio.

North Western Reporter (N.W.), North Western Reporter, Second Series (N.W.2d). The opinions of the highest state court and some intermediate appellate courts in the following states: Iowa, Mich., Minn., Neb., N.D., S.D., Wis.

Pacific Reporter (P.), Pacific Reporter, Second Series (P.2d). The opinions of the highest state court and some intermediate appellate courts in the following states: Alaska, Ariz., Cal., Colo., Haw., Idaho, Kan., Mont., Nev., N.M., Okla., Or., Utah, Wash., Wyo.

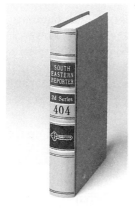

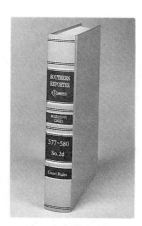

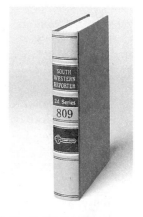

South Eastern Reporter (S.E.), South Eastern Reporter, Second Series (S.E.2d). The opinions of the highest state court and some intermediate appellate courts in the following states: Ga., N.C., S.C., Va., W. Va.

Southern Reporter (So.), Southern Reporter, Second Series (So.2d). The opinions of the highest state court and some intermediate appellate courts in the following states: Ala., Fla., La., Miss.

South Western Reporter (S.W.), South Western Reporter, Second Series (S.W.2d). The opinions of the highest state courts and some intermediate appellate courts in the following states: Ark., Ky., Mo., Tenn., Tex.

Major Characteristics of West Reporters

- The reporters contain the full context of court opinions.
- The opinions are arranged in roughly chronological order according to the date of decision.

- The reporters have advance sheets that come out before the bound volumes.
- There is a Table of Cases at the beginning of each reporter volume.
- There is a Table of Statutes Construed in many reporters, listing the statutes interpreted within an individual reporter volume.
- There is *no* traditional subject-matter index in any reporter volume (the main index to the opinions in reporters is the separate set of books called digests).
- At the beginning of each opinion there are small-paragraph summaries of the opinion. As we will see later, these are headnotes which are also printed in digests, and at the beginning of the advance sheet containing the opinion, and at the end of the reporter volume containing the opinion.

Casebook

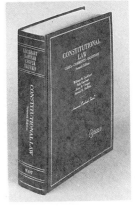

A *casebook* is a law school textbook. It consists mainly of a collection of edited court opinions and other materials relating to a particular area of the law, e.g., Lockhart, Kamisar, Choper, and Shiffrin, *Constitutional Law: Cases, Comments, Questions.*

CD ROM

CD ROM ("computer disc read-only memory") is an optical information-storage system that operates much like a compact disc sold in music stores. Through your computer system, you gain access to the vast amount of information stored on the disc. Up to 60 large volumes of law books can be stored on one disc! Users cannot add any information to the disc; they can only read the information on it through their computer screen or monitor. (Hence the phrase *read only.*) Unlike more traditional computer-assisted research systems, you do not need a modem (see Chapter 13) to use CD ROM. Everything you need is on the disc.

Century Digest

A digest that is part of the American Digest System. *See* Digests (p. 498).

A CD ROM product of
West Publishing Co.

Citation

A *citation* (also called a cite) is a reference to any written material, such as a case, statute, law review article, treatise, treaty, annotation or report. It is the "address" where that material can be found in the library. The reference tells you how to locate the item by volume number, name of book, edition, page number, or section number. A *parallel cite* is an additional reference to the *same* material. If there are two parallel cites to a case, for example, you will be able to find the same case—word for word—in two different reporters. The major book on citation form is A Uniform System of Citation.

Citator

A *citator* is a book containing lists of citations that serve two functions: first and foremost, to help you assess the current validity of a case, statute, or other law; and secondarily, to provide you with leads to additional laws. Citators often provide other features as well, e.g., they will give you a parallel citation. The major citator in legal research is Shepard's. The columns of Shepard's contain nothing but citations that are relevant to whatever you are "shepardizing" (pp. 509, 563). There are also citators on computer systems, such as Insta-Cite and Auto-Cite.

Code of Federal Regulations

Code

A code is a collection of laws or rules classified by subject matter. To *codify* something means to rearrange it by subject matter. The arrangement of *uncodified* material is chronological by date of enactment; the arrangement of *codified* material is by subject matter or topic. When statutes are first passed by the legislature, they are placed in uncodified books called Session Laws, Acts and Resolves, Statutes at Large, etc. Most of these statutes are later codified into statutory codes. (See Statutory Code.) Administrative regulations are also often codified. (See Administrative Code.)

Code of Federal Regulations (C.F.R.)

The C.F.R. is a set of pamphlets containing many of the regulations of federal agencies. *See* Administrative Code.

Congressional Record

The *Congressional Record* is an official collection of the day-to-day happenings of Congress. It is one source of legislative history (p. 596) for federal statutes. It also contains many relatively trivial items that are relevant only to the districts of individual legislators.

Corpus Juris Secundum

Corpus Juris Secundum (C.J.S.)

Corpus Juris Secundum (C.J.S.) is a national legal encyclopedia (published by West) that summarizes almost every area of the law. (C.J.S. is the second edition of *Corpus Juris*.) It is very useful (a) as background reading before beginning legal research on a topic and (b) as a case finder because of the extensive footnotes. Its main competitor is *American Jurisprudence 2d*.

Cumulative

Cumulative means that which repeats earlier material and consolidates it with new material. A cumulative supplement, for example, is a pamphlet or volume that repeats, updates, and consolidates all earlier pamphlets or volumes. Because of the repetition, the earlier pamphlets or volumes can be thrown away. Similarly, pocket parts (containing supplemental material at the end of a book) are often cumulative. When the most recent pocket part comes out, the old one can be thrown away.

UNITED STATES CODE
ANNOTATED

Title 28
Judiciary and Judicial Procedure
§§ 171 to 1250

Cumulative Annual Pocket Part

For Use in 1986

Replacing prior **pocket part** in **back** of volume

Decennial Digest

A digest that is part of the American Digest System. *See* Digests.

Digests

Our goals in this section are to define *digest,* to identify the major digests, and to explain the relationship between digests and reporters. Later in the chapter, we will cover the techniques of using digests in research (page 553).

Digests are volumes containing small-paragraph summaries of court opinions organized by subject matter. (These summaries are sometimes called *abstracts* or *squibs.*) The primary purpose of digests is to serve as case finders. The major publisher of digests is West. Its *key topic and number system* is the organizational principle used to classify the millions of small-paragraph summaries in the digests. Every topic and subtopic in the law is assigned a key topic and number by West. For example:

⚷290. Strikes and lockouts.

⚷984. Sentence on conviction on different counts.

⚷406.3(9). Clearly erroneous findings of court or jury.

Once you find a key topic (and subtopic)—plus its key number—relevant to your research problem, you are given paragraph summaries of cases under that topic and number. For example, the following excerpt from a digest contains cases that are digested under the topic of "Obscenity" and the subtopics of "Nature and elements of offenses in general" and "Statutory provisions":

OBSCENITY

⚷1. Nature and elements of offenses in general.

Ill.App. 1973. Obscenity vel non is not constitutionally protected. People v. Rota, 292 N.E.2d 738.

Iowa 1973. Knowledge of obscene material is an essential element in obscenity prosecutions. I.C.A. § 725.5. State v. Lavin, 204 N.W.2d 844.

⚷2. Statutory provisions.

D.C.Md. 1972. Although Maryland motion picture censorship statute did not provide disseminator of motion picture film with an adversary hearing before board of censors on issue of obscenity, disseminator was not constitutionally prejudiced in this regard because the statute requires an adversary judicial determination of obscenity with circuit court for Baltimore City exercising de novo review of the board's finding of obscenity, and with burden of proving that the film is unprotected expression resting on the board. Code Md. 1957, art. 66A, §§ 6(c, d), 19(a); 28 U.S. C.A. § 100. Star v. Preller, 352 F.Supp. 530.

Beneath each summary paragraph is a citation to the case being summarized. For example, see the citation for *People v. Rota* in the first paragraph listed.

There are a few digests that are *not* published by West. For example, the United States Supreme Court Digest, L. Ed. is published by Lawyers Co-op. Such digests also contain small-paragraph summaries of court opinions, but since they are not published by West, they are not organized by the key topic system. They use their own organizational principle. (See photo at top of page 500.)

We now turn to an overview of the West digests. There are four main kinds:

- A national digest covering most state and federal courts
- Federal digests covering only federal courts
- Regional digests covering the courts found in the regional reporters
- Digests of individual courts or states

National Digest   There is one national digest: the *American Digest System* published by West. This massive set (containing over 100 volumes) gives you small-paragraph summaries of the court opinions of most appellate state and federal courts and some lower state and federal courts. The American Digest System has three main units: (a) *Century Digest,* (b) *Decennial Digests,* and (c) *General Digests.*

Federal Digests Covering Only Federal Courts   There are five large digests that cover the main federal courts: the U.S. Supreme Court, the U.S. Courts of Appeal, and the U.S. District Courts:

- *Federal Digest*
- *Modern Federal Practice Digest*
- *Federal Practice Digest* 2d
- *Federal Practice Digest* 3d
- *Federal Practice Digest* 4th

(a) Here is a sample volume from the **Century Digest,** covering summaries of opinions written between 1658 and 1896 (part of the American Digest System).

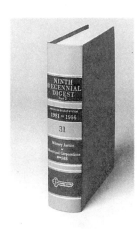

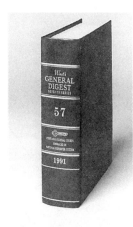

(b) The **Decennial Digests** cover summaries of opinions for ten-year periods starting in 1897. Here is a sample volume from the Ninth Decennial. It is printed in two parts, each covering five years. Part I covers the period from 1976 to 1981. Part II covers 1981–1986. (Prior to the Ninth Decennial, all of the *Decennial Digests* were issued in one part only—covering the entire ten years.)

(c) The **General Digests** cover summaries of opinions since the last Decennial was published. The *General Digest* volumes are kept on the shelf only until they are eventually consolidated (cumulated) into the next *Decennial Digest* unit. At that time, all of the General Digest volumes are thrown away.

Modern Federal Practice Digest. Contains small-paragraph summaries of federal cases decided between 1939 and 1961.

Federal Practice Digest 2d. Contains small-paragraph summaries of federal cases decided from 1961 to 1975.

Federal Practice Digest 3d. Contains small-paragraph summaries of federal cases decided from 1975.

Federal Practice Digest 4th. This is the most recent set. Its coverage begins where *Federal Practice Digest 3d* leaves off.

Finally, West publishes a number of special digests that cover specific federal courts or specific topics of federal law:

- West's *Bankruptcy Digest*
- West's *Military Justice Digest*
- *United States Claims Court Digest*

Given the tremendous importance of the U.S. Supreme Court, there are two extensive digests covering only its opinions. These two digests (shown at the top of page 500) are published by competing companies.

Regional Digests   A regional digest contains small-paragraph summaries of those court opinions that are printed in its corresponding regional reporter. The opinions in the *Pacific Reporter*, for example, are digested in the *Pacific Digest*. As we shall see in Figure 11.5, only four of the seven regional reporters have corresponding regional digests. Those digests are: *Atlantic Digest, North Western Digest, Pacific Digest,* and *South Eastern Digest.* (Regional digests for the other three regions either do not exist or have been discontinued.)

One of the regional digests

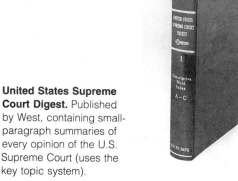

United States Supreme Court Digest. Published by West, containing small-paragraph summaries of every opinion of the U.S. Supreme Court (uses the key topic system).

United States Supreme Court Digest, L. Ed. Published by Lawyers Co-op., containing small-paragraph summaries of every opinion of the U.S. Supreme Court (does not use key topic system).

Digests of Individual States   A state digest contains small-paragraph summaries of the opinions of the state courts within that state, as well as the opinions of the federal courts that are relevant to that state. The following are examples of state digests:

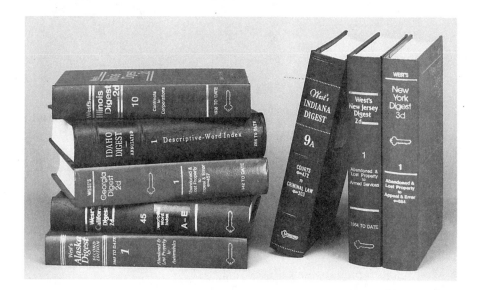

Now let us summarize. In Figure 11.5, there is a list of reporters, the names of the courts whose full opinions are currently printed in those reporters, and the names of the digests that give small-paragraph summaries of those opinions.

Federal Cases

Federal Cases is the name of the reporter that contains very early opinions of the federal courts (up to 1880) before F., F.2d, and F. Supp. came into existence.

Federal Digest

See Digests.

FIGURE 11.5

Reporters and
Digests:
A Checklist

NAME OF REPORTER	THE COURTS WHOSE OPINIONS ARE CURRENTLY PRINTED IN FULL IN THIS REPORTER	THE DIGESTS THAT CONTAIN SMALL-PARAGRAPH SUMMARIES OF THE OPINIONS IN THIS REPORTER
United States Reports (U.S.) Supreme Court Reporter (S. Ct.) United States Supreme Court Reports, Lawyers Edition (L. Ed.) United States Law Week (U.S.L.W.) United States Supreme Court Bulletin (CCH)	United States Supreme Court	American Digest System United States Supreme Court Digest (West) United States Supreme Court Digest, L. Ed. Federal Digest Modern Federal Practice Digest Federal Practice Digest, 2d Federal Practice Digest, 3d Federal Practice Digest, 4th Individual state digests (for Supreme Court cases relevant to that state)
Federal Reporter, 2d (F.2d)	United States Courts of Appeal	American Digest System Federal Digest Modern Federal Practice Digest Federal Practice Digest, 2d Federal Practice Digest, 3d Federal Practice Digest, 4th Individual state digests (for federal cases relevant to that state)
Federal Supplement (F. Supp.)	United States District Courts United States Court of International Trade	American Digest System Federal Digest Modern Federal Practice Digest Federal Practice Digest, 2d Federal Practice Digest, 3d Federal Practice Digest, 4th Individual state digests (for federal cases relevant to that state)
Atlantic Reporter 2d (A.2d)	The highest state court and some intermediate appellate courts in Conn., Del., D.C., Me., Md., N.H., N.J., Pa., R.I., Vt.	American Digest System Atlantic Digest Individual state digests for Conn., Del., D.C., Me., Md., N.H., N.J., Pa., R.I., Vt.
North Eastern Reporter 2d (N.E.2d)	The highest state court and some intermediate appellate courts in Ill., Ind., Mass., N.Y., Ohio	American Digest System Individual state digests for Ill., Ind., Mass., N.Y., Ohio (There is *no* North Eastern Digest)
North Western Reporter 2d (N.W.2d)	The highest state court and some intermediate appellate courts in Iowa, Mich., Minn., Neb., N.D., S.D., Wis.	American Digest System North Western Digest Individual state digests for Iowa, Mich., Minn., Neb., N.D., S.D., Wis.

Continued

FIGURE 11.5

Reporters and
Digests:
A Checklist
—Continued

NAME OF REPORTER	THE COURTS WHOSE OPINIONS ARE CURRENTLY PRINTED IN FULL IN THIS REPORTER	THE DIGESTS THAT CONTAIN SMALL-PARAGRAPH SUMMARIES OF THE OPINIONS IN THIS REPORTER
Pacific Reporter, 2d (P.2d)	The highest state court and some intermediate appellate courts in Alaska, Ariz., Cal., Colo., Haw., Idaho, Kan., Mont., Nev., N.M., Okla, Or., Utah., Wash., Wyo.	American Digest System Pacific Digest Individual state digests for Alaska, Ariz., Cal., Colo., Haw., Idaho, Kan., Mont., Nev., N.M., Okla, Or., Utah., Wash., Wyo.
South Eastern Reporter, 2d (S.E.2d)	The highest state court and some intermediate appellate courts in Ga., N.C., S.C., Va., W. Va.	American Digest System South Eastern Digest Individual state digests for Ga., N.C., S.C., Va., W. Va.
Southern Reporter, 2d (So.2d)	The highest state court and some intermediate appellate courts in Ala., Fla., La., Miss.	American Digest System Individual state digests for Ala., Fla., La., Miss. (There is *no* Southern Digest)
South Western Reporter, 2d (S.W.2d)	The highest state court and some intermediate appellate courts in Ark., Ky., Mo., Tenn., Tex.	American Digest System Individual state digests for Ark., Ky., Mo., Tenn., Tex. (There is *no* South Western Digest)

Federal Practice Digest 2d; Federal Practice Digest 3d; Federal Practice Digest 4th

See Digests.

Federal Register (Fed.Reg.)

The *Federal Register* is a daily publication of the federal government that prints proposed regulations of the federal administrative agencies; executive orders and other executive documents; and news from federal agencies, such as announcements calling for applications for federal grants. Many of the proposed regulations that are adopted by the federal agencies are later printed in the *Code of Federal Regulations* (C.F.R.). (See photo at top of page 503.)

Federal Reporter

A reporter containing opinions of the United States Courts of Appeal. *See* Cases.

Federal Rules Decisions (F.R.D.)

A reporter containing opinions of United States District Courts on issues of

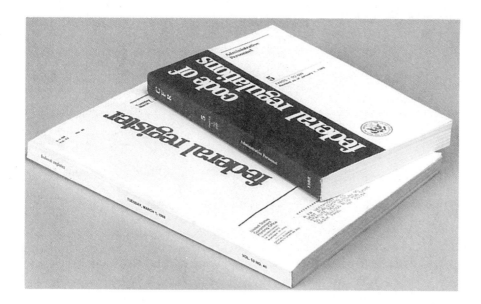

civil and criminal procedure, plus articles and speeches on procedural issues. *See* Cases.

Federal Supplement

A reporter containing opinions of the United States District Courts. *See* Cases.

Formbook

A *formbook* is a manual written by private individuals (or by a public official writing in a private capacity) giving practical information on how to practice law in a given area. It contains summaries of the law, checklists, sample forms, etc. Formbooks are how-to-do-it texts. They can be single-volume or multi-volume. Other names for a formbook are *practice manual, handbook,* etc.

General Digest

A digest that is part of the American Digest System. *See* Digests.

Handbook

A practical text on an area of the law. See *formbook.*

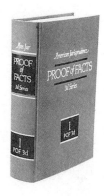

Example of a formbook

Headnote

A headnote is a summary of a portion of an opinion, printed just before the opinion begins. In West reporters, each headnote is numbered consecutively and is assigned a key topic and number. The headnote is later printed in the digests of West.

Here is the third headnote printed at the beginning of an opinion from a West reporter. It summarizes a portion of the opinion. West also prints this headnote in one or more of its digests. If you went to these digests and looked up Libel and Slander 28, you would find this headnote plus headnotes from other opinions on the same point of law.

> **3. Libel and Slander** ☞ 28
>
> One may not escape liability for defamation by showing that he was merely repeating defamatory language used by another person, and he may not escape liability by falsely attributing to others the ideas to which he gives expression.

Hornbook

A hornbook is a treatise (page 515) that summarizes an area or topic of the law. It may contain commentaries, extensive footnote references, etc. Hornbooks differ somewhat from formbooks in that hornbooks are often less practical than formbooks.

Interstate Compact

An *interstate compact* is an agreement between two or more states governing a problem of mutual concern, such as the resolution of a boundary dispute. The compact is passed by the legislature of each state and is therefore part of the statutes of the states involved. Also, Congress must give its approval.

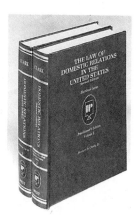

Example of a hornbook

Kardex

Kardex is a file in which the library records the volume numbers and dates of incoming publications that are part of subscriptions. If, for example, you are not sure whether certain volumes or supplements on the shelf are the most current ones received by the library, you would ask the library staff to check Kardex. Not all libraries use Kardex. A library might use another system of recording subscription material received by the library.

Legal Dictionary

A *legal dictionary* contains definitions of words and phrases used in the law. Examples include: *Black's Law Dictionary* (West), *Ballentine's Law Dictionary* (Lawyers Co-op.), and *Statsky's Legal Thesaurus/Dictionary* (West). The major multivolume legal dictionary is *Words and Phrases* from West. The definitions in this set consist of thousands of excerpts from court opinions that have treated the word or phrase. Hence, this set of volumes can also serve as an excellent case finder.

Multivolume legal dictionary

Legal Encyclopedia

A *legal encyclopedia* is a multivolume set of books that summarizes almost every legal topic (page 582). It is valuable (a) as background reading for a research topic that is new to you, and (b) as a case finder (due to its extensive footnotes). The two competing national encyclopedias are *American Jurisprudence 2d* published by Lawyers Co-op., and *Corpus Juris Secundum* published by West. A number of states have their own encyclopedias covering the law of that state, e.g. *Florida Jurisprudence* and *Michigan Law and Practice*.

Legal Newspaper

A *legal newspaper* is a local newspaper published (often daily) by a private company that lists court calendars, legal announcements, the full text of some opinions of local courts, new court rules, job announcements, etc. Most large cities have their own legal newspaper. It may be called the daily law journal, the daily law reporter, etc.

Legal Periodical

A *legal periodical* (often called a *law review* or a *law journal*) is an ongoing publication of scholarly commentary published by law students of specific law schools. In addition, there are some periodicals published by private companies and by bar associations that tend to be more practice-oriented (and more expensive). Periodicals are first published as small pamphlets, and are later bound by most libraries.

As we will see later (page 578), the major general indexes to legal periodical literature are:

- Index to Legal Periodicals (ILP)
- Current Law Index (CLI)
- Legal Resource Index (LRI)

In addition, there are special indexes to legal periodical literature on topics such as tax law.

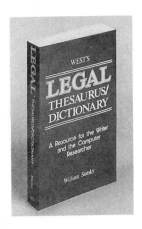

Legal Thesaurus

A *legal thesaurus* provides word alternatives for words used in legal writing. The thesaurus may also be helpful in forming queries for computer-assisted legal research (page 655). Two examples: Burton's *Legal Thesaurus* (Macmillan, 1980); and Statsky's *Legal Thesaurus/Dictionary: A Resource for the Writer and Legal Researcher* (West, 1985).

Legislation

Legislation is the process of making statutory law by the legislature. The word legislation also refers to the statutes themselves.

LEXIS

LEXIS is a legal research computer system. (See pages 585 and 656.)

Loose-Leaf Service

Most law books come in one of three forms:

- Pamphlet
- Bound volume
- Loose-leaf

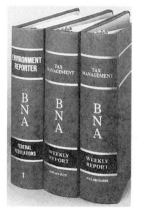

A *loose-leaf* text or *service* is a three-ring (or post) binder containing pages that can easily be inserted or taken out. As new material is written covering the subject matter of the loose-leaf text, it is placed in the binder, often replacing the pages that the new material has changed or otherwise supplemented. Since this kind of updating can sometimes occur as often as once a week, loose-leaf services frequently contain the most current material available.

There are few areas of the law that are *not* covered by one or more loose-leaf services. Examples of such services include: *Employment Practices Guide, Standard Federal Tax Reports, United States Law Week, Criminal Law Reporter, Family Law Reporter, Media Law Reporter, Sexual Law Reporter, Environmental Law Reporter, Labor Relations Reporter.*

While some loose-leaf services do little more than print the most current cases in their speciality, most have more varied features:

- The full text plus summaries of court opinions in the area of the specialty
- The full text plus summaries of administrative regulations and decisions in the area of the specialty (some of which may not be available elsewhere)
- Summaries of the major statutory provisions of the specialty
- Suggestions on how to practice in the specialty

Examples of a loose-leaf service

The major publishers of loose-leaf services are Commerce Clearing House (CCH), Bureau of National Affairs (BNA), Prentice-Hall (PH), and Matthew Bender.

Martindale-Hubbell Law Directory

The *Martindale-Hubbell Law Directory* (see excerpt on page 140) is a multivolume set of books that serves three major functions:

- Gives an alphabetical listing of attorneys and law firms by state and city (for some firms, the listing includes paralegals and other nonattorney personnel)
- Gives short summaries of the law of all fifty states (in its separate Digest volume)
- Gives short summaries of the law of many foreign countries (in its separate Digest volume)

Microforms

Microforms are images or photographs that have been reduced in size. Among the material stored on microforms are pages from reporters, codes, trea-

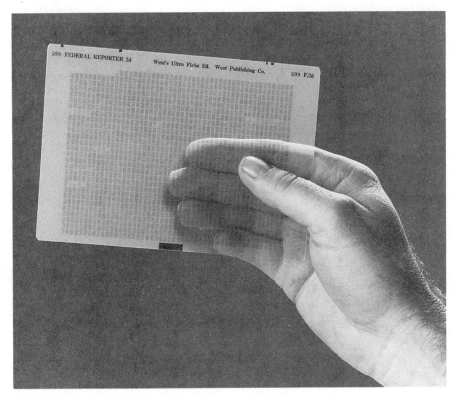

Example of West's ultrafiche, containing a volume of the *Federal Reporter 2d*

tises, periodicals, etc. Vast amounts of material can be stored in this way. An entire volume of a 1,000-page law book can fit on a single plastic card! Special machines (reader-printers and fiche readers) magnify the material so that it can be read. Several kinds of microforms are available. (a) *Microfilms* store the material on film reels or cassettes. (b) *Microfiche* stores the material on single sheets of film. (c) *Ultrafiche* is microfiche with a considerably greater storage capacity.

New York Supplement (N.Y.S.)

A reporter containing New York cases. *See* Cases.

North Eastern Reporter 2d (N.E.2d)

A regional reporter. *See* Cases.

North Western Digest

A digest that summarizes cases in the North Western Reporter. *See* Digests.

North Western Reporter 2d (N.W.2d)

A regional reporter. *See* Cases.

Pacific Digest

A digest that summarizes cases in the Pacific Reporter. *See* Digests.

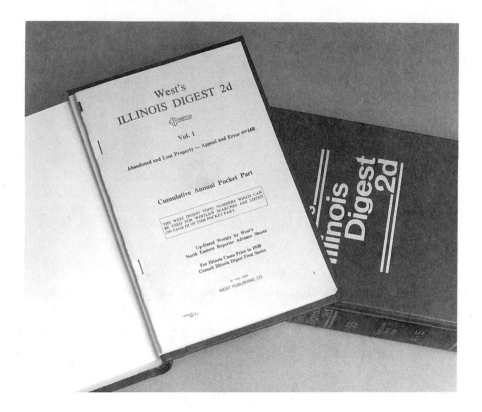

Example of a law book
with a pocket part

Pacific Reporter 2d (P.2d)

A regional reporter. *See* Cases.

Pocket Part

A *pocket part* is a small-pamphlet addition placed in a special pocket built into the inside cover of a bound volume. The purpose of the pamphlet is to update the material in the bound volume.

Record

When referring to a trial, the *record* is the official collection of what happened during the trial. It includes a word-for-word transcript of what was said, the pleadings, all the exhibits, etc.

Regional Digest

A digest that summarizes cases in a regional reporter. *See* Digest.

Restatements

Restatements are scholarly *treatises* (see page 515) published by the American Law Institute (ALI) which attempt to formulate (that is, restate) the existing law of a given area. Occasionally the Restatements also state what the ALI thinks the law *ought* to be.

Examples of Restatements:

Restatement of Agency

Restatement of Conflicts of Law

Restatement of Contracts

Restatement of Foreign Relations Law

Restatement of Judgments

Restatement of Property

Restatement of Restitution

Restatement of Security

Restatement of Torts

Restatement of Trusts

Restatements are not law, but they are extensively relied on and cited by courts.

Rules of Court

Rules of Court, also called *Court Rules,* are the rules of procedure that govern the conduct of litigation before a particular court. They are often found in the statutory code and in separate volumes or pamphlets.

Series

An *edition* is a *revision* of an earlier version of a book or set of books. The word *series,* on the other hand, refers to a new numbering order for new volumes within the *same* set of books. Reporters, for example, come in series. Federal Reporter, First Series (abbreviated "F.") has 300 volumes. After the last volume was printed, the publisher decided to start a new series of the same set of books—Federal Reporter, Second Series (abbreviated "F.2d"). The first volume of F.2d is volume 1. After a large number of F.2d volumes are printed, we will probably see an F.3d, which will begin again with volume 1. There is no consistent number of volumes that a publisher will print before it decides to start a new series for a set of books.

Session Law

An uncodified printing of statutes. *See* Act; Acts and Resolves.

Shepard's

Our goal here is to provide a brief overview of Shepard's and sheparizing by identifying the major sets of Shepard's volumes that exist. Later in the chapter we will learn how to use Shepard's—how to *shepardize.* (See page 563.)

	– 327 –	
	ICT§2.16	622F2d³₁.
₄n89		492FS³774
	– 365 –	
– 946 –	Cir. 4	– 485
Cir. 9	623F2d¹²891	W V:
23F2d⁴561	Cir. 5	268S℞3(
	623F2d¹⁰359	
– 953 –	623F2d¹¹359	– 5F
Cir. 4	623F2d¹²359	C
₁24F2d³510	623F2d¹³359	613P2
	623F2d¹⁴359	
– 995 –	623F2d¹⁵359	– !
Cir. 7	623F2d¹⁶359	(
491FS⁴970	f623F2d³360	4BR
e491FS¹²972	f623F2d⁷360	
	623F2d¹⁰397	–
– 1010 –	623F2d¹¹397	
DC	j623F2d403	492′
412A2d35	f623F2d	
	[¹⁰1088	
3	f623F2d	
	[¹²1089	⁄
–	f624F2d¹³539	
d490FS⁹1218	f624F2d¹⁰554	
	f624F2d¹¹155⁄	
242	f624F2d¹²5⁵	
– 1209 –	f624F2d¹¹	
Kan	f624F2d¹¹	
615P2d135	f624F2²	
′–	f624F2·	
5		

Excerpt from a page in a Shepard's volume

Shepard's Citations are citators (page 496). To *shepardize* an item means to use the volumes of Shepard's to collect the research references provided for that item. The references differ depending on what you are shepardizing. If, for example, you are shepardizing a case, you will be given the parallel cite (if one exists) for this case, the history of the case, such as appeals within the same litigation, other cases that have interpreted or mentioned the case you are shepardizing, legal periodical literature on the case, etc. If you are shepardizing a statute, you may be given the session law cite for the statute, amendments, repeals or additions to the statute, court opinions that have interpreted the statute, legal periodical literature on the statute, etc.

What can you shepardize? Here is a partial list:

- Court opinions
- Statutes
- Constitutions
- Some administrative regulations
- Some administrative decisions
- Ordinances
- Charters

- Rules of court
- Some executive orders
- Some treaties
- Patents, trademarks, copyrights
- Restatements
- Some legal periodical literature

As we shall see later, the items in this list constitute the *cited* material—that which you are shepardizing. When you go to the references to these cited materials in the volumes of Shepard's, you will be given a variety of other references on the cited materials, such as cases that have interpreted statutes, amendments to statutes, and cases that have overruled prior cases. These other references are called the *citing* material. (See page 565.)

On pages 511–513, there is an overview of some of these items that can be shepardized with the appropriate sets of Shepard's that you would use to shepardize them.

Shepard's Citations are also available online through WESTLAW and LEXIS.

Slip Law

A *slip law* is a single act passed by the legislature. It is printed separately, often in a small pamphlet. It is the first official publication of the act. All slip laws are later printed in volumes that may be called Session Laws, Acts, Statutes at Large, etc. Finally, if the slip law is a public law or statute, it is also printed in a *statutory code*.

Example of
a slip law

Public Law 87-17
87th Congress, H. R. 4363
April 7, 1961

AN ACT   75 STAT. 41.

To amend Public Law 86–272 relating to State taxation of interstate commerce.

Be it enacted by the Senate and House of Representatives of the United States of America in Congress assembled, That section 201 of Public Law 86–272 (73 Stat. 556) is amended to read as follows: Interstate commerce.
"Sec. 201. The Committee on the Judiciary of the House of Representatives and the Committee on Finance of the United States Senate, acting separately or jointly, or both, or any duly authorized subcommittees thereof, shall make full and complete studies of all matters pertaining to the taxation of interstate commerce by the States, territories, and possessions of the United States, the District of Columbia, and the Commonwealth of Puerto Rico, or any political or taxing subdivision of the foregoing."   Taxation studies.
15 USC 381 note.

Approved April 7, 1961.

An Overview of Major Items That Can Be Sheypardized

Assume that you want to shepardize an opinion of the United States Supreme Court:

Supreme Court Reporter

Assume that you want to shepardize opinions found in *Federal Reporter, 2d:*

Federal Reporter, 2d (F.2d)

Assume that you want to shepardize opinions found in *Federal Supplement:*

Federal Supplement (F. Supp.)

Here is the set of Shepard's you use to shepardize an opinion of the United States Supreme Court:

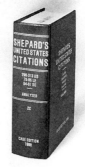

Shepard's United States Citations, Case Edition

Here is the set of Shepard's you use to shepardize an F.2d opinion:

Shepard's Federal Citations

Here is the set of Shepard's you use to shepardize an F. Supp. opinion:

Shepard's Federal Citations

An Overview of
Major Items That
Can Be
Shepardized
—*Continued*

Assume that you want to shepardize a federal statute of Congress: a statute found in U.S.C.A. *(United States Code Annotated)* or in U.S.C.S. *(United States Code Service)* or in U.S.C. *(United States Code):*

Assume that you want to shepardize a regulation of a federal agency found in C.F.R.:

Assume that you want to shepardize opinions found within the following regional reporters:

Atlantic Reporter 2d

Pacific Reporter 2d

South Western Reporter 2d

South Eastern Reporter 2d

North Eastern Reporter 2d

At right are the sets of Shepard's that you use to shepardize the opinions in these regional reporters.

Here is the set of Shepard's that you use to shepardize a federal statute·

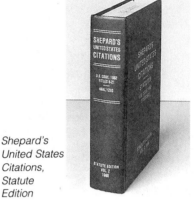

*Shepard's
United States
Citations,
Statute
Edition*

Here is the set of Shepard's that will enable you to shepardize a regulation in C.F.R.:

*Shepard's
Code of
Federal
Regulations
Citations*

You want to shepardize the following:

A Rhode Island court opinion

A Rhode Island statute

A Rhode Island constitutional provision

A New Hampshire court opinion

A New Hampshire statute

A New Hampshire constitutional provision

Here are the sets of Shepard's that you would use:

Note: Every state has its own set of Shepard's similar to Shepard's Rhode Island Citations and Shepard's New Hampshire Citations above.

Slip Opinion

When a court first announces a decision, it is usually published in what is called a *slip opinion* or slip decision. It contains a single case in pamphlet form. The slip opinions are later printed in advance sheets for reporters, which in turn become bound reporters.

South Eastern Digest

A digest that summarizes cases in the South Eastern Reporter. *See* Digests.

South Eastern Reporter 2d (S.E.2d)

A regional reporter. *See* Cases.

Southern Reporter 2d (So.2d)

A regional reporter. *See* Cases.

South Western Reporter 2d (S.W.2d)

A regional reporter. *See* Cases.

Statutes at Large

An uncodified printing of statutes. *See* Act; Acts and Resolves. *See also* United States Statutes at Large.

Statutory Code

A *statutory code* is a collection of the statutes of the legislature organized by subject matter. For example, the statutes on murder are together, the statutes on probate are together, etc. Statutory codes are often annotated, meaning that there are research references provided along with the full text of the statute. The references might include summaries of cases that have interpreted the statute and information on the legislative history of the statute such as the dates of earlier amendments.

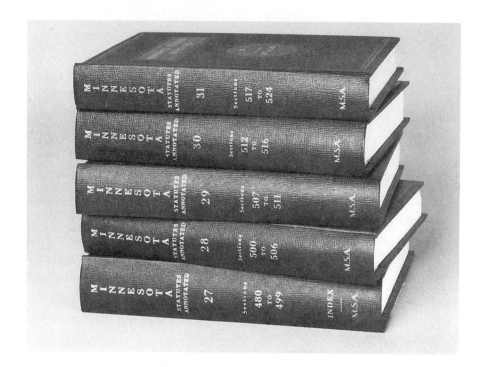

Example of a state
statutory code

The three major federal
statutory codes

U.S.C.A.—United States Code Annotated (published by West)
U.S.C.S.—United State Code Service (published by Lawyers Co-op.)
U.S.C.—United States Code (published by the U.S. Government Printing Office)

Supreme Court Reporter (S. Ct.)

An unofficial reporter that prints every opinion of the United States Supreme Court. *See* Cases.

Total Client-Service Library

The *Total Client-Service Library* is the system by which Lawyers Co-op. refers you to many of the books and materials it publishes. If, for example, you are reading an annotation in A.L.R., A.L.R.2d, A.L.R.3d, A.L.R.4th, or A.L.R. Fed, you may be referred to other Lawyers Co-op. books on the same subject matter, such as *American Jurisprudence 2d,* U.S.C.S. (United States Code Service), *Am Jur Pleading and Practice Forms,* etc. Note that the following example also refers you to the Auto-Cite computer service of Lawyers Co-op., which we will examine later.

Total Client-Service Library® References

50 Am Jur 2d, Landlord and Tenant §§ 1168–1171

Annotations: See the related matters listed in the annotation, infra.

16 Am Jur Pl & Pr Forms (Rev). Landlord and Tenant §§ 161:724–161:727

US L Ed Digest, Landlord and Tenant § 10

ALR Digests, Landlord and Tenant §§ 52.57

L Ed Index to Annos, Buildings; Landlord and Tenant; Real Property

ALR Quick Index, Adequacy Sufficiency; Buildings; Extension or Renewal; Landlord and Tenant; Leases; Perpetuities and Restraints on Alienation; Real Property

Federal Quick Index, Buildings; Landlord and Tenant; Leases; Real Property; Renewal

Auto-Cite®: Any case citation herein can be checked for form, parallel references, later history, and annotation references through the Auto-Cite computer research system

---

Treatise, Legal

A *treatise* (not to be confused with treaty) is any book written by a private individual (or by a public official writing as a private citizen) that provides an overview, summary, or commentary on a topic of law. The treatise will usually attempt to give an extensive treatment of that topic. Hornbooks and formbooks are also treatises.

Ultrafiche

See microforms.

United States Code (U.S.C.)

Volumes containing federal statutes. *See* Statutory Code.

United States Code Annotated (U.S.C.A.)

Volumes containing federal statutes. *See* Statutory Code.

U.S. Code Congressional and Administrative News (USCCAN)

USCCAN, published by West, will enable you to:

- Obtain the complete text of public laws or statutes of Congress before they are published in U.S.C./U.S.C.A./U.S.C.S.

- Obtain the complete text of some congressional committee reports (important for legislative history)

- Translate a Statute at Large cite into a U.S.C./U.S.C.A./U.S.C.S. cite (through Table 2)

- Obtain leads to the legislative history of federal statutes (primarily through its Table 4)

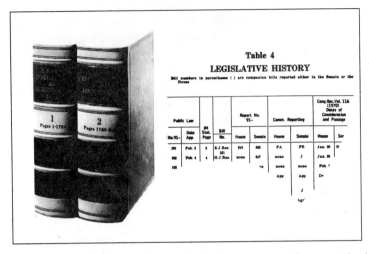

- Obtain the complete text of some federal agency regulations (duplicating what is found in the *Federal Register—F.R.*, and in the *Code of Federal Regulations—C.F.R.*)
- Obtain the complete text of executive orders and other executive documents
- Obtain the complete text of all current United States Statutes at Large (see below)

United States Code Service (U.S.C.S.)

Volumes containing federal statutes. *See* Statutory Code.

United States Law Week (U.S.L.W.)

U.S.L.W is a loose-leaf service published by the Bureau of National Affairs (BNA) that prints the full text of every U.S. Supreme Court case on a weekly basis. It also prints other data on cases in the Supreme Court and summarizes important cases from other courts.

United States Reports (U.S.)

An official reporter that prints every opinion of the United States Supreme Court. *See* Cases.

United States Statutes at Large

The United States Statutes at Large (abbreviated "Stat.") contains the full text of every public law or statute and every private law or statute of Congress. The statutes within it are printed chronologically. All current statutes at large are now also printed in *U.S. Code Congressional and Administrative News* as well as in separate Stat. volumes. (The public laws of general interest are later codified and printed in each of the three sets of codified federal statutes: U.S.C., U.S.C.A., U.S.C.S.)

United States Supreme Court Reports, L. Ed.

An unofficial reporter that prints every opinion of the United States Supreme Court. *See* Cases.

WESTLAW

WESTLAW is a legal research computer system. (See pages 585 and 656).

 # Section H. Authority in Research and Writing

1. Introduction

Authority

Authority is anything that a court can rely on in reaching its conclusion.

Primary and Secondary Authority.   *Primary authority* is any *law* that the court can rely on in reaching its conclusion. Examples include statutes, regulations, constitutional provisions, executive orders, charters, ordinances, treaties, and other court opinions.

Secondary authority is any *nonlaw* that the court can rely on in reaching its conclusion. Examples include legal and nonlegal periodical literature, legal and nonlegal encyclopedias, legal and nonlegal dictionaries, legal and nonlegal treatises.

Mandatory Authority and Persuasive Authority.   *Mandatory authority* is whatever the court *must* rely on in reaching its conclusion. Only primary authority, such as another court opinion, a statute, a constitutional provision, can be mandatory authority. A court is never required to rely on secondary authority, such as a law review article or legal encyclopedia. Secondary authority cannot be mandatory authority.

Persuasive authority is whatever the court relies on when it is not required to do so. There are two main kinds of persuasive authority: (a) a prior court opinion that the court is not required to follow but does so because it finds the opinion persuasive and (b) any secondary authority that the court is not required to follow but does so because it finds the secondary authority persuasive.

Nonauthority.   *Nonauthority* is (a) any primary or secondary authority that is not "on point" because it does not cover the facts of the client's case, (b) any invalid primary authority, such as an unconstitutional statute, or (c) any book that is solely a finding aid, such as Shepard's Citations or digests.

2. Mandatory Authority

Courts *must* follow mandatory authority. There are two broad categories of mandatory authority: (a) *enacted law* such as a statute, a constitutional provision, an ordinance, or a regulation, and (b) other court opinions. Each category will be considered separately.

(a) *Enacted Law as Mandatory Authority*

Any enacted law is mandatory authority and must be followed if the following two tests are met:

- It was the intention of the authors of the enacted law (e.g., the legislature that wrote the statute) to cover the facts that are currently before the court; and

- The application of this enacted law to these facts does not violate some other law that is superior in authority (e.g., the statute does not violate the constitution).

Suppose that Smith is arrested for burglarizing a house. Section 14 of the state code provides, "It shall be a felony to break and enter a dwelling for the purpose of stealing property therein." Section 14 is mandatory authority for the court as long as it is clear that the statute was intended to cover this kind of situation, and the statute does not violate a higher law—the constitution. Suppose, however, that Smith was arrested for breaking into a car. Is a car a "dwelling" for purposes of § 14? Did the legislature intend to include motor vehicles within the meaning of "dwellings?" Would it depend on whether the owner ever slept in the car? These are questions of legislative intent. If the statute was not intended to cover these facts, it is not applicable; it cannot be mandatory authority.

Even if the enacted law was intended to cover the facts before the court, it is not mandatory authority if it violates some higher law. The authors of a regulation, for example, may intend to cover a particular individual's activities, but if this regulation is inconsistent with the statute that the regulation is supposed to be carrying out, the regulation is not mandatory authority; it is invalid. Similarly, a statute may clearly cover a given set of facts but be invalid because the statute is unconstitutional. For example, a statute that prohibits marriage between the races is clearly intended to prevent whites from marrying blacks, but the statute is not mandatory authority because it is in violation of the constitution.

State enacted law is usually mandatory only in the state that enacted that law. Suppose, however, that a state court is considering a *federal* enacted law.

Federal enacted law can sometimes be mandatory authority in *state* courts. The United States Constitution is the highest authority in the country. If a provision of this Constitution applies, it controls over any state law to the contrary. Federal statutes and the regulations of federal agencies are also superior in authority to state laws in those areas entrusted to the federal government by the United States Constitution, such as the regulation of interstate commerce, patents, bankruptcy, or foreign affairs. Federal statutes and regulations in these areas are mandatory authority in state courts.

Can the enacted law of one state ever be mandatory authority in another state? Generally no, with two exceptions involving the principles of conflict of law, and full faith and credit. We will consider these principles when we examine court opinions as mandatory authority.

(b) Court Opinions as Mandatory Authority

When is a court *required* to follow an opinion? Two conditions must be met:

- The opinion must be *on point,* that is, it must be *analogous* and
- The opinion must have been written by a court that is superior to the court currently considering the applicability of the opinion.

For an opinion to be on point, or analogous, there must be a sufficient similarity between the key facts of the opinion and the facts of the client's case, and between the rule of law (e.g., statute, common-law principle) that was interpreted and applied in the opinion and the rule of law that must be interpreted and applied in the client's case.

If the opinion is not on point or is not analogous because the similarity listed above does not exist, then the opinion cannot be mandatory authority; it is nonauthority.

The second condition for the existence of mandatory authority requires us to examine the relationship between the court that wrote the opinion and the court that is currently considering that opinion. Six variations will be covered briefly:

1. The highest court in the judicial system is considering an opinion written by a lower court in the same judicial system.

2. A lower court is considering an opinion written by the highest court in the same judicial system.

3. A court is considering an opinion written in the past by the same court.

4. A court in one state is considering an opinion written by a court from another state.

5. A state court is considering an opinion written by a federal court.

6. A federal court is considering an opinion written by a state court.

In each of these six situations a court is attempting to determine whether a prior opinion is binding in the litigation currently before the court. Assume that each opinion *is* analogous: the facts currently before the court are similar to the key facts in the opinion under consideration, and the rules of law are also the same or similar.

1. The highest court is considering an opinion written by a lower court in same judicial system.   A higher court is never required to follow an opinion written by a lower court in the same judicial system, whether or not the opinion is analogous. If the opinion is analogous, it can only be persuasive authority; the higher court can follow it if it chooses to do so.

2. A lower court is considering an opinion written by the highest court in the same judicial system.   An opinion written by the highest court in a judicial system is mandatory on every lower court in the same judicial system—if that opinion is analogous. An analogous opinion by the Supreme Court of Montana, for example, must be followed by every lower state court in Montana.

3. A court opinion is being considered by the same court that wrote the opinion.   Does a court have to follow its *own* prior opinions? If, for example, the Florida Supreme Court wrote an opinion in 1970, is that opinion mandatory authority for the Florida Supreme Court in 1992 if the opinion is analogous? No. A court is always free to *overrule* its own prior opinions.

Suppose that the opinion was written by an intermediate or middle appeals court. Does that same court have to follow this opinion later if the opinion is analogous? No. *Any* court can later overrule itself and reach a holding that differs from the holding it reached in the earlier opinion as long as there is no opinion in existence written by a higher court that is contrary to the result the middle appeals court now wants to reach.

4. One state court is considering an opinion written by a state court in another state.   One state court, generally, does not have to follow an opinion written by another state court no matter how similar the opinion is. An Idaho court, for example, does not have to follow an opinion written by a Massachusetts court.

There are two main exceptions to the principle that an opinion of one state is not mandatory authority in another state. The first involves conflicts of law and the second, full faith and credit:

(a) *Conflicts of Law.* Suppose that an accident occurs in New York, but the negligence suit based on this accident is brought in an Ohio state court. Assume that the Ohio court has subject-matter jurisdiction over the dispute and personal jurisdiction over the parties. What negligence law does the Ohio court apply? Ohio negligence law or New York negligence law? The negligence law of the two states may differ in significant respects. This is a conflicts-of-law problem. Under the principles of the conflicts of law, a court of one state may be required to apply the law of another state. For example, the law to be applied may be the law of the state where the injury occurred or the law of the state that is at the center of the dispute. If this state is deemed to be New York, then the Ohio court will apply New York negligence law. Analogous opinions of New York courts on the law of negligence will be mandatory authority in the Ohio court.

(b) *Full Faith and Credit.* The United States Constitution provides that "Full Faith and Credit shall be given in each State to the public Acts, Records, and judicial Proceedings of every other State." Art. IV, § 1. Suppose that Richards sues Davis for breach of contract in Delaware. Davis wins. Richards cannot go to another state and bring a breach-of-contract suit arising out of the same facts against Davis in the other state. If the Delaware court had proper jurisdiction when it rendered its judgment, the Delaware opinion must be given full faith and credit in every other state. The case cannot be relitigated. The Delaware opinion is mandatory authority in every other state.

5 and 6. A state court is considering an opinion written by a federal court and vice versa. The general rule is that state courts have the final say on what the state law is, and federal courts have the final say on what the federal law is. State courts do *not* have to follow opinions written by federal courts *unless* the issue before the state court involves a federal question—one arising out of the United States Constitution or out of a statute of Congress. Federal courts do not have to follow state court opinions *except to the extent that* the federal court needs to know what the state law is on a given topic.

3. Court Opinions as Persuasive Authority

Review the two conditions mentioned earlier on when an opinion is mandatory authority: the opinion must be analogous, or on point, *and* it must have been written by a court that is superior to the court currently considering that opinion. If *both* these tests are not met, the opinion is either nonauthority or it might be *persuasive authority.*

Assume that the holding in the *X v. Y* opinion is not analogous to the legal issues currently being considered by a court in the *A v. B* litigation. Assume also that within *X v. Y* there is some *dictum* that has relevance or some bearing on the issues before the *A v. B* court. By definition, the dictum cannot be part of the *X v. Y* holding, since dictum is a statement by a judge that was not necessary to resolve the narrow legal issues before the court in *X v. Y.* Dictum, therefore, can never be mandatory authority. The *A v. B* court is not *required* to follow the *X v. Y* dictum. The *A v. B* court, however, has the discretion of adopting the *X v. Y* dictum, since it does relate to the issues before the *A v. B* court. If the court does adopt it, it has become persuasive authority.

Suppose that you are reading an opinion that *is* analogous, or on point, but is not mandatory because:

- It was written by an inferior court and is now being considered by a court within the same judicial system that is superior to the court that wrote the opinion; or

- It was written by a court from a judicial system that is different from the judicial system where the court considering that opinion sits.

If either of these two situations exists, the court, as we have seen, does *not* have to follow the opinion; it is not mandatory authority. If, however, the opinion is on point, the court would be free to adopt it as persuasive authority.

A number of factors go into a court's determination of whether a prior opinion is persuasive enough to adopt. A judge will usually be interested in knowing how many other courts have adopted the result of this opinion. Is there a "majority rule" or school of thought that has developed around that result? Has the opinion been frequently cited with approval? How well reasoned is the opinion? These considerations will help a judge decide whether to adopt an opinion as persuasive. Finally, it is human nature for judges to gravitate toward those opinions that are most in tune with their personal philosophies and biases—although preferences on this basis are never acknowledged.

4. Secondary Authority as Persuasive Authority

Secondary authority is not the law itself. It is *not* written by the legislature, a court, an agency, a city council, etc. Secondary authority can never be mandatory authority; it can only be persuasive. The chart in Figure 11.6 provides an overview of the major kinds of secondary authority that a court could decide to rely on in reaching its conclusion.

Some of these secondary authorities quote from the law itself, that is, they quote primary authority. As a general rule, *you should never use someone else's quotation of the law.* Quote *directly* from the primary authority. Use the secondary authority to bolster your arguments on the interpretation of the primary authority. This is the main function of secondary authority: to help you persuade a court to adopt a certain interpretation of primary authority. You are on very dangerous ground when you use secondary authority as a substitute for primary authority.

Secondary authority will frequently *paraphrase* or summarize primary authority, e.g., a hornbook or legal encyclopedia will summarize the law of a particular state on a topic. You will be *very* tempted to use such summaries in your own legal writing. There are serious dangers, however, in relying on excerpts containing such summaries. While they can be used and sometimes *should* be used (with proper citation to avoid the charge of plagiarism), the difficulties with using quotes from such excerpts are as follows:

- The excerpts are secondary authority, and the goal of your writing is to use primary authority to support your arguments.

- The excerpts may contain summaries of court opinions; these opinions should be *individually* analyzed before you use any of them in your writing.

- The excerpts may be based on opinions from different states, and your legal writing must focus on the law of the state in which the client is litigating the case.

In short, too much reliance on such excerpts from secondary authority amounts to laziness in legal research and analysis. It is sometimes difficult to find and

FIGURE 11.6

Categories of
Secondary
Authority

KIND	CONTENTS	EXAMPLES
1. Legal encyclopedias	Summaries of the law, organized by topic	*Corpus Juris Secundum* *American Jurisprudence 2d*
2. Nonlegal encyclopedias	Summaries of many topics on science, the arts, history, etc.	*Encyclopedia Britannica*
3. Legal Dictionaries	Definitions of legal terms taken almost exclusively from court opinions	*Words and Phrases*
4. Legal Dictionaries	Definitions of legal terms that come from a variety of sources	*Black's Law Dictionary* *Ballentine's Law Dictionary* West's *Legal Thesaurus/ Dictionary*
5. Nonlegal Dictionaries	Definitions of all words in general use	*Webster's Dictionary*
6. Legal Periodicals (general)	Pamphlets (later often bound) containing articles written on a variety of legal topics	*Harvard Law Review* *American Bar Association Journal*
7. Legal Periodicals (specialized)	Pamphlets (later often bound) containing articles written on a specialized area or aspect of the law	*Journal of Family Law* *Journal of Legal Education*
8. Nonlegal Periodicals	Pamphlets on general topics	*Newsweek* *Foreign Affairs*
9. Legal Treatises	Summaries of and commentaries on areas of the law	*McCormick on Evidence* Johnstone and Hopson, *Lawyers and Their Work* *Restatement of the Law of Torts*
10. Nonlegal Treatises	Perspectives on a variety of topics	Samuelson, *Economics*
11. Loose-Leaf Services	Collections of materials in three-ring binders covering current law in designated areas	*Pollution Control Guide* *Accountancy Law Reports* *Products Liability Reporter*
12. Formbooks, Manuals, Practice Books	Same as legal treatises with a greater emphasis on the "how-to-do-it" practical dimensions of the law	Dellheim, *Massachusetts Practice* Moore's *Federal Practice* *Am Jur Pleading and Practice Forms Annotated*
13. Legal Newspapers	Daily or weekly compilations of information relevant to practice	*Daily Washington Law Reporter* *National Law Journal*
14. Nonlegal Newspapers	General circulation newspapers	*New York Times* *Detroit Free Press*

apply the law. If someone else at least appears to have done all the work for you in secondary authority, why not use it? The answers to this question are found in the three difficulties mentioned above.

Before covering the *proper* use of secondary authority in your legal writing, the value of secondary authority *as a research tool* should be reemphasized. Often the most valuable parts of these texts are the footnotes. The citations in the footnotes to court opinions (and to other authority) can be invaluable to you as you pursue your search for relevant law. If the secondary authority has led you to laws that you eventually use in your writing (after proper legal analysis), the secondary authority will have been of tremendous service to you.

Secondary authority can provide another service, independent of whether you use it directly in your writing. You will often be doing legal research in areas of the law that are new to you. You may need help trying to make sense of what might appear to be quite formidable and esoteric areas of the law—with or without the inevitable Latin phrases. One approach is to read a chapter in a hornbook, a section in a legal encyclopedia, or material in any other secondary authority in order to obtain an overview of the law. Armed with this general understanding, you will be better equipped to resume your research and analysis in the unfamiliar area of law. See page 550 on doing such background research.

Suppose that you want to *use* a quote from the secondary authority *in your legal writing*. What steps must you take in order to do so properly? What is the proper *foundation* for the use of secondary authority in legal writing? Figure 11.7 presents the steps that provide this foundation. The secondary authority mentioned in the chart is a treatise, although the steps apply equally to *any* type of secondary authority that you are thinking about using in your legal writing as possible persuasive authority. You cannot avoid extensive research and analysis simply by quoting from secondary authority—no matter how tempting. Unless you have researched and analyzed the relevant *mandatory* authority, you will be unable to establish the necessary foundation to use *secondary* authority.

Many well-written and comprehensively researched legal memoranda and appellate briefs make very few references to secondary authority. Experienced advocates know that judges are suspicious of secondary authority. It is true that some secondary authorities are highly respected (such as *Prosser on Torts* or any of the *Restatements* of the American Law Institute). Yet even these must be used with caution. The preoccupation of a court is on primary authority. Before you use secondary authority in your writing, you must be sure that (a) the secondary authority is not used as a substitute for the primary authority, (b) the

---

FIGURE 11.7

The Foundation for the Use of Secondary Authority in Legal Writing as Possible Persuasive Authority

1. You must satisfy yourself through independent legal research that the quote from the treatise that you want to use does not contradict any law (opinion, statute, constitutional provision, etc.) that exists in the jurisdiction where the client is litigating the case. Stated more simply: there must be no contrary mandatory authority.

2. If the quote from the treatise *does* contradict any such law, you cannot use the quote *unless* you satisfy yourself:

   - that the court before which the client is litigating the case has the power to change the law that contradicts what the treatise says and, in effect, adopt the treatise's statement as new law in the jurisdiction, and

   - that there is a reasonable likelihood that a court with such power is inclined to change the law.

secondary authority is not unduly repetitive of the primary authority, (c) the secondary authority will be helpful to the court in adopting an interpretation of primary authority, particularly when there is not a great deal of primary authority on point, (d) you discuss the secondary authority after you have presented the primary authority, and (e) the foundation for the use of secondary authority (see Figure 11.7) can be demonstrated if needed.

 ## Section I. Citation Form

A citation, or cite, is a reference to any written material. The cite gives you the "address" where you can go in the library to find the cited document.

Are there any consistent rules on citation form? If you pick up different law books and examine the citations of similar material within them, you will notice great variety in citation form. You will find that people abbreviate things differently, they do not include the same order of information in the cite, they use parentheses differently, they use punctuation within the cite differently, they include different amounts of information in the same kind of cite, etc. There does not appear to be any consistency. Yet, in spite of this diversity and confusion, you are often scolded by supervisors for failing to use "proper citation form." What, you may well ask, is "proper"?

Start by checking the court rules of the court that will have jurisdiction over the problem you are researching. There may or may not be citation rules within them. If such rules exist, they must obviously be followed in spite of what any other citation rule book may say. These are, in effect, citation *laws*.

Suppose, however, that there are no official citation laws in the court rules for your court or that these citation rules do not cover the citation question that you have. In such circumstances, *ask your supervisor what citation form you should use.* You will probably be told, "Use the Bluebook." This is a reference to A Uniform System of Citation we looked at earlier (page 490). It is a small blue pamphlet (although in earlier editions, white covers were used). The Bluebook is published by a group of law students on the law reviews of their law schools. Caution is needed, however, in using the Bluebook. It is a highly technical and sometimes difficult-to-use pamphlet because it packs so much information in a relatively small space. Primary users of the Bluebook are law

---

GENERAL GUIDELINES ON CITATION FORM

1. Find out if there are citation laws in the rules of court.

2. Ask your supervisor if he or she has any special instructions on citation form.

3. Consult the Bluebook.

4. Consult the basic citation rules presented below (I–VII). Most of these rules are based on the Bluebook.

5. Remember that the *functional* purpose of a citation is to enable readers to locate your citation in a library. You must give enough information in the cite to fulfill this purpose. Courtesy to the reader in providing this help is as important as compliance with the niceties of citation form.

6. Often a private publisher of a book will tell you how to cite the book. ("Cite this book as. . . .") Ignore this instruction! Instead, follow guidelines 1–5 above.

7. When in doubt about whether to include something in a citation after carefully following guidelines 1–5 above, resolve the doubt by including it in the cite.

schools that wish to have their law reviews typeset by professional printers. What about those of us who use regular typewriters or word processors and do not typeset what we produce? While the Bluebook does cover many of our citation needs, keep in mind that we are not the main audience of the Bluebook. Also, be aware that many courts do *not* follow the Bluebook even if there are no court rules on citation form for that court. Judges often simply use their own "system" of citation without necessarily being consistent.

Basic Citation Rules

Use the following citation forms unless General Guidelines 1–3 above tell you otherwise:

  I. Citing Opinions

  II. Citing Constitutions and Charters

  III. Citing Federal Statutes

  IV. Citing State Statutes

  V. Citing Administrative Regulations

  VI. Citing the Documents of Legislative History

VII. Citing Secondary Authority

I. Citing Opinions

The following are the most common kinds of opinions and decisions that you will be citing:

Example A: Format of a Citation to an Opinion of the Highest Federal Court (the United States Supreme Court):

> *Taglianetti v. United States,* 394 U.S. 316, 89 S. Ct. 1099, 22 L. Ed.2d 302 (1969). [As indicated below, there is a disagreement over the proper citation form for this Court. The Bluebook says the correct cite would be: *Taglianetti v. United States,* 394 U.S. 316 (1969).]

Example B: Format of a Citation to an Opinion of a Federal Middle Appeals Court (the United States Court of Appeals, Second Circuit):

> *Sterling Nat'l Bank & Trust Co. of N.Y. v. Fidelity Mortgage Investors,* 510 F.2d 870 (2d Cir. 1975).

Example C: Format of a Citation to an Opinion of a Federal Trial Court (the United States District Court, Western District in Wisconsin):

> *Stone v. Schmidt,* 398 F. Supp. 768 (W.D. Wisc. 1975).

Example D: Format of a Citation to an Opinion of the Highest State Court (New Jersey Supreme Court):

> *Petlin Associates, Inc. v. Township of Dover,* 64 N.J. 327, 316 A.2d 1 (1974).

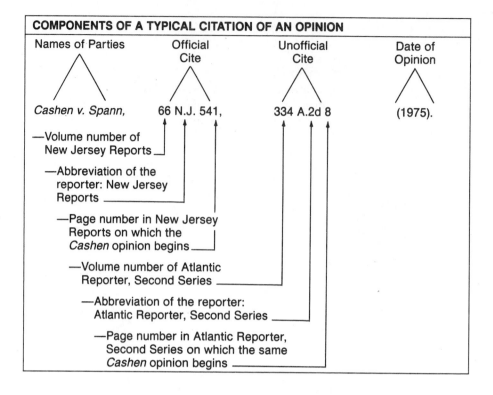

COMPONENTS OF A TYPICAL CITATION OF AN OPINION

Names of Parties	Official Cite	Unofficial Cite	Date of Opinion
Cashen v. Spann,	66 N.J. 541,	334 A.2d 8	(1975).

—Volume number of New Jersey Reports

—Abbreviation of the reporter: New Jersey Reports

—Page number in New Jersey Reports on which the *Cashen* opinion begins

—Volume number of Atlantic Reporter, Second Series

—Abbreviation of the reporter: Atlantic Reporter, Second Series

—Page number in Atlantic Reporter, Second Series on which the same *Cashen* opinion begins

Example E: Format of a Citation to an Opinion of a Lower State Court (Connecticut Superior Court, Appellate Session):

> *Huckabee v. Stevens,* 32 Conn. Supp. 511, 338 A.2d 512 (Super. Ct. 1975).

Example F: Format of a Citation to an Administrative Decision (National Labor Relations Board):

> *Standard Dry Wall Products, Inc.,* 91 N.L.R.B. 544 (1950).

Example G: Format of a Citation to an Opinion of the Attorney General:

> 40 Op. Att'y Gen. 423 (1945).

Guidelines:

1. You will note that some of the citations in the above examples have *parallel cites* (see Examples A, D, and E) and some do not. Before examining the rules of providing parallel cites and the techniques of finding such cites, some basics need to be covered.

2. The same opinion can be printed in more than one reporter. A parallel cite is a reference to an *additional* reporter where the same opinion (word-for-word) can be found. In Example D, the *Petlin* opinion can be found in New Jersey Reports (abbreviated "N.J.") and in Atlantic 2d ("A.2d").

3. Do not confuse (a) the parallel cite with (b) the same case on appeal. Examine the following three citations:

- *Smith v. Jones,* 24 Mass. 101, 19 N.E.2d 370 (1920).
- *Jones v. Smith,* 26 Mass. 228, 21 N.E.2d 1017 (1922).
- *Smith v. Jones,* 125 F.2d 177 (2d Cir. 1925).

Assume that these three opinions involve the same litigation—the same parties and the same issues. The case went up on appeal three times: twice to the Massachusetts Supreme Judicial Court and once the United States Court of Appeals for the Second Circuit. The first two opinions have parallel cites. For example, the first opinion is printed in both Massachusetts Reports (24 Mass. 101) and in North Eastern Reporter, 2d (19 N.E.2d 370). The third opinion has no parallel cite. The second and third opinions are citations to the "same case on appeal." They are *not* parallel cites to the first opinion. While the same litigation is involved, the citations are to three distinct opinions, two of which have parallel cites.

4. There are four main techniques of finding a parallel cite:

- Shepardize the case. The first cite in parentheses in Shepard's is the parallel cite. If you find no cite in parenthesis, it means (a) that no parallel cite exists, (b) that the reporter containing the parallel cite has not been printed yet, or (c) the parallel cite was given in one of the earlier volumes of Shepard's and was not repeated in the volume you are examining.

```
– 717 –
(439US438)      | 0
592F2d²288      | e61
f615F2d¹739     | f473t
f615F2d²739     | 94Æ318
f615F2d⁵739     | 94Æ319
471FS⁵101       | 94Æ211
f476FS¹92       | 94Æ324
477FS961        |
ᴵ77FS⁴969       |

      ᵀ33
```

Finding a parallel cite through Shepard's

- *National Reporter Blue Book.* Go to this set of books published by West to try to locate a parallel cite. The National Reporter Blue Book will also tell you which official reporters have been discontinued. (If your state has a Blue and White Book, you can also use it to try to find a parallel cite.)

- Top of the caption. Go to the reporter that contains the opinion. At the beginning of the opinion, there is a caption giving the names of the parties, the court, etc. At the top of this caption, see if there is a parallel cite. (This technique does not always work, but it is worth a try.)

```
169 Conn. 677

Application of Verne Freeman SLADE
for Admission to the Bar.

Supreme Court of Connecticut.

Dec. 2, 1975.
```

Finding a parallel cite by checking the top of the caption

■ Table of Cases in Digest. Go to every digest that gives small-paragraph summaries of court opinions for the court that wrote the opinion, e.g., the American Digest System. Go to the table of cases in these digests. See if there is a parallel cite for your case. In the following excerpt from a digest table of cases, you find two cites for *Ames v. State Bar*—106 Cal.Rptr. 489 and 506 P.2d 625:

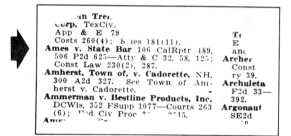

Finding a parallel cite by checking the table of cases in digests

5. When should you provide a parallel cite? The general answer is, whenever one exists. As we shall see in a moment, however, there are some important exceptions to this guideline.

6. Although an opinion may eventually be printed in more than one reporter, the reporters are rarely, if ever, printed at the same time. The publication of an official reporter, for example, can be as much as a year behind the unofficial reporter. At the time you want to cite a recent opinion, you may have only the unofficial reporter available. Hence, you could not provide a parallel cite. Simply provide the cite that you have.

7. As indicated earlier, loose-leaf services often provide the most current legal material available. Some services will send out opinions within a week of their issuance by the court. Generally, however, you do *not* include the citation to the loose-leaf service *unless* no other citation to the opinion is available at the time.

8. Court opinions are found in traditional library volumes (reporters) and on computerized legal research services. Some opinions, however, are found *only* online in these services. An example is *Bucknum v. Bucknum*, which was decided on February 19, 1991 by the Minnesota Court of Appeals. Its docket number is No. C6-90-1798. This opinion is found on WESTLAW and on LEXIS but not in a traditional library reporter volume. Here is how the case is cited in WESTLAW and LEXIS respectively:

Bucknum v. Bucknum, 1991 WL 17881 (Minn. App.).

Bucknum v. Bucknum, 1991 Minn. App. LEXIS 145.

The number 17881 is an internal WESTLAW number, and 145 is an internal LEXIS number.

The Bluebook does *not* follow these citation formats. The Bluebook has its own format for citing cases found in WESTLAW and LEXIS:

Bucknum v. Bucknum, No. C6–90–1798, 1991 WL 17881 (Minn. App. Feb. 19, 1991).

Bucknum v. Bucknum, No. C6–90–1798, 1991 Minn. App. LEXIS 145 (Feb. 19, 1991).

Note that in these Bluebook cites, the docket number and the WESTLAW/LEXIS cite are given, along with the full date of the decision in parentheses at the end. You should not cite a case in WESTLAW or LEXIS unless it is not readily available in traditional library volumes such as reporters.

9. There is some disagreement as to whether parallel cites are needed for opinions of the U.S. Supreme Court. The Bluebook says you should not provide a parallel cite for such opinions if you have the official cite ("U.S.") available, even if the parallel cites in "S. Ct." and "L. Ed." are also available. The better view, however, is to give all three cites when they are available. (See Example A.)

10. When parallel cites are to be cited, always place the official cite first before the unofficial cite. (See Examples A, D, and E.)

11. There is no parallel cite for Federal Reporter 2d cases (F.2d). (See Example B.) Abbreviate the circuit in parentheses at the end of the cite before the year. 2d Cir. means the opinion was decided by the U.S. Court of Appeals for the Second Circuit. D.C. Cir. would mean the case was decided by the U.S. Court of Appeals for the District of Columbia Circuit. The caption of the opinion will tell you which circuit court wrote the opinion.

12. There is no parallel cite for Federal Supplement cases (F. Supp.). (See Example C.) Abbreviate the U.S. District Court in parentheses at the end of the cite before the year. W.D. Wisc. means the opinion was written by the United States District Court, Western District, sitting in Wisconsin. The caption of the opinion will tell you which U.S. District Court wrote the opinion.

13. In Example D, the parentheses at the end of the cite to the *Petlin* case contain the date of the decision, but nothing more. There is no need to indicate the name of the court in the parentheses if the court is the highest court of the state, and if it is clear from the reporter abbreviation what state is involved. In Example D, the *Petlin* case was written by the highest court (the Supreme Court) in the state of New Jersey. You know this by examining the abbreviation of the official reporter in the cite (64 N.J. 327). When the abbreviation of the reporter (here, N.J.) is the abbreviation of the state, you can assume that the case was written by the highest court in that state. Suppose, however, that you did not have this official reporter cite. If all you had was the unofficial Atlantic 2d cite (316 A.2d 1), you would cite the case as follows:

Petlin Associates, Inc. v. Township of Dover, 316 A.2d 1 (N.J. 1974).

By looking at the abbreviation of the reporter (A.2d), you cannot tell which state wrote this opinion. Therefore, you must indicate the name of the state in the parentheses before the date. Since the case was written by the highest court in the state, there is no need to abbreviate the name of this court. Using the abbreviation of the state alone (N.J.) tells you that it was the highest.

14. In Example E, there is an abbreviation of the court that wrote the opinion (Superior Court) in parentheses before the date at the end of the cite. This is necessary because the opinion was written by a state court other than the highest court in the state. Note that it is not necessary to tell the reader

that this court is in Connecticut because it is clear from the abbreviation of the reporter (32 Conn. Supp. 511) that it is a Connecticut case.

15. Include only the last name of parties who are people. For example, if the parties are listed as "Frank Taylor v. Mary Smith" by the court, your cite should list them as *Taylor v. Smith*.

16. If a party is a business, use the full name of the business, but abbreviate words such as Corporation (Corp.), Incorporated (Inc.), Company (Co.), Limited (Ltd.), and Brothers (Bros.). If, for example, a party is listed by the court as "John J. Dover, Incorporated," your cite would read *John J. Dover, Inc.* (If, however, John J. Dover was a party suing or being sued as human person rather than as a business, your cite would simply list this party as *Dover*.)

17. When the United States is a party, do not use the abbreviation "U.S." See Example A.

18. Assume that New York State is a party. Your cite should say "State" (rather than "State of New York" or "New York") *if and only if* the opinion was written by a New York state court. Suppose, however, that New York is a party in a case written by an Ohio court. In such a case, use "New York" (not "State of New York" or "State") in your cite as the name of this party. This same guideline applies for the words "Commonwealth" and "People." These words are used alone in a cite only if the court that wrote the opinion you are citing is in the same state referred to by the words "Commonwealth" and "People." Example: You are citing an opinion of the California Supreme Court, which describes the parties as follows:

People of California v. Gabriel S. Farrell

Your cite of this opinion would be *People v. Farrell*.

19. If your printer can print in italics, you should italicize the names of the parties. For example:

Steck v. Farrell

If you cannot italicize, underline or underscore. For example:

<u>Steck v. Farrell</u>

20. Some opinions consolidate more than one litigation. A supreme court, for example, may use one opinion to resolve similar issues raised in several different lower court cases. The caption of the opinion written by the supreme court will probably list all the parties from these different lower court cases, for example, *A v. B; C v. D; E v. F.* When you cite this opinion, include only the *first* set of parties listed in the caption—here, *A v. B*. On the other hand, the court may not list all the multiple parties but may simply say *et al.* (and others) after the name of a party. Do not include the phrase *et al.* in your cite.

21. Often the court will tell you the litigation status of the parties, such as plaintiff, defendant, appellant, or appellee. Generally, you should not include this information in your cite.

22. Titles of individual parties (such as administrator or secretary) should be omitted from your cite. One exception is the Commissioner of Internal Revenue. Cite this party simply as "Commissioner"—for example, *Jackson v. Commissioner*.

23. Include the phrase *in re* (meaning "in the matter of") in your cite—for example, *In re Jones.*

24. Include the year of the decision at the end of the cite in parentheses. If more than one date is given in the caption of the opinion, use the year from the date the opinion was decided.

25. Do not include the *docket number* of the case in the cite unless the case is not printed in a traditional reporter (see guideline #8), or unless the case is still pending.

26. The reporter volumes that contain current opinions are conveniently arranged by volume number. All the volumes of the same set have the same name, e.g., Atlantic Reporter, 2d. There was a time, however, when life was not this simple. Volumes of opinions were identified by the name of the individual person who had responsibility for compiling the opinions written by the judges. These individuals were called reporters. "7 Cush. 1," for example, refers to an opinion found on page 1 of volume 7 of Massachusetts cases when Mr. Cushing was the official reporter. When he ended his employment, Mr. Gray took over, and the cite of an opinion in the volume immediately after "7 Cush." was "1 Gray." Simply by looking at the cover of the volume, you *cannot* tell what court's opinions were inside unless you happen to be familiar with the names of these individuals and the courts for which they worked. These volumes are called *nominative reporters* because they are identified by the name of the individual person who compiled the opinions for the court.

27. Assume that all you know are the names of the parties and the name of the court that wrote the opinion. How do you obtain the full cite?

    ■ Go to every digest that covers that reporter. Check its table of cases.

    ■ Call the court clerk for the court that wrote the opinion. If it is a recent case, the clerk may be able to send you a copy. Occasionally, the clerk will give you the cite of the case. (It will help if you can tell the clerk the docket number of the case.)

    ■ Go to the reporter volumes that cover the court that wrote the opinion. Since you do not have a volume number, you cannot go directly to the volume that has the opinion. If, however, you can *approximate* the date of the case, you can check the table of cases in each reporter volume that probably covers that year. You may have to check the table of cases in 10 to 15 volumes before achieving success. The opinions are printed in the reporters in roughly chronological order.

28. When quoting from or referring to specific language in an opinion, you must list both the number of the page on which the opinion begins *and* the number of the page on which the quoted language begins. The latter page number is inserted in the citation immediately following the former and is set off with a comma. If a parallel cite is included, do the same for the parallel cite. In the following example, the quote is from page 20 of *Maryland Reports* ("Md.") and from p. 379 of Atlantic 2d ("A.2d"):

EXAMPLE

"Even though laches may not apply, one must use reasonable promptness when availing himself of judicial protection." *Bridgeton Educ. Ass'n v. Bd. of Educ.,* 147 Md. 17, 20, 334 A.2d 376, 379 (1975).

II. *Citing Constitutions and Charters*

Constitutions and charters are cited to (a) the abbreviated name of the constitution or charter, (b) the article, and (c) the section.

EXAMPLE

U.S. Const. art. I, § 9.
N.M. Const. art. IV, § 7.

In citing constitutions and charters, the date of enactment should *not* be given unless the provision you are citing has been amended or repealed.

III. *Citing Federal Statutes*

1. All federal statutes of Congress are collected in chronological order of passage as session laws in the *United States Statutes at Large.* If the statute is of general public interest, it is also printed in *each* of three codes:

   - United State Code (U.S.C.)
   - United States Code Annotated (U.S.C.A.)—West Publishing Co.
   - United States Code Service (U.S.C.S.)—Lawyers Co-operative Publishing Co.

   The preferred citation format is to U.S.C. For example:

   42 U.S.C. § 3412(a)(1970).
   or
   Narcotic Rehabilitation Act of 1966, 42 U.S.C. § 3412(a)(1970).

   While it is not necessary to give the popular name of the statute (as in the second version of the above example), citing the popular name when known is often helpful.

2. A new edition of the U.S.C. comes out every six years. The date you use in citing a statute in U.S.C. is the date of the edition you are using unless your statute is found in one of the annual Supplements to the U.S.C., which come out in between editions. If your statute is in a Supplement, you cite the volume and year of this Supplement. Suppose your statute is found in the sixth Supplement published in 1983. Your cite would be as follows:

   29 U.S.C. § 169 (Supp. VI 1983).

   The date you use in citing a statute in U.S.C. is not the year the statute was enacted or passed by the legislature. It is the date of the edition of the code or of the Supplement year.

3. Although citation to U.S.C. is preferred, it is not uncommon to find citations to the other codes: U.S.C.A. and U.S.C.S. (There is never a need, however, to cite more than one of the three codes.) The format is as follows:

   29 U.S.C.A. § 169 (West 1983).
   29 U.S.C.S. § 169 (Law. Co-op. 1982).

   In parentheses before the date, include the name of the publisher. Use the year that appears on the title page of the volume, or its latest copyright year, in this order of preference. If your statute is in one of the annual pocket parts of either of these two codes, include "Supp." and give the year of the pocket part—for example, (West Supp. 1984).

4. There is one instance in which you *must* cite to the *United States Statutes at Large* (abbreviated Stat.) rather than to U.S.C. The rule is as follows: Cite to the statute in Statutes at Large if (a) there is a difference in the language of the statute in Stat. and in the U.S.C. and (b) the statute in U.S.C. is in a title that has *not* been enacted into positive law by Congress.

It is highly unlikely that you will find a difference in language between Stat. and U.S.C. Yet the conscientious researcher must check this out before relying on any statutory language.

All the statutes in U.S.C. fall within one of fifty titles—for example, title 11 on Bankruptcy, title 39 on the Postal Service. If Congress goes through all the statutes in a particular title and formally declares that all of them are valid and accurate, then that title has been enacted into positive law. You can rely exclusively on the language of such statutes even if the language is different from the statute as it originally appeared in Statutes at Large. At the beginning of the first volume of U.S.C., you will be told which titles of the U.S.C. have been enacted into positive law.

5. A Statute at Large cite, when needed, should include (a) the name of the statute if one exists; if one does not exist, include "Act of" and give the full date of enactment—month, day, and year, (b) the Public Law number of the statute or its chapter number, (c) the section of the statute you are citing, (d) the volume number of the Statutes at Large used, (e) the abbreviation "Stat.," (f) the page number on which your statute is found in the Stat. volume, (g) in parentheses, the year the statute was enacted or passed by the legislature. Do not include the year, however, if you used the "Act of" option referred to in (a).

EXAMPLE

Narcotic Addict Rehabilitation Act, Pub. L. No. 80–793, § 9, 80 Stat. 1444 (1966).

Note that the year in parentheses at the end of the cite is the year the statute was passed. Guideline 2 above said that you do not use the date of enactment when citing a statute in U.S.C. The rule is different when giving a Stat. cite.

Note the section number (9) of this Public Law in the example. The statute might also have several title numbers. If so, § 9 would be found within one of these titles. Assume, for example, that § 9 is in title III of the Public Law. It is important to remember that these section and title numbers are found in the original *session law* edition of the statute. When this statute is later printed in U.S.C. (assuming it is a public law of general interest), it will *not* go into § 9 of the third title. The U.S.C. has its own title and section number scheme. (For example, title III, § 9 of the above statute might be found in title 45, § 1075(b) of the U.S.C.) This can be very frustrating for the researcher new to the law. If you are reading a statute in its original session or Public Law form, you cannot find this statute under the same title and section number in U.S.C. You must *translate* the Public Law or Stat. cite into a U.S.C. cite. Phrased another way, you must translate the session law cite into a code cite. Later, we will see that this is done by using one of two tables: Table III in a special Tables volume of USC/USCA/USCS, or Table 2 in U.S. Code Congressional and Administrative News.

6. Of course, if the statute is a private law or is a public law that is deemed to be of no general public interest, it will not be printed in the U.S.C. It will be found only in Statutes at Large.

7. The Internal Revenue Code is within the U.S.C. Hence, you use guideline 1 above in citing a tax statute. For example:

26 U.S.C. § 1278 (1976).

For tax statutes in the Internal Revenue Code (I.R.C.), however, there is *another* option that is considered acceptable:

I.R.C. § 1278 (1976).

8. There is a special format for citing Federal Rules of Civil Procedure, Federal Rules of Criminal Procedure, Federal Rules of Appellate Procedure, and the Federal Rules of Evidence. Examples:

Fed. R. Civ. P. 15
Fed. R. Crim. P. 23
Fed. R. App. P. 3
Fed. R. Evid. 310

IV. Citing State Statutes

1. Like federal statutes, the statutes of the various states are compiled in two kinds of collections: state *codes* (arranged by subject matter) and *session laws* (arranged in chronological order of enactment).

2. Citations to state codes vary from state to state. On page 535, there are examples of standard citation formats. Use these as guides unless local rules of court dictate otherwise. The year at the end of the cite should be the year that appears on the spine of the code, or the year that appears on the title page, or the latest copyright year—in this order of preference.

V. Citing Administrative Regulations

1. Federal administrative regulations are published in the *Federal Register* (Fed. Reg.). Many of these regulations are later codified by subject matter in the *Code of Federal Regulations* (C.F.R.).

2. Federal regulations that appear in the *Code of Federal Regulations* are cited to (a) the title number in which the regulation appears, (b) the abbreviated name of the code, (c) the number of the particular section to which you are referring, and (d) the date of the code edition which you are using.

EXAMPLE

29 C.F.R. § 102.60(a)(1975).

3. Federal regulations that have not yet been codified into the *Code of Federal Regulations* are cited to the *Federal Register* using (a) the volume in which the regulation appears, (b) the abbreviation "Fed. Reg.," (c) the page on which the regulation appears, and (d) the year of the *Federal Register* you are using.

EXAMPLE

27 Fed. Reg. 2,092 (1962).

Examples of State Statutory Code Citations

Alabama:	Ala. Code § 37–10–3 (1977).
Alaska:	Alaska Stat. § 22.10.110 (1962).
Arizona:	Ariz. Rev. Stat. Ann. § 44–1621 (1956).
Arkansas:	Ark. Code Ann. § 20–316 (Michie 1968).
California:	Cal. Prob. Code § 585 (West 1956). Cal. Prob. Code § 585 (Deering 1956).
Colorado:	Colo. Rev. Stat. Ann. § 32–7–131 (West 1971). Colo. Rev. Stat. § 32-7-131 (1971).
Connecticut:	Conn. Gen. Stat. § 34–29 (1989). Conn. Gen. Stat. Ann. § 53a–135 (West 1972).
Delaware:	Del. Code Ann. tit. 18, § 2926 (1974).
District of Columbia:	D.C. Code Ann. § 16–2307 (1981).
Florida:	Fla. Stat. ch. 2.314 (1986). Fla. Stat. Ann. ch. 6.341 (Harrison 1985).
Georgia:	Ga. Code Ann. § 110–118 (Michie 1973). Ga. Code Ann. § 22–1414 (Harrison 1977).
Hawaii:	Haw. Rev. Stat. § 431:19–107 (1988).
Idaho:	Idaho Code § 18–3615 (1987).
Illinois:	Ill. Rev. Stat. ch. 85, para. 8–103 (1985). Ill. Ann. Stat. ch. 40, para. 501 (Smith-Hurd 1980).
Indiana:	Ind. Code § 9–8–1–13 (1976). Ind. Code Ann. § 9–8–1–13 (Burns 1983). Ind. Code Ann. § 9–8–1–13 (West 1979).
Iowa:	Iowa Code § 455.92 (1958). Iowa Code Ann. § 98.14 (West 1984).
Kansas:	Kan. Stat. Ann. § 38–1506 (1986). Kan. Corp. Code Ann. § 17–6303 (Vernon 1975).
Kentucky:	Ky. Rev. Stat. Ann. § 208.060 (Baldwin 1988). Ky. Rev. Stat. Ann. § 44.072 (Michie/Bobbs-Merrill 1986).
Louisiana:	La. Rev. Stat. Ann. § 15:452 (West 1981). La. Code Civ. Proc. Ann. art. 3132 (West 1961).
Maine:	Me. Rev. Stat. Ann. tit. 36, § 1760 (West 1964).
Maryland:	Md. Fam. Law Code Ann. § 7–106 (1984). Md. Ann. Code art. 78, § 70 (1957).
Massachusetts:	Mass. Gen. L. ch. 106, § 2–318 (1984). Mass. Gen. Laws Ann. ch. 156, § 37 (West 1970). Mass. Ann. Laws ch. 123, § 15 (Law. Co-op. 1988).
Michigan:	Mich. Comp. Laws § 550.1402 (1980). Mich. Comp. Laws Ann. § 211.27 (West 1986). Mich. Stat. Ann. § 28.1070 (Callaghan 1987).
Minnesota:	Minn. Stat. § 336.1–101 (1988). Minn. Stat. Ann. § 104.08 (West 1987).
Mississippi:	Miss. Code Ann. § 19–13–57 (1972).
Missouri:	Mo. Rev. Stat. § 545.010 (1986). Mo. Ann. Stat. § 334.540 (Vernon 1989).
Montana:	Mont. Code Ann. § 37–5–313 (1989).
Nebraska:	Neb. Rev. Stat. § 44–406 (1983).
Nevada:	Nev. Rev. Stat. § 463.150 (1987). Nev. Rev. Stat. Ann. § 679B.180 (Michie 1986).

Continued

Examples of State Statutory Code Citations—*Continued*

New Hampshire:	N.H. Rev. Stat. Ann. § 318:25 (1984).
New Jersey:	N.J. Rev. Stat. § 40:62–127 (1961).
	N.J. Stat. Ann. § 14A:5–20 (West 1969).
New Mexico:	N.M. Stat. Ann. § 31–6–2 (Michie 1978).
New York:	N.Y. Penal Law § 155.05 (McKinney 1988).
	N.Y. Town Law § 265 (Consol. 1978).
North Carolina:	N.C. Gen. Stat. § 15A–1321 (1988).
North Dakota:	N.D. Cent. Code § 23–12–11 (1989).
Ohio:	Ohio Rev. Code Ann. § 2935.03 (Anderson 1987).
	Ohio Rev. Code Ann. § 2305.131 (Baldwin 1975).
Oklahoma:	Okla. Stat. tit. 42, § 130 (1979).
	Okla Stat. Ann. tit. 21, § 491 (West 1983).
Oregon:	Or. Rev. Stat. § 450.870 (1987).
Pennsylvania:	1 Pa. Cons. Stat. § 1991 (1972).
	18 Pa. Cons. Stat. Ann. § 3301 (1983).
	Pa. Stat. Ann. tit. 24, § 7–708 (1949).
Puerto Rico:	P.R. Laws Ann. tit. 7, § 299 (1985).
Rhode Island:	R.I. Gen. Laws § 34–1–2 (1956).
South Carolina:	S.C. Code Ann. § 16–23–10 (Law. Co-op 1976).
South Dakota:	S.D. Codified Laws Ann. § 15–6–54(c) (1984).
Tennessee:	Tenn. Code Ann. § 33–1–204 (1984).
Texas:	Tex. Penal Code Ann. § 19.06 (West 1989).
	Tex. Rev. Civ. Stat. Ann. art. 5336 (West 1962).
Utah:	Utah Code Ann. § 41–3–8 (1953).
Vermont:	Vt. Stat. Ann. tit. 19, § 708 (1987).
Virginia:	Va. Code Ann. § 18.2–265.3 (Michie 1950).
Washington:	Wash. Rev. Code § 7.48A.010 (1987).
	Wash. Rev. Code Ann. § 11.17.110 (West 1967).
West Virginia:	W. Va. Code § 23–1–17 (1985).
Wisconsin:	Wis. Stat. § 52.28 (1967).
	Wis. Stat. Ann. § 341.55 (West 1971).
Wyoming:	Wyo. Stat. § 26–18–113 (1977).

VI. *Citing the Documents of Legislative History*

1. The main documents of legislative history (page 596) are: copies of the bills and amendments introduced, copies of the reports and hearings of congressional committees, the *Congressional Record* that contains transcripts of floor debates and material submitted from the floor, etc.

2. Bills and amendments are cited by referring to (a) the number assigned to the bill by the House or Senate, (b) the number and session of Congress during which the bill was introduced, and the year of the bill.

EXAMPLES

H.R. 3055, 94th Cong., 2d Sess. (1976).
S. 1422, 101st Cong., 1st Sess. (1989).

3. Reports of congressional committees are cited by reference to (a) the number of the report, (b) the number and session of the Congress during which the report was published, (c) the number of the page to which you are referring, and (d) the year in which the report was published.

EXAMPLES

H.R. Rep. No. 238, 92d Cong., 1st Sess, 4 (1979)
S. Rep. No. 415, 92d Cong., 1st Sess., 6 (1971).

4. Hearings held by congressional committees are cited by reference to (a) the title of the hearing, (b) the number and session of Congress during which the hearing was held, (c) the number of the page in the published transcript to which you are referring, and (d) the year in which the hearing was held.

EXAMPLE

Hearings on S. 631 Before the Subcomm. on Labor of the Senate Comm. on Labor and Public Welfare, 92d Cong., 1st Sess., 315 (1971).

5. The *Congressional Record* is issued on a daily basis and later collected into bound volumes. The *bound* volumes are cited by referring to (a) the number of the volume in which the item appears, (b) the abbreviation "Cong. Rec.," (c) the number of the page on which the item appears, and (d) the year. The *unbound* daily volumes are cited in the same manner except that (a) the page number should be preceded by the letter "H" or "S" in order to indicate whether the item appeared in the House pages or the Senate pages of the volume, (b) the date should include the exact day, month, and year, and (c) the phrase "daily ed." should go before the date.

EXAMPLES

Bound volumes:
103 Cong. Rec. 2,889 (1975).
Unbound volumes:
122 Cong. Rec. S2,395 (daily ed. Feb. 26, 1976)
132 Cong. Rec. H1,385 (daily ed. Mar. 13, 1990).

VII. *Citing Secondary Authority*

1. Treatises and other books are cited to (a) the number of the volume being referred to (if part of a set), (b) the full name of the author, (c) the full title of the book as it appears on the title page, (d) the number of the section and/or page to which you are referring, (e) the edition of the book, if other than the first, and (f) the date of publication. The title of the book should be italicized or underscored. The name of the publisher is almost never given.

EXAMPLES

6 Melvin Belli, *Modern Trials* § 289 (1963).
George Osborne, *Handbook on the Law of Mortgages* 370 (2d ed. 1970).

2. Law review *articles* are cited by reference to (a) the full name of the author, (b) the title of the article, (c) the number of the volume in which the article appears, (d) the abbreviated name of the law review, (e) the number of the page on which the article begins, and (f) the year of publication. The title of the article should be italicized or underscored.

EXAMPLE

Robert Catz & Susan Robinson, *Due Process and Creditor's Remedies,* 28 Rutgers L.Rev. 541 (1975).

3. Law review *notes* and *comments* written by law students are cited in the

same manner as the law review articles (see #2) except that the word "Note," "Comment," or "Special Project" is placed after the author's name just before the title.

4. Legal encyclopedias are cited by reference to (a) the number of the volume, (b) the abbreviated name of the encyclopedia, (c) the subject heading to which you are referring—in italics or underscored, (d) the number of the section to which you are referring, and (e) the date of publication of the volume you are citing.

EXAMPLES

83 C.J.S., *Subscriptions* § 3, (1953)
77 Am. Jur. 2d, *Vendor and Purchaser* § 73 (1975).

6. *Restatements of the Law* published by the American Law Institute are cited by reference to (a) the title of the Restatement, (b) the edition being referred to (if other than the first edition), (c) the number of the section being referred to, and (d) the date of publication.

EXAMPLE

Restatement (Second) of Agency § 37 (1957).

7. Annotations in A.L.R., A.L.R.2d, A.L.R.3d, A.L.R.4th, and A.L.R. Fed. are cited by (a) the full name of the author, if available, (b) the word, "Annotation," (c) the title of the annotation—in italics or underscored, (d) the volume number, (e) the abbreviation of the A.L.R. unit, (f) the page number where the annotation begins, and (g) the date of the volume.

EXAMPLE

James J. Watson, Annotation, *Attorney's Fees: Cost of Services Provided by Paralegals or the Like as Compensable Element in Award in State Court,* 73 A.L.R.4th 938 (1989).

■ ASSIGNMENT 11.2

There is one or more things wrong with each of the following citations. Describe the errors and gaps in format. For example, a parallel cite is missing or something is abbreviated incorrectly. You do not have to go to the library to check any of these cites. Simply use the guidelines presented above.

(a) Smith v. Jones, 135 Mass. 37, 67 N.E.2d 316, 320 (1954).

(b) *Paul Matthews v. Edward Foley, Inc.,* 779 F.2d 729 (W.D.N.Y., 1979).

(c) *Jackson v. Jackson,* 219 F.Supp. 1276, 37 N.E.2d 84 (1980).

(d) *Davis v. Tompson,* et al, 336 P.2d 691, 210 N.M. 432 (1976).

(e) *Washington Tire Company v. Jones,* 36 N.J.Super. 222, 351 A.2d 541 (1976).

(f) *State of New Hampshire v. Atkinson,* 117 N.H. 830, 228 A.2d 222 (N.H.Super., 1978).

(g) *Richardson v. U.S.,* 229 U.S. 220 (1975).

(h) American Law Institute, *Restatement of Torts* (2d ed 1976).

(i) U.S.Const. Art. III (1797).

(j) Smith, F., Products Liability (3rd ed. 1985).

(k) 42 USC 288 (1970).

(l) 17 U.S.C.A. 519 (1970).

(m) 40 Fed. Reg. § 277 (1976).

■ ASSIGNMENT 11.3

(a) For your state, check the state code and rules of court of the highest state court in the state to find out whether there are any special citation rules that must be followed in documents submitted to the courts.

(b) Find a court opinion written by any state court in your state. (See Figures 11.4 and 11.5.) Pick an opinion that is at least ten pages long.

    (i)   Write down every citation in this opinion (up to a maximum of twenty-five).

    (ii) State whether these citations conform to the Bluebook citation rules outlined in this section of Chapter 11. Point out any differences.

    (iii) State whether these citations conform to the special citation rules, if any, you identified in answering question (a) above. Point out any differences.

Note on the Maroon Book

For years, many have criticized *A Uniform System of Citation*—the Bluebook. People find its citation rules too arbitrary and the book itself difficult to use. In 1989, a major challenger to the Bluebook appeared: *The University of Chicago Manual of Legal Citation,* also known as the Maroon Book because of the color of its cover. Whereas the Bluebook tries to include citation rules for almost every situation, the Maroon Book adopts a substantially different point of view. Because "it is neither possible nor desirable to write a particular rule for every sort of citation problem that might arise," the citation rules in the Maroon Book "leave a fair amount of discretion to practitioners, authors, and editors." To a devotee of the Bluebook, such discretion is very distasteful. It is too early to tell what impact the Maroon Book will have on the world of citation. Because the Bluebook is so firmly entrenched, it is unlikely that a competitor will replace it any time soon.

Section J. Cite Checking

In a *cite-checking* assignment, you are given a document written by someone else and asked to check the citations provided by the author of the document. The assignment is quite common in law firms, particularly when the document to be checked is an appellate brief. Students on law review in law school also do extensive cite checking on the work of fellow students and outside authors.

While our focus in this section will be the writing of others, the guidelines discussed here are in large measure equally applicable to your own writing.

Guidelines for Cite Checking

1. The first step is to obtain clear instructions from your supervisor on the scope of the assignment. Should you do a "light check" or a comprehensive one? Should you focus solely on citation form, or should you determine the accuracy of all quotes used by the writer of the document? On citation form, what Rules should you use? The Bluebook?

. . . .

The following guidelines assume that you have been asked to undertake a comprehensive check.

2. Make sure that you have a *copy* of the document on which you can make comments. Avoid using the original.

3. If the pages of the document already have pencil or pen markings made by others (or by the author who made last-minute insertions), use a pencil or pen color that is different from any other markings on the pages. In this way it will be clear to any reader which corrections, notations, or other comments are your own. If you find that you do not have enough room to write in the margins of the pages, use separate sheets of paper. You can increase the size of the margins by photocopying the document on a machine that will reduce the size of what is copied.

4. If the document is an appellate brief, be sure that you have in front of you any citation rules that are required by the court where the brief will be submitted. If such rules exist, they must be followed. Then determine from your supervisor what citation system should be used for citations that are not governed by court rules, e.g., the Bluebook.

5. Before you begin, try to find a model. By going through the old case files of the office, you may be able to locate a prior document, such as an old appellate brief, that you can use as a general guide. Ask your supervisor to direct you to such a document. While it may not cover all the difficulties you will encounter in your own document, you will at least have a general guide approved by your supervisor.

6. Check the citation form of *every* cite in the document. This includes any cites in the body of the text, the footnotes, appendix material, and in the introductory pages of the document, such as the Table of Authorities (page 627) at the beginning of a brief.

7. For longer documents, you need to develop your own system for ensuring the completeness of your checking. For example, you might want to circle every cite that you have checked and found to be accurate, and place a small box around (or a question mark next to) every cite that is giving you difficulties. You will want to spend more time with the latter, seeking help from colleagues and your supervisor.

8. When you find errors in the form of the citation, make the corrections in the margin of the pages where they are found.

9. For some errors, you will not be able to make the corrections without obtaining additional information, such as a missing date or a missing parallel cite. If you can obtain this data by going to the relevant library books, do so. Otherwise make a notation in the margin of what is missing or what still needs correction.

10. Consistency in citation format is extremely important. On page 2 of the document, for example, the author may use one citation form, but on page 10, he or she may use a completely different format for the same kind of legal material. You need to point out this inconsistency, and make the corrections that are called for.

11. Often your document will quote from legal materials such as cases, statutes, etc. Check the accuracy of these quotations. Go to the material being quoted, find the quote, and check it against the document line by line, word by word, and punctuation mark by punctuation mark. Be scrupulous about the accuracy of quotations.

12. Shepardize anything that can be shepardized, such as cases and statutes. Examples of what you need to determine through shepardizing:

   ▪ Whether any of the cited cases have been overruled

- Whether any of the cited statutes have been repealed, amended, or changed in any way

13. Check the accuracy of all "*supra*'s" and "*infra*'s." The word *supra* means "above" or "earlier." It is a reference to something mentioned earlier in the document. For example, on page 23 of the document, there might be a footnote that says, "See *Smith v. Jones, supra* p. 9." Go to page 9 and verify that *Smith v. Jones* is discussed or mentioned there. *Infra* means "below" or "later" and refers the reader to something that will come later in the document. In the same manner as you checked the *supra*'s, determine whether the *infra* references are accurate.

Cite-Checking Software

Two kinds of cite-checking software have been produced by computer companies. First, there is *format* software that tells you whether a particular citation conforms to *A Uniform System of Citation*—the Bluebook. The developers placed the entire Bluebook into the program so that it can recognize discrepancies between the rules of the Bluebook and citations that are typed into the computer. In addition to pointing out citation errors, the program will refer you to specific rules in the Bluebook that have been violated. Two examples of such software are Cite Checker from Legal Software, Inc., and CiteRite II from Jurisoft, Inc. The second kind of cite-checking software provides *validation* data on citations. You will be told, for example, whether a particular court opinion has been overruled and whether a particular statute has been repealed. Two examples of such software are WESTcheck, used in conjunction with WESTLAW, and CheckCite, used in conjunction with LEXIS. Unlike the format cite-checking software, the validation programs are online and hence are used through a modem.

Section K. Components of a Law Book

There are similarities in the structure of many law books. To be sure, some books, such as *Shepard's Citations,* are totally unique. In the main, however, there is a pattern to the texts. The following is a list of components that are contained in many:

1. Outside Cover.   On the outside cover you will find the title of the book, the author(s) or editor(s), the name of the publisher (usually at the bottom), the edition of the book (if more than one edition has been printed), and the volume number (if the book is part of a series of books). After glancing at the outside cover, the researcher should ask the following questions:

- Is it a book *containing* law (written primarily by a court, a legislature, or an administrative agency), or is it a book *about* the law (written by a scholar who is commenting on the law)? Is the book a combination of both?

- Is this book the most current available? Look at the books on the shelf in the area where you found the book that you are examining. Is there a replacement volume for your book? Is there a later edition of the book? Check your book in the card catalog to see if other editions are mentioned.

2. Publisher's Page.   The first few pages of the book often include a page or pages about the publisher. The page may list other law books published by the same company.

3. Title Page.   The title page repeats most of the information contained on the outside cover: title, author, editor, publisher. It also contains the date of publication.

4. Copyright Page.   The copyright page (often immediately behind the title page) has a copyright mark © plus a date or series of dates. The most recent date listed indicates the timeliness of the material in the volume. Given the great flux in the law, it is very important to determine how old the text is. If the book has a pocket part (see item 14 below), it has been updated to the date on the pocket part.

COPYRIGHT © 1974, 1979, 1985, 1989 WEST PUBLISHING CO.

———

COPYRIGHT © 1992
By
WEST PUBLISHING CO.

The dates on this copyright page indicate that the material in the book is current up to 1992, the latest copyright date.

5. Foreword, Preface, or Explanation.   Under such headings, the reader may find some basic information about the book, particularly material on how the book was prepared and guidance on how to use it.

6. Summary Table of Contents.   On one or two pages, the reader may find the main topics treated in the book.

7. Detailed Table of Contents.   When provided, the detailed table can be very extensive. The major headings of the summary table of contents are repeated, and detailed subheadings and sub-subheadings are listed. This table can be used as an additional index to the book.

8. Table of Cases.   The table of cases lists, alphabetically, every case that is printed or referred to in the text, with the page(s) where the case is found or discussed. This table is sometimes printed at the end of the book.

9. Table of Statutes.   The table of statutes gives the page numbers where every statute is interpreted or referred to in the text. This table is sometimes printed at the end of the book.

10. List of Abbreviations.   The abbreviation list, if provided, is critical. A reader who is unfamiliar with law books should check the list immediately. It may be the only place in the book that spells out the abbreviations used in the body of the text. In *Shepard's Citations,* for example, abbreviations are found in the first few pages of bound volumes and in most of the pamphlets covering case citations. (See example at the top of page 543.)

11. Statutory History Table.   In statutory codes, there may be a table that lists every statute cited in the book and indicates whether it has been repealed or whether there is a new section number and title for the statute. The legislature may have changed the entire name of the statutory chapter (from Prison Law to Correction Law, for instance) and renumbered all the sections. Without this table, the researcher can become lost. In the example below, note that former Prison Law sections 10–20 are now found in Correction Law sections 600–610. You may find a citation to a Prison Law section in a book that was published

```
History of Case
  a   (affirmed)       Same case affirmed on appeal.
  cc  (connected       Different case from case cited but arising out of same
          case)          subject matter or intimately connected therewith.
  D   (dismissed)      Appeal from same case dismissed.
  m   (modified)       Same case modified on appeal.
  r   (reversed)       Same case reversed on appeal.
  s   (same case)      Same case as case cited.
  S   (superseded)     Substitution for former opinion.
  v   (vacated)        Same case vacated.
  US cert den          Certiorari denied by U. S. Supreme Court.
  US cert dis          Certiorari dismissed by U. S. Supreme Court.
  US reh den           Rehearing denied by U. S. Supreme Court.
  US reh dis           Rehearing dismissed by U. S. Supreme Court.
Treatment of Case
  c   (criticised)     Soundness of decision or reasoning in cited case criticised
                         for reasons given.
  d   (distinguished)  Case at bar different either in law or fact from case cited
                         for reasons given.
  e   (explained)      Statement of import of decisions in cited case.  Not merely
                         a restatement of the facts.
  f   (followed)       Cited as controlling.
  h   (harmonized)     Apparent inconsistency explained and shown not to exist.
  j   (dissenting      Citation in dissenting opinion.
          opinion)
  L   (limited)        Refusal to extend decision of cited case beyond precise
                         issues involved.
  o   (overruled)      Ruling in cited case expressly overruled.
  p   (parallel)       Citing case substantially alike or on all fours with cited
                         case in its law or facts.
  q   (questioned)     Soundness of decision or reasoning in cited case ques-
                         tioned.
```

Example of abbreviations used by Shepard's

TABLE OF PRISON LAW SECTIONS

Showing the distribution of those sections of the former Prison Law in effect prior to the general amendment by L.1929, c. 243, which are contained wholly or in part in the Correction Law, or which have been omitted or repealed.

Prison Law Section	Correction Law Section
1	1
10–20	600–610
21	Repealed
22 L.1919, c. 12	611
22 L.1920, c. 933	612
23–32	613–622
40–50	40–50

Example of a statutory history table

before the state changed to Correction Law sections. When you go to look up the Prison Law section, you will find nothing unless you have a way to translate the section into a Correction Law section. The statutory history table may be one way to do it.

12. Body of the Text. The fundamental characteristic of the body of many legal texts is that it is arranged according to units such as parts, subparts, divisions, subdivisions, chapters, subchapters, sections, subsections, etc. Often each unit covers a similar subject matter, and is numbered or lettered in sequence. You should thumb through the entire book to obtain a feel for the numbering and classification system used by the author or editor.

13. Footnotes. Footnotes are very important in law books; researchers place great emphasis on them. They often give extensive citations to cases and other cross-references, and hence can be an excellent lead to additional law.

14. Pocket Parts. A unique and indispensable feature of many law books is the pocket part. It is a small-booklet addition to the text, placed at the very end of the text in a specially devised "pocket" built into the inside of the rear cover. (See page 508.) The pocket part is published after the book is printed and is designed to bring the book up-to-date with the latest developments in the field covered by the book. Of course, a pocket part can also grow out of date. Normally it is replaced once a year. On the front cover of the pocket-part booklet, there is a date telling you what period is covered. The title page (see above) may say that the last edition of the book was published in 1990, but the front page of the pocket part may say "for use during 1992–1993."

Normally the organization of the pocket part exactly parallels the organization of the main text. To find out, for example, if there has been anything new in the area covered by chapter 7, part 2, section 714 of the main text, you go to chapter 7, part 2, section 714 of the pocket part. If nothing is found there, then nothing new has happened. If changes or additions have occurred, they will be found there.

Pocket parts are cumulative in that, whenever a pocket part is replaced by another pocket part, everything in the early pocket part is consolidated into the most recent one. The earlier pocket part is thrown away.

15. Appendix.   The text may include one or more appendixes. Normally, they include tables, charts, or the entire text of statutes or regulations, portions of which are discussed in the body of the book.

16. Glossary.   The book may include a glossary, which is a dictionary that defines a selected number of words used in the body of the book.

17. Bibliography.   A brief or extended bibliography of the field covered by the book may be included at the end of each chapter or at the end of the book.

18. Index.   The index is a critical part of the book. Unfortunately, some books either have no index or do a sloppy job of indexing. (Some sets of administrative regulations and loose-leaf services fall into this category.) The index is arranged alphabetically and should refer the reader to the page number(s) or to the section number(s) where the item is treated in the body of the text. The index is found at the end of the book. If there are many volumes in the set, you may find more than one index. For example, there may be a general index for the entire set and a series of smaller indexes covering individual volumes.

■ Section L. The CARTWHEEL: A Technique of Using Indexes and Tables of Contents

We now come to one of the most important skills in legal research: the creative use of indexes and tables of contents in law books. If you have mastered this skill, 70 percent of the research battle is won. The CARTWHEEL is a technique designed to assist you in acquiring the skill. (See Figure 11.8.)

The objective of the CARTWHEEL can be simply stated: to develop the habit of phrasing every word involved in the client's problem *fifteen to twenty different ways!* When you go to the index or table of contents of a law book, you naturally begin looking up the words and phrases that you think should lead you to the relevant material in the book. If you do not find anything relevant to your problem, two conclusions are possible:

■ There is nothing relevant in the law book.

■ You looked up the wrong words in the index and table of contents.

While the first conclusion is sometimes accurate, nine times out of ten, the second conclusion is the reason you fail to find material in a law book that is relevant to the client's problem. The solution is to be able to phrase a word in

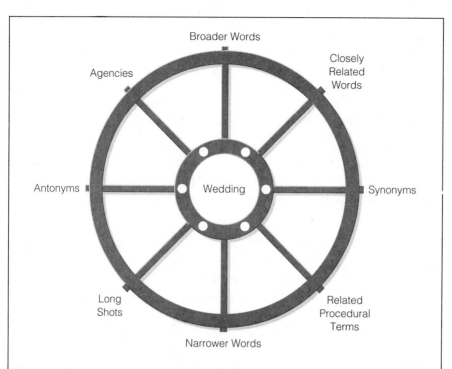

FIGURE 11.8

The CARTWHEEL:
Using the Index
and Table of
Contents of
Law Books

1. Identify all the *major words* (such as *wedding*) from the facts of the client's problem. (Most of these facts can be obtained from the intake memorandum (see page 366) written following the initial interview with the client.) Place each word or small set of words in the center of the CARTWHEEL.

2. In the index and table of contents, look up all of these major words.

3. Identify the *broader* categories of the major words.

4. In the index and table of contents, look up all of these broader categories.

5. Identify the *narrower* categories of the major words.

6. In the index and table of contents, look up all of these narrower categories.

7. Identify all *synonyms* of the major words.

8. In the index and table of contents, look up all of these synonyms.

9. Identify all of the *antonyms* of the major words.

10. In the index and table of contents, look up all of these antonyms.

11. Identify all words that are *closely related* to the major words.

12. In the index and table of contents, look up all of these closely related words.

13. Identify all *procedural* terms related to the major words.

14. In the index and table of contents, look up all of these procedural terms.

15. Identify all *agencies,* if any, with some connection to the major words.

16. In the index and table of contents, look up all of these agencies.

17. Identify all *long shots.*

18. In the index and table of contents, look up all of these long shots.

Note: The above categories are not mutually exclusive.

as many different ways and in as many different contexts as possible. Hence, the CARTWHEEL.

Suppose that the problem of the client involved, among other things, a wedding. The first step would be to look up the word *wedding* in the index and table of contents of any law book. Assuming that you are not successful with this word (either because the word is not in the index and table or because the page or section references do not lead you to relevant material in the body of the book), the next step is to think of as many different phrasings and contexts of the word *wedding* as possible. This is where the eighteen steps of CARTWHEEL can be useful.

If you applied the steps of the CARTWHEEL to the word *wedding*, here are some of the words and phrases that you would check:

- *Broader words:* celebration, ceremony, rite, ritual, formality, festivity, etc.
- *Narrower words:* civil wedding, church wedding, golden wedding, proxy wedding, sham wedding, shotgun wedding, etc.
- *Synonyms:* marriage ceremony, nuptial, etc.
- *Antonyms:* alienation, annulment, divorce, separation, legal separation, judicial separation, etc.
- *Closely related words:* remarriage, antenuptial, prenuptial, matrimony, marital, conjugal, domestic, husband, wife, bride, license, anniversary, custom, children, blood test, premarital, spouse, relationship, family, home, consummation, cohabitation, sexual relations, betrothal, minister, wedlock, consent, oath, contract, religion, community property, name change, domicile, residence, etc.
- *Procedural terms:* action, suit, statute of limitations, complaint, discovery, defense, petition, jurisdiction, court, superior court, county court, etc.
- *Agencies:* Bureau of Vital Statistics, County Clerk, Department of Social Services, License Bureau, Secretary of State, Justice of the Peace, etc.
- *Long shots:* dowry, common law, single, blood relationship, fraud, illegitimate, alimony, bigamy, pregnancy, gifts, chastity, impotence, incest, virginity, support, custody, paternity, etc.

As indicated in Figure 11.8, there may be some overlapping of categories; they are not mutually exclusive. Also, it is not significant whether you place a word in one category or another so long as the word comes to your mind as you comb through the index and table of contents. The CARTWHEEL is, in effect, a *word association game* that should become second nature to you with practice. Perhaps some of the word selections seem a bit far-fetched. You will not

---

■ ASSIGNMENT 11.4

CARTWHEEL the following words or phrases:

1. Paralegal
2. Woman
3. Rat bite
4. Rear-end collision
5. Monopoly

---

know for sure, however, whether a word is fruitful until you try it. Be imaginative, and take some risks.

Indexes and tables of contents are often organized into headings, subheadings, sub-subheadings and perhaps even sub-sub-subheadings. In the following excerpt from an index, "Burden of proof" is a sub-subheading of "Accidents" and a subheading of "Unavoidable accident or casualty." The latter is a subheading of "Accidents," which is the main heading of the index entry. If you were looking for law on burden of proof, you might be out of luck unless you *first* thought of looking up "accidents" and "unavoidable accident."

```
Accidents
    Opportunity to avoid accident, application of last
        clear chance doctrine, § 137(5), pp. 154–160
    Parents' responsibility, attractive nuisance doc-
        trine, § 63(76)
    Pleading unavoidable accident as defense, § 197
    Precautions against injury from dangerous place,
        agency, etc., §§ 84–89, pp. 1016–1034
    Presumption of negligence from happening, § 220.1,
        pp. 506–512
    Proximate cause of injury, § 115, pp. 1231–1234
    Res ipsa loquitur, accident and defendant's rela-
        tion thereto, §§ 220.10–220.15, pp. 551–578
    Restaurant patron's injuries, liability, § 63(131)
    Storekeeper's liability, § 63(121), p. 892
    Unavoidable accident or casualty, § 21, pp. 647,
        649
        Burden of proof, § 204, p. 450, n. 86; § 209,
            p. 482
        Consistency between general verdict and find-
            ings, § 304, p. 1072, n. 5
```

Suppose that you identify the following words to check in an index:

minor	sale
explosion	warranty
car	damage

The index may have no separate heading for "minor," but "minor" may be a subheading under "sale." If so, you would not find "minor" unless you first thought of checking "sale." Under each of the above six words, you should be alert to the possibility that the other five words may be subheadings for that word. Hence the process of pursuing these six words in an index (or table of contents) would be as follows: (The word in bold letters is checked first and then the five words *under it* are checked to see if any of them are subheadings.)

Car	**Damage**
damage	car
explosion	explosion
minor	minor
sale	sale
warranty	warranty

Explosion	**Minor**
car	car
damage	damage
minor	explosion
sale	sale
warranty	warranty

Sale	**Warranty**
car	car
damage	damage
explosion	explosion
minor	minor
warranty	sale

■ ASSIGNMENT 11.5

One way to gain an appreciation for the use of indexes is to write one of your own. Be sure to use headings, subheadings, sub-subheadings, etc. in each index you write.

(a) Write a comprehensive index of your present job or the last job that you had.

(b) Pick one area of the law that you have covered in class or read about. Write your own comprehensive index on what you have learned.

(c) Write a comprehensive index of the following statute:

§ **132. Amount of force.** The use of force against another for the purpose of effecting the arrest or recapture of the other, or of maintaining custody of him, is not privileged if the means employed are in excess of those which are reasonably believed to be necessary.

FIGURE 11.9

Excerpt from Index

EVIDENCE

Dealers,
  Securities, judicial notice, § 29, p. 890
  Value,
    Household goods, opinion evidence, § 546(121), p. 479, n. 95
    Property, § 546(115), p. 430
      Opinion evidence, § 546(122), p. 483
Death,
  Autopsy, generally, ante
  Best evidence rule, § 803, p. 136
  Book entries,
    Entrant, proof of handwriting, § 693, p. 942
    Supplemental testimony respecting entries by clerks and third persons, § 693, p. 939
    Supporting entries by deceased persons by oath of personal representative, § 684, p. 910
  Clerk or employee making book entries, § 692
  Copy of record, certification by state registrar, § 664, p. 865, n. 69
  Declaration against interest, death of declarant, § 218, p. 604
  Declarations, § 227, p. 624
    Death of declarant as essential to admission, § 230
  Dying declarations, generally, post
  Experiments, object or purpose, § 588(1)
  Former evidence, death of witness, § 392
  General reputation, § 1048
  Hearsay, § 227, p. 624
    Death certificates, § 194, pp. 561, 562; § 766, p. 66
    Death of declarant, § 205
    Impossibility of obtaining other evidence, § 204
  Letters, § 703, p. 976
  Maps and diagrams of scenes of occurrence, § 730(1), p. 1045
  Memorandum, § 696, p. 955
  Mortality tables, generally, post
  Newspaper announcement, § 227, p. 625
  Opinion evidence,
    Animals, § 546(68)
    Cause and effect, § 546(11), p. 129
    Effect on human body, § 546(97), p. 374
    Fixing time, § 546(91), n. 16
  Owners, admissions, § 327
    Personal property, § 334
  Parol or extrinsic evidence, rule excluding, action to recover for, § 861, p. 230
  Photographs, personal appearance or identity, § 710
  Presumptions, ancient original public records, official making, § 746, p. 37
  Prima facie evidence, record of, § 644
  Private documents, recitals, § 677
  Public records and documents, registers of, § 623
  Reputation, § 227, p. 626
  Res gestae, statements, § 410, p. 991
  Rumor, § 227, p. 625
  Self-serving declarations, effect of death of declarant, § 216, p. 591
  Services, value, opinion evidence in death action, · § 546(124), p. 489, n. 96
  Statements, weight of evidence, § 266
  Value of service rendered by claimant, opinion evidence, § 546(125), p. 493, n. 41

Death—Continued
  Witness, unsworn statements, circumstances tending to disparage testimony, § 268
  Wrongful death,
    Admissions, husband and wife, § 363
    Admissions of decedent, privity, § 322, n. 96.5
    Declarations against interest, § 218, p. 607
    Loss of life, value, opinion evidence, § 546(121), p. 473, n. 54
    Municipal claim, evidence of registry, § 680, n. 21
    Value of decedent's services, opinion evidence, § 546(124), p. 489, n. 96
Death certificates,
  Certified copies, § 651, p. 851
    Officer as making, § 664, p. 865, n. 69
    Prima facie evidence, § 773
  Church register, competency, § 727
  Conclusiveness, § 766, p. 64
  Expert testimony, supporting opinion, § 570
  Foreign countries, authenticated copies, § 675, p. 885
  Hearsay, § 194, pp. 561, 562; § 766, p. 66
  Kinship, § 696, p. 949, n. 2
  Official document, § 638, pp. 823, 824
  Prima facie case or evidence, post
Debate, judicial notice, United States congress, § 43, p. 995
Debs, judicial notice, § 67, p. 56, n. 17
Debtor and creditor, admissions, § 336
Debts. Indebtedness, generally, post
Decay,
  Judicial notice, vegetable matter, § 88
  Opinion evidence, buildings, § 546(73), p. 290
Decedents' estates,
  Judicial admissions, claim statements, § 310
  Judicial records, inferences from, § 765
  Official documents, reports and inventories of representatives, § 638, p. 818
  Value, opinion evidence, § 546(121), p. 478
Deceit. Fraud, generally, post
Decisions, judicial notice, sister states, § 18, p. 861
Declaration against interest, §§ 217–224, pp. 600–615
  Absence of declared from jurisdiction, § 218, p. 604
  Account, § 224
  Admissions, distinguished, § 217, p. 603
  Adverse character, § 222
  Affirmative proof as being best evidence obtainable, § 218, p. 604
  Apparent interest, § 219, p. 608
  Assured, § 219, p. 611
  Best evidence obtainable, necessity of, § 218, p. 604
  Boundaries, § 219, p. 611
  Coexisting, self-serving interest, § 221
  Contract, § 224
  Criminal prosecution, statement subjecting declarant to, § 219, p. 608
  Death action, § 218, p. 607
  Death of declarant, § 218, p. 605
  Dedication to public use, § 219, p. 611
  Deeds, § 224
  Disparagement of title, § 219, p. 611
  Distinctions, § 217, p. 603
  Enrollment of vessel, § 224

■ ASSIGNMENT 11.6

Examine the index in Figure 11.9 from a legal encyclopedia. It is an excerpt from the heading of "Evidence." "Death" is the subheading of "Evidence." What sub-subheadings or sub-sub-headings of "Evidence" would you check to try to find material on the following?

(a) Introducing a death certificate into evidence.

(b) The weight that a court will give to the personal conclusions of a witness.

(c) Introducing the last words of a decedent into evidence.

(d) A statement by the person who died disclaiming ownership of land around which he or she had placed a fence.

■ Section M. The First Level of Legal Research: Background

There are three interrelated levels of researching a problem:

Background Research provides you with a general understanding of the area of law involved in your research problem.

Specific Fact Research provides you with primary and secondary authority that covers the specific facts of your research problem.

Validation Research provides you with the most up-to-date information on the current validity of all the primary authority you intend to use in your research memorandum on the problem.

. . . .

At times all three levels of research go on simultaneously. If you are new to legal research, however, it is recommended that you approach your research problem in the three stages just listed. Our concern in this section is the first level: background research. See Figure 11.10. The other two levels are covered throughout the remainder of the chapter.

Our assumption here is that you are researching a topic that is totally new to you. Spend an hour or two (depending on the complexity of the area) doing some reading in law books that will provide you with an overview—a general understanding of the area. This will help you identify the major terminology, the major agencies involved, if any, and some of the major issues. Of course, while doing this background research, you will probably also come up with leads that will be helpful in the second and third levels of research.

All this background research will be in the secondary sources—legal encyclopedias, treatises, legal periodical literature, legal dictionaries, etc. Caution must be exercised in studying these materials. As we have seen, they must never be used as a substitute for mandatory primary authority, which is the objective of your research. In your research memorandum, try to avoid quoting from a legal dictionary or a legal encyclopedia. Many courts do not consider them very persuasive. Treatises and periodical literature are considered somewhat more persuasive (depending on the author), but again, even these secondary sources should be quoted infrequently once you have laid the proper foundation for their use. (See Figure 11.7 on when you can use secondary authority.) As we noted, judges want to know what the primary authority is—opinions, statutes, constitutional provisions, regulations, etc. Use the secondary material for the

FIGURE 11.10

Techniques for
Doing Background
Research on
a Topic

---

1. LEGAL DICTIONARY

Have access to a legal dictionary throughout your research. For example:

> *Black's Law Dictionary*
> *Ballentine's Law Dictionary*
> *Oran's Law Dictionary*
> Statsky's *Legal Thesaurus/Dictionary*

Look up the meaning of all important terms that you come across in your research. These dictionaries are starting points only. Eventually you want to find primary authority that defines these terms.

---

2. LEGAL ENCYCLOPEDIAS

Find discussions of your topic in the major national legal encyclopedias:

> *American Jurisprudence 2d*
> *Corpus Juris Secundum*

Also check encyclopedias, if any, that cover only your state. Use the CARTWHEEL to help you use their indexes and tables of contents.

---

3. TREATISES

Find discussions of your topic in legal treatises. Go to your card catalog. Use the CARTWHEEL to help you locate cards on treatises such as hornbooks, handbooks, formbooks practice manuals, scholarly studies, etc. Many of these books will have KF call numbers. Use the CARTWHEEL to help you use the indexes and tables of contents of these books.

---

4. ANNOTATIONS

Find discussions of your topic in the annotations of A.L.R., A.L.R.2d, A.L.R.3d, A.L.R.4th, and A.L.R. Fed. Use the Quick Index and the Index to Annotations. The CARTWHEEL will help you use these indexes.

---

5. LEGAL PERIODICAL LITERATURE

Find discussions of your topic in legal periodical literature. The three main indexes to such literature are:

> *Index to Legal Periodicals*
> *Current Law Index*
> *Legal Resource Index*

Use the CARTWHEEL to help you use these indexes to locate legal periodical literature on your topic. (Later we will cover computer index systems.)

---

6. AGENCY REPORTS/BROCHURES

If your research involves an administrative agency, call or write the agency. Find out what brochures, reports, or newsletters the agency has available to the public. Such literature often provides useful background information.

---

7. COMMITTEE REPORTS

Before statutes are passed, committees of the legislature often write reports that comment on and summarize the legislation. In addition to being good sources of legislative history on the statute, the reports are excellent background reading. If practical, contact both houses of the legislature to find out which committees acted on the statute. If the statute is fairly recent, they may be able to send you copies of the committee reports or tell you where to obtain them. If you live near the library of the legislature, you may be able to find committee reports there. The committee reports of many federal statutes are printed in *U.S. Code Congressional and Administrative News.*

Continued

---

8. REPORTS/STUDIES OF SPECIAL INTEREST GROUPS

There are special interest groups for almost every area of the law, e.g., unions, bar associations, environmental associations, tax associations, insurance and other business associations. They often have position papers and studies that they could send you. Although one-sided, such literature should not be ignored.

9. MARTINDALE-HUBBELL LAW DIRECTORY

The Digest volume of Martindale-Hubbell provides concise summaries of the law of the fifty states and many foreign countries. (See page 506.)

FIGURE 11.10

Techniques for Doing Background Research on a Topic
—*Continued*

limited purposes of (1) background reading and (2) providing leads to primary authority—particularly through the footnotes in the secondary sources. Of course, you will not have time to use all of the nine techniques on background research presented in Figure 11.10. Usually one or two of the techniques is sufficient for the limited purpose of providing an overview and getting you started.

◼ Section N. Checklists for Using the Ten Major Search Resources

We have said that the main objective of legal research is to locate mandatory primary authority. There are three levels of government—federal, state, and local. An overview of their primary authority is as follows:

KINDS OF PRIMARY AUTHORITY		
FEDERAL LEVEL OF GOVERNMENT	**STATE LEVEL OF GOVERNMENT**	**LOCAL LEVEL OF GOVERNMENT (CITY, COUNTY, ETC.)**
U.S. Constitution	State constitution	Charter
Statutes of Congress	State statutes	Local ordinances
Federal court opinions	State court opinions	Local court opinions
Federal agency regulations	State agency regulations	Local agency regulations
Federal administrative decisions	State administrative decisions	Local administrative decisions
Federal rules of court	State rules of court	Local rules of court
Executive orders of the president	Executive orders of the governor	Executive orders of the mayor
Opinions of the U.S. attorney general	Opinions of the state attorney general	Opinions of the corporation counsel
Treaties		

Later in this chapter, we examine methods of finding most of these kinds of primary authority. Throughout our examination, you will be referred back to the ten checklists for the major finding tools presented in this section. These ten findings tools (or search resources) are often useful for locating more than one kind of primary authority. Hence they are presented together here.

Many of the ten search resources are also helpful in doing background research in the secondary sources. Indeed, some of the search resources *are* secondary sources themselves. Finally, some of the search resources are helpful in doing the third level of research—validation research, particularly Shepard's.

In short, the following ten search resources, or finding tools, are the foundation of legal research itself:

1. Card catalog
2. Digests
3. Annotations
4. Shepard's
5. Loose-leaf services
6. Indexes to legal periodical literature
7. Legal encyclopedias
8. Treatises
9. Phone and mail
10. Computers

The tenth resource—computers—will be introduced here, but covered in greater depth in Chapter 13.

1. Card Catalog

A well-organized card catalog is one of the researcher's best friends. If the law library has not switched over to a completely computerized catalog, you need to learn some of the basics of the manual card catalog. Most law libraries use the Library of Congress (LC) classification system. Under this system, many law books have KF call numbers. The following is an example of a card from a card catalog:

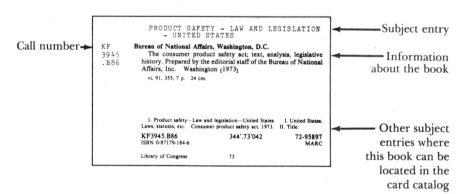

Checklist #1

Checklist for Using the Card Catalog
1. Find out if your law library has more than one card catalog. Is there a catalog with entries by subject matter and another with entries by author? Are there different catalogs for different topics or areas of the law?
2. Find out if the library has any descriptive literature on how to use the catalog.
3. Pull out a tray from the catalog at random. Thumb through the KF cards in this tray. Put a paper clip on an example of each kind of card that appears to be organized differently or that contains different kinds of information. Pick any two of these cards. Try to figure out why the cards are different. If you can't, ask a staff member of the library to briefly explain the differences.

Continued

Checklist #1—*Continued*

Checklist for Using the Card Catalog—*Continued*
4. Be sure you understand all the information on the cards that tells you where the books are located in the library. Some books may be on reserve, in special rooms, or in other buildings.
5. Select several KF cards at random, particularly of books housed in different locations. Try to find these books. Ask for help if you cannot locate them.
6. Now try the reverse process. Select at random three different kinds of books from the library shelves (not the same books you looked at in #5 above). Take these books to the card catalog and try to find their card. Your goal is to become as proficient in the structure and use of the card catalog as possible. Steps #3–6 are designed to help you achieve this goal before you experience the pressure of actual research.
7. Ask a staff member what kinds of research material, if any, are *not* cataloged, such as microfilm, ultrafiche, appellate briefs, or old exams.
8. Ask a staff member what special lists of law books, if any, are in the library (lists of legal periodicals, lists of reserve books, etc.).
9. Ask a staff member to explain the difference between the library's card catalog and Kardex. (The latter is the place where many libraries keep records of current serial publications that come into the library every day.) If the library does not use Kardex, ask what it uses instead.
10. When using any card catalog, the CARTWHEEL will help you think of words and phrases to check.
11. Never antagonize the employees of a law library! You are going to need all the help you can get! But do not abuse their availability. For example do not ask any questions until you first try to find the answer on your own.

■ **ASSIGNMENT 11.7**

Assignment 11.1 asked you to organize a system of three-by-five-inch index cards for each of the legal research words and phrases listed there. For each card that contains the name of a law book on it, find out where the book or set of books is located in a law library near you. Obtain this information from the card catalog or other library list, and enter it on the index cards.

2. Digests

We have already examined the major digests and the names of reporters whose opinions are summarized (in small paragraphs) in the digests. You should review this material now. See Figure 11.5.

Our focus here is on the digests of West, which are organized by the key topic and number system. Lawyers Co-operative Publishing Company also has digests for Supreme Court opinions and for its annotations in A.L.R., A.L.R.2d, etc., which are organized differently.

The beauty of the West digests is that once you know how to use one of the digests, you know how to use them all. A good way to begin this understanding is to follow the journey of a court opinion from the time it arrives at West. (See Figure 11.11.)

Keep the following points in mind about Figure 11.11:

■ Most state court opinions printed in the reporters of West go through the same process or journey as outlined in the *first* column of Figure 11.11. Of

FIGURE 11.11

Journey of a
Court Opinion

JOURNEY OF A STATE COURT OPINION, e.g., CALIFORNIA	JOURNEY OF A FEDERAL COURT OPINION, e.g., A U.S. COURT OF APPEALS
1. The California Supreme Court sends a copy of its opinion to West Publishing Company in Minnesota.	1. The U.S. Court of Appeals sends a copy of its opinion to West Publishing Company in Minnesota.
2. West editors write brief paragraph headnotes for the opinion. Each headnote summarizes a portion of the opinion.	2. West editors write brief paragraph headnotes for the opinion. Each headnote summarizes a portion of the opinion.
3. The headnotes go at the beginning of the full text of the opinion in the reporter—here, the Pacific Reporter 2d (P.2d). The editors assign each of these headnotes a key topic and number, e.g., Criminal Law ☞ 1064(5).	3. The headnotes go at the beginning of the full text of the opinion in the reporter—here, the Federal Reporter 2d (F.2d). The editors assign each of these headnotes a key topic and number, e.g., Appeal and Error ☞1216.
4. In addition to being printed at the beginning of the opinion in P.2d, the headnotes will *also* be printed at the beginning of the advance sheet for P.2d that contains the opinion, and in the back of the P.2d volume that contains the opinion.	4. In addition to being printed at the beginning of the opinion in F.2d, the headnotes will *also* be printed at the beginning of the advance sheet for F.2d that contains the opinion, and in the back of the F.2d volume that contains the opinion.
5. This headnote is *also* printed in the appropriate digests of West. The above example will go in the "C" volume of these digests where "Criminal Law" is covered. The headnote will be placed under key number 1064(5) of Criminal Law along with summaries of other opinions on the same or similar point of law. In what digests will such headnotes from a recent California opinion be printed? The list follows: ■ All headnotes of P.2d cases go into the *American Digest System*. First, the headnote goes into a General Digest volume. After a ten-year period (in two five-year intervals), all the General Digests are thrown away, with the material in them printed in the next Decennial Digest. ■ All headnotes of P.2d cases are *also* printed in its regional digest—the Pacific Digest. ■ All headnotes of California cases in P.2d are *also* printed in the individual state digest—the California Digest.	5. This headnote is *also* printed in the appropriate digests of West. The above example will go in the "A" volume of these digests where "Appeal and Error" is covered. The headnote will be placed under key number 1216 of Appeal and Error along with summaries of other opinions on the same or similar point of law. In what digests will such headnotes from a recent F.2d opinion be printed? The list follows: ■ All headnotes of F.2d cases go into the *American Digest System*. First, the headnote goes into a General Digest volume. After a ten-year period (in two five-year intervals), all the General Digests are thrown away, with the material in them printed in the next Decennial Digest. ■ All headnotes of F.2d cases are *also* printed in the most current federal digest—the Federal Practice Digest 4th. ■ If our F.2d case dealt with a particular state, the headnotes of the F.2d case will *also* be printed in the individual state digest of that state.
6. Hence, the headnote from the California opinion will be printed: ■ at the beginning of the opinion in P.2d.	6. Hence, the headnote from the opinion of the U.S. Court of Appeals will be printed:

Continued

FIGURE 11.11

Journey of a
Court Opinion
—*Continued*

- at the beginning of the P.2d advance sheet containing the opinion.
- at the end of the bound P.2d volume containing the opinion.
- in the *American Digest System* (first the General Digest and then the Decennial Digest).
- in the regional digest—*Pacific Digest*.
- in the individual state digest—*California Digest*.

In all the above digests, the headnote will be printed in the "C" volume for Criminal Law under number 1064(5) along with headnotes from other opinions on the same or similar area of the law.

- at the beginning of the opinion in F.2d.
- at the beginning of the F.2d advance sheet containing the opinion.
- at the end of the bound F.2d volume containing the opinion.
- in the *American Digest System* (first in the General Digest and then in the Decennial Digest).
- in the *Federal Practice Digest* 4th.
- in a state digest if the F.2d case dealt with a particular state.

In all the above digests, the headnote will be printed in the "A" volume for Appeal and Error under number 1216 along with headnotes from other opinions on the same or similar area of the law.

course, different states have their own reporters and digests (see Figure 11.5), but the process is the same.

- All U.S. District Court opinions printed in *Federal Supplement* (F. Supp.) go through the same process or journey as outlined in the *second* column of Figure 11.11.
- All U.S. Supreme Court opinions printed in *Supreme Court Reporter* (S. Ct.) go through the same process or journey as outlined in the *second* column of Figure 11.11. (For additional digests that summarize all U.S. Supreme Court opinions, see Figure 11.5.)

Assume that you are doing research on the right of a citizen to speak in a public park. You find that the digests of West cover this subject under the following key topic and number:

Constitutional Law ☞ 211

West publishes about sixty digests—state, federal, and national. You can go to the "C" volume of *any* of these sixty digests, turn to "Constitutional Law" and find number "211" under it. Do you want only Idaho case law? If so, go to Constitutional Law ☞ 211 in the *Idaho Digest*. Do you want only case law from the states in the western United States? If so, go to Constitutional Law ☞ 211 in the *Pacific Digest*. Do you want only current federal case law? If so, go to Constitutional Law ☞ 211 in the *Federal Practice Digest 4th*. Do you want only U.S. Supreme Court cases? If so, go to Constitutional Law ☞ 211 in the *U.S. Supreme Court Digest* (West).

Do you want the case law of *every* court in the country? If so, trace Constitutional Law ☞ 211 through the three units of the *American Digest System*:

- Go to Constitutional Law ☞211 in every General Digest volume.
- Go to Constitutional Law ☞211 in every Decennial Digest.
- Go to the equivalent number for Constitutional Law ☞211 in the Century Digest.

To *trace a key topic and number* through the *American Digest System* means to find out what case law, if any, is summarized under that key topic and number in every unit of the American Digest System. (For the Century Digest, you will need an equivalent number, since there are no key topics and numbers in the Century Digest. See step 8 in the following checklist.)

Checklist #2

Checklist for Using the Digests of West

1. Locate the right digests for your research problem. This is determined by identifying the kind of case law you want to find. State? Federal? Both? Review pages 498 ff. on the American Digest System, the four regional digests, the five major federal digests, the two digests for U.S. Supreme Court cases (only one of which is a West digest), the individual state digests, etc. You must know what kind of case law is contained in each of these digests. See the chart in Figure 11.5.

2. Find a key topic and number to cover your research problem. There are thousands of topics and subtopics in the digests. How do you find the ones relevant to your research problem? There are four techniques:

- Descriptive Word Index (DWI). Every digest has a DWI. Use the CARTWHEEL to help you locate key topics and numbers in the DWI.
- Table of Contents. There are approximately 400 main topics (e.g., Constitutional Law, Criminal Law), which are scattered throughout the volumes of the digest you are using. At the beginning of each main topic you will find a table of contents. If you can find one of these main topics in the general area of your research, you then use its table of contents to locate specific key numbers. These tables of contents have different names: "Scope Note," "Analysis," or "Subjects Included." Use the CART-WHEEL to help you locate key topics and numbers in them.
- Headnote in West Reporter. Suppose that you already have an opinion on point. You are reading its full text in a West reporter. Go to the headnotes at the beginning of this opinion. Each headnote has a key topic and number. Use this key topic and number to go to any of the digests to try to find *more* case law on that topic and number.
- Table of Cases in the Digests. Suppose again that you already have an opinion on point. You are reading its full text in a reporter. Go to the table of cases in the *American Digest System* or in any other digest that covers the reporter. Look up the name of the case in this table of cases. There you will find out what key topics and numbers that case is digested under in the digest. Go to those topics and numbers in the body of the digest to find that case summarized along with *other* cases under the same topics and numbers. (Note: the Table of Cases in some West digests is called Plaintiff-Defendant Table *or* Defendant-Plaintiff Table, depending on which party's name comes first. The Defendant-Plaintiff Table is useful if you happen to know only the name of the defendant or if you want many cases where the same party was sued, e.g., General Motors. Defendant-Plaintiff Tables usually refer you back to the Plaintiff-Defendant Table, where the key topics and numbers are listed.)

3. Assume that while using the Descriptive Word Index (DWI) in any of the digests, you come across a key topic and number that appears to be relevant to your research problem. But when you go to check that topic and number in the body of the digest, you find no case law, and the phrase "See Scope Note for Analysis." The DWI has, in effect, led you to nonexistent case law! The editors are telling you that there are no cases digested under this topic and number *at this time*. Go to the table of contents for the main topic you are in (see step #2 above). Check the Scope Note there to see if you can find a more productive key topic and number. Or, go to a different digest to see if you can be more lucky with your original key topic and number.

4. The West editors occasionally add new key topics and numbers to its system. Hence, you may find topics and numbers in the later digests that are not in the earlier digests.

Continued

Checklist #2—*Continued*

Checklist for Using the Digests of West—*Continued*

5. The first key number under most topics and subtopics is often labeled "In General." This is obviously a broad category. Many researchers make the mistake of overlooking it in their quest for more specific topic headings. Go after more specific key numbers, but do not neglect this general one.

6. The West digests obviously duplicate each other in some respects. The *American Digest System,* for example, contains everything that is in all the other digests. A regional digest will duplicate everything found in the individual state digests covered in that region. (See the chart in Figure 11.5.) It is wise, nevertheless, to check more than one digest. Some digests may be more up-to-date than others in your library. You may miss something in one digest that you will catch in another.

7. Be sure you know all the units of the most comprehensive digest—the *American digest System:* Century Digest, Decennial Digests, General Digests. These units are distinguished solely by the period of time covered by each unit. Know what these periods of time are: Century Digest (1658–1896), Decennial Digests (ten-year periods), General Digests (the period since the last Decennial Digest was printed).

8. At the time the Century Digest was printed, West had not invented the key number system. Hence, topics are listed in the Century Digest by *section* numbers rather than by key numbers. Assume that you started your research in the Century Digest. You located a relevant section number and you now want to trace this number through the Decennial Digests and General Digests. To do this you need a corresponding *key* number. There is a parallel table in volume 21 of the First Decennial that will tell you the corresponding *key* topic number for any section number in the Century Digest. Suppose, however, that you started your research in the Decennial Digests or the General Digests. You have a key topic and now want to find its corresponding section number in the Century Digest. In the First and Second Decennial, there is a "see" reference under the key topic number that will tell you the corresponding section number in the Century Digest.

9. Tricks of the trade are also needed in using the General Digests, which cover the most recent period since the last Decennial Digest was printed. When the current ten-year period is over, all the General Digests will be thrown away. The material in them will be consolidated or cumulated into the next Decennial Digests (which is issued in two parts beginning with the Ninth Decennial). When you go to use the General Digests, there may be twenty to thirty bound volumes on the shelf. To be thorough in tracing a key topic and number in the General Digests, you must check *all* these bound volumes. There is, however, one shortcut. Look for the "Table of Key Numbers" within the General Digests. This table tells you which General Digests contain anything under the key topic and number you are searching. You do not have to check the other General Digests.

3. Annotations

An annotation is a collection of notes or commentary on something. It is, in effect, a research paper. The most extensive annotations are those of the Lawyer's Co-operative Publishing Company in the following sets of books:

A.L.R.
American Law Reports, First

A.L.R.4th
American Law Reports, Fourth

A.L.R.2d
American Law Reports, Second

A.L.R. Fed.
American Law Reports, Federal

A.L.R.3d
American Law Reports, Third

All five sets are reporters in that they print opinions in full. They are *annotated* reporters in that notes or commentary is provided after each case in the form of an annotation. Unlike West reporters, only a selected number of opinions are printed in these A.L.R. volumes. The editors select opinions raising novel or interesting issues, which then become the basis of an annotation. The following is an example of an annotation found on page 1015, volume 91 of A.L.R.3d:

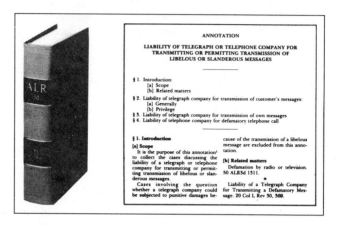

One of the joys of legal research is to find an annotation on point. A wealth of information is contained in annotations, such as a comprehensive, state-by-state survey of law on an issue. It would not be uncommon for a single annotation to contain hundreds of citations to court opinions. Picture yourself having the capacity to hire your own team of researchers to go out and spend weeks finding just about everything there is on a particular point of law. While none of us are likely to have this luxury, we do have a close equivalent in the form of annotations in the five sets of *American Law Reports*. They are a gold mine of research references. Since there are hundreds of volumes in these five sets, the chances are very good that we will find an annotation that is on point, i.e., that covers the facts of our research problem.

Most of the references in the annotations are to case law. Their primary service, therefore, is to act as a case finder. Because of this, the annotation system of Lawyers Co-operative Publishing Company is the major competitor of the other massive case finders—the digests of West. It is to our advantage that each system claims to do a better job than the other. Their competition has led to a rich source of material at our disposal.

The annotations cover both federal and state case law. A.L.R. First, A.L.R.2d, and most of A.L.R.3d cover both state and federal case law. The later volumes of A.L.R.3d and all of A.L.R.4th cover mainly state case law. A.L.R. Fed. covers only federal case law. The annotations in these five sets do not follow any particular order. There may be an annotation on burglary, for example, followed by an annotation on defective wheels on baby carriages. The annotations in A.L.R. First and A.L.R.2d are older than the annotations in the other sets, but this is not significant because all of the annotations can be updated.

We turn now to the two major concerns of the researcher:

- How do you find an annotation on point?

- How do you update an annotation that you have found?

Index Systems for A.L.R. First	Index Systems for A.L.R.2d	Index Systems for A.L.R.3d, A.L.R.4th, A.L.R. Fed.
■ *A.L.R. First Series Quick Index* ■ *Permanent A.L.R. Digest*	■ *Index to Annotations* ■ *A.L.R.2d Digest* ■ LEXIS	■ *Index to Annotations* ■ *A.L.R. Digest to 3d, 4th, Federal* ■ LEXIS

FIGURE 11.12

Finding Annotations When You Have No Leads

It is much easier to find and update annotations in A.L.R.3d, A.L.R.4th, and A.L.R. Fed. than in the earlier A.L.R. First and A.L.R.2d.

(a) Finding an Annotation on Point

The major ways of finding annotations on point are outlined in Figure 11.12. These methods are most useful when you are at the very beginning of your search and have no leads.

Annotations in A.L.R. First are found by using a single-volume Quick Index.[1] The multivolume *Index to Annotations* is used to find annotations in A.L.R.2d, A.L.R.3d, A.L.R.4th, and A.L.R. Fed. There are also sets of digests that can be used as indexes, although they are somewhat more awkward. The digest for A.L.R. First is the *Permanent A.L.R. Digest.* The digest for A.L.R.2d is the *A.L.R.2d Digest.* There is a single digest that covers all of A.L.R.3d, A.L.R.4th, and A.L.R. Fed. It is called the *A.L.R. Digest to 3d, 4th, Federal.* Finally, you can search for annotations by computer through LEXIS, which covers all annotations except those in A.L.R. First.

Figure 11.13 tells you what to do if you are further along in your research and you already have an opinion (state or federal), a statute (state or federal), or a regulation (federal) that is on point, or potentially on point. Use the methods listed in the second column of Figure 11.13 to try to find any annotations that discuss or mention that opinion, statute, or regulation.

As we will see later, annotations are one of the "citing materials" in Shepard's. This simply means that the annotations have discussed or mentioned whatever you are shepardizing. Hence if you shepardize the items in the first column of Figure 11.13, you will be led to all annotations, if any, that have mentioned that item. If you have access to Auto-Cite (page 586), this computer service will tell you what annotations have mentioned your federal or state court opinion. Finally, use the "Table of Laws, Rules, and Regulations" to find annotations on a federal statute (in U.S.C., U.S.C.A., or U.S.C.S.), or on a federal administrative regulation (in C.F.R.). This excellent table is located in the last volume of the Index to Annotations referred to in Figure 11.12.

As indicated earlier, some of the annotations in the five sets are very long and comprehensive. How do you find the law of a *particular* state or court within an annotation without having to read the entire annotation? At the beginning of annotations in A.L.R.3d and A.L.R.4th, you will find a "Table of

---

[1]There is also a multivolume index to the annotations in A.L.R. First. It is called *A.L.R. Word Index to Annotations.* It is seldom used today even though many libraries still keep it on the shelf. This set is different from the other multivolume index, called *Index to Annotations,* which *is* widely used today. The latter covers A.L.R.2d, A.L.R.3d, A.L.R.4th, and A.L.R. Fed.

FIGURE 11.13

Finding
Annotations When
You Already Have
a Lead

IF YOU ALREADY HAVE A CITATION TO:	USE THE FOLLOWING METHODS OF FINDING ANNOTATIONS THAT MENTION THAT CITATION:
A State Court Opinion	▪ Shepardize the opinion ▪ Check Auto-Cite
A Federal Court Opinion	▪ Shepardize the opinion ▪ Check Auto-Cite
A State Statute	▪ Shepardize the statute
A Federal Statute	▪ Shepardize the statute ▪ Check the "Table of Laws, Rules, and Regulations" in the *Index to Annotations*
A Federal Regulation	▪ Shepardize the regulation ▪ Check the "Table of Laws, Rules, and Regulations" in the *Index to Annotations*

Jurisdictions Represented," which will direct you to specific sections of the annotation that cover the law of your state. At the beginning of annotations in A.L.R. Fed. there is a "Table of Courts and Circuits," which will direct you to sections of the annotation dealing with certain federal courts. In addition to these tables, there will usually be other indexes or tables of contents found at the beginning of the annotations.

TABLE OF JURISDICTIONS REPRESENTED

Consult POCKET PART in this volume for later cases

US: §§ 2[b], 3, 4[a], 5[b], 6[a], 7[a], 10[b]
Ala: §§ 2[b], 4[a], 6[a], 7[a], 8, 10[b]
Cal: §§ 4[a, b], 7[a, b], 10[b], 11
Fla: §§ 5[a]
Ga: §§ 3, 4[b], 5[b], 6[b], 10[a]
Ill: §§ 4[b], 5[a, b], 6[a, b], 10[a]
Ind: §§ 4[a], 5[b], 6[a], 7[a, b], 8, 9, 10[b]
Iowa: §§ 7[a], 8
Ky: §§ 3, 4[a], 5[b]
La: §§ 5[b], 7[a, b]
Me: §§ 5[b], 7[a], 10[b]
Md: §§ 4[b]
Mich: §§ 4[a], 10[b]

Miss: §§ 4[a]
Mo: §§ 4[a], 6[a], 10[b]
NH: §§ 3, 4[b]
NC: §§ 7[a]
Ohio: §§ 4[a, b], 6[a], 7[a, b], 10[b]
Or: §§ 4[a], 10[b]
Pa: §§ 4[a], 7[a], 10[b]
Tenn: §§ 4[a], 5[b], 6[a]
Tex: §§ 4[a], 7[a], 10[b]
Vt: §§ 9
Wash: §§ 6[a], 7[a], 8
Wis: §§ 7[a], 8, 10[b], 11

TABLE OF COURTS AND CIRCUITS

Consult POCKET PART in this volume for later cases and statutory changes

Sup Ct: §§ 2[a], 3[a], 5, 6, 14
First Cir: §§ 5[b], 6[b], 15[b], 16[a], 18[a]
Second Cir: §§ 2[b], 3[a, b], 5[a], 12[a], 16[a], 18[a]
Third Cir: §§ 3[a], 5[a], 7, 11[b], 12[b], 13[a], 15[b]
Fourth Cir: §§ 2[b], 3[a], 4[b], 5[a, b], 8, 9, 10[b], 12[a, b], 13[b], 14, 15[a, b], 16[a], 17, 18[a]
Fifth Cir: §§ 3[a], 5[a, b], 8, 10[a], 11[a, b], 13[a], 15[a], 16[b], 18[b]

Sixth Cir: §§ 5[b], 6[b], 10[a, b], 12[a], 13[a], 15[b]
Seventh Cir: §§ 2[a, b], 4[b], 5[b], 10[b], 15[b]
Eighth Cir: §§ 3[a], 4[a, b], 5[a, b], 6[a], 12[a], 13[a], 15[b], 16[a], 17, 19
Ninth Cir: §§ 2[a, b], 3[a], 4[a], 5, a, 6[b], 7, 8, 10[a], 11[a, b], 12[a, b], 13[a, b], 15[a, b], 16[b], 17, 18[a, b]
Tenth Cir: §§ 2[b], 3[a], 5[a, b], 6[a, b], 9, 11[a, b], 12[a], 14, 17, 18[b]
Dist Col Cir: §§ 3[b], 5[b], 6[b], 10[a, b]
Ct Cl: § 16[a]

(b) Updating an Annotation

Suppose that you have found an annotation on point. It has led you to very useful law. This annotation, however, may be ten, twenty, thirty, or more years old. How do you update this annotation to find the most current law on the points covered in the annotation? Of course, any opinion or statute found within the annotation can be shepardized as a technique of finding more law. But our focus here is the updating systems within A.L.R. itself. Figure 11.14 outlines these systems.

If the annotation you want updated is in A.L.R. First, you use the *A.L.R. Blue Book of Supplemental Decisions.* (Check each volume of this Blue Book.) If the annotation you want updated is in A.L.R. 2d, you use the *A.L.R. 2d Later Case Service.* (Check the volume that covers your annotation, plus the pocket part of this volume of the Later Case Service.) If the annotation you want updated is in A.L.R. 3d, or in A.L.R. 4th, or in A.L.R. Fed., you check the pocket part of the volume containing the annotation.

There are no pocket parts to the volumes of A.L.R. First and A.L.R. 2d. Hence you need the Blue Book and Later Case Service in order to perform needed updating. Thankfully, the volumes of A.L.R. 3d, A.L.R. 4th, and

Updating an Annotation in A.L.R. First	Updating an Annotation in A.L.R.2d	Updating an Annotation in A.L.R.3d, A.L.R.4th, and A.L.R. Fed.
■ *A.L.R. Blue Book of Supplemental Decisions* ■ "Annotation History Table" in *Index to Annotations*	■ *A.L.R.2d Later Case Service* ■ "Annotation History Table" in *Index to Annotations*	■ Pocket Part of volume containing the annotation ■ "Annotation History Table" in *Index to Annotations*
Note: any case you find in an annotation can also be updated by shepardizing that case.		

FIGURE 11.14

How to Update an Annotation

A.L.R. Fed. *do* have pocket parts that can be used to update annotations in them. The existence of these pocket parts makes it much easier to update annotations in A.L.R. 3d, A.L.R. 4th, and A.L.R. Fed. than to update annotations in A.L.R. First or A.L.R. 2d.

There is a toll-free number that can be used to obtain additional updating information on the annotations in A.L.R. 2d, A.L.R. 3d, A.L.R. 4th, and A.L.R. Fed. Any member of the public can use this number; you do not have to be a subscriber. Currently, the number is 1-800-225-7488.

One final updating feature must be covered: the Annotation History Table. Note that Figure 11.14 lists this Table as a further method of updating annotations in all five sets of A.L.R. The law in some annotations may become so outdated that it is replaced by another annotation. The outdated annotation is called a *superseded annotation,* which should not be read. If, however, an annotation is substantially updated but not totally replaced by another annotation, the older annotation is called a *supplemented annotation,* which can be read along with the newer annotation. There are two ways to find out which annotations have been superseded or supplemented. Check the "Annotation History Table" found in the last volume of the *Index to Annotations.* Of course, you should also check the standard method for updating annotations in A.L.R. First (the Blue Book), in A.L.R. 2d (Later Case Service), in A.L.R. 3d (pocket parts), in A.L.R. 4th (pocket parts), and in A.L.R. Fed. (pocket parts).

Note on Another Annotated Reporter of Lawyers Co-op.   Lawyers Co-op. publishes *United States Supreme Court Reports, Lawyers' Edition* (abbreviated L.Ed.). This is also an annotated reporter in that it prints the full text of opinions (those of the U.S. Supreme Court) with annotations on issues following some of these opinions. (See photo of this reporter at the top of page 492.)

Checklist #3

Checklist For Finding and Updating Annotations in A.L.R., A.L.R.2d, A.L.R.3d, A.L.R.4th, and A.L.R. Fed.
1. Your goal is to use the five sets to find annotations on your research problem. The annotations are extensive research papers on numerous points of law.
2. The most current annotations are in A.L.R.3d, in A.L.R.4th, and in A.L.R. Fed. Start with these sets. Then try to find annotations in A.L.R.2d, and in A.L.R. First. Use the CARTWHEEL to help you locate annotations in the following index resources:

Continued

Checklist #3—*Continued*

**Checklist For Finding and Updating Annotations
in A.L.R., A.L.R.2d, A.L.R.3d, A.L.R.4th, and A.L.R. Fed.**

(a) To find annotations in A.L.R.3d, in A.L.R.4th, and in A.L.R. Fed.:
- Use *Index to Annotations*
- Use *A.L.R. Digest to 3d, 4th, Federal*
- Use LEXIS

(b) To find annotations in A.L.R.2d:
- Use *Index to Annotations*
- Use *A.L.R.2d Digest*
- Use LEXIS

(c) To find annotations in A.L.R. First:
- Use *A.L.R. First Series Quick Index*
- Use *Permanent A.L.R. Digest*

---

3. If you already found a particular law and you want to know if there is an annotation that mentions that law, check the following resources:

(a) If you already have a federal opinion or a state opinion:
- Shepardize that opinion
- Check Auto-Cite

(b) If you already have a state statute:
- Shepardize that statute

(c) If you already have a federal statute:
- Shepardize that statute
- Check the "Table of Laws, Rules, and Regulations" in the last volume of *Index to Annotations*

(d) If you already have a federal administrative regulation:
- Shepardize that regulation
- Check the "Table of Laws, Rules, and Regulations" in the last volume of *Index to Annotations*

---

4. Use the tables or other indices at the beginning of the annotation to help you locate specific sections of the annotation. (Before you spend much time with the annotation, however, check the "Annotation History Table" to determine if it has been superseded or supplemented by another annotation. See step 5 below.)

---

5. Update all annotations that are on point.

(a) To update an annotation in A.L.R. First:
- Check the *A.L.R. Blue Book of Supplemental Decisions*
- Check the "Annotation History Table" in the last volume of *Index to Annotations*

(b) To update an annotation in A.L.R.2d:
- Check the *A.L.R.2d Later Case Service*
- Check the "Annotation History Table" in the last volume of *Index to Annotations*

(c) To update an annotation in A.L.R.3d, in A.L.R.4th, or in A.L.R. Fed.:
- Check the pocket part
- Check the "Annotation History Table" in the last volume of *Index to Annotations*

4. Shepard's

There have been four great research inventions in the law:

- The key topic and number system of the West digests
- The annotations in A.L.R., A.L.R.2d, A.L.R.3d, A.L.R.4th, and A.L.R. Fed
- Computers (CALR: Computer Assisted Legal Research)
- Shepard's

The first three are extensively used as case finders. While Shepard's is not primarily designed to be a case finder, it can serve this function, along with other functions, as we shall now see.

Before we examine Shepard's and the techniques of *shepardizing,* you should review the material starting on page 511 covering the kinds of Shepard's volumes that exist, the material on page 527 covering the use of Shepard's as one of the four techniques of finding a parallel cite, and the material on page 487 describing an advance sheet for Shepard's.

Shepard's is a citator, which means that its function is to provide you with relevant citations to whatever you are shepardizing. We will examine Shepard's through the following topics:

(a) The units of a set of Shepard's

(b) Determining whether you have a complete set of Shepard's

(c) The distinction between "cited material" and "citing material"

(d) Abbreviations in Shepard's

(e) Shepardizing a case (court opinion)

(f) Shepardizing a statute

(g) Shepardizing a regulation

We will limit ourselves to shepardizing cases, statutes, and regulations. Knowing how to shepardize these items, however, will go a long way toward equipping you to shepardize other items as well (such as constitutions, administrative decisions, charters, and rules of court).

(a) The Units of a Set of Shepard's

By "set of Shepard's" we mean the group of volumes of Shepard's that cover whatever you are trying to shepardize. There are two main units to every set of Shepard's: (a) *bound* red volumes and (b) white, gold, yellow or red *pamphlet* volumes. The bound volumes and pamphlets are sometimes broken into parts, e.g., Part 1, Part 2. The white pamphlet is the advance sheet (page 487) that is later thrown away and cumulated (or consolidated) into a larger pamphlet. Eventually all the pamphlets are thrown away and cumulated into bound red volumes. The pamphlets contain the most current shepardizing material.

(b) Determining Whether You Have a Complete Set of Shepard's

You should not try to shepardize anything until you are satisfied that there is a complete set of Shepard's on the shelf in front of you. As we saw above, Shepard's comes in sets, e.g., the set of Shepards for United States statutes, the set for New Mexico laws. You need a complete set in order to shepardize. To determine whether you have a complete set, go through the following four steps:

1. Pick up the advance sheet or the most recently dated pamphlet for that set of Shepard's (the date is on top of the pamphlet).

2. What month and year is at the top of this advance sheet or other pamphlet? If the month is not the month of today's date or the immediately preceding month, ask the librarian for the date of the most recent pamphlet the library has received for the set of Shepard's you are using. (The librarian will check the office Kardex, (page 504), or other system of recording serial or subscription material that the library has received.)

3. Once you are satisfied that the advance sheet or latest pamphlet is the most current the library has, find the following statement on its front cover: "What Your Library Should Contain." Here you will be told what constitutes a complete set of Shepard's for the set you are using. Go down the list and make sure that the library has on the shelf everything you are told should be there.

4. The last entry in the list is always the advance sheet or other pamphlet that contains the list you are reading.

Here, for example, is the list that will allow you to shepardize the cases and statutes of the state of Kansas:

WHAT YOUR LIBRARY SHOULD CONTAIN:

- 1986 Bound Volume, Cases (Parts 1 and 2)*
- 1986 Bound Volume, Statutes*

*Supplemented with January, 1989 Cumulative Supplement Vol. 60 No. 5 and February, 1989 Advance Sheet Vol. 60 No. 6

DESTROY ALL OTHER ISSUES

To be complete, the following units of *Shepard's Kansas Citations* should be on the shelf:

- a 1986 bound volume of *Shepard's Kansas Citations* covering cases (Part 1); *and,*

- a 1986 bound volume of *Shepard's Kansas Citations* covering cases (Part 2); *and,*

- a 1986 bound volume of *Shepard's Kansas Citations* covering statutes; *and,*

- a January 1989 Cumulative Supplement pamphlet of *Shepard's Kansas Citations,* Vol. 60, No. 5.; *and,*

- A February 1989 Advance Sheet of *Shepard's Kansas Citations,* Vol. 60, No. 6.

The last item on the list is always the pamphlet that contains the list you are reading. Hence, the above list is found on the February 1989 Advance Sheet pamphlet of *Shepard's Kansas Citations,* Vol. 60, No. 6.

Occasionally the list can become quite involved. For example, you may find two lists on the pamphlet. One list tells you what should be on the shelf before a certain bound Shepard's volume is received by the library, and a second list tells you what should be on the shelf after that bound volume is received by the library. Yet the same process is followed. Carefully go through the list (or lists) one unit at a time, checking to see if the library has on the shelf what the list says should be present.

(c) The Distinction Between "Cited Material" and "Citing Material"

- Cited Material: whatever you are shepardizing, such as a case, statute, or regulation.

- Citing Material: whatever mentions or discusses the cited material, such as another case, a law review article, an annotation in A.L.R., A.L.R.2d, A.L.R.3d, A.L.R.4th, A.L.R. Fed, etc.

Suppose you are shepardizing the case found in 75 F.2d 107 (a case that begins on page 107 of volume 75 of Federal Reporter 2d). While reading through the columns of Shepard's, you find the following cite: f56 S.E.2d 46. The *cited* material is 75 F.2d 107. The *citing* material is 56 S.E.2d 46, which followed (f) or agreed with the decision in 75 F.2d 107.

Suppose you are shepardizing a statute: 22 U.S.C. § 55.8 (section 55.8 of title 22 of the United States Code). While reading through the columns of Shepard's, you find the following cite: 309 U.S. 45. The *cited* material is 22 U.S.C. § 55.8. The *citing* material is 309 U.S. 45, which interpreted or mentioned 22 U.S.C. § 55.8.

Shepard's always indicates the cited material by the black bold print along the top of every page of Shepard's and by the black bold print numbers that are the volume or section numbers of the cited material. In the following excerpt, the cited material is 404 P.2d 460. The citing material follows the number **460**:

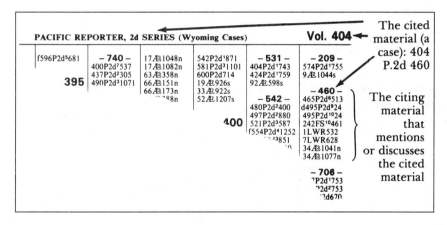

In the following excerpt, the cited material is a statute: § 37–31 of the Wyoming Statutes. The citing material is indicated beneath § 37–31.

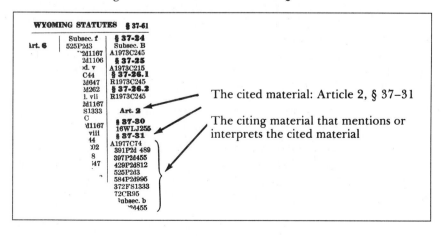

(d) Abbreviation in Shepard's

Shepard's packs a tremendous amount of information (the cites) into every one of its pages. Each page contains about eight columns of cites for the cited and the citing materials. For the sake of economy, Shepard's uses many abbreviations that are peculiar to Shepard's. For example:

FS → means Federal Supplement   * → means that a regulation of a
                                             particular year was discussed

A → means American Law   Δ → means that a regulation was
       Reports 3d   discussed without mentioning
                                         the year of the regulation

Most researchers do not know the meaning of every abbreviation and signal used by Shepard's. *But you must know where to find their meaning.* There are two places to go:

■ The abbreviations tables at the beginning of most of the units of Shepard's (for an example, see page 543).

■ The preface or explanation pages found at the beginning of most of the units of Shepard's

Many researchers neglect the latter. Buried within the preface or explanation pages may be an interpretation of an abbreviation or symbol that is not covered in the abbreviation tables.

(e) Shepardizing a Case (Court Opinion)

Almost every reporter has a corresponding Shepard's set, which will enable you to shepardize cases in that reporter (page 511). For example, if the case you want to shepardize is 193 Mass. 364, you go to the set of Shepard's that covers cases in Massachusetts Reports—*Shepard's Massachusetts Citations.* If the case you want to shepardize is 402 F.2d 1064, you go to the Shepard's set that covers F.2d cases—*Shepard's Federal Citations.*

Of course, many cases have parallel cites—the case is found word-for-word in more than one reporter. You can shepardize the case through *either* reporter for most cases with parallel cites. Assume you want to shepardize the following case:

Welch v. Swasey, 193 Mass. 364, 79 N.E. 745 (1907).

This case is found in two reporters: *Massachusetts Reports* and *North Eastern Reporter.* Hence, you can shepardize the case and obtain the same citing material from two different sets of Shepard's: **Shepard's Massachusetts Citations** and **Shepard's Northeastern Citations.**

To shepardize a *case* means to obtain the following six kinds of information about the cited case (the case you are shepardizing):

1. The parallel cite of the case. The first entry in parenthesis is the parallel cite. (See page 527 for the reasons why you may find no parallel cite here.)

2. The history of the case. Here you will find all cases that are part of the same litigation, e.g., appeals, reversals.

3. Citing cases that have mentioned or discussed the cited case—for example, followed it, distinguished it, or just mentioned it.

4. Citing legal periodical literature (articles or case notes) that has analyzed or mentioned the cited case.

5. Citing annotations in A.L.R., A.L.R.2d, A.L.R.3d, A.L.R.4th, or A.L.R. Fed. that have analyzed or mentioned the cited case.

6. Citing opinions of the attorney general that have analyzed or mentioned the cited case.

The great value of Shepard's as a case finder comes thorough items 3 to 5. If a citing case mentions or discusses the cited case, the two cases probably deal with similar facts and law. All citing cases, therefore, are potential leads to more case law on point. Similarly, a citing law review article or annotation will probably discuss a variety of cases in addition to the discussion of the cited case. Hence again, you are led to more case law through Shepard's.

Items 2 and 3 above also enable you to do validation research (page 606). They tell you if the cited case is still good law. Has it been reversed? Has it been discussed with approval by citing cases? Has it been ignored by other courts?

One final point before examining an excerpt from a Shepard's page. Recall that cases in reporters are broken down into headnotes at the beginning of the case (page 503). These headnotes are written either by the private publisher (such as West) or by the court clerk in official editions of the case. Shepard's calls these headnotes of the case the *syllabus* of the case—small-paragraph summaries of portions of the case found at the beginning of the case.

A case can involve many issues, only a few of which may be relevant to your research problem. Is it possible to narrow your sheparding to those parts of the case that are most relevant to your research problem? Yes. It is possible to shepardize a portion of a case through its headnote or syllabus numbers. In effect, you are shepardizing the headnote! How is this done?

■ Every headnote or syllabus paragraph of the *cited* case has a consecutive number: 1, 2, 3, 4, etc.

■ When the editors of Shepard's come across a *citing* case that deals with only one of the headnotes or syllabus paragraphs of the *cited* case, they include the number of this headnote or syllabus paragraph as part of the reference to the *citing* case in the columns of Shepard's.

■ The number is printed as a small raised, or elevated, number—called a small superior figure—within the reference to the *citing* case.

Be careful. It is easy to become confused. The superior figure refers to the headnote or syllabus number of the *cited* case, not the citing case.

For example, assume again that you are shepardizing Welch v. Swasey, 193 Mass. 364. In the columns of Shepard's you find the following:

$$f193Mas^8476$$

The *citing* case is 193 Mass. 476. This case follows (agrees with) the *cited* case: Welch v. Swasey, 193 Mass. 364. Note the raised number 8—the superior figure. This 8 refers to the eighth headnote or syllabus of the *cited* case, *Welch v. Swasey*. The *citing* case dealt with that portion of *Welch* that was summarized in the eighth headnote or syllabus of the *Welch* case. Again, do not make the mistake of thinking that the small raised number refers to a headnote or syllabus in the citing case. It refers to a headnote or syllabus number of the *cited* case.

We now look at a sample or specimen page from *Shepard's Massachusetts Citations* (see Figure 11.15), where we will begin to shepardize Welch v. Swasey, 193 Mass. 364. Read the oval inserts on this specimen page now—before carefully studying the following comments.

Let us assume that in your legal research you have located the case of *Welch v. Swasey,* reported in volume 193 of Massachusetts Reports at page 364. This again is the cited case that we want to shepardize.

FIGURE 11.15

Excerpt from Shepard's Page (Cases)

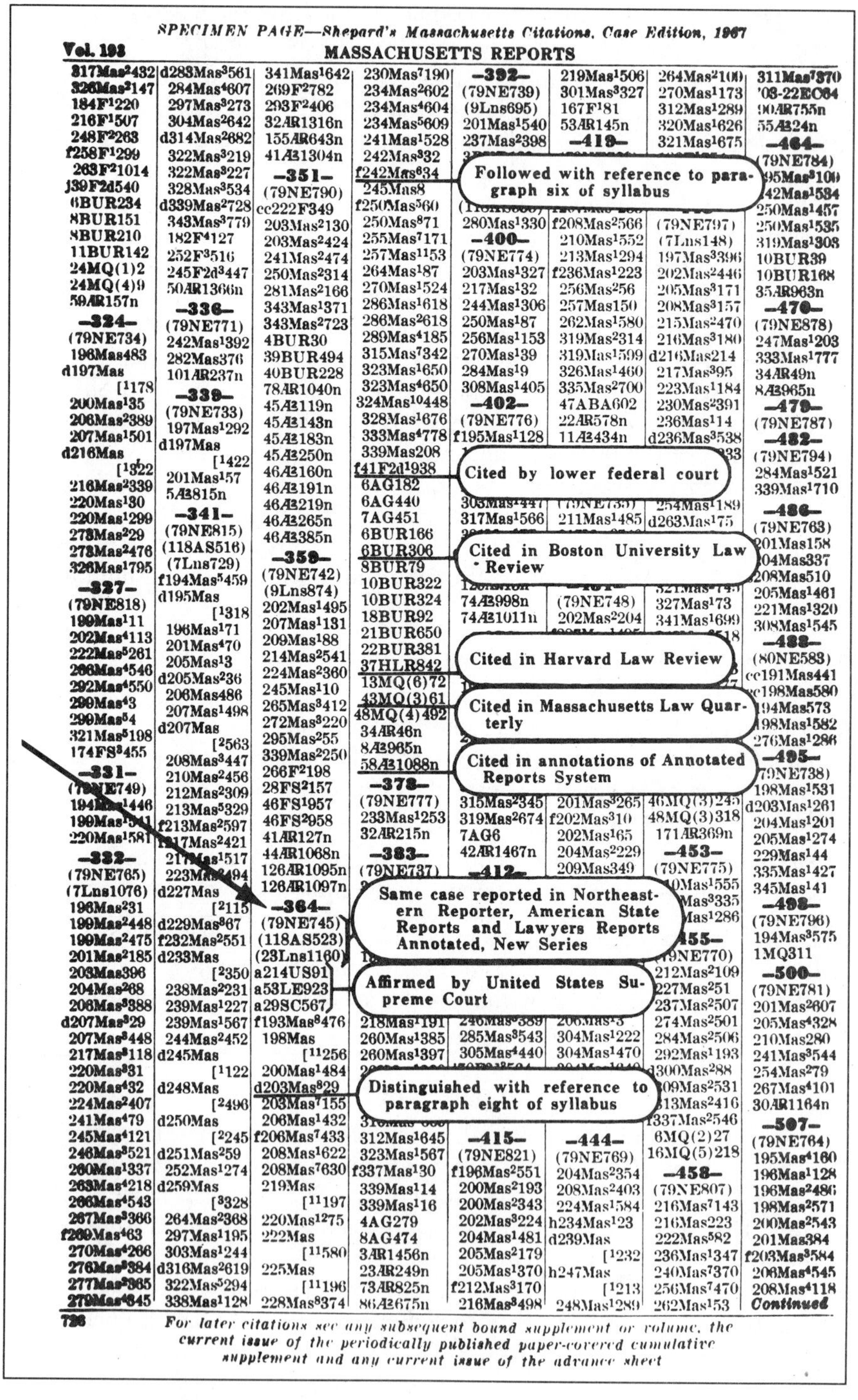

SPECIMEN PAGE—Shepard's Massachusetts Citations, Case Edition, 1967

Vol. 193

MASSACHUSETTS REPORTS

The specimen page contains columns of Shepard's citation entries with oval callout boxes labeled:

- Followed with reference to paragraph six of syllabus
- Cited by lower federal court
- Cited in Boston University Law Review
- Cited in Harvard Law Review
- Cited in Massachusetts Law Quarterly
- Cited in annotations of Annotated Reports System
- Same case reported in Northeastern Reporter, American State Reports and Lawyers Reports Annotated, New Series
- Affirmed by United States Supreme Court
- Distinguished with reference to paragraph eight of syllabus

For later citations see any subsequent bound supplement or volume, the current issue of the periodically published paper-covered cumulative supplement and any current issue of the advance sheet

The specimen page contains a reproduction of page 726 in the 1967 Case Edition of *Shepard's Massachusetts Citations*. Note the number of the volume of reports, "Vol. 193," in the upper left corner of the page.

Find our page number in bold print "—364—" in the third column. See the arrow. This is the initial page of our cited case under consideration. Following this page number you will find the citations "(79NE745)," "(118AS523)," "(23Lns1160)," indicating that the same case is also reported in 79 *North Eastern Reporter* 745, 118 *American State Reports* 523, and 23 *Lawyers Reports Annotated, New Series* 1160. These are parallel citations. As indicated earlier, abbreviations are explained at the beginning of Shepard's volumes.

Next comes the history of the cited case. On appeal to the United States Supreme Court, our cited case was affirmed "a" in 214US91 (also printed in 53LE923 and in 29SC567). Also, the cited case has been followed "f" and distinguished "d" in subsequent cases of the Massachusetts and federal courts.

In the citation "f242 Mas⁶34" (see top of next column), the small superior figure 6 before the citing page number 34 indicates that the principle of law brought out in the sixth paragraph of the syllabus (i.e., of the headnotes) of 193 Mass. 364 has been followed in 242 Mass. 34.

This case has also been cited in several legal periodicals: *Harvard Law Review* "HLR," *Boston University Law Review* "BUR," and *Massachusetts Law Quarterly* "MQ."

The citations appearing in annotations of the *American Law Reports* are grouped together after the legal periodical citing references.

By examining the same volume and page number of the cited case in the other units of *Shepard's Massachusetts Citations,* more citing material for this case will be found.

Checklist #4a

Checklist for Shepardizing a Case
1. You have a case you want to shepardize. In what reporter is this case found? Go to the set of Shepard's in the library that covers this reporter.
2. If the case you want to shepardize has a parallel cite that you already have, find out if the library has a set of Shepard's for the other reporter volumes in which the case is also found. You may be able to shepardize the case through more than one set of Shepard's. (There are sets of Shepard's for the individual state official reports and for all the reporters of West's unofficial National Reporter System.)
3. Know whether you have a complete set of Shepard's in front of you by reading the "What Your Library Should Contain" list on the most recent pamphlet of that set.
4. The general rule is that you must check the cite of the case you are sheparddizing (the cited case) in *every* unit of a set of Shepard's. With experience you will learn, however, that it is possible to bypass some of the units of the set. There may be information on the front cover of one of the Shepard's volumes, for example, that will tell you that the date or volume number of the reporter containing your cited case will not be covered in that Shepard's volume. You can bypass it and move on to other units of the set.
5. In checking all the units of Shepard's, it is recommended that you work *backward* by examining the most recent Shepard's pamphlets first so that you obtain the latest citing materials first.
6. Suppose that in one of the units of a set of Shepard's, you find nothing listed for the cited case. This could mean one of three things:

Continued

Checklist #4a—*Continued*

Checklist for Shepardizing a Case—*Continued*
(a) You are in the wrong set of Shepard's.
(b) You are in the right set of Shepard's, but the Shepard's unit you are examining does not cover the particular volume of the reporter that contains your cited case. (See #4 above.)
(c) You are in the right set of Shepard's. The silence in Shepard's about your cited case means that since the time of the printing of the last unit of Shepard's for that set, nothing has happened to the case—there is nothing for Shepard's to tell you.
7. Know the six kinds of information that you can obtain when shepardizing a case: parallel cites, history of the cited case, citing cases, citing legal periodical literature, citing annotations, citing opinions of the attorney general.
8. The page number listed for every citing case is the page on which the cited case is mentioned. It is not the page on which the citing case begins.
9. Use the abbreviations tables and the preface pages at the beginning of most units of Shepard's—and use them often.
10. A small "n" to the right of the page number of a citing case (e.g., 23ALR198n) means the cited case is mentioned within an annotation. A small "s" to the right of the page number of a citing case (e.g., 23ALR198s) means the cited case is mentioned in a supplement to or pocket part of the annotation.
11. Item #2 above said that cases with parallel cites can often be shepardized through more than one set of Shepard's. There is, however, only one set of Shepard's for U.S. Supreme Court opinions *(United States Citations, Case Edition)*. The question arises as to whether you can shepardize the Supreme Court opinion through any one of the three cites within this set of Shepards. For older opinions, the answer is *no;* you must shepardize through the U.S. cite. Today, you can shepardize through any of the three cites. It is recommended, however, that you shepardize *only* through the U.S. cite, since you may pick up some citing material through the U.S. cite that is not available when you shepardize through the S.Ct. or L.Ed. cites.
12. You can also shepardize a case online through either WESTLAW or LEXIS.

(f) Shepardizing a Statute

You shepardize a *statute* in order to try to find the following seven kinds of information:

- A parallel cite of the statute (found in parentheses immediately after the section number of the statute). The parallel cite (if given) is to the *session law* edition of the statute (see the discussion that follows)
- The history of the statute in the legislature, such as amendments, new sections added, sections repealed, renumbered, etc.
- The history of the statute in the courts, such as citing cases that have analyzed or mentioned the statute, declared it unconstitutional, etc.
- Citing administrative decisions, such as agency decisions that have analyzed or mentioned the statute
- Citing legal periodical literature, such as law review articles that have analyzed or mentioned the statute
- Citing annotations in A.L.R., A.L.R.2d, A.L.R.3d, A.L.R.4th, and A.L.R. Fed. that have analyzed or mentioned the statute

■ Citing opinions of the attorney general that have analyzed or mentioned the statute

When a statute is passed by the legislature, it comes out as a slip law (page 510) and then is printed in volumes called Session Laws, Laws, Acts, Acts and Resolves, Statutes at Large, etc. (For convenience, all the latter items will be referred to below as session laws.) Session laws are arranged chronologically by year—the statutes are not arranged by subject matter in the session law volumes. Finally, many but not all of the session laws are later printed in statutory codes. The are *codified,* which means that they *are* organized by subject matter rather than chronologically. As indicated earlier, not all session laws are codified. The statute may not be considered of sufficient general interest to be codified. If codification has occurred, there will be two cites for the same statute. Here are examples of codified and session law cites of a state statute (Ohio) and of a federal statute.

Session Law Cite	**Codified Cite**
↓	↓
1975 Ohio Laws, C. 508	Ohio Rev. Code Ann. § 45 (1978)
87 Stat. 297 (1965)	34 U.S.C. § 18(c) (1970)

Notice the totally different numbering system in the codified and session law cites—yet they are the same statutes. Section 45 of the Ohio Revised Code Annotated is found word-for-word in Chapter (C.)508 of the 1975 session laws of Ohio. And section 18(c) of title 34 of the United States Code is found word-for-word in volume 87 of Statutes at Large (Stat.) on page 297. Notice also the different years for the same statute. The year in the *session law cite* is the year the legislature passed the statute. The year in the *codified cite,* however, is usually the year of the edition of the code.

Now the question becomes: when do you shepardize a statute through its session law cite and when do you shepardize it through its codified cite?

There are two instances when you *must* shepardize the statute through its session law cite:

■ If the statute will never be codified because it is not of general public interest and

■ If the statute has not yet been codified because it is so recent (codification will come later)

If the statute *has* been codified, you must shepardize it through its latest codified cite. But suppose you know only the session law cite of the statute. How do you find its codified cite? Go to the current code that will contain your statute. Look for special tables at the beginning or end of the code. For federal statutes in the United States Code, for example, there is a Tables volume in which you will find Table III. It will enable you to translate a session law cite into a codified law cite (page 533). (A Tables volume also exists for U.S.C.A. and for U.S.C.S.)

Shepard's has its own abbreviation system for session laws. Suppose that you are shepardizing Kan Stat Ann. § 123 (1973)—a codified cite. Section 123 is the cited statute—what you are shepardizing. In the Shepard's columns for Kansas statutes, you might find:

Section 123
(1970C6)
A1972C23
Rp1975C45

The parallel cite in parentheses is 1970C6, which means the 1970 Session Laws of the state of Kansas, Chapter 6. The mention of a year in Shepard's for statutes usually refers to the sessions laws for that year. (You find the meaning of "C" by checking the abbreviations tables at the beginning of the Shepard's volume.)

Immediately beneath the parentheses in the above example you find two other references to session laws:

A1972C23	In the 1972 Session Laws of Kansas, Chapter 23, there was an amendment to section 123 (which is what "A" means according to Shepard's abbreviation tables)	Rp1975C45	In Chapter 45 of the 1975 Session Laws of Kansas, section 123 was repealed in part (which is what "Rp" means according to Shepard's abbreviation tables)

You will note that Shepard's does *not* tell you what the amendment was, nor what was repealed in part. How do you find this out? Two ways. First, you go to the actual session laws if your library has them. Second, you go to the cited statute (§ 123) in the codified collection of the statutes (here the Kansas Statutes Annotated). At the bottom of the statute in the code, there may be historical or legislative history notes which will summarize amendments, repeals, etc. (Also check the same kind of notes for the cited statute in the pocket part of the code volume you are using.)

Other citing material given in Shepard's for a statute is less complicated. For example, there are cites to citing cases, citing law review articles, etc., that follow a very similar pattern to the citing material for cases you are shepardizing (see Checklist #4a on shepardizing a case).

FIGURE 11.16

Excerpt from a Shepard's Page (Federal Statutes)

United States Code, 1970 Edition and Supplement, 1972 TITLE 18 § 700	Citations to section "§" 700 of Title 18 of the United States Code, 1970 Edition and the 1972 Supplement are shown in the left margin of this page.

Citations to section "§" 700 of Title 18 of the United States Code, 1970 Edition and the 1972 Supplement are shown in the left margin of this page.

Citations for each cited statutory provision are grouped as follows:
1. amendments, repeals, etc. by acts of Congress;
2. citing cases of the United States Supreme Court and the lower federal courts analyzed as to constitutionality or validity;
3. other citing cases;
4. citing legal periodical literature;
5. citing annotations;
6. citing material for specific subdivisions of the statute.

For the purpose of illustration only, this grouping has been indicated by brackets. It will be noted that as yet there is no citing material in group four.

The first citation shown indicates that section 700 of Title 18 was added "Ad" by an act of Congress printed in 82 United States Statutes at Large "St" at page 291. This section is next shown to have been held constitutional "C" by a lower federal court in a case reported in 302 Federal Supplement "FS" 1112 and to have been cited in several cases before the federal courts and the United States Supreme Court. The section was also cited in an annotation "n" of the American Law Reports, Third Series "A3".

Citing references to specific subdivisions of the section are then shown. Subsection (Subsec) "a" of section 700, for example, was held constitutional in two lower federal court cases reported in 454 F2d 972 and 462 F2d 96.

TITLE 18
§ 700

Ad82St291   1
C302FS1112   2
394US604
22LE592
89SC1372
445F2d226
462F2d96
479F2d1177   3
313FS49
317FS138
322FS593
324FS1278
343FS165

41Æ3504n   5

Subsec. a
C454F2d972
C462F2d96
445F2d226
479F2d1179
324FS1278
Subsec. b   6
C462F2d96
445F2d226
Subsec. c
394US598
22LE588
89SC1360
322FS585

Assume that you want to shepardize a federal statute—in the United States Code (U.S.C.). As with the sheparadizing of every statute, you must shepardize through the most current edition of the code. A new edition of the U.S.C. comes out every six years, e.g., 1970 Edition, 1976 Edition. In between editions, the U.S.C. is supplemented by annual Supplement volumes, e.g., Supplement 1972, Supplement 1973. Shepardize your statute through the latest code edition *and* through any of the Supplement years indicated at the top of the pages used to shepardize a federal statute in *Shepard's United States Citations, Statute Edition* (page 512).

Assume that the most current code edition is the 1970 edition and that the latest Supplement year is 1972. You want to shepardize 18 USC § 700 (1970). You trace this cite through all the units of *Shepard's United States Citations, Statute Edition*. In Figure 11.16, there is an excerpt containing one column from a page in one of these units.

Checklist #4b

Checklist for Sheparadizing a Statute
1. Go to the set of Shepard's that will enable you to shepardize your statute. For federal statutes, it is *Shepard's United States Citations, Statute Edition*. For state statutes, go to the set of Shepard's for your state. This set of Shepard's may cover both state cases and state statutes in the same units or in different case and statute editions of the set.
2. If the statute has been codified, shepardize it through its latest codified cite. If all you have is the session law cite of the statute, translate it into a codified cite by using the tables in the current code, such as Table III of the Tables volume of U.S.C./U.S.C.A./U.S.C.S. (page 533).
3. If the statute has not been codified, you can shepardize it through its session law cite.
4. Know whether you have a complete set of Shepard's in front of you by reading the "What Your Library Should Contain" list on the most recent pamphlet of that set.
5. Check your cite in *every* unit of Shepard's. It is recommended that you work *backward* by examining the most recent Shepard's pamphlets first so that you obtain the latest citing material first.
6. At the top of a Shepard's page, and in its columns, look for your statute by the name of the code, year, article, chapter, title, or section, however the statute is identified in its cite. Repeat this for every unit of Shepard's.
7. Know the seven kinds of information you can try to obtain by shepardizing a statute: parallel cite (not always given), history of the statute in the legislature, history of the statute in the courts, citing administrative decisions, citing legal periodical literature, citing annotations, citing opinions of the attorney general.
8. The history of the statute in the legislature will give you the citing material in session law form, e.g., A1980C45. This refers to an amendment (A) printed in the 1980 Laws of the legislature, chapter (C) 45. Another example: A34St.654. This refers to an amendment (A) printed in volume 34, page 654, of the Statutes at Large. If you want to locate these session laws, find out if your library keeps the session laws. Also, check the historical note after the statute in the statutory code (page 591).
9. The notation "et seq" means "and following." The citing material may be analyzing more than one statutory section.
10. Use the abbreviation tables and the preface material at the beginning of most of the units of the set of Shepard's.

Continued

Checklist #4b—*Continued*

Checklist for Sheparidizing a Statute—*Continued*
11. If your state code has gone through revisions or renumberings, read the early pages in the statutory code and in the Shepard's volumes to try to obtain an explanation of what has happened. This information may be of considerable help to you in interpreting the data provided in the Shepard's units for your state code.

(g) *Shepardizing a Regulation*

You cannot shepardize regulations of state agencies. No sets of Shepard's cover state regulations. Until recently, the same was true of most federal regulations. Today, however, it is possible to shepardize federal regulations in the Code of Federal Regulations (C.F.R.). This is done through *Shepard's Code of Federal Regulations Citations.* (See page 512). (It will also allow you to shepardize executive orders and reorganization plans.)

The C.F.R. comes out in a new edition every year. All the changes that have occurred during the year are incorporated in the new yearly edition. Two kinds of changes can be made:

■ Those changes made *by the agency* itself, e.g., amendments, repeals, renumbering—this is the history of the regulation in the agency.

■ Those changes forced on the agency *by the courts,* e.g., declaring the regulation invalid—this is the history of the regulation in the courts.

Unfortunately, Shepard's will give you only the history of the regulation *in the courts* (plus references to the regulation in legal periodical literature and in annotations). The columns of Shepard's will *not* give you the history of the regulation in the agency. (To obtain the latter, you must check elsewhere, e.g., the "CFR Parts Affected" tables in the Federal Register.) The main value of the Shepard's for C.F.R. is that it will tell you what *the courts* have said about the regulation (plus the periodical and annotation references).

When shepardizing through the Shepard's C.F.R. Citations, the cited material, of course, is the federal regulation—which we refer to as the cited regulation. There are two kinds of *citing* material provided by Shepard's:

■ Citing cases, periodicals, and annotations that refer to the cited regulation *by year,* that is, by C.F.R. edition.

■ Citing cases, periodicals, and annotations that refer to the cited regulation *without* specifying the year or edition of the regulation in the C.F.R.

To indicate the first kind of citing material, Shepard's gives you a small elevated asterisk just before a given year. If, for example, the cited regulation you were shepardizing is 12 C.F.R. § 218.111(j), you might find the following:

§ 218.111(j)
420F2d90*1965

The citing material is a citing case—420 F.2d 90. The small asterisk means that this case specifically identified the year of the cited regulation—1965. This year is *not* the year of the citing case. It is the year of the cited regulation. We are not given the year of the citing case.

Now let us examine the second kind of citing material mentioned above. There may be citing material that mentions the regulation but does *not* tell us

FIGURE 11.17
Excerpts from a
Shepard's Page
(C.F.R.)

```
CFR
TITLE
42
§53.111
323F2d965 △1963
458F2d1117 △1972
551F2d333 *1972
Va559F2d973 △1977
327FS113 △1971
359FS911 *1973        1
Vp373FS551 △1974
373FS559 1974
409FS711 △1976
Up453FS410 *1973
453FS680 *1976
Mass
382NE1043 *1977
NY
413S2d88 △1979        2
Ore
582P2d48 *1976
88YLJ277 *1977        3
11ALRF684n △1972      4
```

Code of Federal Regulations

Shepard's Code of Federal Regulation Citations gives citations to the Code of Federal Regulations and to Presidential Proclamations, Executive Orders, and Reorganization Plans as cited by the United States Supreme Court, by the lower federal courts, and by state courts in cases reported in any unit of the National Reporter System, and in annotations of American Law Reports. In addition, citations appearing in articles in legal periodicals are shown.

If the citing material mentioned the year of the cited CFR regulation, that year is preceded by the symbol *. When you find a year preceded by the symbol △, the year is the date of the citing material.

Citations to each provision of the Code of Federal Regulations are grouped as follows:

1. citing federal cases;

2. citing state cases;

3. citing legal periodical literature;

4. citing annotations.

The 1973 edition of section 53.111 was held unconstitutional in part "Up" by a United States District Court case reported in 453 Federal Supplement "FS" 410. Another United States District Court decision held § 53.111 void or invalid in part "Vp." The United States Court of Appeals in 1977 determined that § 53.111 was valid, "Va."

Section 53.111 has also been cited by the Courts of Massachusetts, New York, and Oregon. A citing legal periodical is shown by the reference 88 Yale Law Journal "YLJ" 277, and a citing annotation "n" is shown by the reference 11 American Law Reports, Federal "ALRF" 684.

the specific year or edition of that regulation. Shepard's uses a triangle in such situations. If, for example, the cited regulation you were sheparizing is 12 C.F.R. § 9.18(a)(3), you might find the following:

$$§9.18(a)(3)$$
$$274FS628△1967$$

The citing material is a citing case—274 F. Supp. 628. The small triangle means that the citing case did not refer to the year or edition of section 9.18(a)(3). When this occurs, the year next to the triangle is the year of the citing case and not the year of the cited regulation. The citing case of 274 F. Supp. 628 was decided in 1967.

Checklist #4c

Checklist for Shepardizing a Federal Regulation
1. Go to *Shepard's Code of Federal Regulations Citations.*
2. Know whether you have a complete set of Shepard's in front of you by reading the "What Your Library Should Contain" list on the most recent pamphlet in that set.
3. Shepardize your regulation through every unit of this set of Shepard's.
4. This set of Shepard's will give you two kinds of information: **(a)** Citing material that analyzes a regulation and mentions the specific year or edition of that regulation (indicated by an asterisk next to the year)

Continued

Checklist #4c—*Continued*

Checklist for Shepardizing a Federal Regulation—*Continued*
(b) Citing material that analyzes a regulation without referring to the specific year or edition of the regulation (indicated by a triangle next to the year)   The citing material includes citing cases, citing legal periodical literature, and citing annotations.
5. This set of Shepard's does not directly tell you what amendments, revisions, or other changes were made *by the agencies* to the regulations. You are told only what *the courts* have said about the regulations. (To find out what the agencies have done to the regulations, you must check sources such as the "CFR Parts Affected" tables in the *Federal Register.)*
6. Check the abbreviation table and preface at the beginning of most of the Shepard's units.
7. All regulations in C.F.R. are based on statutes of Congress. As we will see later, you can find out what statutes in U.S.C. are the authority for particular regulations in C.F.R. by checking the "authority" reference under many of the regulations in C.F.R. Once you know the statute that is the basis for the regulation, you might want to shepardize that statute for more law in the area. (See Checklist 4b on shepardizing a statute.)

5. Loose-Leaf Services

Loose-leaf services are law books with a three-ring or post-binder structure. Additions to these services are made frequently—monthly or sooner. The major publishers of the services are Bureau of National Affairs (BNA), Commerce Clearing House (CCH), Prentice-Hall (PH), and Matthew Bender. They cover numerous areas of the law, such as criminal law, taxes, corporate law, and unions. You should assume that one or more loose-leaf services exist for the topic of your research problem until you prove to yourself otherwise. The contents of loose-leaf services often include the following:

- Recent court opinions or summaries of opinions
- Relevant legislation—usually explained in some detail
- Administrative regulations and decisions, or summaries of them (some of this material may not be available elsewhere)
- References to relevant studies and reports
- Practice tips

In short, the loose-leaf services are extremely valuable. Unfortunately, however, they are sometimes awkward to use. Occasionally, library users of the loose-leaf services misfile pages that they take out for photocopying.

There is no standard format to the loose-leaf books. You may find the following, for example:

- One volume or multivolume
- Organization by page number, organization by section number, organization by paragraph number, or a combination of these
- Different colored pages to indicate more recent material
- Indexes at the end, in the middle, or at the beginning of the volumes
- Bound volumes that accompany the three-ring volumes
- Transfer binders that contain current material

You should approach the structure of each loose-leaf service as a small puzzle sitting on the shelf waiting for you to unravel.

Checklist #5

Checklist for Finding and Using Loose-Leaf Services
1. Divide your research problem into its major topics, such as family law, tax law, antitrust law, etc. Assume that one or more loose-leaf services exist for these topics until you have demonstrated to yourself otherwise.
2. Find out where the loose-leaf services are located in your library. Are they all together? Are they located in certain subject areas? Does the library have a separate list of them?
3. Check the card catalog. Look for subject heading cards on your topics to see if loose-leaf services are mentioned. Check the names of the major publishers of loose-leaf services—Bureau of National Affairs, Commerce Clearing House, Prentice-Hall, Matthew Bender.
4. Ask library staff members if they know of loose-leaf services on the major topics of your research.
5. Call other law libraries in your area. Ask the staff members there if they know of loose-leaf services on the major topics of your research. See if they can identify loose-leaf services that you could not identify through your own library.
6. Speak to experts in the area of the law, e.g., professors. (See Checklist #9.) Ask them about loose-leaf services.
7. Once you have a loose-leaf service in front of you, you must figure out how to use it: **(a)** Read any preface or explanatory material in the front of the volumes of the loose-leaf service **(b)** Ask library staff members to give you some help **(c)** Ask teachers who are experts in the area if they can give you a brief demonstration on its use **(d)** Ask a fellow student who is familiar with the service **(e)** Read any pamphlets or promotional literature by the publishers on using their loose-leaf services **(f)** Do the best that you can to struggle through the set on your own For each loose-leaf service, you need to know the following: ■ What it contains and what it does not contain ■ How it is indexed ■ How it is supplemented ■ What its special features are ■ How many volumes or units it has and the interrelationship among them You obtain this information through techniques (a) to (f) above.
8. In your research memo, you rarely cite a loose-leaf service unless the material you found there does not exist elsewhere. Use the loose-leaf service mainly as background research and as a search tool for leads to find cases, statutes, regulations, etc.—in other words, to find primary authority.

6. Legal Periodical Literature

Legal periodical literature consists of the following:

- Lead articles and comments written by individuals who have extensively re-searched a topic
- Case notes that summarize and comment on important court opinions
- Book reviews.

Most periodicals are published by law students who are "on law review" or "on the law journal" at their law school. There are hundreds of legal periodicals containing a wealth of information for the researcher.

How can you locate legal periodical literature on point? What index systems exist for the hundreds of periodicals and the tens of thousands of articles, case notes, comments, and other material in them? There are three major index systems:

- Index to Legal Periodicals (ILP), published by H. W. Wilson Co.
- Current Law Index (CLI), published by Information Access Corporation
- Legal Resource Index (LRI), published by Information Access Corporation

While all three systems are extensive, CLI and LRI are more comprehensive than ILP. Comprehensiveness is determined by the number of periodicals in-dexed. The benefit of a comprehensive index is that you obtain access to many periodicals. Unfortunately, most law libraries will *not* have all the periodicals mentioned in the index. You may be obtaining cites to periodicals that your library does not have. If so, you need to check other libraries in the area.

(a) Index to Legal Periodicals (ILP)

- The ILP first comes out in pamphlets that are later consolidated (i.e., cumu-lated) into bound volumes.
- You must check each ILP pamphlet and each ILP bound volume for whatever years you want.
- ILP regularly adds new periodicals to be indexed.
- Every ILP pamphlet and bound volume has four indexes:
  - (1) A subject-and-author index
  - (2) A table of cases commented on
  - (3) A table of statutes commented on (added recently)
  - (4) A book review index
- There are abbreviations tables at the beginning of every pamphlet and bound volume.
- The "subject" portion of the subject-and-author index is easy to use; you are given full bibliographic references to periodical literature under the subjects relevant to your research topics.
- Beginning in 1983, the "author" portion of the subject-and-author index also has full bibliographic references to periodical literature by that author. Prior to 1983, however, the use of the "author" portion was more complex. If you know the name of an author but not the title of his or her article, you look for that author's name in the subject-and-author index. Under that

name you will find one or more subjects and capital letters in parentheses after the topics. Go to those subjects in the subject-and-author index. Under those subjects, look for articles beginning with the capital letters you initially found in parentheses until you locate the article by the author you want. This awkward procedure applies only to pre-1983 ILP volumes.

■ Toward the end of every ILP pamphlet and bound volume there is a Table of Cases Commented Upon. Suppose that elsewhere in your research you come across an important case, and you now want to know if that case was ever commented on (i.e., noted) in the legal periodicals. Go to the ILP pamphlet or bound volume that covers the year of the case and check the Table of Cases Commented Upon.

■ The Table of Statutes Commented Upon will tell you where you can find periodical literature analyzing certain statutes.

■ At the end of every pamphlet and bound ILP volume there is a book review index. If you are looking for a review of a law book you have come across elsewhere in your research, go to the ILP pamphlet or bound volume that covers the year of publication of the book for which you are seeking reviews.

■ ILP is also available:

    (1) On WILSONLINE, the publisher's online research system

    (2) On WILSONDISC, a CD-ROM system (page 495)

    (3) On WESTLAW

    (4) On LEXIS

(b) Current Law Index (CLI)

■ The CLI first comes out in pamphlets that are later consolidated (i.e., cumulated) into bound volumes.

■ CLI indexes more periodical literature than ILP.

■ CLI regularly adds new periodicals to be indexed.

- Check all current pamphlets and all annual issues for the years you want.
- There are four indexes within each CLI unit:
  - A subject index
  - An author-title index
  - A table of cases
  - A table of statutes
- There are abbreviation tables at the beginning of every CLI unit.
- The subject index gives full citations to periodicals under a topic and under an author's name.
- Book reviews are included under the author-title index along with cites to periodical literature by the authors.
- The table of cases is valuable if you already know the name of a case located elsewhere in your research. To find out if that case was commented on, check the table of cases in the CLI unit that covers the year of the case.
- The table of statutes is equally valuable. If you already have the name of a statute from your other research (such as Atomic Energy Act; California Fair Employment Practices Act), look for the name of that statute in the table of statutes for the CLI unit that covers the approximate time the statute was passed.

- The CLI began in 1980; it does not index periodicals prior to this date. The ILP must be used for this period.

(c) Legal Resource Index (LRI)

- LRI provides the same material as CLI; they are both published by Information Access Corporation.
- LRI can be used in several ways:
  - On microfilm with a special viewer machine (see photo below)
  - On LegalTrac, a computer using CD-ROM (page 495)
  - On WESTLAW
  - On LEXIS

Other Index Systems.

A number of other periodical index systems exist:

- Index to Federal Tax Articles
- Index to Foreign Legal Periodicals
- Index to Canadian Legal Periodical Literature
- Jones-Chipman Index to Legal Periodical Literature (covering periodical literature up to 1937 only)
- Index Medicus (covers medical periodicals—available in medical libraries)
- MEDLINE (a computer search system for medical periodicals—available in medical libraries)

Checklist #6

Checklist for Finding Legal Periodical Literature
1. Use legal periodical literature for background research and for leads to primary authority, particularly through the extensive footnotes in this literature. Scholarly articles can also be cited in your research memo.
2. There are three major index systems: Index to Legal Periodicals (ILP), Current Law Index (CLI), and Legal Resource Index (LRI).
3. The CARTWHEEL will help you locate material in these index systems.
4. Within ILP there are separate indexes. Within CLI and LRI there are also separate indexes. You should become familiar with all these internal index features.
5. Start with the subject headings index within ILP, CLI, and LRI.
6. Identify the name and date of every important case that you have found in your research thus far. Go to the table of cases in ILP, in CLI, and in LRI to find out if there is any periodical literature that has commented on that case. (Go to the ILP, CLI, and LRI units that would cover the year the case was decided. To be safe, also check their units for two years after the date of the case.)
7. If you are researching a statute, find out if there is any periodical literature that has commented on the statute. This is done in two ways: **(a)** Check the table of statutes in ILP, CLI, and LRI. **(b)** Break your statute down into its major topics. Check these topics in the subject indexes of ILP, CLI, and LRI to see if any periodical literature has been written on these topics.
8. If you have the name of an author who is known for writing on a particular topic, you can also check for literature written by that author under his or her name in ILP, CLI, and LRI.
9. Ask library staff members if the library has any other indexes to legal periodical literature, particularly in specialty areas of the law.
10. It is possible to shepardize some legal periodical literature. If you want to know whether the periodical article, note, or comment was ever mentioned in a court opinion, go to *Shepard's Law Review Citations.*
11. It is possible to search for legal periodical literature online in WESTLAW, LEXIS, and WILSONLINE.

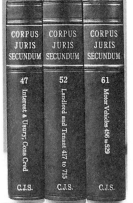

7. Legal Encyclopedias

Here our main concern is using the major national encyclopedias: *American Jurisprudence 2d* (Am. Jur. 2d), and *Corpus Juris Secundum* (C.J.S.).

Checklist #7

Checklist for Using Legal Encyclopedias
1. Use both Am. Jur. 2d and C.J.S. for the following purposes: **(a)** As background research for areas of the law that are new to you **(b)** For leads in their extensive footnotes to primary authority, such as cases, statutes, etc.

Continued

Checklist #7—*Continued*

Checklist for Using Legal Encyclopedias—*Continued*
2. Both legal encyclopedias have multivolume general indexes at the end of their sets. Use the CARTWHEEL to help you locate material in them. In addition to these general indexes, Am. Jur. 2d and C.J.S. have a separate index to many of the individual volumes.
3. There is no table of cases in either Am. Jur. 2d or C.J.S.
4. There is no table of statutes in C.J.S. In Am. Jur. 2d, however, there is a separate volume called *Table of Statutes, Rules, and Regulations Cited.* Check this table if you have found a relevant statute, regulation, or rule of court from your other research that you want to find discussed in Am. Jur. 2d.
5. Am. Jur. 2d is published by Lawyers Co-op. C.J.S. is published by West. Within these legal encyclopedias, the publishers provide cross-references to other research books that they publish. In Am. Jur. 2d, for example, Lawyers Co-op will refer you to annotations in A.L.R., A.L.R.2d, A.L.R.3d, A.L.R.4th, and A.L.R. Fed. In C.J.S., West will refer you to its key number digests.
6. Find out if your library has a *local* encyclopedia that is limited to the law of your state. Among the states with such encyclopedias are California, Florida, Illinois, Maryland, Michigan, New York, Ohio, Pennsylvania, and Texas.

8. Treatises

As mentioned, a treatise is any book written by private individuals (or by public officials writing in a private capacity) on a topic of law. Some treatises are scholarly while others are more practice oriented. The latter are often called hornbooks, handbooks, formbooks, and practice manuals. Treatises give overview summaries of the law, and references to primary authority. There are single-volume treatises such as *Prosser on Torts,* as well as multi-volume treatises such as *Moore's Federal Practice, Collier on Bankruptcy,* etc.

Checklist #8

Checklist for Finding and Using Treatises
1. Always look for treatises on the topics of your research problem. Assume, until you prove to yourself otherwise, that three or four such treatises exist and are relevant to your problem.
2. Treatises are useful for background research, and for leads to primary authority.
3. Many treatises are updated by pocket parts, supplemental volumes, and page inserts if the treatise has a three-ring or post-binding structure.
4. Start your search for treatises in the card catalog. See Checklist #1 on using the catalog.
5. Check with experts in the area of law in which you are interested, e.g., teachers, for recommendations on treatises you should examine. See Checklist #9.
6. If your library has open stacks, find the treatise section (with KF call numbers, for example). Locate the areas containing treatises on your topic. Browse through the shelves in these areas of the stacks to try to find additional treatises. (Some treatises that you need may be on reserve.)
7. Once you have found a treatise, check that author's name in the Index to Legal Periodicals (ILP), the Current Law Index (CLI), and the Legal Resource Index (LRI) to try to find periodical literature on the same topic by this author. You can also use these indexes to see if there are any book reviews on the treatises. (See Checklist #6 on finding legal periodical literature.)

9. Phone and Mail—Speak with the Experts

Don't be reluctant to call recognized experts on the topics of your research. If you can get through to them and if you adopt a sufficiently humble attitude, they may give you leads to important laws and may even discuss the facts of your research problem. Many experts are quite willing to help you free of charge, as long as you are respectful and do not give the impression that you want more than a few moments of their time. You do not ask to come over to spend an afternoon!

Checklist #9

Checklist for Doing Phone and Mail Research
1. Your goal is to contact someone who is an expert in the area of your research problem. You want to try to talk with him or her briefly on the phone. (You can try to contact experts through the mail, but this route is seldom as successful as phone contact.)
2. Do not try to contact an expert until you have first done a substantial amount of research on your own. For instance, you should have already checked the major cases, statutes, regulations, treatises, legal periodical literature, annotations, etc., that are readily available in the library.
3. Prepare the questions you want to ask the expert. Make them short and to the point. For example, "Do you know of any recent case law on the liability of a municipality for . . .?" "Could you give me any leads to literature on the doctrine of promissory estoppel as it applies to . . .?" "Do you know anyone who has done any empirical research on the new EPA regulations whom I could contact?" "Do you know of anyone currently litigating § 307?" Do *not* recite all the facts of the research problem to the expert and say, "What should I do?" If the expert wants more facts from you, let him or her ask you for them. You must create the impression that you want no more than a few moments of the expert's time. If the experts want to give your request more attention, they will let you know.
4. Introduce yourself as a student doing research on a problem. State how you got their name (see guideline below) and then state how grateful you would be if you could ask them a "quick question."
5. Your introductory comments should state how you came across their name and learned of their expertise. For example, say "I read your law review article on . . . ." "I saw your name as an attorney of record in the case of . . . ." "Mr./Ms. _____ told me you were an expert in this area and recommended that I contact you."

6. Where do you find these experts? A number of possibilities exist:
 	
(a) *Special interest groups and associations*
   Contact attorneys within groups and associations such as unions, environmental groups, and business associations. Ask your librarian for lists of such groups and associations, for example, the *Encyclopedia of Associations,* the *Directory of Directories.*
 	
(b) *Government agencies*
   Contact the law departments of the agencies that have something to do with the topics of your research problem.
 	
(c) *Specialty libraries*
   Ask your librarian for lists of libraries, such as the *Directory of Special Libraries and Information Centers.*
 	
(d) *Law professors*
   Ask a librarian if the library has the *AALS Law Teachers Directory,* which lists teachers by name and specialty across the country.
 	
(e) *Attorneys of Record*
   If you have found a recent court opinion on point, the names of the attorneys for the case are printed at the beginning of the opinion (see page 354). Try to

Continued

Checklist #9—*Continued*

Checklist for Doing Phone and Mail Research—***Continued***
obtain the phone number and address of the attorneys in *West's Legal Directory* or *Martindale-Hubbell Law Directory*. These attorneys may be willing to send you a copy of appellate briefs on the case. Also try to find out about ongoing litigation in the courts.   Often you are permitted to go to the court clerk's office and examine pleadings, appellate briefs, etc., on pending cases. Finally, don't forget to check the closed case files of your own office for prior research that has already been done in the same area as your problem.
(f) *Authors of legal periodical literature and of treatises*   Try to contact the author of a treatise or law review article that is relevant to your research. The author's business address can often be found in sources such as the *Law Teacher's Directory, West's Legal Directory, Martindale-Hubbell*, etc.

10. Computers

If you have access to any of the computerized legal research services, ask for a demonstration on how to operate the computer from the librarian or from the company that produces the computer. *CALR* (Computer Assisted Legal Research) is becoming more and more common and essential. An overview of some legal research computer services are listed below. We will return to the major ones in Chapter 13.

WESTLAW® by West Publishing Company

WESTLAW contains a great deal of material. Here are some examples: federal court opinions; state court opinions; United States Code; state statutes; the Code of Federal Regulations; administrative decisions; treatises published by West, Commerce Clearing House, Bureau of National Affairs, Prentice-Hall, and other publishers; legal periodical literature; a *West's Legal Directory* containing the addresses of attorneys throughout the United States; nonlegal data from Dow Jones and DIALOG, etc. You can check the current validity of cases and statutes by using Insta-Cite, QuickCite, Shepard's Preview, and Shepard's online—without leaving the computer. There are also special databases in many areas, such as international law, professional responsibility (ethics), taxation, securities, medicine, etc. Other special databases that can be of unique value to litigators contain the names and addresses of experts in the fields of science, engineering, economics, etc. Each day more material is added to WESTLAW.

LEXIS® by Mead Data Central

LEXIS is also a massive source of *online* data. Examples include: federal and state court opinions; federal and state statutes; Code of Federal Regulations; administrative decisions; treatises, *Martindale-Hubbell Law Directory*; annotations in A.L.R.2d, A.L.R.3d, A.L.R.4th, A.L.R. Fed., and in Lawyers' Edition 2d; special libraries on taxation, insurance, and international law; treatises published by Commerce Clearing House and the Bureau of National Affairs; nonlegal databases covering medicine, patents, current news, etc.; validation data through Shepard's and Auto-Cite, etc. As with WESTLAW, materials are being added to LEXIS regularly.

In Chapter 13 when we discuss databases in general, we will examine WESTLAW and LEXIS in greater detail. In particular, we will cover the critical skill of formulating a *query*, or question to ask WESTLAW and LEXIS.

Auto-Cite and VERALEX by Lawyers Cooperative Publishing Company

Auto-Cite permits you to check the accuracy of a legal citation. It provides parallel cites and cites to other opinions in the same litigation. Auto-Cite also gives you citations to annotations in A.L.R., A.L.R.2d, A.L.R.3d, A.L.R.4th, and A.L.R. Fed. The full text of any of these annotations can be found and read online through two computer services: LEXIS and VERALEX.

WILSONLINE by H.W. Wilson Co.

H.W. Wilson publishes a number of periodical indexes, such as *Index to Legal Periodicals* (ILP) and *Reader's Guide*. If you want to use these indexes online, you can do so through a service called WILSONLINE. (The indexes are also available on CD-ROM as well as on a service called WILSONDISC.)

DIALOG by Dialog Information Services

This online service provides access to a large volume of material, such as the complete text of articles from over 800 newspapers, magazines, newsletters, and trade journals; MEDLINE, a massive index to articles in medical periodicals; the complete text of selected newswires and encyclopedias; psychological abstracts; information on numerous corporations via Dun & Bradstreet, Standard & Poor's, Moody's; employee benefits data via EBIS; patent and trademarks; etc. DIALOG is also available through WESTLAW.

NEXIS by Mead Data Central

NEXIS contains the full text of daily newspapers such as the *New York Times* and the *Los Angeles Times,* numerous magazines and trade journals, newsletters, etc.

 ## Section O. Finding Case Law

In Chapter 7, we covered the structure of a court opinion, the briefing of an opinion, and the application of an opinion to a set of facts. Here our focus is *finding* these opinions in the library—finding case law.

In searching for case law, you will probably find yourself in one or more of the following situations:

- You already have one opinion on point (or close to being on point) and you want to find additional ones.

- You are looking for opinions interpreting a statute, constitution, charter, ordinance, court rule, or regulation that you already have.

- You are starting from square one. You want to find case law when you do not have a case, statute, or other law to begin with. You may be looking for opinions containing common law (judge-made law in the absence of controlling statutory or constitutional law), and you have no such opinions to begin with.

The following search techniques are not necessarily listed in the order in which they should be tried. Your goal is to know how to use all of them. In practice, you can vary the order.

First, a reminder about doing the first level of legal research: background research. You should review the checklist for background research presented in Figure 11.10. While doing this research, you will probably come across laws that will be of help to you on the specific facts of your problem (which is the second level of research). If so, you may already have some case law. You now want to find more.

Techniques for Finding Case Law
When You Already Have One Case on Point

1. *Shepardize the case that you have.* (See Checklist #4a on shepardizing cases, page 569.) In the columns of Shepard's, look for cases that have mentioned your case. Such cases will probably cover similar topics.

2. *Go to the West digests.* There are two ways to do this:

    (a) Go to the table of cases in all the digests covering the court that wrote the case you already have, such as the table of cases in the *American Digest System*. The table of cases will tell you what key topics and numbers your case is digested under in the main volumes of the digest. Find your case digested under those key topics and numbers. Once you have done so, you will probably be able to find other case law under the same key topics and numbers.

    (b) Go to the West reporter that contains the full text of the case you already have. At the beginning of this case in the reporter, find the headnotes and their key topics and numbers. Take the key topics and numbers that are relevant to your problem into the digests of West to find more case law.

    (See Checklist #2 on using digests, page 556.)

3. *Find an annotation.* First identify the main topics or issues in the case you already have. Look up those topics in the *Quick Index* (to find annotations in A.L.R. First), and in the *Index to Annotations* (to find annotations in A.L.R.2d, A.L.R.3d, A.L.R.4th, and A.L.R. Fed.). Other ways to find annotations include shepardizing the case you have and using Auto-Cite. Once you have such an annotation, you will be given extensive citations to more case law. (See Checklist #3 on finding annotations, page 561.)

4. *Find a discussion of your case in the legal periodicals.* Go to the table of cases in the Index of Legal Periodicals (ILP), the Current Law Index (CLI), and the Legal Resource Index (LRI). There you will be told if your case was analyzed (noted) in the periodicals. If so, the discussion may give you additional case law on the same topic. (See Checklist #6 on finding legal periodical literature, page 582.)

5. *Go to Words and Phrases.* Identify the major words or phrases that are dealt with in the case you have. Check the definition of those words and phrases in the multivolume legal dictionary, *Words and Phrases*. By so doing you will be led to other cases defining the same words or phrases.

Now let us assume that you already have a statute and you want case law interpreting that statute. The techniques for doing so (many of which are the same when seeking case law interpreting constitutions, regulations, etc.) are as follows:

Techniques for Finding Case Law Interpreting a Statute

1. *Shepardize the statute that you have.* (See Checklist #4b on shepardizing statutes, page 573.) In the columns of Shepard's, look for cases that have mentioned your statute.

2. *Examine your statute in the statutory code.* At the end of your statute in the statutory code, there are paragraph summaries of cases (often called Notes of Decisions) that have interpreted your statute. Check these summaries in the bound volume of the code, in the pocket part of this volume, and in any supplemental pamphlets at the end of the code. (For federal statutes, the codes to check are U.S.C.A. and U.S.C.S. The U.S.C. will not have such case summaries.)

Continued

Techniques for Finding Case Law Interpreting a Statute—*Continued*

3. *Find an annotation on your statute.* To find out if there is an annotation in A.L.R, A.L.R.2d, etc. that mentions your statute, shepardize that statute. Such annotations are among the "citing materials" of Shepard's. (Also, if the statute is federal, check the Table of Laws, Rules, and Regulations in the last volume of the *Index to Annotations.* See page 559.) Such annotations will probably lead you to more case law on the statute.

4. *Find legal periodical literature on your statute.* There are three ways to do this:

   (a) Shepardize the statute. (See technique 1 above.) Citing material for a statute includes legal periodical literature.

   (b) Check the table of statutes in the Current Law Index (CLI), the Legal Resource Index (LRI), and the Index to Legal Periodicals (ILP).

   (c) Go to the subject indexes in ILP, CLI, and LRI and check the topics of your statute.

5. *Go to loose-leaf services on your statute.* Find out if there is a loose-leaf service on the subject matter of your statute. Such services often give extensive cites to cases on the statute. (See Checklist #5 on loose-leaf services, page 577.)

6. *Go to treatises on your statute.* Most major statutes have treatises on them that contain extensive cites to cases on the statute. (See Checklist #8 on treatises, page 583.)

7. *Shepardize any cases you found through techniques 1–6 above.* You may be led to additional case law on the statute.

Finally, we assume that you are starting from scratch. You are looking for case law and you do not have a starting case or statute with which to begin. You may be looking for common law or for cases interpreting statutes that you have not found yet.

Techniques for Finding Case Law When You Do Not Have a Case or Statute to Begin With

1. *West digests.* Try to find key topics and numbers in the Descriptive Word Indexes (DWI) of the West digests. (See Checklist #2 on using digests of West, page 556.)

2. Annotations. Try to locate annotations through the index systems for A.L.R., A.L.R.2d, A.L.R.3d, A.L.R.4th, and A.L.R. Fed. (See Checklist #3 on finding annotations, page 561.)

3. *Treatises.* Try to find treatises in the card catalog. (See Checklist #8 on finding treatises, page 583.)

4. *Loose-leaf services.* Find out if there are loose-leaf services on the topics of your research. (See Checklist #5 on finding loose-leaf services, page 577.)

5. *Legal periodical literature.* Try to find legal periodical literature in the subject indexes of ILP, CLI, and LRI. (See Checklist #6 on finding legal periodical literature, page 582.)

6. *Legal encyclopedias.* Go to the indexes on Am. Jur. 2d and C.J.S. Try to find discussions in these legal encyclopedias. (See Checklist #7 on using legal encyclopedias, page 582.)

7. *Computers* (page 585).

8. *Phone and mail research.* Find an expert. (See Checklist #9 on doing phone and mail research, page 584.)

Continued

Techniques for Finding Case Law When You Do Not Have a Case or Statute to Begin With—*Continued*
9. *Words and Phrases.* Identify all the major words or phrases from the facts of your research problem. Look up these words or phrases in the multivolume legal dictionary, *Words and Phrases*, which gives case law definitions.
10. *Shepardizing.* If techniques 1–9 lead you to any case law, shepardize what you have found in order to look for more cases. (See Checklist #4a on shepardizing a case, page 569.)

■ P. Reading and Finding Statutes

Reading Statutes

On page 591, there is an example of a statute from a New York statutory code. Here is an explanation of the circled numbers in this excerpt:

① This is the section number of the statute. The mark "§" before "146" means section.

② This is a heading summarizing the main topic of the statute. Section 146 covers who can visit state prisons in New York. This summarization was written by the private publishing company, not by the New York state legislature.

③ Here is the body of the statute written by the legislature.

④ At the end of a statutory section you will often find a reference to session laws (page 571), using abbreviations such as L. (laws), P.L. (Public Law), Stat. (Statutes at Large), etc. Here you are told that in the Laws (L) of 1962, chapter (c) 37, § 3, this statute was amended. The Laws referred to are the session laws. See the Historical Note ⑥ below for a further treatment of this amendment.

⑤ The amendment to § 146 was effective ("eff.") on February 20, 1962. The amendment may have been passed by the legislature on an earlier date, but the data on which it became the law of New York was February 20, 1962.

⑥ The Historical Note provides the reader with some of the legislative history (page 596) of § 146. First, the reader is again told that § 146 was amended in 1962. Note that in the second and third lines of the body of the statute, the title "commissioner of general services" is found. The 1962 amendment simply changed the title from "superintendent of standards and purchase" to "commissioner of general services."

⑦ Also, part of the Historical Note is the "Derivation" section. This tells the reader that the topic of § 146 of the Corrections Law was once contained in § 160 of the Prison Law, which dates back to 1847. In 1929 there was another amendment. The Historical Note was written by the private publisher, not by the New York state legislature.

⑧ The "Cross References" refer the reader to other statutes that cover topics similar to § 146.

⑨ The "Library References" refer the reader to other texts that address the topic of the statute. On the lefthand side, there are two topics, "Prisons" and "Reformatories," each followed by key numbers. The key numbers refer the reader to the digests of West Publishing Company. On the right column there is the abbreviation C.J.S. (*Corpus Juris Secundum*), a legal encyclopedia.

① ②

§ 146. Persons authorized to visit prisons

The following persons shall be authorized to visit at pleasure all state prisons: The governor and lieutenant-governor, commissioner of general services, secretary of state, comptroller and attorney-general, members of the commission of correction, members of the legislature, judges of the court of appeals, supreme court and county judges, district attorneys and every minister of the gospel having charge of a congregation in the town wherein any such prison is situated. No other person not otherwise authorized by law shall be permitted to enter a state prison except under such regulations as the commissioner of correction shall prescribe. The provisions of this section shall not apply to such portion of a prison in which prisoners under sentence of death are confined.

③

⑤

As amended L.1962, c. 37, § 3, eff. Feb. 20, 1962.

④

Historical Note

⑥

L.1962, c. 37, § 3, eff. Feb. 20, 1962, substituted "commissioner of general services" for "superintendent of standards and purchase".

⑦

Derivation. Prior to the general amendment of this chapter by L.1929,

c. 243, the subject matter of this section was contained in former Prison Law, § 160; originally derived from R.S., pt. 4, c. 3, tit. 3, § 159, as amended L.1847, c. 460.

Cross References

⑧

Promoting prison contraband, see Penal Law, §§ 205.20, 205.25.

Library References

⑨

Prisons ⟂13.
Reformatories ⟂7.

C.J.S. Prisons §§ 18, 19.
C.J.S. Reformatories §§ 10, 11.

⑩

Notes of Decisions

1. Attorneys

Warden of maximum security prison was justified in requiring that interviews of prisoners by attorney be conducted in presence of guard in room, in view of fact that attorney, who sought to interview 34 inmates in a day and a half, had shown no retainer agreements and had not stated purpose of consultations. Kahn v. La Vallee, 1961, 12 A.D.2d 832, 209 N.Y.S.2d 591.

Supreme court did not have jurisdiction of petition by prisoner to compel prison warden to provide facilities in prison which would not interfere with alleged violation of rights of prisoner to confer in private with his attorney. Mummiani v. La Vallee, 1959, 21 Misc.2d 437, 199 N.Y.S.2d 263, affirmed 12 A.D.2d 832, 209 N.Y.S.2d 591.

Right of prisoners to confer with counsel after conviction is not absolute but is subject to such regulations as commissioner of correction may prescribe, and prisoners were not entitled to confer with their attorney privately within sight, but outside of hearing of a prison guard, when warden insisted on having a guard present in order to insure against any impropriety or infraction of prison rules and regulations during interview. Id.

⑩ The most important research reference is the "Notes of Decisions." It includes a series of paragraphs that briefly summarize every court decision that has interpreted or applied § 146. Of course, the decisions cover cases decided before the book was published. For later decisions, the reader must look to the pocket part of the code volume that contains § 146, and to any supplemental pamphlets at the end of the code. The first decision that you are given is *Kahn v. La Vallee.* Next is *Mummiani v. La Vallee.* At the end of the final paragraph, you will find "Id.," which means that the paragraph refers to the case cited in the immediately preceding paragraph, the *Mummiani* case. (Of course, another way to find later decisions is to shepardize § 146. See Checklist #4b on shepardizing a statute.)

With this perspective of what an annotated statute looks like, we turn to some general guidelines on understanding statutes:

1. Statutory codes are heavily stratified.   A statutory code can contain anywhere from 5 to 150 volumes. If you are unfamiliar with a code, you should examine the first few pages of the first volume. There you will usually find the subject matter arrangement of all the volumes, e.g., "agency," "corrections," "corporations." Different states often have varied labels and categorization schemes.

An individual subject matter in a code may be further broken down into titles, parts, articles, or chapters, which are then broken down into sections and subsections. Here is an example of a possible categorization for the state of "X":

<u>X Code Annotated</u>

Title 1. Corporate Law

Chapter 1. Forming a Corporation

Section 1. Choosing a Corporate Name

Subsection 1(a). Where to File the Name Application

Subsection 1(b). Displaying the Name Certificate

Subsection 1(c). Changing the Corporate Name

Section 2 . . . .

Chapter 2 . . . .

Etc.

Note again, however, that each jurisdiction may adopt its own classification terminology. What is called a chapter in one state may be called a title in another.

You also need to be sensitive to the internal context of a particular statutory section. A section is often a sub-sub-subunit of larger units.

Example: Examine § 1183 in Figure 11.18. § 1183 is within Part II which is within Subchapter II, which is within chapter 12, which is within title 8.

As indicated earlier, a legislature may completely revise its labeling system (page 542). What was once "Prison Law," for example, may now fall under the topic heading of "Correction Law." What was once section 73(b) of "Corporations Law" may now be section 13(f) of the "Business and Professions Law." If such a reordering has occurred, you should be able to find out about it either in a transfer table at the beginning of one of the code volumes or in the Historical Note at the bottom of the section.

2. A common sequence of statutes on administrative agencies.   Statutes are carried out mainly by administrative agencies. The agency may be a grant-making or service agency (such as the Social Security Administration) or a regulatory agency (such as the Federal Power Commission, the State Utilities Com-

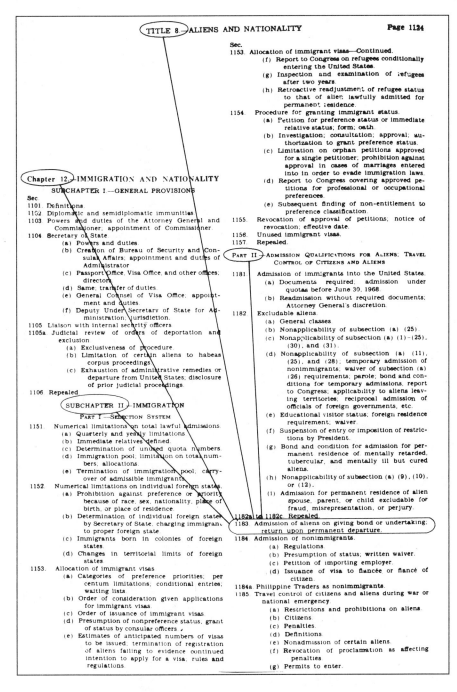

FIGURE 11.18

Sections, Parts, Subchapters, Chapters, and Titles in a Statutory Code

mission, etc.). Statutes that cover agencies are sometimes organized in the following sequence:

■ The agency is created and named.

■ The major words and phrases used in this cluster of statutes are defined.

■ The administrators of the agency are given titles and powers.

■ The budgetary process of the agency is specified.

- The method by which the public first comes into contact with the agency is established, such as applying for the benefits or services of the agency.
- The way in which the agency must act when a citizen complains about the agency's actions is established.
- How the agency must go about terminating a citizen from its services is established.
- The way in which a citizen can appeal to a court, if not satisfied with the way the agency handled his or her complaint, is established.

3. *All statutes must be based on some provision in the Constitution that gives the legislature the power to pass the statute.* Legislatures have no power to legislate without constitutional authorization. The authorization may be the general constitutional provision vesting all legislative powers in the legislature, or, more often, it will be a specific constitutional provision such as the authority to raise revenue for designated purposes.

4. *Statutory language tends to be unclear.* Seldom, if ever, is it absolutely clear what a statute means or how it applies to a given set of facts. Because of this, statutory language regularly requires close scrutiny and interpretation.

5. *Statutes are to be read line by line, pronoun by pronoun, punctuation mark by punctuation mark.* Statutes cannot be speed read. They should be read with the same care that you would use if you were translating a foreign language to English. Sentences sometimes appear endless, and there are often so many qualifications and exceptions built into the statute that it appears incomprehensible. Don't despair. The key is perseverance and a willingness to tackle the statute slowly, piece by piece.

6. *Check to see if a statutory unit has a definition section.* At the beginning of a cluster of statutes, look for a definition section. If it exists, the section will define a number of words used in the remaining sections of the unit. Here is an example of such a definition section:

> **§ 31.   Definitions.**—As used in this article, unless the context shall require otherwise, the following terms shall have the meanings ascribed to them by this section:
>
> 1. "State" shall mean and include any state, territory or possession of the United States and the District of Columbia.
>
> 2. "Court" shall mean the family court of the state of New York; when the context requires, it shall mean and include a court of another state defined in and upon which appropriate jurisdiction has been conferred by a substantially similar reciprocal law.
>
> 3. "Child" includes a step child, foster child, child born out of wedlock or legally adopted child and means a child under twenty-one years of age, and a son or daughter twenty-one years of age or older who is unable to maintain himself or herself and is or is likely to become a public charge.
>
> 4. "Dependent" shall mean and include any person who is entitled to support pursuant to this article.

7. *Statutes should be briefed.* Briefing a statute simply means outlining it and breaking it down into its elements (page 347). The following are some of the questions that you should ask yourself in briefing a statute:

(a) What is the citation (the name of the statutory code, volume of the code, number of the section, date of the code edition)?

(b) To whom is the statute addressed? (To everybody? To the director of an agency? To citizens who want to do certain things?) Who is the audience?

(c) Does the statute make reference to other statutes? (If so, then the statute may be unintelligible to you unless you also study the other statutes.)

(d) Is there a condition that will make the statute operative? (Very often the statute will have a "whenever" or a "wherever" clause indicating that whenever or wherever a certain set of facts occur, the statute will be applied; without the occurrence of such facts, the statute may not apply.)

(e) What or whom does the statute specifically *include* in its provisions?

(f) What or whom does the statute specifically *exclude* from its provisions?

(g) Is the statute mandatory or discretionary? (Does it say or imply that someone "must" or "shall" do something, or does it say or imply that someone "may" or "can" do something?)

Finding Statutes

Techniques for Finding Statutes
1. Go to the statutory code in which you are interested. Some states have more than one statutory code. For federal statutes, there is the United States Code (U.S.C.), the United States Code Annotated (U.S.C.A.), and the United States Code Service (U.S.C.S.). Know how to use all available statutory codes that cover the same set of statutes. While they contain the same statutes, the index and research features may differ.
2. Read the explanation or preface pages at the beginning of the first volume of the statutory code. Also read the comparable pages at the beginning of the Shepard's volumes that will enable you to shepardize statutes in that code. These pages can be very helpful in explaining the structure of the code, particularly if there have been new editions, revisions, or renumberings.
3. Most statutory codes have general indexes at the end of the set as well as individual indexes for separate volumes. Use the CARTWHEEL to help you use these indexes. Also check any tables of contents that exist. Some statutes have popular names, such as the Civil Rights Act of 1964. If you know the popular name of a statute, you can find it in the statutory code through a Popular Name Table that often exists within the code itself.
4. While reading one statute in the code, you may be given a cross-reference to another statute within the same code. Check out these cross-references.
5. Loose-leaf services. Find out if there is a loose-leaf service on the topics of your research. Such services will give extensive references to applicable statutes. (See Checklist #5 on finding and using loose-leaf services, page 577.)
6. Treatises. Find out if there are treatises on the topics of your research. Such treatises will often give extensive references to applicable statutes. (See Checklist #8 on finding and using treatises, page 583.)
7. Legal periodical literature. Consult the Index to Legal Periodicals (ILP), the Current Law Index (CLI), and the Legal Resource Index (LRI). Use these indexes to locate periodical literature on the topics of your research. This literature will often give extensive references to applicable statutes. (See Checklist #6 on finding legal periodical literature, page 582.)
8. Annotations. Use the index systems for A.L.R., A.L.R.2d, A.L.R.3d, A.L.R.4th, and A.L.R. Fed. to help you locate annotations. Annotations will sometimes refer you to statutes—particularly in A.L.R. Fed. for federal statutes. (See Checklist #3 on finding and updating annotations, page 561.)

Continued

Techniques for Finding Statutes—*Continued*
9. Legal encyclopedias. Occasionally, legal encyclopedias such as Am.Jur.2d and C.J.S. will give you references to statutes. (See Checklist #7 for using legal encyclopedias, page 582.)
10. Computers. (see page 585.)
11. Phone and mail research. Try to find an expert. (See Checklist #9 on doing phone and mail research, page 584.)
12. For every federal statute that you find, determine whether there are federal regulations on that statute. To find out, check the Parallel Table of Authorities and Rules in the *C.F.R Index and Finding Aids* volume.
13. Shepardize any statute that you locate through techniques 1–11 above. (See Checklist #4b on shepardizing a statute, page 573.)
14. Check the legislative history of important statutes (page 596).
15. Also update any statute that you find in the statutory code by checking the pocket part of the volume you are using, supplementary pamphlets at the end of the code, bound supplement volumes, etc.
16. Occasionally in your research you will come across a statute that is cited in its session law form (page 571). To find this statute in the statutory code, you must translate the session law cite into the codified cite. This is done by trying to find transfer tables in the statutory code. For federal statutes, a session law or Statute at Large cite is translated into a U.S.C./U.S.C.A./U.S.C.S. cite by: **(a)** Checking Table III in the Tables volume of U.S.C./U.S.C.A./U.S.C.S. **(b)** Checking Table 2 in *U.S. Code Congressional & Administrative News* Some session laws, however, are never printed in the statutory code. Hence there is no codified cite for such statutes. You must go directly to the session laws in the library—if the library has them. (For federal statutes, the session laws are in *United States Statutes at Large,* page 516.) It is also possible to shepardize session laws that are not codified, page 571.

 ## Section Q. Legislative History

In Chapter 6, we examined the six stages of the legislative process during which a bill becomes law. The documents and events of this process constitute the *legislative history* of a statute. Here we consider two themes:

- Why researchers search for legislative history
- Finding legislative history

1. Why Search for Legislative History: Advocacy Objectives

Problem: In 1975 the state legislature enacts the Liquor Control Act. Section 33 of this Act provides that "Liquor shall not be sold on Sunday or on any day on which a local, state, or federal election is being held." The Fairfax Country Club claims that § 33 does not apply to the sale of liquor on Sunday or on election day *by membership clubs;* it applies only to bars that provide service to any customers that come in off the street. The question, therefore, is whether the legislature intended to include membership clubs within the restrictions of § 33. The state liquor board says that it did. The Fairfax Country Club argues that it did not.

How can the legislative history of § 33 help resolve this controversy? An advocate has two objectives while researching the legislative history of a statute:

- To determine whether the specific facts currently in controversy were ever discussed by the legislature while it was considering the proposed statute, and

- To determine the broad or narrow purpose that prompted the legislature to enact the statute and to assess whether this purpose sheds any light on the specific facts currently in controversy

For example, when the legislature was considering § 33, was there any mention of country or membership clubs in the governor's message, in committee reports, in floor debates, etc.? If so, what was said about them? What was said about the purpose of § 33? Why was it enacted? What evil or mischief was it designed to combat? Was the legislature opposed to liquor on moral grounds? Did it want to reduce rowdyism that comes from the overuse of liquor? Did it want to encourage citizens to go to church on Sunday and to vote on election day? Were there complaints made to the legislature about the use of liquor by certain groups in the community? If so, what groups? Answers to such questions might be helpful in formulating arguments on the meaning and scope of § 33. The advocate for the Fairfax Country Club will try to demonstrate that the legislature had a narrow objective when it enacted § 33: to prevent neighborhood rowdyism at establishments that serve only liquor. The legislature, therefore, was not trying to regulate the more moderate kind of drinking that normally takes place at membership clubs where food and liquor are often served together. The opponent, on the other hand, will argue that the legislature had a broader purpose in enacting § 33: to decrease the consumption of liquor by all citizens on certain days. The legislature, therefore, did not intend to exclude drinking at a membership club.

2. Finding Legislative History

In tracing legislative history, you are looking for leads to the documents of this history, such as bills, hearing transcripts, proposed amendments, and committee reports. Unfortunately, it is often very difficult to trace the legislative history of *state* statutes. The documents are sometimes poorly preserved, if at all.

Techniques for Tracing the Legislative History of State Statutes
1. Examine the historical data beneath the statute in the statutory code (page 591). Amendments are usually listed there.
2. For an overview of codification information about your state, check the introductory pages in the first volume of the statutory code, or the beginning of the volume where your statute is found, or the beginning of the Shepard's volume that will enable you to shepardize the statutes of that state.
3. Ask your librarian if there is a book (sometimes called a legislative service) that covers your state legislature. If one exists, it will give the bill numbers of statutes, proposed amendments, names of committees that considered the statute, etc. If such a text does not exist for your state, ask the librarian how someone finds the legislative history of a state statute in your state.

Continued

**Techniques for Tracing the Legislative History
of State Statutes—*Continued***

4. Contact the committees of both houses of the state legislature that considered the bill. Your local state representative or state senator might be able to help you identify these committees. If your statute is not too old, staff members on these committees may be able to give you leads to the legislative history of the statute. Ask if any committee reports were written. Ask about amendments, etc.

5. Ask your librarian (or a local politician) if there is a law revision commission for your state. If so, contact it for leads.

6. Is there a state law library in your area? If so, contact it for leads.

7. Check the law library and drafting office of the state legislature for leads.

8. Cases interpreting the statute sometimes give the legislative history of the statute, or portions of it. To find cases interpreting a statute, check the Notes of Decisions after the statute in the statutory code (page 591), shepardize the statute, etc. (See also Checklist #4b on shepardizing a statute, page 573.)

9. You may also find leads to the legislative history of a statute in legal periodical literature on the statute (see Checklist #6, page 582), in annotations on the statute (see Checklist #3, page 561), in treatises on the statute (see Checklist #8, page 583), and in loose-leaf services on the statute (see Checklist #5, page 577). Phone and mail research might also provide some leads (see Checklist #9, page 584).

It is easier to trace the legislative history of a *federal* statute, since the documents are generally more available.

Techniques for Tracing the Legislative History of a Federal Statute

1. Examine the historical data at the end of the statute in the United States Code (U.S.C.), in the United States Code Annotated (U.S.C.A.), and in the United States Code Service (U.S.C.S.).

2. You will also find the PL number (Public Law number) of the statute at the end of the statute in U.S.C./U.S.C.A./U.S.C.S. This PL number will be important for tracing legislative history. (Note that each amendment to a statute will have its own PL number.)

3. Step one in tracing the legislative history of a federal statute is to find out if the history has already been compiled by someone else. Ask your librarian. The Library of Congress compiles legislative histories. If the statute deals with a particular federal agency, check with the library or law department of that agency in Washington, D.C., or in the regional office nearest you to see if it has compiled the legislative history. Also check with special interest groups or associations that are directly affected by the statute. They may have compiled the legislative history, which might be available to you. (One question you can ask through phone and mail research is whether the expert knows if anyone has compiled the legislative history of the statute. See Checklist #9 on doing phone and mail research, page 584.) Ask your librarian if there is a *Union List of Legislative Histories* for your area. This list tells you what area libraries have compiled legislative histories on federal statutes.

4. The following texts are useful in tracing the legislative history of federal statutes:

- *U.S. Code Congressional & Administrative News* (see table 4)
- *CCH Congressional Index*
- *Congressional Information Service (CIS) Annual*
- Information Handling Service (legislative histories on microfiche)
- *Digest of Public General Bills and Resolutions*

Continued

Techniques for Tracing the Legislative History of a Federal Statute—*Continued*

- *Congressional Record* (see Index and the History of Bills and Resolutions for House and Senate)
- House and Senate Journals
- *Congressional Quarterly*
- *Congressional Monitor*
- *Monthly Catalog of U.S. Documents*

5. Contact both committees of Congress that considered the legislation. Ask for leads to legislative history. (They may be able to send you committee reports, hearing transcripts, etc.)

6. Cases interpreting the statute sometimes give the legislative history of the statute. To find cases interpreting the statute, check the notes of decisions after the statute in the U.S.C.A. and in the U.S.C.S. Also, shepardize the statute (see Checklist #4b on shepardizing a statute, page 573).

7. Find out if there is an annotation on the statute. See the "Table of Laws, Rules, and Regulations" in the last volume of *Index to Annotations*. (See Checklist #3 on finding and updating annotations, page 561.)

8. You may also find leads to the legislative history of a statute in legal periodical literature (see Checklist #6, page 582), in treatises on the statute (see Checklist #8, page 583), in loose-leaf services on the statute (see Checklist #5, page 577), and through phone and mail research (see Checklist #9, page 584).

9. To try to find a discussion of your statute in Am.Jur.2d, a legal encyclopedia, check a separate volume called *Table of Statutes, Rules, and Regulations Cited.*

10. Examine your statute in its session law form in *United States Statutes at Large* for possible leads (page 516).

 ## Section R. Monitoring Proposed Legislation

Occasionally you will be asked to *monitor* a bill currently before the legislature that has relevance to the caseload of the law office where you work. To monitor a bill means to determine its current status in the legislature and to keep track of all the forces that are trying to enact, defeat, or modify the bill.

Techniques for Monitoring Proposed Legislation

1. Begin with the legislature. Find out what committee in each house of the legislature (often called the Senate and House) is considering the proposed legislation. Also determine whether there are more than two committees considering the entire bill or portions of it.

2. Ask committee staff members to send you copies of the bill in its originally proposed form and in its amended forms.

3. Determine whether the committees considering the proposed legislation have written any reports on it and, if so, whether copies are available.

4. Determine whether any hearings have been scheduled by the committees on the bill. If so, try to attend. For hearings already conducted, see if they have been transcribed (a word-for-word recording).

Continued

Techniques for Monitoring Proposed Legislation—*Continued*

5. Find out the names of people in the legislature who are working on the bill: legislators "pushing" the bill, legislators opposed to it, staff members of the individual legislators working on the bill, and staff members of the committees working on the bill. Ask for copies of any position papers or statements.

6. The local bar association may have taken a position on the bill. Call the association. Find out what committee of the bar is involved with the subject matter of the bill. This committee may have written a report on the position of the bar on the bill. If so, try to obtain a copy.

7. Is there an administrative agency of the government involved with the bill? Identify the agency with jurisdiction over the subject matter of the bill. Find out who in the agency is working on the bill and whether any written reports of the agency are available. Determine whether the agency has a Legislative Liaison Office.

8. Who else is lobbying for or against the bill? What organizations are interested in it? Find out if they have taken any written positions.

9. What precipitated consideration of the bill by the legislature? Was there a court opinion that prompted the legislative action? If so, you should know what the opinion said.

10. Are any other legislatures in the country contemplating similar legislation? Some of the ways of finding out include the following:

    (a) Look for legal periodical literature on the subject matter of the bill (see Checklist #6, page 582).

    (b) Check loose-leaf services, if any, covering the subject matter of the bill (see Checklist #5, page 577) — these services often cover proposed legislation in the various legislatures.

    (c) Check treatises on the area (see Checklist #8, page 583).

    (d) Organizations such as bar associations, public interest groups, business associations, etc. often assign staff members to perform state-by-state research on what the legislatures are doing. Such organizations may be willing to share this research with you.

    (e) Find out if there is a Council of State Governments in your area. It may have done the same research mentioned in (d) above.

    (f) Contact an expert for leads to what other legislatures are doing (see Checklist #9, page 584).

■ Section S. Reading and Finding Constitutional Law

Reading Constitutional Law

The constitution sets out the fundamental ground rules for the conduct of the government in the geographical area it covers. It defines the branches of the government, establishes basic rights of citizens, and covers matters that the framers considered important enough (such as limitations on the power to tax) to be included in the constitution. The United States Constitution does this for the federal government, and the state constitution does it for the state government. In reading constitutional law, a number of guidelines can be helpful:

1. Thumb through the headings of the constitution or glance through the table of contents. How is the document organized? What subjects did the framers want covered by the constitution? A quick scanning of the section headings or table of contents is a good way to obtain an overview of the structure of the text.

2. *The critical sections or articles are those that establish and define the powers of the legislative, judicial, and executive branches of government in the geographic area covered by the Constitution.*   Who passes, interprets, and executes the law? For the United States Constitution, "all legislative Powers granted herein shall be vested in a Congress" (art. I, § 1); "the judicial Power of the United States, shall be vested in one supreme Court, and in such inferior Courts as the Congress may from time to time ordain and establish" (art. III, § 1); and "the executive Power shall be vested in a President of the United States of America" (art. II, § 1). The exact scope of these powers, as enunciated elsewhere in the Constitution, has been and continues to be an arena of constant controversy and litigation.

3. *The amendments to the Constitution change or add to the body of the text.*   The main vehicle for changing the constitution is the amendment process, which itself is defined in the constitution. Some constitutions, for example, can be amended by a vote of the people in a general election. A condition for most amendments is that they must be approved by one or more sessions of the legislature. Constitutional amendments usually appear at the end of the document.

4. *Constitutions are written in very broad terms.*   There are, of course, exceptions to this, particularly with respect to the constitutions of local governments. In the main, however, a common characteristic of constitutional provisions is their broad language. How would you interpret the following section?

> Congress shall make no laws respecting an establishment of religion, or prohibiting the free exercise thereof; or abridging the freedom of speech, or of the press; or of the right of the people to assemble, and to petition the Government for a redress of grievances.

How many words in this provision do you *not* understand? What is an "establishment?" If the school board requires a "moment of silence" at the beginning of each day, is the school board establishing a religion? What does "abridging" mean? If a government official leaks secret documents to the press, and the government tries to sue the press to prevent the publication of the documents, has the "freedom" of the press been abridged? If the people have a right to "assemble," could the government pass a law prohibiting all gatherings of three or more people at any place within one thousand yards of the White House gates? The questions arising from the interpretation of constitutional law are endless; tens of thousands of court opinions exist on questions such as these. The broader the language, the more ambiguous it is, and therefore the greater the need for interpretation.

5. *A central question for the interpreter of constitutional law is, what meaning did the authors intend?*   Common sense dictates that when language is ambiguous, the ambiguity may be resolved in part by attempting to determine what the author of the language intended by it. What was the author's meaning? In what context was the author writing? Does the context shed any light on what any light on what was meant? This kind of analysis is fundamental to legal reasoning whether the document is a constitution, a statute, a regulation, or a case. It is particularly difficult to do, however, for a constitution written over a hundred years ago.

Finding Constitutional Law

Techniques for Finding Constitutional Law
1. Start with the text of the constitution itself. It is usually found at the beginning of the statutory code of the jurisdiction. (The federal Constitution is in U.S.C./U.S.C.A./U.S.C.S.).
2. Use the CARTWHEEL to help you use the general index of the statutory code and the separate index for the constitution itself. Also check the table of contents material for the constitution in the statutory code.
3. Following the text of individual constitutional provisions there are often Notes of Decisions containing summaries of cases interpreting the constitution. Some of these notes can run hundreds of pages. Check the separate index material for these notes.
4. Shepardize the constitutional provision. The set of Shepard's to use is the same set you use for shepardizing a statute. (See Checklist #4b on shepardizing a statute.)
5. Annotations. Find annotations in A.L.R., A.L.R.2d, etc. on the constitutional provisions in which you are interested. (See Checklist #3 on finding and updating annotations, page 561.)
6. Digests. Go to the *United States Supreme Court Digest* (West) (page 500). Also use the various digests of West that cover other jurisdictions. (The *American Digest System,* of course, covers all jurisdictions.) Use the Descriptive Word Index (DWI) of a digest to locate key topics and numbers on point. (See Checklist #2 on using West digests, page 556.) (For cases on the U.S. Constitution, you can also go to the non-West digest—the *United States Supreme Court Digest, Lawyers Ed.,* page 492.)
7. Treatises. Find treatises on the entire constitution or on the specific portions of the constitution in which you are interested. (See Checklist #8 on finding treatises, page 583.)
8. Legal periodical literature. Go to the three indexes to legal periodical literature: ILP, CLI, and LRI. Use them to help you locate periodical literature on the constitution. (See Checklist #6 on finding legal periodical literature, page 582.)
9. Loose-leaf services. Find out if there are loose-leaf services on the area of the constitution in which you are interested. (See Checklist #5 on loose-leaf services, page 577.)
10. Phone and mail research. Contact an expert. (See Checklist #9 on phone and mail research, page 584.)
11. *Words and Phrases.* Identify specific words or phrases within the constitutional provision you are examining. Find court definitions of these words or phrases in the multi-volume legal dictionary, *Words and Phrases.*
12. Legal encyclopedias. Find discussions of constitutional law in Am.Jur.2d and in C.J.S. (See Checklist #7 on legal encyclopedias, page 582.)
13. Shepardize every case you found that interprets the constitution. (See Checklist #4a on shepardizing a case, page 569.)

■ Section T. Finding Administrative Law

A regulation is an official rule or law of an administrative agency which explains or carries out the statutes and executive orders that govern the agency.

There are many agencies writing regulations, but few of them have coherent systems of organizing and distributing the regulations. A major exception is the federal agencies whose regulations are first published in the *Federal Register;* many are then codified in the *Code of Federal Regulations.*

Normally an agency does not have the power to write regulations unless it has specific statutory authority to do so. An examination of the statute giving the agency this authority can be helpful in understanding the regulations themselves. In theory, the legislature in its statutes sets out the purpose of the agency and defines its overall policies, but leaves to the agency (through its regulations) the task of filling in the specifics of administration. Regulations, therefore, tend to be very detailed.

The other major kind of administrative law is the administrative decision, which is a written resolution of controversies brought before the administrative agency. Not many agencies publish their decisions in any systematic order; some agencies do not publish them at all. Regulatory agencies, such as the Federal Communications Commission and state environmental agencies, often do a better job at publishing their decisions than other agencies.

Techniques for Finding Administrative Law

1. Start with the agency itself. Call or visit the agency. There may be a regional or district office near you. Contact the library, the law department, or the public information section. Ask for a list of the publications of the agency, such as regulations, decisions, annual reports. Also ask where these materials are located. Find out if you can come to the agency and use the materials. Ask about brochures describing the agency's functions, which can be sent to you.

2. Whenever an agency official is reluctant to let you have access to any publications of the agency, you may have to do separate research to find out whether you are entitled to access—under the federal Freedom of Information Act and its state equivalents, for example.

3. Many federal administrative regulations are printed in the *Code of Federal Regulations* (C.F.R.), which are usually printed first in their proposed form in the *Federal Register* before they are enacted by the agency. The C.F.R. comes out in a new edition every year. There are four main ways to locate regulations in the C.F.R.:

    (a) The *C.F.R. Index and Finding Aids* volume. This is a single-volume pamphlet that is reissued every year.

    (b) The *Index to the Code of Federal Regulations* published by Congressional Information Service (CIS).

    (c) The *Code of Federal Regulations Index* published by R. R. Bowker.

    (d) Loose-leaf services. As indicated earlier, there are numerous loose-leaf services covering many federal agencies and some state agencies. These services usually give extensive references to administrative regulations and decisions. (See Checklist #5, page 577.)

    Also check the monthly and annual indexes within the Federal Register.

       If you find no federal regulations on point in the C.F.R. or in the Federal Register, you should check whether the agency has regulations, rules, bulletins, etc., that are published elsewhere. (See technique 1.)

4. Once you have found a federal regulation on point in the C.F.R., do the following:

    (a) Shepardize the regulation. (See Checklist #4c on shepardizing a regulation, page 575.)

    (b) Find the statute that is the authority for that regulation. Read this statute in U.S.C./ U.S.C.A./U.S.C.S. Make sure the regulation does not contradict, go beyond the scope of, or otherwise violate the statute that the regulation is supposed to implement. There are two ways to find the statutory authority of a regulation:

Continued

Techniques for Finding Administrative Law—*Continued*

- Look for an "Authority" reference beneath the specific regulation in C.F.R. *or* at the beginning of the cluster of regulations of which your regulation is a part.
- Check the Parallel Table of Authorities and Rules (Table II) in a volume called *Index and Finding Aids to Code of Federal Regulations,* published by Lawyer's Co-op.

(c) Once you have found a regulation in the C.F.R., you must find out if the regulation has been *affected* in any way (changed, added to, renumbered) by subsequent material printed in the *Federal Register.* This is done by checking your C.F.R. cite in:

- The monthly LSA pamphlet (List of Sections Affected).
- The lists of "CFR Parts Affected" in the daily *Federal Register* from the date of the LSA pamphlet to the current date

The LSA pamphlet and the "CFR Parts Affected" will tell you what pages of the *Federal Register* contain material that affects your regulation in the C.F.R. (You need to do this only until the next annual edition of the C.F.R. comes out, since anything affecting the regulation during the preceding year will be incorporated in the next edition of C.F.R.)

(d) Find out if there is an annotation on your regulation. Shepardize the regulation. Annotations in A.L.R., A.L.R.2d etc. are among the "citing materials" of Shepard's. Also, check the Table of Laws, Rules, and Regulations in the last volume of the *Index to Annotations* (page 559.)

---

5. State administrative agency regulations are much more difficult to find and update. Very few states have an administrative code similar to the C.F.R. For most state agencies, you must check with your law library and with the agency itself (see technique 1 above) on how the regulations are printed, found, and updated.

---

6. When federal or state administrative *decisions* are printed, they will often be found in separate volumes for each agency. Also check loose-leaf services that cover a particular agency. (See Checklist #5, page 577.)

---

7. The *Federal Register* and the C.F.R. can also be found on WESTLAW and LEXIS.

■ Section U. Finding Local Law

Find out if there is a municipal code for your city or county containing local charters, ordinances, etc. Many charters are also printed in the state's statutory code. Check with your law librarian. Also call city hall, the city council, or the county commissioner's office. Speak with the public information officer or the law department. Ask about the local publications of your city or county. What is printed? Where is it found? How often is it printed? How is it updated?

The following are other items to check:

- Legal periodical literature on local issues such as zoning, municipal bonds, etc. (see Checklist #6 on legal periodical literature, page 582).
- The Shepard's volumes for a particular state will enable you to shepardize local charters and ordinances.
- Digests can be used to find case law on charters and ordinances (see Checklist #2 on digests, page 556).
- Annotations on local law in A.L.R., A.L.R.2d, A.L.R.3d, A.L.R.4th, and A.L.R. Fed (see Checklist #3 on annotations, page 561).
- Treatises on local law (see Checklist #8 on treatises, page 583).

- Am.Jur.2d and C.J.S. discussions on local law (see Checklist #7 on legal encyclopedias, page 582).

- Loose-leaf services cover aspects of local law (see Checklist #5 on loose-leaf services, page 577).

- Phone and mail research; contact an expert (see Checklist #9 on phone and mail research, page 584).

- *Ordinance Law Annotations* (published by Shepard's) summarizes court opinions that have interpreted ordinances.

Section V. Finding Rules of Court

You must always check the rules of court governing practice and procedure before a *particular* court. These rules will tell you how to file a request for an extension of time, the number of days a defendant has to answer a complaint, the format of a complaint or appellate brief, etc.

Techniques for Finding Rules of Court

Rules of Court for State Courts:

- Check your state statutory code for the text of the rules.

- Ask your librarian if there is a service company that publishes an updated edition of state rules of court.

- Find out if the court itself publishes its own rules.

- Shepardize rules of court in the same set of Shepard's you use to shepardize a statute (page 573).

- For case law on the rules of court, check the digests for your state (see Checklist #2 on digests, page 556).

- Check local practice books, formbooks, or other treatises (see Checklist #8 on treatises, page 583).

- Check with an expert (see Checklist #9 on phone and mail research, page 584).

Rules of Court for Federal Courts:

- Check the U.S.C./U.S.C.A./U.S.C.S., such as title 28, title 18 (appendix).

- Shepardize federal rules of court in *United States Citations, Statute Edition* (page 512).

- For case law on rules of court, check the digests, such as *Federal Practice Digest* 4th (see Checklist #2 on digests, page 556).

- Check the Federal Rules Service.

- Check special treatises on the federal rules such as:
  Moore's Federal Practice
  Wright and Miller, *Federal Practice and Procedure*

- Find annotations on the federal rules of court. Check the "Table of Laws, Rules, and Regulations" in the last volume of the *Index to Annotation* (see Checklist #3, page 561).

- Check legal periodical literature on the federal rules of court (see Checklist #6 on legal periodical literature, page 582).

- Check Am. Jur. 2d and C.J.S. on the federal rules of court (see Checklist #7 on legal encyclopedias, page 582).

- Check with an expert (see Checklist #9 on phone and mail research, page 584).

Section W. Finding International Law

Techniques for Finding International Law
1. In general, check: ■ The yearly U.S. Statutes at Large (page 516) contain U.S. treaties (page 329) ■ *United States Treaties and Other International Acts* ■ *Treaties and Other International Acts Series* ■ *United States Treaties and Other International Agreements* ■ Blaustein and Flanz, *Constitutions of the Countries of the World* ■ *CCH Tax Treaties* ■ *Treaties in Force* ■ *Department of State Bulletin* ■ United Nations Treaty Series ■ Catalog of U.S. publications ■ *International Legal Materials* ■ Szladits, *Bibliography on Foreign and Comparative Law: Books and Articles in English* For other texts summarizing and commenting on treaties and international law generally, see Checklist #8 on treatises, page 583.
2. Legal periodical literature. There is extensive periodical literature on international law, both in general legal periodicals and in specialty periodicals devoted to international law exclusively. (See Checklist #6, page 582.)
3. Loose-leaf services, such as CCH Tax Treaties, mentioned above. (See Checklist #5 on loose-leaf services, page 577.)
4. American case law on international law. Check the digests. (See Checklist #2 on digests, page 556.)
5. Case law of foreign countries. Statutory law of other countries. Go to the international law section of a large law library.
6. Annotations on international law. (See Checklist #3 on annotations, page 561.)
7. Legal encyclopedias. For material on international law in Am. Jur. 2d and in C.J.S., see Checklist #7, page 582.
8. Phone and mail research. (See Checklist #9 on contacting experts, page 584.)
9. See *Restatement (Second) of Foreign Relations Law of the United States.*
10. Shepardize all treaties. Go to *Shepard's United States Citations, Statute Edition* (page 512).
11. *Martindale-Hubbell Law Dictionary*—Digest volume. Contains brief summaries of the law of many countries (page 506).

Section X. The Third Level of Research (Validation): Ending Your Research

Earlier (page 549) we mentioned the three levels of legal research:

■ Background research

- Specific fact research
- Validation research

We already examined the steps for conducting background research on an area of law that is new to you (page 550). We also examined the techniques of specific fact research through the checklists (pages 552 ff.) presented above in section N through W of this chapter. If you have done a comprehensive job on the first two stages of research, you may also have completed most of the third stage—*validation research.*

At the validation stage, you ensure that everything you want to use from your research is still good law. This means making sure that the law is current and has not been affected by any later laws that you have not yet found. A good way to approach validation research is to take the perspective of the other side. Suppose that you have written an appellate brief. It has been filed in court and served on the attorney for the other side. Your brief is handed over to a researcher in the law office of your opponent. That person will do the following:

- Read the full text of all primary authority (page 517) on which you rely in order to see if you have interpreted the statutes, cases, regulations, etc., properly; to see whether you have taken quotations out of the context, etc.

- Shepardize the statutes, cases, regulations, etc., that you cite in order to find out whether the law is still valid (page 563)

- Read the secondary authority (page 517) that you cite in order to see whether you have interpreted the treatise, law review article, etc., properly; to see whether you have taken quotations out of context, etc.

- Look for other applicable primary authority that you failed to mention

- Look for other applicable secondary authority that you failed to mention

Proper validation research means that you will be able to predict what this imaginary researcher will find when he or she checks your research through these steps. In short, at the validation stage of your research you must ask yourself:

- Have I found everything I should have found?
- Is everything I found good law?
- Have I properly interpreted what I found?

The answer to the first two questions should be *no* if:

- You did an incomplete job of CARTWHEELING the indexes and tables of contents of all the sets of books mentioned in the checklists and techniques in this chapter.

- You failed to shepardize cases, statutes, constitutional provisions, rules of court, ordinances, treaties, etc., as called for in the checklists and techniques listed above.

- You failed to take other standard validation steps, such as checking the List of Sections Affected (LSA) material to update a regulation in the C.F.R. (page 604).

At the outset of your research, the difficulty you face is often phrased as: "Where do I begin?" As you resolve this difficulty, another one emerges: "When do I stop?" Once the research starts flowing, you are sometimes faced with a mountain of material, and yet you do not feel comfortable saying to yourself that you have found everything there is to be found. The only guidance that can be given to you is this: be comprehensive in following all the checklists and techniques presented in this chapter. With experience, you will begin to acquire a sense of when it is time to stop. But it is rare for you to know this with any certainty. You will always have the suspicion that if you pushed on just a little longer, you would find something new and more on point than what you have come up with to date. Also, there is no way around the reality that comprehensive research requires a substantial amount of time. It takes time to dig. It takes more time to dig comprehensively.

Section Y. Annotated Bibliography

An *annotated bibliography* is a report giving a list of library material on a particular topic, with a brief description of how the material relates to the topic. An annotated bibliography on contributory negligence, for example, would list the major cases, statutes, periodical articles, etc. and would explain in a sentence or two what each says about contributory negligence. The same would be true of an annotated bibliography on a set of facts that you are researching. If the facts present more than one research issue, you would do an annotated bibliography for each issue, or you would subdivide a single annotated bibliography into sections so that it would be clear to the reader which issue you are covering at any given place in the bibliography. The annotated bibliography is, in effect, a progress report on your research. It will show your supervisor the status of your research. (The following instructions mainly cover the preparation of an annotated bibliography for a topic that requires the application of state and local law. The same instructions, however, would be used when doing the bibliography on a federal topic. The exception would be instruction #9, which calls for local ordinances. For all other instructions below, replace the word *state* with the word *federal* when researching a federal topic.)

Instructions for Preparing an Annotated Bibliography

1. CARTWHEEL the topic of your annotated bibliography.

2. *Annotated* simply means that you provide some description of everything you list in the bibliography—not a long analysis, just a sentence or two explaining why you included it. If you find no relevant material in any of the following sets of books, specifically say so in your report.

3. Hand in a report that will cover what you find on the topic in the sets of books mentioned in the following instructions.

4. Statutes. Go to your state code. Make a list of the statutes on the topic. For each statute, give its citation and a brief quotation from it to show that it deals with the topic.

5. Constitutions. Go to your state constitution (usually found within your state code). Make a list of the constitutional provisions on the topic. For each provision, give its citation and a brief quotation from it to show that it deals with the topic.

6. Cases. If you found statutes or constitutional provisions on the topic, check to see if there are any cases summarized in the Notes of Decisions (page 591) *after* these statutes or provisions. Also go to the digests (page 497). Select several cases that you found through the Notes of Decisions and the digests that deal with the topic. For each case you select, give its citation and a brief quote from the case summary to show that it deals with the topic.

Continued

Instructions for Preparing an Annotated Bibliography—*Continued*

7. Key topics and numbers. In instruction #6, you went to the digests. Make a list of the key topics and numbers that you found most productive. (See page 497.)

8. Rules of court. Go to the rules of court that cover courts in your state (page 605). Make a list of the rules, if any, that deal with the topic. For each rule, give its citation and a brief quotation from it to show that it deals with the topic.

9. Ordinances. Go to the ordinances that cover your city or county (page 604). Make a list of the ordinances, if any, that deal with the topic. For each ordinance, give its citation and a brief quotation from it to show that it deals with the topic.

10. Agency regulations. Are there any state agencies that have jurisdiction over any aspect of the topic? If so, list the agencies. If your library has the regulations of the agencies, make a list of the regulations, if any, that deal with the topic. For each major regulation, give its citation and a brief quote from it to show that it deals with the topic (page 603).

11. A.L.R., A.L.R.2d, A.L.R.3d, A.L.R.4th, A.L.R. Fed. Go to these five sets of books (page 557). Try to find one annotation in *each* set that deals with your topic. Give the citation of the annotations in each set. Flip through the pages of each annotation and try to find the citation of one case from a state court of your state, or from a federal court with jurisdiction over your state. Give the citation of the case.

12. Legal periodical literature. Use the *Index to Legal Periodicals*, the *Current Legal Index*, and the *Legal Resource Index* to locate three law review articles that deal with the topic (page 578). Try to find at least one relevant article in each index. Give the citation of the articles. Put a check mark next to the citation if your library has the law review in which the article is located.

13. Treatises. Go to your card catalog (page 552). Find any two treatises (page 583) that cover your topic. Give the citation of the treatises. Sometimes you may not find entire books on the topic. The topic may be one of many subjects in a broader treatise.

14. Loose-leaf texts. Are there any loose-leaf services on this topic (page 577)? Check the card catalog and ask the librarian. For each loose-leaf, give its citation and explain how it covers the topic.

15. *Words and Phrases*. Go to this multivolume legal dictionary (page 504). In this dictionary, locate definitions, if any, of the major words and phrases involved in your topic. Limit yourself to definitions from court opinions of your state, if any.

16. Shepardize every case, statute, or constitutional provision you find to make sure it is still valid, and to locate other material on the topic (page 563).

17. Other material. If you come across other relevant material not covered in the above instructions, include it in the bibliography as well.

18. When in doubt about whether to include something in the bibliography, include it.

19. There is no prescribed format for the bibliography. One possible outline format you can use is as follows:
    Topic: _____

    A. Statutes (Instructions 4 and 16)
    B. Constitutions (Instructions 5 and 16)
    C. Cases (Instructions 6 and 16)
    D. Key topics and numbers (Instruction 7)
    E. Rules of court (Instruction 8)
    F. Ordinances (Instruction 9)
    G. Agency regulations (Instruction 10)

Continued

Instructions for Preparing an Annotated Bibliography—*Continued*

H. A.L.R., A.L.R.2d, A.L.R.3d, A.L.R.4th, A.L.R. Fed. (Instruction 11)

I. Legal periodical literature (Instruction 12)

J. Treatises (Instruction 13)

K. Loose-leaf texts (Instruction 14)

L. *Words and Phrases* (Instruction 15)

M. Other material (Instruction 17)

■ **ASSIGNMENT 11.8**

Prepare an annotated bibliography on the following topics:

(a) Common-law marriage

(b) Negligence liability of a driver of a car to his or her guest passenger

(c) Negligence liability of paralegals

(d) Overtime compensation for paralegals

(e) Sex discrimination

(f) The felony-murder rule

(g) Default judgment

(h) Worker's compensation for injury on the way to work

(i) Fact situation assigned by your instructor

■ **ASSIGNMENT 11.9**

In the problems that follow, include citations that support every position you take in your responses. In analyzing and researching some of the problems below, you may find it difficult to proceed unless you know more facts about the problem. In such situations, clearly state the missing facts that you need to know. In order to proceed with the analysis and research, you can assume that certain facts exist as long as you state what your factual assumptions are, *and* your assumptions are reasonable given the facts that you have.

(a) In your state, what entity (e.g., legislature, committee, court, agency) has the authority to prescribe rules and regulations on who can and who cannot practice law?

(b) List the kinds (or levels) of courts (local, state, or federal) that sit in your state and identify the major powers of each court, i.e., what kinds of cases can each court hear.

(c) In your state, find a statute or court opinion that defines the following words or phrases:

　(i) Summons

　(ii) In personam

　(iii) Mandamus

　(iv) Exhaustion of administrative remedies

　(v) Judgment

(vi) Jurisdiction

(vii) Warrant

(d) Mary Adams works for a National Welfare Rights Organization chapter in your state. She is a paralegal. An N.W.R.O. member, Mrs. Peterson, has a complaint against a local welfare department branch concerning her welfare check. Mary Adams goes to a hearing with Mrs. Peterson to represent her. The hearing officer tells Mary that she cannot represent Mrs. Peterson since she (Mary) is not an attorney. Is the hearing officer correct?

(e) Using as many statutory codes of different states as are available in your law library (do not go beyond five different codes, however), find out how old a male and female must be in order to marry without consent of parent or guardian in each of the states.

(f) Go to any statutory code that has a pocket part. Starting with the first few pages of the pocket part, identify any three statutes that have totally repealed *or* partially modified the corresponding three statutes in the body of the bound text. Describe what the modification was. (*Note:* You may have to compare the new section in the pocket part with the old section in the body of the text in order to be able to describe the change.)

· · · · · · · · · · · · · ·

In the following problems, use the state law *of your state* whenever you determine from your research that state law governs the problem.

(g) John Jones was sent to a state mental hospital after being declared mentally ill. He has been institutionalized for the last five years. In his own view, he is not now mentally ill. The hospital disagrees. What can John do? What steps might he take to try to get out?

(h) Peter Thomas is convicted of petty larceny. At the time of sentencing, his attorney asks the court to grant probation in lieu of a prison term. The judge replies, "Since Mr. Thomas has had three prior felony convictions (one of them for attempted rape), I could not grant him probation even if I wanted to. I sentence him to a year in prison." On appeal, the attorney argues that the judge was incorrect when he ruled that he had no power to grant probation to a person with three prior convictions. Is the attorney correct?

(i) Mrs. Peterson invites a neighbor to her house for dinner. Mrs. Peterson's dog bites the neighbor. Is Mrs. Peterson responsible for the injury?

(j) Sam, age fifteen, goes to a used car lot. He signs a purchase agreement on a used car: $500 down and $100 a month for the next ten months. One day after the purchase, Sam allows a friend to drive the car. The friend demolishes the car in an accident. When Sam tells the used car dealer about the accident, he is told that he must still make all payments until the purchase price has been paid. Is the dealer right?

(k) An elderly woman presented the following facts to you during a legal interview. She and her husband moved into their house in 1946. Next to the house is a vacant lot. She does not know who owns the lot. She planted a small vegetable and flower garden on this lot. She built a small fence around the garden. She has continued to cultivate this garden for the past twenty-seven years. Neighbors regard this garden as hers. Since her husband's death last fall, men in the neighborhood have been trying to use the garden area as a place to store their old car parts. She is troubled by this. What are her rights?

(l) Dorothy Rhodes and John Samualson are the parents of Susan Samualson. (Dorothy married Robert Rhodes after divorcing John Samualson.) Dorothy died after separating from Robert Rhodes. Susan's father has disappeared.

Mr. and Mrs. Ford were neighbors of the Rhodes. Susan lived with the Fords for a long period of time while her mother was having marital difficulties. A court granted the Fords custody and guardianship in 1988. The Social Security Administration sent Susan the Social Security benefits she was entitled to on the death of her mother. In 1990, the Fords formally adopted Susan, but did not inform the Social Security office of this; they did not know that they had to. When the Social Security office learned of the adoption, they terminated the payments for Susan and informed the Fords that the money she had received since the adoption would have to be returned.

The Fords and Susan want to know what substantive and procedural rights they have.

(m) Jane Smith owns a small shoe repair shop. The city sanitation department determines that Jane is a carrier of a typhoid germ. She herself does not have typhoid fever, but others could become infected with the fever by coming in contact with her. The city orders Jane's shop to be closed. She and her husband are not allowed to leave the shop until arrangements can be made to transfer them to a hospital.

     (i)   Can the city quarantine Jane and her husband?

     (ii)   If the Smiths enter a hospital quarantine, can they be forced to pay the hospital bill?

     (iii)   Can the Smiths recover loss of profits due to the closing of their business?

(n) The Henderson family owns a $140,000 home next door to a small grocery store. The store catches fire. In order for the firefighters to get at the fire from all angles, they decide that they must break through the Henderson home, which is not on fire. Damage to the Henderson home from the activity of the firefighters comes to $40,000. Who pays for this damage?

(o) Bill and Mary are married with two children. They are happily married except for one constant quarrel. Bill is upset with Mary because she goes bowling every Friday night. Mary is disturbed with Bill because he plays cards every Tuesday night. To resolve their difficulty, they reach the following agreement: Bill will give up his Tuesday night cards if Mary will give up her Friday bowling. On Friday, Mary stays home. On the following Tuesday, however, Bill plays cards. He declares that he wants to continue the card playing. Mary, on the other hand, wants him to live up to his agreement. She brings a suit in court against him, charging breach of contract. (Assume that neither wants a divorce.) What result?

(p) After a series of serious accidents in which numerous riders are hurt, a bill is placed before the city council that would require all motorcyclists to wear protective helmets whenever riding. Is the bill constitutional?

(q) As a measure to enforce a standard of dental care, a bill is proposed that all the drinking water in the state be fluoridated and every citizen be required to visit a dentist at least once a year. Is this bill constitutional?

(r) Tom Jones has terminal lung cancer. Modern technology, however, can keep him alive indefinitely. Tom requests that the hospital official no longer use the technology. He wants to die. What are his rights?

(s) Alice Brown is seventeen years old. She is a self-styled hippie. She refuses to work. Alice's parents tell her that they will fully finance a college education for her. She refuses. The parents go to court and ask that their daughter be forced to go to college and avoid ruining her life. What result?

(t) In 1942 James Fitzpatrick died, leaving an estate of $50,000. The executor tried to locate the heirs. In 1943 the probate court closed the estate and distributed the money to the heirs who were known at the time. In 1986, an individual claiming to be an heir appears. He wants to go to court to reopen the estate and claim his share of the inheritance. What result?

(u) Mary is the sole beneficiary of her father's will. Another sister is intentionally left out of the will by her father. There are no other heirs. Mary murders her father. Who gets his estate?

(v) The board of education is alarmed over increasing disturbances in the public schools. A board regulation currently exists that permits school principals to administer corporal punishment to unruly pupils. The superintendent of schools proposes that the board adopt a regulation that would authorize the school nurse, under the direction of the principal, to administer an oral tranquilizer to disruptive pupils so that they could be rendered "relatively passive" and responsive to school guidance. Discuss the legality of the regulation.

(w) The state claims that welfare costs are bringing the finances of the state to the brink of bankruptcy. It is proposed that all children of welfare parents be required to attend vocational classes as part of their regular school curriculum. Discuss the legality of the regulation.

(x) The United Kosher Butchers Association (UKBA) is accepted by most of the kosher meat stores as the authoritative certifier that "all the religious requirements have been thoroughly observed." Associated Synagogues (AS) certifies caterers as authentic carriers of kosher food. AS refuses to certify caterers who buy meat from stores certified by the UKBA because the latter refuses to submit to supervision by the rabbinical committee of AS. Many caterers then withdraw their patronage from stores supervised by UKBA. What legal action, if any, can UKBA take?

(y) The town of Salem has a population of 2,000. A group of avowed homosexuals moves into the area. They begin to run for public offices, with some success. The old-time townspeople become very upset. A state law gives courts the power to hospitalize mentally ill individuals. The mayor of Salem files petitions in court to have the homosexuals declared mentally ill and institutionalized. Discuss any law that might apply to these facts.

(z) Mary Perry belongs to a religion that believes that medical problems can be resolved through spiritual meditation. Her son Paul is ten years old. One day at school, Paul is rushed to a hospital after collapsing. Mrs. Perry is called at home. When she arrives at the hospital, she is told that Paul will require emergency surgery. She refuses to give her consent. The doctor tells that her if the operation is not performed within the next twenty-four hours, Paul will die. Mrs. Perry responds by saying that "God will cure my son." What legal action, if any, can be taken to protect Paul's rights and to protect Mrs. Perry's rights?

State Legal Research References

Alabama Practice Materials by L. Kitchens, 82 Law Library Journal 703 (1990).

Alaska Legal and Law-Related Publications by A. Ruzicka (American Association of Law Libraries, 1984).

Arizona Practice Materials by A. Torres, 80 Law Library Journal 577 (1988).

Survey of Arizona State Legal and Law-Related Documents by R. Teenstra (American Association of Law Libraries, 1984).

Arkansas Legal Bibliography by L. Foster (American Association of Law Libraries, 1988).

Arizona Practice Materials by K. Fitzhugh, 81 Law Library Journal 277 (1989).

Continued

State Legal Research References—*Continued*

California Current State Practice Materials by B. Ochal, 74 Law Library Journal 281 (1981).

California Law Guide by D. Henke (2d ed. Parker, 1976).

Legal Research Guide for California Practice by T. Dabagh (Hein, 1985).

Research in California Law by M. Fink (2d ed. Dennis, 1964).

Colorado Legal Resources by G. Alexander, et al. (American Association of Law Libraries, 1987). 16 Colorado Lawyer 1795 (1987).

Colorado Legal Source Materials—1981 by S. Weinstein, 10 Colorado Lawyer 1816 (August 1981).

Connecticut State Legal Documents by D. Voisinet (American Association of Law Libraries, 1985).

Sources of Connecticut Law by S. Bysiewicz (Butterworth, 1987).

Selected Information Sources for the District of Columbia by C. Ahearn (2d ed. American Association of Law Libraries, 1986).

Florida Legislative Histories by C. Roehrenbeck (D&H, 1986).

Guide to Florida Legal Research by R. Reinersten & R. Brown (2d ed. Florida, Bar, 1986).

Research in Florida Law by H. French (2d ed. Oceana, 1965).

Reference Guide to Georgia Legal History and Legal Research by L. Chanin (Michie, 1980).

How To Research Constitutional, Legislative, and Statutory History in Hawaii by R. Kahle (Hawaii Legislative Reference Bureau, 1986).

Idaho Law-Related State Documents by P. Cervenka (American Association of Law Libraries, 1989).

Illinois Legal Research Manual by L. Wendt (Butterworth, 1988).

Illinois State Documents by C. Nyberg (American Association of Law Libraries, 1986).

Researching Illinois Legislative Histories: A Practical Guide by L. Wendt, 1982 Southern Illinois University Law Journal 601.

An Introduction to Indiana State Publications . . . by L. Fariss (American Association of Law Libraries, 1982).

A Guide to Kansas Legal Research by F. Snyder (Kansas Bar Association, 1986).

Kansas State Documents for Law Libraries by M. Wisnecki (American Association of Law Libraries, 1984).

Guide to Kentucky Legal Research by W. Gilmer (2d ed. State Law Library, 1985).

Louisiana Legal Documents . . . by C. Corneil (American Association of Law Libraries, 1984).

Louisiana Legal Research by W. Chiang (2d ed. Butterworth, 1990).

Maine Legal Research Guide by W. Wells (Tower, 1989).

An Introduction to Maryland State Publications . . . by L. Davis (American Association of Law Libraries, 1981).

Ghost Hunting: Finding Legislative Intent in Maryland by M. Miller (Maryland State Law Library, 1984).

Annual State Bibliography (Massachusetts) by L. McAuliffe (American Association of Law Libraries, 1985).

Handbook of Legal Research in Massachusetts by M. Botsford, et al. (Massachusetts Continuing Legal Education, 1988).

Michigan Citation Manual by J. Doyle (1986).

Michigan Legal Documents by D. Yoak (American Association of Law Libraries, 1982).

Michigan Legal Literature and Annotated Guide by R. Beer & J. Field (2d ed. Hein, 1991).

Michigan Practice Materials by D. Johnson, 73 Law Library Journal 672 (1980).

Legal Research Guide for Michigan Libraries (Michigan Association of Law Libraries, 1982).

Minnesota Legal Research Guide by A. Soderberg & B. Golden (Hein, 1985).

Continued

State Legal Research References—*Continued*

Guide to Minnesota State Documents . . . by M. Baum (American Association of Law Libraries, 1986).

Mississippi Legal Documents . . . by B. Cole (American Association of Law Libraries, 1987).

Mississippi Legal Research Bibliography by C. Bunnell (1983).

A Law Librarian's Introduction to Missouri State Publications by P. Aldridge (American Association of Law Libraries, 1980).

A Guide to Montana Legal Research by S. Jordan (Montana State Law Library, 1991).

Nebraska State Documents Bibliography by M. Fontent (American Association of Law Libraries, 1988).

Nebraska Legal Research and Reference Manual by P. Hall (Mason, 1983).

Nevada State Documents Bibliography . . . by K. Henderson (American Association of Law Libraries, 1984).

A Guide to New Jersey Legal Bibliography and Legal History by C. Allen (Rothman, 1984).

New Jersey Legal Research Handbook by P. Axel-Lute (New Jersey Institute for Continuing Legal Education, 1985).

New Jersey State Publications by C. Senezak (American Association of Law Libraries, 1984).

Guide to New Mexico State Publications by P. Wagner (American Association of Law Libraries, 1983).

Manual for Effective New Mexico Legal Research by A. Poldervaart (University of New Mexico Press, 1955).

New York Legal Documents by S. Dow (American Association of Law Libraries, 1985).

New York Legal Research Guide by E. Gibson (Hein, 1988).

An Annotated Bibliography of Current New York State Practice Materials by Brown, 73 Law Library Journal 28 (1980).

Guide to North Carolina Legal Research by I. Kavass (Hein, 1973).

Survey of North Carolina State Legal and Law-Related Documents by T. Steele (American Association of Law Libraries, 1988).

For All Intents and Purposes: Essentials in Researching Legislative Histories (North Dakota Legislative Council, 1981).

Ohio Legal Research by S. Schaefgen & M. Putnum (Professional Education Systems, 1988).

Ohio State Legal Documents . . . by C. Corcos (American Association of Law Libraries, 1986).

Oklahoma Legal and Law-Related Documents . . . by C. Corcos (American Association of Law Libraries, 1983).

Bibliography of Law Related Oregon Documents by L. Buhman (American Association of Law Libraries, 1984).

An Introduction to Pennsylvania State Publications . . . by J. Fishman (American Association of Law Libraries, 1985).

Pennsylvania Practice Materials by S. Fishman, 78 Law Library Journal 74 (1986).

Research in Pennsylvania Law by C. Moreland & E. Surrency (2d ed. Oceana, 1965).

Legal Research in Rhode Island (Rhode Island Law Institute, 1989).

South Carolina Legal Research Handbook by R. Mills (Hein, 1976).

South Dakota Legal Documents by D. Jorgensen (American Association of Law Libraries, 1988).

South Dakota Legal Research Guide by D. Jorgensen (Hein, 1988).

Law and Government Publications of . . . Tennessee by D. Picquet (American Association of Law Libraries, 1988).

Tennessee Legal Research Handbook by L. Laska (Hein, 1977).

Continued

State Legal Research References—*Continued*

An Annotated Bibliography of Texas Practice Materials by K. Gruben, 74 Law Library Journal 87 (1981).

A Reference Guide to Texas Law . . ., Gruben & J. Hambleton, editors (2d ed. Butterworth, 1987).

Texas State Documents for Law Libraries by M. Allison (American Association of Law Libraries, 1983).

A Bibliographical Guide to the Vermont Legal System by V. Wise (American Association of Law Libraries, 1989).

A Guide to Legal Research in Virginia, D. Eure, ed. (Virginia Law Foundation, 1989).

A Law Librarian's Introduction to Virginia State Publications by J. Lichtman (American Association of Law Libraries, 1988).

A Guide to Specialized Resources and Methods for Conducting Legal Research in Washington State by J. Quinn, 44 Washington State Bar News 9 (October 1990).

Legal Research Guide (University of Washington Law School, 1980).

Washington State Law-Related Publications by S. Burson (American Association of Law Libraries, 1984).

An Introduction to Wisconsin State Documents . . . by J. Oberla (American Association of Law Libraries, 1987).

Legal Research in Wisconsin by R. Danner (University of Wisconsin, Extension Law Department, 1980).

Wyoming State Legal Documents by N. Greene (American Association of Law Libraries, 1985).

☐ Chapter Summary

The law is changing every day. The only dependable way to find out about all of these changes is through legal research. Research skills will take time and determination to master. A useful first step is to compile a list of definitions or functions of the major research terms (such as citation, citator, cumulative, and headnote), and the major sets of research materials (such as A.L.R., Corpus Juris Secundum, Federal Reporter 2d, U.S.C.A., and WESTLAW).

You need to know where to find law libraries in your community, particularly depository libraries. Within these libraries, you will find the following kinds of authority that courts consider in reaching a decision: primary authority, which consists of laws such as statutes and cases; secondary authority, which consists of nonlaws such as law review articles and legal encyclopedias; mandatory authority, which a court *must* rely on; and persuasive authority, which a court has discretion to accept or reject.

A citation is an "address" where authority can be found in a library. *A Uniform System of Citation*—the "Bluebook," tells you what to abbreviate in the citation, where spaces and commas must be inserted, in what order the information in the citation must be provided, etc. Most courts do not follow the Bluebook; a court may have its own rules of citation that it follows. Yet a very large number of supervising attorneys and teachers will ask you to follow the Bluebook. When cite checking, you identify inaccuracies in citation form, shepardize the authorities cited, check the accuracy of any quotations referred to in the citations, etc.

There are standard features of many law books. Each time you come across a new law book or set of law books, you should check features such as the copyright page, which contains the latest copyright date; and the forward or preface, which may give a general description of how to use the book. The tables or lists at the beginning of the book will help you understand terms, symbols, or signals used in the book. Check also for updating features, (such as pocket-parts), various tables of contents, and index features that may be available.

The CARTWHEEL is a technique that helps you use the often poorly organized tables of contents and indexes of law books. The technique assumes

(Continued on next page)

☐ **Chapter Summary** *(Continued)*

that the entry you first check in the table or index leads you nowhere, and that you must now think of some other entries to check that might be more productive. The CARTWHEEL is designed to help you identify these other entries.

There are three levels of legal research: background research, in which you start identifying the basic vocabulary and the major principles of an area of the law that is relatively new to you; specific fact research, in which you look for primary and secondary authority covering the facts of a client's case; and validation research, in which you check the current validity of whatever authority you initially believed was relevant to the problem you are researching. Occasionally, aspects of all three levels of research will be going on simultaneously.

A competent legal researcher knows how to use the major search tools or resources:

■ Card catalog (or the computer catalog) to find what is available in the library you are using

■ Digests to find case law

■ Annotations to find case law

■ Shepard's to shepardize cases, statutes, and

regulations in order to validate cited material and to find citing material such as case law

■ Loose-leaf services to give you leads to, and explanations of, primary authority

■ Legal periodical literature to give you leads to, and explanations of, primary authority

■ Legal encyclopedias to give you leads to, and explanations of, primary authority

■ Treatises to give you leads to, and explanations of, primary authority

■ Phone and mail research to give you leads to, and explanations of, primary authority.

Major CALR (computer-assisted legal research) tools include WESTLAW, LEXIS, Auto-Cite, VERA-LEX, WILSONLINE, DIALOG, and NEXIS. (In Chapter 13, we will cover WESTLAW and LEXIS in greater detail.)

These major search tools or resources will often lead you to more than one kind of primary authority: opinions, statutes (plus legislative history), constitutions, administrative law, local law, rules of court, and international law. (See Figure 11.1.)

Key Terms

depository library	special edition state reporter	interstate compact
act	casebook	kardex
administrative code	CD-ROM	legal dictionary
advance sheet	citation/cite	legal newspaper
legal encyclopedia	parallel cite	legal periodical
annotate	citator	law review
annotated	code	law journal
annotation	codify	legal thesaurus
annotated code	uncodified	legislation
annotated statutes	cumulative	loose-leaf service
bill	cumulative supplement	law directory
Bluebook	digest	microform
West	abstracts	microfilm
appellate brief	squibs	microfiche
amicus curiae brief	key topic and number	ultrafiche
case	regional digest	pocket part
opinion	formbook	record
official reporter	practice manual	Restatements
unofficial reporter	handbook	rules of court
star paging	headnote	edition
regional reporter	hornbook	series

shepardize
slip law
slip opinion
statutory code
treatise
authority
primary authority
secondary authority
mandatory authority
persuasive authority
nonauthority
enacted law
on point
analogous
conflicts of law
full faith and credit
dictum
caption of opinion
reporters
online
italicize
et al.
litigation status
in re
docket number
nominative reporter

popular name
enacted into positive law
cite checking
supra
infra
title page
copyright
table of cases
table of statutes
statutory history table
footnotes
appendixes
CARTWHEEL
background research
validation research
KF call number
Library of Congress
    classification system
trace a key topic and number
DWI
scope note
superseded
supplemented
cited material
citing material
syllabus (Shepard's)

small raised number
codified cite
session law cite
et seq.
case note
online
query
CALR
common law
notes of decisions
section (§)
historical note
legislative history
Id.
mandatory statute
discretionary statute
monitoring legislation
legislative service
PL number
transcribed
constitution
regulation
validation research
annotated bibliography

12

Legal Writing

■ Chapter Outline

■ Section A. Kinds of Legal Writing

There are a number of different kinds of writing within a law office:

- Letters
- Instruments
- Pleadings
- Memoranda of law
- Appellate briefs

1. Letters

Many garden-variety letters are written in a law office every day, such as a letter requesting information, a letter demanding payment, or a letter notifying someone of the fact that the office represents a particular person or company.

In an *opinion letter,* the office writes to its client to explain the application of the law and advise the client what to do. Such letters try to clarify technical material. Unlike a brief or memorandum, the opinion letter does not make extensive reference to court opinions or statutes. The client's need is for clear, concise, practical advice.

2. Instruments

An *instrument* is a formal document that gives expression to a legal act or agreement. Examples of instruments are contracts, deeds, wills, leases, bonds, notes, mortgage agreements, etc. Many formbooks and computer programs provide models for drafting such instruments. Rarely will anyone write an instrument from scratch. The starting point is almost always a standard form or model, which is adapted to the particular facts of the client.

3. Pleadings

Pleadings are formal statements of claims and defenses that are exchanged between parties involved in litigation. The major pleadings are the complaint, answer, counterclaim, reply to counterclaim, cross-claim, and third party complaint. Formbooks are also often used as the starting point in drafting pleadings. Some high-volume litigation firms use computers or word-processing equipment to help prepare repetitive pleadings.

 ## Section B. Memorandum of Law

A *memorandum of law* is an analysis of legal authority governing one or more legal issues. It is generally the product of a fairly extensive research effort. There are two kinds of legal memoranda:

- The *internal* or *interoffice* memorandum
- The *external* or *adversary* memorandum

The audience of an *interoffice* memorandum is your own office. Its primary feature is its objectivity. It must present the strengths *and* weaknesses of the client's case so that the senior members of the office can make intelligent decisions based on all aspects of the law. The memo will certainly attempt to show how the law can be interpreted in the light most favorable to the client, but it must go beyond this level. The memo also must try to anticipate what the strongest arguments of the *opponent* will be. Such arguments must be presented with precision and honesty. When this is done, the reader of the memo within the office will be in the best position to design a realistic strategy.

An *external* memorandum, by contrast, is not an objective document at all. It is an *adversary* document that attempts to persuade the reader to adopt a decision favorable to the client. The audience of your external memorandum may be a hearing officer in an administrative agency (if so, it will often be called a hearing memorandum or a *points and authorities memorandum*) or a trial court judge (if so, it will often be called a *trial memorandum*). A trial memorandum is like an appellate brief (discussed below) in that both are advocacy documents directed to a court. An appellate brief, however, is more stylized in format and is not written for an agency or a trial court.

The distinguishing features of the two kinds of memoranda are outlined in the chart in Figure 12.1.

Structure of an Interoffice Memo

Not all supervisors agree on the preferred structure of the interoffice memorandum of law. The following are common features of many memos:

1. Heading
2. Statement of the assignment
3. Legal issues
4. Facts
5. Discussion or analysis
6. Conclusion
7. Recommendations
8. Appendix

1. Heading

At the top of the page, state the kind of document you are writing (interoffice memorandum of law). Then list:

- The person to whom the memo is addressed
- The name of the author of the memo
- The date the memo was prepared
- The name of the client and the opponent
- The office file number of the case
- The court docket number, if the case has already been filed in court
- A very brief subject-matter entry (following the notation "RE:") in which you state what the memo is about

The following sample heading illustrates how this information might be set forth in a heading for a memorandum written on behalf of client Brown, who is suing Miller:

Interoffice Memorandum

TO: Jane Patterson, Esq.   RE: Availability of the contribu-
FROM: John Jackson, Paralegal   tory negligence defense to
DATE: April 30, 1991   Miller
CASE: Brown v. Miller
OFFICE FILE NUMBER: 91-42
DOCKET NUMBER: CIV. 1-91-307

Note that the subject-matter description in this sample (RE:) briefly indicates the nature of the question that will be treated in the memorandum. This information is needed for at least two reasons. First, the average law office case file contains a large number of documents, often including several legal memoranda. A heading that at least briefly indicates the nature of the subject of each memorandum makes it much easier to locate the memorandum in the client's file. Second, it is unlikely that the usefulness of your memorandum will end when the client's case is closed. Some law offices maintain fairly extensive libraries of old office memoranda, which are cataloged and filed by subject matter for reference in future cases. This avoids unnecessary and costly duplication of research time in the event that a similar question arises in a future client's case. The subject-matter heading on your memorandum facilitates the cataloging and filing of your memorandum in such a library.

The inclusion of the date on which the memorandum was completed and submitted is important for similar reasons. While your analysis and conclusions may have been very accurate at the time the memorandum was written, subsequent changes in the law may have occurred by the time the memorandum is

INTEROFFICE MEMORANDUM OF LAW	EXTERNAL MEMORANDUM OF LAW
■ Emphasizes both the strengths and the weaknesses of the client's position on each issue (objective)	■ Emphasizes the strengths but minimizes or ignores the weaknesses of the client's position on each issue
■ Emphasizes both the strengths and the weaknesses of the opposing party's probable position on each issue	■ Emphasizes the weaknesses but minimizes or ignores the strengths of the opposing party's position on each issue
■ Predicts the court's or the agency's probable decision on each issue	■ Argues for a favorable decision on each issue
■ Recommends the most favorable strategy for the client to follow	

FIGURE 12.1

Characteristics of Interoffice and External Memoranda of Law

next referred to. On seeing the date of the memorandum, a reader will know from what date subsequent legal research is needed.

2. Statement of the Assignment

It is a good idea early in the memo to provide an explicit statement of what your supervisor has asked you to do.

3. Statement of the Legal Issue(s)

On phrasing issues, see page 350.

Often you must state and discuss certain issues *on the assumption* that the court or agency will decide against you on prior issues that you discuss early in the memorandum. Suppose that the client is a defendant in a negligence action. The first issue may concern the liability of the defendant: was the defendant negligent or not? In the first issue, the defendant will be covering the liability question and will attempt to demonstrate in the discussion or analysis on this issue why the defendant is *not* liable. All the evidence and authority supporting nonliability will be examined under this issue. At the time that the memorandum is written, there will, of course, be no resolution of the first issue. Hence, you must be prepared for issues that will arise *on the assumption* that the client will lose the first issue. For example, all issues concerning damages (how much money must be paid to a plaintiff who has successfully established liability) need to be anticipated and analyzed in the event that the liability issue is lost. The statement of the damage issue in the memorandum should be prefaced by language such as:

In the event that we lose the first issue, then we must discuss the issue of . . . .

or

On the assumption that the court finds for [the other party] on the liability issue, the damages question then becomes whether . . . .

No matter how firmly you believe in your prediction of what a court or agency will do on an issue, be prepared for what will happen in the event that your prediction eventually proves to be erroneous. This must be done in an internal memorandum, in an external memorandum (hearing or trial), and in an appellate brief.

4. Statement of the Facts

Your statement of the facts of the client's case is one of the most important components of the memorandum. You should take great pains to see that it is concise, highly accurate, and well organized.

Conciseness.   An unduly long fact statement will only frustrate the reader. Try to eliminate any unnecessary facts from the statement. One way of doing this is to carefully review your fact statement *after* you have completed your analysis of the issues. If there are facts in your statement that are not subsequently referred to in your analysis, it may be that those facts are not particularly relevant to your memorandum and can be eliminated in your final draft.

Accuracy.   In many instances you will be drafting the memorandum for an attorney who is preparing to go before a court or agency for the first time; there may be no prior proceedings. Hence, there will be no record and no official

findings of fact. The temptation will be to indulge in wishful thinking—to ignore adverse facts and to assume that disputed facts will be resolved in favor of
the client. Do not give in to this temptation. You must assess the legal consequences of favorable *and* unfavorable facts. If a particular fact is presently un-
known, put aside your writing, if possible, and investigate whatever evidence
exists to prove the fact one way or the other. If it is not practical to conduct an
investigation at the present time, then you should provide an analysis of what
law will apply based on your most reasonable estimate of what an investigation
may uncover. The need for accuracy does not mean that you should fail to state
the facts in the light most favorable to the client. It simply means that you must
be cautious in doing so in order to avoid making false or misleading statements
of fact.

Organization.   A disorganized statement of facts not only prevents the reader
from understanding the events in question but also interferes with an understanding of your subsequent analysis. In general, it is best to start with a short
one- or two-sentence summary of the nature of the case, followed by a *chronologically* ordered statement of the detailed facts. Occasional variations from
strict chronological order can be justified as long as they do not interfere with
the flow of the story.

5. Discussion or Analysis

Here you present the law and explain its applicability to the facts. In other
words, you try to answer the issues. For memos that require interpretation of
statutes, a suggested organizational structure is as follows:

- State the entire section or subsection of the statute that you are analyzing.
  Include only what must be discussed in the memo. If the section or subsection
  is long, you may want to place it in an appendix to the memo. If you are
  going to discuss more than one section or subsection, treat them separately
  in different parts of the memo unless they are so interrelated that they must
  be discussed together.

- Break the statute into its elements. (An element is a portion of a rule that is a
  precondition of the applicability of the entire rule. See page 347.) List each
  element separately.

- Briefly tell the reader which elements will be in contention and why. In effect,
  you are telling him or her why you have phrased the issue(s) the way you did
  earlier in the memo.

- Go through each element you have identified, one at a time, spending most
  of your time on the elements that are most in contention.

- For the elements not in contention, simply tell the reader why you think there
  will not be any dispute about them. For example, you anticipate that both
  sides probably will agree that the facts clearly support the applicability or
  nonapplicability of the element.

- For the elements in contention, present your interpretation of each element;
  discuss court opinions that have interpreted the statute, if any; discuss regulations and administrative decisions that have interpreted the statute, if any;
  discuss the legislative history of the statute, if available (page 596); discuss
  scholarly interpretation of the statute, if any.

- Give opposing viewpoints for the elements in contention. Try to anticipate
  how the other side will interpret these elements. For example, what counter-

arguments will the other side probably make through court opinions or legislative history?

6. *Conclusion*

Give your personal opinion on which side has the better arguments. Do not state any new arguments in the conclusion. Simply state your own perspective on the strengths and weaknesses of your arguments.

7. *Recommendations*

State recommendations you feel are appropriate in view of the analysis and conclusion that you have provided. For example, further facts should be investigated, further research should be undertaken, a letter should be written to the agency involved, the case should be litigated or settled, etc.

8. *Appendix*

At the end of the memo, include special items, if any, that you referred to in the memo, such as photographs, statistical tables, or the full text of statutes.

. . . .

What follows is an interoffice memorandum of law that conforms with this structure. Assume that the supervisor wants this memorandum within a few hours after it is given to you. You are asked to provide a preliminary analysis of a statute. Hence, at this point there has been no time to do any research on the statute, although the memo should indicate what research will be needed.

INTEROFFICE MEMORANDUM OF LAW

TO: Mary Jones, Esq.   RE: Whether Donaldson has
FROM: Tim Farrell, Paralegal   violated § 17
DATE: March 13, 1990
CASE: Department of Sanitation v. Jim Donaldson
OFFICE FILE NUMBER: 90-114
DOCKET NUMBER: (none at this time; no action has been filed)

A. ASSIGNMENT
   You have asked me to do a preliminary analysis of 23 State Code Ann. § 17 (1980) to assess whether our client, Jim Donaldson, has violated this statute. No research on the statute has been undertaken thus far, but I will indicate where such research might be helpful.

B. LEGAL ISSUE
   When a government employee is asked to rent a car for his agency, but uses the car for personal business before he signs the lease, has this employee violated § 17, which prohibits the use of "property leased to the government" for nonofficial purposes?

C. FACTS
   Jim Donaldson is a government employee who works for the State Department of Sanitation. On February 12, 1990, he is asked by his supervisor, Fred Jackson, to rent a car for the agency for a two-year

---

Continued

period. At the ABC Car Rental Company, Donaldson is shown several cars available for rental. He asks the manager if he could test drive one of the cars for about 15 minutes before making a decision. The manager agrees. Donaldson then drives the car to his home in the area, picks up a TV, and takes it to his sister's home. When he returns, he tells the manager that he wants to rent the car for his agency. He signs the lease and takes the car to the agency. The supervisor, however, finds out about the trip that Donaldson made to his sister with the TV. He is charged with a violation of § 17. Since he is a new employee at the agency, he is fearful that he might lose his job.

D. ANALYSIS

Donaldson is charged with violating 23 State Code Ann. § 17 (1980), which provides as follows:

§17. Use of Government Property

An employee of any state agency shall not directly or indirectly use government property of any kind, including property leased to the government, for other than officially approved activities.

To establish a violation of this statute, the following elements must be proven:

(1) An employee of any state agency
(2) (a) shall not directly use government property of any kind including property leased to the government, or
    (b) shall not indirectly use government property of any kind including property leased to the government
(3) for other than officially approved activities

The main problem in this case will be the second element.

(1) Employee of a state agency

Donaldson works for the State Department of Sanitation, which is clearly a "state agency" under the statute.

(2) Use of property leased to the government

The central issue is whether Donaldson used property leased to the government. (The rented car was not owned by the government. Hence it was not "government property." And Donaldson acted "directly" rather than "indirectly," such as by causing someone else to drive the car.) There should be no dispute that when Donaldson drove the car to his sister's, he directly used property. But was it "property leased to the government"?

Donaldson's best argument is a fairly strong one. His position will be that when he made the trip to his sister, he had not yet signed the lease. He would argue that "leased" means contractually committed to rent. Under this definition, the car did not become property leased to the government until after he returned from his sister's house. No costs were incurred by the government because of the test drive. Rental payments would not begin until the car was rented through the signing of the lease.

The supervisor, on the other hand, will argue for a broader definition of "leased"—that it means the process of obtaining a contractual commitment to rent, including the necessary steps leading up to that commitment. Under this definition, the car

Continued

was leased to Donaldson when he made the unauthorized trip. The test drive was arguably a necessary step in making the decision to sign a long-term leasing contract.

The goal of the legislature in enacting § 17 should be kept in mind when trying to determine the meaning of any of the language of § 17. The legislature was trying to avoid the misuse of government resources. Public employees should not take advantage of their position for private gain. To do so would be a violation of the public trust. Yet this is what Donaldson did. While on the government payroll, he obtained access to a car and used it for a private trip. Common sense would lead to the conclusion that leasing in § 17 is not limited to the formal signing of a leasing contract. Anything that is necessarily part of the process of signing that contract should be included. The legislature wanted to prevent the misuse of government resources in all necessary aspects of the leasing of property.

It is not clear from the facts whether the manager of the ABC Rental Company knew that Donaldson was considering the rental on behalf of a government agency when he received permission to take the test drive. The likelihood is that he did know it, although this should be checked. If the manager did know, then Donaldson probably used the fact that he was a government employee to obtain the permission. He held himself out as a reliable individual because of the nature of his employment. This reinforces the misuse argument under the broader definition of "leased" presented above.

I have not yet checked whether there are any court opinions or agency regulations interpreting § 17 on this point. Nor have I researched the legislative history of the statute. All this should be done soon.

(3) Officially Approved Activities

Nothing in the facts indicates that Donaldson's supervisor, Fred Jackson, gave him any authorization to make the TV trip. Even if Jackson had authorized the trip, it would probably not be "officially" approved, since the trip was not for official (i.e., public) business.

E. CONCLUSION

Donaldson has the stronger argument based on the language of the statute. The property simply was not "leased" at the time he made the TV trip. I must admit, however, that the agency has some very good points in its favor. Unlike Donaldson's technical argument, the agency's position is grounded in common sense. Yet on balance, Donaldson's argument should prevail.

F. RECOMMENDATIONS

Some further investigation is needed. We should find out whether the ABC Rental Company manager knew that Donaldson was a government employee at the time he asked for the test drive. In addition, legal research should be undertaken to find out if any court opinions and agency regulations exist on the statute. A check into the legislative history of § 17 is also needed.

Finally, I recommend that we send a letter to Donaldson's supervisor, Fred Jackson, explaining our position. I have attached a draft of such a letter for your signature in the event you deem this action appropriate. [See page 628.]

Continued

> There is one matter that I have not addressed in this memo. Donaldson is concerned that he might lose his job over this incident. Assuming for the moment that he did violate § 17, it is not at all clear that termination would be an appropriate sanction. The statute is silent on this point. Let me know if you want me to research this issue.

■ ASSIGNMENT 12.1

The Pepsi Cola Bottling Company is authorized to do business in Florida. It wishes to prevent another Florida company from calling itself the Pepsi Catsup Company because this name violates § 225.25. The Pepsi Catsup Company denies that its name is in violation of this statute. The Secretary of State has the responsibility of enforcing this statute.

48 State Code Ann. § 225.25 (1979). The name of a company or corporation shall be such as will distinguish it from any other company or corporation doing business in Florida.

Your supervisor asks you to prepare a preliminary memorandum of law on the applicability of this statute. The office represents the Pepsi Catsup Company. Do no legal research at this time, although you should point out what research might be helpful. After you complete the memo, draft a letter to the Secretary of State giving the position of your office on the applicability of the statute. (You can make up the names and addresses of the people involved as well as any dates that you need.)

■ Section C. Appellate Brief

The word *brief* has several meanings.

First, to *brief* a case is to summarize its major components, such as key facts, issues, reasoning, disposition. (See Chapter 7.) Such a brief is your own summary of a court opinion for later use.

Second, a *trial brief* is an attorney's set of notes on how to conduct the trial. The notes will be on the opening statement, witnesses, exhibits, direct and cross-examination, closing argument, etc. This trial brief is sometimes called a trial manual or trial notebook (see page 470). It is not submitted to the court nor to the other side. A *trial memorandum* on points of law might be submitted, but not the trial brief, which contains counsel's strategy. (This trial memorandum, however, is sometimes referred to as a trial brief. In such instances, the trial brief consists of arguments of law rather than the tactical blueprint for the conduct of the trial.)

Third, the *appellate brief* is the formal written argument to a court of appeals on why a lower court's decision should be affirmed, modified, or reversed. It is submitted to the appellate court and to the other side. The appellate brief is one of the most sophisticated kinds of legal writing in a law office.

The first appellate brief that is usually submitted is the *appellant's* brief. The appellant is the party initiating the appeal. Then the *appellee's* brief is filed in response. The appeal is taken against the appellee (sometimes called the *respondent*). Finally, the appellant is often allowed to submit a *reply brief* to counter the position taken in the appellee's brief.

Occasionally a court will permit a nonparty to the litigation to submit an appellate brief. This is referred to as an *amicus curiae* (friend of the court) brief

Farrell, Grote, & Schweitzer
Attorneys at Law
724 Central Plaza Place
West Union, Ohio 45693
513-363-7159

March 15, 1990

Frederick Jackson
Field Supervisor
Department of Sanitation
3416 34th St. NW
West Union, Ohio 45693

RE: James Donaldson
90-114

Dear Mr. Jackson:

Our firm represents Mr. James Donaldson. As you know, some question has arisen as to Mr. Donaldson's use of a car prior to the time he was asked to rent it for your agency on February 12, 1990. Our understanding is that he was asked to go to the ABC Car Rental Company in order to rent a car that was needed by your agency, and that he did so satisfactorily.

Your agency became responsible for the car at the moment Mr. Donaldson signed the lease for the car rental. What happened prior to the time the lease was signed is not relevant. The governing statute (§ 17) is quite explicit. It forbids nonofficial use of property "leased" to the government. Such use did not occur in this case. No one has questioned Mr. Donaldson's performance of his duty once he "leased" the car.

If additional clarification is needed, we would be happy to discuss the matter with you further.

Sincerely,

Mary Jones, Esq.

wps: TF

(page 491). The *amicus* brief advises the court on how to resolve the controversies before it.

Not all appellate briefs have the same structure. Rules of court often specify what structure or format the brief should take, the print size, number of copies to be submitted, etc. The following are the major components of many appellate briefs:

(a) Caption. The caption states the names of the parties, the name of the court, the court file or docket number, and the kind of appellate brief it is. The caption goes on the front cover of the brief (page 491).

(b) The Statement of Jurisdiction. In this section of the brief, there is a short statement explaining the subject-matter jurisdiction of the appellate court. For example:

This Court has jurisdiction under 28 U.S.C. § 1291 (1967).

The jurisdiction statement may point out some of the essential facts that relate to the jurisdiction of the appellate court, such as how the case came up on appeal. For example:

On January 2, 1978, a judgment was entered by the U.S. Court of Appeals for the Second Circuit. The U.S. Supreme Court granted certiorari on February 6, 1978. 400 U.S. 302.

Later in the brief there is a Statement of the Case in which more detailed jurisdictional material is often included.

(c) Table of Contents.   The table of contents is an outline of the major components of the brief, including *point headings,* and the pages in the brief on which everything begins. A point heading is the party's conclusion it wants the court to adopt for a particular issue. The function of the table of contents is to provide the reader with quick and easy access to each portion of the brief. Because the page numbers will not be known until the brief is completed, the table of contents is the last section of the brief to be written. The following excerpt from the respondent's brief illustrates the structure of a table of contents which includes the point headings as part of the "argument."

TABLE OF CONTENTS

(d) Table of Authorities.   This table lists all the cases, statutes, regulations, administrative decisions, constitutional provisions, charter provisions, ordinances, court rules, and secondary authority relied on in the brief. All the cases are listed in alphabetical order, all the statutes are listed in alphabetical and numerical order, etc. The page numbers on which each of these authorities is discussed in the brief are presented so that the table acts as an index to these authorities.

Example:

Table of Authorities

	Page
CASES:	
Smith v. Jones, 24 F.2d 445 (5th Cir. 1974)	2, 4, 12
Thompson v. Richardson, 34 Miss. 650, 65 So. 109 (1930)	3, 9
Etc.	
CONSTITUTIONAL PROVISIONS	
Art. 5, Miss. Constitution	12, 17
Art. 7, Miss. Constitution	20
Etc.	
STATUTES	
Miss. Code Ann. § 23(b) (1978)	2, 8, 23
Miss. Code Ann. § 45 (1978)	7
Etc.	
LAW REVIEW ARTICLES	
Colom, *Sex Discrimination in the 1980's,* 35 Miss. Law Journal 268 (1982)	19
ETC.	

(e) Questions Presented. The label used for this part of the brief varies. It may be called "Questions Presented," "Points Relied on for Reversal," "Points in Error," "Assignments of Error," "Issues Presented," etc. Regardless of the label, its substance is essentially the same: it is a statement of the legal issues that the party wishes the appellate court to consider and decide.

(f) Statement of the Case. Here, the dispute and lower court proceedings to date are summarized, the essential facts of the case are presented, and (often) jurisdictional data is included.

Example:

These are actions based upon the Federal Tort Claims Act, 28 U.S.C. § 1346(b), initiated by the appellants, Garrett Freightlines, Inc. and Charles R. Thomas in the United States District Court for the District of Idaho. The appellant alleged that appellee's employee, Randall W. Reynolds, while acting within the scope of his employment, negligently caused injury to appellants. The United States denied that the employee was acting within the scope of his employment.

On March 27, 1973, appellant Garrett made a motion for limited summary judgment as to whether Reynolds was acting within the scope of his employment when the collision occurred. The actions of Garrett and Thomas were consolidated by order of the court, and appellee later moved for summary judgment (see trial transcript, page 204).

The District Court held that under the authority of dicta in *Berrettoni v. United States,* 436 F.2d 1372 (9th Cir. 1970), Reynolds was not within the scope of his employment when the accident occurred and granted appellee's motion for summary judgment. It is from that order and judgment that the injured now appeals.

Staff Sergeant Reynolds was a career soldier in the United States Military and, until November 9, 1970, stationed at Fort Rucker, Alabama. On or about July 30, 1970, official orders directed that Reynolds be reassigned to the Republic of Vietnam. . . .

(g) Summary of Argument.   The major points to be made in the brief are summarized in this section.

(h) Argument.   Here the attorney explains the legal positions of the client. All the primary and secondary authority relied on is analyzed.

(i) Conclusion.   The conclusion states what action the attorney is asking the appellate court to take.

(j) Appendixes.   The appendixes contain excerpts from statutes, or other primary authority, excerpts from the trial, charts, descriptions of exhibits entered into evidence at the trial, etc.

Section D. Some Writing Guidelines

1. Words and Phrases to Avoid

■ Avoid the following terms altogether:

> above (as an adjective)
>
> aforementioned
>
> aforesaid
>
> and/or (say "A or B," or say "A or B or both")
>
> beforementioned
>
> provided that
>
> said (as a substitute for "the," "that," or "those")
>
> same (as a substitute for "it," "he," "her," etc.)
>
> to wit
>
> whatsoever
>
> whensoever
>
> wheresoever

■ Avoid circumlocutions, which are pairs of words having the same effect:

alter and change	full force and effect
any and all	made and entered into
authorize and empower	null and void
by and with	order and direct
each and all	over and above
each and every	sole and exclusive
final and conclusive	type and kind
from and after	unless and until
full and complete	

■ Avoid expressions such as:

none whatever

make application, make a determination

shall be considered to be, shall be deemed to be, may be treated as, have the effect of (unless a fiction is intended)

2. *Preferred Expressions*

Unless there are special reasons to the contrary:

Do Not Say	*Say*
(1) accorded	(1) given
(2) adequate number of	(2) enough
(3) admit of	(3) allow
(4) afforded	(4) given
(5) all of the	(5) all the
(6) a person is prohibited from	(6) a person shall not
(7) approximately	(7) about
(8) at least	(8) not less than (when referring to two or more)
(9) at such time as	(9) when
(10) attains the age of _____	(10) becomes _____years of age
(11) attempt (as a verb)	(11) try
(12) at the time	(12) when
(13) by means of	(13) by
(14) calculate	(14) compute
(15) category	(15) kind, class, group
(16) cause it to be done	(16) have it done
(17) contiguous to	(17) next to
(18) corporation organized under the laws of Ohio	(18) Ohio corporation
(19) deem	(19) consider
(20) does not operate to	(20) does not
(21) during such time as	(21) while
(22) during the course of	(22) during
(23) endeavor (as a verb)	(23) try
(24) enter into a contract with	(24) to contract with
(25) evince	(25) show
(26) expiration	(26) end
(27) for the duration of	(27) during
(28) for the purpose of holding (or other gerund)	(28) to hold (or comparable infinitive)
(29) for the reason that	(29) because
(30) forthwith	(30) immediately
(31) in accordance with	(31) pursuant to, under
(32) in case	(32) if
(33) in cases in which	(33) when, where
(34) in order to	(34) to
(35) in sections 2023 to 2039 inclusive	(35) in sections 2023 to 2039

Do Not Say	*Say*
(36) in case of	(36) when, if
(37) in the event of	(37) if
(38) in the event that	(38) if
(39) in the interest of	(39) for
(40) is able to	(40) can
(41) is applicable	(41) applies
(42) is authorized to	(42) may
(43) is binding upon	(43) binds
(44) is directed to	(44) shall
(45) is empowered to	(45) may
(46) is entitled (in the sense of "has the name")	(46) is called
(47) is entitled to	(47) may
(48) is hereby authorized and it shall be his or her duty to	(48) shall
(49) is hereby authorized to	(49) shall
(50) is not prohibited from	(50) may
(51) is permitted to	(51) may
(52) is required to	(52) shall
(53) is unable to	(53) cannot
(54) it is directed	(54) shall
(55) it is his or her duty to	(55) shall
(56) it is the duty of	(56) shall
(57) it shall be lawful	(57) may
(58) it shall be unlawful for a person to	(58) a person shall not
(59) no later than June 30, 1990	(59) before July 1, 1990
(60) on or after July 1, 1991	(60) after June 30, 1991
(61) on or before June 30, 1989	(61) before July 1, 1989
(62) on the part of	(62) by
(63) or, in the alternative	(63) or
(64) paragraph (5) of subsection (a) of section 2097	(64) section 2097(a)(5)
(65) per annum	(65) a year
(66) per centum	(66) percent
(67) period of time	(67) use period *or* time
(68) provision of law	(68) law
(69) render (in the sense of give)	(69) give
(70) State of Massachusetts	(70) Massachusetts
(71) subsequent to	(71) after

Do Not Say	Say
(72) suffer (in the sense of permit)	(72) permit
(73) under the provisions of	(73) under
(74) until such time as	(74) until

3. Action Verbs

Wherever possible, draft your sentences to use action verbs instead of participles, gerunds, and other noun or adjective forms. Action verbs are shorter and more direct.

Do Not Say	Say
(1) give consideration to	(1) consider
(2) give recognition to	(2) recognize
(3) have knowledge of	(3) know
(4) have need of	(4) need
(5) in the determination of	(5) to determine
(6) is applicable	(6) applies
(7) is dependent on	(7) depends on
(8) is in attendance at	(8) attends
(9) make an appointment of	(9) appoint
(10) make application	(10) apply
(11) make payment	(11) pay
(12) make provision for	(12) provide for

4. Active Voice

Avoid the passive voice whenever possible.[1]

Do Not Say	Say
It was decided by the plaintiff.	The plaintiff decided . . .
The motion is filed by defendant.	Defendant files the motion.

Compare the following versions of the same sentence:[2]

In neither the motion nor appellant's brief was there any reliance on ORC § 2943.39.	Appellant did not rely on ORC § 2943.39 in either his motion or his brief.
The testimony of the defendant was contradicted by the fact that he had the receipt showing partial payment.	The receipt showing partial payment contradicted defendant's testimony.

---

[1]State Bar of California, *Are You Misunderstood?* (March 1990).

[2]Grey, *Writing a Good Appellate Brief*, 88 Case and Comment 44, 48–50 (No. 6, November–December 1983). Reprinted by special permission. Copyrighted © 1983 by the Lawyers Cooperative Publishing Co.

The result obtained from a properly administered breathalyzer test is the percentage by weight of alcohol in a person's blood.	A properly administered breathalyzer test shows the percentage by weight of alcohol in a person's blood.

5. Positive Form

Phrase something positively rather than negatively whenever possible.

Do Not Say	*Say*
It is not difficult to imagine.	It is easy to imagine.
The paper is not without flaws.	The paper has flaws.

6. Verbosity

Avoid unnecessary words. Compare the following versions of the same sentence:

He consulted *with* a doctor *in regard* to his injuries.	He consulted a doctor *about* his injuries.
He drove to the left *due to the fact* that the lane was blocked.	He drove to the left *because* the lane was blocked.
This product is used for *hair-dyeing purposes.*	This product is used to *dye hair.*
The continuance was requested *in order to obtain the presence of a witness who was not then available.*	The continuance was requested *because a witness was unavailable.*

Read these sentences, with and without the italicized words.

The court directed a verdict in favor of defendant *and against the plaintiff.* (Verdicts for defendants usually are against the plaintiff.)

The car was green *in color.* (This distinguishes it from the car that was green in size!)

A stipulation by *all of* the parties. (A stipulation by some of the parties is not of much use.)

A delivery was made every Tuesday *on a regular weekly basis.* (What does *every Tuesday* mean?)

7. Shorter Sentences

Use short sentences. A short precise sentence is often more comprehensible and more effective. What is the writer saying in the following sentence?

The Appellee contends that there is not reversible error in the trial court's sustaining the Appellant's objections given the immediate corrective instructions of the trial court as well as the weight of the evidence against the Appellant.

Divide such sentences into a series of shorter sentences:

There is no reversible error. The trial court sustained the objection and immediately cautioned the jury. Considering all the evidence, there is no prejudice to Appellant.

Compare these versions:

The deicer spray had admittedly been sprayed on the inside of the windshield. However, without knowing the name of the manufacturer or having an independent analysis made of the deicer spray, it could not possibly be ascertained what quantity of methanol was in the product and that would be essential to ascertaining what effect, if any, having breathed the chemical would have upon the intoxilizer test.

The deicer sprayed on the inside windshield contained methanol. It was not possible to analyze the product and determine the amount of methanol without knowing the name of the manufacturer. It was not possible to learn what effect, if any, inhaling the methanol would have on the intoxilizer test.

The defendant, ABC, an Ohio Corporation for profit, is engaged in the subsidized housing business and incident thereto is the owner of six dwelling units containing 46 apartment units housing 100 people. To provide for the culinary and sanitary needs of the occupants the defendant purchases from LeAx approximately 5300 gallons (22 tons) of water per day, and since opening for business in July 1975 has purchased 11,308,000 gallons of water which is all collected following use, placed in a sewage plant, treated, and discharged into a drainage ditch, which in turn discharges onto the plaintiff's property.

The defendant, ABC Corp., owns and operates a 46-unit apartment complex containing 100 residents. Water for the apartments is supplied by LeAx at the rate of 5300 gallons, 22 tons, per day. All waste water from the apartments is treated in defendant's sewage plant and discharged into a drainage ditch that runs across plaintiff's property.

This case involves an incident which occurred on November 16, 1988. The plaintiff, Oilcorp, was the owner of a drilling rig which was located in a rural section of Athens County for the purpose of drilling for petroleum. Prior to November 16, 1988, it has been determined that the drilling was completed and it was necessary to move the rig to another location. The defendant was notified of this need and was requested to bring equipment to the drill site for the purpose of moving the drilling rig and associated apparatus from that location to a new location.

The plaintiff, Oilcorp, owned an oil drilling rig located in rural Athens County. It was necessary to move the rig to another location. Oilcorp requested defendant to bring his equipment to the drill site to move the drilling rig.

8. Pronoun Reference

Use pronouns only where the nouns to which the pronouns refer are unmistakably clear. Using pronouns with ambiguous referents can confuse the meaning of a sentence. If the pronoun could refer to more than one person or object in a sentence, repeat the name of the person or object to avoid ambiguity.

Do Not Say: After the administrator appoints a deputy assistant, he shall supervise the . . .. [Who does the supervising? The administrator or the deputy? If the latter is intended, then:]

Say: After the administrator appoints a deputy assistant, the deputy assistant shall supervise the . . ..

9. Sexism in Language

Avoid gender-specific language when the intent is to refer to both sexes. If neutral language is not available, rewrite the sentence to avoid the problem.

Gender-Specific Language	*Gender-Neutral Alternatives*
(1) businessman	(1) executive, member of the business community
(2) chairman	(2) chairperson, chair
(3) draftsman	(3) drafter
(4) man	(4) person, human, humankind
(5) man-hours	(5) worker hours
(6) mankind	(6) humanity
(7) manpower	(7) work force, personnel
(8) workmen's compensation	(8) worker's compensation

☐ Chapter Summary

A law office prepares many different kinds of written documents. Opinion letters provide legal advice to a client. Instruments such as deeds, contracts, and other agreements are more formal documents that accomplish specific legal results. Pleadings such as complaints, answers, and cross-claims state claims, defenses, and other positions of parties in litigation. An internal memorandum of law analyzes primary and secondary authority for other members of the office. An external memorandum of law (for example, a "points and authorities" memorandum) analyzes the law for someone outside the office, such as a hearing officer. A case brief is a summary of the major parts of a court opinion. A trial brief (often called a trial manual or trial notebook) is an attorney's set of notes on how he or she intends to conduct a trial. An appellate brief is an argument submitted to an appellate court on why the decision of a lower court should be affirmed, modified, or reversed.

The major components of an internal memorandum of law are the heading, the statement of the assignment, the legal issues, the facts, the discussion or analysis, the conclusion, and the recommendations.

The major components of an appellate brief are the caption, the statement of jurisdiction, the table of contents, the table of authorities, the questions presented, the statement of the case, the summary of the argument, the argument, the conclusion, and the appendices.

There are a number of important guidelines that will increase the clarity and effectiveness of any kind of writing. Avoid overly formal language, such as aforesaid, to wit, and wheresoever. Avoid circumlocutions like "any and all," "each and every," and "unless and until." Prefer words and expressions that are less pompous and often shorter. For example, instead of saying "at such time as," say "when." Prefer action verbs. For example, instead of saying "give consideration to," say "consider." In addition, prefer the active voice to the passive voice, phrase things positively rather than negatively, avoid verbosity, use shorter sentences, make all pronoun references clear, and avoid sexism in language.

Key Terms

opinion letter
instrument
formbook
pleading
memorandum of law
internal/interoffice
    memorandum of law
external/adversary
    memorandum of law
hearing memorandum
points and authorities
    memorandum

trial memorandum
heading
RE
legal issue
trial brief
trial manual
trial notebook
trial memorandum
appellate brief
appellant
appellee
respondent

reply brief
amicus curiae
caption of appellate brief
statement of jurisdiction
point heading
table of authorities
questions presented
statement of the case
circumlocution

13

Computer Literacy for Paralegals: An Introduction to the Use of Computers in a Law Office

with Dale Hobart*

■ Chapter Outline

▮ Section A. Law Offices, Computers, and Paralegals

It is very doubtful that you will work in an office without computers. For many medium and large law offices, computers dominate the practice of law and the management of the law office. If you flipped through the pages of a bar association magazine or legal newspaper, you would probably find that two-thirds of the advertising is from computer manufacturers, vendors, and consultants. Paralegals are an integral part of this computer environment, as demonstrated by the surveys presented in Figures 13.1 and 13.2 and by the comments of paralegals that follow these surveys.

How do paralegals feel computers have affected their professional lives? The following comments, while not representative of all paralegals, help provide an answer.

---

*Director of Legal Assistant Program and Assistant Director of Academic Computing, Ferris State College

FIGURE 13.1

Survey on Computer Use

Employment and Salary Survey 1990 (Rocky Mountain Legal Assistants Association, 1990) Question: Do you personally use a computer for any of the following? (Answer based on 470 responses from paralegals.)	Task	Yes	Percent Responding
	▪ Word Processing	331	77
	▪ Docketing	94	22
	▪ Conflicts Check	24	6
	▪ Litigation Support	181	42
	▪ Timekeeping/Billing	87	20
	▪ Other	95	22

PARALEGAL COMMENTS:
General

"These amazing little machines are filled with micro-chips, circuit boards, disks, and many other magical parts about which I know nothing! What I do know is how much more efficient I am with my PC." [1]

"In the last few years, the computer has become a desirable, if not indispensable, tool of the legal profession, and, in fact, it is somewhat ironic that this new tool has caused typing skills to enjoy a comeback in popularity. Efficient use of the computer keyboard not only facilitates drafting of legal pleadings but also the use of a variety of software programs. While word processing programs are the programs most widely used by legal assistants, [other software used includes:] programs for file organization, document retrieval, calculation, spreadsheet formulation, and research. . . ." [2]

Corporate Law

Some paralegals have become adept at tailoring general business programs, such as spreadsheet and database management programs, to different areas of legal practice. "When I worked . . . for a major corporation, I was responsible for the shareholder relations program. This required monthly analysis of the company's shareholder base. Rather than have a transfer agent compile the information for a handsome fee, I prepared the report on an IBM PC using Lotus 1-2-3." [3]

Criminal Law

"We were confronted with more than 300 boxes of documents stored in a depository in Houston" that contained evidence that had to be classified so that it would be available for the trial attorney. To do that, the attorney "started building a data base, using teams of paralegals to code and input the information." The judge allowed the attorney to connect his computer and fax machine

▪
Not so many years ago, computers were fancy tools only big firms could afford. Even firms with computers were inclined to keep them out of sight, off the polished oak desks of their lawyers, many of whom made it a point of pride not to be able to type. Those days are gone forever.
Paul Reidinger, American Bar Association Journal (1991).
▪

---

[1] Eastwick, *JLA's Seminar/Workshop on Personal Computers in the Law Office,* JLA News 4, Issue 12 (Jacksonville Legal Assistants, January 1988).
[2] Schueneman, *Software Brings Typing Back to the Future,* 3 TALAFAX 3, No. 3 (Tucson Ass'n of Legal Assistants, 1991).
[3] B. Bernardo, *Paralegal* (Peterson's Guides, 1990).

FIGURE 13.2

Computers in the Law Office

Results of 1989 Wage, Benefit & Utilization Survey

(Legal Assistants of New Mexico, 1989)

Question: What types of tasks do you use your computer for? (Answer based on 103 responses. Paralegals could check more than one task.)

71 Word Processing
49 Document Control
41 Case Evaluation and Management
39 Document Assembly/Forms Fill-in
39 Preparing Charts and Exhibits
36 Database Research (WESTLAW & LEXIS)
33 Full-text Data Storage and Retrieval
29 Database Research (nonlegal)
22 Calendaring/Date Reminder (tickler) System
13 Networking/E-Mail (Electronic Mail)
13 Accounting/Billing
 9 Calculating/"Number Crunching"
 5 Desktop Publishing
 4 Conflicts Checking
 5 Other

Question: Which computer do you use? (Answer based on 96 responses from paralegals.)

Number	Computer Used
62	IBM or Compatible PC
4	Apple PC
1	IBM Displaywriter
9	Portable and/or laptop
20	Other

Question: Does your firm provide you with your own PC or terminal, or do you share it with other users? (Answer based on 101 responses.)

60 Use own PC or terminal
17 Share a PC or terminal
24 N/A

Question: Which word processing software program does your office use? (Answer based on 80 responses.)

Number	Software Used
47	WordPerfect
14	Wang
4	Microsoft Word
3	Displaywrite
18	Other (e.g., DEC, Lanier)

Question: Does your firm use a computerized litigation support system? (Answer based on 103 responses.)

71 YES
29 NO
 3 N/A

Question: When your firm orders the transcript of a hearing or a deposition, it is provided on disk so that it can be used with your in-house database system? (Answer based on 95 responses.)

50 YES
40 NO
 5 N/A

Question: Has your firm used an outside computer consultant when acquiring computer hardware and/or software? (Answer based on 95 responses.)

66 YES
27 NO
 2 N/A

---

in the courtroom with the computer and fax machine in the law office. In effect, the attorney was "wired into the network back at the office, which is staffed with paralegals who have access to all kinds of information which can be faxed or sent by computer back into the courtroom immediately."[4]

---

[4]Keeva, *Document Analysis in Criminal Litigation*, 76 American Bar Ass'n Journal 80 (May 1990).

Estates and Trusts

Ann Cook, legal assistant at Pepper, Hamilton & Scheetz of Philadelphia, saw a demonstration of a software package for fiduciary accounting and immediately began urging her firm to move in that direction. "After seeing it, I was no longer satisfied writing the same information several times for each different purpose when all I had to do was input it once and then push buttons. . . . We've now expanded our system to do estate planning calculations which manually were cumbersome and expensive to produce. Eventually, we would like to connect our system into a data bank like Standard & Poors, so that we can get instant evaluations of stock and bond values." [5]

Insurance

In the case management area, Norman Strizek works with insurance firms. He's "created databases so they can track separately every litigation case they're involved in, and [identify] which law firm is handling each part; what they're billed each quarter; the status of the litigation; responsible attorneys and paralegals, with phone numbers; due dates of different filings and who is handling each. It helps the insurer manage all their litigation." [6]

Litigation

"When the portable PC is not used for data retrieval, the legal assistant can use it to take notes." Julie Hoff, a litigation legal assistant for ten years, "cites an example of a legal assistant who put her portable to work in an efficient manner during a recent trial in Minneapolis. While the witness was testifying, the legal assistant summarized the proceedings on her portable computer. At the end of each day, she printed her notes and they were used in the preparation of [cross] examination for the next day and for future witnesses." [7]

"I never leave home without my laptop!" says Laurie Roselle, the Litigation Paralegal Manager at Rogers & Wells in New York. She "types in taxis, commutes with her desktop portable, pulls cases and does actual memos." She says, "You have to use every minute—and you can bill the time." [8]

Professional Responsibility

Jane Palmer is the conflict-of-interest specialist at Hogan and Hartson in Washington D.C. Working under the supervision of an attorney, Jane spends "more than half her time at the computer on requests for information." She "does all the research on every prospective client" for the firm's offices in Washington D.C., Maryland, Virginia, London, and Brussels "to find out who are the related parties in the matter they are bringing." She "uses her database to see if Hogan and Hartson has ever represented any party on any side of the matter, or been adverse to them. The databases are a client list, accounting and

---

[5]Troop, *Paralegals Are Taking the Lead Through Computers,* 2 Legal Assistant Today 21 (Winter 1985).

[6]Milano, *Novel Way Paralegals Are Using Computers,* 8 Legal Assistant Today 22, 110 (March/April 1991).

[7]*Law Office Trends: Portable PCs in the Courtroom,* Merrill Advantage, 6 (Spring 1989).

[8]Milano, see footnote 6 at p. 23.

billing information, and addresses." "I draw on that for searches, and add to it every day, updating the information." Building on the accounting department's database, Palmer uses Informatics, software designed for conflicts, which connects to accounting and is used for both functions.[9]

Torts

"Moving on to a tetracycline case involving five pharmaceutical firms, he computerized 40,000 documents. . . ." His "team did the coding." [10]

McCarthy, Palmer, Volkema & Becker is a plaintiff's tort litigation firm in Columbus Ohio. "Computers are an important part of the legal assistants' daily work environment. In place of the message slips and paper memos, the desks of the attorneys and paralegals are adorned with personal computers. Since the firm's beginning, all of the attorneys, legal assistants, secretaries and receptionists have been networked. All telephone messages are transferred from the receptionist via E-mail (Electronic Mail). The main function of the computer, however, is as a warehouse for client file information. The attorney and legal assistant can access the computer from the name and phone number of the judge, opposing counsel, adjuster, treating physician or expert, without pulling a large file from the filing cabinet. An electronic calendar is also available on the system. Firm members now have a means for scheduling meetings with more than one attorney and/or legal assistant without leaving their desks. The computer will notify the person . . . of any conflicts. No more telephone tag or running from one calendar to another.[11]

 ## Section B. Survival Strategies

When you walk into your first paralegal job, be prepared to encounter some sophisticated equipment. Our goal in this chapter is not to make you an expert in any particular product or system, rather the goal is to provide you with some of the fundamentals so that you will be in a better position to benefit from the inevitable on-the-job training in the computer products and systems used by a particular law office. We will assume in this chapter that you are a beginner. Even if you are well-versed in computers generally, you'll be a beginner with respect to computer programs that have been (and will be) designed for law offices. Our starting point is a series of survival strategies presented in Figure 13.3. As we begin our exploration of computer use in the practice of law, keep these strategies in mind.

 ## Section C. Terminology

The world of the computer, like the world of law, has its own language. Initially, this language can be very confusing. Persistence and time, however, will help rectify this problem.

---

[9]Milano, see footnote 6 at p. 24.

[10]Milano, see footnote 6 at p. 24.

[11]Overly, *Innovations in Law Office Automation,* 6 LACO Letter 12 (Legal Assistants of Central Ohio, December 1990).

FIGURE 13.3

Computer Survival Strategies: A Paralegal Tackles a New Program in the Law Office

Stage I: Identify Your "Help" Resources

- Find out whether there is anyone in the office who already knows how to use the program who would be willing to answer your questions about it. If possible, this should be someone other than—or in addition to—your supervisor.

- Ask if the program you will be using has an 800 number that you can call for assistance.

- Ask if the program has an *online tutorial* which explains the basics. If so, ask someone to start the tutorial for you.

- Ask if the program has a *"HELP" key* that can be used while you are running the program. If so, ask how to use it.

- Find the manual for the program (called the *documentation*). Turn to the index, if one exists. Select some familiar terms in the index, such as capitalization. Turn to the pages for such items and try to follow the instructions provided for them.

- Start a computer notebook in which you write definitions of new terms, steps to follow for certain tasks, steps you took just before you seemed to make a mistake, questions that you want to ask someone later, etc.

- Expect to learn a new vocabulary. (*Boot*, for example, has nothing to do with what goes on your foot.)

Stage II: Learn the Big Seven Tasks

Learn the seven essential tasks that apply to most programs:

- How to turn on the computer, *load* the program, and start using it

- How to create a new document or file with the program

- How to save a document or file

- How to call up (or retrieve) a document or file that

- was created and saved earlier

- How to make a copy of the document or file

- How to turn on the printer and print a document or file

- How to exit from the program and turn the computer off

Stage III: Take the Initiative

- Find out if your local paralegal association is offering a seminar on computer use. Attend it. If none is planned, call the president of the association and suggest that one be offered.

- Read the local bar association journals to find out what computer seminars are offered by the bar or by CLE (Continuing Legal Education). Attend some that are relevant to your job.

- Photocopy a chapter from the computer manual at the office. Take the chapter home and read it over the weekend.

- Ask librarians in your area how you can find magazine reviews of the program that you use. Read these reviews.

- Find out if there is a *users group* in your area that meets every month to discuss the program, such as a WordPerfect Users Group. Attend the meetings of this group.

- Organize a "specialty section" of your paralegal association that consists of paralegals who use the program. Members of this section would meet periodically to learn from each other and to discuss common problems with the program.

First we begin with some basic definitions:

Hardware.   The computer and its physical parts. Hardware is what you take out of the box and plug together when you purchase a computer system. It is any part of the system that can be physically touched.

Backup.   To copy information that a computer uses. The copy is made regularly just in case the original is destroyed.

Command.   A word or character typed into the computer to tell the computer what to do next.

Data.   Information of any type that can be used by computers. The data may consist of numbers, words, or pictures.

Typical desktop computer system

Disk Drive (also called a disk).   In this chapter, we will use the term *disk drive* (rather than disk) to describe the part of your hardware that is used to store and retrieve programs and information to and from diskettes (see next definition). The disk drive has the capability of placing program information on a diskette. This is often referred to as *writing information to the diskette*. The disk drive also has the capability of "reading" the information from the diskette into the computer. If the information is a program, the program can then be "run" (see definition below) by the computer. Disk drives can be hard or floppy. A *floppy disk* drive is one that can use diskettes. The diskettes can be easily inserted and removed from the disk drive. *Hard disks,* on the other hand, cannot be removed without taking the hardware apart. Furthermore, they have a much greater memory capacity than diskettes. A 40 megabyte hard disk, for example, will be

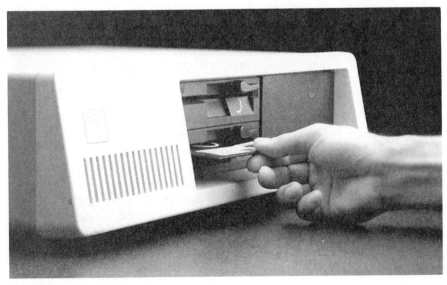

Diskette being inserted into a floppy disk drive

able to hold approximately 40 million *bytes* of information—about 20,000 pages of text. (One byte is the storage equivalent of one letter of the alphabet, or one punctuation mark, or one blank space.) It would take over one hundred regular-sized diskettes to store the same amount of data.

Diskette.   Sometimes these are also called disks, floppy disks, or just floppies. In this chapter, the term *diskette* will be used. A diskette is a flat piece of plastic, 3½ inch or 5¼ inch in size, that is covered with the same magnetic substance used on a magnetic tape. Information is placed on the diskette in a manner similar to the way music is stored on a cassette. The information can be a program or data to be used by a program. This information can then be read into the computer for the computer to use.

3½-inch and 5¼-inch diskettes

File.   A file refers to any information that a computer can use and that is stored or kept together as a group. A file can consist of data or a program. (For the meaning of file in a database program, see Figure 13.5.)

k.   A measure of capacity. Each k equals one kilobyte, which is 1,024 bytes (see definition of byte above). The letter k often refers to the amount of information that can be kept on your diskette. It can also refer to the work area in the computer. The work area is the amount of space available to the computer for keeping programs and information that will be used. When microcomputers were new, 64k was considered a great deal of memory (see definitions below). Today, however, many of the programs require 640k or more to function properly.

Language.   A program that allows a computer to understand commands and carry them out. BASIC, COBAL, and PASCAL are among the most common computer languages.

Laptop.   A portable computer that can be powered by rechargeable batteries.

Typical laptop computer system

Load.   To move or transfer a program or information from a disk drive into the computer.

Memory.   The area inside a computer that contains programs, and data that programs help generate.

Microcomputer.   A computer that is small enough to fit on a desk. The term is not clearly defined because the power of small computers has increased dramatically in the past few years.

Monitor.   A TV-like device that is part of the hardware of the computer. On the screen the monitor displays whatever commands you type at the keyboard—and displays information in response to those commands.

Operating System.   A program that is in charge of what is displayed on the screen, what is sent to the printer, and all other facets of the operation of a computer. In effect, the operating system serves the function of traffic cop or central manager. There are a variety of operating systems available, such as DOS or MS-DOS, OS/2, UNIX, GEOS, HFS (Macintosh), and NextStep. In some of the systems, you type certain commands on the keyboard. In others, you use a small pointer device called a *mouse* to point to pictures (graphics or icons) on the screen that stand for the same kind of commands that you would otherwise "type in." To execute the command, you push (or *click*) a button on the mouse. An important development in this area is *Windows* from Microsoft. This is a mouse-pointer program that allows a user to run several large programs (such as word processing, database management, spreadsheet) simultaneously. To take advantage of this *multitasking* capacity, a number of the older operating systems are issuing what they call their *windows-based* operating system. Furthermore, many software manufacturers are rushing to release versions

A monitor displaying text on screen

of their products for the *windows environment*, e.g., WordPerfect for Windows.

Run.   To cause a program to be loaded into the computer from a disk drive and to begin performing its task.

Save.   To cause a program or data that is in the computer memory to be moved or stored on a diskette or hard drive.

Computer with mouse

Software.   The programs that allow you to perform tasks such as word processing, database management, and spreadsheet calculations. To use a program, you must get it into the computer. This is usually done by transferring the program from a diskette or from the hard drive.

Section D. Hardware

Many people make the mistake of buying a computer first and then trying to figure out what to do with it. This is not the best approach. If you know what you want to do, you should *first find the software* that can do the job and *then buy the computer* that will run that software.

When investigating available programs, you will probably discover that we live in an IBM world. At the present time, most business application programs are designed first for an IBM or *compatible* computer and then are developed for others. There are many computers that are IBM compatible.

The word *compatible,* or compatible computer, is used in several senses. At a minimum, the word simply means that the information or data files created on an IBM computer can also be used by another computer. At the other end of the spectrum of compatibility, some non-IBM computers not only will use information or data from an IBM computer but will also run most software designed for an IBM computer.

Once software has been selected, the next step is to choose a computer. One of the first considerations is how much memory should be purchased for the computer. Most come with a minimum of 640k. For multipurpose software, it is advisable to obtain considerably more.

The next item of hardware to consider is the disk drive. Disk drives are used to load programs into the computer and to store letters, documents, and other information. There are several combinations of disk drives for a microcomputer, but only two that make sense for business applications.

One choice is two floppy drives (a disk drive that uses diskettes to store data). These are disk drives that use removable diskettes that are usually 3½ or 5¼ inches in diameter. The disk drives should be *dual sided,* meaning that the disk drive is capable of writing on both sides of the diskette. It should also be able to store information on a diskette in *condensed* mode. This mode is referred to as *double-density.* Therefore, a two-floppy-drive machine should have dual-sided, double-density disk drives. This will often be abbreviated DS DD. Two disk drives are needed to make the use of a computer faster and easier. If only one disk drive is available, the user is often required to change the diskette in the drive while using the computer. This is time-consuming and frustrating.

The more common choice for business purposes is a computer with one floppy disk drive and one hard disk drive. A hard disk normally used in a microcomputer can hold much more information than a diskette. This means that most of the programs and data that are used from day to day can be kept on the hard disk, making use of the computer more convenient. There is no need to locate and insert a new diskette to change programs on a hard disk system. All the programs that you normally need can be stored on the hard disk and accessed directly. Unlike a diskette, a hard disk cannot be easily removed from the machine. If finances allow, a hard disk is preferable either in the computer itself or externally as part of a network. (A *network,* as we will see below, is created when several computers are connected together.) You will find that it is nearly impossible to have too much disk storage capacity.

You'll need a monitor as part of your system. Monitors usually come in one of two formats: monochrome or color. The monochrome may be either black and white, green, or amber. Most users prefer the green or amber screen monitors. Color is tempting, but unless the computer is going to be used for color graphics or presentations, monochrome is better. Color can be hard on the eyes, though this is beginning to change. As computers become more sophisticated, color quality will improve.

To obtain a printed copy of what has been entered into the computer, you need a printer. There are many different kinds of printers available:[12]

- *Dot Matrix Printer.* This printer uses tiny pins that press against or punch a ribbon to create a pattern of dots.

Daisy wheel

- *Daisy Wheel Printer.* This printer uses a "daisy wheel," a device (resembling a flower) that contains the alphabet and other characters on spokes. The printer spins the wheel to find the character, which then strikes the ribbon.
- *Ink Jet Printer.* This printer uses a stream of ink sprayed on paper to produce the print. The ink comes from a cartridge rather than a ribbon.

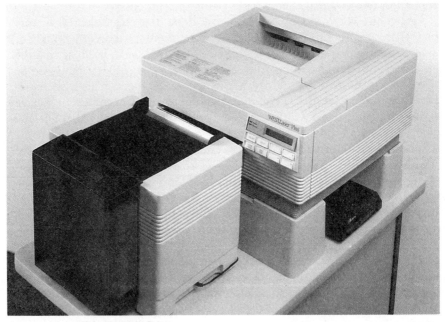

Laser printer: HP LaserJet III Printer

[12]Electronic Industries Association, *How to Buy a Personal Computer,* 14 (1990).

■ *Laser Printer.* This printer uses a laser beam of light to reproduce images. Special cartridges are needed to print text or graphics. It operates very much like a copy machine. Because of their versatility, speed, and high quality, laser printers have become standard in law offices.

A *network* is another important hardware item used by law offices. It will allow you to connect many computers together, enabling them to share (a) information, (b) a hard disk, or (c) printers. For example, a network can make it possible for everyone in a law office to have access to wills, pleadings, or other frequently used documents without each person needing separate copies on individual diskettes. A network can be cost-efficient since it can provide the means for many computers to share some of the more expensive parts of a system.

A *modem* is needed for any law office wishing to use its computer for communications. The modem makes it possible for a computer to send and receive information using regular telephone lines.

An external modem

Many other hardware options are available. The list just given covers the basics and is sufficient to satisfy the needs of most users.

Section E. Software

There are four basic types of software available:

■ Word processing
■ Database management
■ Spreadsheets
■ Communications
■ The fifth and latest kind of software consists of a combination of all four

There are two ways of making a rational choice when selecting software. One is to try out the programs *before* purchasing them. This will work best for someone with experience who knows what to look for. Testing software yourself can be very time consuming. If you have neither the background nor the time to develop the needed expertise (months are needed), consult an expert. Generally the expert should *not* be someone connected with the local computer store who has an interest in selling you the software that is in stock. A person within your own office is often the best expert. There are a surprising number of people who develop such expertise on their own.

1. Word Processing Software

Use a *word processor* instead of a typewriter for writing. It makes little sense to use a typewriter for anything other than addressing one envelope or filling in a simple printed form. Any letter, memo, pleading, brief, or other typed material is easier to prepare with word processing. Once you have used a good word processor, you will be very reluctant to sit at a traditional typewriter again. Since a large volume of writing is done in the law office, a word processor can be a great productivity tool.

Many law offices have used *dedicated word processing* for a long time. A dedicated word processor is one that can do only word processing and none of the other functions that a computer can perform. It is not a computer. The capabilities of the dedicated word processor, however, are now available on computers that can do word processing and other jobs for less cost than the single-purpose or dedicated word processors of old.

The most elemental difference between a word processor and the familiar manual or electric typewriter becomes apparent when you prepare a document for the first time. For example, unlike a traditional typist, the computer user does not listen for a bell in order to know whether he or she is at the end of a line. The computer will automatically move a word down to the next line when the end of a line is reached. This feature is called *word wrap*. There is no need to pause or slow down. The only time you strike the carriage return key is at the end of a paragraph. When a typing error is made at the computer keyboard, there is no need to reach for the bottle of "white out." Nor is there ever a need to worry about a messy final draft caused by insertions or corrections. With the computer you simply go back and correct the error(s). If you left out a letter or sentence, you can easily insert it. The line, in effect, opens up to allow this insertion. If you typed the wrong letter, you can quickly type the correct one directly over the wrong one. If there are too many letters, just press the delete key over the excess letters. Furthermore, there is no need to worry about what such changes will do to paragraph alignment. The computer will take care of it. The task of typing becomes infinitely easier. Someone with limited typing skills soon becomes a confident and competent typist. (See Figure 13.4 for a list of common word-processing terms.)

Easy text entry is just the beginning. Once a document has been put into the computer, it can be used over and over again. Standard paragraphs can be saved, modified, and inserted whenever needed. Documents can be designed so that names are entered once and then automatically included in the final output at fifty different locations. Standard documents can be rearranged by moving paragraphs and sentences within the document. Large or small parts of a document may be moved, deleted, or duplicated to create the final document.

A helpful feature on many word processors is the spelling checker. After a document has been typed, you can activate a spelling program. Different types of spelling programs exist, all of which are based on a large number of words in the program's dictionary. The simpler programs place a mark on any word *not* contained in the program's dictionary. You have probably misspelled such words. You can then review and correct the marked words as needed. More sophisticated spelling programs not only mark a word that is not in the program's dictionary, but also present several possible correct spellings. Spelling

TERM	DEFINITION
Automatic pagination	A feature that enables a word processor to number the pages of the printed copy automatically.
Block	A group of characters, such as a sentence or paragraph.
Block movement	A feature that allows the user to define a block of text and then perform a specific operation on the entire block. Common block operations include block move, block copy, block save, and block delete..
Boldface	Heavy type; for example, **this is boldface**.
Character	A letter, number, or symbol.
Character enhancement	Underlining, boldfacing, subscripting, and superscripting.
Control character	A coded character that does not print but is part of the command sequence in a word processor.
Cursor	The marker on the display screen indicating where the next character can be displayed.
Default setting	A value used by the word processor when it is not instructed to use any other value.
Deletion	A feature by which a character, word, sentence, or larger block of text can be removed from the existing text.
Editing	The act of changing or amending text.
Format	The layout of a page; for example, the number of lines and the margin settings.
Global	An instruction that will be carried out throughout an entire document. For example, change the word ''avenue'' to ''street'' everywhere in the document.
Header	A piece of text that is stored separately from the text and printed at the top of each page.
Incremental spacing	A method by which the printer inserts spaces between words and letters to produce justified margins; also called microspacing.
Insertion	A feature in which a character, word, sentence, or larger block of text is added to the existing text.
Justification	A feature that makes lines of text even at the margins.
Menu	A list of commands or prompts on the display screen.
Print formatting	The function of a word processor that communicates with the printer to tell it how to print the text on paper.
Print preview	A feature that enables the user to view a general representation on the screen of how the document will look when printed.
Screen formatting	A function of a word processor that controls how the text will appear on the screen.
Scrolling	Moving a line of text onto or off the screen.
Search and find	A routine that searches for, and places the cursor at, a specified series or string of characters.
Search and replace	A routine that searches for a specified character string and replaces it with the specified replacement string. See global.
Status line	A message line above or below the text area on a display screen that gives format and system information.

FIGURE 13.4

Frequently Encountered Word Processing Terms

Continued

FIGURE 13.4

Frequently Encountered Word Processing Terms —*Continued*

TERM	DEFINITION
Subscript	A character that prints below the usual text baseline.
Superscript	A character that prints above the usual text baseline.
Text buffer	An area set aside in memory to hold text temporarily.
Text editing	The function of a word processor that enables the user to enter and edit text.
Text file	A file that contains text, as opposed to a program.
Virtual representation	An approach to screen formatting that enables the user to see on the screen exactly how the printed output will look.
Word wrap	The feature in which a word is moved automatically to the beginning of the next line if it goes past the right margin.
WYSIWYG	What you see (on the screen) is what you get (when the screen is printed).

Source: S. Mandell, *Introduction to Computers Using the IBM and MS-DOS PCs with Basic,* 3d ed., 216 (West, 1991).

checkers are great for catching transposed letters, easily overlooked by a proof-reader. (You will be told, for example, that you need to change the spelling of th*ie*r to th*ei*r.) Be aware that a spelling checker will not tell you that you used "to" when you should have used "two" or "too." Since all these words are correctly spelled, they will not be marked by the program.

Word processors can print out a document in many formats. You can change formats if you discover that you are not satisfied with the format of your document. A variety of formats or formatting styles can be selected. The type can be *right justified* (meaning that the right-hand margin of the text is even) or have a ragged right edge. Left margins can be set at many different places throughout the document. Pages can be numbered or unnumbered, and the numbering can start with any digit you choose. Most word processors can include footnotes and keep the textual material that has been footnoted on the same page with the footnote even if you later insert a lot of material on this page. Many word processors can place the same heading at the top of each page without your having to retype the heading for all the pages in the document. A few word processors come with the capability of creating indexes for the document. You simply mark the word or phrase that is to be included in the index and run the index part of the program. An index is then created with all the page numbers for the location of the word or phrase.

Probably the most powerful capability of a word processor is called *merge printing*. It allows you to combine several whole files and to place data from one file into specific locations in another.

Merge printing whole files is very useful in creating documents with standard paragraphs. Each paragraph is usually saved in a computer file with its own name. When you wish to include the paragraph in a document, you simply enter the proper code and the name of the file. When you print out the document, the paragraph will be included at the location indicated without the necessity of retyping it.

Merging data from one file into another allows the creation of letters or other documents with appropriate names and addresses included in the finished document at all the proper places. This can be particularly useful in mailing the same document to many people. Code words are used for the placement of each bit of information such as the street address, the city, and the state. Once the code words are created, the street address, city, or whatever is represented by the code word, will be included in the final document wherever the code word is found.

When selecting a word processing program, the first step is to determine what current tasks could be done better and more efficiently with a word processing program. If the law office uses standard forms or standard language in documents or mass mailings (such as billings), a word processor with good merge capabilities is very helpful.

If you already have word processing capabilities, you may be considering a change in your system. It is critical to determine whether the current system performs all the tasks you need. If it does, you probably shouldn't change your system. The current system is known by the current users, and retraining can be very disruptive. Do not buy new software just to have the latest program. When new programs are first sold, they frequently have defects *(bugs)*. Some of the defects can be serious. If the new features are not critical to your operation, wait six months. After that time, most of the bugs will be found and fixed by the manufacturer (and the price may go down). Let someone else be the guinea pig.

Many magazines review word processors and other software programs. Go to the library and find at least three reviews on a software program that you are thinking of purchasing. Read them carefully. Usually you will find a consensus within the reviews.

Examples of computer magazines that review software programs

2. Databases

Database software is used to store and organize information. The information is entered into the database in an organized manner so that the computer can extract it, reorganize it, consolidate it, summarize it, and create reports from it. As a business management tool in a law office, a database is used for timekeeping, calendars, ticklers, billing, and client records. (See Figure 13.5.) As a case management tool, it can be used for document control in cases that have a large number of documents that must be indexed and cross-referenced. Also, as we shall see, WESTLAW and LEXIS are services that consist of hundreds of databases used for legal research.

Entering information into the database usually requires someone to sit at a terminal and manually type in the information. (Machines called *scanners* are able to enter text without typing, but they are generally more effective in taking in graphics than text.) If the database is to contain documents, each document entered will need an ID code, a brief description of the document, and index words for it. One of the major features of a database is that it can serve as a large index, thereby allowing rapid retrieval of information.

Once all the data has been entered, the database can be used to retrieve, compare, or compile information. To perform any of these functions, you need to search the database. There are two ways to search a database: *key word* searches and *full text* searches.

A *key word* search is like looking through the index of a book. The data base program will build an index using information that it is told to use for the index. The computer searches through this index and displays all information associated with the key word. For example, assume that you create a database to keep the membership list for your paralegal association, and you instruct the database program that you want an index created using the state in the address of members of the association. You could then ask the computer to list all members from Ohio or any other state. This type of search can be completed very quickly. The quality of the results of such a search depends on how well indexed the database is. If the person who made the list of index words for each document did not do a very good job, the search will not be very productive. Poor

FIGURE 13.5

Frequently Encountered Database Management Terms

TERM	DEFINITION
Database	A grouping of independent files into one integrated whole that can be accessed through one central point; a database is designed to meet the information needs of a wide variety of users within an organization.
Data Manager	A data management software package that consolidates data files into an integrated whole, allowing access to more than one data file at a time.
Data Redundancy	The repetition of the same data in several different files.
Field	A subdivision of a record that holds a meaningful item of data, such as an employee number.
Record	A collection of related data fields that constitute a single unit, such as an employee record.
File	A group of related data records, such as employee records.

Source: S. Mandell, *Introduction to Computers Using the IBM and MS-DOS PCs with Basic,* 3d ed., 514–15 (West, 1991).

indexing causes either too little or too much information to be reported from the search.

The second way to search a database is called a *full-text* search. With this type of search, the computer will examine *all* the information stored by the database program, not just the contents of an index. You might, for example, create a document-control database that contains a summary of the document, including important dates, names, and events. A full-text search would be a search of all the words in the summaries of the documents that were entered in the database. The computer will look through the summaries and display a list of documents that meet the search criteria. If, for example, the documents that were entered into the database concerned an automobile accident and you wished to find all the documents that referred to Helen Johnson (who is the chief witness for the opposition), you could make a full-text search of the document summaries and receive a list of all the documents that mention Helen Johnson.

To make a search, the computer must be told what to search for and where to search for it. This is called the *search criteria*. Many large databases allow search criteria that use the words AND, OR, and NOT. A search criteria using such words might be:

GUN AND ROBBERY AND NOT BANK

This would cause a search of the database to return a list of documents in which the summary had the words *gun* and *robbery* but exclude any summary that also contained the word *bank*. The problem with this type of search is that if the word *holdup* were used instead of *robbery* in the summary of one document, that document would not be found by the search. To find that document, the following search criteria must be used

GUN AND (ROBBERY OR HOLDUP) AND NOT BANK

The parentheses show that the OR applies only to *robbery* and *holdup*. If you did not think of the word *holdup* at the time you phrase your search request, an important document would be missed because you did not use the same words as the person who wrote the summary for the database. In a moment, we will examine how search requests are made on the major legal research services, WESTLAW and LEXIS.

Most database programs can perform several simple tasks. Calendar control is one of them. A database is very efficient in keeping trial and appointment calendars for a law office. Each attorney can receive a printed calendar of appointments for the day. All office calendars can be kept on one computer so that scheduling can be done without creating time conflicts among the attorneys.

A database could also be designed to print out a list of all the cases for the office where the statute of limitations is due to expire during the coming month.

Name, address, family status, phone numbers, case type, and other pertinent information for all the clients of a law firm can be kept in a database. This information could be used for mass mailings of informational letters about certain types of cases to those clients. The database can also be used to identify the types of cases handled by different attorneys in the office and the completion time for each type. This information is very helpful in making management and marketing decisions for the law firm.

For more complex tasks, the usefulness of the computer increases. Time-keeping and billing can be made more efficient with a good database program. There are many database programs designed specifically to perform timekeeping and billing tasks. For different clients, these programs can handle multiple rates for attorneys and paralegals. We will examine this in more detail in Chapter 14 on law office administration.

The database also makes it possible to analyze which types of cases are more profitable to the law firm and which people are more productive in terms of billed hours. Of course there are other factors that must still be evaluated subjectively. The attorney who brings in new clients for the law firm could very well show up poorly on a billable-hours evaluation. Like all other tools, the numbers produced by a computer must be evaluated in perspective.

Databases can be very useful for document control. For example, they can keep track of the content and location of thousands of documents in an antitrust case. Document-control programs were once available only for large computers and were very expensive. Consequently, document control with computers was used only in very large cases. Today, programs have been developed that enable small computers to perform many document control functions.

WESTLAW and LEXIS

(See also page 585 in Chapter 11.) WESTLAW and LEXIS are commercial services that are available to anyone who wishes to perform (and pay for) CALR—Computer-Assisted Legal Research. As we saw in Chapter 11, these services can give you access to a vast amount of material, such as the full text of federal and state court opinions, federal and state statutes, federal and state administrative regulations, loose-leaf services, treatises, law review articles, directories of attorneys, and financial data. West Publishing Company, which offers WESTLAW,[13] and Mead Data Company, which offers LEXIS, have user agreements which must be signed before you will be allowed to use their services. The agreement establishes the fees to be paid for the different services available. You gain access to these services by using your PC, personal computer (or a custom terminal), which is connected by telephone lines to computers with vast storage capacities. Data is thereby searched *online*.

Assume that you are working on a case in which a client developed cancer after smoking for many years. You want to know if the client can bring a product-liability claim against the tobacco industry. You would need to formulate a question—called a *search query*—for the computer. The query would ask the computer to find cases involving product liability and cigarettes. Here is an example of such a query used in WESTLAW:

```
cigar! tobacco smok! /p product strict! /5 liab!
```

Later, we will examine the meaning of such queries and how to write them. For now, we simply want to give you an overview of what is available.

The screen in Figure 13.6 shows a recent case *(Forster v. R. J. Reynolds Tobacco Co.)* that would be retrieved by WESTLAW, using the above query. After looking at a large number of such cases, you might want to ask the computer to give you a list of citations of every case that fits your query. The screen in Figure 13.7 presents such a list. (It includes the *Forster* case as well as others that fit the query.) If you have a printer connected to your computer, you can ask for a printout of any of these screens.

Every citation to a case that you obtain through CALR can be taken to a traditional law library where you can read the case in a reporter volume. Of

---

[13]The assistance of Laura C. Mickelson is gratefully acknowledged for the material on WESTLAW.

FIGURE 13.6

				PAGE 1

Citation	Rank(R)	Rank(P)	Database	Mode
437 N.W.2d 655	R 2 OF 8	P 1 OF 37	MN–CS	T

57 U.S.L.W. 2604, 8 UCC Rep. Serv.2d 370
(Cite as: 437 N.W:2d 655)

John FORSTER, et al., Respondents,

v.

R.J. REYNOLDS TOBACCO COMPANY, Erickson Petroleum Corporation, d/b/a Holiday
Station Stores, Inc., Petitioners, Appellants.
No. C1-87-2170.
Supreme Court of Minnesota.
April 14, 1989

Smoker who developed lung cancer brought **products liability** action against manufacturer and retailer of **cigarettes**. The District Court, Hennepin County, Jonathan Lebedoff, J., granted motion of manufacturer and retailer for summary judgment on ground that claims were preempted, and appeal was taken. The Court of Appeals, 423 N.W.2d 691, reversed. On further review, the Supreme Court, Simonett, J., held that: (1) state tort claims based on state-imposed duty to warn are impliedly preempted by Federal **Cigarette** Labeling and Advertising Act, while other state tort claims are not preempted, and (2) federal Act does not preempt state tort claims based on failure to warn which predate its effective date.
Affirmed in part, reversed in part, and remanded for further proceedings.

COPR. (C) WEST 1991 NO CLAIM TO ORIG. U.S. GOVT. WORKS

Case retrieved in WESTLAW, with search words in bold print

course, you can also read the case on the computer screen or you can read a printout of the case, but it is usually cheaper to read material in a library volume than to read it online. The computer is excellent for searching, not necessarily for extensive reading.

The *Forster* case was decided in 1989. Suppose that you wanted to know what has happened to the case since 1989. Has it been overruled? Has it been cited by other courts? There are three different updating or validation services on WESTLAW that can give you further information about cases like *Forster*. They are Insta-Cite (see Figure 13.8), Shepard's Preview (see Figure 13.9), and Shepard's Citations (see Figure 13.10).

In litigation, there is often a need to find experts who may be able to provide consultation and, if needed, deposition or trial testimony.[14] One of the specialized searches that can be performed by computer is a search for such experts. Figure 13.11 presents an example of the results of this kind of search from the Forensic Services Directory (FSD) database in WESTLAW.

LEXIS works in a similar way, with many of the same features. Suppose, for example, that you wanted cases in which a juror concealed his or her bias.

---

[14]See Runde, *Computer Assisted Legal Research*, 10 Facts and Findings 13 (NALA, July/August 1983).

FIGURE 13.7

CITATIONS LIST   Total Documents: 8
Database: MN-CS

   1. Minn.App., 1991.
Andren v. White-Rodgers Co., a Div. of Emerson Elec. Co.
(To be reported at: 465 N.W.2d 102)

   2. Minn. 1989. Forster v. R.J. Reynolds Tobacco Co.
437 N.W.2d 655, 57 U.S.L.W. 2604, 8 UCC Rep.Serv.2d 370

   3. Minn.App. 1988. Forster v. R.J. Reynolds Tobacco Co.
423 N.W.2d 691, 56 U.S.L.W. 2664

   4. Minn.App. 1988. Holstad v. Southwestern Porcelain, Inc.
421 N.W.2d 371, 5 UCC Rep.Serv.2d 912

   5. Minn. 1985. Bixler by Bixler v. J.C. Penney Co., Inc.
376 N.W.2d 209

   6. Minn.App. 1984. Dalager v. Montgomery Ward & Co., Inc.
350 N.W.2d 391

   7. Minn. 1979. Armstrong v. Mailand 284 N.W.2d 343, 11 A.L.R.4th 583
188 N.W.2d 426, 290 Minn. 321

   8. Minn. 1971. LEE v. CROOKSTON COCA-COLA BOTTLING COMPANY
188 N.W.2d 426, 290 Minn. 321

END OF CITATIONS LIST
       COPR. (C) WEST 1991 NO CLAIM TO ORIG. U.S. GOVT. WORKS

List of cases retrieved in WESTLAW

You would instruct LEXIS to find cases in which the word *bias* appears in proximity to the words *juror* and *conceal* or *concealing*. See Figure 13.12.

Once you have examined a number of these cases, you can ask the service to display a list of citations of all the cases discovered when LEXIS fulfilled your search request. See Figure 13.13.

Formulating a Query

We turn now to one of the critical skills in using WESTLAW and LEXIS: formulating a research question or *query*. Our examination of this skill will explore the following topics:

(a) Universal Character (*) and Root Expander (!) for WESTLAW and LEXIS
(b) WESTLAW Queries:
- The OR connector
- The AND connector (&)
- The sentence connector (/s)
- The paragraph connector (/p)
- The BUT NOT connector (%)

FIGURE 13.8

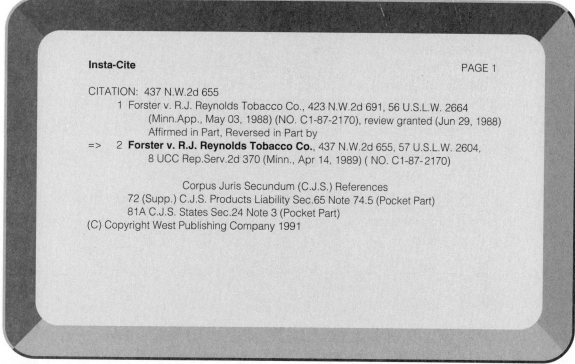

Insta-Cite PAGE 1

CITATION: 437 N.W.2d 655
   1 Forster v. R.J. Reynolds Tobacco Co., 423 N.W.2d 691, 56 U.S.L.W. 2664
     (Minn.App., May 03, 1988) (NO. C1-87-2170), review granted (Jun 29, 1988)
     Affirmed in Part, Reversed in Part by
=> 2 **Forster v. R.J. Reynolds Tobacco Co.**, 437 N.W.2d 655, 57 U.S.L.W. 2604,
     8 UCC Rep.Serv.2d 370 (Minn., Apr 14, 1989) (NO. C1-87-2170)

     Corpus Juris Secundum (C.J.S.) References
   72 (Supp.) C.J.S. Products Liability Sec.65 Note 74.5 (Pocket Part)
   81A C.J.S. States Sec.24 Note 3 (Pocket Part)
(C) Copyright West Publishing Company 1991

Insta-Cite, an updating or validation service in WESTLAW

- The numerical connector (/n)
- Phrase searching (" ")

(c) LEXIS Queries:

- The OR connector
- The AND connector
- The numerical connector (w/n)
- The AND NOT connector
- Phrase searching

(d) Field Searches:

- Title search
- Synopsis search
- Topic search
- Digest search
- Judge search

(e) Find and Read

(a) Universal Character (*) and Root Expander (!) for WESTLAW and LEXIS

An important technique in the formulation of queries in either WESTLAW or LEXIS is the proper use of the asterisk (*) as a universal character, and the exclamation mark (!) as a root expander. The discussion below of these and

FIGURE 13.9

```
Shepard's PreView

                    SHEPARDS PREVIEW              PAGE 1 OF 2
Citations to:  437 N.W.2d 655
               Forster v. R.J. Reynolds Tobacco Co., (Minn. 1989)

Retrieval
   No.      --------- Citation ----------
    1       458 N.W.2d 417, 419

                  Mass
    2       556 N.E.2d 1025, 1031
    3       556 N.E.2d 1025, 1033
    4       556 N.E.2d 1025, 1034

                  NJ
    5       577 A.2d 1239, 1246
    6       577 A.2d 1239, 1247
    7       577 A.2d 1239, 1256
    8       577 A.2d 1239, 1257

Note:  Citing references are only from West Reporters.  See SCOPE for a list.
       Check Shepard's, Insta-Cite, and WESTLAW as a Citator.
Copyright (c) 1991 Shepard's/McGraw-Hill, Inc. and West Publishing Company
```

Shepard's PreView in WESTLAW

other query-formulation techniques will cover searches for cases, although the techniques are generally applicable when searching any kind of document available in the databases and files of WESTLAW and LEXIS.

The Universal Character (*)   Suppose that you asked the computer to find cases that contained the following word anywhere in the case:

marijuana

This search will not find a case that spelled the word *marihuana*. If, however, you changed your query to:

mari*uana

you would pick up cases under both spellings. The asterisk stands for any character or letter. Hence the above search will also pick up cases that contained the words *maribuana, marituana,* or *marizuana*—if such words existed in any of the cases in the database or file you are searching. Since the asterisk stands for any character, it is called the universal character. It is most commonly used when searching for cases that contain a proper name you are having trouble

FIGURE 13.10

```
Shepard's

                    SHEPARD'S (Rank 1 of 4)              PAGE 1 of 1
CITATIONS TO:  437 N.W.2d 655
CITATOR:  NORTHWESTERN REPORTER CITATIONS
COVERAGE:  First Shepard's volume through May 1991 Supplement

Retrieval                                                 Headnote
   No.       -- Analysis --      --------- Citation ----------     No.
    1        SC Same Case        423 N.W.2d 691
    2                            458 N.W.2d 417, 419
    3                            721 F.Supp. 1058, 1063            1


    4                                    Mass
                                 556 N.E.2d 1025, 1031


    5                                     NJ
    6                            577 A.2d 1239, 1246
                                 577 A.2d 1239, 1256


    7                                     Pa
                                 578 A.2d 417, 420
             N  Anno                97 A.L.R.Fed. at 896


Check Shepard's PreView, Insta-Cite, and WESTLAW as a Citator or QuickCite.
Copyright (c) 1991 McGraw-Hill, Inc.; Copyright (c) 1991 West Publishing Co.
```

Shepard's in WESTLAW

spelling. If, for example, you were looking for cases decided by a judge whose name is spelled *Falen* or *Falon*, you can enter the query as:

                          fal*n

You are not limited to one universal character per word. For example, the following search:

                        int**state

will give you cases containing the word *interstate* and cases containing the word *intrastate*. Similarly, the query:

                       s****holder

will give you cases containing the word *stockholder*, cases containing the word *stakeholder*, and cases containing the word *shareholder*.

Root Expander (!)   Next we consider the exclamation mark (!) as a root expander. When this mark is added to the root of a word, it acts as a substitute for one or more characters or letters. If your query is:

                          litig!

FIGURE 13.11

Citation	Rank(R)	Database	Mode
Chapman, Judy-Anne W.	R 8 OF 14	FSD	P

GENERAL PROFESSIONAL DISCIPLINES
CONSULTING SCIENTISTS
MEDICINE & HEALTH
PHYSICAL HEALTH
Medical Research, Clinical **Trials** & Biostatistics

Chapman, Judy-Anne W.
11 Dayman **Court**
Kitchener, Ontario
Canada N2M 3A1
(519) 579-2996

Specialties: Biometry; **Cancer** research; Mortality or incidence data; Clinical trials; Case-control studies. Affiliations: Independent Consultant. Degrees and Licenses: PhD.
END OF DOCUMENT
COPR. (C) WEST 1991 NO CLAIM TO ORIG. U.S. GOVT. WORKS

Search for expert witnesses in WESTLAW

you will find cases containing one or more of the following words: litig, litigable, litigate, litigated, litigating, litigation, litigator, litigious, litigiousness. The root expander is quite powerful and can be overused. The query:

tax!

will lead you to cases containing any one or more of the following words: tax, taxability, taxable, taxation, taxational, taxes, taxi, taxicab, taxidermy, taxidermist, taxied, taximeter, taxing, taxis, taxiway, taxon, taxonomist, taxonomy, taxpayer. This will undoubtedly lead to cases that are beyond the scope of your research problem.

Plurals.   Finally, it is not necessary to use universal characters or the root extender to obtain the regular plural of a word. The query:

guest

will give you cases containing the word *guest* and cases containing the word *guests*. Entering the singular form of a word will automatically search the plural form of that word.

Next we will focus on special guidelines for formulating WESTLAW queries and LEXIS queries.

(b) WESTLAW Queries

When formulating a query in WESTLAW, *connectors* can be used to show the relationship between the words in the query. Connectors link query words

FIGURE 13.12

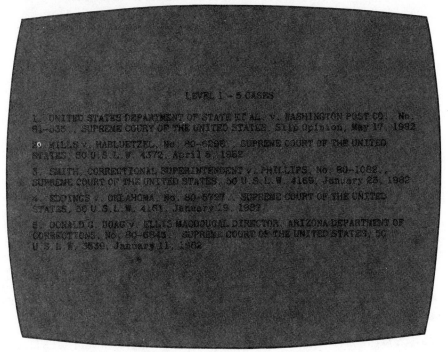

Case retrieved in LEXIS, with search words highlighted

FIGURE 13.13

List of cases retrieved in LEXIS

together to give the query more direction. The main connectors in WESTLAW are:

- The OR connector
- The AND connector (&)

- The sentence connector (/s)
- The paragraph connector (/p)
- The BUT NOT connector (%)
- The numerical connector (/n)

After explaining how to use each of these connectors, we will examine how to search for phrases on WESTLAW through the use of quotation marks (" ") in queries.

The OR Connector   The simplest connector in WESTLAW is OR, which can be expressed by typing the word *or* between two words, or by leaving a blank space between the words. This connector instructs WESTLAW to treat the two words as alternatives and to find cases that contain either or both words. Hence, the query:

doctor or physician

or the query:

doctor physician

will find the following cases:

- A case that contains the word *doctor,* but not the word *physician*
- A case that contains the word *physician,* but not the word *doctor*
- A case that contains both the word *doctor* and the word *physician*[15]

Similarly, the query:

attorney or lawyer or counsel

or the query:

attorney lawyer counsel

will find the following cases:

- A case that contains the word *attorney* but not the words *lawyer* or *counsel*
- A case that contains the words *attorney* and *lawyer* but not the word *counsel*
- A case that contains the words *attorney* and *counsel* but not the word *lawyer*
- A case that contains the word *lawyer* but not the words *attorney* or *counsel*
- A case that contains the words *lawyer* and *attorney* but not the word *counsel*
- A case that contains the words *lawyer* and *counsel* but not the word *attorney*
- A case that contains the word *counsel* but not the words *attorney* or *lawyer*
- A case that contains the words *counsel* and *lawyer* but not the word *attorney*
- A case that contains the words *counsel* and *attorney* but not the word *lawyer*
- A case that contains all three words: *attorney* and *lawyer* and *counsel.*

The AND Connector (&)   When you use the & connector in your WESTLAW query, you are asking WESTLAW to find cases that contain every word joined by &. The query:

paralegal & fee

---

[15]In all of these examples, remember that the service will retrieve cases containing these words and their plurals, such as physician, physicians; doctor, doctors.

will find cases in which the word *paralegal* and the word *fee* are found. The query will not find cases containing only one of these words.[16]

The Sentence Connector (/s)   The sentence connector (/s) requires the search words to appear in the same sentence in the case.[17] The query:

paralegal /s termin!

will find cases in which the word *paralegal* is found in the same sentence as the word *terminable* or *terminal* or *terminate* or *terminating* or *termination* or *terminator* or *terminology* or *terminus*. Here are examples of two sentences from two different cases that this query would retrieve:

Case #1:
>   "The **paralegal** did not receive notice of the allegation until the letter of **termination** arrived the next day."

Case #2:
>   "The patient's **terminal** condition was negligently diagnosed in a report obtained by the **paralegal** of the opposing counsel."[18]

The Paragraph Connector (/p)   The paragraph connector (/p) requires the search words to appear in the same paragraph in the case. The query:

paralegal /p certif!

will find cases in which the word *paralegal* is found in the same paragraph as the word *certifiable* or *certificate* or *certified* or *certification* or *certifier* or *certify* or *certifying*.

The BUT NOT Connector (%)   The BUT NOT connector (%) excludes everything that follows the percentage mark, %. The query:

paralegal % fee

or

paralegal but not fee

will find every case in which the word *paralegal* appears, except for those cases in which the word *fee* plus the word *paralegal* appear in the case. Perhaps you are looking for every case that mentions the word *paralegal* other than those involving paralegal fees or attorney fees.

The Numerical Connector (/n)[19]   The numerical connector (/n) requires search words to appear within a specified number[20] of words of each other in the case. The query:

paralegal /5 license*

---

[16]It is also possible to write this query as *paralegal and fee* (rather than use the ampersand—&), but this is not recommended.

[17]The sentence connector (/s) and the paragraph connector (/p) are referred to as the *grammatical connectors*.

[18]Note that in case #2, the order in which the search terms appear in the sentence is not the order of the words in the query itself. If you want to limit the search to cases that contain the search words in the sentence in the order presented in the query, you would phrase the query as follows: paralegal +s termin!

[19]The numerical connector can also be expressed as w/n. For example: paralegal w/5 fee. As we will see, LEXIS also uses w/n in its numerical connector. Only on WESTLAW can you use /n.

[20]Up to 255.

will retrieve any case in which the word *paralegal* appears within five words of the word *license,* or within five words of the word *licensed.* Here is an example of a line from a case that this query would retrieve:

"... the **paralegal** had no **license** from the state."[21]

A case with the following line, however, would *not* be retrieved by this query because there are more than five words between the search words of the query:

"... **paralegals** as well as notaries and process servers are not **licensed.**"

Phrase Searching (" ") Thus far, our examples of queries have involved searches for individual words in cases. Suppose, however, that you wanted to search for phrases such as drug addict, habeas corpus, or legal assistant. If your query was:

legal assistant

WESTLAW would interpret the space between these two words to mean OR. hence, it will retrieve

- Any case in which the word *legal* appears but the word *assistant* does not appear
- Any case in which the word *assistant* appears but the word *legal* does not appear
- Any case in which both the word *legal* and the word *assistant* appears

This could lead to thousands of cases, the vast majority of which would have nothing to do with legal assistants.[22] To avoid this problem, we need a way to tell WESTLAW not to interpret the space between the search words to mean OR. This is done by placing quotation marks around any phrase (or group of words) that you want WESTLAW to search as a unit. Hence our query should read:

"legal assistant"

In a moment, we will see that LEXIS does not require quotation marks when conducting a phrase search since LEXIS does not interpret every space as an OR.

(c) LEXIS Queries

When using LEXIS, connectors are also used in formulating a query. While there are some similarities between the connectors in WESTLAW and in LEXIS, the differences are significant. The main connectors in LEXIS are:

- The OR connector
- The AND connector
- The numerical connector (w/n)
- The AND NOT connector

---

[21]In this example, the words in the sentence are presented in the order of the words in the query—paralegal before license. The query, however, would not require this order unless you use a + sign before the number: paralegal + 5 license*. Another way to ensure this order would be to phrase the query: paralegal pre/5 license*.

[22]WESTLAW will probably flash a message on the screen warning you that your search query may retrieve a large number of cases and suggesting that you rephrase your query to make it narrower.

After examining these connectors, we need to compare how to search for phrases in LEXIS and in WESTLAW.

The OR Connector   The OR connector tells LEXIS to treat the two words joined by OR as alternatives. The query:

merger or acquisition

will find the following cases:

- A case that contains the word *merger* but not the word *acquisition*
- A case that contains the word *acquisition* but not the word *merger*
- A case that contains both the word *merger* and the word *acquisition*

Hence the OR connector in LEXIS is similar to the OR connector in WEST-LAW, except that LEXIS does not interpret a space between two words as an OR.

The AND Connector   When you use the AND connector in your LEXIS query, you are asking LEXIS to find cases that contain every word joined by AND. The query:

paralegal and fee

will find cases in which the word *paralegal* and the word *fee* are found. The query will not find cases containing only one of these words. (In WESTLAW, the preferred way to achieve this result is by using the & connector.)

The Numerical Connector (w/n)   The numerical connector (w/n) of LEXIS requires search words to appear within a designated number of words of each other in the case. The query:

paralegal w/5 license

will retrieve any case in which the word *paralegal* appears within five words of the word *license*.[23]

The AND NOT Connector   The AND NOT connector in a LEXIS query excludes everything that follows *and not*. The query:

paralegal and not fee

will find every case in which the word *paralegal* appears, except for those cases in which the word *fee* plus the word *paralegal* appear in the case.[24]

Phrase Searching   Recall that phrase searching in WESTLAW required the use of quotation marks around any phrase, since WESTLAW interprets spaces between words in a phrase to mean OR. This is not so in LEXIS, since LEXIS does not equate spaces with ORs. Hence to search for a phrase in LEXIS, you do not

---

[23]The number (n) of words that can be used as the numerical connector in LEXIS is any number up to 255. But LEXIS does not count words such as *the, be,* and *to.* LEXIS considers them "noise words." The numerical connector in WESTLAW also goes up to 255. See footnote 20. But WEST-LAW counts every word. In the LEXIS numerical query, if you wanted the words in the case to exist in the order in which the words are listed in the query, use the pre/n connector. For example: paralegal pre/5 license. See also footnote 21.

[24]Another way to phrase this query is: paralegal but not fee. The latter phrasing would make this LEXIS connector the same as the connector in WESTLAW that serves this function.

have to use quotation marks around the phrase. Simply state the phrase. The query:

legal assistant

will not lead you to any cases in which the word *legal* appeared but not the word *assistant*, and vice versa.

■ ASSIGNMENT 13.1

Below you will find five separate queries. If they were used in either WESTLAW or LEXIS, what words in the documents would they find?

(a) para!

(b) assign!

(c) crim!

(d) legis!

(e) e****e

■ ASSIGNMENT 13.2

On page 658, the following query was given as an example of a WESTLAW query:

cigar! tobacco smok! /p product strict! /5 liab!

Explain this query. State what the symbols mean. What is the query designed to find? Assume that you are using the query to find cases in one of the databases of WESTLAW.

■ ASSIGNMENT 13.3

You are looking for cases in which a paralegal is charged with the unauthorized practice of law.

(a) Write the query for WESTLAW.

(b) Write the query for LEXIS.

■ ASSIGNMENT 13.4

You are looking for cases in which a law firm illegally failed to pay overtime compensation to its paralegals.

(a) Write the query for WESTLAW.

(b) Write the query for LEXIS.

■ ASSIGNMENT 13.5

You would like to know what judges in your state have said about paralegals.

(a) Write several queries for WESTLAW.

(b) Write several queries for LEXIS.

(d) Field Searches

In addition to full-text searches, both WESTLAW and LEXIS allow you to conduct searches that are limited to information found in certain parts of cases or other documents. On LEXIS, these parts are called *segments*. The segments of cases are: name, court, writtenby, dissentby, counsel, number, etc. On WESTLAW, these parts are called *fields*. The fields of cases are: title, synopsis, topic, digest, judge, etc. Here is a fuller explanation and some examples of field searches on WESTLAW:

Field Searches on WESTLAW

Title (abbreviated *ti*). The title field contains only the names of the parties to a case. Use this field to retrieve a case if you know the case name. The computer will quickly retrieve your case and display it so you can either read it online or print it to read at a later time. Suppose, for example, that the title of the case you wanted to read was *Pennzoil v. Texaco*. Once you select the database you want, a title field search for this case would be as follows:

ti (pennzoil & texaco)

Synopsis (abbreviated *sy*). The synopsis field contains a summary of the case prepared by the editorial staff of WESTLAW. This summary includes the facts presented by the case, the holding of the lower court, the issues on appeal, and the resolution of those issues. The names of majority, concurring, and dissenting judges are also included in the synopsis field. Since general legal concepts are used to describe the issues before the court, this is a good field in which to run a conceptual search. A conceptual search is helpful for finding cases that fall into a legal category or classification, such as domicile, adverse possession, or product liability. The digest field (to be considered below) also allows you to conduct a search via concepts. Hence it is often worthwhile to combine the synopsis and digest fields in a single search. For example:

sy, di ("product liability")

Topic (abbreviated *to*). Each small-paragraph summary in the West digests (page 497) is assigned a topic classification, such as criminal law, bankruptcy, and divorce. West has tens of thousands of cases summarized under these topics. If you already know

a topic classification, you can conduct a WESTLAW search that is limited to this topic field. For example:

to (criminal)
to (bankruptcy)
to (divorce)
to ("product liability")

Digest (abbreviated *di*). In addition to a topic classification, every small-paragraph case summary in a West digest contains the name or title of the case, the name of the court that decided it, the citation of the case, and the rest of the summary itself, known as a headnote (page 503). All of this information (topic, title, court, citation, headnote) is contained within what is called the digest field of WESTLAW. Here is an example of a search in this field:

di (paralegal)

This search will find every case that has the word paralegal anywhere in a small-paragraph case summary of a West digest. To make sure that your search finds cases mentioning legal assistants as well as those mentioning paralegals, the search would be:

di (paralegal "legal assistant")

As indicated above, it is often wise to combine searches in the digest and synopsis fields.

Judge (abbreviated *ju*). If you wanted to find cases written by a particular judge, e.g., Justice William Brennan, you could conduct a search in the judge field:

ju (brennan)

When run in the database containing opinions of the United States Supreme Court (sct), this search will give you every majority opinion written by Justice Brennan.

(e) Find and Read

Suppose that you already have the citation of a case or other document, and you simply want to read it. But you are not in a traditional law library that has the bound volumes you need. If you have access to WESTLAW or LEXIS, there is a relatively easy way to retrieve what you want. On WESTLAW, use the *find* command (abbreviated *fi*). On LEXIS, use the *lexstat* command (abbreviated *lxt*) when you are looking for a statute and the *lexsee* command (abbreviated *lxe*) when you are looking for cases or any other documents available through this route.

Using the *find* command of WESTLAW, here are four examples that retrieve documents in the Supreme Court Reporter (sct), the United States Code Annotated (usca), the Code of Federal Regulations (cfr), and the Federal Register (fr). All of these examples assume that you already know the volume numbers, page numbers, section numbers, etc. indicated. You simply want to find these documents and read them on your computer screen.

```
fi 97 sct 451
fi 18 usca 1968
fi 9 cfr 11.24
fi 52 fr 22391
```

Using the *lexstat* command of LEXIS, here is an example that locates a statute in United States Code Service (uscs); and using the *lexsee* command, here are three examples that locate material in Columbia Law Review (colum l rev), American Law Reports, Federal (alrfed), and an IRS Revenue Ruling (rev rul). Again, all of these examples assume that you already know the volume numbers, pages numbers, section numbers, etc. indicated.

```
lxt 11 uscs 101
lxe 87 colum l rev 1137
lxe 44 alrfed 148
lxe rev rul 88-2
```

3. Spreadsheet Programs

Most law offices can clearly see the usefulness of word processing and database programs. The usefulness of a spreadsheet, however, is a little more difficult to appreciate. A spreadsheet can be helpful for almost any project that requires the use or manipulation of numbers. It is a good management tool for creating budgets and tracking expenses of a law firm. Most spreadsheet programs have built-in functions that will make intricate calculations, such as determining present net value, loan repayment schedules, averages, and many other statistical functions.

A spreadsheet allows you to create large groups of interrelated numbers. Once this is done, changing one of the numbers allows you to see what happens to all the others. A spreadsheet can quickly recalculate the values of all the numbers that are dependent on the one that was changed. (See Figure 13.14.) For example, with a spreadsheet you can create a program that will calculate the size of payments on a loan based on the amount, length, and interest rate that apply to the loan. If you change the numbers displayed on the screen for the amount, for the length, or for the interest rate of the loan, the spreadsheet will recalculate the payment size.

A spreadsheet consists of a series of boxes called cells. Numbers and other information can be placed directly into the boxes from the keyboard. Once the

TERM	DEFINITION
Cell	A storage location within a spreadsheet used to store a single piece of information relevant to the spreadsheet.
Coordinates	The column letter and row number that define the location of a specific cell.
Formula	A mathematical expression used in a spreadsheet.
Label	Information used for describing some aspect of a spreadsheet. A label can be made up of alphabetic or numeric information, but no arithmetic can be performed on a label.
Value	A single piece of numeric information used in the calculations of a spreadsheet.
Window	The portion of a worksheet that can be seen on the computer display screen.

Source: S. Mandell, *Introduction to Computers Using the IBM and MS-DOS PCs with Basic,* 3d ed., 409 (West 1991).

FIGURE 13.14

Terms Associated with Electronic Spreadsheets

information is stored in a box, it can be a source for formulas in other boxes. When a box containing a formula is displayed on the screen, the result of the formula is seen, not the formula itself. If any of the numbers in the boxes used by a formula are changed, the display for the box with the formula will reflect this change. For example, let us assume that we have a small spreadsheet program with three boxes. (Large, sophisticated spreadsheets can have thousands of boxes.) Each of our three boxes has a name that refers to the information in them. We will name our boxes A, B, and C.

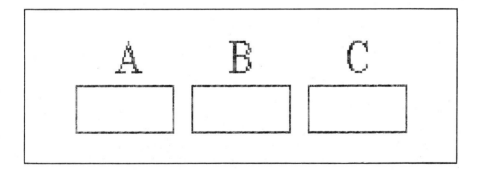

If we placed the number 5 in box A and the number 2 in box B, we could then combine this information in box C by entering the formula A + B into box C.

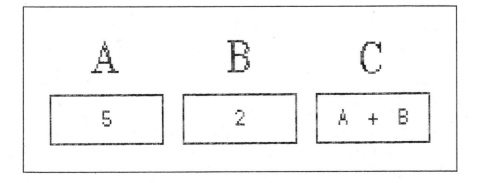

Box C would then display the number 7.

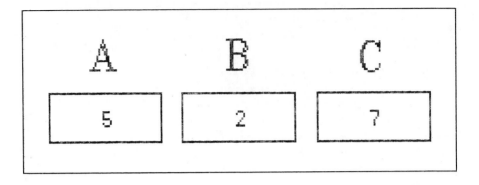

We could change the formula in box C to read (A + B) * 2 (here, the * means *times* on most computers).

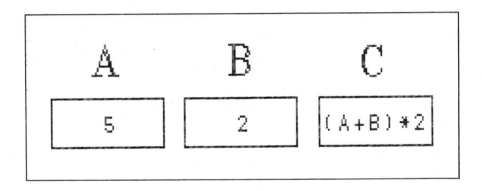

C would now read 14.

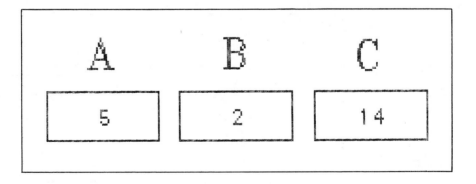

Now if we change the number in box A from 5 to 4, box C would read 12.
[(4 + 2) * 2 = 12.]

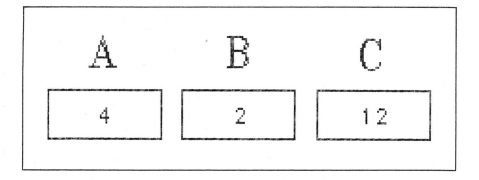

Our small spreadsheet example can be made more complicated. Let us start over. Place the number 2 in box A. Then place the formula A + 2 in box B. Box B will now contain the number 4 [2 + 2 = 4]. We could now place the formula A * B in box C. Box C would now display the number 8 [2 * 4 = 8].

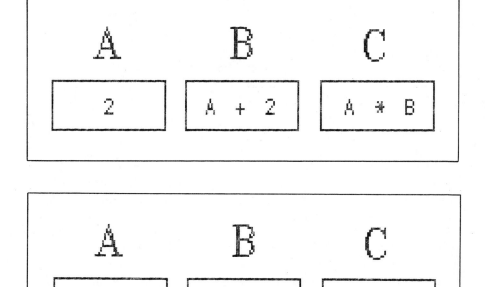

Any time we change the number that is in box A, the numbers displayed in both box B and C will change. If the number 4 is placed in box A, box B will show the number 6 [4 + 2 = 6], and box C will display the number 24 [6 * 4 = 24].

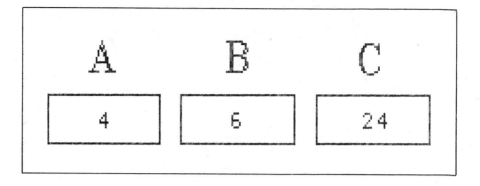

On a large spreadsheet, many cells (boxes) can depend on information from formulas in other cells. Sophisticated models and project formulas, therefore, can be created using a spreadsheet program.

When creating large models you must guard against making circular references. For example, place the formula (A * C) in box B and the formula (A * B) in box C.

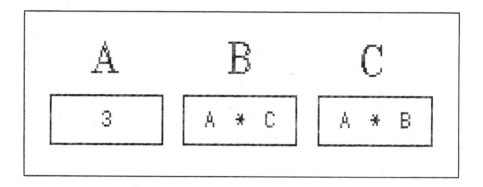

No matter what number is entered in box A, box B looks to box C for information and box C looks to box B for information. Some spreadsheet programs will get stuck on these two formulas and stop dead. Other spreadsheets will run through the calculations for the two boxes ten or twenty times and then stop.

The capability of a spreadsheet to perform a whole series of calculations based on formulas and numbers makes it possible for you to do in minutes or seconds what once took accountants hours or days. The spreadsheet is perfect for doing what users call "what ifs." Suppose you were considering the purchase of a house and wanted to figure out what the monthly payments would be. Three factors determine the size of the payments: the interest rate, the length of the mortgage, and the amount of the loan. Using the proper financial formulas, you could create a spreadsheet that would let you enter an interest rate, the number of years, and the amount that you wished to borrow. In seconds the spreadsheet would display the monthly mortgage payment based on those numbers. You can then play "what if" and change one or more of the numbers to see what happens to the payment level as the interest rate went down, the length of the mortgage increased, the amount of the loan was greater, etc. (See Figure 13.15.)

A spreadsheet used as a "what if" device can be very helpful in a law office for working out damage projections and settlement offers, particularly struc-

FIGURE 13.15

Spreadsheet
Mortgage
Cost Display

```
              Real Estate Financial Analysis

                       Assumptions

        House Price:              $35,900.00
        Downpayment:               1,795.00
                                 ---------------
        Amount Financed:         $34,105.00
        Interest Rate %:              9.75
        Number of Yrs Financed:     20.00
        Calculated Payment:       $323.49
```

tured settlements where the payments are spread over a period of time and take account of the value of money in the future according to an agreed-on formula. Once the relationship of the various elements of damages is determined, different interest and inflation assumptions can be tested. You can determine how these assumptions will influence the amount of damages that would be necessary in a particular case. For example, assume you are trying to project lost wages of an injured plaintiff. Interrelated formulas can be created to determine this damage calculation. One of the formulas would project potential salary over the working life of the person, starting with the current salary and adding increases over time. The increase would be a percent of salary. The formula created can allow for changing the percent increase so that different increase assumptions may be tested quickly. Another formula can take the results from the salary calculations and determine how many dollars would be needed today to create an amount equal to the future income. Various rates of return can be tested with this formula. Used in a similar manner, a spreadsheet can be productive for estate planning and real estate projections.

Most of the current spreadsheet programs have the capability of creating graphs from the numbers they produce. They can create line, bar, and pie charts in many different formats. Bar charts can be made to appear three dimensional or can be stacked one above the other. If the computer has a color monitor, the bars representing different items can be displayed in various colors.[25]

There are many applications for spreadsheets that can be obtained by purchasing a *template* to perform the needed task. A template is a set of formulas sold with instructions on its use. A federal income tax template, for example, will contain all the lines and forms of a tax return. The template covers each part of the tax form on which information must be entered, and calculates the taxes based on the information entered. The template then prints the form as a completed tax return. Templates are available for almost any type of business calculation. There are small bookkeeping programs, purchase-lease comparison programs, linear regression programs, and many others.

Some publishers of spreadsheets claim that bookkeeping and other *database* applications can be performed using their programs. This is true to a limited extent. These bookkeeping and database systems are limited and awkward, however, and hence of little practical use in most law offices. Bookkeeping and

---

[25]When you need a hard copy of the chart, laser printers are often very effective. If high-quality charts are needed in color, a *plotter* can be used. A plotter is a device that will hold a pen to a piece of paper and draw lines as instructed by commands you enter into the computer.

database manipulation should be performed on programs designed for that purpose rather than with spreadsheet programs.

■ ASSIGNMENT 13.6

Barklay is a freelance paralegal. He shares an office with three others: Adams, Cordier, and Davis. The expenses of the office are: rent, phone, electricity, gas, postage meter, and secretarial service. They agree to the following allocation of expenses: rent will be $185 per person; the cost of electricity and gas will be split evenly among the four of them; everything else will be apportioned according to actual use and cost.

The four will have the following bill-paying responsibilities: Barklay will pay the phone and secretarial bills; Adams will pay the rent; Cordier will pay the electricity and gas bills; and Davis will pay the postage bill. At the end of every month, each will make an accounting of what was paid. They will then calculate who owes what to whom based on their agreement of how expenses are to be allocated.

Here are the figures for last month. Adams ran up $122 in phone calls, Barklay $85, Cordier $77, and Davis $19. Postage use was $22.50 for Adams, $14.20 for Barklay, $66.85 for Cordier, and $10.31 for Davis. The bill for secretarial services showed that Adams owes $118.00, Barklay $100.33, Cordier $84, and Davis $44. The electric bill was $29.03. The gas bill was $11.16.

The bills were paid on time. In Parts I and II of this assignment, you will be setting up a spreadsheet to calculate each person's share of the expenses, using the following basic structure as a guide:

	A Adams	B Barklay	C Cordier	D Davis
ROW				
1 Rent				
2 Amt. Paid				
3 Bal. Due				
4 Phone				
5 Amt. Paid				
6 Bal. Due				
7 Electricity				
8 Amt. Paid				
9 Bal. Due				
10 Gas				
11 Amt. Paid				
12 Bal. Due				
13 Postage				
14 Amt. Paid				
15 Bal. Due				
16 Secretarial				
17 Amt. Paid				
18 Bal. Due				
19 Grand Totals Due from Each				

Part I

For each category of expense, fill in the figures you are given for last month. Do not do any math at this time, but state the formulas that you would use to arrive at all of the mathematical calculations. For example, if you must divide $11.16 by 4, phrase the formula as follows: (11.16/4). Or, if you must add Row 13 for all four individuals, phrase the formula as follows: (A13+B13+C13+D13).

Next, do all the calculations based on your formulas.

Part II

Assume that there is a 3 percent tax on the phone calls over and above the amounts stated. Change your spreadsheet setup accordingly.

4. Communications

Finally we come to one of the most recent microcomputer developments. Communications software makes it possible to call up WESTLAW or LEXIS to do legal research over telephone lines. Such programs also make it possible to contact people or businesses and communicate with their computers. You can send or receive letters, statistical information, programs, or insults! Anything that can be put on paper or into a computer can be sent from one computer to another over telephone lines.

For successful computer communications, there are two necessary components: a modem and communications software. A *modem* is a piece of hardware that is plugged into your computer on one end and into your telephone line on the other. The modem controls the transmission of information over telephone lines. The communications software controls the information sent to the modem that is to be transmitted over telephone lines. When two computers are transmitting information to one another over telephone lines, each one must have a modem and a communications program. The two modems transmit the information that they are told to send by the communications software.

For the modems to be able to do this, they must be "speaking" with the same code and "talking" at the same speed. Most modems sold today use the same code, but they do not all communicate at the same speed. Some can communicate at more than one speed. The speed of transmission is stated in terms of *baud* or the *baud rate*. Three hundred baud is the minimum used today; most modems can transmit and receive information at this speed. If large amounts of information are being sent, however, 300 baud is very slow. The higher the baud rate, the less time it takes to send the same information. Twelve hundred baud is today's high-speed standard. As modem technology improves, 2400 baud modems are becoming available. The only drawback with higher (faster) baud rates is that the error rate goes up with the speed. When more information is squeezed into the same space, the equipment used must be more sensitive. Unfortunately sensitive equipment may be less able to distinguish static from the information being sent on the telephone line. Therefore, at higher transmission rates, the information is more likely to become garbled. This problem must be controlled by the communications software.

When selecting communications hardware, keep in mind the amount of information that you wish to send or receive. The greater the amount of bulk transmission used, the greater the need for high-speed modems. If you will be using the communications system mostly for reading or examining materials immediately on screen, 1200 is a sufficient communications speed.

When purchasing software for communications, higher cost does not necessarily mean better software. There are commercial software packages available that are expensive yet difficult to use. You may need a thick instruction manual and a degree in computer science to use them. Other communications packages are available in the *public domain*, meaning that the programs are available to the public without charge. Some are easy to use and will satisfy 90% of users requiring communications software.

Developing the skills necessary for communications can be difficult. Once you have started, however, stopping can be just as hard or harder! It is a fascinating and challenging area of the computer world. A great deal of information about sources of software, user special-interest groups, "adult" bulletin boards, etc. is available through electronic *bulletin boards*. A bulletin board is an inexpensive version of large commercial database information services, such as WESTLAW and Dialog. The bulletin board contains information centered around a common interest. Users can obtain this information, exchange messages to each other, find buyers or sellers for certain products, etc. Your phone bill could become very large if you are addicted to calling bulletin boards around the country.

5. Combinations

We have examined four types of programs: word processing, database management, spreadsheets, and communications. You can now obtain software packages that contain all four types in one program. These are often called *integrated* packages. They are programs that require computers with large amounts of memory. The reason for creating an integrated package is to simplify the process of moving information from one application to another. If, for example, you have information in your database that you wish to manipulate with a spreadsheet program, the task of moving the information from a format that a database understands to one that a spreadsheet understands can be monumental or impossible. An integrated package makes it possible.

The big question is, "Do you really need an integrated package?" If you are not sure, the answer is probably *no*. If you frequently find yourself wishing that you could put a graph from your spreadsheet into a letter or wishing that you could easily get your database information into a spreadsheet, then you do need integrated software.

Section F. The Real Investment: Time

Thus far we have examined the relative expense of some of the hardware and software options. The greatest cost by far, however, is *time*. For the system to be implemented successfully, time must be invested both before and after acquisition of the system. Considerable time must be spent before the purchase of a system to determine what the law office needs. If this is not carefully done, the system will probably not fulfill the office's needs. After the system is acquired, time must be spent implementing the system and training all members of the staff to use its capabilities properly. If the time invested before or after installation is insufficient, the microcomputer system will be a failure.

Another costly but necessary element for the successful implementation of a computer system is a guru. The guru is the one who has a knack for figuring out and solving most of the system's problems. The guru will be a person in the office who has a system at home, or who, when introduced to the training, learns quickly and wants to take the system manuals home to see how the thing "really" works. Encourage this person. Meanwhile, other staff members need to take over some of this person's duties. Having someone present in the office who can respond to a crisis saves time and minimizes frustration.

Other cost factors that must be considered involve "down time" and lost data. *Down time* occurs when the computer breaks. No matter how good, expensive, or reliable your equipment may be, sooner or later it will fail. Many firms have discovered that microcomputers are so inexpensive they purchase one or more to keep in the closet just to replace the unit that breaks down. This is often less expensive than having to wait a day, week, month, or six months for the defective computer to be repaired.

The loss of data can be even more expensive. Some data, of course, is irreplaceable. Other data can be replaced or reconstructed only at great cost. Nothing can compare to the horror of realizing that the diskette you just erased contained the only copy of the brief you have been working on for months. Every system should have regular backup procedures. There should be at least one backup copy of all data, and for particularly valuable or difficult-to-reconstruct data, two backup copies are recommended. If possible, a backup copy of important diskettes should be kept at a place other than where the day-to-day or working copies are located. This backup is an added expense, but it's not nearly as costly as the destruction of data by fire, magnet, or other calamity.

■ ASSIGNMENT 13.7

Each student will make a presentation in front of the class on a computer product—a hardware or software product. You can select your own product, but it must be approved in advance by your teacher.

The setting will be a mock meeting of members of a law firm (attorney, paralegals, and secretaries) who have assembled to listen to you. You have come to the meeting to make a sales presentation on the product.

You have several objectives:

(a) *To introduce yourself.* You are the representative of the company that makes the product. Use your own name. Make up some brief facts about yourself as representative, such as how long you have been with the company.

(b) *To provide something visual about the product.* You do not have to bring the product with you. Try to obtain a brochure on it. If not available, try to obtain a photo of the product. For example, you might be able to photocopy an ad that has a picture of the product. At the very least, you should prepare a diagram or drawing of the product or of some important aspect of it. Circulate the brochure, photo, ad, diagram, or drawing to the group while you are talking.

(c) *To describe the product.* State what the product does. What is its purpose? How is it used in a law office? What are its benefits? Who is supposed to use it in the office? How will the product improve efficiency or increase profit? How does the product compare with competing products on the market? How much does it cost? Try to cover as many of these areas as possible.

The product you select must meet the following characteristics:

- It is a brand product that is currently on the market.
- It is a product that is either designed exclusively for law offices or is widely used in law offices.
- It is not a product that you work with every day (if you already work in a law office). The goal of this assignment is to force yourself to learn about a *new* product and to communicate what you have learned to others.
- It is a product that no one else in the class has covered in a presentation. (The teacher will enforce this guideline by approving the products in advance.)

The best starting point in locating a product is to go to any law library and look through ads in bar association journals (state or national) and ads in legal newspapers (state or national). Many of these ads have 800 numbers you can call for more information. Once you have identified a product, ask a librarian how you can find out if any reviews of that product have been published. (Manufacturers of the product are often very willing to send you copies of favorable reviews.) You might also obtain a lead to products by talking to someone who works in a law office.

No one is expected to have intimate familiarity with the product (although you may want to give a contrary impression as part of your sales presentation).

Your goal is give information about the product that you learn by:

- Reading ads
- Reading brochures
- Talking with company representatives (locally, if available, or via an 800 number)
- Reading reviews
- Talking with someone in a law office in your area that already uses the product

■ ASSIGNMENT 13.8

Smith, Smith & Smith is a forty-attorney law firm that was established thirty years ago. It employs eight paralegals, ten secretaries, a librarian, a receptionist, a file clerk, and a part-time maintenance worker. The firm handles a great variety of cases: personal injury litigation, worker's compensation, government contracts, antitrust, domestic relations, estates and trusts, taxation, bankruptcy, commercial law, etc.

The founder and leader of the firm is John Smith, who practiced law with his father in the 1920s before he set up the present firm with his two children, Mary and David Smith. They are full partners in the firm.

For years, John Smith practiced law "the old fashioned way." "If it was good enough for my father," he is fond of saying, "it's good enough for me." The consequence of this attitude is that Smith, Smith, and Smith is managed today in almost the same manner that it was run thirty years ago. Almost everything is done by hand. All the secretaries have typewriters. John agreed to purchase electric typewriters only five years ago. These machines do nothing but type. There are a few dictaphones, but they are seldom used.

Payroll, billing, document control, etc. are all done by hand. The law firm consists of a suite of fifty rooms, almost half of which contain nothing but records and files.

Six months ago John Smith died. Mary and David are now in full control of the firm. At a recent bar association meeting, Mary and David listened to a presentation on the use of computers in the practice of law. Mary was fascinated by the presentation and is ready to restructure the law firm with the introduction of computers throughout the office. David (who believed that his father and grandfather were incapable of making a mistake) is skeptical. David does not see any reason to change the way the firm practices law. Yet he agrees that the idea of computer use is worth exploring.

Mary and David agree to hire you as a computer consultant. You specialize in giving advice to attorneys in the use of computers in the management of a law firm and in the practice of law.

(a) Name some areas where you think Smith, Smith & Smith might be able to use computers in the office. Explain why.

(b) What do you think some of David's objections might be to the introduction of computers in these areas? How would you respond to these objections?

☐ Chapter Summary

Like almost every other aspect of our society, the law office has been substantially altered by the computer. Since there is a tremendous diversity in computer products available, it is unlikely that any paralegal will walk into a new office, particularly a large one, and be totally familiar with all of the hardware and software programs in use. Hence, you must expect to go through a large and ongoing dose of on-the-job computer training. Standard survival techniques can help, such as finding out if any of the products have an 800-number helpline that you can call, taking advantage of online tutorials, and using help keys.

Fairly soon you should learn a relatively small list of computer terms. The list includes hardware, software, backup, data, hard-disk drive, operating system, modem, laser printer, etc. The four major kinds of software programs are word processing, database management, spreadsheets, and communications. A fifth kind combines the other four.

Word processing software is a substitute for the traditional typewriter, bottle of "white-out," and scissors that were once used to cut-and-paste a report together. Now you can use the word processor to type the text of a report, to insert additional text, to move text around, and to make other corrections on a computer screen (monitor) so that you can see the finished product before the report is printed. This feature, plus many others, makes word processing the most widely used software in offices and homes throughout the country.

Database software allows you to store, organize, and retrieve a large body of information. The office can design its own database, and it can purchase access to commercial databases such as WESTLAW and LEXIS. One of the critical skills in this area is the ability to formulate a question, or query, for the computer to answer. Most queries ask the computer to find data within a designated database. In formulating a query, you need to know how to use the universal character (*) and the root expander (!). You also need to know when to use connectors (such as the OR connector, the AND connector, and the numerical connector) to specify the relationship among the search words in the query in order to give the search more direction. You also need to know how to search for phrases, how to conduct field and segment searches, and how to perform simple "find" searches when you already have the citation to something you want to read.

Spreadsheet software allows you to make financial calculations and solve mathematically oriented problems with much greater ease than with traditional calculators. Endless "what if?" questions can be answered based on variables entered into the program.

Communications software makes it possible for computers to "talk" with each other, through a modem, over telephone lines. Finally, software exists that allows the user to combine or integrate word processing, database management, spreadsheets, and communications capabilities.

Key Terms

online tutorial	file	compatible
help key	k	dual sided
documentation	language	double density
CLE	laptop	network
users group	memory	dot matrix printer
hardware	microcomputer	daisy wheel printer
backup	monitor	ink jet printer
command	operating system	laser printer
data	mouse	modem
disk drive	windows	word processor
floppy disk	multitasking	dedicated word processing
hard disk	run	word wrap
byte	save	spelling checker
diskette	software	automatic pagination
floppy	hardware	block

block movement
boldface
character
character enhancement
control character
cursor
default setting
deletion
editing
format
global
header
incremental spacing
insertion
justification
right justified
menu
print formatting
print preview
screen formatting
scrolling
search and find
search and replace
status line
subscript
superscript
text buffer
text editing
text file

virtual representation
WYSIWYG
merge printing
bugs
database
data manager
data redundancy
field
record
file
scanner
key-word search
full-text search
search criteria
WESTLAW
LEXIS
online search
search query
universal character (*)
root expander (!)
connectors
OR connector
AND connector
sentence connector
paragraph connector
grammatical connector
BUT NOT connector
numeral connector
phrase searching

noise words
AND NOT connector
segment search
field search
title search
synopsis search
topic search
digest search
headnote
judge search
fi
lexstat
lexsee
spreadsheets
cell
coordinates
formula
label
value
window
plotter
template
communications
baud rate
public domain
bulletin board
integrated packages
down time

CHAPTER

14

Introduction to Law Office Administration*

■ Chapter Outline

 Section A. The Practice of Law in the Private Sector

There are over 700,000 attorneys in the United States—one for every 360 citizens. (This is double the number that existed in 1970.) By the year 2000 the number is expected to grow to 1,000,000.[1]

About 70% of attorneys practice in private law offices. Another 10% work for corporations in corporate practice. The remainder practice in the public sector for government, for legal aid and legal service offices, for organizations such as unions, trade associations, and public interest groups, or do not practice law at all. In this chapter, our primary focus will be on attorneys who practice law in relatively large private offices, although other practice settings will also be covered.

In the private sector, law is practiced in a variety of settings:

■ Sole practice

■ Office-sharing arrangement

■ Partnership

---

*Portions of this chapter were originally written with Robert G. Baylor, Business Manager at Manatt, Phelps, Rothenberg, and Tunney, Los Angeles. Others who have reviewed this chapter and provided valuable commentary include Dorothy B. Moore, Kathleen M. Reed, Michele A. Coyne, Patsy R. Pressley, Deborah L. Thompson, and Shawn A. Jones.
[1]Stanton, *Stepping Up to the Bar,* 35 Occupational Outlook Quarterly 3 (Spring 1991).

- Professional corporation
- Corporate law department

Sole Practice

A *sole* (or solo) *practice* often refers to an attorney who practices alone. More accurately, it means a sole proprietorship in which one attorney owns and manages the firm. Anyone who works for this attorney, including another attorney, is an employee who receives a salary. They are not entitled to a share of the profits of the office in addition to a salary.

Sole practitioners are generalists or specialists. A generalist is the equivalent of a doctor in general practice. An attorney who is a *general practitioner* often tries to handle all kinds of cases. If, however, the case is unusually complex or if the attorney is very busy with other cases, he or she might consult with an attorney in another office or refer the case to another attorney. Other sole practitioners specialize. Their practice might be limited, for example, to tax, criminal, or patent and trademark cases, or—more commonly—to personal injury cases.

Most sole practitioners have very few employees. There is a secretary, who often performs many paralegal functions along with the traditional clerical responsibilities of typing, filing, and reception work. He or she may also perform bookkeeping chores. The most common job title of this individual is "legal secretary," although occasionally he or she will be known as a "paralegal/secretary." You will sometimes find job ads for small offices seeking paralegals with clerical skills. These skills are often phrased more positively as administrative or word processing skills, but they are, in essence, clerical. In recent years, however, many sole practitioners have begun to hire one or more paralegals who have minimal or no clerical duties.

The office may employ a part-time law clerk who is a student currently in law school. It may also employ one or more other attorneys. Again, in a sole practice these attorneys do not share in the profits of the office.

Office-Sharing Arrangement

Occasionally, a sole practitioner will allow a newly admitted attorney to use the facilities of the office in exchange for some nonpaid help on the practitioner's cases. A more formal arrangement would be two or more attorneys with independent practices who share the use and cost of administration such as rent, copy machine, other equipment, library, secretarial help, etc. They do not practice law together as a partnership or corporation, although they may assist each other during periods of vacation, illness, or other emergencies. To avoid the conflict-of-interest and confidentiality problems discussed in Chapter 5, they must be careful in the selection of clients and in discussions about their cases with each other.

Partnership

A law partnership is a group of individuals who practice law jointly and who share in the profits and losses of the venture. Its revenues come from client fees. If the partnership is relatively large, it will probably be organized into a series of departments based on client needs (such as an antitrust department, a litigation department, etc.) and will be managed through a series of committees (such as a recruitment committee, a library and records committee, etc.) based on the variety of support services available to the attorneys. See Figure 14.1 for an example of the organization structure of a large law firm.

There are many different categories of attorneys in a large partnership, the most common of which are:

- Partners
- Associates
- Staff attorneys
- Of counsel
- Contract attorneys

1. *Partners*

Partners contribute the capital that is needed to create the firm and to expand it as needed. They decide whether to merge with other firms, and, indeed,

FIGURE 14.1   Large Law Firm Organization Chart: An Example

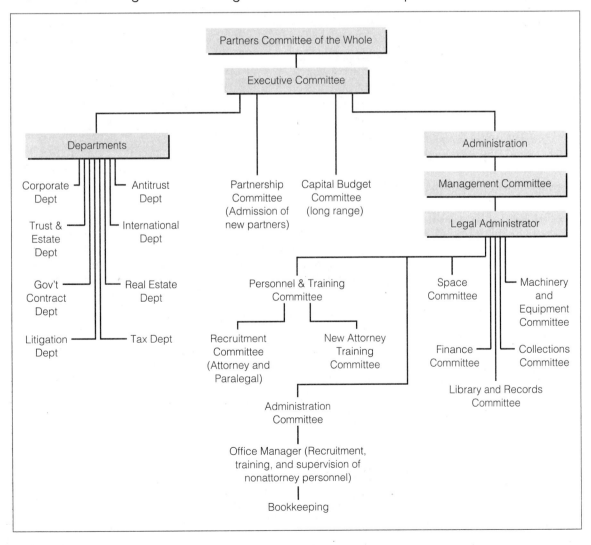

whether to go out of business altogether. Partners share the profits and losses of the firm pursuant to an elaborate partnership agreement. They decide how the firm should be managed, when to take on new partners, what attorneys, paralegals, and other employees to hire, etc. Most of this is done through a variety of administrative staff. In short, the partners own the firm. There may be different categories of partners in a firm (for example, senior partner and junior partner) depending on factors such as the amount of capital the attorney contributed to the firm and how involved he or she is in the firm's management. As we will see, a distinction is also sometimes made between equity and nonequity partners.

Generally, partners are not on salary in the traditional sense, although they do receive a periodic *draw*, which is an advance against profits in some firms and an overhead expense in others.

2. Associates

Associates are attorney employees of the firm. Often, they are hired right out of law school while studying for the bar examination. As students, they may have worked for the firm as a *law clerk*. Other associates, however, are hired from other law firms. They are known as *lateral hires*. (When partners and paralegals switch law firms, they also are referred to as lateral hires.) After a certain number of years at the firm, e.g. seven, associates are usually considered for partnership. If they are *passed over* for partner, they often leave the firm to practice elsewhere, although a few may be invited to stay as a *permanent associate* or a *senior associate*.

In some firms, there is a movement away from the "up-or-out" system that adds great tension to the ranks of associates. To encourage good people to stay, the firms have created different tiers of partners. For example, a firm might create the category of *nonequity partner* or *income partner,* to be distinguished from the *equity partner* or *capital partner*. The latter is a full partner in the sense of owning the firm and sharing in its profits and losses. A nonequity or income partner, on the other hand, is an individual who has not made, or who does not aspire to become, a full partner. In effect, he or she is often little more than a permanent associate with a more inviting title.

(Hence paralegals are not the only workers who are frustrated by a lack of career ladders in the legal profession. As we saw in Chapters 1 and 3, the paralegal field has been slowly developing career ladders, e.g., from case clerk to paralegal to senior paralegal and paralegal supervisor. Attorneys also want career ladders beyond the traditional associate-partner regime. Equally slowly, the profession has been responding to this need.)

3. Staff Attorneys

Staff attorneys (sometimes called *second-tiered attorneys*) are hired with the understanding that they will never be considered for partnership. This is what distinguishes them from associates.

4. Of Counsel

There is no fixed definition of an attorney who is *of counsel* to a firm. He or she may be a semiretired partner, a part-time attorney, or a full-time attorney who is considering a long-term relationship with the firm. Not all firms use the title "of counsel." Some prefer "special counsel" or simply "counsel."

5. Contract Attorneys

Contract attorneys (sometimes called *project attorneys*) are hired when the firm has a temporary shortage of attorneys, or needs expertise in a certain area for a limited period. Often paid on an hourly basis, the contract attorney is not a full-time employee.

Professional Corporations

In most states, it is possible for attorneys to incorporate their practice of law as a *Professional Corporation* (P.C.), e.g., "Jamison & Jamison, P.C." This is done primarily for tax purposes. From a tax and estate-planning perspective, it is often more advantageous to organize as a corporation than as a partnership. Like any corporation, a professional corporation has stockholders (the owners), directors, and officers—all of whom are attorneys. The operation of a professional corporation is practically identical to the operation of a traditional partnership. A client would hardly notice the difference.

Corporate Legal Departments

Many large corporations have a *law department* headed by a *general counsel* who may also be a vice-president of the company. Other attorneys in this office can include deputy or associate general counsel, senior attorneys, staff attorneys, etc. They are the in-house attorneys who handle the day-to-day tasks of advising the company on legal matters. They have one client—the corporation that hires them and that pays them a salary. Frequently, paralegals work with these attorneys. In 1983, the ratio of paralegals to attorneys was 0.15-to-1. In 1990, the ratio increased to 0.21-to-1.[2] Other support personnel may include legal administrators, legal secretaries, word processing and data processing operators, clerks, librarians, and records managers.

There are, of course, no client fees. Funds to operate the department come directly from the corporate treasury. If expertise is needed that is not available in the department, such as trial experience in a certain specialty, the general counsel will hire "outside" attorneys from law firms.

■ Section B. The Legal Administrator and the Legal Assistant Manager: Overview of Administration in a Large Law Firm

The practice of law is a profession, but it is also a business. The larger the practice, the more likely its business component will be managed by individuals whose main or sole responsibility is administration. While the owners of a law firm have ultimate responsibility for administration, they often delegate this responsibility to others. For example, there may be a managing partner, often an attorney with a small case load or none at all. More and more firms are hiring new categories of management personnel who are not attorneys. We will focus on two such individuals: the *legal administrator* and the *legal assistant manager*. One way to obtain an overview of management is to examine the job descriptions of such individuals.

---

[2]Wilber, *Support Staffing Ratios,* National Law Journal S6, col. 2 (May 20, 1991).

The legal administrator works under the supervision of the managing partner or of a management committee of the firm. The range of this person's responsibility, and of the business component of the practice of law, can be seen in the job description in Figure 14.2.

Again, this job description fits an individual who works for a law office that is fairly large. The support staff for such an office can also be quite extensive. Here are some examples:[3]

Administrative Support Staff in a Large Law Office

Legal Administrator	Secretaries
Legal Assistant Manager	Data Processing Operators
Personnel Manager	Word Processing Supervisor
Records/File Manager	Word Processors
Employee Benefits Manager	Proofreaders
Recruiter	Docket Clerks
Director of Marketing	Computer Specialists
Facilities Manager	Equipment Managers
Risk Manager	File Room Clerks
Office Manager	Librarian
Financial Manager	Library Aides
Credit/Collections Manager	Messengers/Pages
Chief Financial Officer/Comptroller	Copy Room Clerks
Bookkeepers	Mail Clerks
Analysts	Purchasing Clerks
Payroll Specialists	Receptionists
Accounts Payable Clerk	Telephone Operators
Accounts Receivable Clerk	Reservation Clerks
Time and Billing Assistants	

Prominent on this list is the legal assistant manager, whose job description is presented in Figure 14.3.

 ## Section C. Expenses

How does a large law firm spend the fee income that it receives? There are a number of organizations that conduct surveys to answer this question. One of the largest is the Altman Weil Pensa Survey of Law Firm Management. Some of the highlights of its 1990 survey are presented in Figure 14.4. The data was collected from 647 law firms with more than 16,000 attorneys.

 ## Section D. Timekeeping

Abraham Lincoln's famous statement that a "lawyer's time is his stock in trade" is still true today. Effective timekeeping is therefore critical to the success of a law firm. In some firms, it is an obsession, as typified by the following story. A senior partner in a very prestigious Wall Street law firm walked down the corridor to visit the office of another senior partner. Upon entering the room, he was startled to find his colleague on the floor writhing in pain, apparently

---

[3]R. Green, ed., *The Quality Pursuit* 69 (American Bar Association, 1989).

Summary of Responsibilities

The legal administrator manages the planning, marketing, and business functions, as well as the overall operations, of a law office. He or she reports to the managing partner or the executive committee and participates in management meetings. In addition to general responsibility for financial planning and controls, personnel administration (including compensation), systems, and physical facilities, the legal administrator also identifies and plans for the changing needs of the organization, shares responsibility with the appropriate partners for strategic planning, practice management, and marketing, and contributes to cost-effective management throughout the organization.

WHETHER DIRECTLY OR THROUGH A MANAGEMENT TEAM, THE LEGAL ADMINISTRATOR IS RESPONSIBLE FOR MOST OR ALL OF THE FOLLOWING:

Financial Management:

☐ Planning
☐ Forecasting
☐ Budgeting
☐ Variance analysis
☐ Profitability analysis
☐ Financial reporting
☐ Operations analysis
☐ General ledger accounting
☐ Rate analysis
☐ Billing and collections
☐ Cash flow control
☐ Banking relationships
☐ Investment
☐ Tax planning and reporting
☐ Trust accounting
☐ Payroll and pension plans
☐ Other related functions

Systems Management:

☐ Systems analysis
☐ Operational audits
☐ Procedures manual
☐ Cost-benefit analysis
☐ Computer systems design
☐ Programming and systems development
☐ Information services
☐ Records and library management
☐ Office automation
☐ Document construction systems
☐ Information storage and retrieval
☐ Telecommunications
☐ Litigation support
☐ Conflict-of-interest docket systems
☐ Legal practice systems
☐ Other related services

Facilities Management:

☐ Lease negotiations
☐ Space planning and design
☐ Office renovation
☐ Purchasing and inventory control
☐ Reprographics
☐ Reception/switchboard services
☐ Telecommunications
☐ Mail messenger services
☐ Other related functions

Human Resource Management:

☐ Recruitment, selection, and placement
☐ Orientation, training, and development
☐ Performance evaluation
☐ Salary and benefits administration
☐ Employee relations
☐ Motivation and counseling
☐ Discipline
☐ Termination
☐ Worker's compensation
☐ Personnel data systems
☐ Organization analysis
☐ Job design, development of job descriptions
☐ Resource allocation
☐ Other human resource management functions for the legal and support staff

AS A MEMBER OF THE LEGAL ORGANIZATION'S MANAGEMENT TEAM, THE LEGAL ADMINISTRATOR MANAGES AND/OR CONTRIBUTES SIGNIFICANTLY TO THE FOLLOWING:

General Management:

☐ Policymaking
☐ Strategic and tactical planning
☐ Business development
☐ Risk management
☐ Quality control
☐ Organizational development
☐ Other general management functions

FIGURE 14.2

Legal Administrator: Job Description (Association of Legal Administrators)

Continued

FIGURE 14.2

Legal
Administrator:
Job Description
(Association of
Legal
Administrators)
—*Continued*

Practice Management:	Marketing:
☐ Attorney recruiting	☐ Management of client-profitability analysis
☐ Attorney training and development	
☐ Legal assistant supervision	☐ Forecasting of business opportunities
☐ Work-product quality control	☐ Planning client development
☐ Professional standards	☐ Marketing legal services: enhancement of the firm's visibility and image in the desired markets
☐ Substantive practice systems	
☐ Other related functions	

Job Requirements

Knowledge: Has familiarity with legal or other professional service organizations, and experience managing business operations, including planning, marketing, financial and personnel administration, and management of professionals.

Skills and Abilities: Able to identify and analyze complex issues and problems in management, finance, and human relations, and to recommend and implement solutions. Able to manage office functions economically and efficiently, and to organize work, establish priorities, and maintain good interpersonal relations and communications with attorneys and support staff. Excellent supervisory and leadership skills, as well as skills in written and oral communication. Demonstrated willingness and ability to delegate.

Education: Graduation from a recognized college or university with major coursework in business administration, finance, data processing, or personnel management, or comparable work experience.

due to a heart attack. Standing there, he could think of only one thing to say to him: "Howard, are your time sheets in?" [5]

In some firms, the pressures of the clock on attorneys and paralegals can be enormous:

[Y]oung lawyers often are shocked to discover their new employer's time expectations. Many firms in major cities require as many as 2,400 billable hours

FIGURE 14.3   Legal Assistant Manager

**Legal Assistant Manager: Job Description
Attorneys' Guide to
Practicing with Legal Assistants**
(State Bar of Texas, 1986)[4]

General Responsibilities:

The legal assistant manager has overall responsibility for administration of the program. Formal training programs responsive to the needs of the various sections and to the professional development of legal assistants are identified and established by this individual. He or she works with the supervising attorneys, providing assistance in staffing and in resolving legal assistant-related conflicts between sections and between individuals.

Specific Duties:

A. Development and utilization of legal assistant skills

  1. Work with the supervising attorneys. Become and remain familiar with the nature and amount of work done by each lawyer in the firm.

  2. Work with the supervising attorney. Develop and submit to the Practice Management Committee a written analysis of each

---

[4]The job title used in the Guide is Legal Assistant Coordinator. Legal Assistant Manager or Paralegal Manager, however, is more common.

[5]Margolis, *At the Bar*, New York Times B13 (September 7, 1990).

FIGURE 14.3 Legal Assistant Manager—*Continued*

lawyer's work, identify the portions which should be performed by a legal assistant, and update this information on an annual basis.

3. Develop a training program for the supervising attorneys.

4. Develop a short introductory presentation for lawyers in each section to demonstrate the types of tasks for which legal assistants should be used.

5. Meet with each new attorney in the firm to explain the legal assistant program, thus ensuring the utilization of legal assistants by new attorneys.

6. Develop an orientation program for new legal assistants and conduct orientation sessions with each new legal assistant.

7. Develop an in-house training program for all new legal assistants and conduct or supervise the training provided by others.

8. Receive notice of each lawsuit docketed in the Litigation Section and assign a legal assistant to each lawsuit.

9. Assign legal assistants to all files which require the assistance of a legal assistant.

10. Receive notice of the assignment of all or major parts of "Special Projects" to attorneys, and assign a legal assistant to each "Special Project."

11. Monitor the progress of legal assistant use in each section and develop changes in the legal assistant support program as needed.

12. Consult with each legal assistant and each supervising attorney individually at appropriate intervals, perhaps quarterly, to identify problems and possible solutions.

13. Conduct monthly meetings of the legal assistants to keep them informed.

14. Work with the supervising attorney in the development of written procedures for inclusion in the firm's manual concerning the use of legal assistants.

15. Evaluate the need for support staff for legal assistants and work with firm administrator to ensure that legal assistants have adequate support.

B. Legal assistant supervision

1. Supervise the development of procedure manuals for legal assistants in each section for review by the supervising attorneys.

2. Review legal assistant time records to ensure proper preparation and to monitor workloads.

3. Coordinate evaluations of legal assistants.

4. With the respective supervising attorneys, conduct a performance interview with each legal assistant.

5. Ensure that all section staff meetings and similar meetings are open to legal assistants.

6. Monitor both quality and quantity of work assignments to legal assistants.

C. Reporting

Prepare and submit to the Practice Management Committee a quarterly report showing:

1. Approximate hours spent by each legal assistant on work from each lawyer.

2. The number of assignments carried out by each assigned legal assistant for each lawyer.

3. The same information for backup work done by the legal assistants in each section.

D. Professional development for legal assistants

1. Set objectives for and help plan in-house professional instruction for legal assistants.

2. Review all notices received in the firm regarding seminars.

3. Develop and implement schedules of continuing in-house and outside training for each legal assistant to ensure timely completion of required formal and enhancement instruction.

E. Personnel

1. Recruit, interview, and hire legal assistants.

2. Maintain a personnel file for each legal assistant.

3. Anticipate and correct unsatisfactory assignments and inadequate or inappropriate staffing.

4. Assign backup responsibility after consultation with legal assistants and supervising attorneys.

5. Provide assistance in resolving legal assistant conflicts between individuals.

6. Evaluate office space requirements for legal assistants and work with firm administration in providing office space for legal assistants.

FIGURE 14.4

1990 Survey of Law Firm Economics

During the past five years, the average overhead costs per attorney was $93,648, an increase of 51%. The average law firm spent:

- $34,121 per attorney for support staff (excluding paralegals). This constituted 16.5% of the gross revenue of the firm. This is the same percentage that existed in 1984. (Apparently, the large investment in law office automation between 1984 and 1990 did *not* result in significant net staff cost savings.)

- $28,718 per attorney for general expenses, such as insurance of all kinds, printing, meetings, postage, and office supplies not charged to clients. This constituted 13.9% of the gross revenue of the firm, an increase of 69% between 1985 and 1990.

- $8,323 per attorney for paralegals. This constituted 4.0% of gross revenue, an increase of 67% between 1984 and 1990.

- $15,462 per attorney for occupancy expenses. This constituted 7.5% of gross revenue, an increase of 49% between 1985 and 1990.

- $4,672 per attorney for equipment. This constituted 2.3% of gross revenue, an increase of 10% between 1985 and 1990.

- $2,352 per attorney for library and reference expenses. This constituted 1.1% of gross revenue, an increase of 33% between 1984 and 1990.

The median number of billable hours were:

- 1,706 for partners/shareholders (up from, 1,571 in 1984)

- 1,820 for associates (up from 1,738 in 1985)

- 1,400 for paralegals in 1989

The median billing rates were:

- $150 per hour for partners/shareholders

- $100 per hour for associates

- $55 per hour for paralegals

per year. When one considers that many full-time employees outside of the law only *work* 2,000 hours per year, the time commitment required by these firms is staggering.[6]

The cry for billable hours is thought by many to be at the heart of much of the problem. Many legal assistants as well as attorneys have quotas of billable hours. Zlaket [the President of the State Bar of Arizona] stated that some firms require 2,200 hours a year and he deems this to be outrageous. He suggested that this only leads to padding of bills and time sheets, and it leads to unnecessary work that will be paid by somebody.[7]

The ethical dimensions of this problem are considered in Chapter 5. Here our concern is the administration of the timekeeping and billing system.

· · · · · · · · · · · · · ·

After the initial client interview, the accounting starting point can be a *New File Worksheet* (see Figure 14.5). It is also sometimes referred to as a *New Matter Sheet* or a *New Business Sheet*. The New File Worksheet becomes the source document for the creation of all the necessary accounting records involved in working on the case or matter of a client.

Attorneys and paralegals must keep an accurate account of the time they spend on behalf of a client. An example of a form they can use is the *Daily Time*

---

[6]Walljasper, *I Quit!*, Wisconsin Lawyer 16 (March 1990).

[7]Morris, *Join the Effort to Restore Respect to the Legal Profession*, The Digest 3 (Arizona Paralegal Ass'n, April 1989).

FIGURE 14.5

New File Worksheet

Billing No. _____

Date _____ Opened _____ Closed

New File

Client (Check one)

___ INDIVIDUAL   _____
                          Last   First   Middle Initial

___ ENTITY   _____
                  (Use complete name & common abbreviations; place articles [e.g., The] at end.)

___ CLASS ACTION _____
                              (File Name, ex.: Popcorn Antitrust Litigation)

Matter (Check One)

___ NON-LITIGATION _____

___ LITIGATION   _____
    _____ Approved for litigation by—MUST BE INITIALED by submitting attorney!!

Nature of the Case

   Area of law code _____   Summary of work or dispute: _____
   _____

Client Contact (N/A for Class Actions)

   Name: _____
   Company: _____
   Street: _____
   City, State, Zip: _____
   Telephone: _____

Billing Address (N/A for Class Actions)

   Name: _____
   Company: _____
   Street: _____
   City, State, Zip: _____
   Telephone: _____

Team Information (Use initials)

   ___ ___ ___   Managing Attorney(s) (for non-litigation cases only)
   ___ ___ ___   Bill Review Attorney(s)
   ___ ___ ___   Originating Attorney(s)
   _____   Calendar Attorney (for litigation cases only)
   _____   Legal Assistant (for litigation cases only)
   _____   Secretary to Calendar Attorney (for litigation cases only)

Referral Source (Check one)

___ Existing Client   _____
                                        (Name)

___ Non-Firm Attorney   _____
                                        (Name)

___ Firm Attorney or Employee _____

___ Martindale-Hubbell

___ Other   _____

Continued

FIGURE 14.5   New File Worksheet—*Continued*

Fee Agreement (Check those that apply)

___ Hourly

___ Contingent _____%

___ Fee Petition

___ Fixed Fee $_____ or Fixed Range from $_____ to $_____

___ Retainer $_____

___ Letter of Retainer sent by _____ on _____

___ ___   (Initials)   (Date)

Statement Format (Check those that apply)

Do you want identical disbursements grouped?   _____ Yes _____ No

Do you want attorney hours reflected on *each* time entry?   _____ Yes _____ No

Do you want fees extended on *each* time entry?   _____ Yes _____ No

Conflict Check

Conflict Check Completed By: _____   **Date:**_____

                                    (Initials)

Conflict Check Not Needed: _____

                    (Initials of Submitting Person)

Check One:

_____ No conflicts

_____ Potential conflict with the following existing parties (from computer system):

_____

_____

(Or attach computer printout from Conflict Check System.)

*New Adverse Parties:

_____

_____

_____

*New Related Parties (for Class Actions, Named Plaintiffs Only):

_____

_____

_____

*Will be entered into computer system by Bus. Dept. *AFTER* approval by Managing Partner.

Closed File

Date Closed: _____   **Atty. or Sec. Initials:** _____

_____ Attach Pleadings and/or File Indexes. If indexes are not available, attach brief description of what is contained in the file(s). SEND FILES, THIS FORM, AND INDEX TO FILE ROOM.

Routing Lists

(Initial)

	New File:	Date:	Closed File:	Date:
Submitted by	_____	_____	_____	_____
Sec. of Submitting Person	_____	_____	_____	_____

Continued

FIGURE 14.5   New File Worksheet—*Continued*

Managing Partner	——	——	——	——
Business Department	——	——	——	——
File Department	——	——	——	——
Firm Newsletter	——	——	——	——
Docket for Litigation	——	——	——	——

EnviroLaw (Computer Center) Add?   ——

IdeaLaw (Computer Center)   Add?   ——

JobLaw (Computer Center)   Add?   ——

Pulse—See Fred Farrell

Sheet (see Figure 14.6). This sheet becomes the journal from which all time entries are posted to individual client ledger pages.

Law firms normally use tenths of an hour (in increments of six minutes) as the base unit for the measurement of time, although a few firms still use one-fourth of an hour as their base for recording time. *Hourly Time and Rate Charts* (see Figure 14.7) can later be used to translate these time fractions into dollars and cents for billing purposes; or this can be quickly accomplished by computer. Attorneys and paralegals note their activities on the Daily Time Sheet each time during the day that they work on a particular matter. The information from these Daily Time Sheets can then be typed on *time tickets* (see Figure 14.8) or into a computer database.

These time tickets are usually perforated or shingled. For offices still using a manual system, this facilitates easy separation so that they can be subsequently sorted into alphabetical order for quick posting to client ledger cards. The tickets can be processed in several different ways. One is to retain the individual tickets in an open tray in alphabetical order for eventual retrieval and tabulation for billing; another would be to use gummed backs for pasting directly onto a client ledger card; or the ticket may be used as a source document for transcribing onto a *Master Ledger Card* (see Figure 14.9); or the ticket could

FIGURE 14.6

Daily Time Sheet

DAILY SERVICE REPORT OF: _____   DATE: _____

ANS	–Answer	DEPO	–Deposition	K	–Contract	O	–Order	RES	–Research
APP	–Appearance or Attending	DIC	–Dictation	L	–Legal	OP	–Opinion	REV	–Revision
ARG	–Argue or Argument	DOC	–Document	LT	–Letter to	P	–Preparation	S	–Settlement
BR	–Brief	DR	–Drafting	LF	–Letter from	PL	–Plaintiff	TF	–Telephone from
COMP	–Complaint	F	–Facts	MT	–Memorandum to	PR	–Praecipe	TT	–Telephone to
CW	–Conference–Office	FL	–File	MF	–Memorandum from	PRT	–Pretrial	TR	–Trial
CWO	–Conference–Outside Office	H	–Hearing	MOT	–Motion	R	–Reading and Review	TRV	–Travel
DEF	–Defendant	INV	–Investigation	NEG	–Negotiation	REL	–Release	W	–Witness
DEM	–Demurrer	INT	–Interview						

CLIENT (State billing division or department)	MATTER	DESCRIPTION OF WORK (Use abbreviations above)	TIME	
			Hours	10ths

FIGURE 14.7

Hourly Time ×
$ Hourly Rate

TIME: / RATE:	$20	$25	$30	$35	$40	$45	$50	$55	$60	$65	$70	$75
0.10 hour	2.00	2.50	3.00	3.50	4.00	4.50	5.00	5.50	6.00	6.50	7.00	7.50
0.20	4.00	5.00	6.00	7.00	8.00	9.00	10.00	11.00	12.00	13.00	14.00	15.00
0.30	6.00	7.50	9.00	10.50	12.00	13.50	15.00	16.50	18.00	19.50	21.00	22.50
0.40	8.00	10.00	12.00	14.00	16.00	18.00	20.00	22.00	24.00	26.00	28.00	30.00
0.50	10.00	12.50	15.00	17.50	20.00	22.50	25.00	27.50	30.00	32.50	35.00	37.50
0.60	12.00	15.00	18.00	21.00	24.00	27.00	30.00	33.00	36.00	39.00	42.00	45.00
0.70	14.00	17.50	21.00	24.50	28.00	31.50	35.00	38.50	42.00	45.50	49.00	52.50
0.80	16.00	20.00	24.00	28.00	32.00	36.00	40.00	44.00	48.00	52.00	56.00	60.00
0.90	18.00	22.50	27.00	31.50	36.00	40.50	45.00	49.50	54.00	58.50	63.00	67.50
1.00 hour	20.00	25.00	30.00	35.00	40.00	45.00	50.00	55.00	60.00	65.00	70.00	75.00
2.00	40.00	50.00	60.00	70.00	80.00	90.00	100.00	110.00	120.00	130.00	140.00	150.00
3.00	60.00	75.00	90.00	105.00	120.00	135.00	150.00	165.00	180.00	195.00	210.00	225.00
4.00	80.00	100.00	120.00	140.00	160.00	180.00	200.00	220.00	240.00	260.00	280.00	300.00
5.00	100.00	125.00	150.00	175.00	200.00	225.00	250.00	275.00	300.00	325.00	350.00	375.00
6.00	120.00	150.00	180.00	210.00	240.00	270.00	300.00	330.00	360.00	390.00	420.00	450.00
7.00	140.00	175.00	210.00	245.00	280.00	315.00	350.00	385.00	420.00	455.00	490.00	525.00
8.00	160.00	200.00	240.00	280.00	320.00	360.00	400.00	440.00	480.00	520.00	560.00	600.00
9.00	180.00	225.00	270.00	315.00	360.00	405.00	450.00	495.00	540.00	585.00	630.00	675.00
10.00 hours	200.00	250.00	300.00	350.00	400.00	450.00	500.00	550.00	600.00	650.00	700.00	750.00

FIGURE 14.8

Time Ticket

DATE	NAME	CLIENT	MATTER	CLIENT REFERENCE NUMBER	TIME

DESCRIPTION:

Posted:

FIGURE 14.9

Master
Ledger Card

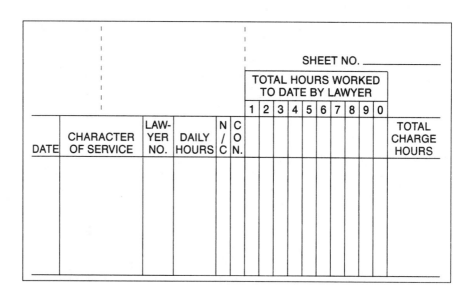

be keyed directly from the Daily Time Sheet of the attorney or paralegal and used as an input document for the firm's computerized system.

If you have never kept close track of your time, you will find that the task requires a great deal of effort and discipline; it does not come naturally to most of us. The key to performing the task effectively is to do it consistently and comprehensively until it becomes second nature. Even nonbillable activities should be accounted for, such as performing administrative chores, helping to develop standard forms, or taking a lunch break. A senior attorney or other supervisor will then be in a better position to determine the best allocation of an employee's efforts, now and in the future.

Tory Barcott, a Certified Legal Assistant in Anchorage, makes a number of important points about timekeeping:[8]

> It "sometimes" scares me a little to contemplate clients paying" $10.00 or more "for every six minutes of our time." To survive in this world, the legal assistant must possess the accuracy and efficiency of a Swiss watch. "I keep one of those small, cheap, adhesive digital clocks where it can't be missed or covered with paperwork. Sticking it to my phone, in the middle of my desk, works best for me. The first step in performing any task is to record the time on my time sheet. I do this before retrieving the file, making a phone call," or going to meet a supervising attorney. The clock is also helpful in recording the time when a task is interrupted by anything unrelated to the current client matter. "I take notes on the start and stop times exactly as displayed on my digital clock." Some Saturdays, while absently attending to household chores, "I'll glance at the clock and catch myself thinking, 'that floor took only 0.4 to clean.' " This is a sure sign that the discipline of timekeeping has been internalized!

For other recommendations on effective timekeeping, see Figure 14.10.

Computer programs have been developed to provide assistance in keeping track of time. In one program, for example, there is a menu on the screen that you use to tell the computer the following information (with relatively few keystrokes): what project you are working on, whether the time is billable, what client the project is for, the nature of the work you are doing, the time you begin the project, the times you are interrupted, and the completion time. An internal computer clock keeps track of the time until you tell it to stop and resume. You can also "input" costs connected with the case, such as postage and photocopying charges. The data you enter into the computer can be sent to the accounting department and to the supervising attorney for eventual billing. The computer can use the data in other ways as well, as the following discussion demonstrates.

> Computers . . . can take an initial item of data such as a specific transaction:
>
> Attorney RLR Met with client ACME to discuss research needs, 2 hours, July 2
>
> and use the data over and over again in various ways. For example, the data may be sorted by attorney to give a listing of all the hours worked by the attorney on that day, or in that month for all clients. It may be sorted by client to give a listing of all the hours worked for a particular client. It may be used to produce a preliminary or final bill. The data may be merged with other data to price the hours spent and to provide additional billing information. The same data may be matched with other data to list the total hours billed for the client that year or even total hours still unbilled. The Meeting With Client might be encoded as MWC and the firm, for whatever reason, might build statistics on how much meeting with clients occurred for all clients. . . .
>
> Computerization not only allows one entry to provide a great deal of output but it speeds the entry. Special codes can be used for such items as the name of the lawyer (RLR), the name of the client (ACME) and the type of work done (e.g., MWC, above). The user may not even need to enter a billing rate ($100 per hour) since some systems can automatically search the lawyer or client information to find a rate. Or the system may look at the transaction code (Processed Application for State Trademark abbreviated as AST) and disregard all hourly rates, using the $175 fixed fee automatically associated with that type of work. Some computer systems can keep track of the hours spent on all trade-

---

[8]Barcott, *Time Is Money*, AALA News (Alaska Ass'n of Legal Assistants, April 1990).

FIGURE 14.10

Effective Timekeeping Techniques[9]

- Always have your time sheet and pen at your side, ready for entries.

- If available, use a dictating machine for time only. Regularly tell the machine what you are doing—for example, as soon as you hang up the phone.

- When you begin a project, make a list of each task involved. Note the time you begin each task. Note the time of interruptions and the completion time. If additional tasks are needed for the project, add them to the list.

- In addition to a project list of tasks to be completed over a period of days, weeks, or longer, compile a **daily to-do list.** This will help you organize your day and focus on the time dimensions of what you do.

- Whenever possible, complete a project before moving on to another one. This facilitates timekeeping.

- Conduct your own study of your nonbillable hours, such as interruptions, pro bono work, interoffice conferences on administrative matters, breaks, clerical work, lunch. At the end of a pre-determined period, e.g., two weeks, identify the largest categories of your non-billable time. Determine whether you can do anything to cut this time down. You may want to show your study to a supervisor to encourage him or her to delegate some of your nonbillable tasks to others who do not bill by the hour, or who bill at a lower rate than you do.

mark cases, multiply by the lawyer's basic rate and determine at the end of the year if the $175 fee is profitable for this type of work.

Entry by computer is also faster and easier. Computers prompt the operator for information and require it before allowing the operator to move on. The details are often immediately verified to see if they are consistent with other data in the computer. Correction speed is also improved. If a lawyer sees a printout of the work done for a client and realizes that there was an error, it can be easily corrected without much retyping. For example if an entry were made for a meeting with a client, when the meeting was actually with the client's witness, the error can usually be changed with a single entry. And all other places where the data are used are automatically changed as well.[10]

 ## Section E. Billing

There are least nine different methods of billing, according to the Law Practice Management Section of the American Bar Association. See Figure 14.11.

In addition to fees for services, a law firm usually recovers out-of-pocket expenses (called *disbursements* or costs) that the firm incurs while working on the case, e.g., court filing costs, witness fees, copying charges, long-distance phone calls, out-of-town transportation, and lodging for attorneys and paralegals.

The fees and costs to be paid by the client should be spelled out in the *retainer.* Unfortunately, not everyone uses this word in the same way. Its meaning should be made clear in the agreement between attorney and client. In a general sense, a retainer is the contract of employment between the attorney and client. More specifically, it sometimes refers to an amount of money paid to assure that an attorney will be available to work for a particular client, and

---

[9]Rucker, *Effective Timekeeping: A Legal Assistant's Point of View,* Newsletter (Houston Legal Assistants Ass'n, August 1987); Serrano, *The Member Connection,* Facts & Findings 7 (NALA, December 1986).

[10]P. Maggs & J. Sprowl, *Computer Applications in the Law,* 172–74 (1987).

- *Hourly Rate.* A designated amount per hour. An hourly rate is "bundled" if overhead is included in this rate. It is "unbundled" if the various charges are broken out separately.
- *Fixed Fee.* A flat fee for services.
- *Full Contingent Fee.* The amount of the fee is based on a percentage of the recovery, if any. This arrangement is often used in personal-injury cases.
- *Hourly Plus Fixed Fee.* A specified hourly rate is used until the nature and scope of the problem are defined, and a fixed fee is used thereafter.
- *Hourly Reduced or with Contingent.* A discounted hourly rate, sometimes combined with a contingent fee.
- *Blended Hourly Rate.* One rate is set depending on the mix of partners and associates working on the case.
- *Lodestar.* A lodestar is a mathematical formula used by federal courts and some state courts. It is based on a multiplier and relies on hourly rates and various other factors.
- *Value Billing.* The bill is not based solely on the time required to do the work. Instead, the amount to be paid is based on the complexity of a legal problem, the expertise it demands of an attorney, and on the sheer number of hours devoted to the matter. An estimate is often given to the client at the outset. This amount may eventually go higher or lower based on the factors used to determine value.
- *Percentage Fee.* The fee is a percentage of the amount involved in the transaction, such as the assets to be probated in an estate, the cost of real estate to be transferred, or the amount received as damages in a personal-injury case.

FIGURE 14.11

Methods of Billing[11]

hence unavailable to work for the client's competitor. When the attorney does work for the client, the latter pays fees in addition to the retainer, plus the out-of-pocket costs of the attorney. Another meaning of retainer is the amount of money or other assets paid by the client as a form of deposit or advance payment against future fees and costs. Additional money is paid only when the deposit or advance runs out. The agreement should specify whether money or other assets from the client are refundable if the client terminates the relationship because he or she decides not to pursue the matter.

The actual billing process differs from firm to firm, and occasionally differs from case to case within the same firm. Client billing sometimes occurs only after the matter is completed. More commonly, a client is billed monthly, quarterly, or semiannually. An administrator in the firm usually works with the billing attorney to prepare the bill. When a matter is called for billing, the administrator may prepare a billing memorandum (the *draft bill*) which specifies the disbursements of the firm in connection with the matter, plus the amount of time each attorney and paralegal has spent on the matter (along with the billing rate of each). For example:[12]

- *Attorney Jones: $1,000.* This attorney, who has a billing rate of $200 an hour, spent five hours on the matter. (5 × $200 = $1,000).
- *Attorney Smith: $800.* This attorney, who has a billing rate of $100 an hour, spent eight hours on the matter. (8 × $100 = $800).
- *Paralegal Kelly: $500.* This paralegal, who has a billing rate of $50 an hour, spent ten hours on the matter. (10 × $50 = $500).

[11]See Marcotte, *Billing Choices,* 75 American Bar Ass'n Journal 38 (November 1989); and *Value Billing Gaining Popularity,* Tennessee Bar Journal 9 (January/February 1990).
[12]Darby, *Of Firms and Fees: The Administrator's Role,* 8 Legal Management 34, 39 (March/April 1989).

The billing attorney has three choices: (1) Bill the total of the actual amounts. In our example, this would produce a bill of $2,300 ($1,000 + $800 + $500). (2) *Write-down* the matter by subtracting a certain amount, such as $300. This would produce a bill of $2,000. (3) *Write-up* the matter by adding an amount, such as $600. This would produce a bill of $2,900. This adjustment downwards or upwards is known as *valuing the bill.* An increase is sometimes called a premium adjustment; a decrease, a discount adjustment. The decision to adjust is based on factors such as the potential liability exposure of the firm (leading to a write-up) and the relative inexperience of an attorney or paralegal working on the matter (leading to a write-down). If, for example, recently hired attorneys or paralegals take an unusually long time to complete a task they never performed before, a write-down may be appropriate so that the client does not have to bear the full cost of their on-the-job training. See Figure 14.12 for an example of a bill sent to a client covering work of attorneys and paralegals on a matter.

Section F. Administrative Reports

There are different types of administrative reports that naturally "fall out" of the timekeeping and billing process. The more common reports used by law firms are:

1. Billable hours delinquent time reports
2. Billable hours analysis
3. Nonbillable time analysis
4. Accounts receivable reports
   a. Accounts receivable ledger
   b. Cash receipts journal
   c. Open invoice report
   d. Accounts receivable *aging report*[13]
      ■ billing by client (cumulative for a year)
      ■ billing by attorney (cumulative for a year)
   e. Departmental profitability analysis

These reports could be available on a regular schedule such as weekly, monthly, annually, or on request as needed. In any event, the raw data will be available and should be developed and stored in such a fashion as to accommodate easy retrieval, tabulation, and display for the legal administrator and managing partner, with summary totals being available for presentation to the entire firm. All this historical data can be compared to the results of the preceding year for the same period to measure quickly "how we are doing this year;" can be compared to the budget or any other acceptable benchmark; can be used as danger signals to prompt remedial action where appropriate; can be be used as

---

[13]An *aging report* is one of the most common reports developed by accountants to provide management with the time outstanding of accounts receivables. For example, an *aged accounts receivable* will set forth how many of the total receivables are less than thirty days old, how many are thirty to fifty-nine days old, how many are sixty to ninety days old, and how many are more than ninety days old. It is a truism that the older an account receivable is, the less collectable it is. Therefore, management needs to know how old the account is in order to put the emphasis on collecting it before it becomes so old that it is worthless.

Rubin, Rinke, Pyeumac & Craigmoyle
1615 Broadway, Suite 1400
Oakland, California 94612-2115
(415) 444-5316
Tax ID 94-2169491

April 10, 1991

IBM Corporation
Norm Savage
3133 Northside Parkway
Atlanta GA 33033

Statement for Professional Services Rendered

Re: Chapter 11   (IBM-1)
     Reorganization

Description of services

04/17/91   Receipt and review of contracts regarding Ar-
           monk home office liquidation.

04/18/91   Meeting with opposing attorney regarding
           court appearance in Atlanta in late October
           of 1991.

04/21/91   Receipt and review of depositions from seven
           hundred forty three (743) claimants to Austin
           plant parking facilities.

04/22/91   Meeting with officers of the corporation to dis-
           cuss liquidation of office furniture in all
           branch offices. Scheduling of 2000 simultane-
           ous garage sales in marketing managers'
           driveways to be advertised during next year's
           Super Bowl.

Total for legal services rendered			$797.50

	Hours	Rate	
Partners	4.00	125	500.00
Paralegals	3.50	85	297.50

Reimbursable expenses

Date	Description	Amount
04/17/91	Lunch meeting with opposing attorney.	185.17
04/27/91	Atlanta Bankruptcy Court filing fee due September 1, 1990.	55.00
04/29/91	Photocopies	5.69
04/29/91	Long distance telephone charges	36.90

	Total expenses	$282.76
	Total current charges	$1080.26

Source: Computer Software for Professionals, Inc., LEGALMASTER

FIGURE 14.12
Bill Sent to Client Involving Attorney and Paralegal Services

the basis for compensation schedules; can provide the firm with all necessary
data for complying with government regulations (such as tax laws governing
the firm's income); and can be used as a general audit and control device.

A well-thought-out system should give the managers of the law firm effective control and provide additional meaningful data for:

1. Firm Management Reports
    a. Firm activity and work status
    b. Summary aging of work in progress
    c. Summary aging of uncollected bills
    d. Summary of billings and realizations
    e. Uncollected bills written off
    f. Nonlegal staff charges to work in progress
2. Practice Analysis Reports[14]
    a. Staff utilization
    b. Attorney practice experience
3. Partner Responsibility Reports
    a. Partners' work in progress summary
    b. Partners' work in progress aging
    c. Partners' uncollected bills
    d. Partners' billing and realizations
4. Work in Progress and Billing Reports
    a. Work in progress ledger—detail
    b. Work in progress disbursements—detail
    c. Billing memorandum
    d. Delinquent diaries
    e. Client billing history
5. Special Purpose Reports
    a. Billings by introducing attorney
    b. Billings by assigned attorney
    c. Allocations to prior partnerships
6. Special Management Reports as Required

One of the reports that could be generated from the basic timekeeping records is an analysis of how much time paralegals are investing in client matters. This analysis is the same kind of analysis that the firm would want regarding time invested by attorneys. Sometimes large firms also keep track of time invested by secretaries and other nonattorneys, but generally this is not done. More commonly, firms keep track of attorney time and paralegal time spent on client matters. Firms need time expenditures in order to evaluate profit centers, costs, allocation of work among attorneys and paralegals, etc.

. . . .

---

[14]A "practice analysis report" can be very helpful to a firm. It analyzes where the firm is investing its time, how much money it is earning from specific areas of the practice, where its costs lie, and hence how much profit is being earned from the various areas of practice. Specifically, a practice analysis could develop such information for probate practice, litigation practice, general corporate practice, banking practice, antitrust practice—any of the "specialties" that are identifiable within a firm. Beyond the economic impact, the firm can use these "practice analysis reports" to be sure that all are carrying their fair share of work.

We will now examine representative formats for some reports that are often used in law office administration.

Work Summary

Each attorney in the firm should routinely complete a form such as that illustrated in Figure 14.13, "Work Summary," so that the managing partner of the firm can evaluate the workload of the firm each week. The managing partner should then be able to assign new work or reallocate work to attorneys on the basis of this Work Summary in conjunction with a review of time utilization reports developed from the timekeeping system. Paralegals also fill out Work Summary sheets, depending on the nature of the work they're doing. If they are working for many attorneys in one department, the department head and the paralegal supervisor, if any, often require copies of the Work Summary report in order to keep track of the work being done.

Cash Flow Projection

Many firms have cash flow problems, but only a few use mathematical methods to determine projected needs. One approach, as suggested by the form in Figure 14.14, is to determine anticipated cash receipts for the period under consideration by adding to the ending cash balance a certain percentage of new billings (the firm can anticipate payment within thirty days from approximately 50% of new billings, with the remaining bills being paid over a sixty-day to one-year period, depending on the firm's attentiveness to receivable collections), plus the anticipated collection from the more than sixty-day old account receivables, to arrive at "total estimated cash resources," from which the firm can subtract out-of-pocket costs anticipated for the time period, and arrive at a "projected cash balance." The firm can then quickly determine whether it needs

[ ] Can Handle More Work
[ ] Have All the Work
   I Can Handle
[ ] Need Help
Report of:
				* C (Work Completed
				       Since Last Report)
				WP (Work in Progress)
				IA (Matter Is Inactive)
				Date:			

Client	Matter	Description of Work [Designate Specialty Work by Symbol (S)]		Date Assgnd.	Part- ner	Sta- tus*	

FIGURE 14.13

Work Summary

FIGURE 14.14

Cash Flow
Projection

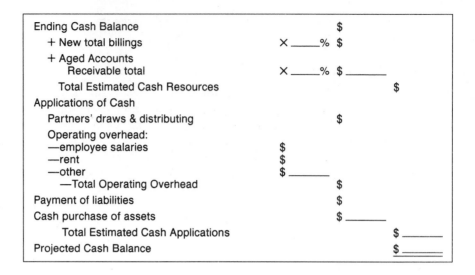

to borrow supplemental cash from the bank, or cut overhead, or take whatever remedial action may be necessary.

Chargeable Hour Schedule

The Chargeable Hour Schedule summarizes the actual hours invested by the attorneys and paralegals on a month-by-month basis (see Figure 14.15). To refine this schedule further and make it more informative, multiply hours by billing rates to arrive at a total dollar value of an attorney's or a paralegal's investment in the practice each month.

Aged Accounts Receivable

A list of clients, showing the amount due from each client as of a specified date, is known as a Schedule of Accounts Receivable. This schedule can be refined to indicate the number of days outstanding since the original billing date, normally into the following categories: 0–29 days old, 30–59 days old, 60–90 days old, and older than 90 days. This now becomes known as the Aged Accounts Receivable report.

The schedule in Figure 14.16 is common throughout most businesses. Law firms generally do not develop such a schedule, yet this can be a critical tool in the collection process. It should be prepared each month so that the managing partner and legal administrator can quickly determine where a special effort may be needed in the collection process, evaluate the status of receivables, and adjust cash-flow predictions in accordance with the status of the receivables.

Budget Reports

The annual budget should be one of the very first items management develops. It can be combined with income statements to give the firm current information on the firm's financial health. See Figure 14.17. Traditionally, law firms have had little understanding or control over their financial destiny and, as a consequence, they generally tend to react to problems on a crisis basis. The use of an annual budget and other such planning tools would virtually eliminate or greatly minimize crises throughout the year. The trend is for law firms to be

FIGURE 14.15

Chargeable Hour Schedule

	Jan.	Feb.	Mar.	April	May	June	July	Aug.	Sept.	Oct.	Nov.	Dec.	Total
Partners:													
A													
B													
C													
D													
Total Partners													
Associates:													
A													
B													
C													
D													
E													
F													
G													
Total Associates													
Paralegals:													
A													
B													
C													
Total Paralegals													
TOTAL FIRM													

more and more businesslike in their management style, and many firms will probably be implementing more sophisticated budgetary procedures.

Section G. The Procedures Manual in a Small Office: Mail, Copying, and Filing

Law offices often have a procedures manual to cover different aspects of law office administration. The following excerpts are from a manual in a relatively small firm.[15]

Incoming Mail

Before touching sophisticated areas, the manual should start with some fairly straightforward routines. A prime candidate is incoming mail. A suggested statement for the manual begins at the top of page 709.

---

[15]Adapted from Light, *The Procedure Manual: Mail, Copying and Filing Rules,* 26 The Practical Lawyer 71 (January 1980). Copyright 1980 by the American Law Institute. Reprinted with permission of The Practical Lawyer.

FIGURE 14.16

Aged Accounts
Receivable
Billed—Not Yet
Collected

Billing Attorney	Client Name	Legal Services	Disburse-ments	Total Due		Current To 30 Days	31–60 Days	61–90 Days	91–180 Days	More Than 6 Mos. Old
	(Alphabetic listing by client)	$	$	$		$	$	$	$	$
	TOTAL, ALL CLIENTS	$	$	$		$	$	$	$	$
	% Distribution	%	%	100%		%	%	%	%	%
	TOTAL RECAP BY BILLING ATTORNEY				% to total					
	(Total by billing lawyer) . . .	$	$	$	% % % %	$	$	$	$	$
	TOTAL ALL LAWYERS				100%					

FIGURE 14.17

Income Statement with Budget

11/16/86		CLARK, LOWREY & SMITH								
PERIOD 9		ATTORNEYS AT LAW							PAGE 1	

INCOME STATEMENT WITH BUDGET

ACCT NO	DESCRIPTION	CURRENT PERIOD				YEAR TO DATE			
		THIS YEAR	%	BUDGET	%	THIS YEAR	%	BUDGET	%
	INCOME								
	INCOME ACCRUAL								
400	FEES: INCOME FROM CLIENTS	42356.00		19000.00		229247.57		228000.00	
460	OTHER INCOME/RECEIPTS	1836.23		700.00		9232.88		8400.00	
480	INCOME PRODUCING PROPERTY	.00		350.00		3790.00		4200.00	
	TOTAL INCOME ACCRUAL	44192.23		20050.00		242270.37		240600.00	
	EXPENSES								
	PAYROLL								
500	SALARY: SECRETARIAL	2975.30	6.7	1500.00	7.5	17851.00	7.4	18000.00	7.5
501	SALARY: WORD/DATA PROC.	1100.00	2.5	650.00	3.2	7556.45	3.1	7800.00	3.2
502	SALARY: PARALG & CLERKS	1875.18	4.2	2000.00	10.0	20632.15	8.5	24000.00	10.0
503	SALARY: ATTORNEYS	11400.00	25.8	6000.00	29.9	68400.00	28.2	72000.00	29.9
504	SALARY: OTH NON-OWN EMPL	1050.00	2.4	700.00	3.5	7804.00	3.2	8400.00	3.5
	TOTAL PAYROLL	18400.48	41.6	10850.00	54.1	122244.40	50.5	130200.00	54.1
	NON-PAYROLL EMPLOYEE COSTS								
510	FICA & UNEMPLOY TAXES	838.77	1.9	420.00	2.1	5038.77	2.1	5020.00	2.1
514	RETIREMENT BENEFITS	746.00	1.7	370.00	1.8	4446.00	1.8	4440.00	1.8
518	TRAINING & EDUCATION	250.00	.6	300.00	1.5	3660.00	1.5	3600.00	1.5
519	OTHER EMPLOYEE COSTS	.00	.0	150.00	.7	1674.00	.7	1800.00	.7
	TOTAL NON-PAYROLL EMPL COST	1834.77	4.2	1240.00	6.2	14818.77	6.1	14860.00	6.2
	OCCUPANCY EXPENSES								
520	OFFICE RENT	2940.00	6.7	750.00	3.7	10290.00	4.2	9000.00	3.7
521	PARKING	240.00	.5	80.00	.4	1003.85	.4	960.00	.4
523	REAL EST TAXES & INS	382.00	.9	185.00	.9	2245.78	.9	2200.00	.9

Source: Computer Legal Systems, Inc.

Mail: Incoming

In addition to sorting mail by addressee, the individual responsible for the morning mail should:

1. Date-stamp *everything* with the "Received" stamp. Exceptions are books received on approval or original documents such as deeds that have been mailed to the office for recording or filing elsewhere. Whenever possible, stamp the date in the same location on every document. This will make it easier for someone to read the dates when perusing through a large file.

2. When an incoming document requires reference to previous papers, place the appropriate file with it.

3. If you can draft a response to the incoming document, prepare a draft and place it with the document.

4. Return receipts for certified mail should be stapled to the copies of the documents to which they correspond.

5. File the following documents immediately without circulation:

   - Pocket parts or supplements to treatises in the library.

   - All loose-leaf page supplements.

   - The paperback supplements to the state statutes and the United States Code Annotated or United States Code Service.

6. For informational purposes, prepare a "Daily Checks and Bills Received" sheet using the format in Figure 14.18.

Incoming mail may have to be photocopied and distributed to others—for example, to paralegals for specific assignments or to clients for their information. In some firms, special stamps are used such as the following:

FOR INFORMATION ONLY—NO ACTION REQUIRED

Copying Charges

Failure to record legitimate copying charges for later billing to the client constitutes a drain on the firm's financial resources.

1. Register on the alphabetical list that is kept on or near the copying machine the client's name, if not already there, and the number of copies.

2. Copies that are not to be charged to any client should be noted as "office" copies or "N/C" copies.

Received on January 6, 1991		
CHECKS		
Hammerlee	(title search)	$380.00
Mid-Penn	136.55 C.A.	3961.43
PNB	164.80 C.A.	724.80
Kalp, Arn	2.25 C.A.	62.25
BILLS		
Wagners	(clips and rubber stamps)	12.72
Rec'd vol. 97 of *Supreme Court Reporter*		N/C

FIGURE 14.18

Daily Checks and Bills Received

3. On at least a monthly basis, the member of the staff who is responsible for copy charges should post them to the respective client accounts.

Filing System

Rules and Comments

The importance of a good filing system cannot be overestimated. Lost and misplaced papers are the obvious result of a poor system. But the damage can run even deeper. Deadlines can be missed, leading to one of the most common causes of malpractice claims against attorneys. Hours may be lost in ferreting through files for crucial documents that cannot be found. Appellate briefs might be poorly prepared because files are not in a readily usable form that would allow drafters to gather information and prepare the briefs in an orderly fashion. Particular tasks might be overlooked because attorneys, often subconsciously, dread having to search for needed information or simply do not know how to tell a member of the staff to compile what is needed.

Some firms use an exclusively *alphabetical filing system*. For example, all the documents for the Allen Construction Corporation case would be filed just before all the documents for the Allenson estate case. Such a system is not as effective as a *numerical filing system* accompanied by an alphabetical card index. Here is an example of the categories of cases (or client matters) that could be used in a numerical filing system:

001–099	Large clients
100–199	Wills and estate planning
200–349	Real estate: purchase and sale
350–399	Estate administration and trusts
400–499	Domestic relations, excluding divorce and custody masterships
500–549	Personal injury, including worker's compensation
600–649	Litigation, excluding personal injury
700–749	Corporations and partnerships
750–799	Financing, bonds, industrial developments, and similar matters
800–849	Tax, excluding estate planning
900–999	Miscellaneous files not appropriate for any other category
1000–1499	Printed forms, applications, and other miscellaneous documents
1500–1999	Bar Association and non-client-related matters
2000–2049	Bankruptcy
2100–2149	Divorce and custody masterships and arbitration panels
2200–2299	Criminal matters

These numerical categories vary widely from office to office according to size and type of practice. Large firms spread the brackets and use higher numbers. A two digit number representing the year would precede each of the number categories. Hence, 92.287 would be a real estate matter opened in 1992. Anytime a significant block of cases does not fit within a particular category, it is relatively easy to create a new category.

A numerical filing system with an alphabetical card index is preferable since it:

■ Reduces the misplacement of files. For some reason, individuals are more likely to place files in correct numerical order than in correct alphabetical order. For example, a purely alphabetical system would have difficulty handling the industrial development project for a client named Jones who owns North Marine Industries involving a local development agency bearing the acronym SIFT. While someone may think of the project as "Jones: SIFT-North Marine Industries," others may look for the file under "North Marine Industries: SIFT." Cross-referencing within a card index (see below) almost eliminates this problem when a numerical filing system is used.

- Permits the grouping of files by subject matter, such as litigation or real estate. Such a system can be useful if, for example, the firm wants to contact all clients for whom wills were prepared within the past five years.

- Allows easier reference on memoranda, correspondence, and client lists. It is certainly simpler to jot "86.267" on a title abstract sheet than "Stankiewicz: Purchase of Real Estate (1986).

- Allows cross-referencing within the card index. The index cards *can* be alphabetical. You can create cards under any variety of headings that you think a user might try to use. Each card would refer to the files under their numerical entry.

- Automatically brings old files to the front of the filing system, acting almost as a tickler system.

- Allows the immediate identification of the year of a particular file by the first two digits of the file index, such as, "86.589" for a 1986 file.

- Facilitates the differentiation of files that may have confusingly similar designations. "Jones: Personal Injury (1981)" and "Jones: Property Settlement Agreement (1983)" would probably be stored next to one another in an *alphabetical* system and would have the tendency not only to be filed in the wrong alphabetical order but to attract each other's papers. But in a *numerical* system, although the index cards would probably be neighbors, the physical separation of the folders in the file cabinet would be more likely to prevent the misplacing of documents among the files.[16]

- Adapts to computerization, when that time comes (see next section).

- Eases the handling of closed files. Under an alphabetical system, when the firm is ready to "retire" a particular file, two choices are available—continue to file alphabetically, or switch to a sequential closed-file numbering system, with files placed one after the other as they are closed, regardless of their alphabetical designations. The first choice leads to the situation in which all the files from I through Z have to be moved if H grows rapidly (for example, nobody anticipated that the Half-Penny National Bank would become the firm's most active client). The second alternative requires an alphabetical card index to allow for the retrieval of particular closed files. It would already exist under the numerical system.

Depending on the size of the office, a library-like system may be needed in which files are checked out of the file room in much the same manner that books are checked out of a library. While administratively burdensome, this system at

---

[16]One possible difficulty with a numerical filing system is the confusion of file 91.325 with file 92.325. The multicolored file folders that are available from stationery suppliers offer a ready solution to this potential problem. If blue folders were used for 1991, red for 1992, and green for 1993, a file is not likely to be misplaced, and if it is in the wrong spot, it will stand out. In order to have the benefit of a fully integrated system, color-matching index cards should be used for the alphabetical index.

least ensures an ability to trace missing files. Overly strict measures, however, might backfire. For example, an attempt to prevent attorneys from ever holding files in their office might discourage them from initially storing any of their files in the filing room.

Closed Files

The filing cabinets in the main office contain only files on which work is being done, on which work is likely to be done in the near future, or that are likely to be used for reference in a current matter. Closed file procedures are designed to save active file space as well as allow for easy retrieval of retired information. Theoretically, if the firm's practice is stable, its main filing cabinets should maintain a constant size, while the real accumulation of paper occurs in the closed file storage area.

Generally, only the billing attorney may declare a file closed. Such a decision is not crucial or irreversible because the file can be retrieved easily. It is better to close a file than to keep it around. The fewer the active files, the more manageable the filing system.

When a file is to be closed, one way to do it is to "Pendaflex" it to the individual responsible for file closings, who then:

1. Assigns a CF (closed file) number to the file. This will be the next number for the year, with the first file closed during the calendar year 1992 receiving the number CF 92.001.

2. Places the CF number on the file's alphabetical index cards.

3. Writes the CF number on the file label.

4. Places the file in the "upstairs" CF filing drawer. The upstairs CF filing drawer contains recently closed files that may be needed. These files are sent upstairs for a time, before being relegated to the basement or other permanent storage area.

The closed files are permanently stored in boxes clearly labeled with the first and last CF file number. To retrieve a closed file, simply check the alphabetical index card, obtain the CF number, and find the file in storage. In some firms, closed files are placed on microfilm after a designated time. Most of the original file is then destroyed. Future access and copying of such files are achieved through microfilm readers and printers.

■ Section H. Computer-Based Records Management System in a Large Office

How One Law Firm Automated Its Records Management

Patricia Patterson, Director of Legal Information Services,
Schiff Hardin & Waite, Chicago, Illinois
21 American Association of Law Libraries Newsletter 291 (April 1991)

By the end of the next decade, it is likely that all records managers will have considered, tested, or installed some sort of computer-based records management system. From the smallest to the most complex central file system, computer automation offers the possibility of a cost-effective method for increasing management efficiency. But for many records information managers, jumping into a computerized system may not be conceptually or economically feasible at this time. Their problems probably fall into one or more of the following categories:

1. Insufficient financial resources to purchase a completely computerized system.

2. A non-standard records system that may require a specially customized computer program.

3. Management reluctant to commit to a new way of doing business.

4. Records personnel must be retrained, at great time and expense, to become computer literate and understand a computer system.

If your situation falls into one of these categories, you can take it upon yourself to solve some of these problems.

First of all, and let me emphasize [that] a successfully Automated Records Management System is:

- User Designed and Implemented
- Easy to Use and Accessible
- Online in Real Time
- Multi-User (Multiple/Simultaneous Users)
- Application Based and Controlled
- Management Supported

Using my own experience as a working example, I would like to discuss each of these criteria.

When I assumed the responsibilities of the Schiff Hardin and Waite Records Department, I inherited a large problem. Data entry operators had been employed three years prior to my arrival to capture our 350,000 3 × 5 card file information onto magnetic tape. The Records Department was behind in its duties of opening new files, tracking file locations, and checking for conflicts of interest. In addition, the Records Department still had two people keying all of the file card and cross reference card information into batches of data onto magnetic type. Management directed me to guide the department into the twenty-first century by installing a computer system capable of using the data that the firm had spent significant time and money on over the previous four years. My background was in library management, and I was responsible for the Schiff library, so I was accustomed to working with large volumes of information.

My first task was to select a computer company to convert the data stored on nine reels of magnetic tape. We needed this data reformatted into a structure that could be loaded to an online database. Over 350,000 records of data had been keyed with very little control over checking the validity of client numbers, dates, attorney numbers, etc. Previous computer consultants employed by Schiff had not thoroughly planned for the next step. That being the case and with the keying of data nearly complete, an implementation decision was needed.

At that time, we contacted the firm of Micom Systems, Inc., of North Muskegon, Michigan. Micom had been doing custom programming and computer services work for law firms since 1969. Their proposal to convert our data to a database format and clean up the duplicate entries and as much of the erroneous

editing as possible was accepted by the firm in the fall of 1987. Micom, using its IBM 4341 computer and IBM assembler language, converted the data by January, 1988.

My next task was to select an online database on which to use our newly converted data. After researching all of the records management software packages on the market, we concluded that they were inappropriate for our application. Because of Micom's knowledge of our data and experience with online law firm systems, we selected them to develop our records management system. With our data now ready for use, and after years of keying in the data, we were naturally anxious for the system to be operational. However, Schiff's two IBM System 36s were filled to capacity with litigation support and accounting functions. There was no room for a 250 million-character records management system on either of our two computer systems. Therefore, we chose to install communications equipment and a dedicated 9600 baud line to Micom's IBM mainframe 200 miles from our Chicago office.

Micom personnel studied our information storage and reporting needs. They then designed our system to meet current, as well as future needs. Operational requirements and key functions of the system included:

1. All data from the conversion loaded and accessible.

2. User-friendly system with a short learning curve.

3. An adaptable system that could be changed quickly and easily.

4. Online interactive with additions, changes, and deletions immediately available.

5. Online conflict of interest searching with results printed on demand.

6. File cards and labels printed online using local printers.

7. Accommodation of the complex structured file identification system Schiff already had in place.

As I will list later on, the records management system has many features that address our information needs. The key ones, previously stated, were the driving force behind Micom selecting IBM CSP (Cross System Product) as its development language. Because of CSP's ability to run across IBM platforms, Micom could develop and initially run the system on their IBM mainframe. Then when Schiff installs an IBM AS/400 or networked IBM PS/2s, Micom can port the system to run on either of these computer systems. This software portability across platforms was a positive factor in our decision to use Micom to develop our system.

The Schiff requirements for an automated records management system originated from attorney needs and expectations. Accurate and thorough conflict checking is a necessity and rates the highest priority. Our system provides timely and complete new client screening based on all of the data stored in the records management system. Our attorneys need rapid opening of new files and swift retrieval of stored files. We have the ability to track folders and identify files easily and quickly with very few keystrokes or screen changes. Quick locating of a client's file folders is important whether the file is located in someone's office or in a box at an off-site storage facility. Attorney and secretary requests for file locations and identifications are handled by our staff of 11 using this system. Most requests of this type are handled by phone. New, revised, or additional file labels are printed on demand by the Records Center staff.

Our system has performed as we had hoped it would, allowing us to proceed with add-on enhancements. For example, we are now in the installation phase of a bar coding subsystem. This will enable us to print a bar code label with a unique client/matter number for each file created in the Records Center. Using a fixed scanner in our Records Department, we will scan the bar codes of all folders that leave the Records Center. Both the location and file folder identification will be scanned online directly into the computer system. All file folders leaving the Records Center at night will be batch-scanned into an IBM PS/2 and transferred to the IBM mainframe the next morning. Periodically we will scan all folders in attorneys'

offices using portable, hand-held scanners. This procedure will give us the ability to track folder movements between attorney offices.

One feature of our system which saves additional time is the box storage system. This system tracks all box storage; both on, and off-site. Folder movement into and out of boxes is monitored, as are all pick-ups and deliveries. This system provides us with reports of all pick-ups and deliveries by date to enable us to verify our warehouse service bill more easily.

The Conflict of Interest System deserves more comment. This system is fully integrated into our Records Management System. Our personnel can hot key to the full text search process at any time. Then, using . . . commands, they can completely search our file records data. The data is displayed in our record structure format with the "hits" highlighted. We also have the ability to print any or all of the occurrences immediately. This efficient system has saved us countless hours of work.

While you may not be ready to adopt the automated records system that I have described, I hope the process we went through at Schiff Hardin and Waite will alert you to the advantages offered by computerized records management systems. Just be certain that the system you select addresses your specific information needs. The future is upon us, and we must knowledgeably embrace the technology on which it is based.

Scanning coded files in records department

■ ASSIGNMENT 14.1

In the practice of law, time is money. Hence you must develop the discipline of recording your time. Supervisors will later decide what portions of your time are billable—and to what clients. Step one is to compile a record of your time.

To practice this discipline, fill out a Daily Time Sheet for a day that you select. On *one* sheet of paper, record (in a chart form that you design) everything (approximately) that you do *in six minute* intervals over a continuous eight-hour period. Once you design your chart, *it should take you no more than about fifteen minutes to fill it out* during the eight-hour period. You do not, however, fill it out at one time; you fill it out at appropriate times throughout the eight hours.

Select an eight-hour period in which you are engaged in a fairly wide variety of activities. If possible, avoid an eight-hour period that contains any single activity lasting over two hours. Draw a chart covering the eight-hour period. At the top of the chart, place your name, the date of the eight-hour period that you used, and the starting/ending times of the eight-hour period. The period can be within a school day, a workday, a day of leisure, etc.

Using abbreviations, make specific entries on your activities within the eight hours—in six-minute intervals. For example, "Reading a chapter in a real estate school text" might be abbreviated as RE-R. "Driving to school" might be abbreviated as D-Sch. "Purely personal matters" (such as taking a shower) might be abbreviated as PPM. You decide what the abbreviations are. On the back of the sheet of paper containing the chart, explain what the abbreviations mean. When an activity is repeated in more than one six-minute interval, simply repeat the abbreviation.

One format for the chart might be a series of vertical and horizontal lines on the sheet of paper. This will give you a small amount of space on which to insert your abbreviations for each six-minute interval. Design the chart any way that you want, keeping in mind the goal of the exercise: to enable someone else to know what you did within the eight-hour period.

On page 697, there is an example of a Daily Time Sheet (Figure 14.6) used in a law office. Note that the last column says "hours" and "10ths." A 10th of an hour is six minutes. Do *not* follow the format in Figure 14.6. Use the guidelines listed above, e.g., place your abbreviations on the other side of the sheet of paper that you submit.

■ ASSIGNMENT 14.2

Mary Davis is a paralegal who has been working at the law firm of Smith & Smith for five years. The firm consists of two attorneys, Sam and Karen Smith, a husband and wife attorney team. There is one other employee, Jane Jones, who has just been hired as a paralegal trainee. This person, a high school graduate, was a homemaker for fifteen years. She has had no outside employment or training. The firm has one secretary who spends most of his time typing bills to be sent to clients and acting as the receptionist.

Smith & Smith has a family-law practice, handling mostly divorces. It takes two main kinds of cases: (1) contested divorces, where the husband and wife cannot agree on one or more critical issues (such as custody, property division, or amount of alimony); and (2) uncontested divorces, where everything is agreed on. While most of the firm's clients are plaintiffs who have filed for divorce, the firm also represents defendants on occasion.

Uncontested cases involve a fair amount of paperwork plus at least one court appearance, where the attorney obtains the approval of the court on what the parties have agreed to do. Contested cases involve extensive paperwork and many court appearances in which the disputed issues are resolved by the court—unless a settlement is eventually reached by the parties.

Almost every case requires the preparation of the following documents:

- Retainer (in which the client hires the firm)
- Intake Interview Report (reporting on a long interview with the client, during which extensive information is obtained about spouses, children, addresses, employment, facts of marriage, length of time in the county, bank accounts, residences, cars, other property owned, family health conditions, kinds of insurance, stocks, bonds, pension plans, debts already incurred, budget data, etc.)
- Complaint (stating the grounds for divorce)
- Answer (responding to the complaint)
- Letters to opposing counsel requesting information
- Motions to the court requesting temporary alimony or maintenance, child custody and support, and attorney fees
- Motion for a Restraining Order (to prevent either side from transferring assets and to prevent harassment)
- Motion to Produce (a formal request that the other side turn over designated items, such as pay stubs, copies of tax returns, bank statements, and insurance policies)
- Agreement on Property Division, Custody, and Support (uncontested cases only, unless a settlement is eventually reached in contested cases)
- Interrogatories (in which one party sends written questions to the other)
- A Notice of Deposition (informing the other to appear at a designated place, such as at the office of one of the attorneys, to answer questions)
- Proposed Final Decree of Dissolution of the Marriage

In the office, Mary prepares the Intake Interview Report based on an interview that she conducts with the client. This occurs after the retainer is signed and one of the attorneys goes over the case with the client. Mary prepares the first draft of all the other documents listed above.

Mary conducts the intake interview with the client alone. Since she has done so many of these interviews, she knows from memory what questions to ask. When she was first hired, she watched the attorneys interview and so learned what to ask and how to conduct an interview on her own. Whenever anything unusual came up during the interview, she left the room to find one of the attorneys for guidance. She took extensive notes on what the client said and later typed her notes for the Intake Interview Report.

Whenever Mary needed to draft one of the documents, she went to the firm's closed-case files to try to find a model that she could adapt. Since she had legal research skills, she also sought help from texts (such as practice books) found in the law library. The more experienced Mary became, however, the less she had to resort to the old files and the law library. The attorneys were amazed at her ability to find and retain whatever she needed to prepare so many different kinds of documents. They developed tremendous trust in Mary. For many cases, the documents never seemed to vary except for the names of the parties and particular financial figures. A fair number of times, however, different situations arose—for example, the parties had prior marriages or a child was retarded and therefore required special care following the divorce. Starting from scratch, Mary used her experience and skills to draft the proper documents to accommodate these situations.

Mary was also responsible for opening case files for all new clients. Each time the firm accepted a client, she took an accordion folder and typed the name of the client on it. Scattered throughout the folder were handwritten notes (from Mary or the attorney in charge of the case) describing some event that was relevant to the case. The documents were not placed in the folder in any particular order. This, however, did not create much difficulty since Mary was so familiar with all of the files. Only occasionally were things lost or misfiled.

The reason that the firm has decided to hire another paralegal is that Mary has announced that in six months she is going to leave the firm for another position. The receptionist also gave notice that he is leaving. Neither is dissatisfied with the firm; it is simply time to move on. The firm tried to find an experienced paralegal to replace Mary, but could not. Hence it just hired Jane Jones who, as indicated, has had no experience or training. The firm will replace the receptionist with a full-time typist and a full-time receptionist who will also be available for messenger assignments.

The firm is in a panic. The caseload is increasing at a rapid pace. There is some talk of hiring an additional attorney who has just graduated from law school and passed the bar, but no definite decision has yet been made. The big worry is the effect of Mary's departure in six months.

Sam Smith's solution is to have Jane Jones, the paralegal trainee, follow Mary around, observing everything Mary does during her last six months in the hope of absorbing as much as possible.

Karen Smith has a different approach. "Why don't we create some management systems and then train everyone on them?" Sam is very skeptical, but willing to listen.

Assume that you work for a law office management consulting firm. Karen and Sam Smith have asked you to prepare a report on how the office can systematize and manage its divorce practice so that Jane Jones—and *anyone* else—can come in, learn the system on their own (or almost on their own), and become functioning members of the team.

State how you would go about handling this task. If you think more than one system is needed, describe what they are. What facts do you want to obtain on how the firm now operates? How would you go about getting these facts? State any problems that you anticipate in obtaining these facts and how these problems might be resolved. Then describe what you would do with what you learn. State how the system or systems would operate. Give examples. Detail any problems you antici-pate in implementing the system or systems and how these problems might be handled. If you feel that the firm needs different kinds of equipment, describe what is needed and how it would be used within the system or systems that you propose. State the benefits that the system(s) might provide. Also describe any difficulties that might exist in the system(s). In short, provide a comprehensive but realistic report. Don't try to oversell what you propose. Assume that the main audience of your report will be attorneys who are uninformed about the management dimensions of a law office.

☐ Chapter Summary

Our examination of law office administration be-gan with an overview of the different settings in which attorneys practice law in the private sector in the United States and of the different kinds of attorneys found in each setting.

A sole practice consists of one attorney who owns the practice even if he or she employs other attorneys. The others do not share in the profits and losses of the firm. To save on expenses, sev-eral sole practitioners may enter into an office-sharing arrangement under which the attorneys share expenses for office space, secretarial help, library materials, etc.

In a partnership, the equity or capital partners share in the profits and losses of the firm and con-trol its management, often through a committee or department structure. Associates are attorneys in the firm who hope one day to be invited to become partners. There are, however, special categories of associates created for those who do not become

(Continued on next page)

☐ **Chapter Summary** (Continued)

partners, such as senior associate and permanent associate.

Other categories of attorneys who might be hired by a law firm include staff attorneys, of-counsel attorneys, and contract attorneys. For tax and estate-planning purposes, many states allow attorneys to practice law as a professional corporation. There is little practical difference, however, between the administration of a partnership and a professional corporation.

Finally, there are attorneys who practice law in the legal departments of corporations. They are employees of the corporation, which is their sole client.

Large law offices may have many nonattorney employees to help manage the office. These employees have become increasingly influential because of the sharp rise in overhead costs in recent years. Among the most prominent is the Legal Administrator. Also, if there are more than a few paralegals in the office, a Legal Assistant Manager is often hired to help administer the office's system for recruiting, hiring, training, and monitoring the progress of paralegals.

There is considerable pressure on attorneys and paralegals to keep track of their time with precision. The accounting records and financial health of the law firm depend on it. At least nine different methods of billing exist: hourly rate, fixed fee, full contingent fee, hourly plus fixed fee, hourly reduced or with contingent, blended hourly rate, lodestar, value billing, and percentage fee. The method of paying this bill (including disbursements) should be spelled out in the retainer. The amount actually paid by a client is not determined until there has been a valuing of the bill, which might result in a write-up, a write-down, or no change.

An efficient law firm uses administrative reports to help it keep track of and manage the practice. Among the most important are the practice analysis report, work summary, cash flow projection, chargeable hour schedule, aged accounts receivable, and budget reports.

A busy law firm receives a great deal of mail, does a great amount of copying, and files a great many documents. It is important for the paralegal to learn what method the firm uses for these tasks. While some offices file alphabetically, many firms have found that numerical filing is more effective. Offices with large caseloads, and hence many documents to file and store, often use a computerized system of record management.

Key Terms

sole practice
general practitioner
law clerk
office sharing
partnership
partner
draw
associate
law clerk
lateral hire
passed over
permanent associate
senior associate
nonequity partner
income partner
equity partner
capital partner
staff attorney
second-tiered attorney
of counsel
contract attorney
project attorney

professional corporation
corporate legal department
general counsel
in-house attorney
legal administrator
legal assistant manager
timekeeping
new file worksheet
new matter sheet
daily time sheet
hourly time and rate chart
time ticket
master ledger card
hourly rate
bundled/unbundled
fixed fee
full contingent fee
hourly plus fixed fee
hourly reduced or with
    contingent
blended hourly rate
lodestar

value billing
percentage fee
disbursements
retainer
billing memorandum
draft bill
write down
write up
valuing the bill
premium adjustment
discount adjustment
aging report
practice analysis report
work summary
cash flow projection
chargeable hour schedule
aged accounts receivable
annual budget
alphabetical filing system
numerical filing system
bar coding

15

Informal and Formal Administrative Advocacy

■ Chapter Outline

■ Section A. The Nature of Advocacy

Advocacy is the process by which an individual attempts to influence the behavior of others according to predetermined goals. Advocacy is a basic component of everyday life; we are frequently advocates for ourselves and for others. Note, for example, the advocacy involved, or potentially involved, in the following circumstances:

1. At a supermarket checkout counter, a clerk tells a customer that the price of tomatoes is 49¢ a pound. The customer replies, "But the sign back there said 39¢ a pound." The clerk says, "I'm sorry, but the price is 49¢."

2. A student goes to the teacher to say that a term paper should have been graded "A" rather than "B."

3. A tenant tells the landlord that a $50 a month rent increase is ridiculous because the building has been steadily deteriorating.

4. An individual applying for a driver's license is told that he filled out his application incorrectly and that he must wait a week before he will be allowed to fill out another one. The individual feels that his application is not incorrect and that even if it is, he should not have to wait a week to do it over.

5. An employee has been laid off from her job. She calls the unemployment insurance bureau and asks to be sent forms so that she can fill out a claim. The clerk tells her that no forms can be sent through the mail. She asks the clerk if an exception can be made in her case because she has not been feeling very well and her doctor has told her to stay in bed. The clerk says there are no exceptions.

6. A homeowner has been away on a vacation. Upon his return, he finds that his house has been burglarized. When he goes to the police station to report

the crime, he asks the desk sergeant why his neighborhood has not been receiving better protection in view of all the burglaries that have been occurring in the area lately. The sergeant replies that there are not enough police available to patrol the neighborhood adequately. The homeowner is not satisfied with this response and asks to see the precinct captain.

. . . .

The customer, student, tenant, applicant, employee, and homeowner all have complaints. They are complainants. They are not satisfied with something. Their natural response it to make an *argument* for better service. In so doing, they become advocates for the goals or objectives that they are seeking. Advocacy does not always require courtrooms, judges, and attorneys; all that is needed is a complaint, a complainant, and someone who should be able to act on the complaint.

The distinction between *formal* and *informal advocacy* is primarily one of degree. Generally, the more the setting looks like a court procedure (for example, with a hearing officer present, evidence or testimony taken, or written decisions issued) the more formal it is. As we saw in Chapter 6, an administrative agency's quasi-judicial powers are often exercised through hearings that have many similarities to courtroom proceedings. A quasi-judicial proceeding is one in which the agency resolves a dispute between a citizen and the agency (such as between welfare recipient and welfare department) or between two or more citizens under the control of the agency (e.g., two students in the same school or two inmates in the same prison who are having a dispute). If you are representing yourself or someone else at such a hearing, you are engaged in formal advocacy.

Our first concern in this chapter is *in*formal advocacy that occurs (a) in connection with administrative agencies not involving formal hearings or (b) outside the realm of administrative agencies altogether, as in the supermarket case in the example at the beginning of this chapter. Our primary focus will be the informal advocacy techniques that can be used when confronting employees of *any* organization—for example, a public agency such as a social security office or a private business such as an insurance company.

Paralegals often have contact with organizations that require the application of informal advocacy techniques. The following list contains several examples:

- Determining the names and addresses of the principal shareholders of a corporation
- Gaining access to the records of an agency or of a company
- Obtaining copies of forms from the Securities and Exchange Commission on the disclosure and reporting requirements of a corporation
- Writing to or visiting an agency or company to obtain its position on a matter involving a client
- Trying to convince a caseworker or a social worker that the action the agency has taken (or that it proposes to take) is illegal or ill-advised

A paralegal can meet resistance in any and all of these situations. The basic techniques of informal advocacy should help in handling this resistance.

Section B. The Techniques of Informal Advocacy

In Figure 15.1, on page 722, there is a summary of nineteen techniques that are sometimes used in trying to obtain action from an administrative agency or from any large organization. As you read the list, think of which ones are more likely to be effective.

Clearly, some of these techniques in Figure 15.1 will be more effective than others. Perhaps some of them should *never* be tried. A great deal would obviously depend on the circumstances confronting the paralegal at the time. In general how would you assess the nineteen techniques? If you were to list the techniques in the order in which you think that the technique would be effective in *most* situations, what would your order be?

The following outline lists the nineteen techniques in one possible order of effectiveness. The outline also presents other considerations relevant to their use: threshold concerns, evaluation of techniques, adaptation, and recording.

Advocacy

I. *Threshold Concerns*

    1. Define your goals in order of priority

    2. Decide when to intervene

II. *Advocacy Techniques*

    1. Put your cards on the table

    2. Insist on service

    3. Ask for authorization

    4. Go up the chain of command

    5. Insist on common sense

    6. Act tired, battered, and helpless

    7. Cite a precedent

    8. Find the points of compromise

    9. Uncover the realm of discretion

    10. Demonstrate the exception

    11. Cite the law

    12. Be a buddy

    13. Make clear that the case is important to you

    14. Redefine the problem

    15. Do a favor

    16. Seek the support of a third party

    17. Preach

    18. Embarrass

    19. Get angry

III. *Evaluate the Techniques Used*

    1. Are you making yourself clear?

FIGURE 15.1

Techniques of Informal Advocacy

1. *Put your cards on the table.* Be direct and completely above board in telling the agency official what your position is and what you want.

2. *Insist on adequate service.* Point out to the agency official that the purpose of the agency is service and that this principle should guide the official's actions.

3. *Seek the support of third parties.* Before you make your position known, gather the support of individuals or groups within and outside the agency so you can demonstrate that you are not alone.

4. *Be a buddy.* Show agency officials that you are not an enemy, that you respect and like them, and that you are aware how difficult their job is.

5. *Find the points of compromise.* Ferret out the negotiable points in the dispute and determine whether you can bargain your way to a favorable result.

6. *Insist on common sense.* Convey to the agency official the impression that common sense dictates your position—in addition to or despite regulations or technicalities that might be cited against you.

7. *Demonstrate the exception.* Insist on the uniqueness of your client's situation. Show agency officials that the general rule they are using to deny your client a benefit is inapplicable.

8. *Uncover the realm of discretion.* Take the position that rules do not exist until they are applied, and that, in the application of rules, agency officials often have wide discretion despite claims that their hands are tied.

9. *Ask for authorization.* Insist that the agency official show you the regulation, law, or authority that supports the action taken or proposed by the agency.

10. *Cite the law.* Show the agency official that you know what administrative regulations apply to the case. Also cite statutes and other laws to demonstrate your point.

11. *Redefine the problem.* If you can't solve a problem, redefine it—as long as you can still achieve what the client seeks. For example, stop trying to qualify the client for program "Z" if program "Y" will serve the client equally well and the problems of qualifying the client for "Y" are not as great as you'll face by continuing to insist on "Z."

12. *Demonstrate anger and hostility.* Be completely open about the bad feelings that you have concerning what is being done or proposed.

13. *Preach.* Lecture the civil servant. Tell the agency what it should or should not be doing.

14. *Climb the chain of command.* Normally everyone has a boss who can overrule decisions made by those beneath him or her. When you are dissatisfied with the decision or action of an employee, "appeal," or complain "up the chain of command," to the employee's supervisor and to the supervisor's supervisor, if needed.

15. *Embarrass the official.* Show the agency official that you do not respect him or her. Do it in such a way that the official is made to look silly.

16. *Make clear that you and your office are going to fight this case all the way up.* Make the agency official aware of how important the case is. Point out that you are thinking about taking the case to a formal agency hearing and that your office may go to court, if necessary.

17. *Take the role of the tired, battered, helpless citizen.* Do not insist on anything. Play dumb; act exhausted; act in such a way that the agency official will think, "This person needs help;" act as if everyone else has given you the runaround and that you are praying that this official (whom you have not dealt with before) will finally give you a sympathetic ear—and some help.

18. *Do a favor to get a favor.* Be willing to do something (within reason) for the person from whom you are seeking something.

19. *Cite a precedent.* Point out to the agency official (if it is true) that your case is not unusual because the agency has granted what you want to others under the same or similar circumstances in the past.

2. Are you creating more problems than you are solving?

3. Are you accomplishing your goal?

IV. *Adaptation.* Are you flexible enough to shift your technique?

V. *Recording*

1. Describe what you saw

2. Describe what you did

The focus of the first threshold concern is the priority of goals. This concern, of course, would not be applicable if the assignment you are given contains only one goal, such as obtaining a copy of a record at the agency. It may be, however, that the assignment contains a variety of objectives at the outset or that a single-objective assignment subsequently blossoms into tasks involving more than one goal. Priorities must be set. If you try to do everything, you may end up accomplishing nothing. Every technique of informal advocacy will probably fail if you have unrealistic expectations of what can be accomplished.

The second threshold issue is to decide when to intervene with the advocacy techniques. The decision to intervene involves a strategic judgment about when it would be most appropriate to seek what you are after at the agency. In most situations, a sense of timing is very important. For example, suppose that you must contact the complaint bureau of an agency that is relatively new to you. One approach would be simply to walk up to the complaint bureau and delve right into the matter that brought you there. Another approach would be to try to find out something about the bureau *before* going to it. There may be some literature available on the structure of the agency that will provide you with at least a general idea of what to expect. You may be able to talk to attorneys or other paralegals who have had prior contact with the bureau. Suppose you learn that there are two agency employees who rotate their work at the bureau and that one employee has a reputation of being more cooperative than the other. You may decide not to go to the bureau until this employee is on duty. In short, you decide to postpone your involvement with, or intervention at, the bureau until circumstances are most favorable to the objective you are seeking.

Next in the outline, the nineteen techniques are listed. Note that the last three are preaching, causing embarrassment, and becoming angry. These are placed at the bottom of the list because they are likely to antagonize the agency employee and perhaps set up roadblocks to your objective. Do you agree? Can you think of circumstances when anger, for example, *would* be appropriate? These questions move us to the next section (III) of the outline: evaluation of the techniques.

As you use any one of the techniques, you must simultaneously judge the *effectiveness* of the technique in light of what you are trying to accomplish. Are you making yourself clear? Are you complicating rather than resolving things? Are you getting through? Are you pacing yourself properly? Is your insistence on immediate success interfering with building a step-by-step road toward progress?

One of the major signs of ineffective advocacy is becoming so involved in the case that you begin to take roadblocks and defeat *personally.* Everyone agrees that objectivity is a good quality—and most of us claim to possess this quality in abundance. The unfortunate fact, however, is that *we tend to lose objectivity as friction increases.* We allow our careers and our lifestyles to be threatened when someone says to us, "You can't do that." Of course, we rarely admit that we can be so threatened. We justify our response by blaming someone else for insensitivity, stupidity, or unfairness.

Of course, evaluation for the sake of evaluation is worthless. Once you have disciplined yourself to identify the techniques you are using and evaluate their effectiveness, you must be flexible enough to *adapt* your techniques and shift to more effective techniques, when needed.

Finally, the paralegal usually will have a recording responsibility. Almost every case you work on will have to be heavily documented in the office files. Your efforts at informal advocacy should be included in those files.

■ ASSIGNMENT 15.1

In each role-playing exercise, there are two characters: P (the paralegal) and AE (the agency employee). Students from the class will be assigned one or the other role. As indicated, P is seeking something from AE. AE is uncooperative. The objective of AE is to antagonize P (within reason) to the point where P loses objectivity. The objective of P is to refrain from losing his or her objectivity.

(a) At 4:30 P.M., P goes to the Department of Motor Vehicles to apply for a license. AE tells P that the office closes at 5:00 P.M. and the application procedure takes forty-five minutes. AE refuses to let P apply.

(b) At the post office, P tries to buy $400.00 worth of 29¢ stamps. AE tells P that no individual customer can buy over $100.00 worth of stamps per day.

(c) P goes to the bureau of vital statistics and requests a copy of his mother's birth certificate. AE tells P that no citizen can obtain the birth certificate of another person without the written permission of the person. P's mother is ill in a hospital a thousand miles away. P wants the record without going through the bother of obtaining this permission.

Those members of the class who are not participating in the role-playing exercises should identify and evaluate the techniques of informal advocacy that P uses.

We now examine some of the informal advocacy techniques in the context of the following fact situation:

> You are in your own home or apartment. You receive a letter from the gas company stating that your gas will be shut off in ten days if you do not pay your bill. Your spouse tells you that the bill has already been paid. You call the gas company and, when you question the clerk, she says to you, "I'm sorry sir, our records reflect an unpaid bill. You must pay the bill immediately." To try to straighten matters out, you take a trip to the utilities office.

In the dialogue that follows the complainant is his own advocate. "C" will stand for complainant and "E" will stand for the various company employees.

E: *Can I help you?*

C: *Yes, I want to see someone about my bill.*

E: *I'm sorry, sir, but the customer complaint division closed at 2 P.M. You'll have to come back or call tomorrow.*

C: *Closed! Well, let me see someone about terminating the gas service altogether.*

E: *All right, would you step right over to the desk?*

Technique: If you can't solve a problem, redefine the problem to manageable proportions if, on balance, it is consistent with your objectives.

The client is taking a risk. He cannot get to the complaint division so he is going to try to achieve his objective through the termination division. He has substituted one problem (getting to the complaint division) for another problem (getting to the termination division) in the hope of expressing his grievances.

E: *Can I help you?*

C: *Yes, I want to terminate my gas if I can't get this problem straightened out.*

E: *You'll have to go over to the bill complaint division, sir.*

C: *Look, stop sending me somewhere else! Either I get this straightened out or else!*

Technique: Demonstrate anger and hostility. This is a dangerous tactic to employ. It is a fact of life, however, that some people respond to this kind of pressure.

C: *Aren't you here to serve the public?*

Technique: Insist on adequate service. Point out that the organization exists to serve and you need better service.

E: *There are rules and procedures that we all must abide by and. . . .*

C: *Your responsibility is to take care of the public!*

Technique: Preach. Perhaps the most common way in which people try to change other people is to lecture them, to tell them what they should or should not be doing.

Technique: Embarrass the official. Make the agency official look silly, unworthy of respect.

At this point, has the complainant lost all objectivity? What risks are being taken? Do you think the complainant is aware of what he is doing? If you asked him whether he's being effective, what do you think his response would be? Is he more involved with the "justice" of his case than with the effectiveness of his approach?

C: *I'd like to speak to your supervisor. Who is in charge of this office?*

E: *Well, Mr. Adams is the unit director. His office is right over there.*

C: *Fine.*

Technique: Climb the chain of command. Everyone has a boss who can overrule his or her subordinate's decisions. If you're unhappy about a decision, complain "up the chain of command," to the top if necessary.

E: *Can I help you?*

C: *I want to speak to Mr. Adams about a complaint. Tell him that it is very important.*

E: *Just a moment. [She goes into Mr. Adams' office for a few moments and then returns.] You can go in, sir.*

C: *Mr. Adams?*

E: *Yes, what can I do for you? I understand you are having a little problem.*

C: *It's about this bill. I have been talking to person after person in this office without getting any response. I'm going in circles. I need to talk to someone who is not going to send me to someone else!*

Technique: Take the role of the tired, battered, helpless citizen.

E: *Well, let me see what I can do. I've asked the secretary to get your file. . . . Here it is. The records say that you haven't paid last month's bill. Our policy here is to terminate utility service if payment is delayed thirty days or more.*

C: *What policy is that? Could I see a copy of this policy and what law it is based on?*

Technique: Ask for authorization. Make the agency show you the regulation, law, or authority that allegedly backs up the action it has taken or says it will take.

What risk is the complainant taking by resorting to this technique? Is the complainant suggesting to Mr. Adams that he does not trust him? How would you have asked for authorization in this situation? Does the request for authorization always have to be made in a hostile manner?

E: *Well, I'll be glad to show you the brochure.*

C: *I would like to see it and also the law it is based on. My position, Mr. Adams, is that my wife paid the bill.*

E: *Well our records don't reflect it.*

C: *The cancelled checks have not yet come back from the bank. I would like a Xerox copy of your file on me. Under the law, I am entitled to it.*

Technique: Cite the law. Demonstrate that you know what regulations and other laws apply to the case.

E: *You do have this right, but only if you make the request in writing.*

C: *Let's be reasonable. I'm making the request in person. That should be sufficient.*

Technique: Insist on common sense. You need to show the agency official your position makes good common sense, even if regulations or technicalities go against you.

C: *Surely, your rule calling for a written request can't apply when the person making the request is right in front of you.*

Technique: Interpret the law. Regulations, statutes, and cases often are susceptible to more than one meaning; identify and argue for the meaning most favorable to your cause.

Technique: Demonstrate the exception. Insist that your situation is unique, not governed by the general rule.

C: *Don't you have the power to waive this rule in such a case?*

Technique: Uncover the realm of discretion. Argue that rules do not exist until they are applied and that in the application of rules, agency officials often have a lot of latitude as to how they interpret them in spite of their claim that their hands are tied by the rules.

E: *Well, all right, I'll see if I can't get a copy run off for you while you are here, but it will take a little time and I must point out that it's highly irregular.*

C: *Now, Mr. Adams, I understand that you are a very busy man and that you have responsibilities more demanding than listening to people like me all day.*

Technique: Be a buddy. Show the agency official that you are not his enemy and that you respect and like him and that you are aware of how difficult his job is.

Here the complainant has obviously shifted his tactic; he is no longer antagonistic. Consciously or unconsciously, he has made an evaluation of how successful his techniques have been thus far and has decided on a different course of action. What risk is he running in making this shift?

C: *All I want is a thirty-day extension of time so that I can collect the proof needed to show you that the bill has been paid.*

Technique: Put your cards on the table. Tell the agency official, directly and openly, what your position is and what you want.

E: *Well, we seldom give extensions. The situation must be extreme. I don't know. . . .*

C: *Mr. Adams, suppose we forget my request for a copy of the records for the time being. All I want is thirty days.*

Technique: Find the points of compromise. Look for the negotiable points and figure out whether you can bargain your way to a good result.

E: *I don't think so.*

C: *Well, Mr. Adams, it's either that or I'm going to go to court. All I'm asking for is some fair treatment. There's a principle involved and I intend to fight for it.*

Technique: Make clear that you are going to fight this case all the way up. Make the agency official aware of how important this case is. When you have grounds to back you, point out that you are thinking about taking the case to a formal hearing and, if necessary, to court.

E: *I'm sorry you feel that way, but we have our rules here. It would be chaos if we broke them every time someone asked for it.*

C: *Good day, Mr. Adams. [You leave the office, resolved never to come back alone.]*

Technique: Seek the support of third parties. Gather the support of individuals or groups within and outside of the agency so that you can demonstrate that you are not alone.

. . . .

Has the complainant failed? Was he a "bad" advocate? Has he accomplished anything? Should he give up? Do you think he will? If he does not, do you think he has learned (or that he should have learned) enough about the utility company to come back next time better equipped to handle his problem? If he comes back, what approach should he take and whom should he see? Should he see the supervisor of Mr. Adams, for example?

■ ASSIGNMENT 15.2

What follows are two exercises for role-playing. The instructor will select students to play the roles indicated. The rest of the class will evaluate the role-playing through questions that follow the statement of the exercises.

(a) A paralegal is asked by his supervisor to file some papers in court. They must be filed by 5:00 P.M. that day. At 4:15 P.M. the paralegal takes the papers to the office of the court clerk. The clerk determines that the papers are in order except that the attorney forgot to sign one of them. It would take the paralegal more than an hour to go back to obtain the signature and return to court. The paralegal asks the clerk to accept the *other* papers. The clerk refuses since all the papers are closely interrelated. The paralegal tells the clerk that this happened once before and the clerk (another one) accepted the papers that were properly executed. The clerk refuses.

(b) A parent (acting as her own advocate) asks the principal for a meeting on her child. The child has been selected by the school to be sent to another school. The parent is opposed to this transfer. The principal tells her that she will have to go talk to an official at the City Board of Education about the matter. The parent persists in demanding a meeting with the principal. She wants to know, for example, the position of the principal on the transfer, but the principal wants to avoid controversy and therefore refers her to the City Board.

Evaluation

1. What advocacy technique did the paralegal start out using?
2. On a scale of 1 to 10, how effective was this technique? ("10" is very effective; "1" is very ineffective.) Give reasons for your score.
3. When the sequence ended, what advocacy technique was the paralegal using? How would you score this technique?
4. What shifts in technique, if any, did the paralegal make? Score each technique.
5. On a scale of 1 to 10, how effective was the paralegal's overall performance?
6. According to the agency official, what was the problem?
7. According to the paralegal, what was the problem?
8. What, if anything, was standing in the way of communication between them?
9. How could this communication problem have been overcome?
10. Was the paralegal objective, or did the paralegal take anything personally? Explain.
11. Was the agency official taking anything personally? Explain.
12. If the agency official took anything personally, how did the paralegal deal with this?
13. What do you think the paralegal *should* have done about this?
14. Describe the most positive aspects of what you saw the paralegal do.
15. Describe the least effective aspects of what you saw the paralegal do.
16. As specifically as possible, list all the advocacy techniques that you observed the paralegal use that you haven't already mentioned.
17. Reexamine the list of nineteen informal advocacy techniques in Figure 15.1. Do you think that any techniques should be added? If so, how would you rate the effectiveness of the techniques that you would add?

Section C. Procedural Due Process

Where paralegals are authorized by law to engage in *formal advocacy* by representing clients at administrative hearings (see Chapter 4), it is one of the great challenges that they enjoy. In this chapter, we will explore some of the skills required to perform this task effectively.

The subject matter of a hearing, as well as its procedure, can range from the very simple to the very complex. Our approach will be to examine a relatively simple hearing, after identifying the components of procedural due process when a government agency and a citizen have a dispute.

. . . .

When a government agency and a citizen have a serious dispute, basic fairness may require a number of procedural safeguards for the citizen. These safeguards are known as *procedural due process*.

> Tom is a civilian employee of the army. One day he receives a call from the assistant manager of his unit who says, "I have finished examining all of the records, and it is clear to me that you have been using the agency car for your own personal use. I have decided to fire you." As a matter of common sense and fairness, what is wrong with the assistant manager's approach? (Assume that Tom denies the charge.)

Note that in this hypothetical situation, the assistant manager wanted to end the entire matter right on the phone. What visceral response would you have (if you were Tom) to the action of the assistant manager? Shock? Anger? Some of Tom's responses might be:

1. "I wasn't given a chance to explain myself before I was fired."
2. "I wasn't given a chance to talk to the assistant manager before I was fired."
3. "I wasn't give a chance to be told what records he was talking about."
4. "I wasn't given a chance to talk to the assistant manager's boss before I was fired."

These four responses can be translated into legal language:

1. Someone who is charged with wrongdoing (or who is told that he or she is not entitled to a particular benefit) should be given the opportunity to be *heard*. The *hearing* is a formal proceeding in which an individual can present his or her position on a dispute.
2. The individual should be allowed to *appear in person* at the hearing. He or she should be allowed to *confront* and *cross-examine* his or her accuser.
3. The individual should be allowed to *examine the evidence against him or her*.
4. The individual should be allowed to *appeal* the initial decision against him or her.

Note that the individual would be asking for these rights *before* the job is taken away.

Tom might have a number of other responses:

5. "Before he called me to say that I was fired, he should have let me know that I was in trouble."

Here the call, in legal terms, is for adequate *notice*. Before the phone call, and certainly before the actual firing, the employee should have been given notice that there was a grievance or complaint against him so that he could prepare a response.

6. "Since the assistant manager was the one who made the charge, he should not be the one to make the decision."

Legally, this response goes to the issue of *legal bias* and the need for an impartial decision-maker. The basic theory is that the accuser should not be the executioner. If the same person wears both hats, the likelihood is that he or she will lose objectivity. While making the ultimate decision (as executioner), his or her tendency will be to reinforce the decision he or she originally made (as accuser) rather than to approach the final decision with an open mind. In short, the person with both hats is likely to have a bias. In the hypothetical situation, the assistant manager made the original charge (accuser) of misusing the agency car and he also made the decision to fire (executioner). He appears, therefore, to have a bias.

7. "When and if I am able to confront the assistant manager, I should be able to have someone help me state my case."

Legally, the call here is for the right of *representation*: counsel or counsel-substitute.

8. "When I am able to confront the assistant manager, I should be able to bring with me some of my co-workers, who will back up my side of the case."

Legally, the call is for the right to bring *your own witnesses* to the hearing and to *present your own* counter *evidence*.

9. "When the army finally makes its decision in my case, they should give me their decision in writing with an explanation of their decision."

Legally, this is a call for a *written opinion* or a *decision with reasons*.

10. "At my hearing, they should focus only on the charge that they raised and not bring up extraneous facts, such as that I am now going through a divorce."

Legally, the call is for only *relevant evidence* to be considered in making the decision.

Hence the ten safeguards (presented in roughly chronological order) are as follows:

- Notice (#5 above)
- Examination of evidence against you (#3)
- Hearing (#1)
- No legal bias in hearing officer (#6)
- Personal appearance at hearing; confrontation and cross-examination of accuser (#2)
- Representation (#7)
- Relevance of evidence (#10)
- Presenting your own witnesses (#8)
- Written decision stating reasons (#9)
- Appeal (#4)

In constitutional law, these safeguards constitute procedural due process. Of course, an agency does not provide all ten every time it has a conflict with a citizen. The safeguards that are required differ from agency to agency, depending on the seriousness of the dispute. In a welfare hearing, for example, all ten safeguards *are* required whenever a welfare recipient wishes to challenge a decision of the welfare department to terminate public assistance. This is so because of the extreme consequences that could result from this termination. The more extreme the possible consequences, the more procedural safeguards the law imposes on the conduct of hearings to determine whether those consequences should be imposed.

Section D. An Agency Problem

Fact Situation

George Temple was born on January 1, 1950. His parents, Mr. and Mrs. Sam Temple, live at 435 West 100th Street, New York, New York. He was graduated from high school in 1967 and spent six months at Wentworth Technical Institute in Boston before dropping out. He came back to live with his parents in February of 1968. But while in Boston, he began using drugs. He smoked pot regularly and experimented with LSD and heroin. After returning to New York on April 15, 1968, he got a job with the Thomas TV Repair Shop at 90 South Side Avenue, Queens. The boss, John Adams, fired George on June 1, 1968, because he suspected George of being an addict and of stealing.

On June 30, 1968, George married Ann Fuller. George began using drugs more often. Ann realized that he was not going to be able to support her and their expected child. When the child was born on January 2, 1969, she decided to go to the Amsterdam Welfare Center to apply for public assistance. She did so on January 10, 1969. The caseworker, Brenda Marshall, asked Ann what her husband did for a living. Ann answered that he took odd jobs "off and on," since he was sick. The caseworker asked if he was an addict. Ann was scared and answered *no*. The caseworker told her that she would need more information about her husband's employment history and condition before her application could be processed and approved. Ann left the center confused and frustrated. She never returned.

In the meantime, George was arrested on March 13, 1969 for possession of a dangerous drug in the third degree. He "took a plea" for attempted petty larceny and spent four months at Green Haven prison. When he got out on July 13, 1969, he went to live with his wife at 758 West 85th Street. While George was in prison, Ann worked as a waitress. During this time, her mother-in-law cared for the child. She was laid off from work on August 1, 1969.

George did not want to settle down with a job. He began using drugs again. He wanted to stop but couldn't.

On September 1, 1969, he went to Exodus House, a voluntary drug rehabilitation center in New York City. He stayed only two days since the program, he claimed, demanded too much from him. For example, he would have had to live at Exodus House, which he refused to do. On September 25, 1969, he went to Reality House, another voluntary rehabilitation center at 2065 Amsterdam Avenue. This was not a live-in program; members stayed there from 9 to 5. On October 1, 1969, he left this program because, when his urine was tested, it came back positive, meaning that he was still using drugs. He left rather than be confronted with the results of this urine test.

On October 2, 1969, he obtained a job with the ABC Truck Company and worked there part-time until February 15, 1970, when he was fired for being late.

On February 16, 1970, he went back to Reality House. But he failed to attend every day. On March 1, 1970, he went to the Amsterdam Welfare Center to apply for welfare for himself and his family. The caseworker, Linda Stout, asked him why he could not get a job. He said he was an addict attending Reality House. Linda Stout was skeptical. She demanded verification that he was regularly attending Reality House. George went back to Reality House to speak to his therapist, John Hughey. Mr. Hughey told him that he could not give him a letter stating that he was a member of the program until he began to attend more often.

On March 15, 1970 Linda Stout contacted Brenda Marshall, the caseworker who previously interviewed George's wife on January 10, 1969. Brenda told Linda that Mrs. Temple told her that her husband was *not* an addict.

In the meantime, George still had trouble getting a letter from Reality House stating that he was a "member" of the program. On March 17, 1970, Linda Stout called John Hughey at Reality House, who told her that George was not coming in every day. On March 18, 1970, she closed George's case, declaring him ineligible for welfare for failure to demonstrate need. She concluded that the welfare regulation authorizing public assistance to addicts attending rehabilitation programs did not apply to George.

Section E. Preliminary Considerations

The first responsibility of the paralegal assigned to this case is to decide when and how to intervene. George comes into the law office and tells you that he wants to fight the decision of the caseworker, Linda Stout. He wants a hearing. Is this an appropriate strategy? What alternatives exist? What about informal advocacy? Would you first want to call or visit Linda Stout? Brenda Marshall? Mrs. Temple? John Hughey? Linda Stout's boss? Brenda Marshall's boss? John Hughey's boss? If so why? Is the time ripe to intervene by asking for a formal hearing?

Suppose that you decide to give informal advocacy a try, but it does not work. The welfare department still refuses to declare George eligible. Therefore, in consultation with your supervisor, you decide to ask for a hearing.

In preparing for a hearing, there are a number of preliminary considerations:

1. Define your issues.   What are the issues in George's case? What would you have to show in order to qualify him for welfare? What are the points in doubt? Two questions should come to mind: (1) Is George an addict? And (2) is he a member of a drug rehabilitation center? If you showed that George was an addict, would he be sent to jail or to a hospital? Is this a real danger? How would you find out? Linda Stout demanded verification from George that he was a member of Reality House. Can you identify two reasons she would ask for this? Is she saying that if George is not a member of a drug rehabilitation program, he probably is not an addict? Or is she saying that he cannot obtain welfare unless he is a member of such a program even if he is an addict? Which is the case? How would you find out? What other issues exist? What legal research should be done?

2. Draft the request for the hearing.   In welfare cases, paralegals often draft the letter to the agency requesting the *hearing*. The client signs this letter. The request is extremely important since it can be a major determinant of what the issues at the hearing will be. How broadly or narrowly should an issue be stated? How many issues should be presented? These are questions of strategy that are answered largely in the light of what the paralegal thinks he or she might be able to prove at the hearing.

When a response to the letter of request is received, the client and paralegal will know whether a hearing has been granted on the issues requested. If not satisfied with this response, the paralegal should consult with his or her supervisor on ways to challenge the response before the hearing. If satisfied, preparation should be geared accordingly.

A careful definition and a thorough understanding of what the issues are can be critical for the following reasons:

a. At the hearing, the other side or the hearing officer may raise matters outside the scope of the issues of the hearing. The paralegal can object, based on the wording of the request for the hearing and the response received to the request.

b. If an office attorney is going to appeal the final decision of the hearing in court, the starting point in preparing for the appeal is often an analysis of what the issues of the hearing were supposed to be.

3. Engage in continuing efforts to resolve the case through informal advocacy. It is almost always preferable to try to solve a problem informally so that the time and expense of formal hearings and court proceedings can be avoided. At the time the paralegal and his or her office decided to request a formal hearing in this case, it was determined that informal advocacy would not be or was not effective. The agency, however, can always change its mind, particularly when it realizes that the client is serious about fighting the case. Throughout preparation for the hearing, the paralegal should try to be in continued contact with employees of the agency involved in the case. In these contacts, the paralegal may be able to bring to the agency's attention new factors that may cause it to reevaluate its position. The result may be a reversal of the agency's decision or the negotiation of a settlement between agency and client, eliminating the need for a hearing altogether. The paralegal must be constantly aware of this option.

4. Familiarize yourself with agency procedures in advance. There is no better way to prepare for a hearing than to see one in operation before you conduct your own. You might "tag along" as the assistant of another advocate conducting a hearing. Give it a try. Take extensive notes on procedure and strategy. Later on, organize your notes into an outline covering the procedures that governed the hearing as well as the strategy that both sides used.

If the agency has more than one type of hearing, you should determine how many exist and whether you want to ask for more than one type. Some agencies have prehearing conferences, during which the advocates for both sides sit down (in advance of the hearing) to narrow the issues and determine whether a solution can be reached without a formal hearing. When available, this can be a valuable meeting. If the agency does not have prehearing conferences as a matter of course, why not ask for one anyway? Besides being a vehicle to attempt a solution, the conference is an excellent way for the paralegal to learn more about the agency's case and hence be better prepared for the hearing, if it is held.

5. Try to respond to the client's emergency needs, if any, while waiting for a hearing decision. In a welfare case, the recipient should not be left destitute while the agency makes a decision following a hearing. Emergency assistance of a temporary nature may be available in the interim. Suppose that the paralegal is representing a client in a worker's compensation case. While the hearing is going on, the paralegal may be able to help this individual obtain public assistance or, possibly, union benefits. To the extent feasible, the paralegal should be alert to a client's total needs and not simply zero in on narrow legal questions. Of course, the paralegal has limited time available and must set priorities on what he or she can do. Very often the paralegal can be of help simply by referring the client to other resources in the community.

6. *Make sure that the client has given you proper authorization to act on his or her behalf.*   The law office may have a standard form for the client to sign authorizing you to represent the client at the agency proceeding. In addition, you should have the client sign a waiver-of-confidentiality statement authorizing you to examine all documents the agency possesses that pertain to the case. A similar statement may permit you to gain access to needed doctor or hospital records.

7. *Make a request in writing that the agency send you, in advance, copies of all documents that it intends to rely on at the hearing.*   Are you curious about what documents the welfare department will be using at the hearing to prove its case against George? Why not ask the department to send you copies of these documents in advance of the hearing? Would this be a fair request? In many situations, the law will back up such a request. (Suppose the agency wanted *you* to send them copies of the documents you will be using? What would you do?)
      What documents would you be interested in seeing? Their entire file on George? Their most recent policy statement on addicts? What else?

8. *Find out as much as you can about the witnesses the agency intends to call at the hearing.*   Usually the agency will tell you in advance what witnesses it will call to support its position. Often these witnesses are willing to talk to you before the hearing, particularly if they are agency employees. This is frequently an excellent way to discover more details about the agency's case and how the agency intends to establish that case at the hearing. Your approach should be casual. Do not say to these witnesses, "What testimony are you going to give at the hearing next week?" Rather, deal with points of information: "I understand that you know George Temple. Could I ask when you last spoke to him?" Etc.

9. *Make sure that you have completed all necessary field investigation before the hearing.*   What facts do you think need to be checked? What are you unsure of? Are you convinced that George is an addict? What *is* an addict? Someone currently using drugs? What kinds of drugs? How would you find out? Are you also unsure about George's relationship with Reality House? What is a "member"? How many definitions of "member" might exist? Do George, Linda Stout, and John Hughey each define it differently? Would you want to check this out? How often does George go to Reality House? What other items should you investigate? Before the hearing, would you want to make a request to the agency that it state its position on George's case in writing? What would you do with such a document? Use *fact particularization* to help identify factual questions that you need to pursue through investigation and subsequent client interviews (see Chapters 8 and 9).

10. *Study the law governing your case.*   It goes without saying that the paralegal must be thoroughly familiar with the law, particularly the agency regulations that may be applicable to the case. A good deal of legal research may be necessary before the paralegal even requests a hearing. Some aspects of the law governing the case may be unclear due to ambiguities in regulations, statutes,

or cases. Part of the task of preparation is to identify these ambiguities and to map out a strategy on how to deal with them if they arise at the hearing.

Bring photocopies of relevant regulations, statutes, or cases with you to the hearing. In addition, summarize, in your own words, the sections of these documents that you believe will be most pertinent.

11. Determine what witnesses you want to call and prepare them. Who should be present at the hearing to help George make his case? Should George be present? Why? Should John Hughey be present? Why? How about the boss of John Hughey? Do you want George's wife to be present? The tests that you should use in deciding whether to ask a witness to be present are: Does the witness have something to say that would help George make his case, and would the witness be able to say it? Someone may have important points to make but be so frightened at the thought of going to a hearing that he or she is, in effect, unavailable. Suppose you have a witness whom you want to call, but the person has an acute stuttering problem. How would you handle this?

Tell your witnesses what the hearing is all about to set their mind at ease. To be willing and valuable participants, they must trust you. Tell them why you want them to come. (You do not have to use words such as "witness" and "testimony" if these would frighten them.) Get them to role-play part of the proceeding with you. A brief role-playing experience can be very helpful. Explain that the other side may want to ask some questions after you introduce them and ask your own questions. Be sure that your witnesses understand what the issues are. They may try to use the occasion to begin a tirade about everything under the sun. This could be damaging, though you may determine as a matter of strategy to let the witnesses "unload" to some extent.

You must be careful not to place your witnesses in embarrassing situations. Whenever you think that a question you want to ask might be embarrassing or damaging to your witnesses, check it out with your supervisor before the hearing. What about George's addiction? Can you think of any questions you might ask that could create difficulties for him?

12. Assemble all the documentary evidence that you want to introduce at the hearing. Determine how you will lay the foundation for each item of evidence— that is, how you will show that it is relevant to the issues of the hearing. What documents do you want to present at the hearing on behalf of George? Do you want a letter from Exodus House stating that he once attended the program? If so, why? What would it prove? Do you want a letter from Reality House? Saying what? Would you ask them to write down all of the dates that George did attend that program? Would it help or hurt to obtain a letter from ABC Truck Company stating that George once worked there? Is it relevant? Suppose that you could arrange a doctor's examination of George. Would you want to use the results of this examination at the hearing? What would it depend on?

13. Draft an outline of how you intend to present your case at the hearing. The great danger of preplanning, of course, is that the unexpected almost always "fouls up" your preliminary plan. It nevertheless is helpful to have a tentative plan in mind, **as long as you do not slavishly try to follow it.** Flexibility is always key.

A useful approach is to arrange all the facts according to a chronological history. Every client's story has a beginning, middle, and end. Your outline should attempt to tell George's story in this way. Simple as this may seem, it is not easy to do. At the hearing, people will raise points out of sequence. These points often have to be dealt with, but if you have prepared your chronology carefully, you at least have something to come back to after this other point is treated.

Draft a preliminary outline of your strategy in conducting George's hearing. What points do you want to make? What documents or witnesses will you use to help you make these points? Arrange the entire sequence chronologically.

Confusion over the precise issue or issues of the hearing is one of the major frustrations you might experience in conducting formal hearings. This can arise in a number of ways: (a) the original request for a hearing or the agency's response to it was not precise enough; (b) the hearing officer refuses to hear testimony on an issue that you were prepared to argue; (c) your own witness raises an issue that you are not prepared to argue; (d) subissues are raised by either side, the relevance of which are dependant on the establishment of other major issues or subissues that have not yet been established; or (e) you make the dangerous assumption that everyone is focused on the same issue.

Issue control, therefore, is critical. How do you identify the issue in the most favorable light for your client? How do you make sure everyone is on the same wavelength with respect to the issues of the hearing? What do you do when new issues are raised? How do you keep from becoming paralyzed when the issue on which you have based your entire case is taken away from you, not by a failure to prove the issue but by a decision of the hearing officer about what's relevant to the hearing? Again, the answer to these questions is "preplanned flexibility." As you prepare for the hearing, you must do such a thorough job of anticipating the unexpected that you are ready to meet *any* new challenge, even if it is your own witness who poses the challenge.

Suppose that at George's hearing, the welfare department begins by making a major issue of George's poor employment record. They want to prove that he should enter a state vocational training program. What do you do? You should have anticipated this during your preparation, particularly due to the informal contacts that you had with the agency before the hearing. If for some reason this new position takes you by surprise, or if any other issue comes up that you feel is irrelevant, you have a number of options:

(a) Argue that the other side is being unfair; the agency should have let you know about its new position in advance.

(b) Argue that the issues at the hearing should conform to the issues defined in the letter granting the hearing.

(c) Ask for a postponement.

(d) After you have made your protest and lost, do the best you can with the issues that the hearing officer decides will be discussed.

14. Make sure that the hearing officer does not have a legal bias.   The hearing officer should not have been involved in the agency's initial decision against the client, the decision that led to the necessity of asking for a hearing. Normally this will not be a problem, since the hearing officer will usually be employed within a separate unit of the agency.

15. If, after you request the hearing, it becomes clear that you need more time to prepare, ask for a postponement of the hearing.   Do not be rushed into a hearing unless it is absolutely necessary. Ask for a postponement and be prepared to back up your request with reasons (e.g., you are waiting for a letter to arrive that you want to produce at the hearing).

16. *Make sure that the client and the witnesses know when and where the hearing is to be held.*

 ## Section F. Hearsay, Opinions, and Relevance

Generally, the technical rules of evidence that are scrupulously followed in court proceedings (see Chapter 10) do not apply to administrative hearings. The standard rule is that hearings are conducted "informally." Nevertheless, you should have an understanding of some concepts of evidence, because they do come up in hearings despite the general rule of informality.

As we shall see when we cover direct and cross-examination, you should (1) know when your witness or a witness for the other side is speaking from firsthand or personal knowledge as opposed to second- or thirdhand knowledge *(hearsay)*, and (2) know when the witness is stating a fact as opposed to an opinion. It is important to know these distinctions not because a hearing officer will exclude hearsay evidence or opinion evidence, but because your case is always strengthened when your own witness speaks from personal knowledge of the facts. You tend to weaken the case of the other side when you can point out (through cross-examination) that a witness for the opposition is speaking from hearsay or is relating opinions as opposed to facts. If you ask your witness to state an opinion or conclusion, be sure your witness has already stated the underlying facts that support the opinion.

■ **ASSIGNMENT 15.3**

For each statement made by the witness below, answer the following questions:

(a) Is the witness talking from firsthand (personal) knowledge? Secondhand? Thirdhand?

(b) Is the witness stating a fact, an opinion, or a conclusion?

(c) What questions would you ask the witness so that the same information would come out in a different way?

    (1) "My case worker is rude."

    (2) "My caseworker called me a liar."

    (3) "I am eligible for public assistance."

    (4) "My son told me that the caseworker reported me to the supervisor."

    (5) "I need welfare."

    (6) "My mother can't pay my rent."

    (7) "I'm too sick to join the job training program."

    (8) "That job does not suit me."

    (9) "My husband does not contribute to the support of my family."

   (10) "I did report to the job employment agency."

   (11) "I was told that no jobs were available."

   (12) "You must give me seven days' notice before you terminate me."

Another critical concern of evidence is relevance: only evidence that is relevant to the issues at the hearing should be considered by the hearing officer. Something is relevant if it (reasonably) tends to prove or disprove a matter in dispute. Very often common sense is a clear guide on whether something is relevant. The fact that I am in Chicago is not at all relevant to whether or not it is raining in New York; but the fact that I am in Chicago is relevant to whether or not I *know* if it is raining in New York. In a large number of situations, however, the borderline between relevance and irrelevance is thin. On the question of whether or not George Temple "regularly attends" a drug rehabilitation center, is it relevant that he often plays in baseball games? Is is relevant he has an ulcer? Is it relevant that he is twenty-four years old? Hearing officers will generally lean in the direction of admitting something into evidence if its relevance is at least probable; they are more inclined to let evidence in than to exclude it.

Whenever the hearing officer or the representative of the other side objects to an item of evidence that you plan to introduce, you must be prepared to argue its relevance by explaining how it will contribute to reaching a resolution of the issues. If this approach does not seem to be successful, make a basic "fairness pitch" by asking that you be allowed to present your client's case in the best manner that you can. In effect you are saying, "Don't push me on technicalities; give me some time to show you why this is important. It may not be clear to you now why it is important, but I'll make it clear to you shortly."

Another consideration is the extent to which the evidence you want to produce would be burdensome on the proceeding. You must be reasonable. You cannot try to introduce one thousand pages of cancelled receipts and bills, for example, if it is not quite clear that every item is needed to make your case.

■ Section G. Introduction to the Examination of Witnesses

Before the examination of witnesses begins, be sure that you know who everyone is in the hearing room. The hearing officer may ask everyone to state his or her name and connection with the case. If the hearing officer does not, you should ask that this be done.

Another preliminary is the opening statement made by each side. When it is your turn to begin, your opening statement should briefly cover the following:

1. Your understanding of what the issues at the hearing are

2. A summary of what you are going to establish at the hearing through your witnesses and other evidence

3. The result the client is seeking from the hearing

After the opening statements, the next step is the examination of witnesses.

You *directly examine* your own witnesses (George, for example) and cross-examine the witnesses presented by the other side (the agency employee, Linda Stout, for example). After you have directly examined your own witnesses, the other side can cross-examine them. After the other side has directly examined their own witnesses, you can cross-examine them. Each side directly examines its own witnesses and cross-examines the witnesses of the other side. When you directly examine a witness, it simply means that you are the first person to ask questions of that witness.

Normally, one side presents its entire case and then the other side presents its case. The main time you talk when the other side is presenting its case is when you are cross-examining its witnesses, and vice versa.

After a side has cross-examined a witness, the other side (the one that originally examined the witness directly) is sometimes allowed to conduct a *redirect examination* to cover points raised in the cross-examination.

Sequence:

I. You Present Your Side

- You direct-examine your own witnesses.
- They cross-examine your witnesses.
- You conduct a redirect examination of your own witnesses to cover points they raised in their cross-examination.

II. They Present Their Side

- They direct-examine their own witnesses.
- You cross-examine their witnesses.
- They conduct a re-direct examination of their own witnesses to cover points you raised in your cross-examination.

This may all sound highly technical. Some hearings are, in fact, conducted this formally. Others are not. You must be prepared to deal with both settings.

To call a witness does not necessarily mean that the person stands in a witness box or is "sworn in." In all probability, everyone will remain in his or her own seat and will not be asked to take an oath. Furthermore, the technical words "direct," "cross," and "redirect" examination may not and need not be used. Simpler language can be used:

> *Direct-Examination*
>
> "Sir (addressed to the hearing officer) I would like to ask (name of witness) a few questions."

> *Cross-Examination*
>
> "I would like the opportunity to ask (name of witness) some questions if (name of advocate on the other side) is finished with her own questions."

> *Re-Direct Examination*
>
> "After I asked (name of witness) some questions, Ms. (name of advocate representing the other side) asked some questions of her own, and while I was listening, a few other important and pertinent points occurred to me. I would like to ask a few final questions of (name of witness), if I could."

It does not make any difference what labels are used, as long as you take every allowable opportunity to make your points.

 ## Section H. Direct-Examination

Reduced to its simplest level, direct examination means nothing more than interviewing or talking to someone concerning what he or she knows about an event. A direct examination has three components:

1. *Introduction:* Who is the witness, where does he or she live, where does he or she go to school or work?
2. *Connection to event:* What relationship does the witness have to the events at issue in the hearing?
3. *Testimony on event:* What does this witness have to say about the events at issue in the hearing?

Guidelines on Conducting Direct-Examination

1. The witness on direct examination is *your* witness. You call this witness to give testimony. You are always very cordial to the witness. You never ask anything that might embarrass him or her.

2. Let the witness tell his or her own story in his or her own words. The story should flow naturally.

3. Ask the witness to speak loudly and clearly. If the witness says something that may not be clear to others, ask him or her to state it again, even though it may have been perfectly clear to *you* what was said.

4. Encourage the witness to let you know when he or she does not understand a question.

5. In the introduction of the witness, let the witness give the basic facts about himself or herself. Instead of saying, "This is John Smith of . . .," you should ask the witness to state his or her name, address, occupation, etc.

6. Before you ask the witness to state what he or she knows about an event, ask questions to establish his or her relationship or connection to the event. If the witness is a doctor, for example, before you ask his or her opinion of the client's medical condition, you should ask if the doctor has treated the patient. Before you ask a neighbor whether or not the client earns money as a private babysitter at home, you should ask the witness questions to establish that he or she is a close neighbor of the client and often visits the client during the day. By so doing, you will be **laying the foundation for the relevance of the witness's testimony.**

7. It is often helpful to structure your questions to the witness so that he or she tells the story chronologically from beginning to end. Discourage jumping from topic to topic if the narrative is becoming confusing.

8. When the witness is stating things from firsthand knowledge, emphasize the fact that it is firsthand, personal knowledge.

9. When the witness is stating things from secondhand (or hearsay) knowledge, de-emphasize the fact that it is not firsthand knowledge. When you prepare a witness to testify, encourage him or her to preface his or her statements by saying "to the best of my knowledge."

10. When your witness must state conclusions or opinions, you should structure your questions so that you first bring out all the supporting facts on which the witness has relied in forming the opinions or conclusions.

11. Be aware of the danger of open-ended questions such as, "Tell us what happened." Very often such questions are invitations to ramble. Confusion can result. The more effective kind of questions are structured to require a brief and concise answer. Use an open-ended question only when you are sure that the witness is able to handle it.

12. Very often a witness, particularly the client, has a need to vent his or her feelings. When this happens, the witness often becomes emotional and raises issues that may not be relevant. You must make a decision when this happens. On the one hand, it is the client's hearing and—as a matter of fairness—he or she should have the opportunity to speak his or her mind. It can be very frustrating if questioners keep steering the client away from what he or she has been waiting a long time to say. On the other hand, you do not want the client to say anything that may be damaging to the case. You must understand the witness psychologically. The best strategy is to determine in advance whether the witness is inclined to become emotional. If so, then the paralegal's responsibility is to make the witness aware of the consequences of this occurring at the hearing.

In the final analysis, the witness must decide; it is his or her case that's on the line, not yours.

13. You may want to introduce certain documents into evidence after you have asked the witness questions that will reveal facts demonstrating the document's relevance. That is, you establish a foundation for the documents through your questioning. Once the foundation has been laid, you *introduce* the document by asking the hearing officer to make it part of the record and by giving a copy to the agency's representative. Then you resume your direct examination of the witness.

14. The hearing officer may interrupt you with questions of his or her own for the witness. The officer, of course, has the right to do this. You may, however, want to tell the hearing officer politely that you will treat the subject matter of his or her question in "just a few moments."

15. The advocate for the other side may try to interrupt you with questions. Normally, he or she does *not* have this right. Politely ask the hearing officer if you can finish your own questions before the other side asks any questions on cross-examination.

16. Try to anticipate what the other side will want to question your witness about on cross-examination, and try to cover these points in your own direct examination.

17. Expect the unexpected. Your witness may say things that you never anticipated. You have to be flexible enough to deal with whatever comes your way.

■ ASSIGNMENT 15.4

Role-play the following situations in class. The instructor will select one student to take the part of the person conducting the direct examination and someone else to role-play the person being questioned. The latter should make up answers that are generally consistent with the situation stated. (Review the material in Chapter 8 on fact particularization as a guide to formulating questions. See Figure 8.4.) Conduct a:

(a) Direct-examination (DE) of another student concerning the most frustrating aspect of his or her last job

(b) DE of a teenager who just drove home the family car with a big dent on the side

(c) DE of a pupil who has been charged with fighting

(d) DE of a caseworker who claims that the recipient gave her permission to enter the client's apartment (client denies it)

(e) DE of a welfare recipient on his claim that he has tried to find suitable work but has been unable to do so

(f) DE of George Temple

Section I. Cross-Examination

Before covering guidelines on cross-examination, you should review Chapter 9 on investigation. Restudy the evaluation of testimonial and physical evidence and the checklist on the validity of physical (tangible) evidence. (See Figures 9.6 and 9.7.) Many of the considerations discussed in the investigation chapter apply to cross-examination at hearings.

Guidelines on Conducting Cross-Examination

1. Be courteous to the witness even though you may be tempted, and indeed baited, into attacking him or her personally.

2. Be sure that it is clear to you who the witness is and what relationship he or she has to the events at issue in the hearing. This may not have been brought out clearly enough while this witness was being direct-examined by the agency representative.

3. If during the direct examination, this witness said something based on secondhand knowledge (or if it was not clear to you whether it was said from personal or secondhand knowledge), ask about it on cross-examination. Be sure that your questions force the witness to admit that no firsthand knowledge exists when this is so.

4. If, during the direct examination, this witness stated conclusions without stating any facts to support them, ask this witness on cross-examination about these conclusions. Probe the underlying facts that support them—according to the witness. Do *not* use this tactic, however (nor the one mentioned in guideline 3 above), if you are absolutely certain that the witness has valid facts to support the conclusions or opinions even though they were not brought out on direct examination. You do *not* want to give an opposing witness the opportunity to *reinforce* damaging evidence.

5. If it is a fact (or if you are reasonable in suspecting that it is a fact) that the witness has a bias (something personal) against the client, you should try to bring this out on cross-examination. This, of course, will be very difficult and somewhat dangerous to do. No one wants to admit that he or she is not being objective. Probably the best that you can do on cross-examination is to raise some doubts about the objectivity of the witness's testimony (by asking questions about any prior hostility that may have existed between the client and the witness, for example) even though you may not be able to establish bias conclusively.

6. The point made about bias *against* someone applies to bias *in favor of* a person. A witness can lose objectivity because of partisanship and friendship as well as because of hostility.

7. If the witness is reading from any papers during cross-examination, politely ask the witness what he or she is reading from and request that you be shown a copy. If needed, ask for a few moments to read it before you continue your cross-examination. If the witness is reading from a document that was not sent to you before the hearing (and you requested that the agency send you *all* records that it was going to rely on at the hearing), you should object.

8. Sometimes the witness will read from official agency records. These records often refer to statements made by individuals who work for the agency but who are not present at the hearing. The agency representative will try to introduce these records into evidence. It has already been said that you should bring out, through your questioning, the fact that the witness is not speaking from firsthand knowledge when referring to records of which he or she is not the author. In addition, you should complain that, as a matter of fairness, authors of critically important statements in the records should be present at the hearing so that you can confront and cross-examine them. If you are not allowed to cross-examine them, you should request that their statements not become part of the hearing proceedings.

9. If, during cross-examination, the witness raises points that surprise you (for a reason other than your own sloppy preparation), you should ask the hear-

ing officer to exclude the matter because of unfair surprise or to postpone the hearing to give you more time to prepare the client's response to the new point.

10. In courtroom proceedings, it is often the rule that you cannot raise new matters on cross-examination; you can cross-examine a witness only within the scope of the testimony this witness gave on direct examination. If, for example, the witness testifies only about food stamp eligibility on direct examination, the attorney conducting the cross-examination cannot ask questions about an invasion of privacy claim. This technical rule, however, almost *never* applies to administrative hearings. You should nonetheless be aware of it, since the advocate for the agency may improperly try to apply the technical rule against you while you are cross-examining a witness. You usually do *not* have to limit your questioning on cross-examination to the scope of what was brought out by the other side on direct examination. Normally, however, it is a good practice not to raise new matters on cross-examination unless you have no alternative. Use direct examination to make all your major points. Use cross-examination as a vehicle to challenge positions of the other side and to buttress the points you have made on direct examination.

11. On cross-examination you are questioning witnesses who are normally hostile to your client, although this is not always so. Do not antagonize them unnecessarily. You may find that on cross-examination the witness is willing, either consciously or not, to make statements that are very favorable to your client.

12. As a corollary to point 11, do not be unduly aggressive or defensive. Make your case positively by direct examination. Do not rely exclusively on establishing your case negatively by trying to show on cross-examination that the witnesses for the other side are fools.

13. Do not help the other side by asking questions on cross-examination that you know (or reasonably anticipate) will produce damaging statements. (See also guideline 4 above.)

14. You do not have to conduct a cross-examination of a witness (a) if nothing he or she said on direct examination is unclear to you or to the hearing officer or (b) if you do not think you can prompt the witness to contradict or discredit his or her position. In such a case, it would be better to rely solely on what you were able to establish on direct examination.

15. Remain loose and flexible; anticipate the unexpected.

■ ASSIGNMENT 15.5

Role-play the following situations in class. The instructor will select students to play the roles involved. The witness should make up answers that are generally consistent with the situation stated. (Review the material in Chapter 8 on fact particularization as a guide to formulating questions. See Figure 8.4.)

(a) On direct examination, the witness testified that Mr. Smith was drunk. Conduct a cross-examination of this witness.

(b) On direct examination, the witness (a social worker) testified that she feels the client is an unfit mother. When she visited the client, the house was dirty, the children were sick, and there was no food in the refrigerator. Conduct a cross-examination of this witness.

(c) On direct examination, the witness (a social worker) testified that an unemployed client should be able to obtain employment for the following reasons: the children are old enough for daycare services, the client is basically healthy in spite of occasional headaches, and jobs are available (or at least job-training programs are available). Conduct a cross-examination of this witness.

■ Section J. Closing the Hearing and Preparing for an Appeal

At the end of all the questioning and presentation of evidence, ask the hearing officer to let you sum up with your version of what happened. State what you think you proved, state what you think the other side failed to prove. Specifically, state again what result you seek for the client. If you think that the hearing was inconclusive because you were unfairly surprised by what the other side did or because the other side failed to bring individuals to the hearing who were sufficiently acquainted with the case, then:

- Ask for a decision for the client because of these factors; or
- At the very least, ask for an adjournment. The hearing can resume after you have had a chance to study the matter that the other side unfairly surprised you with, or after the other side brings individuals to the hearing who should have been there.

Many hearings are either transcribed or tape recorded by the agency. Every word of the hearing, therefore, is preserved. Normally, the law office for which you work will be able to purchase a typed copy of the transcript or a copy of the tape. This record made of the hearing becomes the basis of a court appeal if the client is dissatisfied with the decision. You must understand the relationship between what happens at the hearing and a possible subsequent *court appeal*. To a very large extent, you are responsible for *making a record* for the attorney to use on appeal.

Attorneys who have litigated cases following administrative hearings should acquaint you with the mechanics of the court appeal process. If possible, you should try to read a copy of an old appellate brief that cites testimony taken at an administrative hearing so that you can see the connection between the hearing and the court action.

In some administrative hearings, an advocate waives any objection that he or she has to what takes place at the hearing *unless he or she specifically objects on the record at the agency hearing*. A *waiver* can mean that the attorney cannot later raise the point on appeal in court.

To avoid such waivers, then you must be familiar with the technique of objecting for the record. When you have an objection to make during the hearing, you should do so simply by saying to the hearing officer, "Sir, I would like to object" and briefly state what you are objecting to and the reasons. It is not necessary to object constantly to the same point. If the hearing officer decides against you and you object once, it is usually unnecessary to object again every time the agency representative brings up what you objected to.

With few exceptions, courts do not allow clients to appeal an issue in court unless the agency involved has been given the opportunity to resolve the issue within the agency's own hearing structure. This is the doctrine of *exhausting administrative remedies*. For example, at a welfare hearing, a client might claim that he or she failed to receive a check that was due *and* that the caseworker is harassing him or her with unauthorized home visits. At the hearing, if the only issue discussed concerned the check, then the visitation issue cannot be appealed in court since, as to this issue, the client has not exhausted administrative remedies. Another hearing may have to be brought on the visitation issue before it can be raised in court. You must be aware of this problem as a matter of issue control.

■ ASSIGNMENT 15.6

Read each situation. State whether you would raise any objection. If so, state the reasons for your objection. Also, answer any other questions asked in the problem situation.

(a) On direct examination, a witness of the agency representative says that your client "is a liar."

(b) On direct examination, a witness of the agency representative reads from a piece of paper. You are not sure what the paper is.

(c) On direct examination, a witness of the agency representative says that he or she was told by another caseworker that the client had a secret bank account. On cross-examination of this same witness, what line of questions should you pursue?

(d) Before the hearing began, you requested the agency to send you all the documents that the agency intended to rely on at the hearing. The agency never did. Should you refer to this fact at the beginning of the hearing? If so, how?

(e) Same as (d) above, except that when the you mention at the beginning of the hearing that the records were never sent, the agency representative hands you forty pages of records.

(f) Same as (d) above except that when you mention at the beginning of the hearing that the records were never sent, the agency representative responds by saying that the records are confidential.

(g) On direct examination of your witness, the agency representative keeps interrupting with questions of his or her own.

(h) While the agency representative is talking to the hearing officer, he or she uses some legal language that you do not understand.

(i) While talking to the hearing officer, the agency representative hands him or her a document that announces a new agency regulation.

■ ASSIGNMENT 15.7

Role-play the George Temple hearing in class. As a starting point, use the facts presented on page 731. Participants can make up other facts as they go along, as long as they are generally consistent with the facts given. The instructor will select students to play the parts of the various roles, such as hearing officer, paralegal for George, paralegal for the agency, and witnesses. The paralegals should review the material on fact particularization as a guide in formulating questions (see Chapter 8). The rest of the class should observe and take notes on how the paralegals conduct themselves. What did they do well? What went wrong? How should it have been handled?

☐ Chapter Summary

Advocacy takes place all the time. It is an everyday process by which all citizens—not just attorneys—attempt to influence or change the actions of others at one time or another. Informal advocacy occurs outside of courts or other tribunals where hearings are held to resolve controversies that the participants have not been able to resolve informally.

Advocates try many techniques of informal advocacy, with varying degrees of success. Among the most common are the following: placing your cards on the table; insisting on adequate service;

(Continued on next page)

☐ Chapter Summary *(Continued)*

seeking the support of third parties; being a buddy; finding the points of compromise; insisting on common sense; demonstrating the exception; uncovering the realm of discretion; asking for authorization; citing the law; redefining the problem; showing anger and hostility; preaching; climbing the chain of command; embarrassing the official; making clear that you will fight the case; taking the role of the tired, battered, helpless citizen; doing a favor to get a favor; and citing a precedent. While using any of these techniques, you need to evaluate your effectiveness and modify the techniques based on this evaluation.

Whenever the government takes an action that seriously affects a citizen, such as denying or removing a benefit, basic fairness may require a number of procedural safeguards. These requirements are referred to as *procedural due process*. While not applicable to every situation, the safeguards include notice, hearing, personal appearance at the hearing, the absence of legal bias, representation, relevance of the evidence, opportunity to examine the evidence, opportunity to present your own witnesses, a decision in writing, and an opportunity to appeal.

When paralegals are allowed to represent clients at administrative hearings, preparation re-

quires careful defining of the issues, drafting the requests or demand for the hearing, continuation of informal advocacy, familiarity with the procedures to be used at the hearing and with the substantive law that will govern the client's case, attention to a client's emergency needs, proper authorization from the client, efforts to obtain access to agency documents and witnesses before the hearing, finalizing field investigation, preparation of your own witnesses, organization of documentary evidence, and the design of a flexible outline of your presentation. While most hearings are conducted less formally than a court proceeding, the paralegal should be familiar with the evidentiary difficulties involving hearsay, opinion testimony, and relevance. (These areas are discussed more fully in Chapter 9.)

The standard format of an administrative hearing is as follows: direct examination of a witness by the side that calls the witness; cross-examination of that witness by the other side; and redirect examination of the witness by the side that called the witness. Normally, any objections that are not made during the hearing are waived and hence cannot be the basis of a court appeal after administrative remedies have been exhausted.

Key Terms

advocacy
formal advocacy
informal advocacy
quasi-judicial proceeding
procedural due process
hearing
confrontation
cross examination

appeal
notice
legal bias
representation
relevance
issues
hearsay
direct examination

redirect examination
appeal
making a record
waiver
exhausting administrative
    remedies

Bibliography

Abbreviations:

AAfPE = American Association for Paralegal Education

ABA = American Bar Association

ALA = Association of Legal Administrators

F&F = Facts and Findings (a journal of NALA)

JPE&P = Journal of Paralegal Education and Practice (a journal of the AAfPE)

LAMA = Legal Assistants Management Association

LAT = Legal Assistant Today (a magazine on paralegal issues)

LAU = Legal Assistant Update (a periodical pamphlet of the ABA)

LOEM = Law Office Economics and Management (a journal)

NALA = National Association of Legal Assistants

NALS = National Association of Legal Secretaries

NFPA = National Federation of Paralegal Associations

NPR = National Paralegal Reporter (a journal of NFPA)

Index to Bibliography

■ Articles, Books, Reports, etc. on Paralegals

1. *ABA Approval: Another Viewpoint* by K. Sheehy, 7 NPR 2 (NFPA, Spring 1983).

2. *ABA Associate Membership: A Paralegal's View* by J. Whalen, 10 NPR 1 (NFPA, Spring 1986).

3. *ABA Associate Membership: An Historical Review,* 10 NPR 1 (NFPA, Apr. 1986).

4. *ABA Associate Membership for Legal Assistants,* 3 LAT 32 (Winter 1986). *See also* 10 F&F 5 (Jan./Feb. 1984).

5. *ABA Commission: Historical Overview and Current Status* by R. Major, 11 NPR 18 (NFPA, Spring 1987).

6. *ABA Standing Committee on Legal Assistants: Issues Position Paper on Licensing/Certification* by K. Judd, 12 F&F 8 (NALA, Apr. 1986).

7. *The ABC's of Overtime Pay* by D. Orlik, 4 LAT 37 (July/Aug. 1987).

8. *Activities of Insurance Adjusters as Unauthorized Practice of Law,* 29 American Law Reports 4th 1156 (1967).

9. *Activities of Law Clerks as illegal Practice of Law,* 13 American Law Reports 3rd 1137 (1967).

10. *The Administrative Legal Assistant: A Nuts and Bolts View of Complex Toxic Tort Litigation Management* by B. Gagnon, 16 F&F 24 (NALA, Mar. 1990).

11. *Alternate Career Paths* by B. Van de Mark, 16 F&F 11 (NALA, July 1989).

12. *Alternate Sentencing: A Case Study: What a Paralegal Can Do to Improve the Criminal Justice Process* by M. Courlander, 3 LAT 16 (Winter 1986).

13. *Annual Ethics and Case Law Update,* 17 F&F 36 (NALA, Fall 1990).

14. *Approaches for Continuing Legal Education of Paralegals,* by T. Calvocoressi & R. Villanova, 7 JPE&P 43 (1990).

15. *Are Paralegals Professionals?* by D. Johnson, NPR 26 (NFPA, Fall 1989).

16. *Are They Really Independent Contractors?* by D. Jackson, 17 F&F 20 (NALA, Mar. 1991) (freelance legal assistants).

17. *The Art of Managing Your Support Staff* by the Section of Economics of Law Practice (ABA, 1986).

18. *The Art of Resume Writing* by C. Jett, 7 Legal Professional 91 (renamed LAT) (Sept./Oct. 1989).

19. *Attitudes and Functions of Paralegals: Ten-Year Perspective* by M. Jennings & P. Murranka, 29 LOEM 192 (1988).

20. *Attorney-Client Privilege and the Paralegal* by K. Sheehy, 6 NPR 1 (NFPA, Fall/Winter 1981).

21. *Attorneys' Fees: Cost of Services Provided by Paralegals or the Like as Compensable Element of Award in State Court,* 73 American Law Reports 4th 938 (1989).

22. *Attorneys' Guide to Practicing with Legal Assistants* (State Bar of Texas, 1986).

23. *Attorney's Splitting Fees with Other Attorneys or Laymen as Grounds for Disciplinary Proceedings,* 6 American Law Reports 3rd 1446 (1966).

24. *A Banker with the Soul of a Legal Assistant* by C. Kane, 5 LAT 65 (July/Aug. 1988).

25. *Bar Association Involvement in the Paralegal Profession: Helpful or Harmful?* by J. Polsinelli, 6 NPR 4 (NFPA, Spring 1982).

26. *Bay Area Paralegal Administrators Speak Up About Peronnel Issues* by C. Estrin, 7 Legal Professional 36 (renamed LAT) (Sept./Oct. 1989).

27. *Be Steps Ahead of Other Candidates: Understand the Interview Game* by C. Reitz, 5 LAT 24 (Mar./Apr. 1988).

28. *Better Resumes for Attorneys & Paralegals* by A. Lewis & D. Saltman (Barron's 1986).

29. *Billing for Paraprofessional Services* by T. McCormick, New Jersey Lawyer, 20 (No. 136, Sept./Oct. 1990).

30. *Bridging the Gap from Student to Professional* by R. Sova, 7 Legal Professional 47 (renamed LAT) (Jan./Feb. 1990).

31. *Building a Strong Attorney-Paralegal Team* by N. Cattie & T. Vesper, 27 Trial 24 (Jan. 1991).

32. *Build Respect: Be an Assertive Professional* by L. Bourget, 4 LAT 40 (Jan./Feb. 1987).

33. *Calculating Profit from Associates and Paralegals,* 58 The Journal of the Kansas Bar Ass'n 5 (Apr. 1989).

34. *California Paralegal Magazine* (P.O. Box 6960, Los Osos, CA 93412) (805-772-8806).

35. *California Paralegal's Guide,* 3d ed. by Z. Mack (Parker, 1987).

36. *Canadian Legal Assistants Enjoy Growth & Recognition* by P. Hicks, 15 NPR 4 (NFPA, Spring 1991).

37. *Capitalizing on Legal Assistants in Columbia, South Carolina* by T. Howard, 5 LAT 40 (Nov./Dec. 1987).

38. *Career Paths for Legal Assistants* by D. Patrick, 8 LAT 21 (May/June 1991).

39. *Career Paths for Paralegal Assistants in Corporate Legal Departments* by R. Homes & T. Caples, 14 Legal Economics 59 (ABA, July/Aug. 1988).

40. *Career Progress* by C. Milano, 8 LAT 34 (Sept./Oct. 1990).

41. *Careers in Transition: Paralegals in Progress* by L. Jevahirian, 8 LAT 87 (Nov./Dec. 1990).

42. *The Case for Career in Trademark Law* by S. Wilkinson, 7 Legal Professional 29 (renamed LAT) (Nov./Dec. 1989).

43. *The Case for Temporary Paralegals* by D. Rothfield, 30 LOEM 305 (1989).

44. *CBA [Colorado Bar Association] Legal Assistants Committee Survey Report,* 9 Colorado Lawyer 482 (1980).

45. *Certification: A Professional Goal,* 15 F&F S1 (NALA, May 1989).

46. *Certification of Legal Assistants: A Report of the American Bar Association Survey* by R. Larson, 5 LAU 143 (ABA, 1986).

47. *Certification Proposed in South Dakota* by J. Polsinelli, 7 NPR 12 (NFPA, Spring 1983).

48. *Certification v. Certificate* by L. Klessig, 17 F&F 32 (NALA, Fall 1990).

49. *Challenges of Government Jobs: Opportunities for Paralegals* by T. Howard, 8 LAT 84 (May/June 1991).

50. *Changing Jobs: Ethical Considerations* by V. Voisin, 15 F&F 12 (NALA, Mar. 1989).

51. *CLA (Certified Legal Assistant) Study Guide* by Florida Legal Assistants, Inc. (Butterworths, 1986).

52. *Code of Ethics: Ideals of a Profession? Or Legally Enforceable Law?* by R. Major, 7 NPR 6 (NFPA, Spring 1983).

53. *Colloquium on Nonlawyer Practice Before Federal Administrative Agencies,* 37 Administrative Law Review 359 (1985).

54. *Columbus Bar Association Associate Membership for Paralegals,* 9 NPR 11 (NFPA, Feb. 1985).

55. *Communication Skills Needed by Legal Assistants* by M. Moore, 5 LAU 19 (ABA, 1986). *See also* 12 F&F 28 (NALA, Aug. 1985).

56. *Community Courts* by W. Statsky, 3 Capital University Law Review 1 (1974).

57. *A Computer Training Program for Paralegals* by R. Granat & D. Knight, 14 Legal Economics 40 (ABA, Mar. 1988).

58. *Conducting a CLA [Certified Legal Assistant] Litigation Specialty Study Group* by S. McInnis, 16 F&F 18 (NALA, Jan. 1990).

59. *Conducting an Effective Interview: How to Hire the Right Person for the Job* by J. Bassett, 7 LAT 56 (May/June 1990).

60. *Confessions of a Male Paralegal* by M. Russell, 13 NPR 15 (NFPA, Summer 1988).

61. *Confessions of Starstruck Legal Assistants* by T. Howard, 5 LAT 16 (July/Aug. 1988).

62. *Connie Burke: Legal Assistant Manager . . . Orchestrates 141 Legal Assistants* by J. Murry, 4 LAT 18 (Jan./Feb. 1987).

63. *Conn. Paralegal Wages Near U.S. Average,* 16 The Conneticut Law Tribune 13 (Feb. 26, 1990).

64. *Conoco Inc. Legal Assistant Program Job Description. . . ,* 5 Corporate Counsel's Quarterly 100 (Apr. 1989).

65. *The Corporate Paralegal* by J. Bassett, 8 LAT 21 (Nov./Dec. 1990).

66. *Counsel Behind Bars: Jailhouse Lawyers. . .* by Kroll, 7 Calif. Lawyer, 34 (June 1987).

67. *The Court Appointed Special Advocate Program* by N. Toomey, 17 F&F 16 (NALA, July 1990).

68. *Court-Awarded Paralegal Fees: An Update* by M. Lee, 5 JPE&P 11 (Oct. 1988).

69. *Create Your Own Career Path* by G. Malone, 4 LAT 33 (July/Aug. 1987).

70. *Creating Good Will Through Education: Paralegal Internships* by P. Everett, 15 NPR 10 (NFPA, Summer 1990).

71. *Creative Burnout* by M. Gorkin, 1 LAT 17 (Summer 1984).

72. *Creative Computing: A Paralegal's Key Role in Law Office Automation* by J. Gurdak & C. Bellias, 5 LAT 36 (Sept./Oct. 1987).

73. *Daily Responsibilities of Legal Assistant at Trial,* 15 F&F 24 (NALA, Mar. 1989).

74. *Dallas Paralegal Pro Bono Legal Clinics* by F. Whiteside, 15 NPR 6 (NFPA, Fall 1990).

75. *DAs [District Attorneys]: Consider Legal Assistants,* 9 NDAA Bulletin 4 (National District Attorneys Ass'n, Mar./Apr. 1990).

76. *Dealing Effectively with Divorce Clients* by M. McAuliffe, 3 LAT 39 (Summer 1986).

77. *Defining the Unauthorized Practice of Law* by A. Morrison, 4 Nova Law Journal 363 (1980).

78. *Delegate to Your Legal Assistant* by M. Gaige, 5 Maine Bar Journal 98 (Mar., 1990).

79. *The Delivery of Legal Services by Non-Lawyers* by D. Rhode, 4 Georgetown Journal of Legal Ethics 209 (1990).

80. *Demand for Paralegals Mushrooms* by R. Lee, Texas Lawyer 6 (Jan. 8, 1990).

81. *Designing an Effective Paralegal Performance Evaluation* by M. Cain, 5 LAMA Manager 3 (LAMA, Fall 1989).

82. *Developing Good Working Relations with Corporate Counsel* by E. Hourigan, 8 LAT 35 (Nov./Dec. 1990).

83. *Developing Performance Competencies for Paralegal Programs* by D. Dye, 5 LAU 51 (ABA, 1986).

84. *A Dialogue on the Unauthorized Practice of Law* by Hunter & Klonoff, 25 Villanova Law Review 6 (1979–1980) (licensing).

85. *Disciplinary Action Against Attorney for Aiding or Assisting Another Person in Unauthorized Practice of Law,* 41 American Law Reports 4th 361 (1985).

86. *Discovery Wins Recognition for Legal Assistant Sleuth* by J. Bassett, 7 LAT 71 (July/Aug. 1990).

87. *Do Independent Contractors Have Special Ethical Considerations?* by D. Brookes, 10 F&F 7 (NALA, Nov./Dec. 1982).

88. *Don't Let Your Staff Do Wrong* by D. Walther, 13 Family Advocate 40 (ABA, Spring 1991).

89. *Do You Have a Job or a Career?* by S. Brashear, 6 LAT 25 (Nov./Dec. 1988).

90. *Drafting and Answering Interrogatories* by B. De Mark, 7 LAT 62 (May/June 1990).

91. *Drafting of Will or Other Estate Planning Activities as Illegal Practice of Law,* 22 American Law Reports 3rd 1112 (1968).

92. *Educating Students about the Transition from School to Work* by J. Kaiser, 3 Journal of Paralegal Education 13 (Oct. 1986).

93. *The Education and Utilization of Paralegals in the Practice of Immigration Law* by A. Wernick, 7 JPE&P 23 (1990).

94. *The Education of Legal Paraprofessionals: Myths, Realities and Opportunities* by W. Statsky, 24 Vanderbilt Law Review 1083 (1971).

95. *Education Update 1989: The Legal Assistant & Law Office Dynamics* by G. Malone, 6 LAT 26 (Jan./Feb. 1989).

96. *Effective and Ethical Use of Legal Assistants* by T. Fagan, 15 The Colorado Lawyer 659 (1986).

97. *Effectively Using Paralegals in Commercial Litigation and Creditor's Rights Matters* by S. Stoddard, 8 LAT 74 (Sept./Oct. 1990).

98. *Effective Use of Job Descriptions and Evaluation Forms,* 15 F&F 9 (NALA, Aug. 1988).

99. *The Effective Use of Legal Assistants* by Bennett, 35 The Practical Lawyer 25 (June 1989).

100. *The Effective Utilization of Legal Assistants* by V. Kunz (Western Dakota Ass'n of Legal Assistants, 1990) (North Dakota).

101. *Effective Utilization of Legal Assistants: The Political and Economic Realities* by R. Granat, 7 LAT 25 (May/June 1990).

102. *The Emerging Role of the Case Manager* by M. Kause, 8 LAT 46 (Nov./Dec. 1990).

103. *An Employer's Assessment of Legal Assistant Candidates* by L. Wertheim & S. Sommers, 6 JPE&P 49 (1989).

104. *Employment Law Paralegals* by H. Walker, 7 Legal Professional 69 (renamed LAT) (Sept./Oct. 1989).

105. *The End of the Lawyer Monopoly: What Will It Look Like?* by S. Elias & R. Warner, 12 NPR 20 (NFPA, Spring 1988).

106. *Ensuring Attorney/Paralegal Team Excellence* by G. Green, 38 The North Carolina State Bar Quarterly 33 (Winter 1991).

107. *Entertainment Law: A Growing Industry for the Paralegal* by Birker, 2 Calif. Paralegal Magazine 7 (Apr./June 1990).

108. *Equal Professionalism, Equal Responsibility: Paralegals and Pro Bono* by T. Neiman, 17 F&F 8 (NALA, July 1990).

109. *E$$ential Nonbillable Hours* by H. Peacock, 6 LAT 33 (Jan./Feb. 1989).

110. *Establishing Yourself as a Professional* by J. Bassett, 8 LAT 41 (May/June 1991).

111. *Ethical Considerations in the Use of Paralegals in Your Office* by C. Gilsinan, 30 The St. Louis Bar Journal 14 (Summer, 1983).

112. *Ethical Considerations of Employing Paralegals in Florida* by J. Lehan, 52 The Florida Bar Journal 14 (Jan. 1979). See also *In re Petition to Amend Code of Professional Responsibility*, 327 So.2d 15 (1976).

113. *Ethical Guidelines for Legal Assistants in Iowa* (Iowa State Bar Ass'n, Mar. 1988).

114. *Ethics for the Legal Assistant* by D. Orlik (Scott, Foresman, 1986).

115. *Ethics: How Good Is Your Conflict Check?* by D. Orlik, 5 LAT 23 (July/Aug. 1988).

116. *The Evolving Role of the Paralegal* (New Jersey State Bar Ass'n, 1991).

117. *Exempt/Non-Exempt: The Debate Continues* by I. Korsack, LAMA Newsletter 8 (LAMA, Winter 1989).

118. *The Expanding Role of Legal Assistants in New York State* (N.Y. State Bar Ass'n, Subcommittee on Legal Assistants).

119. *Expanding the Role Your Paralegals Play* by C. Tokumitsu, 8 LAT 33 (Mar./Apr. 1991).

120. *Face to Face: Client Interviewing Techniques for the Legal Assistant* by R. Bilz, 5 LAT 55 (Jan./Feb. 1988).

121. *Facts and Findings* (magazine) (NALA, 1601 S. Main St., Suite 300, Tulsa, OK 74119, 918-587-6828).

122. *Family Law: Visalia's Legal Aid Paralegal* by D. Clements, 3 Calif. Paralegal Magazine 8 (Apr./June 1991).

123. *Fee-Shifting Statutes and Paralegal Services* by A. Piazza, 2 Journal of Paralegal Education 141 (Apr. 1985).

124. *Fee Splitting with Nonlawyers,* 12 Journal of the Legal Profession 139 (1987).

125. *Fitting Paralegals into the Corporate Legal Department,* 11 F&F 24 (NALA, Sept./Oct. 1984).

126. *Florida Ethics Guide for Legal Assistants* by R. Troutman (Florida Bar, Continuing Legal Education, 1986).

127. *Focus on Corporate Practice: Legal Assistants and Legal Opinion Due Diligence* by C. Drozd, 7 JPE&P 63 (1990).

128. *Focus on Law Practice before Administrative Agencies* by W. Robie, 10 NPR 5 (NFPA, Dec. 1985).

129. *The Forming of the Corporate Paralegal* by Zupanovich, 2 Calif. Paralegal Magazine 4 (July/Sept. 1990).

130. *Form Your Own Career Strategy Group: Support Comes from Others Who Are Dissatisfied or Jobless* by A. Scheele, 5 LAT 61 (July/Aug. 1988).

131. *The Free-Lance Legal Assistant and Ethics* by K. Hill, 2 LAT 15 (Winter 1985).

132. *The Freelance Legal Secretary* by P. Garcia, 38 The Docket 13 (NALS, Sept./Oct. 1989).

133. *From the Courts to the Boardroom: Legal Interpreting and Translating* by A. Adelo, 14 NPR 8 (NFPA, Spring 1990).

134. *Functional Division of the American Legal Profession: The Legal Paraprofessional* by Selinger, 22 Journal of Legal Education 22 (1960).

135. *Fundamentals of Paralegalism,* 2d ed. by T. Eimermann (Little Brown, 1987).

136. *The Future of Paralegal Education* by Q. Johnstone, 6 JPE&P 27 (1989).

137. *General Guidelines for the Utilization of the Services of Legal Assistants by Attorneys* (State Bar of Texas, 1981).

138. *The General Practice Paralegal* by I. Edwards, 8 LAT 49 (Mar./Apr. 1991).

139. *Get a Shovel* by D. Villines & L. Stailey, 17 F&F 16 (NALA, Mar. 1991) (freelance legal assistants).

140. *Getting Started as a Freelance Paralegal* by P. Everett, 8 LAT 59 (Sept./Oct. 1990).

141. *Going for Paralegal Gold* by J. Murry, 3 LAT 18 (Fall 1985) (Wash. D.C. paralegals).

142. *Griping vs. Negotiating: Techniques and Tactics for Achieving Your Goals* by S. Wendel, 4 LAT 51 (May/June 1987).

143. *A Guide for Legal Assistants: Roles, Responsibilities, Specializations,* 2d ed. by M. Gowen (Practicing Law Institute, 1991).

144. *Guidelines and Procedures for Obtaining ABA Approval for Legal Assistant Education Programs* (ABA, 1990).

145. *Guidelines for Practicing with Paralegals,* Missouri Rules of Professional Conduct (1987).

146. *Guidelines for Use of Attorney Assistants as Approved by ISBA Assembly* (1977) (Illinois State Bar Ass'n).

147. *Guidelines for Use of Legal Assistants,* Rhode Island Supreme Court, Provisional Order No. 18 (Feb. 1, 1983).

148. *Guidelines for Use of Legal Assistant Services* (State Bar of New Mexico, 1980).

149. *Guidelines for the Utilization by Lawyers of the Service of Legal Assistants,* New York State Bar Ass'n (1976).

150. *Guidelines for the Utilization by Lawyers of the Services of Legal Assistants Under the New Hampshire Rules of Professional Conduct* (Supreme Court Rule 35) (August 1987).

151. *Guidelines for the Utilization by Lawyers of the Services of Legal Assistants,* South Carolina Bar (1981).

152. *Guidelines for the Utilization of Legal Assistants,* Colorado Bar Ass'n Legal Assistant Committee. *See also* 18 Colorado Lawyer 2097 (1989).

153. *Guidelines for the Utilization of Legal Assistants in Kansas,* Kansas Bar Ass'n Committee on Legal Assistants (1988).

154. *Guidelines for Utilization of Legal Assistants Services,* 57 Michigan State Bar Journal 334 (1978).

155. *A Guide to Cite Checking* by C. Kaufman, 8 LAT 44 (Jan./Feb. 1991).

156. *A Guide to Reviewing and Summarizing Medical Records* by K. Appleby, 8 LAT 26 (Sept./Oct. 1990).

157. *Harnessing the Power of Stress* by J. Hosea, 14 NPR 7 (NFPA, Summer 1989).

158. *Helping Legal Assistants to Help Themselves* by P. Saucier, 9 Legal Management 28 (ALA, Sept./Oct. 1990) (billable hours).

159. *Help! Service Companies Come to the Rescue of Drowning Legal Assistants* by C. McKown, 4 LAT 24 (Mar./Apr. 1987).

160. *Hide & Seek for Assets: The Life of a Probate Paralegal* by H. Walker, 5 LAT 38 (Mar./Apr. 1988).

161. *Hiring Legal Staff: Determining Cost and Value* by T. Brooks & W. Hackett (ABA, 1990).

162. *A History of the American Bar* by C. Warren (Little Brown, 1966).

163. *How Much Are You Worth? Putting a Price Tag on Your Performance,* 38 The Docket 26 (NALS, Jan./Feb., 1990).

164. *How NALA Is Governed* by Favinger, 18 F&F 16 (July 1991).

165. *How Satisfied Are You with Your Job?* by J. Gurdak, 3 LAT 19 (Spring 1986).

166. *How to Analyze and Apply Case Law* by C. Smith, 8 LAT 27 (Mar./Apr. 1991).

167. *How to Assign a Task Clearly* by R. Feferman, 13 Legal Economics 62 (ABA, Apr. 1987).

168. *How to Choose a Paralegal Education Program* (AAfPE, 1990). Reprinted in 17 F&F 31 (NALA, Sept. 1990).

169. *How to Create an In-House Legal Assistant Training Program* by R. Rutherford, 7 Legal Professional 29 (renamed LAT) (Sept./Oct. 1989).

170. *How to Create-A-System for the Law Office,* R. Ramo, ed. (ABA, 1975).

171. *How to Effectively Assist at Trial* by Patrick, 8 LAT 17 (Sept./Oct. 1990).

172. *How to Improve Lawyer/Staff Communications* by E. Brown, 5 Legal Administrator 73 (ALA, Nov./Dec. 1987).

173. *How to Locate Elusive Witnesses* by E. Thorp, 8 LAT 60 (Nov./Dec. 1990).

174. *How to Negotiate a Good Raise* by I. Hill, 8 LAT 53 (May/June 1991).

175. *How to Use Legal Assistants to Enforce Commercial Secured Claims* by J. Verellen, 33 The Practical Lawyer 9 (Dec. 1987).

176. *How to Wage Peace* by T. McGowan, 2 LAT 22 (Winter 1985) (friction with secretaries).

177. *Idaho Needs ABA Approved Legal Assistants' School* by H. Moncrief, The Advocate 8 (Dec. 1989).

178. *If You're Smart, Why Aren't You in Law School?* by L. Hardwick, 4 LAT 27 (May/June 1987).

179. *Illinois State Bar Association Position Paper on Use of Attorney Assistants in Real Estate Transactions* (May 16, 1984).

180. *The Immigration Paralegal* by J. Mason, 8 LAT 76 (Nov./Dec. 1990).

181. *Impact of ABA Associate Membership,* 15 F&F 24 (NALA, Fall 1988).

182. *In California, It's Better to Stay Put Than to Switch: A Paralegal's Past Forces New Boss to Drop Cases* by B. Motamedi, 7 LAT 37 (May/June 1990).

183. *Income Up in Legal and Paralegal Fields,* 26 LOEM 489 (1986).

184. *Independent Paralegals: Entrepreneurs or Imposters?* by B. Motamedi, 7 Legal Professional 16 (renamed LAT) (Mar./Apr. 1990).

185. *The Independent Paralegal's Handbook: How to Provide Legal Services Without Going to Jail* by R. Warner (Nolo Press, 1991).

186. *The Information Resource Manager: A New Career for Legal Assistants?* by C. Griffith, 5 LAT 52 (Mar./Apr. 1988).

187. *Inmate Involvement in Prison Legal Services* by W. Statsky (ABA Resource Center on Correctional Law and Legal Services, 1974).

188. *Innovative Training Techniques* by D. Patrick, 8 LAT 31 (Jan./Feb. 1991).

189. *In Praise of the CLA* [Certified Legal Assistant] by Villines, 18 F&F 28 (July 1991).

190. *The Institute of Legal Executives* by G. Schrader, 4 JPE&P 19 (Oct. 1987) (England).

191. *Intellectual Property: Trademarks, Patents, Copyrights* by J. Cone, 5 LAT 26 (Jan./Feb. 1988).

192. *Interviewing: The Employer Perspective* by C. Kauffman, 7 The LAMA Manager 11 (LAMA, Winter 1991).

193. *Interviews and Statements* by K. Andrews, 13 NPR 14 (NFPA, Spring 1989) (interviewing and investigation).

194. *An Interview with Clark Durant* by B. Albert, 12 NPR 6 (NFPA, Winter 1988) (deregulation of the legal profession).

195. *Introducing Student [Paralegal] Associations* by C. Cattie, 15 NPR 10 (NFPA, Spring 1991).

196. *Investigation Techniques: Locating People* by S. Peterson, 13 NPR 14 (NFPA, Winter 1989).

197. *Issues in Paralegalism: Education, Certification, Licensing, Unauthorized Practice* by Haskell, 15 Georgia Law Review 631 (1981).

198. *Is There Life After the Law Firm?* by C. Estrin, 8 LAT 65 (May/June 1991).

199. *Is There Room for a Paralegal on L.A. Law?* by Hangley, 12 NPR 7 (NFPA, Spring 1988).

200. *It's Not Easy Being Second Chair: A Basic Approach to Trial Assistance* by R. Sova, 5 LAT 45 (Jan./Feb. 1988).

201. *Job-Hunting: How to Bag the Big One* by F. Grones, 5 LAT 48 (Sept./Oct. 1987).

202. *Job Satisfaction: Mental and Environmental Improvements* by Y. Garman, 6 LAMA Manager 14 (LAMA, Fall 1990). Reprinted in 17 F&F 10 (Nov. 1990).

203. *Journal of Paralegal Education and Practice* (AAfPE, P.O. Box 40244, Overland Park, KS, 66204).

204. *Judging Credentials: Nonlawyer Judges and the Politics of Professionalism* by D. Provine (Univ. of Chicago Press, 1986).

205. *Kentucky Supreme Court Rule 3.700* (Provisions Relating to Paralegals, 1979).

206. *Labor Department Groups Paralegals with "Crafts, Sales, Secretarial," Attempts to Avoid Aptitude Testing* by M. Dick, 13 NPR 9 (NFPA, Fall 1988).

207. *Landmark Ethics Case Takes Toll on Paralegal's Career, Family* by B. Motamedi, 7 LAT 39 (May/June 1990).

208. *Law Clerks and the Unauthorized Practice of Law*, 46 Chicago-Kent Law Review 214 (1969).

209. *Law Firm Diversification and Affiliation Between Lawyers and Nonlaywer Professionals* by D. Pitofsky, 3 Georgetown Journal of Legal Ethics 885 (1990).

210. *Law Office Management: Leveraging with Legal Assistants* by E. Clark, 25 Arizona Attorney 36 (Oct. 1989).

211. *Law Office Staff Manual* by B. Rolston (ABA, 1982).

212. *Law School: Legal Education in America from the 1850s to the 1980s* by R. Stevens (Univ. of North Carolina Press, 1983).

213. *The Lawyer from Antiquity to Modern Times* by R. Pound (West, 1953).

214. *Lawyers Aiding Nonlawyers in the Unlawful Practice of Law*, Oregon State Bar Bulletin, 37 (Feb./Mar. 1990).

215. *Lawyers, Clients Gain from Paralegals' Legal Expertise*, Kansas City Business Journal (Aug. 21, 1989).

216. *Lawyer's Professional Obligations Concerning Paralegals* by Conn. Bar Ass'n Inter-Committee Group to Study the Role of Paralegals, 59 Conn. Bar Journal 425 (1985).

217. *The Lay Advocate* by Sparer, 43 University of Detroit Law Journal 493 (1966).

218. *Layman's Assistance to Party in Divorce Proceeding as Unauthorized Practice of Law*, 12 American Law Reports, 4th 656 (1982).

219. *Lay Practice Before Administrative Tribunals: Clarification Needed* by Pollack, 66 Michigan Bar Journal 675 (1987).

220. *The Legal Assistant & Preparing Deposition Summaries*, 15 F&F S1 (NALA, Jan. 1989).

221. *Legal Assistant as Law Librarian* by J. Lewek, 17 F&F 28 (NALA, Mar. 1991).

222. *The Legal Assistant as Librarian* by N. Wendt, 6 LAT 19 (Sept./Oct. 1988).

223. *Legal Assistant as the Office Manager* by C. Amira, 11 F&F 25 (NALA, Jan./Feb. 1985).

224. *Legal Assistant at the Computer Forefront* by M. George, 5 LAT 49 (Nov./Dec. 1987).

225. *Legal Assistant Charges as Recoverable Attorney Fees: An Arizona Case,* 27 LOEM 453 (1986–87).

226. *Legal Assistant Education* by D. Dye, 38 Journal of the Missouri Bar 111 (Mar. 1982).

227. *Legal Assistant Hiring Techniques* by M. Coyne, 6 LAMA Manager 10 (LAMA, Summer 1990).

228. *The Legal Assistant in Corporations* by D. Templeton, 5 LAT 35 (July/Aug. 1988).

229. *A Legal Assistant Is Elected Probate Judge* by T. Howard, 5 LAT 32 (Mar./Apr. 1988).

230. *Legal Assistant Manager Discusses Hiring and Firing* by C. Gibson, 11 NPR 22 (NFPA, Spring 1987).

231. *Legal Assistant Manager Improves Bottom Line (Deborah Wahl)* by T. Howard, 8 LAT 34 (Jan./Feb. 1991).

232. *Legal Assistant Managers Enhance Productivity* by P. Curtis, 15 NPR 28 (NFPA, Summer 1990).

233. *A Legal Assistant of Note* by H. Kaufman, 6 LAT 56 (May/June 1989) (copyright paralegal).

234. *The Legal Assistant Profession: National Utilization and Compensation Survey Report* (NALA, 1991).

235. *A Legal Assistant Program Evaluation Design* by J. Snell & D. Green, 4 JPE&P 53 (Oct. 1987).

236. *Legal Assistant Programs: A Guide to Effective Program Implementation and Maintenance* (ABA, 1978).

237. *Legal Assistants* (NY, Practicing Law Institute) (annual).

238. *Legal Assistants: A Case of Uncertain Identity* by D. Parker, 7 Legal Professional 10 (renamed LAT) (Sept./Oct. 1989).

239. *Legal Assistants: A Growing Role in the Practice of Law in Alabama* by K. Rasmussen, 52 The Alabama Lawyer 214 (July 1991).

240. *Legal Assistants as Law Office Managers* by Kreipe, 59 The Journal of the Kansas Bar Ass'n 19 (July 1990).

241. *Legal Assistants Can Increase Your Profits* by P. Ulrich, 69 ABA Journal 1634 (1983).

242. *Legal Assistants Division Proposes Voluntary Certification Program,* 49 Texas Bar Journal 886 (1986).

243. *Legal Assistants: Even a Small Firm Can Use Them* by Simpson, 15 Legal Economics 20 (ABA, Apr. 1989).

244. *Legal Assistants Going Freelance* by L. Jevahirian, 17 F&F 22 (NALA, Mar. 1991).

245. *The Legal Assistant's Handbook,* 2d ed. by T. Brunner et al. (Bureau of National Affairs, 1988).

246. *Legal Assistants Increase Productivity* by M. Douglass, 45 The Alabama Lawyer 334 (Nov. 1984).

247. *Legal Assistants in Northern Michigan* by C. Andary, 68 Michigan Bar Journal 398 (May 1989).

248. *Legal Assistants in Probate Administration* by M. Mulligan & S. Grabert, 30 The St. Louis Bar Journal 28 (Summer, 1983).

249. *Legal Assistants in Public Law: Their Role in Attorney Generals' Offices* by N. Helmich & R. Larson, 5 LAU 109 (ABA, 1986).

250. *Legal Assistants in the Courtroom* by Hogan, 18 F&F 24 (July 1991).

251. *Legal Assistants: Measuring Profitability* by Green, 14 Legal Economics 26 (ABA, Mar. 1988). *See also* 14 F&F 10 (NALA, Apr. 1988).

252. *Legal Assistants of New Mexico: Statement of Professional Standards* (Dec. 1989).

253. *Legal Assistants: Sample Job Descriptions,* 12 F&F 21 (NALA, Apr. 1986).

254. *Legal Assistants Share the Spotlight at Historic Minneapolis Firm* by T. Howard, 4 LAT 16 (Mar./Apr. 1987).

255. *Legal Assistants Supervising Lawyers* by T. Howard, 4 LAT 28 (July/Aug. 1987).

256. *Legal Assistant's Time to Be Included in Award of Reasonable Attorney Fees in Florida,* 13 F&F 24 (NALA, Aug. 1986).

257. *Legal Assistants Will Increase Your Income* by H. Draper, 62 Michigan Bar Journal 1083 (Dec. 1983).

258. *Legal Assistants Will Increase Your Income* by P. Ulrich, 69 ABA Journal 1634 (Nov. 1983).

259. *Legal Assistant Time in Attorney Fee Awards* by K. Judd, 14 F&F 10 (NALA, June 1988).

260. *Legal Assistant Today* (James Publishing Co., 3520 Cadillac Ave., Suite E, Costa Mesa, CA 92626).

261. *Legal Assistant Utilization in Connecticut Law Firms* by S. Endleman, 55 Connecticut Bar Journal 324 (Aug. 1981).

262. *Legal Assistant Wise* by J. Gish (Professional Publishing Group, 1990).

263. *The Legal Assistant: Your Profit Center* by A. Callum, 69 Michigan Bar Journal 558 (1990).

264. *Legal Investigation & Informal Discovery* by K. Andrews, 7 LAT 36 (July/Aug. 1990).

265. *Legal Malpractice: Prevention through Automation* by H. Snyder, 7 LAT 34 (May/June 1990).

266. *Legal Paraprofessionals and Unauthorized Practice,* Note, 8 Harvard Civil Rights–Civil Liberties Law Review 104 (1973).

267. *Legal Skills Training for the Non-Lawyer Advocate in the Public Sector* by R. Hoffman, 2 LAT 27 (Fall 1984).

268. *Legal Technician: Friend of the People* by S. Braverman, 15 NPR 28 (NFPA, Fall 1990).

269. *Legal Technician: Friend or Foe?* by S. Lewis, 14 NPR 22 (NFPA, Spring 1990).

270. *The Leveraged Legal Assistant* by L. Werthheim & R. Berkow, 5 LAT 22 (Nov./Dec. 1987) (profitability).

271. *Life in a Corporate Law Department* by E. McCann, 6 LAMA Manager 4 (LAMA, Spring 1990).

272. *The Limited Practice Rule: Its Track Record after Four Years* by Fuller, 40 Washington State Bar News 15 (Oct. 1986).

273. *The Litigation Manager* by C. Kaufman, 7 Legal Professional 551 (renamed LAT) (July/Aug./Oct. 1989).

274. *The Litigation Paralegal* by J. McCord (West, 1988).

275. *Long-Term Legal Assistant Job Enrichment* by P. Ulrich, 24 LOEM 366 (1983). *See also* 4 LAU 37 (ABA 1984).

276. *Look Before You Leap into Law School* by C. Bruno, 7 Legal Professional 22 (renamed LAT) (Sept./Oct. 1989).

277. *Looking for a Job Is a Job* by K. Allen, 15 NPR 22 (NFPA, Spring 1991).

278. *Make the Most of Legal Assistants in Tax Practice* by F. Berall, 2 Practical Tax Lawyer 59 (Winter 1988).

279. *Management and Motivation Can Improve Your Legal Assistant Program* by P. Ulrich, 3 LAT 31 (Spring 1986).

280. *Management of Legal Assistants: The Ethical Obligations of the Attorney,* 26 Arizona Attorney, 27 (Jan. 1989).

281. *Managing Paralegals as a Human Resource* by M. George, 4 LAT 26 (Jan./Feb. 1987).

282. *Managing Temporary Legal Aids* by L. Hill, National Law Journal p. 15 (Aug. 15, 1988).

283. *Manual for Legal Assistants,* 2d ed. by NALA (West, 1992).

284. *Manual for the Lawyer's Assistant,* 2d ed. by NALS (West, 1988).

285. *Marching to a Different Drummer: Paralegal Work in the Military* by D. Richards, 2 Calif. Paralegal Magazine 8 (Oct./Dec. 1990).

286. *Mediation and the Legal Assistant* by W. Evarts, 2 LAT 29 (Fall 1984).

287. *Minnesota Parental Leave Law Extends Coverage to Law Firms* by M. Jacobs, 13 NPR 25 (NFPA, Summer 1988).

288. *Missouri Guidelines for Practicing with Paralegals* (Missouri Bar Ass'n, 1987).

289. *Missouri v. Jenkins,* 491 U.S. 274, 109 S.Ct. 2463, 105 L.Ed.2d 229 (1989) (paralegal fees).

290. *Model Guidelines for the Utilization of Legal Assistant Services* (ABA, Standing Committee on Legal Assistants, Mar. 1, 1991) (tentative draft).

291. *Model Standards and Guidelines for Utilization of Legal Assistants Annotated,* 17 F&F 48 (NALA, Fall 1990).

292. *Modern Legal Ethics* by C. Wolfram (West, 1986).

293. *More Firms Use Paralegal Managers* by L. Jevahirian, 13 National Law Journal 23 (Feb. 25, 1991).

294. *Mortgage Foreclosure Litigation: Avoiding the Pitfalls* by R. Hubbell, 16 F&F 10 (NALA, Nov. 1989).

295. *Motivation: The Manager's Approach* by M. Seeley, LAMA Newsletter 5 (LAMA, Winter 1989).

296. *NALA and Arizona Affiliates File Brief on Work Product,* 17 F&F 18 (NALA, Jan. 1991) (attorney-client privilege and paralegal work product).

297. *NALA and NFPA State Positions on Issues,* 12 NPR 20 (NFPA, Fall 1987).

298. *NALA Model Standards and Guidelines* by K. Sanders-West, 2 LAT 9 (Summer 1985).

299. *National Paralegal Reporter* (magazine) (NFPR, 5700 Old Orchard Rd., Skokie, IL, 60077, 708-966-6066).

300. *Nature of Legal Services or Law-Related Services Which May Be Performed for Others by Disbarred or Suspended Attorney,* 87 American Law Reports 3rd 279 (1978).

301. *New Career Opportunities in the Paralegal Profession* by R. Berkey (Arco, 1983).

302. *New Mexico Rules Governing the Practice of Law,* Rule 20-102 (A) (1989) (defining legal assistant).

303. *The New Model Rules: How Will They Apply to the Legal Assistant?* by R. Cleary, 10 F&F 9 (NALA, Jan./Feb. 1984).

304. *New Responsibilities Being Given to Paralegals* by C. Milano, 8 LAT 27 (Nov./Dec. 1990).

305. *NFPA Affirms Self-Direction for Paralegal Profession* by R. Major, 12 NPR 1 (NFPA, Summer 1987).

306. *NFPA Delegates Define Limited Licensure* by A. Retz, 13 NPR 6 (NFPA, Summer 1988).

307. *Nine Factors to Consider in Managing Case Documents* by S. Mohney, 8 LAT 91 (Mar./Apr. 1991).

308. *1990 Index of NALA Files of State Bar Activity,* 17 F&F 26 (NALA, Fall 1990) (paralegal ethics).

309. *The Nixon, Hargrave Environmental Team Walks a Fine Line Between Legal and Technical Advice* by J. Bassett, 7 Legal Professional 26 (renamed LAT) (Jan./Feb. 1990).

310. *The Nonlawyer Partner: Moderate Proposals Deserve a Chance* by S. Gilbert & L. Lempert, 2 Georgetown Journal of Legal Ethics 383 (1988).

311. *Nonlawyer Practice before Federal Administrative Agencies Should Be Discouraged* by Heiserman, 37 Administrative Law Review 375 (1985).

312. *Nonlawyer Practice before Federal Administrative Agencies Should Be Encouraged* by Rose, 37 Administrative Law Review 363 (1985).

313. *Nonlawyers in the Business of Law* by R. Andrews, 40 Hastings Law Journal 577 (1989).

314. *Nontraditional Paralegal Careers* by M. Rattermann, 8 LAT 60 (Jan./Feb. 1991).

315. *Notice of Public Hearings: Texas Voluntary Certification of Legal Assistants,* 48 Texas Bar Journal 1358 (1985).

316. *Novel Ways Paralegals Are Using Computers* by C. Milano, 8 LAT 22 (Mar./Apr. 1991).

317. *Nurses Give Medical Litigation a Booster Shot* by T. Howard, 7 Legal Professional 41 (renamed LAT) (July/Aug./Oct. 1989).

318. *N.Y. Court Questions Use of Paralegal to Screen Documents,* 12 NPR 8 (NFPA, Spring 1988).

319. *Obtaining ABA Approval: A Reference Manual for Legal Assistant Educators* (ABA, 1989).

320. *Occupational Regulation: Issues of Particular Importance to the Paralegal Profession* by R. McManus, 10 NPR 8 (NFPA, Aug. 1986).

321. *Office Politics* by A. Stern, 7 LAT 61 (May/June 1990).

322. *$100,000 a Year for Paralegals?* by P. Marcotte, 73 ABA Journal 19 (Oct. 1987).

323. *The Online Legal Assistant: Legal Databases* by C. Griffith, 4 LAT 39 (Mar./Apr. 1987).

324. *Opportunities in Paralegal Careers* by A. Fins (National Textbook Co., 1979).

325. *Order in the Court: Trial Management and Assistance* by C. Smith, 14 NPR 6 (NFPA, Spring 1990).

326. *Oregon State Bar Certifies Legal Assistants,* 17 LOEM 118 (Sept. 1976).

327. *Organizing and Digesting Depositions* by B. Piatz, 7 LAT 45 (July/Aug. 1990).

328. *Organizing, Developing and Managing a Legal Assistant Program* by P. Ulrich, 22 LOEM 197 (1981). Reprinted in 1981 LAU, 103 (ABA).

329. *Organizing Reorganization: The Legal Assistants Role in Initiating a Chapter 11 Case* by K. Morzak, 5 LAT 33 (Jan./Feb. 1988).

330. *Overcoming the Fear of Legal Writing* by S. McInnis, 17 F&F 38 (NALA, Jan. 1991).

331. *Overcrowding Plagues Field* by G. Sea, Houston Chronicle, pp. 1L & 4L (Oct. 2, 1988).

332. *Parajudges and the Administration of Justice* by Clark, 24 Vanderbilt Law Review 1167 (1971).

333. *Paralegal Advisory Boards Influence Education* by B. King, 15 NPR 24 (NFPA, Summer 1990).

334. *Paralegal Advocacy before Administrative Agencies* by W. Statsky, 4 University of Toledo Law University Review 439 (1973).

335. *The Paralegal and the Principle of Confidentiality* by G. Davis, 3 Journal of Paralegal Education 23 (Oct. 1986).

336. *The Paralegal: An Effective Part of the Legal Service Team* by J. Harwell, 23 Tennessee Bar Journal 37 (July/Aug. 1987).

337. *The Paralegal: A New Career* by R. Deming (Elsevier/Nelson Books, 1980).

338. *Paralegal: An Insider's Guide to the Fastest-Growing Occupation in the 1990s* by B. Bernardo (Peterson's Guides, 1990).

339. *The Paralegal Boom,* by K. Liebler, 12 Pennsylvania Lawyer 12 (Apr. 1990).

340. *Paralegal Burnout: Challenging Work Wanted* by Frank, 70 ABA Journal 30 (Dec. 1984).

341. *Paralegal Career Advancement* by J. Reinard, 6 JPE&P 1 (1989).

342. *Paralegal Careers* by W. Fry & R. Hoopes (Enslow Publishers, 1986).

343. *Paralegal Degree Program Offers Prisoners Hope,* New York Times 40 (Dec. 1, 1985).

344. *Paralegal Education: Advice from the Experts* by J. Bassett, 8 LAT 21 (Jan./Feb. 1991).

345. *Paralegal Education in Prison* by A. Wolk, 4 LAT 49 (Jan./Feb. 1987).

346. *Paralegal Education in the United States* by T. Cannon, 15 F&F 42 (NALA, May 1989).

347. *Paralegal Education: Who Will Control the Future of the Profession?* by B. Albert, 6 LAT 36 (Jan./Feb. 1989).

348. *Paralegal Educators Identify Trends* by T. Cannon, 12 NPR 28 (NFPA, Spring 1988).

349. *Paralegal Employment Opportunities in State Government* by M. Baker & T. Eimmermann, 6 JPE&P 9 (1989).

350. *The Paralegal Factor* by B. Palermo, 9 Calif. Lawyer 47 (June 1989) (paralegal billing).

351. *Paralegal Growth Paralleled 1980s Law-Firm Expansion* by M. Goldberg, 26 Trial 97 (May 1990).

352. *The Paralegal: Key Link on the Team* by J. Harwell, Tennessee Bar Journal (July/Aug. 1987).

353. *The Paralegal in Army Legal Practice* by R. Black, Army Lawyer 70 (Nov. 1990).

354. *The Paralegal in Practice* by A. Clinton, 23 The Arkansas Lawyer 22 (Jan. 1989).

355. *A Paralegal in the Courthouse: An Answer to Crowded Dockets?* by T. Howard, 3 LAT 51 (Summer 1986).

356. *The Paralegal Job-Hunting Handbook* (National Capital Area Paralegal Ass'n, 1982, 1985).

357. *Paralegal Litigation Handbook* by C. Bruno (Institute for Business Planning, 1980).

358. *Paralegal Malpractice: New Profession, New Responsibility* by M. Moon, 18 Trial 40 (Jan. 1982) *See also* 6 NPR 1.

359. *Paralegal Medical Records Review* by K. Appleby & J. Tarver (James, 1989).

360. *Paralegal Opportunities in Environmental Law* by A. Parisi, 8 LAT 83 (Jan./Feb. 1991).

361. *Paralegal Paradox: Job Satisfaction* by J. Whalen, 12 F&F 17 (NALA, June 1986).

362. *Paralegal Parallax: Are Legal Technicians Parasites? Or Are Lawyers Just Paranoid?* by D. Olin, 10 Calif. Lawyer 20 (Nov. 1990).

363. *Paralegal Personnel for Attorneys General's Offices* (National Ass'n of Attorneys General, May 1976).

364. *Paralegal Placement Executive Speaks Out* by J. Hosea, 14 NPR 14 (NFPA, Spring 1990).

365. *Paralegal Practice and Procedure,* 2d ed. by D. Larbalestrier (Prentice Hall, 1986).

366. *Paralegal Pride: Is There Such a Thing?* by J. Mandla, 12 NPR 12 (NFPA, Winter 1988).

367. *The Paralegal Profession* by N. Shayne (Oceana, 1977).

368. *The Paralegal Profession* by Brown, 19 Howard Law Journal 117 (1976).

369. *Paralegal Profitability Analysis* by T. Hemnes, 25 LOEM 100 (1984).

370. *Paralegal Profitability Enhancement* by L. Leraul, 27 LOEM 448 (1987).

371. *Paralegal Programs: An Educational Alternative for Law Librarians* by C. Harris, 77 Law Library Journal 171 (1984–85).

372. *Paralegal Regulation and the New Professionalism* by E. Wheat, 3 Journal of Paralegal Education 1 (Oct. 1986).

373. *Paralegal Representation of Persons before State Administrative Agencies* by T. Aaron, 10 NPR 4 (NFPA, Oct. 1985).

374. *Paralegals' Acceptance and Utilization Increasing in Indy's Legal Community* by D. Brandt, 1 The Indiana Lawyer 1 (No. 5, June 20–July 3, 1990).

375. *Paralegal Salary and Job Function Survey of 1980—Arizona* by B. Childers & M. Jennings, 21 LOEM 506 (1981).

376. *Paralegals and Administrative Assistants for Prosecutors* by J. Stein & B. Hoff (National District Attorneys Ass'n, 1974).

377. *Paralegals and Sublegals: Aids to the Legal Profession* by Holme, 46 Denver Law Journal 392 (1969).

378. *Paralegals and the Imputed Disqualification Rule* by M. Schairer, 7 JPE&P 1 (1990).

379. *Paralegals Are Invaluable Pro Bono Resource* by W. Dean, 15 NPR 10 (NFPA, Winter 1991).

380. *Paralegals: A. Resource for Defenders and Correctional Services* by J. Stein (U.S. Gov't Printing Office, No. 027-000-00399-1) (Dec. 1976).

381. *Paralegals Average $14,000 to Start, Bring Profits to Firm* by Reskin, 70 ABA Journal 52 (Dec. 1984).

382. *Paralegals Can Be More Profitable than Associates* by A. Jones, 16 The Montana Lawyer 7 (Dec. 1990).

383. *Paralegal Serves as Bailiff of Probate Court* by C. Hunt, 10 NPR 18 (NFPA, Spring 1986).

384. *Paralegal Services and Awards of Attorneys' Fees* by Stahl & Smith, Arizona Bar Journal 21 (Oct./Nov. 1984).

385. *Paralegals: Firms Respond to Their Changing Role* by L. Myrick, 8 Of Counsel 3 (Apr. 3, 1989) (corporate paralegals).

386. *Paralegal's Guide to Dallas/Fort Worth Law-Related Careers* (Scrivener Publications, 1989).

387. *Paralegal's Guide to Manhattan Law Firms* by G. Pirozzi (West Heath Press, 1988).

388. *The Paralegal's Guide to U.S. Government Jobs: How to Land a Job in 70 Law-Related Careers,* 3rd ed. by J. Harris (Federal Reports, 1988).

389. *Paralegals in Australia* by J. Johnson, 15 NPR 8 (NFPA, Spring 1991).

390. *Paralegals in the Bush* by Conn & Hippler, 3 UCLA-Alaska Law Review 85 (1973).

391. *Paralegals in the Corporate Setting* by J. Campbell, 30 The St. Louis Bar Journal 22 (Summer, 1983).

392. *Paralegals in the Federal Government* by C. Perko, 4 LAU 75 (ABA 1984).

393. *Paralegals Move Up to Management* by R. Granat & D. Saewitz, National Law Journal p. 19 (Jan. 30, 1989).

394. *Paralegals Needed in Pro Bono Projects* by I. Woody, 15 NPR 12 (NFPA, Fall 1990).

395. *Paralegals: Out of the Shadows and into the Light* by D. Vitucci, Report 22 (Cincinnati Bar Ass'n, Feb. 1991).

396. *A Paralegal Speaks on Professional Issues* by J. Hughbanks, 2 Probate and Property 33 (May/June 1988).

397. *Paralegal Splitting Fees* by J. Unrath, 12 NPR 12 (NFPA, Winter 1988).

398. *Paralegals: Progress and Prospects of a Satellite Occupation* by Q. Johnstone & M. Wenglinsky (Greenwood Press, 1985).

399. *A Paralegal's Role in Insurance Defense Litigation* by S. Bullock, 17 F&F 60 (NALA, May 1990).

400. *Paralegals Seen Taking Jobs from Associates* by Winter, 68 ABA Journal 527 (1982).

401. *Paralegals: Should Legal Technicians Be Allowed to Practice Independently?* by D. Chalfie, 77 ABA Journal 40 (Mar. 1991).

402. *Paralegals: The Making of a Profession* by C. Gilsinan & S. Pope, 30 The St. Louis Bar Journal 6 (Summer, 1983).

403. *Paralegals: The National and State Outlook* by R. Beard, 18 Arkansas Lawyer 189 (Oct. 1984).

404. *Paralegal Survey Reveals Rising Salaries,* 27 Arizona Attorney 9 (Nov. 1990).

405. *Paralegals Use Their Heads and Hearts in Pro Bono Programs* by D. Barr, 15 NPR 4 (NFPA, Fall 1990).

406. *Paralegals Volunteer Pro Bono to Alternative Dispute Resolution Program* by G. Fitleberg, 15 NPR 10 (NFPA, Fall 1990).

407. *Paralegal Trial Handbook* by B. Hutson (James, 1991).

408. *Paralegal: Wills, Trusts and Estates* by P. Carter (D&E Publishers, 1982) (Florida).

409. *Paraprofessionals: Expanding the Legal Service Delivery Team* by W. Statsky, 24 Journal of Legal Education 397 (1972).

410. *Participation of a Legal Assistant in a Commercial Real Estate Transaction* by J. Kauffold, 16 F&F 14 (NALA, Nov. 1989).

411. *Partners in Performance: The Corporate Legal Assistant and the Service Company* by H. Rosenberg, 5 LAT 38 (July/Aug. 1988).

412. *Patricia Coleman of Chicago Creates Her Niche in Taxes, Trusts and ERISA* by T. Howard, 3 LAT 40 (Winter 1986).

413. *Perry Mason They're Not: But "Legal Technicians" Are Cutting into the Establishment's Market* by M. Shao, Business Week, p. 83 (Nov. 20, 1989) (independent paralegals).

414. *Personnel Management Techniques for the First-Time Supervisor* by A. Guinn, 8 LAT 56 (Mar./Apr. 1991).

415. *Policing the Professional Monopoly: A Constitutional and Empirical Analysis of Unauthorized Practice Prohibitions* by D. Rhode, 34 Stanford Law Review 1 (1981).

416. *Polish Your People Skills to Specialize in Family Law* by R. Bilz, 6 LAT 47 (Jan./Feb. 1989).

417. *Position Yourself for Success* by A. Wagner, 7 Legal Professional 16 (renamed LAT) (July/Aug./Oct. 1989).

418. *The Positive Side of Associate Membership* by D. Prehm, 10 NPR 1 (NFPA, Spring 1986).

419. *Practical Considerations in Establishing an Independent Practice* by D. Secol, 16 F&F 18 (NALA, Sept. 1989).

420. *Practice before Administrative Agencies and the Unauthorized Practice of Law* by Vom Baur, 15 Federal Bar Journal 103 (1955).

421. *Practice by Non-Lawyers before the National Labor Relations Board* by Gall, 15 Federal Bar Journal 222 (1955).

422. *Practice by Non-Lawyers before the United States Patent Office* by Bailey, 15 Federal Bar Journal 211 (1955).

423. *Practice with a Paralegal: Making an Educated Choice* by C. Dietrich, 13 Legal Economics 51 (ABA, Oct. 1987).

424. *Practicing with Paralegals* (Missouri Bar Legal Assistants Committee, 1989).

425. *Preparing for the First-Time Teaching Experience* by C. McKernan & A. Stover, 15 NPR 6 (NFPA, Summer 1990).

426. *Preparing for the Job Interview* by J. Penrose, 7 Legal Professional 48 (renamed LAT) (Nov./Dec. 1989).

427. *Preparing for Trial* by C. Wilson, 8 LAT 45 (Sept./Oct. 1990).

428. *Pretrial Preparation Procedures* by M. Farrington, 7 LAT 60 (July/Aug. 1990).

429. *Preventive Law and the Paralegal* by L. Brown, 24 Vanderbilt Law Review 1181 (1971).

430. *The Price of Success* by P. Zavalney, 6 Texas Lawyer 10 (Jan. 21, 1991).

431. *Prisoner Access to Justice and Paralegals* by B. Kempinen, 14 New England Journal on Crim. & Civil Confinement 67 (Winter 1988).

432. *Private Investigator* by T. McGowan, 2 LAT 24 (Fall 1984).

433. *Pro Bono Is for Legal Assistants, Too* by R. Yegge & W. Moore, 15 NPR 8 (NFPA, Fall 1990). Reprinted in 17 F&F 12 (NALA, July 1990).

434. *Pro Bono Opportunities for Nonlawyers,* 17 F&F 38 (NALA, July 1990).

435. *Pro Bono Program* by L. Olmstead, 17 F&F 30 (NALA, July 1990).

436. *Pro Bono Publico: How Paralegal Associations Can Contribute,* 12 NPR 11 (NFPA, Fall 1987).

437. *The Professionalization of the Legal Assistant* by D. Green et al., 7 JPE&P 35 (1990).

438. *Professional Negligence, Paralegals and Modern Legal Ethics between the Bookends* by H. Cohen, 11 The Journal of the Legal Profession 143 (1986).

439. *Professional Teamwork between Attorney and Secretary* by Ralston, 14 Legal Economics 25 (ABA, Sept. 1988).

440. *Profiles of Highly Successful Paralegals* by K. Garrett, 5 LAU 95 (ABA, 1986).

441. *Profitability Formulas and Paralegal/Associate Comparisons* by J. Tate, 15 NPR 18 (NFPA, Spring 1991).

442. *Progressive Paralegal Planning* by C. Acree, 29 The Colorado Lawyer 725 (1991).

443. *The Proper Scope of Nonlawyer Representation in State Administrative Proceedings* by G. Stevens, 43 Vanderbilt Law Review 245 (1990).

444. *Proposed Guidelines for the Utilization of Legal Assistants,* 15 The Colorado Lawyer 183 (1986).

445. *Rate Your Resume* by R. Nesbit, 16 F&F 43 (NALA, July 1989).

446. *The Real Estate Paralegal* by D. Johnson, 8 LAT 73 (Mar./Apr. 1991).

447. *Recognition and Opportunity: The Genesis for a Growing Profession* by S. Keaton, 10 F&F 13 (NALA, May/June 1984) (Texas Legal Assistants Division).

448. *Reflections on the Law Firm Environment* by C. Gorden, 13 NPR 7 (NFPA, Fall 1988).

449. *Registering Legal Assistants* by J. Noll & K. Buss, 5 Bar Bulletin, Issue 7 (Seattle-King County Bar Ass'n, Mar. 1987).

450. *Regulation: A New Forecast on a Timeworn Question* by S. Kaiser, NPR 14 (NFPA, Winter 1990).

451. *Regulation: The Sleeping Giant Awakens* by Murry, 4 LAT 16 (Sept./Oct. 1986).

452. *Removing the Veil of Mystery From the CLA Exam* [Certified Legal Assistant] by Dunn, 18 F&F 38 (July 1991).

453. *The Right Stuff* by T. Howard, 7 Legal Professional 36 (renamed LAT) (July/Aug./Oct. 1989) (upward mobility).

454. *Report from the Committee of Expansion of Professional Responsibilities* by Y. Spiegel, 10 NPR 4 (NFPA, Spring 1986).

455. *Report of the Connecticut Bar Association Special Inter-Committee Group to Study the Role of Paralegals* (12/11/85).

456. *Report of the State Bar of California Commission on Legal Technicians* (State Bar of Calif., July 1990).

457. *Representation of Clients before Administrative Agencies: Authorized or Unauthorized Practice of Law?* 15 Valparaiso University Law Review 567 (1981).

458. *Resumes for Paralegals and Other People with Legal Training* by R. Berkey (Arco, 1984).

459. *Revitalization of the Legal Profession through Paralegalism,* 30 Baylor Law Review 841 (1978).

460. *The Rhode Island Paralegal Association Hosts Conference,* 33 Rhode Island Bar Journal 43 (June/July, 1985).

461. *Rhode Island Supreme Court Provisional Order No. 18* (1983) (covering legal assistants).

462. *A Risky Stand-in? Paralegals at Realty Closings* by Silas, 69 ABA Journal 1812 (Dec. 1982).

463. *The RMLAA [Rocky Mountain Legal Assistants Association] Employment and Salary Survey: A 1990 Paralegal Profile* by B. Lilly, 19 The Colorado Lawyer 2213 (Nov. 1990).

464. *The Role of Accreditation and the Public Interest* by C. Chambers, 11 NPR 15 (NFPA, Spring 1987).

465. *The Role of Paralegals in Inmate Litigation* by F. Devine, 5 JPE&P 1 (Oct. 1988).

466. *The Role of Paralegals in Real Estate Transactions,* 68 Illinois Bar Journal 391 (Feb. 1980).

467. *The Role of the Legal Assistant [Paralegal] in Iowa* by the Iowa State Bar Ass'n (1979).

468. *The Role of the Legal Assistant in Real Estate/ Franchise Transactions* by B. Sacks, 16 F&F 36 (NALA, Nov. 1989).

469. *The Role of the Paralegal in the Civil Commitment Process* by R. Lockwood, 10 Capital University Law Review 721 (Summer 1981).

470. *The Role of the Paralegal in Corporate Acquisition* by S. Decker, 11 NPR 8 (NFPA, 1987).

471. *Running with Hares and Chasing with the Hounds: The Emerging Dilemma of Paralegal*

Mobility by R. Marquardt, 2 Journal of Legal Education 57 (Oct. 1984).

472. *Salaried Personnel: Are They Really Exempt from Minimum Wage and Overtime Requirements?* by P. Stewart, 9 Legal Management 11 (ALA, Jan./Feb. 1990).

473. *Salary Survey Results* by C. Milano, 8 LAT 27 (May/June 1991).

474. *The Salary Wars: Paralegals Could Come Out the Winners* by R. McCroskey, 4 LAT 37 (May/June 1987).

475. *Sale of Books or Forms. . .As Unauthorized Practice of Law,* 71 American Law Reports 3rd 1000 (1976).

476. *School Trains Jail-House Lawyers* by D. Horine, p. 20. The Los Angeles Daily Journal (Mar. 26, 1991).

477. *Searching for a Job? Here Are Some Helpful Hints* by M. Vaneecke, 13 F&F 20 (NALA, Apr. 1987).

478. *Secretary to Paralegal: A Career Manual and Guide* by L. Prendergast (Institute for Business Planning, 1984).

479. *Self-Help for the "Frustrated" Legal Assistant* by L. Fiegener, 15 F&F 20 (NALA, May 1989).

480. *Senior Legal Assistants: How to Keep Them* by M. Coyne, 3 LAMA Manager 7 (LAMA, Summer 1989).

481. *"Senior Paralegal" Is More Than Just a Title* by B. Grajski, 125 New Jersey Law Journal 14 (Apr. 19, 1990).

482. *Senior Paralegals Counsel Newcomers: Computer Litigation Support Can Help* by D. Bernhard, 9 Legal Management 48 (ALA, Mar./Apr. 1990).

483. *$etting Compensation* by M. Reger & L. Doll, 14 NPR 23 (NFPA, Summer 1989).

484. *SFALA Job Hunt Skills: Career Guide* (San Francisco Ass'n of Legal Assistants).

485. *A Short Course in Human Relations I for Legal Assistants* by L. Barth, 17 F&F 52 (NALA, May 1990).

486. *Should Lawyers Compete with Paralegals?* by E. Tronsrue, 12 NPR 4 (NFPA, Fall 1987).

487. *Should Paralegals Have More Responsibility?* by D. Austern, 23 Trial 19 (May 1987).

488. *Should Paralegals Prepare Wills?* 24 Maryland Bar Journal 38 (Jan./Feb. 1991).

489. *Should the ABA Appeal Process Be the Only Game in Town?* by M. Pener, 11 NPR 9 (NFPA, Spring 1987).

490. *Should the ABA or Anyone Else Be Involved in Approving or Accrediting Paralegal Training Programs?,* 1 LAT 14 (Spring 1984).

491. *Show and Tell: The Legal Assistant as Demonstrative Exhibit Specialist* by D. Filter, 5 LAT 26 (Sept./Oct. 1987).

492. *Six Legal Assistant Service Firms: How They Use Technology Creatively* by M. George, 6 LAT 37 (Nov./Dec. 1988).

493. *Slugging It Out for Justice* by J. Murry, 1 LAT 20 (Summer 1984) (Rosemary Furman and the Florida Bar).

494. *Statement to State Bar of California,* 17 F&F 18 (NALA, Fall 1990) (limited licensing).

495. *Strategies for Developing a Successful Computerized Conflict of Interest Management System* by S. Craig, 4 LAT 45 (May/June 1987).

496. *Strategies for Organizing Everyday Cases* by S. Mohney, 8 LAT 86 (Mar./Apr. 1991).

497. *Strategies for Paralegal Career Development* by T. Coyne, NPR 20 (NFPA, Winter 1990).

498. *Strategies for Working with Challenging People* by T. Howard, 8 LAT 54 (Sept./Oct. 1990).

499. *Stress Busters* by T. Howard, 6 LAT 16 (Mar./Apr. 1989).

500. *Success and Survival in a Law Firm* by B. Morgan, 7 LAT 65 (July/Aug. 1990).

501. *Successful Interviewing* by R. Berkey, 5 LAT 64 (Sept./Oct. 1987).

502. *Survey of Legal Assistants Shows Field Increasing in Numbers,* 31 LOEM 94 (1990).

503. *Survey on Law Office Compensation of Legal Assistants/Administrative Support Staff* (Michigan, Institute on Law Office Management; Institute on Continuing Legal Education).

504. *Survey Results of Non-Traditional Paralegal Responsibilities* by P. Ruse & J. Whelan, NPR 18 (NFPA, Winter 1990).

505. *Survey Results of Paralegal Instructors* by J. Hosea, 15 NPR 8 (NFPA, Summer 1990) (paralegals as teachers).

506. *Survival Kit for a New Paralegal* by M. Rosetti, 1 LAT 24 (Winter 1984).

507. *Surviving a Large Document Case,* 15 F&F 24 (NALA, Aug. 1988).

508. *Sweet-Talking Clients and Intransigent Bureaucrats: Immigration Paralegals Know Them All* by M. Myers & K. Raman, 15 NPR 4 (NFPA, Winter 1991).

509. *Systematic Trial Preparation* by B. Kidder, 8 LAT 103 (May/June 1991).

510. *A System for Managing Small to Medium-Sized Cases* by D. Bruegl, 8 LAT 71(Sept./Oct. 1990).

511. *Systemization and the Legal Assistant in the Law Office* by Endacott, 54 Nebraska Law Review 46 (1975).

512. *Teaching Corrections Law to Corrections Personnel* by W. Statsky, 37 Federal Probation 42 (June 1973).

513. *The Team Approach to Practice Development: Substantive and Procedural Guidelines for Law Office Staff* (Professional Education Systems, 1989).

514. *The Teaming of Legal Assistants and Librarians* by M. Wallace, 6 LAT 30 (May/June 1989).

515. *Team Teaching: The Role of Paralegals in Teaching Practical Skills* by S. DiLullo, 7 Legal Professional 45 (renamed LAT) (Jan./Feb. 1990).

516. *Technician, Attorney & Manager* by R. Granat, 7 Legal Professional 53 (renamed LAT) (Mar./Apr. 1990).

517. *Techniques for Supervising Paralegals* by W. Statsky, 22 The Practical Lawyer 81 (No. 4, 1976). (Reprinted in Law Office Management Manual No. 5, p. 27 (ABA-ALI, 1984).

518. *Television Commercial Portrays Paralegal in a Negative Light* by B. Schultz, 13 NPR 7 (NFPA, Winter 1989).

519. *Temporary Employment* by C. Toncray, 15 NPR 9 (NFPA, Winter 1991).

520. *Ten Tips for Effectively Assisting at Trial* by D. Patrick, 8 LAT 22 (Sept./Oct. 1990).

521. *Ten Ways to Make Paralegals More Profitable* by E. Wesemann, 134 Pittsburgh Legal Journal 20 (Apr. 1986).

522. *Texas Certification,* 10 NPR 6 (NFPA, Spring 1986).

523. *The Texas Division Rides Again, but Which Way?* by J. Murry, 3 LAT 42 (Summer 1986) (certification).

524. *Texas Opts for NALA CLA by Default* by J. Browning, 15 F&F 27 (NALA, Fall 1988).

525. *Time Management* by J. Hosea, NPR 2 (NFPA, Winter 1990).

526. *Tips and Traps for the New Paralegal* by A. Wagner, 8 LAT 78 (Mar./Apr. 1991).

527. *Tips on Hiring and Training Paralegals* by C. Tupis, 7 LAT 53 (July/Aug. 1990).

528. *To Be or Not to Be* by D. Villines, 17 F&F 12 (NALA, Mar. 1991) (freelance legal assistants).

529. *Tools for the Successful Paralegal Job Search* by E. Moorer, 6 LAT 20 (Jan./Feb. 1989).

530. *Tort Liability of Legal Paraprofessionals and Lawyers Who Utilize Their Services* by Wade, 24 Vanderbilt Law Review 1133 (1971).

531. *Training Paralegals In-House* by C. Bruno, 27 LOEM 184 (1986–87).

532. *Training the Legal Assistant for Litigation Practice in a Large Law Firm* by J. Goodman, 57 New York State Bar Journal 34 (Apr. 1985).

533. *The Training of Community Judges* by W. Statsky, 4 Columbia Human Rights Law Review 401 (1972).

534. *Turnabout: The Male Perspective of the Paralegal Profession* by D. Sesit, 4 LAT 21 (Nov./Dec. 1986).

535. *Twalla DuPriest: Bankruptcy Trustee [and Paralegal]* by J. Basset, 7 Legal Professional 73 (renamed LAT) (Sept./Oct. 1989).

536. *Unauthorized Practice and Legal Assistants* by Whidden, 13 The Journal of the Legal Profession 327 (1988).

537. *Unauthorized Practice and Pro Se Divorce: An Empirical Analysis,* 86 Yale Law Journal 104 (1976).

538. *The Unauthorized Practice of Law and the Legal Assistant* by D. Orlik, 2 Journal of Legal Education 120 (Apr. 1985).

539. *Unauthorized Practice of Law by Insurance Claims Adjusters* by Jordan, 10 The Journal of the Legal Profession 171 (1985).

540. *The Unauthorized Practice of Law: Do Good Fences Really Make Good Neighbors?* by Christensen, 1980 American Bar Foundation Research Journal 159.

541. *Unionization: Raising the Issue* by S. Peeples, 6 NPR 4 (NFPA, Summer 1982).

542. *Use of Lay Representatives,* 58 Michigan Law Review 456 (1960).

543. *The Use of Legal and Technical Assistants by Administrative Law Judges in Administrative Proceedings* by Mathias, 1 The Administrative Law Journal 107 (1987).

544. *Use of Legal Assistants in a Plaintiff's Trial Practice* by T. Boyer & T. Arington, 5 F&F 10 (NALA, Apr. 1988).

545. *The Use of Legal Assistants in a Small Office* by V. Nicholas & J. Kirk, Arizona Bar Journal 36 (Oct. 1978).

546. *The Use of Paralegal Assistants in Divorce Practice* by P. Grove & M. Binter, 4 American Journal of Family Law 41 (Spring 1990).

547. *Use of Paralegals in Probate Administration* by D. Kennedy, 32 Res Gestae 501 (Apr. 1989).

548. *Use of Paralegals Makes Good Economic Sense,* 69 ABA Journal 1626 (1983).

549. *Using Computers in Litigation Support* by M. Moses, 8 LAT 38 (Nov./Dec. 1990).

550. *Using Legal Assistants in Estate Planning* by G. Cohen, 30 The Practical Lawyer 73 (Oct. 1984).

551. *Using Paralegals in Pre-Trial Litigation* by L. Zimet, 14 Legal Economics 63 (ABA, Mar. 1988).

552. *Using Paralegals in Small and Mid-Sized Law Firms* by D. Howard, 5 JPE&P 67 (Oct. 1988).

553. *Utilization of Legal Assistants* by Y. Garman, 17 F&F 32 (NALA, July 1990). [*See also* 6 LAMA Manager 10 (Winter 1990)].

554. *Utilization of Legal Assistants in the Private Law Firm* by Klessing, 58 Wisconsin Bar Bulletin 33 (1985).

555. *Validity of Will Drawn by Layman Who, in So Doing, Violated Criminal Statute Forbidding Such Activities by One Other Than Licensed Attorneys,* 18 American Law Reports, 2d 918 (1951).

556. *Vertical Expansion of the Legal Service Team* by Smith, 56 ABA Journal 664 (July 1970).

557. *View [of Paralegals] from the Bench,* 17 F&F 36 (NALA, July 1990).

558. *Wage and Hour Law Applications for Paralegals* by J. Jeffries, 7 Legal Administrator 10 (ALA, Mar./Apr. 1988).

559. *Walt Disney World Company's Legal Assistants: Their Role in the Show* by Miquel, 16 F&F 29 (NALA, Jan. 1990).

560. *Washington's Paralegals: An '80s Takeoff Becomes a '90s Institution* by M. Marklein, The Washington Lawyer 26 (Jan./Feb. 1990).

561. *The Weekend Retreat: A New Benefit for Paralegals* by C. Estrin, 6 LAT 26 (Mar./Apr. 1989).

562. *What Activities of Stock or Securities Broker Constitute Unauthorized Practice of Law,* 34 American Law Reports 3d 1305 (1970).

563. *What Are You Worth?* by S. Yost, 7 Legal Professional 33 (renamed LAT) (Sept./Oct. 1989).

564. *Whatever Happened to Paralegal Paradise?* by Boardman, Texas Lawyer (Jan. 7, 1991).

565. *What Is LAMA? The Legal Assistant Management Association* by J. Murry, 4 LAT 13 (May/June 1987).

566. *What Is the Profit from Associates and Paralegals?* 62 Wisconsin Lawyer 6 (Apr. 1989).

567. *What to Consider When Drafting Simple Wills* by C. Carter, 8 LAT 63 (Mar./Apr. 1991).

568. *What Your Law Office Management Professor Never Told You* by C. Elwell, 5 LAT 66 (Nov./Dec. 1987).

569. *When Is a Paralegal Really a Paralegal?* by R. Lais, 32 Orange County Lawyer 6 (May 1990).

570. *When to Hire a Lawyer; When to Hire a Legal Assistant* by L. Dmytryk, 6 LAT 32 (Sept./Oct. 1988).

571. *Who Gets the Best Jobs?* by C. Milano, 8 LAT 39 (Sept./Oct. 1990).

572. *Winds of Change in the Paralegal Profession* by F. Setterberg, 7 Calif. Lawyer 26 (Jan. 1987).

573. *Witnesses: Who, Where, When, Why, How* by V. Nichols, 14 F&F 52 (NALA, Oct./Nov. 1987) (investigation).

574. *Working Effectively with Legal Assistants* by A. Olson, 62 Wisconsin Lawyer 25 (Nov. 1989).

575. *Working with Legal Assistants,* Ulrich & Mucklestone, eds. (ABA, 1980, 1981).

576. *Working with Legal Assistants: Professional Responsibility* by Ulrich & Clarke, 67 ABA Journal 992 (1981).

577. *Write a Letter: Letter Writing in a Law Office* by R. Bilz, 7 Legal Professional 44 (renamed LAT) (Nov./Dec. 1989).

578. *You're the Best: Esteem Building for Paralegals* by R. Roepp, 3 LAT 14 (Summer 1986).

579. *Your Secretary: Paralegal in Disguise* by Sternin, 88 Case & Comment 12 (July/Aug. 1983).

B

Paralegal Associations and Related Organizations

 PARALEGAL ASSOCIATIONS (NATIONAL)

(Membership statistics, where known, are presented in brackets.)

National Association of Legal
   Assistants [15,000]
1601 S. Main St., Suite 300
Tulsa, OK 74119
918-587-6828

National Federation of Paralegal
   Associations [17,500]
P.O. Box 33108

Kansas City, MO 64114
816-941-4000

(NALA and NFPA have numerous affiliated local paralegal associations. NALA affiliates are indicated by one asterisk (*) below; NFPA affiliates are indicated by two asterisks below (**). The addresses of these local associations change frequently. If the address given below turns out to be unproductive, contact the national office of NALA or NFPA for a more current address. Local associations without an asterisk are unaffiliated at this time.)

 PARALEGAL ASSOCIATIONS (STATE)

ALABAMA

Alabama Association of Legal
   Assistants (*) [215]
P.O. Box 55921
Birmingham, AL 35255

Huntsville Association of
   Paralegals
P.O. Box 244
Huntsville, AL 35804-0244

Mobile Association of Legal
   Assistants [75]
P.O. Box 1988
Mobile, AL 36633

ALASKA

Alaska Association of Legal
   Assistants (**) [130]
P.O. Box 101956
Anchorage, AK 99510-1956

Fairbanks Association of Legal
   Assistants (*)
P.O. Box 73503
Fairbanks, AK 99707

Juneau Legal Assistants Association
   (**) [20]
P.O. Box 22336
Juneau, AK 99802

ARIZONA

Arizona Association of Professional
   Paralegals (**) [50]
P.O. Box 25111
Phoenix, AZ 85002

Arizona Paralegal Association (*)
P.O. Box 392
Phoenix, AZ 85001
602-258-0121

Legal Assistants of Metropolitan
   Phoenix (*)

P.O. Box 13005
Phoenix, AZ 85002

Southeast Valley Association of
   Legal Assistants (*)
% Sandy Slater
1707 N. Temple
Mesa, AZ 85203

Tucson Association of Legal
   Assistants (*)
P.O. Box 257
Tucson, AZ 85702-0257

ARKANSAS

Arkansas Association of Legal
   Assistants (*)
P.O. Box 2162
Little Rock, AR 72203-2162

CALIFORNIA

California Alliance of Paralegal
   Associations [4000]

P.O. Box 2234
San Francisco, CA 94126
415-576-3000

California Association of Freelance
 Paralegals [94]
P.O. Box 3267
Berkeley, CA 94703-0267
213-251-3826

Central Coast Legal Assistant
 Association (**) [70]
P.O. Box 93
San Luis Obispo, CA 93406

Central Valley Paralegal
 Association
P.O. Box 4086
Modesto, CA 95352

East Bay Association of Paralegals
 [200]
P.O. Box 29082
Oakland, CA 94604

Inland Counties Paralegal
 Association
P.O. Box 292
Riverside, CA 92502-0292

Kern County Paralegal Association
 [63]
P.O. Box 2673
Bakersfield, CA 93303

Legal Assistants Association of
 Santa Barbara (*)
P.O. Box 2695
Santa Barbara, CA 93120
805-965-7319

Los Angeles Paralegal Association
 (**) [1150]
P.O. Box 241928
Los Angeles, CA 90024
213-251-3755

Marin Association of Legal
 Assistants
P.O. Box 13051
San Rafael, CA 94913-3051
415-456-6020

Orange County Paralegal
 Association (**) [490]
P.O. Box 8512
Newport Beach, CA 92658-8512
714-744-7747

Paralegal Association of Santa
 Clara County (*)

P.O. Box 26736
San Jose, CA 95159

Redwood Empire Association of
 Legal Assistants
1275 4th St. Box 226
Santa Rosa, CA 95404

Sacramento Association of Legal
 Assistants (**) [271]
P.O. Box 453
Sacramento, CA 95812-0453

San Diego Association of Legal
 Assistants (**) [450]
P.O. Box 87449
San Diego, CA 92138-7449
619-491-1994

San Francisco Association of Legal
 Assistants (**) [975]
P.O. Box 26668
San Francisco, CA 94126-6668
415-777-2390

San Joaquin Association of Legal
 Assistants
P.O. Box 1306
Fresno, CA 93715

Sequoia Paralegal Association
P.O. Box 3884
Visalia, CA 93278-3884

Ventura County Association of
 Legal Assistants (*)
P.O. Box 24229
Ventura, CA 93002

COLORADO

Association of Legal Assistants of
 Colorado (*) [106]
% Alma Rodrigues
4150 Novia Dr.
Colorado Springs, CO 80911

Rocky Mountain Legal Assistants
 Association (**) [440]
P.O. Box 304
Denver, CO 80201
303-369-1606

CONNECTICUT

Central Connecticut Association of
 Legal Assistants (**) [290]
P.O. Box 230594
Hartford, CT 06123-0594

Connecticut Association of
 Paralegals, Fairfield County (**)
 [135]
P.O. Box 134
Bridgeport, CT 06601

Connecticut Association of
 Paralegals, New Haven (**)
 [100]
P.O. Box 862
New Haven, CT 06504-0862

Legal Assistants of Southeastern
 Connecticut (**) [55]
P.O. Box 409
New London, CT 06320

DELAWARE

Delaware Paralegal Association
 (**) [295]
P.O. Box 1362
Wilmington, DE 19899

DISTRICT OF COLUMBIA

National Capital Area Paralegal
 Association (**) [620]
1155 Connecticut Ave. N.W.
Wash. D.C. 20036-4306
202-659-0243

FLORIDA

Broward County Paralegal
 Association
% Leigh Williams
Ruden, Barnett, McClosky
P.O. Box 1900
Ft. Lauderdale, FL 33302

Dade Association of Legal
 Assistants (*)
% Maxine Stone
14027 S.W. 84th St.
Miami, FL 33183

Florida Legal Assistants (*)
% Nancy Martin
P.O. Box 503
Bradenton, FL 34206

Jacksonville Legal Assistants (*)
P.O. Box 52264
Jacksonville, FL 32201

Orlando Legal Assistants (*)
% Roxane MacGillivray
Akerman, Senterfitt & Eidson

P.O. Box 231
Orlando, FL 32802

Pensacola Legal Assistants (*)
% Deborah Johnson
Levin, Middlebrooks & Mabie
226 S. Palafox St.
Pensacola, FL 32581

Volusia Association of Legal
   Assistants (*)
P.O. Box 15075
Daytona Beach, FL 32115-5075

GEORGIA

Georgia Association of Legal
   Assistants (**) [820]
P.O. Box 1802
Atlanta, GA 30301

Southeastern Association of Legal
   Assistants of Georgia (*)
% Debra Sutlive
2215 Bacon Park Drive
Savannah, GA 31406

South Georgia Association of Legal
   Assistants (*)
% Martha Tanner
L. Andrew Smith, P.C.
P.O. Box 1026
Valdosta, GA 31603-1026

HAWAII

Hawaii Association of Legal
   Assistants (**) [150]
P.O. Box 674
Honolulu, HI 96809

IDAHO

Idaho Association of Legal
   Assistants (*) [54]
P.O. Box 1254
Boise, ID 83701

ILLINOIS

Central Illinois Paralegal
   Association (*)
% Debra Monke
GTE North Inc.
1312 E. Empire St.
Bloomington, IL 61701

Illinois Paralegal Association (**)
   [1059]

P.O. Box 857
Chicago, IL 60690
312-939-2553

Independent Contractors
   Association of Illinois
6400 Woodward Ave.
Downers Grove, IL 60516

Peoria Paralegal Association
% Sharon Moke
1308 Autumn Lane
Peoria, IL 60604

INDIANA

Indiana Legal Assistants (*)
% Dorothy French
14669 Old State Rd.
Evansville, IN 47711

Indiana Paralegal Association (**)
   [300]
P.O. Box 44518, Federal Station
Indianapolis, IN 46204

Michiana Paralegal Association
   (**) [40]
P.O. Box 11458
South Bend, IN 46634

IOWA

Iowa Association of Legal
   Assistants [400]
P.O. Box 335
Des Moines, IA 50302-0337

Paralegals of Iowa, Ltd.
P.O. Box 1943
Cedar Rapids, IA 52406

KANSAS

Kansas Association of Legal
   Assistants (*) [138]
% Jimmie Sue Marsh
Foulston & Siefkin
700 Fourth Financial Center
Wichita, KS 67202

Kansas City Association of Legal
   Assistants (**)
P.O. Box 13223
Kansas City, MO 64199
913-381-4458

Kansas Legal Assistants Society
   (**) [190]
P.O. Box 1657
Topeka, KS 66601

KENTUCKY

Kentucky Paralegal Association
   [232]
P.O. Box 2675
Louisville, KY 40201-2657

Lexington Paralegal Association
   (**) [80]
P.O. Box 574
Lexington, KY 40586

Louisville Association of Paralegals
   (**) [182]
P.O. Box 962
Louisville, KY 40201

LOUISIANA

Baton Rouge Paralegal Association
P.O. Box 306
Baton Rouge, LA 70821

Lafayette Paralegal Association
P.O. Box 2775
Lafayette, LA 70502

Louisiana State Paralegal
   Association [200]
P.O. Box 56
Baton Rouge, LA 70821-0056

New Orleans Paralegal Association
   (**) [190]
P.O. Box 30604
New Orleans, LA 70190

Northwest Louisiana Paralegal
   Association (*)
P.O. Box 1913
Shreveport, LA 71166-1913

Southwest Louisiana Association of
   Paralegals
P.O. Box 1143
Lake Charles, LA 70602-1143

MAINE

Maine Association of Paralegals (*)
P.O. Box 7554
Portland, ME 04112

MARYLAND

Baltimore Association of Legal
   Assistants (**) [140]
P.O. Box 13244
Baltimore, MD 21203
301-576-BALA

MASSACHUSETTS

Berkshire Association for
    Paralegals and Legal Secretaries
% Nancy Schaffer
Stein, Donahue & Zuckerman
54 Wendell Ave.
Pittsfield, MA 01201

Central Massachusetts Paralegal
    Association (**) [80]
P.O. Box 444
Worcester, MA 01614

Massachusetts Paralegal
    Association (**) [440]
P.O. Box 423
Boston, MA 02102
617-642-8338

Western Massachusetts Paralegal
    Association (**) [50]
P.O. Box 30005
Springfield, MA 01102-0005

MICHIGAN

Legal Assistants Association of
    Michigan (*)
% Cora Webb
Woll, Crowley, Berman
315 S. Woodward
Royal Oak, MI 48067

Legal Assistant Section [400]
State Bar of Michigan
440 E. Congress, 4th Fl.
Detroit, MI 48226

Legal Assistants Section
State Bar of Michigan
306 Townsend St.
Lansing, MI 48933-2083
517-372-9030

MINNESOTA

Minnesota Association of Legal
    Assistants (**) [972]
P.O. Box 15165
Minneapolis, MN 55415

Minnesota Paralegal Association
    (*)
% Tracy Blanshan
Kennedy Law Office
724 SW First Ave.
Rochester, MN 55902

MISSISSIPPI

Gulf Coast Paralegal Association
942 Beach Drive
Gulfport, MS 39507

Mississippi Association of Legal
    Assistants (*)
P.O. Box 996
600 Heritage Bldg.
Jackson, MS 39205

Paralegal Association of Mississippi
P.O. Box 22887
Jackson, MS 39205

MISSOURI

Gateway Paralegal Association
P.O. Box 50233
St. Louis, MO 63105

Kansas City Association of Legal
    Assistants (**) [470]
P.O. Box 13223
Kansas City, MO 64199
913-381-4458

Southwest Missouri Paralegal
    Association [80]
2148 South Oak Grove
Springfield, MO 65804-2708

St. Louis Association of Legal
    Assistants (*) [434]
P.O. Box 9690
St. Louis, MO 63122

MONTANA

Big Sky Paralegal Association
P.O. Box 2753
Great Falls, MT 59403

Montana Paralegal Association
P.O. Box 693
Billings, MT 59101

NEBRASKA

Nebraska Association of Legal
    Assistants (*)
P.O. Box 24943
Omaha, NE 68124

NEVADA

Clark County Organization of
    Legal Assistants (*)
% Angel A. Price

3800 S. Nellis #235
Las Vegas, NV 89121

Sierra Nevada Association of
    Paralegals (*)
P.O. Box 40638
Reno, NV 89504

NEW HAMPSHIRE

Paralegal Association of New
    Hampshire (*)
% Frances Dupre
Wiggin & Nourie
P.O. Box 808
Manchester, NH 03105

NEW JERSEY

Central Jersey Paralegal
    Association
P.O. Box 1115
Freehold, NJ 07728

Legal Assistants Association of
    New Jersey (*) [260]
P.O. Box 142
Caldwell, NJ 07006

South Jersey Paralegal Association
    (**) [160]
P.O. Box 355
Haddonfield, NJ 08033

NEW MEXICO

Legal Assistants of New Mexico
    (**) [200]
P.O. Box 1113
Albuquerque, NM 87103-1113
505-260-7104

NEW YORK

Adirondack Paralegal Association
% Maureen Provost
Bartlett, Pontiff, Stewart
One Washington Street
Box 2168
Glen Falls, NY 12801

Legal Professionals of Dutchess
    County
51 Maloney Rd.
Wappingers Falls, NY 12590

Long Island Paralegal Association
    (**) [130]

P.O. Box 31
Deer Park, NY 11729

Manhattan Paralegal Association
[515]
200 Park Ave., Suite 303 East
New York, NY 10166
212-986-2304

Paralegal Association of Rochester
(**) [170]
P.O. Box 40567
Rochester, NY 14604

Southern Tier Association of
Paralegals (**) [45]
P.O. Box 2555
Binghamton, NY 13902

Western New York Paralegal
Association (**) [275]
P.O. Box 207
Buffalo, NY 14202
716-862-6132

West/Roc Paralegal Association
[130]
Box 101
95 Mamaroneck Ave.
White Plains, NY 10601

NORTH CAROLINA

Cumberland County Paralegal
Association
P.O. Box 1358
Fayetteville, NC 28302

Metrolina Paralegal Association
P.O. Box 36260
Charlotte, NC 28236

North Carolina Paralegal
Association (*)
% T. William Tewes
Fuller & Corbett
P.O. Box 1121
Goldsboro, NC 27533-1121

Professional Legal Assistants
P.O. Box 31951
Raleigh, NC 27622
919-821-7762

Raleigh Wake Paralegal
Association
P.O. Box 1427
Raleigh, NC 27602

Triad Paralegal Association
Drawer U
Greensboro, NC 27402

NORTH DAKOTA

Red River Valley Legal Assistants
(*)
P.O. Box 1954
Fargo, ND 58106

Western Dakota Association of
Legal Assistants (*)
P.O. Box 7304
Bismarck, ND 58502

OHIO

Cincinnati Paralegal Association
(**) [380]
P.O. Box 1515
Cincinnati, OH 45201
513-244-1266

Cleveland Association of Paralegals
(**) [480]
P.O. Box 14247
Cleveland, OH 44114

Greater Dayton Paralegal
Association (**) [160]
P.O. Box 515, Mid City Station
Dayton, OH 45402

Legal Assistants of Central Ohio
(**) [270]
P.O. Box 15182
Columbus, OH 43215-0812
614-224-9700

Northeastern Ohio Paralegal
Association
P.O. Box 9236
Akron, OH 44305

Toledo Association of Legal
Assistants (*) [176]
P.O. Box 1322
Toledo, OH 43603

OKLAHOMA

Oklahoma Paralegal Association
(*)
P.O. Box 18476
Oklahoma City, OK 73154

Tulsa Association of Legal
Assistants (*)
P.O. Box 1484
Tulsa, OK 74101

OREGON

Oregon Legal Assistants
Association (**) [340]

P.O. Box 8523
Portland, OR 97207

Pacific Northwest Legal Assistants
(*)
P.O. Box 1835
Eugene, OR 97440

PENNSYLVANIA

Berks County Paralegal Association
544 Court St.
Reading, PA 19601
215-375-4591

Central Pennsylvania Paralegal
Association (**) [70]
P.O. Box 11814
Harrisburg, PA 17108

Keystone Legal Assistant
Association (*)
% Catrine Nuss
3021 Guineveer Drive, Apt. B4
Harrisburg, PA 17110

Lancaster Area Paralegal
Association
% Rosemary Merwin
Gibble, Kraybill & Hess
41 East Orange St.
Lancaster, PA 17602

Paralegal Association of
Northwestern Pennsylvania (**)
[40]
P.O. Box 1504
Erie, PA 16507

Philadelphia Association of
Paralegals (**) [775]
1411 Walnut St., Suite 200
Philadelphia, PA 19102
215-564-0525

Pittsburgh Paralegal Association
(**) [400]
P.O. Box 2845
Pittsburgh, PA 15230

Wilkes-Barre Area Group
% Tom Albrechta
6 East Green St.
West Hazelton, PA 18201

RHODE ISLAND

Rhode Island Paralegal Association
(**) [200]
P.O. Box 1003
Providence, RI 02901

SOUTH CAROLINA

Charleston Association of Legal
  Assistants
P.O. Box 1511
Charleston, SC 29402

Columbia Association of Legal
  Assistants (**)
P.O. Box 11634
Columbia, SC 29211-1634

Greenville Association of Legal
  Assistants (*)
P.O. Box 10491 F.S.
Greenville, SC 29603

Paralegal Association of the Pee
  Dee [31]
P.O. Box 5592
Florence, SC 29502-5592

SOUTH DAKOTA

South Dakota Legal Assistants
  Association (*) [61]
% Louise Peterson
May, Johnson, Doyle
P.O. Box 1443
Sioux Falls, SD 57101-1443

TENNESSEE

Memphis Paralegal Association
  (**) [105]
P.O. Box 3646
Memphis, TN 38173-0646

Middle Tennessee Paralegal
  Association (**) [145]
P.O. Box 198006
Nashville, TN 37219

Southeast Tennessee Paralegal
  Association
% Calecta Veagles
P.O. Box 1252
Chattanooga, TN 37401

Tennessee Paralegal Association (*)
P.O. Box 11172
Chattanooga, TN 37401

TEXAS

Alamo Area Professional Legal
  Assistants [245]
P.O. Box 524
San Antonio, TX 78292

Capital Area Paralegal Association
  (*) [252]
% Chris Hemingson
Pope, Hopper, Roberts & Warren
111 Congress, Suite 1700
Austin, TX 78701

Dallas Association of Legal
  Assistants (**) [799]
P.O. Box 117885
Carrollton, TX 75011-7885

El Paso Association of Legal
  Assistants (*) [106]
P.O. Box 121
El Paso, TX 79941-0121

Fort Worth Paralegal Association
  [226]
P.O. Box 17021
Fort Worth, TX 76102

Houston Legal Assistants
  Association
P.O. Box 52266
Houston, TX 77052

Legal Assistant Division [2046]
State Bar of Texas
P.O. Box 12487
Austin, TX 78711
512-463-1383

Legal Assistants Association/
  Permian Basin (*)
P.O. Box 10683
Midland, TX 79702

Legal Assistants Professional
  Association (Brazos Valley)
P.O. Box 925
Madisonville, TX 79702

Northeast Texas Association of
  Legal Assistants (*) [29]
P.O. Box 2284
Longview, TX 75606

Nueces County Association of
  Legal Assistants (*)
% Joyce Hoffman
Edwards & Terry
P.O. Box 480
Corpus Christi, TX 78403

Southeast Texas Association of
  Legal Assistants (*) [130]
% Janie Boswell
8335 Homer
Beaumont, TX 77708

Texarkana Association of Legal
  Assistants (*) [40]
P.O. Box 6671
Texarkana, TX 75505

Texas Panhandle Association of
  Legal Assistants (*) [63]
% Lisa Clemens
Morgan, Culton
P.O. Box 189
Amarillo, TX 79105

Tyler Area Association of Legal
  Assistants [94]
P.O. Box 1178
Tyler, TX 75711-1178

West Texas Association of Legal
  Assistants (*) [44]
P.O. Box 1499
Lubbock, TX 79408

UTAH

Legal Assistants Association of
  Utah (*)
P.O. Box 112001
Salt Lake City, UT 84147-2001
801-531-0331

VERMONT

Vermont Paralegal Association [80]
% Trudy Seeley
Langrock, Sperry & Wool
P.O. Drawer 351
Middlebury, VT 05753

VIRGINIA

American Academy of Legal
  Assistants
1022 Paul Avenue N.E.
Norton, VA 24273

Peninsula Legal Assistants (*)
% Diane Morrison
Jones, Blechman, Woltz & Kelly
P.O. Box 12888
Newport News, VA 23612

Richmond Association of Legal
  Assistants (*) [318]
% Vicki Roberts
McGuire, Woods, Battle & Boothe
One James Center
Richmond, VA 23219

Roanoke Valley Paralegal
  Association (**) [70]

P.O. Box 1505
Roanoke, VA 24001
703-224-8000

Tidewater Association of Legal
  Assistants (*)
% Claire Isley
Wilcox & Savage
1800 Sovran Center
Norfolk, VA 23510

VIRGIN ISLANDS

Virgin Islands Paralegals (*)
% Eloise Mack
P.O. Box 6276
St. Thomas, VI 00804

WASHINGTON

Washington Legal Assistants
  Association (**) [453]
2033 6th Ave., Suite 804
Seattle, WA 98121
206-441-6020

WEST VIRGINIA

Legal Assistants of West Virginia
  (*)
% Mary Hanson
Hunt & Wilson
P.O. Box 2506
Charleston, WV 25329-2506

WISCONSIN

Paralegal Association of Wisconsin
  (**) [380]
P.O. Box 92882
Milwaukee, WI 53202
414-272-7168

WYOMING

Legal Assistants of Wyoming (*)
% Nancy Hole
Brown & Drew
123 West First St.
Casper, WY 82601

OTHER ORGANIZATIONS

Alberta Association of Legal
  Assistants
% Mackimme Mathews
700, 401 9th Ave. SW
P.O. Box 2010
Calgary, AB Canada T2P 2M2

American Association for Paralegal
  Education
10100 Santa Fe Dr., Suite 105
P.O. Box 40244
Overland Park, KS 66204
913-381-4458

American Association of Law
  Libraries
53 W. Jackson Blvd., Suite 940
Chicago, IL 60604
312-939-4764

American Association of Petroleum
  Landsmen
4100 Fossil Creek Blvd.
Fort Worth, TX 76137
817-847-7700

American Bar Association
750 N. Lake Shore Dr.
Chicago, IL 60611
312-988-5000
312-988-5618 (Standing
  Committee on Legal Assistants)
202-331-2200 (Wash. D.C. office)

American Paralegal Association
P.O. Box 35233
Los Angeles, CA 90035

American Society of Notaries
918 16th St., NW
Wash. D.C. 20006
202-955-6162

American Society of Questioned
  Document Examiners
1432 Esperson Bldg.
Houston, TX 77002
713-227-4451

Association of American Law
  Schools
1201 Connecticut Ave., NW
Wash. D.C. 20036
202-296-8851

Association of Federal Investigators
1612 K. ST., NW, Suite 506
Wash. D.C. 20006
202-466-7288

Association of Legal
  Administrators
175 E. Hawthorn Parkway
Vernon Hills, IL 60061-1428
312-816-1212

Association of Transportation
  Practitioners
1211 Connecticut Ave., NW
Wash. D.C. 20036
202-466-2080

Canadian Association of Legal
  Assistants
P.O. Box 967
Station "B"

Montreal, Quebec, Canada H3B
  3K5

Coalition for Paralegal and
  Consumer Rights
1714 Stockton St., Suite 400
San Francisco, CA 94133

Federal Criminal Investigators
  Association
P.O. Box 1256
Detroit, MI 48231
512-229-5610

HALT (Help Abolish Legal
  Tyranny)
1319 F. St. NW, Suite 300
Wash. D.C. 20004
202-347-9600

Independent Association of
  Questioned Document
  Examiners
403 W. Washington
Red Oak, IA 51566
712-623-9130

Institute of Law Clerks of Ontario
Suite 502, 425 University Avenue
Toronto, ON Canada M5G 1T6

Institute of Legal Executives
Kempston Manor
Kempston, Bedford England

International Association of Arson
  Investigators
5428 Del Maria Way

Louisville, KY 40291
502-491-7482

International Association of Auto
  Theft Investigators
255 S. Vernon
Dearborn, MI 48124
313-561-8583

Legal Assistant Management
  Association
P.O. Box 40129
Overland Park, KS 66204
913-381-4458

National Association for Law
  Placement
166 Conn. Avenue, Suite 450
Wash. D.C. 20009
202-667-1666

National Association of Document
  Examiners
20 Nassau St.
Princeton, NJ 08542
609-924-8193

National Association of Enrolled
  Agents
6000 Executive Blvd., Suite 205
Rockville, MD 20852
800-424-4339

National Association for
  Independent Paralegals

635 5th St. West
Sonoma, CA 95476
800-542-0034
800-332-4557

National Association of Law Firm
  Marketing Administrators
60 Revere Drive, #500
Northbrook, IL 60062
708-480-9641

National Association of Law
  Placement
1666 Connecticut Ave. NW
Wash. D.C. 20009
202-667-1666

National Association of Legal
  Secretaries
2250 East 73d St., Suite 550
Tulsa, OK 74136-6864
918-493-3540

National Association of
  Professional Process Servers
306 H. St. NE
Wash. D.C. 20002
202-547-5710

National Indian Paralegal
  Association
7524 Major Ave.
Brooklyn Park, MN 55443

National Legal Assistant
  Conference Center
2444 Wilshire Blvd., Suite 301
Santa Monica, CA 90403

National Notary Association
8236 Remmet Ave.
Canoga Park, CA 91304-7184
818-713-4000

National Organization of Social
  Security Claimants
  Representatives
19 E. Central Ave., 2nd F1.
Pearl River, NY 10965
800-431-2804

National Paralegal Association
P.O. Box 406
Solebury, PA 18963
215-297-8333

National Resource Center for
  Consumers of Legal Services
1444 Eye St. NW
Wash. D.C. 20005
202-842-3503

National Shorthand Reporters
  Association
118 Park St., SE
Vienna, VA 22180
703-281-4677

Associations of Attorneys

 ## STATE AND LOCAL BAR ASSOCIATIONS

ALABAMA

Alabama State Bar
P.O. Box 671
Montgomery, AL 36104
205-269-1515

Birmingham Bar Association
109 N. 20th St., 2nd Fl.
Birmingham, AL 35203
205-251-8006

ALASKA

Alaska Bar Association
P.O. Box 100279
Anchorage, AK 99501
907-272-7469

ARIZONA

Maricopa County Bar Association
333 W. Roosevelt St.
Phoenix, AZ 85003
602-257-4200

State Bar of Arizona
363 N. 1st Ave.
Phoenix, AZ 85003
602-252-4804

ARKANSAS

Arkansas Bar Association
400 W. Markham
Little Rock, AR 72201
501-375-4605

CALIFORNIA

Alameda County Bar Association
405 14th St., Suite 208
Oakland, CA 94612
415-893-7160

Bar Association of San Francisco
685 Market St., #700
San Francisco, CA 94105
415-764-1600

Beverly Hills Bar Association
300 S. Beverly Dr., #201
Beverly Hills, CA 90212
213-553-6644

Lawyers Club of Los Angeles
700 S. Flower St.
Los Angeles, CA 90017
213-624-2525

Lawyers' Club of San Francisco
685 Market St., #750
San Francisco, CA 94105
415-882-9150

Los Angeles County Bar
  Association
617 S. Olive St.
Los Angeles, CA 90014
213-627-2727

Orange County Bar Association
601 Civic Center Dr. West
Santa Ana, CA 92701
714-541-6222

San Diego County Bar Association
1333 7th Ave.
San Diego, CA 92101
619-231-0781

Santa Clara County Bar
  Association
2001 Gateway Pl., #220 West
San Jose, CA 95110
408-453-3448

State Bar of California
555 Franklin St.
San Francisco, CA 94102
415-561-8200

COLORADO

Colorado Bar Association
1900 Grant St., #950
Denver, CO 80203-4309
303-860-1115

Denver Bar Association
1900 Grant St., Suite 950
Denver, CO 80201-4309
303-860-1115

CONNECTICUT

Connecticut Bar Association
101 Corporate Pl.
Rocky Hill, CT 06067
203-721-0025

DELAWARE

Delaware Bar Association
708 Market Street
Wilmington, DE 19899
302-658-5278

DISTRICT OF COLUMBIA

Bar Association of the District of
  Columbia
1819 H. St. NW, 12th Fl.
Wash. D.C. 20006
202-293-6600

District of Columbia Bar
1707 L. St. NW, 6th Fl.

Wash. D.C. 20036
202-331-3883

FLORIDA

Florida Bar
650 Apalachee Parkway
Tallahassee, FL 32399-2300
904-561-5600

Dade County Bar Association
111 N.W. First Ave.
Miami, FL 33128
305-371-2220

GEORGIA

Atlanta Bar Association
100 Peachtree St. NW
Atlanta, GA 30303
404-521-0781

State Bar of Georgia
800 The Hurt Bldg.
Atlanta, GA 30303
404-527-8700

HAWAII

Hawaii State Bar
1001 Bishop St., Suite 950
Honolulu, HI 96813
808-537-1868

IDAHO

Idaho State Bar
P.O. Box 895
Boise, ID 83702
208-342-8958

ILLINOIS

Chicago Bar Association
321 S. Plymouth Ct.
Chicago, IL 60603-1575
312-782-7348

Chicago Council of Lawyers
220 S. State St., Rm. 800
Chicago, IL 60604
312-427-0710

Illinois State Bar Association
424 S. Second St.
Springfield, IL 62701
217-525-1760
800-252-8908
312-726-8775 (Chicago)
800-442-ISBA

Illinois Trial Lawyers Association
110 W. Edwards St.
P.O. Box 5000
Springfield, IL 62705
217-798-0755
800-252-8501

INDIANA

Indianapolis Bar Association
10 West Market St.
Indianapolis, IN 46204
317-632-8240

Indiana State Bar Association
230 E. Ohio St., 6th Fl.
Indianapolis, IN 46204
317-639-5465

IOWA

Iowa State Bar Association
1101 Fleming Bldg.
Des Moines, IA 50309
515-243-3179

KANSAS

Kansas Bar Association
1200 Harrison St.
Topeka, KS 66612
913-234-5696

KENTUCKY

Kentucky Bar Association
West Main at Kentucky River
Frankfort, KY 40601
502-564-3795

Louisville Bar Association
707 W. Main St., #200
Louisville, KY 40202
502-583-5314

LOUISIANA

Louisiana State Bar Association
601 St. Charles Ave.
New Orleans, LA 70130
504-566-1600

Louisiana Trial Lawyers
 Association
442 Europe St.
P.O. Drawer 4289
Baton Rouge, LA 70821
504-383-5554

MAINE

Maine State Bar Association
124 State St.
P.O. Box 788
Augusta, ME 04330
207-622-7523

MARYLAND

Bar Association of Baltimore City
111 N. Calvert St.
Baltimore, MD 21202
301-539-5936

Maryland State Bar Association
520 W. Fayette St.
Baltimore, MD 21201
301-685-7878

MASSACHUSETTS

Boston Bar Association
16 Beacon St.
Boston, MA 02108
617-742-0615

Massachusetts Bar Association
20 West St.
Boston, MA 02111
617-542-3602

MICHIGAN

Detroit Bar Association
2380 Penobscot Bldg.
Detroit, MI 48226
313-961-6120

Michigan Trial Lawyers
 Association
501 S. Capitol Ave., Suite 405
Lansing, MI 48933-2327
517-482-7740

Oakland County Bar Association
1200 N. Telegraph Rd., Suite 532
Pontiac, MI 48053
313-338-2100

State Bar of Michigan
306 Townsend St.
Lansing, MI 48933-2083
517-372-9030

MINNESOTA

Hennepin County Bar Association
430 Marquette Ave., No. 402
Minneapolis, MN 55487
612-340-0022

Minnesota State Bar Association
430 Marquette Ave., Suite 403
Minneapolis, MN 55401
612-333-1183
800-292-4152

MISSISSIPPI

Mississippi State Bar
643 N. State St.
Jackson, MS 39202
601-948-4471

MISSOURI

Bar Association of Metropolitan
Saint Louis
One Mercantile Center #3600
St. Louis, MO 63101
314-421-4134

Kansas City Metropolitan Bar
Association
1125 Grand Ave.
Kansas City, MO 64106
816-474-4322

Missouri Bar
326 Monroe
Jefferson City, MO 65102
314-635-4128

MONTANA

State Bar of Montana,
46 N. Last Chance Gulch
P.O. Box 577
Helena, MT 59624
406-442-7660

NEBRASKA

Nebraska State Bar Association
635 S. 14th St.
Lincoln, NE 68508
402-475-7091

NEVADA

State Bar of Nevada
295 Holcomb Ave., Suite 2
Reno, NV 89502-1085
702-382-0502

NEW HAMPSHIRE

New Hampshire Bar Association
112 Pleasant Street
Concord, NH 03301
603-224-6942

NEW JERSEY

Essex County Bar Association
5 Becker Farm Road
Roseland, NJ 07068
201-622-6207

New Jersey State Bar Association
1 Constitution Sq.
New Brunswick, NJ 08901-1500
201-249-5000

NEW MEXICO

State Bar of New Mexico
121 Tijeras St. NE
Albuquerque, NM 87102
505-842-6132
800-876-6227

New Mexico Trial Lawyers'
Association Foundation
P.O. Box 301
Albuquerque, NM 87103
505-243-6003

NEW YORK

Association of the Bar of the City
of New York
42 W. 44th St.
New York, NY 10036
212-382-6600

New York County Lawyers
Association
14 Vesey St.
New York, NY 10007
212-267-6646

New York State Bar Association
1 Elk St.
Albany, NY 12207
518-463-3200

New York State Trial Lawyers
Association
132 Nassau St.
New York, NY 10038
212-349-5890

NORTH CAROLINA

North Carolina Bar Association
1312 Annapolis Dr.
Raleigh, NC 27611
919-828-0561

North Carolina State Bar
1312 Annapolis Dr.
Raleigh, NC 27611
919-828-0561

NORTH DAKOTA

State Bar Association of North
Dakota
515½ E. Broadway, Suite 101
Bismarck, ND 58501
701-255-1404
800-472-2685

OHIO

Cincinnati Bar Association
35 E. 7th St., 8th Fl.
Cincinnati, OH 45202-2411
513-381-8213

Cleveland Bar Association
118 St. Clair Ave., NE
Cleveland, OH 44114-1523
216-696-3525

Columbus Bar Association
40 S. 3rd St., 6th Fl.
Columbus, OH 43215-5134
614-221-4112

Cuyahoga County Bar Association
1228 Euclid Ave., No. 370
Cleveland, OH 44115
216-621-5112

Ohio State Bar Association
33 W. 11th Ave.
Columbus, OH 43201
614-421-2121

OKLAHOMA

Oklahoma Bar Association
1901 N. Lincoln
Oklahoma City, OK 73105
405-524-2365
800-522-8065

Oklahoma County Bar Association
119 W. Robinson #240
Oklahoma City, OK 73102
405-236-8421

Tulsa County Bar Association
1446 S. Boston
Tulsa, OK 74119-3613
918-584-5243

OREGON

Multnomah Bar Association
711 SW Adler, Suite 311
Portland, OR 97205
503-222-3275

Oregon State Bar
5200 S.W. Meadows Rd.

P.O. Box 1689
Lake Oswego, OR 97035
503-620-0222

PENNSYLVANIA

Allegheny County Bar Association
420 Grant Bldg.
Pittsburgh, PA 15219
412-261-6161

Pennsylvania Bar Association
100 South St.
P.O. Box 186
Harrisburg, PA 17108
717-238-6715

Philadelphia Bar Association
One Reading Bldg.
Philadelphia, PA 19107
215-238-6300

PUERTO RICO

Puerto Rico Bar Association
P.O. Box 1900
San Juan, PR 00908
809-721-3358

Puerto Rican Bar Association
888 Grand Concourse, Suite 1-0
Bronx, NY 10451
212-292-8201

RHODE ISLAND

Rhode Island Bar Association
91 Friendship St.
Providence, RI 02903
401-421-5740

SOUTH CAROLINA

South Carolina Bar Association
950 Taylor St.
Columbia, SC 29202
803-799-6653

SOUTH DAKOTA

State Bar of South Dakota
Pierre, SD 57501
605-224-7554

TENNESSEE

Tennessee Bar Association
3622 Westend Ave.
Nashville, TN 37205
615-383-7421

TEXAS

Dallas Bar Association
2101 Ross Ave.
Dallas, TX 75201
214-969-7066

Houston Bar Association
1001 Fannin, Suite 1300
Houston, TX 77002
713-759-1133

State Bar of Texas
1414 Colorado
Austin, TX 78711
512-463-1463

UTAH

Utah Bar Association
645 S. 200 East
Salt Lake City, UT 84111
801-531-9077

VERMONT

Vermont Bar Association
P.O. Box 100
Montpelier, VT 05602
802-223-2020
800-642-3153

VIRGINIA

Virginia Bar Association
701 E. Franklin St., Suite 1515
Richmond, VA 23219
804-644-0041

Virginia State Bar
801 E. Main St., Suite 1000
Richmond, VA 23219
804-786-2061

VIRGIN ISLANDS

Virgin Islands Bar Association
46 King St.
Christiansted, VI 00822
809-778-7497

WASHINGTON

Seattle-King County Bar
900 4th Ave., #600
Seattle, WA 98164
206-624-9365

Washington State Bar Association
2001 6th Ave.
Seattle, WA 98121-2599
206-448-0441

WEST VIRGINIA

West Virginia Bar Association
100 Capitol St.
Charleston, WV 25301
304-342-1474

West Virginia Sate Bar
E-400 State Capitol
Charleston, WV 25305
304-346-8414

West Virginia Trial Lawyers
  Association
P.O. Box 3968
Charleston, WV 25339
304-344-0692

WISCONSIN

Milwaukee Bar Association
533 E. Wells St.
Milwaukee, WI 53202
414-274-6760

State Bar of Wisconsin
402. W. Wilson
Madison, WI 53703
608-257-3838
800-362-8906

WYOMING

Wyoming State Bar
500 Randall Ave.
Cheyenne, WY 82001
307-632-9061

OTHER ATTORNEY ASSOCIATIONS

American Academy of Hospitals
  Attorneys
American Hospital Association
840 N. Lake Shore Dr.
Chicago, IL 60611
312-280-6601

American Academy of Matrimonial
  Lawyers
20 N. Michigan Ave., Suite 540
Chicago, IL 60602
312-263-6477

American Association of Public
  Welfare Attorneys
810 1st St. NE, Suite 500
Wash. D.C. 20002
202-682-0100

American Bar Association
750 N Lake Shore Dr.
Chicago, IL 60611
312-988-5000
202-331-2200 (Wash. D.C. office)

American Blind Lawyers
  Association
1010 Vermont Ave., NW
Wash. D.C. 20005
202-393-3666
800-424-8666

American Board of Professional
  Liability Attorneys
175 E. Shore Rd.
Great Neck, NY 11023
516-487-1990

American Board of Trial Advocates
16633 Ventura Blvd., Suite 1015
Encino, CA 91436
818-501-3250

American College of Probate
  Counsel
2716 Ocean Park Blvd., Suite 1080
Santa Monica, CA 90405
213-450-2033

American College of Trial Lawyers
10886 Wilshire Blvd.
Los Angeles, CA 90024
213-879-0143

American Corporate Counsel
  Association
1225 Connecticut Ave., Suite 302

Wash. D.C. 20036
202-296-4522

American Immigration Lawyers
  Association
1000 16th St., NW, Suite 604
Wash. D.C. 20036
202-331-0046

Association of Defense Trial
  Attorneys
600 Jefferson Bank Bldg.
Peoria, IL 61602
309-676-0400

Association of Life Insurance
  Counsel
201 Park Ave. South
New York, NY 10003
212-679-1110

Association of Trial Lawyers of
  America
1050 31st St. NW
Wash. D.C. 20007
202-965-3500
800-424-2727

Black Entertainment & Sports
  Lawyers Association
111 Broadway
New York, NY 10006
212-587-0300

Decalogue Society of Lawyers
179 W. Washington St., Suite 350
Chicago, IL 60602
312-263-6493

Federal Bar Association
1815 H. St., Suite 408
Wash. D.C. 20006
202-638-0252

Federal Communications Bar
  Association
1150 Connecticut Ave., NW
Wash. D.C. 20036
202-833-2684

Federal Energy Bar Association
1900 M. St. NW, Suite 620
Wash. D.C. 20006
202-223-5625

Federation of Insurance &
  Corporate Counsel
15 Ridge Rd.

Marblehead, MA 01945
617-639-0698

Hispanic National Bar Association
100 W. Randolph
Chicago, IL 60601
312-814-3813

Incorporated Society of Irish/
  American Lawyers
15140 Farmington Rd.
Livonia, MI 48154
313-522-5900

Inter-American Bar Association
1889 F. St. NW, Suite LL-2
Wash. D.C. 20006
202-789-2747

International Academy of Trial
  Lawyers
210 S. 1st St., Suite 206
San Jose, CA 95113
408-275-6767

International Association of
  Defense Counsel
20 N. Wacker Dr., Suite 3100
Chicago, IL 60606
312-368-1494

International Federation of Women
  Lawyers
186 5th Ave.

New York, NY 10010
212-206-1666

International Legal Defense
  Counsel
111 S. 15th St., 24th Fl.
Philadelphia, PA 19102
215-977-9982

International Trade Commission
  Trial Lawyers Association
815 Connecticut Ave. NW
Wash. D.C. 20006
202-659-5070

Maritime Law Association of the
  United States
1 Battery Park Plaza
New York, NY 10004
212-422-7585

Mexican-American Legal Defense
  and Education Fund

1430 K. St. NW
Wash. D.C. 20005
202-628-4074

NAACP Legal Defense and
Education Fund
1275 K. St. NW
Wash. D.C. 20005
202-682-1300

National Academy of Elder Law
Attorneys
1730 E. River Rd., Suite 107
Tucson, AZ 85718

National American Indian Court
Judges Association
1000 Connecticut Ave., NW
Wash. D.C. 20036
202-296-0685

National Association of Attorneys
General
444 N. Capitol St. NW, Suite 403
Wash. D.C. 20001
202-628-0435

National Association of Black
Women Attorneys
3711 Macomb St. NW
Wash. D.C. 20016
202-966-9693

National Association of Bond
Attorneys
P.O. Box 397
Hinsdale, IL 60522
312-920-0160

National Association of College &
University Attorneys
1 Dupont Circle, NW, Suite 620
Wash. D.C. 20036
202-833-8390

National Association of Counsel
for Children
1205 Oneida St.
Denver, CO 80220
303-321-3963

National Association of County
Civil Attorneys
440 1st St. NW
Wash. D.C. 20001
202-393-6226

National Association of Criminal
Defense Lawyers
1110 Vermont Ave., Suite 1150
Wash. D.C. 20005
202-872-8688

National Association of Railroad
Trial Counsel
88 Alma Real Dr., Suite 103A
Pacific Palisades, CA 90272
213-459-7659

National Association of Women
Judges
300 Newport Ave.
Williamsburg, VA 23185
804-253-2000

National Association of Women
Lawyers
750 N. Lake Shore Dr.
Chicago, IL 60611
312-988-6186

National Bar Association
1225 11th St., NW
Wash. D.C. 20001
202-842-3900

National Conference of Black
Lawyers
126 W. 119th St.
New York, NY 10026
212-864-4000

National Conference of Women's
Bar Associations
113 W. Franklin St.
Baltimore, MD 21201
504-835-6705

National District Attorneys
Association
1033 N. Fairfax St., Suite 200

Alexandria, VA 22314
703-549-9222

National Gay Rights Advocates
540 Castro St.
San Francisco, CA 94114
415-863-3624

National Lawyers Guild
55 6th Ave.
New York, NY 10013
212-966-5000

National Legal Aid & Defender
Association
1625 K. St., Suite 800
Wash. D.C. 20006
202-452-0620

National Women's Law Center
1616 P. St. NW
Wash. D.C. 20036
202-328-5160

Native American Rights Fund
1712 N. St. NW
Wash. D. C. 20036
202-785-4166

Puerto Rican Legal Defense &
Education Fund
99 Hudson St., 24th Fl.
New York, NY 10013
212-219-3360

Sports Lawyers Association
P.O. Box 5684
Lakeland, FL 33807
813-646-5091

Transportation Lawyers
Association
3310 Harrison
Topeka, KS 66611
913-266-7014

Volunteer Lawyers for the Arts
1285 Avenue of the Americas
New York, NY 10019
212-977-9270

MISCELLANEOUS

American Arbitration Association
140 W. 51st St.
New York, NY 10020
212-484-4100

American Prepaid Legal Services
Institute
750 N. Lake Shore Dr.

Chicago, IL 60611
312-988-5751

Legal Services Corporation
400 Virginia Ave. SW
Wash. D.C. 20024
202-863-1820

National Clients Council
2617 Martha St.

Philadelphia, PA 19125
215-686-2913

National Conference of Bar
Examiners
333 N. Michigan, Suite 1025
Chicago, IL 60601
312-641-0963

D

Federal Government Organization Chart

The Government of the United States

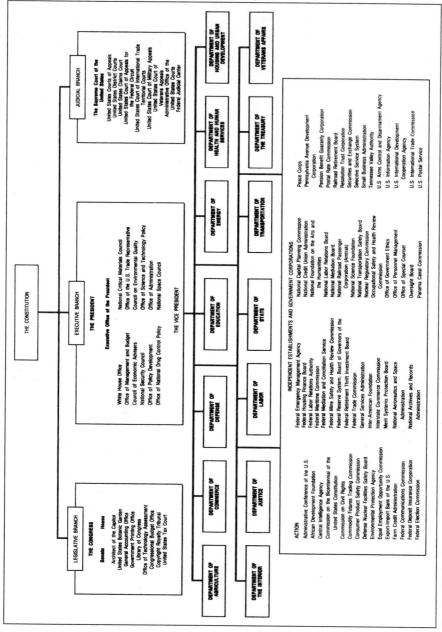

Source: United States Government Manual 1989-90.

E

Survey of Nonlawyer Practice before Federal Administrative Agencies

Standing Committee on Lawyers' Responsibility for Client Protection and the American Bar Association Center for Professional Responsibility

February, 1985

I. Background

The American Bar Association Standing Committee on Lawyers' Responsibility for Client Protection disseminated this survey to thirty-three (33) federal administrative agencies in late August, 1984. The survey was intended to provide background information on the experiences of agencies permitting nonlawyer practice (other than for purposes of self-representation). During September and October ninety-seven percent (97%) of the agencies responded either over the phone or by mail following initial contact with their Offices of General Counsel. The ABA Center for Professional Responsibility tabulated the results in October, 1984.

II. Brief Analysis and Conclusions

We found that the overwhelming majority of agencies studied permit nonlawyer representation in both adversarial and nonadversarial proceedings.* However, most of them seem to encounter lay practice very infrequently (in less than 5% of adjudications), while only a few encounter lay practice as often as lawyer practice. Thus, although universally permitted, lay practice before federal agencies rarely occurs.

Few of the responding agencies comprehensively monitor or control the lay practice that does occur. Only about twenty percent (20%) require nonlawyers to register with the agency before permitting them to practice. Registration procedures may range from simply listing nonlawyers' names to more formalized certifying or licensing procedures which may include testing and character reviews. Proceedings in most of these agencies tend to require highly technical or specialized knowledge. Registration insures that lay representation meets an appropriate level of quality and competence. In at least one agency, registration insures that nonlawyer representatives will charge only nominal fees or no fees at all.

---

*A proceeding is adversarial if there is an opposing side in the controversy, whether or not the other side is represented. A proceeding is nonadversarial if only one side is appearing before the agency official.

CHART I Regulations Governing Nonlawyer Representation, Frequency, and Type of Practice

Agency	Statute/ Regulation Permitting Appearance	Permits Nonlawyer Adversarial Representation	Permits Nonlawyer Nonadversarial Representation	Provisions Limiting or Governing Practice	Frequency of Nonlawyer Representation	Change in Frequency of Nonlawyer Rep. w/in Past 6 Years	Most Common Type(s) of Nonlawyer Representation
Bd. of Immigration Appeals: Immigration and Naturalization Serv.	8 CFR § 292.1-3	Yes	Yes	"Accredited representative"[1] working for "recognized organization"[2] may charge only nominal fees. "Reputable individual"[3] may not charge fees	No statistics available	No statistics available	One time only by family member/friend; charitable, religious or social service organization
Civil Aeronautics Bd.	14 CFR § 300.1-6 14 CFR § 302.11	Yes	Yes	None	Fewer than 6 appearances per yr., less than 1% of appearances[4]	None	Economic consultants for corporations
Comptroller of the Currency	12 CFR § 19.3	Yes[5]	Yes	Nonlawyer may be required to file a power of attorney or show to the satisfaction of the Comptroller the possession of requisite qualifications	None	None	None
Consumer Product Safety Comm'n	16 CFR § 1025.61 et seq.	Yes	Yes	Filing and approval of proof of qualifications. See 16 CFR § 1025.65	Very infrequent, 2–5% of appearances	None	Non-fee by industry rep., consultant, or private service agency

Dep't of Agric., Agricultural Marketing Serv.	7 CFR § 50.27	Yes	Yes	None	Fewer than 3 appearances per yr., less than 1% of appearances	Decreased,[6] no statistics available	Economist/ accountant providing assistance prior to appearance
Dep't of Commerce, Office of Secretary	Those of other agencies governing appearances before administrative bodies, e.g., MSPB, 5 CFR Part 1201	Yes	Yes	Reasonable atty's fees for litigated matters set by agency; maximum atty's fees for settlement set at $75./hr.; government pays fees to winning atty	No statistics available	No statistics available	Non-fee by union reps.
Dep't of Commerce, Patent and Trademark Office	35 U.S.C. §§ 31-33	Yes	Yes	Only registered[7] practitioners permitted to practice	Less than 16% of appearances[8]	None	Repeated practice for a fee by registered agents

[1] May become accredited by the Department of Immigration Appeals (D.I.A.) by submitting an application through a recognized organization for review of character and fitness and experience with and knowledge of immigration law. No formal testing requirement or licensing fee.

[2] Typically a religious, charitable or social service organization becomes recognized by submitting an application for approval to the D.I.A. assuring that it will charge only nominal fees and assess no representation charges.

[3] Typically a family member or friend submits declaration that he or she charges no fee, has a preexisting relationship with immigrant-applicant, and appears only on individual basis at request of immigrant-applicant.

[4] Although nonlawyer practice [is] not discouraged, complexity of agency proceedings tends to require specialized legal practice. Typical parties, large corporations or businesses, tend to hire lawyers.

[5] Permitted but lay representation rare because of complex proceedings and substantial rights or amounts of money involved.

[6] In agency's early history, economists provided a substantial amount of representation because of the economic nature of agency proceedings. As proceedings become more sophisticated, economists began aiding lawyers rather than assuming primary responsibility for legal representation. Representation by economists is now rare, and lawyers handle the bulk of representation.

[7] Nonlawyers become registered by passing a character and fitness review and an examination. Nonlawyers having served four years in the examining corps of the Patent and Trademark Office (P.T.O.) may waive the exam. See 57 CFR § 1.341.

[8] Nonlawyers comprise about 16% of registered practitioners appear before P.T.O., but not all registered practitioners appear before P.T.O., so that nonlawyers probably appear in less than 16% of patent applications filed with P.T.O.

CHART I Regulations Governing Nonlawyer Representation, Frequency, and Type of Practice—*Continued*

Agency	Statute/ Regulation Permitting Appearance	Permits Nonlawyer Adversarial Representation	Permits Nonlawyer Nonadversarial Representation	Provisions Limiting or Governing Practice	Frequency of Nonlawyer Representation	Change in Frequency of Nonlawyer Rep. w/in Past 6 Years	Most Common Type(s) of Nonlawyer Representation
Dep't of Health and Human Services, Food and Drug Admin.	32 CFR §§ 12.40, 12.45	Yes	Yes	None	No appearances in recent years	None	None
Dep't of Justice, Drug Enforcement Admin.	21 CFR § 1316.50	Yes	N/A, all proceedings adversarial	None	2 to 3 appearances per yr., 5% of appearances[9]	None	One time only by officer/employee of small family-owned business
Dep't of Justice, Foreign Claims Settlement Comm'n	45 CFR § 500.1-6	No	No[10]	Lawyer's fees set by statute at 10% of claim award and deducted from award	N/A[11]	N/A[11]	Family member providing assistance prior to appearance
Dep't of Labor, Benefits Review Bd.	20 CFR § 802.201(b) 20 CFR § 802.202	Yes	N/A, all proceedings adversarial	Employer pays fee for successful claimant represented by lawyer; claimant pays fee when represented by nonlawyer; lawyer may acquire lien against award; nonlawyers may not.[12] Professional status is criterion for determining fees.[13]	2–4% of appearances	None	Repeated practice for fee
Dep't of Labor, Employees Compensation Appeals Bd.	20 CFR § 501.11	Yes	N/A, all proceedings adversarial	All fees approved by board	Appear as frequently as lawyers	None	One time only by family member/ friend; repeated practice for a fee

Dept't of Labor, National Railroad Adjustment Bd.	45 U.S.C. § 3153	Yes	N/A	Only entities identified in 45 U.S.C. § 151 allowed to practice	Almost 100% of appearances	None	Industry employees
Dept't of Labor, Wage and Appeals Bd.	20 CFR § 725.362(a) 20 CFR § 725.365 20 CFR § 725.366(b)	Yes	N/A	Fees must be reasonably commensurate with services performed;[14] attorney's fee deducted from award; employer pays fee for successful claimant represented by lawyer; claimant prep fee when represented by nonlawyer; lawyer may require lien against award, nonlawyers may not.[15]	3% of appearances; as in 180 case/yr.	Decrease due to investigations by Office of Inspector General into unauthorized receipt of fees	One time only by family member or friend; repeated practice for fee; assistance prior to appearance

[9] Appearances are by the employees or officers of small family-owned businesses, analogous to pro se appearances.

[10] The agency only allows "representation" by bar members. Family members may sometimes assist in preparation of claims or at oral hearings, typically where elderly parent has language barrier problems.

[11] No nonlawyer representation allowed.

[12] These policies may tend to discourage lay representation.

[13] Typically approved rates for nonlawyers are less than half of those attorneys receive.

[14] See 20 CFR § 725.366(b) (black lung) and 20 CFR § 702.132 (longshore).

[15] These policies may tend to discourage lay representation.

CHART I Regulations Governing Nonlawyer Representation, Frequency, and Type of Practice—*Continued*

Agency	Statute/ Regulation Permitting Appearance	Permits Nonlawyer Adversarial Representation	Permits Nonlawyer Nonadversarial Representation	Provisions Limiting or Governing Practice	Frequency of Nonlawyer Representation	Change in Frequency of Nonlawyer Rep. w/in Past 6 Years	Most Common Type(s) of Nonlawyer Representation
Dep't of Transportation, Maritime Admin.	46 CFR § 201.21	Yes	Yes	Only registered nonlawyers permitted to practice	Very infrequent	None	
Federal Deposit Ins. Corp.	12 CFR § 308.04	Yes	Yes	Only qualified nonlawyers permitted to represent	10 to 20 appearances per yr., 5% of appearances	50% decrease	One time only by family member/ friend; nonlawyer assistance prior to appearance
Federal Energy Regulatory Comm'n	18 CFR § 385.2101	Yes	Yes	None	1 or 2 per yr.	None	Engineering firm assisting in technical nonadversarial proceeding
Federal Maritime Comm'n	46 CFR § 502.30	Yes	Yes	Only registered nonlawyers permitted to appear[16]	.5 to 1% of appearances	None	One time only by family member/ friend; non-fee by industry rep., consultant or private service agency
Federal Mine Safety & Health Review Comm'n	29 CFR § 2700.3(b)	Yes, at trial hearings before Administrative Law Judges (ALJ); at appellate reviews before commissioners	N/A	Nonlawyer may practice only if party, "representative of miners,"[17] or owner, partner, full time officer or employee of party-business entity; otherwise permitted to appear for limited purpose in special proceedings	5–10% of appearances	None	Non-fee by industry rep., consultant or private service agency

General Accounting Office	31 U.S.C. § 731-732; 4 CFR §§ 11 and 28; GAO Orders 2713.2, 2752.1, and 2777.1	Yes, in adverse actions, grievance proceedings, and discrimination complaints	Yes	Nonlawyers not permitted fees; government pays fees to winning representatives[18]	Very infrequent	Not aware of any	Repeated practice for fee by certified public accountant or enrolled agent
Internal Revenue Serv.	13 CFR Part 10; 31 U.S.C. § 330; Treasury Dept. Circular 230	Yes	Yes	Noncertified public accountant and nonlawyer must become enrolled agent[19] to practice	As frequent as lawyer representation[20]	Increased, no statistics available	
Interstate Commerce Comm'n	49 CFR § 1103	Yes	Yes	Fee limitations;[21] only registered nonlawyer permitted to practice,[22] however, self-representation is allowed without registration	1,600 nonlawyers now registered and account for 5% of appearances.[23]	Decreased,[24] no statistics available	Repeated practice for a fee
National Credit Union Admin.	12 CFR § 747	Yes	Yes	None	No statistics available	Decreased, no statistics available	Credit union representatives

[16] Certificates of registration are issued on payment of $13.00 processing fee and completion of application form indicating sufficient educational qualifications and recommendations. There is no testing or formal licensing.

[17] See generally 30 CFR § 40.1(b).

[18] As provided in discrimination statutes, backpay act, and appeals authorized by law.

[19] Nonlawyers and noncertified public accountants become enrolled agents by 1) passing a character and fitness review, and 2) successful completion of special enrollment examination testing on federal taxation and related matters, or 3) former employment with the IRS, provided duties qualify the individual. Lawyers and certified public accountants may practice without enrollment.

[20] Includes representation by certified public accountants as well as enrolled agents.

[21] Practitioners may not overestimate the value of services, accept compensation from party other than client, make contingent fee arrangements or divide fees with laypersons. See 49 CFR § 1103.70.

[22] To become registered applicant must 1) meet educational and experience requirements, 2) undergo character and fitness review, 3) pass exam administered by the agency testing knowledge in the field of transportation, and 4) take an oath. See 49 CFR § 1103.3.

[23] Figure includes appearances in rulemaking as well as adjudicatory proceedings.

[24] Deregulation has reduced the caseload while proceedings have become more complex, creating a greater need for legal expertise.

CHART I Regulations Governing Nonlawyer Representation, Frequency, and Type of Practice—*Continued*

Agency	Statute/ Regulation Permitting Appearance	Permits Nonlawyer Adversarial Representation	Permits Nonlawyer Nonadversarial Representation	Provisions Limiting or Governing Practice	Frequency of Nonlawyer Representation	Change in Frequency of Nonlawyer Rep. w/in Past 6 Years	Most Common Type(s) of Nonlawyer Representation
National Labor Relations Bd.		Yes	Yes	None	Infrequent	None	
National Mediation Bd.	None, agency governed by 29 CFR § 1200 *et seq.*	N/A, all proceedings adversarial	Yes	None	200 appearances per yr., appear twice as frequently as lawyers	Decreased, no statistics available	Union representatives
National Transportation Safety Bd.	49 CFR § 821 49 CFR § 831 49 CFR § 845	Yes	Yes	In adjudication lawyer representation encouraged; in investigation lawyer participation discouraged because technical expertise required; parties[25] participate in investigations	Very infrequent except at investigatory levels	None	Manufacturers at investigatory levels
Occupational Safety and Health Review Comm'n	29 CFR § 2200.22	Yes	N/A, all proceedings adversarial	Optional simplified procedures to encourage self-representation by small businesses	20% of appearances[26]	20% decrease[27]	Nonlegal employee representing employer; union representative
Small Business Admin.	13 CFR § 121.11 13 CFR § 134.16	Yes	N/A, all proceedings adversarial	None	Less than 1% of appearances[28]	None	

Social Security Admin.	42 USC § 406(a) 29 CFR	Yes, tentatively as part of experiment; generally agency has no adversarial proceedings	Yes	Claimants advised of advantages of representation at hearing level;[29] fees set by agency;[30] attorneys' fees withheld from awards[31]	Appear in 13% of total hearings or in 25–30% of hearings with representation	None, although lawyer representation increased by 56% since 1978[32]	One time only by family member/friend; repeated practice for fee; non-fee rep. by legal services paralegal
U.S. Customs Serv.	None	Yes	Yes	None	5 to 15% of caseload volume	None	Repeated practice for fee by licensed customs brokers and former customs officials
U.S. Environmental Protection Agency	40 CFR § 124 40 CFR § 164.30 40 CFR § 22.10	Yes	N/A	None	No appearances	None	None

25 "Parties" includes manufacturers, unions, operators and other regulatory agencies.

26 Statistic includes pro se representation.

27 Nonlawyer practice accounted in 1980 for 40% of the agency's caseload but decreased in 1982–83 to 20%. Decrease may result from increasing complexity in cases causing claimants to seek legal representation.

28 Figure excludes pro se appearances in size and Standard Industrial Classification (SIC) Appeals. Approximately 50% of size and SIC appeals are conducted pro se by nonlawyers.

29 When hearing request [is] filed, agency sends a letter to unrepresented claimant describing advantages of representation. Attached to letter is a list of organizations which may provide representation. The list includes lawyer referral services, legal aid groups, law schools, etc.

30 The agency sets all fees based on criteria listed in 20 CFR § 404.1725(b), including extent and type of services, complexity of case, level of skill and competence required in performing services, time spent, results achieved, level at which representative became involved, and amount requested.

31 When decision is entered in favor of a claimant represented by a lawyer in a Title II or Black Lung case, normally 25% of the benefits awarded are withheld. After agency has set the fee it forwards fee directly to the lawyer from the amount withheld. If attorney's fees exceed the amount withheld, the lawyer must seek the remainder from the claimant. If the attorney's fees are less than the amount withheld, the claimant receives the remainder. Nonlawyer representatives do not have this withholding benefit.

32 In fiscal year 1978 lawyers appeared in 32% of hearings; nonlawyers in 12%. In fiscal year 1983 lawyers appeared in 50% of hearings; nonlawyers in 13%. Though the letter discussed in footnote 29 does not exclusively reference lawyers' services, this list may attribute to the increase in lawyer representation. Lawyers also have a high success rate before the agency as well as the advantage of award withholdings to secure fees in Title II and Black Lung cases (see footnote 31).

No agencies indicated that they would discipline nonlawyers differently from lawyers, although they clearly have an additional ability to pursue sanctions against lawyers through external disciplinary mechanisms. Only a few agencies indicated any special need for nonlawyer discipline. Most reported they had not encountered any problems with misconduct by nonlawyers or any inability of nonlawyers to meet appropriate ethical standards (though fewer than a third of the agencies studied have actually defined any specific ethical standards). Of those that voiced complaints about nonlawyers' skills in representation, most indicated that the problem they encounter most frequently is nonlawyers' lack of familiarity with procedural rules and tactics. The majority of responses suggest that nonlawyers do not pose any special practice problems, nor do they receive any special disciplinary consideration. Overall, the concern for nonlawyers' competence and ethical conduct seems limited, perhaps because nonlawyer practice is not widespread.

III. Methodology

Throughout the survey our questions focused on lay representation (other than self-representation) occurring in adjudicatory proceedings. In question 1, in which we asked whether agencies permitted nonlawyer representation, we attempted to distinguish between adversarial and nonadversarial proceedings. Our distinction did not prove particularly informative because all agencies permitting nonlawyer practice (97%) allow such practice in both arenas.

Question 2 sought the methods by which agencies control or limit those practicing before them. The responses vary considerably from agency to agency. Questions 3 and 4 requested statistics concerning the frequency of nonlawyer practice. Many of the agencies indicated that statistics were unavailable. These responses also vary considerably. The results of questions 1 through 4 are tabulated in Chart I beginning on page 782.

F

State Survey: Ethics Opinions, Rules, and Reports Involving Paralegals

The following ethics summary covers paralegals and other nonattorneys in each state. The purpose of the summary is to give an overview of the kinds of issues that have arisen. It is *not* meant to provide the current state of the law or the current ethics regulations of any particular state. Keep in mind that the rules governing paralegals are undergoing considerable change. See Section D of Chapter 5 on how to do legal research to determine the current ethics rules that apply to your state.

 Alabama

Under Rule 7.6 of the Rules of Professional Conduct, the title "Legal Assistant" is acceptable on a business card that also contains an attorney's or a law firm's name. The title of the nonattorney employee should be legibly and prominently displayed in close proximity to the employee's name. Cards that present an attorney's or law firm's name so prominently that they obscure the employee's nonattorney status are prohibited. An earlier ethics opinion preferred the title, "non-lawyer assistant," since "paralegal" could be a misleading title. *Alabama State Bar Opinion 86–04 (3/17/86).* See also *Opinion 86–120 (12/2/86).*

When a paralegal signs a letter to a nonattorney, the paralegal's name should be followed by one of these titles: "nonlawyer assistant," "nonlawyer paralegal," or "nonlawyer investigator." *Alabama State Bar Opinion 87–77 (6/16/87).*

It is improper to include the name of a nonattorney assistant on the letterhead of law firm stationery. *Alabama State Bar Opinion 83–87 (5/23/83).*

The business card of a legal secretary can list the fact that he or she has been certified by passing an examination of the National Association of Legal Secretaries. *Alabama State Bar Opinion 90–01 (1/17/90).*

When a plaintiff's law firm hires an investigator who worked for a defense law firm, the plaintiff's law firm must withdraw from all cases in which the investigator previously worked, unless the defense law firm and its clients consent. Screening the investigator from such cases is not enough. *Alabama State Bar Opinion 89–41 (4/5/89).* See also *Opinion 89–91 (8/7/89)* on job switching by a secretary and the effectiveness of a Chinese Wall (screening) around her.

Paralegals may draft documents if supervised by an attorney, but they cannot make court appearances or give legal advice. *Alabama State Bar Opinion 86–120* (12/2/86).

An attorney engaged in collection work may not pay his lay employees on a commission basis. *Opinion of the General Counsel* (2/3/88, revised 2/14/90).

Nonattorney independent contractors who sell legal research services to attorneys are not engaged in the unauthorized practice of law. *Alabama State Bar Opinion 90–04* (1/18/90).

Other Alabama State Bar Opinions involving nonattorneys: *86–101* (10/30/86); *86–124* (12/15/86); *87–31* (5/20/87); *87–38* (3/6/87); *87–129* (12/31/87); *87–135* (10/30/87); *75–151* (2/4/88); *88–03* (2/4/88); *89–92* (9/25/89); *89–94* (10/5/89); *98–18* (2/21/90). See also *Birmingham Bar Ass'n Opinion 88–4* (7/8/88).

 # Alaska

A suspended attorney may work as a paralegal, but only under the supervision of an attorney in good standing. He or she may not have a direct relationship with a client. *Alaska Bar Ass'n Ethics Opinion 84–6* (8/25/84).

Under the supervision or review of an attorney, a legal assistant can investigate claims and have contact with insurance agents regarding the settlement of claims in worker's compensation cases. *Alaska Bar Ass'n Ethics Opinion 73–1* (10/6/73).

Paralegal employees of attorneys may not conduct worker's compensation hearings. *Alaska Bar Ass'n Ethics Opinion 84–7* (8/25/84). Note: this Opinion was suspended 11/9/84 pending reconsideration.

 # Arizona

The letterhead of an attorney or law firm can list nonattorney support personnel if their nonattorney status is made clear. *Ethics Opinion 90–03* (3/16/90). This overrules *Opinion 84–14* (10/5/84), which held to the contrary. (The latter opinion also said that separate letterhead for paralegals is not allowed).

A corporation consisting of independent contractor paralegals and a salaried attorney employee is impermissible. *Opinion 82–18* (12/1/82).

Other State Bar of Arizona Opinions involving nonattorneys: *86–7* (2/26/86); *87–13* (6/17/87).

 # Arkansas

"The paralegal should never be placed in a position to decide what information takes priority over other information or to make decisions which affect the client." This function should never be delegated to a paralegal, even though "sometimes a fine line exists in the area of professional judgment." Paralegals need "specific guidelines," preferably in writing, in carrying out responsibilities. *The Paralegal in Practice* by A. Clinton, chairperson of the Paralegal Committee of the Arkansas Bar Ass'n, 23 Arkansas Lawyer 22 (January 1989).

 California

When a paralegal is authorized to represent a client before the Workers' Compensation Appeals Board, a law firm can use its paralegal to represent a client of the firm before this Board if the client consents and the firm supervises the paralegal. *State Bar of California Opinion 1988–103.*

A paralegal who switches jobs might cause the disqualification of his or her new employer to represent clients about whom the paralegal obtained confidential information while working at a prior (opposing) law firm. A rebuttable presumption exists that the paralegal shared this information with the new employer. The most likely way for the new employer to rebut this presumption, and hence to avoid the disqualification, is to show that when the paralegal was hired, a Chinese Wall was built around the paralegal with respect to any cases that are substantially related to cases the paralegal worked on while at the prior employment. *In re Complex Asbestos Litigation,* ____Cal.App.3d ____, 283 Cal. Rptr. 732 (Cal. Ct. App. 1991).

A nonattorney may use a business card if it is used for identification rather than for solicitation of business. *Los Angeles County Bar Ass'n Opinion 381.*

A law firm can pay a bonus to its paralegal as long as the bonus does not involve a sharing of legal fees. *Los Angeles County Bar Ass'n Opinion 457* (11/20/89).

A nonprofit legal services center for the elderly cannot advertise in a local newspaper the availability of "legal help" from "para-legal aides" trained by a local attorney. Legal help implies legal services. *San Diego Bar Ass'n, Opinion 1976–9* (7/1/76).

A business that provides paralegal services to the public should have attorney supervision except for some purely ministerial tasks. *San Diego Bar Ass'n, Opinion 1983–7.*

Other State Bar of California Opinion involving nonattorneys: *Opinion 1988–97.* Other Los Angeles County Bar Ass'n Opinions involving nonattorneys: *Opinion 391, Opinion 444.*

■ Colorado

The names of support personnel can be printed on law firm letterhead, and these employees can have their own business cards as long as they reveal clearly that they are not attorneys. *Colorado Bar Ass'n, Formal Ethics Opinion 84* (4/90).

Paralegals must disclose their nonattorney status to everyone at the outset of any professional relationship. They should be given no task that requires the exercise of unsupervised legal judgment. They can write letters and sign correspondence on attorney letterhead as long as their nonattorney status is clear and the correspondence does not contain legal opinions or give legal advice. They can have their own business cards with the name of the law firm on them if their nonattorney status is made clear. The services performed by the paralegal must supplement, merge with, and become part of the attorney's work product. *Colorado Bar Ass'n, Guidelines for the Utilization of Legal Assistants* (1986).

A law firm can use a paralegal to represent clients at administrative proceedings when authorized by statute and when the practice of law is not involved. To ensure competent representation, the attorney must train and supervise the paralegal. *Colorado Bar Ass'n Opinion 79* (2/18/89).

An attorney may not participate with nonattorneys in preparing and marketing estate planning documents when the venture consists of the unauthorized practice of law. *Colorado Bar Ass'n Opinion 87* (7/14/90).

An attorney shall continually monitor and supervise the work of assistants to assure that the services they render are performed competently and efficiently. *Colorado Bar Ass'n Ethics Opinion 61* (10/23/82).

 # Connecticut

The names of paralegals can be printed on law firm letterhead, and they may have their own business cards if their nonattorney status is made clear. *Ethics Committee Opinion 85–17* (11/20/85).

Paralegals can communicate the legal advice of attorneys if they refrain from interpreting or expanding on that advice. They can attend a real estate closing to distribute or receive documents or funds, but they may not attend as the sole representative of a client. They can attend a deposition but may not conduct one. They may not supervise the execution of a will, but they can act as witnesses to such execution. In contacts with clients, courts, and agencies, paralegals must disclose at the outset that they are not attorneys. Paralegals should not accept or reject cases or set fees if these tasks entail any discretion on their part. *Connecticut Bar Ass'n.*

 # Delaware

A law firm cannot allow its paralegal to represent a client before the Industrial Accident Board on a worker's compensation case. *Delaware State Bar Ass'n Opinion 1985–3.*

A nonattorney law clerk cannot work on a case where the other side is represented by the clerk's former employer. The clerk must be screened from involvement in the case. *Delaware State Bar Ass'n Opinion 1986–1.*

 # District of Columbia

Rule 5.4 of the Model Rules of Professional Conduct has been modified to permit a nonattorney to be a partner of a law firm. Hence the firm can share fees with nonattorneys under the guidelines of Rule 5.4. For example, a lobbyist or an economist could form a partnership with an attorney. The nonattorney must agree to abide by the Rules of Professional Conduct.

Nonattorneys can have a business card that prints the name of the law firm where they work as long as their nonattorney status is made clear. *D.C. Bar Ethics Opinion 19.* See also *Speaking of Ethics, Bar Report, p. 2* (February/March 1988).

Other ethical opinions involving nonattorneys: *172* (4/15/86); *176* (10/21/86); *182* (5/19/87); *201* (4/18/89); *203* (6/20/89).

Florida

An attorney can allow a nonattorney to conduct a real estate closing if certain conditions are met, e.g., an attorney is available (in person or by telephone) to answer legal questions, the nonattorney only performs ministerial acts, and the client consents to having the closing handled by a nonattorney. *Florida Bar Opinion 89–5* (11/89) (overruling *Opinion 73–43*).

It is ethically improper for lawyers to delegate to laypersons the handling of negotiations with adjusters on claims of clients of the lawyers. *Florida Ethics Opinion 74–35.* But the nonlawyer employee can transmit information from the attorney. "For example, the nonlawyer employee may call the adjuster and inform the adjuster that the attorney will settle the matter for X. If the adjuster comes back with a counteroffer, the nonlawyer employee must inform the attorney. The employee cannot be given a range in which to settle." *Ethically Speaking* 15, The Florida Bar News (9/15/91).

Paralegals can have their own business cards. They may also be listed on a law firm's letterhead, but a title indicating their nonattorney status should appear beneath their name. Attorneys should not hold their paralegals out as "certified" if they are not. *Florida Bar Opinion 86–4* (8/1/86).

When a nonattorney changes jobs to an opposing law firm, the old and new employer must admonish him or her not to reveal any confidences or secrets obtained during prior employment. *Florida Bar Opinion 86–5* (8/1/86).

Attorneys cannot authorize a nonattorney to sign their name on pleadings. *Florida Bar Opinion 87–11.*

An attorney can allow a supervised nonattorney to conduct an initial interview of a prospective client if his or her nonattorney status is disclosed to the client and only factual information is obtained. *Florida Bar Opinion 88–6.*

Other Florida Bar Opinions involving nonattorneys: *62–26* (12/15/86); *64–40* (5/1/87); *87–8* (7/1/87); *89–43; 88–15.*

An attorney was suspended for failing to supervise his nonattorney personnel. *Florida Bar v. Carter,* 502 So.2d 904 (FL, 1987).

Nonattorneys from the Health & Rehabilitative Services Department can no longer draft documents or represent the Department in court. *Florida Bar re Advisory Opinion HRS Nonlawyer Counselor,* Fla SupCt, No. 70,615 (5/25/89) Earlier opinion in the case: 518 So.2d 1270.

Georgia

It is the unauthorized practice of law for a law firm to allow a nonattorney to conduct a real estate closing. *State Bar of Georgia Opinion 86–5* (5/12/89).

An attorney should not allow a paralegal to correspond with an adverse party (or the party's agents) on the attorney's letterhead if the letter discusses legal matters that suggest or assert claims. (Routine contacts with opposing counsel not involving the merits of the case are, however, permitted.) *Advisory Opinion 19* (7/18/75).

An attorney may delegate tasks to a paralegal which ordinarily comprise the practice of law, but only if the attorney has direct contact with the client and maintains "constant supervision" of the paralegal. The paralegal can render specialized advice on scientific or technical topics. The paralegal cannot negotiate with parties or opposing counsel on substantive issues. The paralegal's name may not appear on the letterhead or office door. The paralegal must not sign any pleadings, briefs, or other legal documents to be presented to a court. The paralegal can have a business card with the name of the firm on it if the word *paralegal* is clearly used to indicate nonattorney status. Unless previous contacts would justify the paralegal in believing that his or her nonattorney status is already known, the paralegal should begin oral communications, either face-to-face or on the telephone, with a clear statement that he or she is a paralegal employee of the law firm. *Advisory Opinion* 21 (9/16/77).

Other State Bar Opinion involving nonattorneys: *82–2* (11/10/88).

Hawaii

An attorney may list a paralegal on professional cards, letterhead, and professional notices or announcement cards as long as the employee is identified as a paralegal or a legal assistant. A paralegal can use business cards identifying himself or herself as an employee of the law firm. A paralegal can sign correspondence as a paralegal. *Hawaii Supreme Court Disciplinary Board, Formal Opinion 78–8–19.* (6/28/84). See also *Opinion 78–8–19–Supp.*

Idaho

An attorney must not share fees with nonattorneys. The attorney can request compensation for the work of a paralegal or other laymen acting under his or her supervision as long as the request specifies that laymen performed the work. *Formal Ethics Opinion 125.*

A law firm cannot list legal assistants on its letterhead. *Formal Opinion 109* (11/30/81).

Other Idaho State Bar Opinion involving nonattorneys: *117* (3/14/86).

Illinois

Paralegal names can be printed on a firm's letterhead; the nonattorney status of the employee must be indicated. *Illinois State Bar Ass'n Opinion 87–1* (9/8/87).

An attorney can charge an hourly rate for paralegal work but not for "expenses" that includes an hourly rate for a salaried paralegal. *Illinois State Bar Ass'n Opinion 86–1* (7/7/86).

A paralegal cannot handle phone calls involving legal matters of her law firm while at a collection agency that is one of the clients of the law firm. The law firm would not be able to supervise the paralegal. *Illinois State Bar Ass'n Opinion 88–8* (3/15/89).

Sharing fees with a nonattorney via profit-sharing is proper provided the sharing is based on a percentage of overall firm profits and is not tied to fees in a particular case. *Illinois State Bar Ass'n Opinion 89–5* (7/17/89).

A paralegal can conduct a real estate closing without his or her attorney-supervisor present if no legal advice is given, if all the documents have been prepared in advance, if the attorney-supervisor is available by telephone to provide help, and if the other attorney consents. *Chicago Bar Ass'n (1983).*

Legal assistants can be listed on law firm letterhead or on the door as long as their nonattorney status is made clear. *Chicago Bar Ass'n Opinion 81–4.*

Disqualification of a law firm is not required simply because it hired a law office manager–secretary who had worked for opposing party at another law firm. *Kapco Mfg. Co., Inc. c. C&O Enterprises, Inc.,* 637 F. Supp. 1231 (N.D. Ill., 1985).

 # Indiana

Paralegal names can be printed on a firm's letterhead if their nonattorney status is clear. The attorneys and nonattorneys must be distinguished clearly. *Indiana Bar Ass'n Legal Ethics Committee Opinion 9* (1985) (which overrules *Opinion 5*).

Paralegals may have a business card as long as their capacity is stated and the identity of their employing attorney is disclosed. *Indiana Bar Ass'n Legal Ethics Committee Opinion 8* (1984).

 # Iowa

A legal assistant who has passed the CLA exam (Certified Legal Assistant) of the National Association of Legal Assistants may not sign law firm correspondence with the designation "CLA, Legal Assistant" or "Certified Legal Assistant," since the public might be misled about his or her nonattorney status. (A reader might think that CLA was a legal degree.) *Iowa State Bar Ass'n Opinion 88–5* (9/9/88) and *Opinion 88–19* (6/8/89). It is proper, however, to sign the letter with the titles "Legal Assistant" or "Paralegal." *Opinion 89–22* (12/8/89).

Paralegals and other nonattorney employees may not be listed on the law firm letterhead. *Iowa State Bar Ass'n Opinion 87–18* (2/2/88). The office of the county public defender may not list the names of nonattorney personnel on its letterhead. *Opinion 89–35* (12/14/89).

A sign outside the door of a law firm may not list the name of nonattorney employees even if they are called legal assistants. *Iowa State Bar Ass'n Opinion 89–23* (12/26/88).

In oral communications, a paralegal should disclose his or her nonattorney status at the outset of the conversation. *Iowa Code of Professional Responsibility, EC 3–6, subparagraph 5.*

A law firm can pay a paralegal a percentage of the total income it earns as long as the compensation relates to the firm's profits and not the receipt of specific legal fees. *Iowa State Bar Ass'n Opinion 90–9* (8/23/90).

It would be the unauthorized practice of law for a paralegal to represent a client in Small Claims Court. *Iowa State Bar Ass'n Opinion 89–30* (12/8/89).

Other Iowa State Bar Ass'n Opinions involving nonattorneys: *87–28* (5/16/88); *88–16* (2/17/89); *88–25* (6/8/89); *89–3* (9/6/89); *90–20* (8/23/90).

Kansas

An attorney cannot include the name of a legal assistant on its letterhead. *Kansas Bar Ass'n Ethics Advisory Committee Opinion 88–02* (7/15/88). See also *Opinion 82–38* (11/4/82).

A legal assistant can use a business card that prints the name of his or her law firm if the legal assistant is identified as such. *Kansas Bar Ass'n Ethics Advisory Committee, Opinion 85–4.* Overrules *Opinion 84–18.*

Clients must be fully informed that the legal assistant is not an attorney. An attorney shall not share legal fees with a legal assistant, meaning that no form of compensation must be tied to a particular fee. A legal assistant shall not be compensated for recommending an attorney. At the beginning of a professional contact, the legal assistant should disclose that he or she is not an attorney. A legal assistant can sign correspondence on law firm letterhead if the signature is followed by a designation that makes clear that he or she is not an attorney. If an attorney accepts a case in which the legal assistant has a conflict of interest, the attorney should exclude the legal assistant from participating in that case. The client must be told of this conflict. *Standards and Guidelines for the Utilization of Legal Assistants in Kansas* (Kansas Bar Ass'n Committee on Legal Assistants, 12/2/88).

Kentucky

The letterhead of an attorney can include the name of a paralegal. An attorney's name can appear on the business card of a paralegal if the latter's non-attorney status is clear. An attorney shall not share, on a proportionate basis, legal fees with a paralegal. When dealing with a client, a paralegal must disclose at the outset that he or she is not an attorney. This disclosure must be made to anyone who may have reason to believe that the paralegal is an attorney or is associated with an attorney. *Kentucky Paralegal Code, Supreme Court Rule 3.700.*

Without client consent, it is unethical for an attorney to charge a client for paralegal services when the attorney's contract with the client calls for a statutory-set fee, a lump-sum fee, or a contingent fee. The attorney who charges an hourly rate *can* charge for paralegal services which may be separately stated. *Kentucky Bar Ass'n Opinion E–303* (5/85).

A suspended attorney may work in a law firm as a paralegal after the period of his suspension has expired, even if he has not been reinstated. *Kentucky Bar Ass'n Opinion E–336.*

A paralegal cannot appear in court on motion day or for the motion docket. *Kentucky Bar Ass'n Opinion E–266.*

A nonlawyer may not represent a corporation in a court other than the small claims court. *Kentucky Bar Ass'n Opinion E–345.*

A lay assistant cannot take (i.e., conduct) a deposition. *Kentucky Bar Ass'n Opinion E–341.*

Louisiana

An attorney can be disbarred for delegating too much to a paralegal and for failing to supervise the paralegal. *Louisiana State Bar v. Edwins,* 540 So.2d

294 (LA 1989). See also *Louisiana State Bar v. Lindsay,* 553 So.2d 807 (LA 1989) (an attorney charged with professional misconduct tries to shift the blame to his paralegal).

Maine

The names of paralegals can be printed on a firm's letterhead as long as this is not misleading. *Maine Professional Ethics Comm'n Opinion 34 (1/17/83).*

An attorney cannot form a partnership or professional corporation with a nonattorney to provide legal and nonlegal services to clients. *Maine Professional Ethics Comm'n Opinion 79 (5/6/87).*

Other Opinions of the Maine Professional Ethics Comm'n involving nonattorneys: *69 (3/17/86); 99 (9/6/89); 102 (2/2/90).*

Maryland

Legal assistants can have business cards as long as their legal assistant status is designated. *Maryland Bar Ass'n Ethics Opinion 77–28 (10/18/76).*

An attorney can list the names of paralegals on office letterhead or on the office door as long as their nonattorney status is designated. *Maryland Bar Ass'n Ethics Opinion 81–69 (5/29/81).*

A nonattorney once worked for attorney #A. She now works for attorney #B. These attorneys are opponents on a case in litigation. This case was underway when the nonattorney worked for attorney #A. If effective screening (i.e., a Chinese Wall) is used to insulate the nonattorney from the case, attorney #B does not have to withdraw from the litigation. *Maryland Bar Ass'n Ethics Docket 90–17 (1990).*

An attorney can hire a freelance paralegal as long as he or she is supervised at all times by the attorney. *Maryland Bar Ass'n Opinion 86–83 (7/23/86).*

An attorney cannot divide a fee with a nonattorney. *Maryland Bar Ass'n Opinion 86–59 (2/12/86).* A legal assistant cannot be paid a percentage of the recovery in a case on which the assistant works. *Maryland Bar Ass'n Opinion 84–103 (1984).*

An attorney can rent office space to a nonattorney as long as confidentiality of the attorney's clients is not compromised. *Maryland Bar Ass'n Opinion 89–45 (6/12/89).*

Other Maryland Bar Ass'n Opinions involving nonattorneys: *84–6 (7/20/76); 86–45 (9/11/86); 86–57 (2/12/86); 86–69 (7/15/86); 86–45 (9/11/86); 88–56 (3/13/88); 89–18 (3/23/89); 89–64 (8/11/89); 90–26 (2/21/90).*

Massachusetts

Paralegal names can be printed on a firm's letterhead if their nonattorney status is clear. *Massachusetts Bar Ass'n Ethics Opinion 83–10 (11/29/83).*

A paralegal can sign his or her name on law firm letterhead. *Massachusetts Bar Ass'n Ethics Opinion 73–2.*

A law firm cannot pay its office administrator, a nonattorney, a percentage of the firm's profits in addition to his fixed salary. *Massachusetts Bar Opinion 84–2 (1984).*

Michigan

It is not possible for an attorney to give quality supervision to twenty-four paralegals located at six separate sites in the state. *State Bar of Michigan Opinion R–1* (12/16/88).

When nonattorney employees with access to the files move to another law firm, a Chinese Wall may have to be erected around them to prevent the imputed disqualification of the new firm. *State Bar of Michigan Formal Opinion R–4* (9/22/89).

Business cards and law firm letterhead can list the name of nonattorney employees with titles such as *legal assistant* or *paralegal.* The public must not be confused as to their nonattorney status. *State Bar of Michigan Informal Opinion RI–34* (12/15/89).

A paralegal works for a legal service organization that represents a plaintiff in a case against a potential defendant, who is the paralegal's fiance. The organization is not disqualified if the paralegal is screened from the case and the client (the plaintiff) is made aware of this relationship and consents. *State Bar of Michigan Informal Opinion CI–1168* (12/10/86).

Other State Bar of Michigan Informal Opinions involving nonattorneys: *CI–1155* (7/25/86); *CI–1203* (8/5/88); *R–6* (12/15/89); *RI–36* (11/20/89); *RI–55* (8/1/90).

 Minnesota

Paralegal names can be printed on a firm's letterhead, on professional cards, on professional announcement cards, office signs, telephone directory listings, law lists, and legal directory listings, if their nonattorney status is clear. Paralegals, so identified, may sign correspondence on behalf of the law firm if acting under an attorney's direction. But they cannot be named on pleadings under any identification. *Minnesota Bar Ass'n Ethics Opinion 8* (6/26/74, amended 6/18/80). On letterheads, see also *Opinion 93* (6/7/84).

 Mississippi

Paralegal names can be printed on a firm's letterhead if their nonattorney status is made clear. The paralegal should not be called a *paralegal associate,* since in common usage the term *associate* carries a connotation of being an attorney in the firm. *Mississippi Bar Ass'n Ethics Opinion 93* (6/7/84).

An attorney can pay a paralegal a bonus based on the number of her hours billed and collected in excess of a designated minimum. A nonattorney compensation or retirement plan can be based in whole or in part on a profit-sharing arrangement. *Mississippi State Bar Opinion 154* (9/12/88).

A disbarred or suspended attorney cannot work as a paralegal. *Mississippi State Bar Opinion 96* (6/7/84).

 Missouri

At the outset of any professional dealings for the attorney, the paralegal must disclose to clients, the public, or other attorneys that he or she is a paralegal. The name of a paralegal may appear on the letterhead of a law firm and on business cards. A paralegal can sign correspondence on law firm letterhead provided the signature is followed by a title that identifies him or her as a paralegal. Under the supervision of an attorney, a paralegal can handle real estate closings. An attorney cannot share legal fees with a paralegal, but a paralegal can be included in a compensation or retirement plan that is based in whole or part on a profit-sharing arrangement. A bonus cannot be tied to the existence or amount of any particular legal fee. A paralegal cannot participate in a stock ownership plan, since a paralegal cannot become a part-owner of a professional corporation. A paralegal cannot be compensated for recommending an attorney's services. A copy of these guidelines and the ethical rules governing attorneys shall be delivered to or discussed with the paralegal immediately upon employment. *Guidelines for Practicing with Paralegals,* Missouri Bar Ass'n (1987).

Montana

An attorney must not split a fee with a nonattorney. *State Bar of Montana Opinion (1) (9/13/85).*

Nebraska

Paralegals can be listed on law firm letterhead if their nonattorney status is made clear. *Nebraska State Bar Ass'n Advisory Committee Opinion 88–2.*

Several attorneys who are not partners, associates, or otherwise affiliated with each other share office space and share nonattorney personnel. They represent clients who are opposite each other in cases. This is not improper if the clients are aware of and consent to the arrangement. Steps must be taken to ensure confidentiality—such as preventing common access to case files and preventing the nonattorneys from working for both sides on a case. *Nebraska State Bar Ass'n Advisory Committee Opinion 89–2.*

New Hampshire

According to New Hampshire Supreme Court Rules: *Rule 1.* Paralegals must not give legal advice, but they can, with adequate attorney supervision, provide information concerning legal matters. *Rule 3.* A paralegal shall not be delegated any task that requires the exercise of professional legal judgment. *Rule 5.* An attorney shall not form a partnership with a paralegal if any part of the partnership consists of the practice of law. *Rule 6.* An attorney shall not share fees with a paralegal but can include the paralegal in a retirement plan based on a profit-sharing arrangement. *Rule 7.* A paralegal's name may not be included on the letterhead of an attorney. A paralegal can have a business card that prints the name of the law firm where he or she works, if the card indicates the paralegal's nonattorney capacity and the firm does not use the paralegal to solicit business for the firm improperly. *Rule 8.* When dealing with clients, attorneys, or the public, the paralegal must disclose at the outset that he or she is not an attorney.

A law firm cannot list legal assistants on its letterhead. *New Hampshire Bar Ass'n Ethics Opinion 1982–3/20 (3/17/83).*

New Jersey

New Jersey has added an additional subsection to Rule 5.3 of the Model Rules of Professional Conduct. The addition is (c)(3): Attorneys must make a "reasonable investigation of circumstances that would disclose past instances of conduct by the nonlawyer" that are "incompatible with the professional obligations of an attorney, which evidence a propensity for such conduct."

Attorneys cannot hire paralegals as independent contractors because of the difficulty of providing them with needed day-to-day supervision. The required "direct supervision" is not always provided when attorneys use such paralegals in areas where the attorneys have no expertise. And there is an increased danger of conflict-of-interest; independent paralegals might offer services to two opposing attorneys. Furthermore, an attorney using an independent paralegal for a single transaction would not interview him or her with the same care (for instance, regarding level of training and experience) as during a regular interview for full-time traditional employment. *New Jersey Unauthorized Practice of Law Committee Opinion 24* (11/15/90).

A paralegal can have a business card as long as the name of the employing law firm is also printed on it. *New Jersey Advisory Committee on Professional Ethics Opinion 647* (1990).

Nonattorney employees of the county welfare agency may represent litigants before the Office of Administrative Law. *New Jersey Advisory Committee on Professional Ethics Opinion 580* (2/27/86).

Paralegals can sign law firm correspondence concerning routine tasks such as gathering factual information and documents. They should not sign correspondence to clients, adverse attorneys, or tribunals. Minor exceptions are allowed such as "a purely routine request to a court clerk for a docket sheet." *New Jersey Advisory Committee on Professional Ethics Opinion 611* (2/23/88).

A law firm litigating tobacco cases can hire a nonattorney who had been involved in tobacco litigation at another firm, if the nonattorney had no substantial responsibility in the tobacco litigation at the other firm, obtained no confidential information concerning the litigation, and is screened from such litigation at the present firm. *New Jersey Advisory Committee on Professional Ethics Opinion 633* (11/2/89).

A law firm currently in litigation cannot hire a paralegal who formerly worked for the opposing attorney's law firm. There is an irrebuttable presumption that confidences gained in a prior employment have been revealed to the new employer. The disqualification of the law firm where the paralegal now works is automatic. *New Jersey Advisory Committee on Professional Ethics Opinion 546* (1984).

Other New Jersey Advisory Committee on Professional Ethics Opinions involving nonattorneys: *296* (2/6/75); *296 Supplement* (2/12/76); *598* (3/26/87); *631* (10/12/89).

An attorney cannot share fees with an investigator–paralegal. *Infante v. Gottesman,* 233 N.J. Super 310, 558 A.2d 1338 (1989).

New Mexico

A paralegal shall disclose to all persons with whom he or she communicates—at the beginning of any dealings with them—that the paralegal is not an attorney. The word *associate* should not be used when referring to a paralegal since it might be interpreted as an attorney–associate. An attorney shall not share fees with a paralegal. The compensation of a paralegal shall not include a percentage of profits or fees received from clients referred to the attorney by the paralegal. A paralegal's name cannot be printed on the letterhead of an attorney. A paralegal can have a business card that prints the name of the law firm as long as his or her nonattorney status is made clear. A paralegal can sign correspondence on attorney letterhead as long as his or her nonattorney status is disclosed by a title such as *legal assistant* or *paralegal*. "In addition, a lawyer should explain to the legal assistant that the legal assistant has a duty to inform the lawyer of any assignment which the assistant regards as beyond his capability." *New Mexico Rules Governing the Practice of Law* (Judicial Pamphlet 16).

Attorneys must tell clients how much services to be rendered by office nonattorneys will cost. *Advisory Opinions Committee of the State Bar of New Mexico 1990–4.*

Another opinion of the Advisory Opinions Committee of the State Bar of New Mexico involving nonattorneys: *Opinion 1983–3.*

An attorney was suspended for failing to supervise a paralegal; the attorney failed to ensure that the conduct of the paralegal complied with the ethical obligations of the attorney. *In the Matter of Martinez,* 754 P.2d 842 (N.M. 1988).

 New York

An attorney cannot form a partnership with, or share legal fees with, a paralegal. An attorney's name can be printed on the business card of a paralegal as long as the latter's legal assistant status is clearly indicated. When dealing with a client, the paralegal must disclose at the outset that he or she is not an attorney. The same is true when dealing with a court, an agency, or the public if there is any reason for believing he or she is an attorney or associated with an attorney. *Guidelines for Utilization of Legal Assistants by Attorneys* (N.Y. State Bar Assn., 1976).

A paralegal cannot conduct a deposition or supervise the execution of a will. *New York State Bar Ass'n Ethics Opinions 304, 343.*

An attorney can give recognition to a nonattorney for work performed in the preparation of a brief as long as his or her nonattorney status is clear. *New York State Bar Ass'n Ethics Opinion 299.*

Paralegal names can be printed on a firm's letterhead if their nonattorney status is clear. *New York State Bar Ass'n Ethics Opinion 500* (12/6/78) (52–78).

An attorney cannot allow a nonattorney to engage in settlement negotiations or to appear at a pretrial conference. *Committee of Professional Ethics of the Bar Ass'n of Nassau County Opinion 86–40* (9/12/89).

A nonattorney can attend a real estate closing to perform ministerial functions involving mere formalities. His or her nonattorney status must be disclosed at the closing. *Committee of Professional Ethics of the Bar Ass'n of Nassau County Opinion 86–43* (10/21/86); reaffirmed in *Opinion 90–13* (3/18/90).

An attorney cannot divide a fee with a paralegal who brings clients to the attorney. *Committee of Professional Ethics of the Bar Ass'n of Nassau County Opinion 37–87* (10/1/87).

Nonattorneys cannot be referred to as *associates* of an attorney. *Committee of Professional Ethics of the Bar Ass'n of Nassau County 88–34* (9/29/88).

An attorney may not represent a defendant in a criminal case when the complainant in the case is an investigator whom the attorney used in an unrelated case. There would be an appearance of impropriety in such a representation. *Committee of Professional Ethics of the Bar Ass'n of Nassau County 89–1 (1/18/89).*

An attorney cannot form a partnership with a nonattorney to practice law. *Committee on Professional Ethics of the Ass'n of the Bar of the City of New York Opinion 1987–1 (2/23/87).*

Paralegals can be listed on the letterhead of a law firm and on a business card that prints the name of the law firm (without printing the name of the supervising attorney) as long as their nonattorney status is indicated. *Committee on Professional Ethics of the New York County Lawyers' Ass'n Opinion 673 (12/23/89).*

North Carolina

When acting on behalf of an attorney, a paralegal should disclose at the outset to clients, courts, attorneys, or the public that he or she is not an attorney. If an attorney accepts a matter in which a paralegal may have a conflict of interest, the attorney should exclude the paralegal from participating in any services performed in connection with that matter. The client should be told of this conflict. When using independent paralegals, the attorney must use special care to ensure that they are performing competently and ethically. An attorney shall not share fees with a paralegal. The compensation of a paralegal shall not include a percentage of the fees received by the attorney. A paralegal shall receive no compensation for referring matters to the attorney. The letterhead of an attorney shall not include the names of paralegals, but the latter may have business cards that print the name of their employer provided the paralegal's nonattorney capacity is clearly indicated. A paralegal can sign correspondence on an attorney's letterhead as long as his or her title, such as *paralegal* clearly indicates his or her nonattorney status. North Carolina Paralegal Committee, *Proposed Guidelines for Use of Non-Attorneys in Rendering Legal Services.*

Paralegals can negotiate with the claims adjuster of an insurance company of an opposing party as long as they do not exercise independent legal judgment and are supervised by an attorney. *Ethics Committee of the North Carolina State Bar Ass'n Opinion 70 (7/13/89).*

An attorney is not disqualified from representing a defendant even though his paralegal once worked for the attorney who now represents the plaintiff in the same case *if* the paralegal is screened from the case at his or her current office. *Ethics Committee of the North Carolina State Bar Ass'n Opinion 74 (7/13/89).*

Ohio

A legal assistant can sign law firm correspondence on law firm stationery as long as his or her nonattorney status is clearly indicated. *Board of Commissioners on Grievances and Discipline Opinion 89–11 (4/14/89).*

Nonattorneys cannot be listed on law firm letterhead. They can, however, have business cards as long as their nonattorney status is made clear. *Board of Commissioners on Grievances and Discipline Opinion 89–16 (6/16/89).*

Law firm letterhead *can* print the names and titles of nonattorney employees as long as their nonattorney status is indicated and they are listed separately from the attorneys. *Professional Ethics Committee of the Columbus Bar Ass'n Opinion (6)* (11/71/88).

Law firm letterhead *can* print the names and titles of nonattorney employees, and the latter can also have their own business cards as long as their nonattorney status is made clear. *Professional Ethics Committee of the Cleveland Bar Ass'n Opinion 89–1* (2/25/89).

Oregon

Nonattorneys in an estate-planning service are engaged in the unauthorized practice of law when they give legal advice to clients in connection with the service, even if an attorney reviews and executes the documents involved. *Legal Ethics Committee of the Oregon State Bar Opinion 523* (3/89).

Nonattorney employees can have their own business cards which contain the name of their employer–attorney. *Legal Ethics Committee of the Oregon State Bar Opinion 295* (7/75).

A paralegal can write and sign letters on attorney letterhead. *Legal Ethics Committee of the Oregon State Bar Opinion 349* (6/77).

A paralegal cannot take depositions. *Legal Ethics Committee of the Oregon State Bar Opinion 449* (6/77).

Other relevant opinions of the Legal Ethics Committee of the Oregon State Bar: *Opinion 208* (6/6/72); *Opinion 435.*

Pennsylvania

Paralegals can sign letters on attorney letterhead if their nonattorney status is indicated. A supervised paralegal can correspond with the attorney for the opponent. *Committee on Legal Ethics and Professional Responsibility of the Pennsylvania Bar Ass'n Opinion 80–46.*

An attorney's letterhead can print the name of paralegals or other nonattorneys if their nonattorney status is indicated. *Committee on Legal Ethics and Professional Responsibility of the Pennsylvania Bar Ass'n Opinion 85–145* (11/14/85).

A paralegal can have a business card with the title of *legal assistant* and listing the name of the law firm. *Committee on Legal Ethics and Professional Responsibility of the Pennsylvania Bar Ass'n Opinion 80–15.*

A law student who has not taken and passed the bar examination is a paralegal and cannot practice law. *Committee on Legal Ethics and Professional Responsibility of the Pennsylvania Bar Ass'n Opinion 86–97* (5/27/87).

An attorney cannot hire an independent paralegal to do accident investigations if the paralegal is not a licensed private detective. *Committee on Legal Ethics and Professional Responsibility of the Pennsylvania Bar Ass'n Opinion 87–31* (6/87).

An attorney cannot allow a paralegal to conduct a deposition even if the attorney prepares the questions to be asked. *Committee on Legal Ethics and Professional Responsibility of the Pennsylvania Bar Ass'n Opinion 87–127* (12/87).

Other opinions of the Committee on Legal Ethics and Professional Responsibility of the Pennsylvania Bar Ass'n involving nonattorneys: *87–102* (1/88); *89–145*.

It is not unethical for an attorney to employ as a paralegal an attorney who is not permitted to practice law in Pennsylvania (because of suspension and later disbarment). Furthermore, the attorney may permit this paralegal to have client contact. *In re Anonymous No. 27 D.B. 89* (January 16, 1990).

A nonattorney cannot sign papers to be filed with the court, ask questions at a deposition, or handle court appearances. *Professional Responsibility for Nonlawyers, Professional Responsibility of the Philadelphia Bar Ass'n* (1989).

A paralegal can use a business card bearing the name of the law firm, provided his or her nonattorney status is clearly designated. *Professional Guidance Committee of the Philadelphia Bar Ass'n Opinion 74–1* (1974).

Law firm letterhead can include the names of paralegals as long as their nonattorney status is made clear. *Professional Guidance Committee of the Philadelphia Bar Ass'n Opinion 87–18* (6/25/87).

A professional corporation that practices law cannot have a nonattorney as a corporate officer. *Professional Guidance Committee of the Philadelphia Bar Ass'n Opinion 86–76* (6/19/86).

An attorney can accept referrals from a bilingual paralegal even though the paralegal charges the client for translation and investigation services. *Professional Guidance Committee of the Philadelphia Bar Ass'n Opinion 88–15* (6/27/88).

Disqualification of a law firm can be avoided if adequate screening devices requiring a nonattorney employee to maintain confidences gained in a prior job are in place. *Professional Guidance Committee of the Philadelphia Bar Ass'n Opinion 80–77; 80–119.*

Other opinions of the Professional Guidance Committee of the Philadelphia Bar Ass'n involving nonattorneys: *81–44* (undated); *86–162* (12/18/86); *87–3* (5/8/87); *87–6* (5/5/87); *87–21* (9/8/87); *89–5* (3/89); *90–5* (6/90).

Rhode Island

In contacts with clients, courts, agencies, attorneys, or the public, paralegals must disclose at the outset that they are not attorneys. They can assist at a real estate closing. They can sign correspondence as long as their nonattorney status is made clear and the letter does not give legal advice or substantive instructions to a client. They can use a business card with the name of the law firm on it if their nonattorney status is disclosed. An attorney shall not form a partnership with a paralegal if any part of the partnership involves the practice of law. A paralegal cannot share legal fees or be compensated for referring matters to an attorney. An attorney cannot hire a suspended or disbarred attorney as a paralegal (or an attorney who has resigned because of a breach of ethics). *Rhode Island Supreme Court Provisional Order No. 18* (2/1/83), Revised 10/31/90.

Other opinions of the Ethics Advisory Panel of the Rhode Island Supreme Court involving nonattorneys: *88–4* (4/15/88); *87–3* (1/8/88); *88–7* (5/13/88).

South Carolina

If a legal assistant has contact with a client, the latter must understand that the legal assistant is not an attorney. This should be disclosed at the beginning of any dealings with the client. It should be disclosed to others if they have any reason to believe the legal assistant is an attorney or is associated with an attorney. An attorney shall not share, on a proportionate basis, legal fees with a legal assistant. The letterhead of an attorney may not include the name of a nonattorney. A legal assistant can sign correspondence on attorney letterhead and can have a business card with the name of his or her law firm printed on it as long as the legal assistant's capacity is clearly indicated. *Guidelines for the Utilization by Lawyers of the Services of Legal Assistants by the South Carolina Bar* (12/11/81).

Nonattorney employees can have their own business cards as long as the title *legal assistant* is used on the card. The name of the law firm can also be printed on the card but only if the legal assistant performs significant duties outside the law office. *Ethics Advisory Committee of the South Carolina Bar Opinion 88–6.*

An attorney can hire a legal assistant with a criminal record for vehicular manslaughter but cannot hire a legal assistant who is a lawyer who has been disciplined. *Ethics Advisory Committee of the South Carolina Bar Opinion 87–6.*

An attorney can hire nonattorneys to fill in preprinted real estate forms and do title searches as long as they are supervised by the attorney and the attorney maintains direct contact with clients. *Ethics Advisory Committee of the South Carolina Bar Opinion 88–2.*

Other opinions of the Ethics Advisory Committee of the South Carolina Bar involving nonattorneys: *86–5; 88–14; 88–18.*

 South Dakota

A law firm can list paralegals on their letterhead (graduates of law school who have not yet passed the bar exam). *Ethics Committee of the State Bar of South Dakota Opinion 90–10* (9/22/90).

 Tennessee

If appropriate screening devices are in place, and Client "A" consents, an entire law firm need not be disqualified from representing that client simply because a "tainted" attorney in the firm once worked at another firm that represented client "B" in a case adverse to client "A." Furthermore, "the disqualification rules and screening procedures are applicable to lawyer, law clerk, paralegal, and legal secretary." *Board of Professional Responsibility of the Supreme Court of Tennessee, Formal Ethics Opinion 89–F–118* (3/10/89). Note: this Opinion may overrule Opinion 87–F–110, which disqualified a law firm because of a tainted paralegal who switched jobs, even though screening mechanisms were in place.

Texas

The client must understand that the legal assistant is not an attorney. An attorney must not share legal fees with a paralegal, and shall not give the latter any compensation for referring business to the attorney. The nonattorney status of the legal assistant must be specifically disclosed at the outset to clients, courts, agencies, etc. Disclosure may be made in any way that avoids confusion. A legal assistant can use a business card containing the name and address of the employing attorney or firm. The card must designate the legal assistant's status. *General Guidelines for the Utilization of the Services of Legal Assistants by Attorneys* (State Bar of Texas, 1981).

Law firm letterhead can print the name of legal assistants and can indicate that they have been certified (with a notation that they are legal assistants and are not licensed to practice law). *Professional Ethics Committee of the State Bar of Texas Opinion 436* (6/20/86), which overrules Opinion 390.

A legal assistant can write a letter on the law firm's letterhead as long as he or she signs as a legal assistant. The letter should not contain legal advice, judgment, strategy, or settlement negotiations. Such letters should be signed by an attorney. *Professional Ethics Committee of the State Bar of Texas Opinion 381* (3/75).

A legal assistant may have a business card with the law firm's name appearing on it provided the status of the legal assistant is clearly disclosed. *Professional Ethics Committee of the State Bar of Texas Opinion 403* (1982).

The name of an employee can be printed on an outdoor sign of a law firm as long as the nonattorney status of the employee is clear on the sign. *Professional Ethics Committee of the State Bar of Texas Opinion 437* (6/20/86).

Other opinions of the Professional Ethics Committee of the State Bar of Texas involving nonattorneys: *438* (3/16/87); *458* (3/11/88).

When an attorney fails to supervise his paralegal, the attorney is responsible for the malpractice of the paralegal, such as the theft of client funds by the paralegal. "In the future, you should establish greater controls over your paralegals," wrote the *Legal Ethics Committee of the Dallas Bar Ass'n, Opinion 1989–5.*

 Vermont

A law firm cannot continue to represent a defendant in a civil case after hiring a nonattorney employee who had previously performed extensive work on the same case while employed by the law firm representing the plaintiff. *Committee on Professional Responsibility of the Vermont Bar Ass'n Ethics Opinion 85–8* (1985).

In a conversation with a nonattorney employee, if a prospective client threatens to kill someone, the employee who believes the threat can warn the potential victim. *Committee on Professional Responsibility of the Vermont Bar Ass'n Opinion 86–3.*

An attorney represents a client in a real estate transaction where the opposing party is the spouse of a paralegal who works for that attorney. The attorney is not disqualified from the case if the client is told about the paralegal's relationship to the spouse and if the paralegal does not work on the case. *Committee on Professional Responsibility of the Vermont Bar Ass'n 87–15.*

A paralegal works for an attorney who represents the plaintiff in a case. The paralegal also works in a court diversion program that processed the brother of the defendant in this case. What this brother did or didn't do is relevant to the case between the plaintiff and defendant. The attorney can still represent this plaintiff, but the paralegal should be screened from the case and must not tell the attorney any secrets he learned in the diversion program. *Committee on Professional Responsibility of the Vermont Bar Ass'n 89–4.*

Other Vermont Bar Ass'n opinions involving nonattorneys: *78–2; 85–9.*

 Virginia

A paralegal shall not communicate with clients, outside attorneys, or the public without disclosing his or her nonattorney status. *Code of Professional Responsibility, DR 3–104(E).*

A "real estate paralegal company" can provide assistance to an attorney in closing real estate loans that have been referred to this company by the closing attorney. This is not the unauthorized practice of law as long as designated procedures are followed. *Unauthorized Practice of Law Opinion 147* (June 1991).

An attorney is not required to withdraw from a case as long as a nonattorney employee does not disclose confidential information learned while she worked for an opposing attorney. *Standing Committee on Legal Ethics of the Virginia State Bar Opinion 745 (1985).*

A law firm can print the names of nonattorney employees on its letterhead as long as their nonattorney status is made clear. These employees can participate in a profit-sharing plan of the firm as part of a compensation or retirement program. *Standing Committee on Legal Ethics of the Virginia State Bar Opinion 762 (1/29/86).*

An attorney must not split fees with nonattorneys, but nonattorneys can be paid a bonus based on profit sharing. *Standing Committee on Legal Ethics of the Virginia State Bar Opinion 806 (6/25/86).*

A law firm engaged in collection work can pay its nonattorney employee a percentage of profits from the collections received, plus a salary. *Standing Committee on Legal Ethics of the Virginia State Bar Opinion 885 (3/11/87).*

An attorney represents a client in a case in which the attorney's former nonattorney employee will testify against this client. The attorney is not disqualified from representing this client as long as the client is informed of this situation and still wants the attorney to represent him. *Standing Committee on Legal Ethics of the Virginia State Bar Opinion 891 (4/1/87).*

It is unethical for a nonattorney employee of a law firm to contact prospective collections clients to suggest that they hire the law firm for their collections work. *Standing Committee on Legal Ethics of the Virginia State Bar Opinion 1290 (10/25/89).*

Other opinions of the Standing Committee on Legal Ethics of the Virginia State Bar involving nonattorneys: *823 (9/19/86); 875 (1/30/87); 909 (4/1/87); 946 (6/25/87); 970 (9/30/87); 1003 (11/24/87); 1054 (3/29/88); 1077 (5/23/88); 1258 (7/25/89); 1276 (10/3/89); 1288 (10/19/89).*

 Virgin Islands

An attorney who has been suspended from practice before a federal court of appeals can work on a federal case as a paralegal if supervised by an attorney in good standing and if there is no contact with clients. *In re Mitchell,* 901 F.2d 1179, 1190 (3rd Cir. 1990).

Washington

A disbarred attorney cannot be employed as a paralegal. *Washington State Bar Ass'n Opinion 184* (1990).

 West Virginia

Anything delegated to a nonattorney must lose its separate identity and be merged in the service of the lawyer. When communicating with persons outside the office, a paralegal "must disclose his status as such." Nonattorneys can sign letters on law firm stationery as long as their nonattorney status is clearly indicated. *Legal Ethics Inquiry No. 76–7* (3 W.Va. State Bar Journal, Spring 1977).

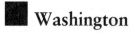 **Wisconsin**

Law firm letterhead can include the names of paralegals as long as their nonattorney status is made clear. *Wisconsin Bar Ass'n Ethics Opinion E–85–6* (10/85).

The office of the district attorney and the office of a circuit judge can share the services of a paralegal as long as the paralegal is supervised so as to maintain the confidentiality of each office. *Committee on Professional Ethics of the State Bar of Wisconsin Opinion E–86–13* (9/24/86).

A paralegal can have a business card containing the law firm's name but cannot be listed on the law firm's letterhead. *Committee on Professional Ethics of the State Bar of Wisconsin Opinion E–75–22.* (Note: Opinion E–85–6 changes the letterhead ruling of E–75–22.)

A paralegal *can* be listed on law firm letterhead. *Committee on Professional Ethics of the State Bar of Wisconsin Opinion E–85–6.*

A paralegal who is a licensed real estate broker cannot appear at a real estate closing. "If a paralegal from the attorney's office appears at the closing, it will *seem* that he is there in a legal capacity." *Committee on Professional Ethics of the State Bar of Wisconsin Opinion E–80–2.*

A law firm can hire a litigation paralegal who will also provide court-reporting services to other attorneys. *Committee on Professional Ethics of the State Bar of Wisconsin Opinion E–86–19* (12/12/86).

 Wyoming

A "lawyer who approaches a represented third party without going through counsel should be severely punished. And this is so though the lawyer uses a law representative or paralegal to do his dirty work." *Brooks v. Zebre,* 792 P.2d 196, 220 (WY 1990).

A suspended attorney shall not participate in the practice of law as an attorney or paralegal. *Medicino v. Whitchurch,* 565 P.2d 460, 478 (WY 1977).

Paralegal Business Cards

Most paralegals have their own business card. As indicated in Chapter 5 and in Appendix F, it is ethical for an attorney to allow a paralegal employee to have a business card which also prints the name of the employer. Here are several examples of such cards in use today:

APPENDIX

Federal Job Information

■ Office of Personnel Management Federal Job Information Centers

Contact the Federal Job Information Center which is nearest the location where you would like to work for information on the job opportunities in that area and the forms needed to apply.

ALABAMA
Huntsville:
Building 600, Suite 341
3322 Memorial Pkwy., South
35801-5311
(205) 544-5802

ALASKA
Anchorage:
222 W. 7th Ave., #22,
99513-7572
(907) 271-5821

ARIZONA
Phoenix:
Century Plaza Bldg., Rm. 1415
3225 N. Central Ave., 85012
(602) 640-5800

ARKANSAS
(See Oklahoma Listing)

CALIFORNIA
Los Angeles:
9650 Flair Drive
Ste. 100A
El Monte, 91731
(818) 575-6510

Sacramento:
4695 Watt Ave., North Entrance
95660-5592
(916) 551-1464

San Diego:
Federal Bldg., Room 4-S-9
880 Front St., 92188
(619) 557-6165

San Francisco:
P.O. Box 7405, 94120
(Located at 211 Main St.,
2nd Floor, Room 235)
(415) 974-5627

COLORADO
Denver:
P.O. Box 25167, 80225
(303) 969-7050
(Located at 12345 W. Alameda
Pkwy., Lakewood)

*For Job Information (24 hours a
day) in the following States, dial:*
Montana: (303) 969-7052
Utah: (303) 969-7053
Wyoming: (303) 969-7054

*For forms and local supplements,
dial:* (303) 969-7055

CONNECTICUT
Hartford:
Federal Bldg., Room 613
450 Main St., 06103
(203) 240-3096 or 3263

DELAWARE
(See Philadelphia Listing)

DISTRICT OF COLUMBIA
Metro Area:
1900 E St., N.W., Room 1416,
20415
(202) 606-2700

FLORIDA
Orlando:
Commodore Bldg., Suite 150
3444 McCrory Pl., 32803-3701
(407) 648-6148

GEORGIA
Atlanta:
Richard B. Russell Federal Bldg.,
Room 940A, 75 Spring St., S.W.,
30303
(404) 331-4315

HAWAII
Honolulu (and other Hawaiian
Islands and Overseas):
Federal Bldg., Room 5316
300 Ala Moana Blvd., 96850
(808) 541-2791
Overseas Jobs—(808) 541-2784

IDAHO
(See Washington Listing)

ILLINOIS
Chicago:
175 W. Jackson Blvd., Room 530
60604
(312) 353-6192
(For Madison & St. Clair Counties,
see St. Louis, MO listing)

INDIANA
Indianapolis:
Minton-Capehart Federal Bldg.,
575 N. Pennsylvania St., 46204
(317) 226-7161

(For Clark, Dearborn, & Floyd Counties, see Ohio listing)

IOWA
(816) 426-7757
(For Scott County see Illinois listing; for Pottawattamie County, See Kansas listing)

KANSAS
Wichita:
One-Twenty Bldg., Room 101
120 S. Market St., 67202
(316) 269-6794
(For Johnson, Leavenworth, and Wyandotte Counties, dial (816) 426-5702)

KENTUCKY
(See Ohio listing: for Henderson County, see Indiana listing)

LOUISIANA
New Orleans:
1515 Poydras St., Suite 680, 70112
(504) 589-2764

MAINE
(See New Hampshire Listing)

MARYLAND
Baltimore:
Garmatz Federal Building
101 W. Lombard Street, 21201
(301) 962-3822

MASSACHUSETTS
Boston:
Thos. P. O'Neill, Jr. Federal Bldg.
10 Causeway St., 02222-1031
(617) 565-5900

MICHIGAN
Detroit:
477 Michigan Ave., Rm. 565, 48225
(313) 226-6950

MINNESOTA
Twin Cities:
Federal Building, Room 501
Ft. Snelling, Twin Cities, 55111
(612) 725-3430

MISSISSIPPI
(See Alabama Listing)

MISSOURI
Kansas City:
Federal Building, Rm. 134
601 E. 12th Street, 64106
(816) 426-5702

(For Counties west of and including Mercer, Grundy, Livingston, Carroll, Saline, Pettis, Benton, Hickory, Dallas, Webster, Douglas, and Ozark)

St. Louis:
400 Old Post Office Bldg.
815 Olive St., 63101
(314) 539-2285
(For all other Missouri counties not listed under Kansas City above)

MONTANA
(See Colorado Listing)

NEBRASKA
(See Kansas Listing)

NEVADA
(See Sacramento, CA Listing)

NEW HAMPSHIRE
Portsmouth:
Thomas J. McIntyre Federal Bldg.
Room 104
80 Daniel Street, 03801-3879
(603) 431-7115

NEW JERSEY
Newark:
Peter W. Rodino, Jr., Federal Bldg.
970 Broad Street, 07102
(201) 645-3673
In Camden, dial (215) 597-7440

NEW MEXICO
Albuquerque:
Federal Building
421 Gold Avenue, S.W., 87102
(505) 766-5583

NEW YORK
New York City:
Jacob K. Javits Federal Bldg.
26 Federal Plaza, 10278
(212) 264-0440, 0441, or 0442

Syracuse:
James M. Hanley Federal Building
100 S. Clinton Street, 13260
(315) 423-5660

NORTH CAROLINA
Raleigh:
P.O. Box 25069
4505 Falls of the Neuse Rd.
Suite 450, 27611-5069
(919) 856-4361

NORTH DAKOTA
(See Minnesota Listing)

OHIO
Dayton:
Federal Building, Rm. 506
200 W. 2nd Street, 45402
(513) 225-2720
(For Van Wort, Auglaize, Hardin, Marion, Crawford, Richland, Ashland, Wayne, Stark, Carroll, Columbiana counties and all counties north of these see Michigan listing)

OKLAHOMA
Oklahoma City:
(Mail or phone only)
200 N.W. Fifth St., 2nd Floor, 73102
(405) 231-4948
TDD-(405) 231-4614
For Forms, dial (405) 231-5208

OREGON
Portland:
Federal Bldg., Room 376
1220 S.W. Third Ave., 97204
(503) 326-3141

PENNSYLVANIA
Harrisburg:
Federal Bldg., Room 168
P.O. Box 761, 17108
(717) 782-4494

Philadelphia:
Wm. J. Green, Jr., Federal Bldg.
600 Arch Street, 19106
(215) 597-7440

Pittsburgh:
Federal Building
1000 Liberty Ave., Rm. 119, 15222
(412) 644-2755

PUERTO RICO
San Juan:
Federico Degetau Federal Building
Carlos E. Chardon Street
Hato Rey, P. R. 00918
(809) 766-5242

RHODE ISLAND
Providence:
Pastore Federal Bldg.
Room 310, Kennedy Plaza, 02903
(401) 528-5251

SOUTH CAROLINA
(See Raleigh, NC Listing)

SOUTH DAKOTA
(See Minnesota Listing)

TENNESSEE
Memphis:
200 Jefferson Avenue
Suite 1312, 38103-2335
(901) 521-3958

TEXAS
Dallas:
(Mail or phone only)
1100 Commerce St., Rm. 6B12,
75242
(214) 767-8035

San Antonio:
8610 Broadway, Rm. 305, 78217
(512) 229-6611 or 6600

UTAH
(See Colorado Listing)

VERMONT
(See New Hampshire Listing)

VIRGINIA
Norfolk:
Federal Building, Room 500
200 Granby St., 23510-1886
(804) 441-3355

WASHINGTON
Seattle:
Federal Building
915 Second Ave., 98174
(206) 442-4365

WEST VIRGINIA
Phone only:
(513) 225-2866

WISCONSIN
For Dane, Grant, Green, Iowa,
Lafayette, Rock, Jefferson,
Walworth, Milwaukee, Waukesha,
Racine, and Kenosha counties call
(312) 353-6189

(For all other Wisconsin counties
not listed above see Minnesota
listing)

WYOMING
(See Colorado Listing)

How to Start a Freelance Paralegal Business

by Linda Harrington

The best way to get into business is to do it, not talk forever about it. In fact, you may be doing it before you know that you are actually running a business.

The conservative approach to getting into freelance business it to take work on the side while you maintain a salaried position. When your side business interferes with your job, then you must decide whether or not the business is enticing enough to promote. If it is not, give up the business, keep the salaried job, and be thankful to have learned a lesson in an undramatic way about running a business.

If the business is satisfying and if you enjoy it, the time has come to devote more time and energy to it. Therefore, you will be resigning your salaried job to tackle a business.

Perhaps you have impressed your current employer enough so that he, she, or it will be your client after you resign.

◼ Preliminary Considerations in Getting Started

What is your area of expertise? Is it likely to generate some cash for you if you go freelance? One of the areas to avoid is claimants' personal injury work where it's contingent, that is, the attorney will get a fee contingent upon success in court. It's been my experience that attorneys will pay you when they get paid on a case. So, if you're working for an attorney who will pay you when that attorney gets paid and that attorney loses the case, then it's likely you won't get paid.

I work in probate. Everyone knows that death and taxes are inevitable. That being the case, I find it a very lucrative and interesting area.

An extremely important aspect of being a freelance paralegal is having a network. A network can be one of two kinds: first, a network of prior employers who respect your skills a lot and will use you when you go freelance; second, the network of your peers that's developed through paralegal associations and contacts. Both are equally important; one does not substitute for the other. I found that my activities in the local association have been extremely rewarding. They have given me leadership opportunities, the ability to learn current law from the people who work in large law firms, and a chance to meet friends who have the same kind of responsibilities I do. For the most part, my job leads have come from people I worked for before I became a freelancer.

The other part of the network to explore is the school system. The local paralegal programs can assist you a great deal in establishing a freelance business. For one thing you can teach there, and that provides some of the income you need when you're first starting a business. (The income does come slowly in a new business.) Second, if you're teaching, you're meeting people who will one day be your peers—and that's expanding your professional network. Third, many paralegal programs have work-study experiences available for the students. The students are placed in offices where they get on-the-job training. I have lots of them come to my office. That keeps my overhead down. I give the student on-the-job training in all aspects of probate and death taxes, and in return, I have people to staff my office. It benefits the school, my office, and the students as well. So there are resources, lots of resources, available from the local schools.

A high level of expertise is something that I would like to stress. I have seen a lot of people come out of paralegal training programs and not get their dream job. They then decide that they're going to open freelance business operations, knowing not too much about the practical reality of dealing with attorneys, not to mention the practical reality of working as a paralegal. *I would think that you'd need about four or five years' experience in your field before attempting to go freelance.* The first reason, of course, is that you want to have strength in your practice area and be able to handle some of the problems that you will later encounter as a freelance paralegal.

The second reason is that you have to know about attorneys. You have to know about their personalities, you have to be able to manage the problems that they often present. I tell all my students that attorneys now have to pass "arrogance" before they are allowed to take the Bar exam, and you have to learn how to deal with this attitude in as cheerful a manner as you possibly can. Dealing with attorneys is just as important an area of expertise to develop as any other aspect of expertise in a practice field. If you're going to go freelance, you have to handle the situation of hundreds of attorneys calling you up, each one considering himself or herself the most important person in the world. You have to deal with that reality.

The most important things I had to learn were to keep a sense of humor and to remember to be compulsive. Some people say that I'm a workaholic; I prefer to state that I work hard. I work very, very hard. The things that most people think are available in freelance work are independence and free time. The reality is that they don't always exist. If your office does not get the work done, the buck stops with you. You can't blame your staff. The final responsibility rests on your shoulders. If everybody else leaves and the computer breaks down, you must still perform. If you don't get it done, you face the possibility of jeopardizing your entire business operation.

Other Practical Suggestions

Step 1.   Have business cards printed. The cards should state your name, specialty area, and telephone number.

Have an answering service. A business answering service provides a real, live voice to a caller, not a recording. It is reassuring to a potential customer to hear "a live one" on the line. Limit the service to the hours 9–5 to keep the cost of the service down.

Have "call waiting" installed by the phone company. This feature enables one line to handle several calls at once by a mere flick of a button.

Have "call forward" installed by the phone company. This feature enables you to have incoming calls automatically forwarded to the telephone number of your choice. If you are waiting for an important call but have a visit to make, you can have your call forwarded to your destination automatically.

Step 2. Systematize your operation immediately. The systems you will need are:

1. Calendar system
2. Timekeeping system
3. Billing system
4. Filing system for both open and closed matters
5. Procedural manual for your specialty area

A *calendar system* should include: a master calendar that is easily spotted among clutter; a pocket calendar, which you must carry at all times; and some sort of statute-of-limitations reminder system. Many companies offer calendar systems at relatively low cost. Two are: Safeguard Business Systems and Lawfax System.

A *timekeeping system* should include: a master time record repository (separate from the case file), time slips, and decision-making on your part concerning standard charges for services and costs. It is easiest to assign a set charge for a particular service, subject to increases for complications or quirks. For example, typical time charges will be incurred for telephone calls. Assign a minimum charge for each call. Each duty should have a minimum charge assigned to it. In this way, your billing will reflect all applicable charges for the particular service involved in the transaction as well as your research, investigation, and other "write up" expenses. Costs such as photocopies should also reflect the time involved to perform the service. Therefore, standard mark-up for costs is advisable. Naturally, these are matters that are internal to the business. Therefore, establish your standards and then keep your mouth shut.

A *billing system* should include a retainer, which is received when the case work comes in, and a statement for services submitted at an advantageous time and in a personal manner which makes it clear that a bill is an important document to the sender. Set up a system for billing that is realistic. If your clients are most likely to pay on the 30th of the month, send your bills on the 25th. If your clients will not pay the bill until the receipts from the case are received, bill at the end of the work. Billing is as much psychology as anything else. Figure out when the client will want to pay and bill at that time.

A *filing system* for open cases will include: a repository for case documents, an identification system for file labels, a spot for the files to be stored; and a case matter sheet that generally describes the client, the case, and the work to be done, as well as the billing arrangements between you and the client. Casework can be stored in file folders, in binders, in boxes, and a number of other places. Make sure that all cases are stored in the same fashion and that the case files are easily located.

Closed cases should be stored and retained. A closed file system should be a numerical system. For this type of system, you need: file folders, a rolodex to store the case name and closed file number (retained in alphabetical order by case), and a central register to show the numbers used for previously closed files, so that the number chosen for a closed file will not have been used previously.

A procedural manual will contain: standard correspondence sent for the particular areas of law you specialize in, standard (completed) court forms used in your field, instructions to others concerning processing the documents. A procedural manual can also contain information concerning special and standard requirements of area courts, if your work involves preparing and filing court papers. The latter will help you avoid procedural errors and will save time, if it is updated regularly.

Step 3.   Fix your goals, make a budget, and prepare to stick to them.

Fixing a goal involves knowing why you want to run a business. There are many reasons to want to be in business for yourself. Some are: ego gratification—now you are going to get recognition for how great you've always known you are; free time—now you can set your own hours and go to the beach whenever you want; money—now you are going to get a piece of the action and get rich.

Caution: be prepared for reality. None of your original goals will be unchanged if you are still in business one year later. Most of the people you work for will never be impressed by your brilliance—you said you could do the work, you did do the work, so what's the big deal? If you are successful, the last thing you will have is free time. Even in the beginning, your clients will want to see you or talk to you when *they* want to do so, not when you want them to. Most attorneys feel that if you only knew that they wanted to talk to you, you would jump to attention at four in the morning and be grateful for the phone call. All the money you earn will be hard earned. When you finally do earn money, some of it will go to your staff, some to your landlord, some to the IRS, and some to you.

To keep your wits about you, you must budget and you must set limits. How much of what you want do you have to receive in order to stick with it? If you want ego gratification, how many clients have to tell you you are great to make the business worthwhile? If you want free time, how much free time do you have to have to make the business worthwhile? If you want money, how much profit must you make to make the business worthwhile? The "how much" is your minimum. Obviously, the sky is the limit.

If you do not get your minimum, are you willing to quit? If not, do not go into business.

You can generally figure out how you are doing by using the following calculation: Monthly gross $\times$ 12 = Year's gross. Do not count on new business to get you by. Count on the status quo as far as income is concerned to figure out how much money you will make by December 31 and budget accordingly. If you need income from the business to pay your personal bills, how much do you need monthly? Does this leave any money to run the business? Of the money that is left, how much will be required for telephone, answering service, supplies, and other fixed expenses? Now how much is left? Use the rest for expansion of your business (equipment purchases, rent, personnel, etc.).

Step 4.   Develop realistic employee relationships.

If you have done everything you can do to avoid hiring your first employee and that is not enough to keep pace with your work or to allow you the time off you desire, then it is time to hire help.

Accept what you are. You are the owner of a very small business and cannot offer big-firm benefits, bonuses, or vacations to your prospective employee.

Also, you are a person who wishes to protect your business position, so you do not want to hand your business over to a potential competitor. Last, you are a person who has certain expectations concerning job performance, productivity, and attendance. You have developed your own ideas about what constitutes a good job in your field.

Do not hire a friend. Being someone's boss does not improve a friendship when you also own the business.

Hire someone trainable. A trainable person is likely to be a recent graduate from a paralegal school. The fact that an applicant has sought education in the field and completed some or all of it is a strong indication that the person has an interest in the field and a desire for practical experience.

Do not hire someone just like you. You are the person who decided to start up the business, who worked (slaved?) to get it going, who knows everything, and who does not want to work so hard now. If you hire someone just like you, you will have two people not wanting to work so hard (you and your employee) *or* one who wants to start a business and has access to all your clients.

Establish a trial employment first. Whether you're hiring a work-study student at minimum wage from a local paralegal program or hiring an experienced person from some other source, set a review period or termination period for the relationship. Tell your employee what that period is and stick to it.

Be realistic about your employee. Because you are a small business, you cannot compete with larger firms that will offer your employee a better deal after the employee has experience and training. Therefore, accept the fact that the employee will probably move on. Tell the employee that you accept this fact and will help the person find a better position after the training has been completed (one to two years, usually). This will motivate the employee to learn as much as possible and to do a good job. This will also avoid you taking personally the job move, which any sensible employee will consider after becoming competent on the job.

Be sure you understand the tax and insurance requirements for your employee. You must have an employer I.D. number, you must withhold taxes and social security and state disability insurance, you must file quarterly reports with the taxing authorities and provide your employee with a W-2 at year end, you must have Worker's Compensation Insurance, and you must contribute as the employer into the unemployment fund and to Social Security. Each employee's salary is hardly your total cost in keeping that employee.

Have your employee work on your premises. This is mandatory during the training period, at bare minimum, so that you can become familiar with the employee's work habits and control work production.

Review the employee's time slips. The time slip review will educate you concerning how long a particular job takes the employee to perform, how many hours during the day the employee devotes to office matters, and how the cases are progressing.

Fire the hopeless. When you know that an employee is not going to work out, do not wait for the realization to come to the employee. It never will. Call the person in to your office, look the person in the eyes, and tell the person how wonderful he or she is and how many fantastic qualities he or she has and how unfortunate it is that the job is so miserable for such a terrific individual and that the job just isn't good enough for such a talented person. *Or* call the person in and tell him or her that the employment is not working out and that you wish to ask for his or her resignation, to avoid the stigma to the employee of being fired. *Or* call the person in and tell him or her that you can no longer tolerate his or her presence and that he or she is fired. In whatever way you can do it, be sure that it gets done as soon as you have given up hope for improvement. That's your money that your employee is taking home every two weeks. Nothing rankles so much as feeling that you are paying for a mistake again and again.

Reward the hearty. Go out to lunch for a chat and pay the bill. Send the employee home early or give him or her a surprise day off after a hard week. Leave town yourself and let him or her have the office to himself or herself. Give bonuses when a difficult case is completed. Give a raise of one-day off a week. Compliment the employee for work well done.

Accept criticism. Your employee will probably be compelled to express criticism of the systems in your office or, perhaps, your own style. So what? This is how good ideas get born. Think about the recommendations and, if they are good ones, change your office systems.

Conclusion

The worst way to get into business is to assume that there is no way you can fail (90% of all new businesses do fail, the Small Business Administration says), to buy the most expensive equipment, rent the most costly office space, get the most sophisticated telephone system, and generally count on the birds in the bushes before they land in your hand. Hope that you are able to start building your business slowly so that you will have time to learn about building and problem solving. Give it a good try. If it works out and if you like it, keep going. If it works out and you do not like it, or if it does not work out, then give it up and congratulate yourself on having given it a good try-out.

"Legal Assistant Day"

In many states, governors and mayors have issued proclamations that set aside a particular day or week to honor paralegals. Here are two examples:

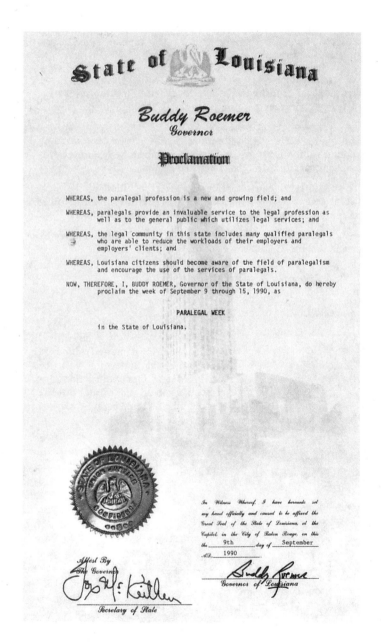

State of Louisiana

Buddy Roemer
Governor

Proclamation

WHEREAS, the paralegal profession is a new and growing field; and

WHEREAS, paralegals provide an invaluable service to the legal profession as well as to the general public which utilizes legal services; and

WHEREAS, the legal community in this state includes many qualified paralegals who are able to reduce the workloads of their employers and employers' clients; and

WHEREAS, Louisiana citizens should become aware of the field of paralegalism and encourage the use of the services of paralegals.

NOW, THEREFORE, I, BUDDY ROEMER, Governor of the State of Louisiana, do hereby proclaim the week of September 9 through 15, 1990, as

PARALEGAL WEEK

in the State of Louisiana.

In Witness Whereof, I have hereunto set my hand officially and caused to be affixed the Great Seal of the State of Louisiana, at the Capitol, in the City of Baton Rouge, on this the ___9th___ day of ___September___ A.D. 1990

Buddy Roemer
Governor of Louisiana

Attest By the Governor

_____
Secretary of State

State of Iowa

Executive Department

IN THE NAME AND BY THE AUTHORITY OF THE STATE OF IOWA

Proclamation

Whereas, the legal assistant profession is an expanding element of the legal community, striving to assist in the delivery of quality and affordable legal services to all citizens; and

Whereas, legal assistants are presently employed with private law firms, corporate legal departments, real estate, banks, insurance, government and public agencies and legal clinics throughout the state of Iowa; and

Whereas, the Legal Assistants Association encourages and provides continuing legal education opportunities for their members by offering workshops, seminars and a monthly newsletter; and

Whereas, there should be a day set aside for the recognition of the legal assistant and to acknowledge the services that they provide to the legal community and the people of the state of Iowa:

Now, Therefore, I, Robert D. Ray, Governor of the State of Iowa, do hereby proclaim August 25, 1982, as

Legal Assistant Day

in Iowa and encourage all Iowans to join in this observance.

In Testimony Whereof, I have hereunto subscribed my name and caused the Great Seal of the State of Iowa to be affixed. Done at Des Moines this 25th day of August in the year of our Lord one thousand nine hundred eighty-two.

Attest

Robert D. Ray
Governor

Deputy Secretary

News Stories, War Stories, and Parting Shots

■ Legal Assistant Elected Probate Judge

In November of 1987, Arlene G. Keegan, a legal assistant, was elected Probate Judge in the town of Litchfield, Connecticut. A law degree is not required to be a Probate Judge in Connecticut. Judge Keegan handles a wide variety of cases. In one case, for example, family members argued that their mother was incompetent when she prepared her will. "It was a tough decision, because I had to get in the middle of a situation with family members pulling against a close friend of the decedent." "I get to deal with a lot of people, and I find people totally intriguing." Howard, *A Legal Assistant Is Elected Probate Judge,* 5 Legal Assistant Today 32 (March/April 1988).

Former Legal Assistant, now Probate Judge Arlene Keegan, at the courthouse in Litchfield, Connecticut

■ Paralegal Appointed Chairman of Bar Association Committee

The Colorado Bar Association has appointed Joanna Hughbanks "to serve as chairman of the Legal Assistants Committee of the Colorado Bar Association." Ms. Hughbanks is an independent paralegal in Denver. She is believed to be the first nonattorney to chair a standing committee of a bar association. Letter from Christopher R. Brauchi, President of the Colorado Bar Association, to Joanna Hughbanks, 6/27/89.

 ## Paralegal Appointed Bankruptcy Trustee

A Fort Worth paralegal, Twalla Dupriest, has been appointed by the Bankruptcy Court as trustee for the estate of T. Cullen Davis, who was one of the wealthiest men in the United States. Twalla will be responsible for gathering all of the assets of Davis for the purpose of repaying creditors, and will preside at the meetings of creditors. *Paralegal Appointed Trustee to Cullen Davis Estate,* Newsletter, Dallas Ass'n of Legal Assistants, (Sept. 1987).

 ## Freelance Paralegal Named Pro Bono Paralegal of the Year

A freelance paralegal, Jim Carrao of Dallas, has been named Pro Bono Paralegal of the Year by the Dallas Bar Association and Legal Services of North Texas, Inc. for donating 176 hours of his time to help provide legal services to the poor. Parchman, *Communiqué,* AAPLA Advocate 17 (Alamo Area Professional Legal Assistants, Inc. July/August 1991).

Paralegal Runs for the Legislature

Rosemary Mulligan, an Illinois paralegal, ran for a seat in the Illinois House of Representatives in 1990 against an incumbent. The election was held in a district in a suburb of Chicago. The vote was so close that it was declared a tie. By law, such elections are decided by lottery—a toss of the coin. Although the paralegal won the toss, a court later declared her opponent the victor after reviewing some disputed ballots. *Toss of Coin to Decide Race in Illinois,* A12 (New York Times, 7/18/90).

 ## Paralegal Sued for Civil Rights Violations

A Kentucky paralegal was sued, along with a prosecutor, for civil rights violations. In the complaint, an automobile dealership alleged that the prosecutor and paralegal fraudulently conspired to obtain the business records of the plaintiff. The paralegal allegedly caused invalid and unenforceable subpoena duces tecum to be issued in order to illegally obtain the records of the dealership. Hectus, *Paralegal Sued for Civil Rights Violations,* One Voice (Kentucky Paralegal Ass'n, March/April 1991).

Paralegal Charged with Insider Trading

A twenty-four old paralegal has been charged with insider trading by the Securities and Exchange Commission. The complaint against the paralegal alleged that she had access to confidential information pertaining to the proposed merger of a client of the firm where she worked. She "tipped" her friends by giving them confidential information. The friends then used this information to earn $823,471 in the purchase of 65,020 shares. A civil complaint seeks damages of $3.29 million. The paralegal has been fired by the law firm. *SEC v. Hurton*, Civ. #89–1070, DC Mass. (5/16/89); *Federal Securities and Corporate Developments*, 21 Securities & Law Report (5/21/89).

A $90,000,000 Mistake!

Several years ago, a paralegal for Prudential inadvertently left off the last three zeros on a mortgage used to secure a $92,885,000 loan made by Prudential to a company that is now bankrupt. As a result of the mistake, Prudential was left with only a $92,885 lien. Litigation is pending before the U.S. Bankruptcy Court in New York City. Prudential's attorneys are trying to convince the Court that Prudential should not be held to the mistake. 17 *At Issue* (San Francisco Legal Assistants Ass'n, Dec. 1990).

Paralegal Convicted

Mershan Shaddy was an independent paralegal in San Diego. He charged clients $180 to handle uncontested divorces, plus $50 if property had to be divided, and $30 for each child. He was arrested after an undercover investigator posed as a divorce client and secretly recorded him giving legal advice in violation of the California law against the unauthorized practice of law. He was convicted and sentenced to forty-five days in jail. *Paralegal's Role in Legal System Stirs a Debate*, San Diego Union B-1 (March 29, 1990).

Law Firm Sues Its Former Paralegal

Richard Trotter once worked as a paralegal for a Denver law firm. He wrote a book called *A Toothless Paper Tiger* about his experiences at the law firm. The book alleges that the firm improperly authorized him and other paralegals at the firm to perform the work of attorneys. The law firm has sought an injunction to prevent the release of the book. Hicks, *Law Firm Fights Book by Former Employee*, National Law Journal 39 (Aug. 6, 1990).

Law Firm Settles Suit Brought by Paralegals

A class action was brought by paralegals and clerical workers who claimed that the Oakland firm where they worked failed to pay them overtime compensation. The case was eventually settled for $170,000 which was distributed among the paralegals and clerical workers. Ziegler, *Firm Settles Suit on Overtime for Paralegals,* San Francisco Banner Daily Journal (1/25/89).

"Will the Legal Assistant Please Tell the Court the Facts of the Case?"

At a paralegal association meeting in Houston, Judge Lynn Hughes, a federal District Court judge, recently drew a "big laugh" concerning an incident in her courtroom. During a hearing, she watched a "Big Gun" senior partner constantly turn to his associate for information on the facts of the case. This associate, in turn, would ask his legal assistant for this information. Finally, Judge Hughes asked the legal assistant to stand up and tell the court the facts of the case! *National News . . . Houston Legal Assistants Association,* 21 Outlook 5 (Illinois Paralegal Ass'n, Spring 1991).

"Then You Should Have Used a Paralegal!"

At oral argument before the United States Supreme Court in a case on paralegal fees, an attorney was interrupted by Justice Thurgood Marshall during the attorney's description of the custom of billing in New Orleans. In the following fascinating excerpt from the transcript of the oral argument, a clearly irritated Justice Marshall suggested that the attorney was unprepared because he did not have a paralegal working with him on the case:

> JUSTICE MARSHALL: Is all that in the record?
> ATTORNEY: I'm sorry. . . .
> JUSTICE MARSHALL: Is that in the record?
> ATTORNEY: I'm not. . . .
> JUSTICE MARSHALL: What you've just said, that the custom of billing and all in New Orleans, is that in the record?
> ATTORNEY: I think it is Justice Marshall.
> JUSTICE MARSHALL: You think? Didn't you try the case?
> ATTORNEY: I tried the case, but whether or not that particular item is in the record, it is certainly in the briefs, but. . . .
> JUSTICE MARSHALL: Then you should have used a paralegal!

Official Transcript Proceedings Before The Supreme Court of the United States, Arthur J. Blanchard, petitioner V. James Bergerson, et al., Case 87–1485, page 25 (11/28/88).

The Perfect Recipe

"To one paralegal, add a pound of variety, eight ounces of flexibility, four ounces of creativity, and a healthy sense of humor. The result? One cost-effective, efficient litigation paralegal." Vore, *A Litigation Recipe,* On Point (Nat'l Capital Area Paralegal Ass'n, Nov. 1990).

Paralegal Trapped

A paralegal, on his way to an assignment on another floor, became trapped in an elevator just after getting on. Fellow employees gathered around the elevator door. The time-conscious paralegal called out from inside the elevator, "Is this billable or nonbillable time?" *A Lighter Note*, MALA Advance 15 (Summer 1989).

Suspense Novel about a Paralegal by a Paralegal

E. P. Dalton has published *Housebreaker*, a novel by David Linzee, who has worked as a litigation paralegal. It is about Megan Lofting. "Megan used to be a probate paralegal at a Connecticut law firm. She used to try hard never to do something wrong. But then she was unjustly fired. Now a big-time criminal is offering her a chance to make a fortune, and to strike back at the client who got her fired, and the lawyer—once her lover—who let it happen." *The First Suspense Novel Ever About a Paralegal . . . by a Former Paralegal*, 4 Viewpoint 10 (Massachusetts Paralegal Association, July/August 1987).

The Cost of What?

Recently, a paralegal was given an unusual assignment by her supervising attorney. She was asked to determine how much it would cost to purchase a penguin! *How Much Does a Penguin Cost?* SJPA Reporter, p. 3 (South Jersey Paralegal Ass'n, Sept. 1990).

Paralegal Watches Exorcism

Kevin McKinley is a paralegal at a West Palm Beach law firm that represented a defendant in a murder case. While working on the case, Kevin found an urn in the room of the defendant where the latter allegedly practiced voodoo and black magic. The family of the defendant was concerned that if the urn was opened in the courtroom, the spirit within it would harm those attending the trial. Hence an exorcism was performed to remove the defendant's control over this spirit. Kevin's assignment was to be a witness at this exorcism. *Columbus Dispatch* (January 6, 1991).

The Paralegal Floral Strategy

A litigation legal assistant was given the task of serving a subpoena on a defendant who was unlikely to open the door. She came up with a creative approach. On her way to the defendant's house, she stopped at a flower shop and picked up a plant. Upon her arrival, she rang the doorbell. The defendant looked out, saw a person with flowers, opened the door, and was presented with a plant . . . and a subpoena! Anderson, *In the Line of Duty*, MALA Advance 17 (Minnesota Ass'n of Legal Assistants, Spring 1991).

◼ I Don't Believe He Said That

- "I told him that I'm a paralegal. He thinks I am a lawyer who jumps out of planes"—in parachutes. *Compendium* (Orange County Paralegal Ass'n, Oct. 1990).
- When asked what to do for your secretary when she needs recognition but doesn't deserve a raise, the attorney answered, "Make her a paralegal!" *The Question of Paralegals,* 20 The Legal Investigator 35 (2/91).
- At a cocktail party, Therese Carey was introduced to a middle-aged businessman. He asked her what she did for a living. Answering that she was a legal assistant, Therese enthusiastically explained her duties. After her response, the man turned to her and earnestly said, "Say, you know, with your background, have you ever considered becoming a paralegal?" Burdett, *Rodney Dangerfield: You're Not Alone,* Newsletter 2, Rhode Island Paralegal Ass'n (Jan. 1987).

◼ Bumper Sticker Award

The Alaska Association of Legal Assistants had a bumper sticker contest. The top three winners were as follows:

"Paralegals Know Their Motions"
"Paralegals Get on Your Case"
"Paralegals Know Briefs"

Paralegals in Tennessee also have a bumper sticker:

Southeastern Paralegal Institute   Nashville, Tennessee   (615) 320-7669

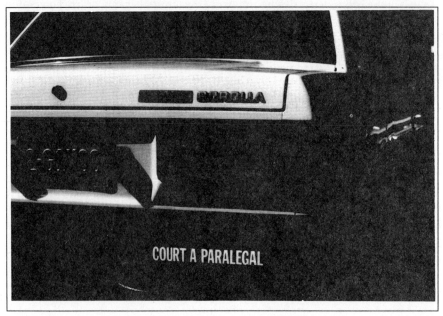

"What It Is That I Do"

A. Pergola, Newsletter, Rocky Mountain Legal Assistants Association (June 1980)

The World of Attorneys

- "I served with General Washington in the legislature of Virginia before the revolution, and during it, with Dr. Franklin in Congress. . . . If the present Congress errs in too much talking, how could it do otherwise in a body to which the people send 150 lawyers, whose trade it is to question everything, yield nothing & talk by the hour?" *Autobiography 1743–1790*, Thomas Jefferson.

- If a man were to give another man an orange, he would say, simply, "Have an orange." But if the transaction were entrusted to an attorney, he would say: "I hereby give, grant, bargain and sell to you, all my right, title and interest in, of, and to said orange, together with all its rind, skin, juice, pulp, and pips, and all rights and advantages therein, with full power to bite, cut, and otherwise eat of the same, or give the same away, with or without the rind, skin, juice, pulp, and pips, anything hereinbefore or hereinafter, or in any other deed or deeds, instrument or instruments, of whatever kind or nature whatsoever to the contrary in any wise notwithstanding." Hirsch, *Pittsburgh Legal Journal*.

■ A document recently filed in the United States Bankruptcy Court in Tennessee contained the following language: "Debtors hereby amend the Amendment to Second Amended and Restated Disclosure Statement, Third Amended and Restated Plan of Reorganization, and Amendment to Third Amended and Restated Plan of Organization as follows. Wherever the name 'Mortgage Company' appears in the Amendment to Second Amended and Restated Disclosure Statement, Third Amended and Restated Plan of Reorganization and Amendment to Third Amended and Restated Plan of Organization, the name 'Bank' shall be inserted in lieu thereof." *The Reporter,* 15 (Delaware Paralegal Association, May/June 1991).

■ Question: How many lawyers does it take to change a light bulb? Answer: Three senior partners to contemplate the history of light; two junior partners to check for conflicts of interest; ten associates to do the research on the antitrust implications of using a particular brand, on the cost-benefits of electric lighting versus candle light, on the health aspects of incandescent versus fluorescent bulb lighting, on the electric components that make light bulbs work, etc. And, of course, a paralegal to screw the bulb into the socket! *On the Lighter Side,* Par·Spectives 5, Paralegal Association of Rochester (May 1990).

Murphy's Law for Paralegals

1. The day you wear comfortable, ugly old shoes is the day you are called into the managing partner's office or have to meet with an important client.

2. The day you wear attractive, stylish pumps that pinch your toes, bite your instep and chafe your heels is the day that you have to serve papers at Nick Tahou's and the Eastern School of Music—before 11 A.M. or after 2 P.M.

3. The night when you have a date, theatre tickets, or fifteen dinner guests due at 7:30 is the night you have to stay late.

4. The day your car is in the garage and you carpooled is the day that you receive a 15-hour project that has to be done before you go home.

5. Your mother, your husband, your boyfriend or your bookie always calls when the boss is standing in your office.

6. Clients that work near you never have to sign anything. The number of documents that need to be signed by a client increases in proportion to the number of miles between their home or office and your office.

7. Whatever you lost is what everyone must have immediately.

8. Whatever can't be found was last in the possession of a paralegal.

9. Whatever needs to be hand delivered or picked up is always beyond the messenger's responsibility.

10. The day you have liverwurst and onion for lunch is the day that you have to attend an unscheduled meeting with an important client or another attorney.

11. The volume of Carmody-Wait 2nd that you require to prepare a motion is always missing from the library.

12. Nobody ever asks you about subjects with which you are familiar. If you are an expert on the mating habits of mosquitoes, you will be asked to digest a deposition or prepare research about the malfunction of the farabus and ullie pin connection in Yugoslavian lawnmowers.

Ciaccia, *Murphy's Laws for Paralegals,* 9 Newsletter 12 (Dallas Ass'n of Legal Assistants, Sept. 1985).

■ Glossary

AAfPE   American Association for Paralegal Education.

ABA   American Bar Association.

Abstracts   *See* Digests.

Accounts Receivable   A list of who owes money to the office, how much, how long the debt has been due, etc.

Accreditation   The process by which an organization evaluates and recognizes a program of study (or an institution) as meeting specified qualifications or standards.

Acquit   To find not guilty.

Act   *See* Statute.

Ad Damnum   The amount of damages claimed in the complaint.

Adjudication   The process by which a court resolves a legal dispute through litigation. The verb is *adjudicate*.

Administrative Agency   A unit of government whose primary mission is to carry out or administer the statutes of the legislature and the executive orders of the chief of the executive branch.

Administrative Code   A collection of administrative regulations organized by subject matter.

Administrative Decision   A resolution of a controversy involving application of the regulations of an administrative agency or its governing statutes and executive orders. Also called a *ruling*.

Administrative Hearing   A proceeding at an administrative agency presided over by a hearing officer (e.g., an Administrative Law Judge) to resolve a controversy.

Administrative Law Judge   A hearing officer who presides over a hearing at an administrative agency.

Administrative Procedure Act   The statute that governs aspects of procedure before administrative agencies.

Administrative Regulation   A law of an administrative agency designed to explain or carry out the statutes and executive orders that govern the agency. Also called a *rule*.

Admiralty Law   An area of the law that covers accidents and injuries on navigable waters. Also called *maritime law*.

Admissible Evidence   Evidence that a judge will allow a jury to consider.

Admission   An out-of-court statement made by a party to the litigation that is inconsistent with a position the party is taking in the litigation. (An exception to the hearsay rule.)

Admonition   A nonpublic declaration that the attorney's conduct was improper. This does not affect his or her right to practice. Also called a private reprimand.

ADR   Alternative dispute resolution.

Advance Sheet   A pamphlet that comes out before (in advance of) a later volume.

Adversarial Hearing   A proceeding in which both parties to a controversy appear before a judge.

Adversarial Memorandum   *See* External Memorandum, Memorandum of Law.

Adversarial System   Justice and truth have a greater chance of emerging when parties to a controversy appear before a neutral judge and jury to argue their conflicting positions.

Adverse Interests   Opposing purposes or claims.

Adverse Judgment   A judgment or decision against you.

Advice   *See* Professional Judgment.

Advocacy   An attempt to influence actions of others.

Affiant   *See* Affidavit.

Affidavit   A written statement of fact in which a person (called the affiant) swears that the statement is true.

Affiliate Member   *See* Associate Member.

Affirmation of Professional Responsibility   A statement of the ethical guidelines of the National Federation of Paralegal Associations.

Affirmative Defense   A defense that is based on new factual allegations by the defendant not contained in the plaintiff's allegations.

Agency Practitioner   An individual authorized to practice before an administrative agency. This individual often does not have to be an attorney.

Aging Report   A listing of accounts receivable indicating the time outstanding on each account.

ALA   Association of Legal Administrators.

Allegation   A claimed fact.

Ambulance Chasing   Aggressively going to individuals with potentially good claims as plaintiffs (e.g., personal-injury victims) to encourage them to hire a particular attorney. If the attorney uses someone else to do the soliciting, the latter is called a *runner*. If this other person uses deception or fraud in the solicitation, he or she is sometimes called a *capper*.

Amicus Curiae Brief A friend-of-the-court brief. An appellate brief submitted by someone who is not a party to the litigation.

Analogous Sufficiently similar in the facts and law being applied. Also referred to as *on point*.

Annotate To provide notes or commentary. A text is annotated if such notes and commentary are provided along with the text.

Annotated Bibliography A bibliography that briefly states why you included each entry in the bibliography.

Annotated Code/Annotated Statutes A collection of statutes organized by subject matter, along with notes and commentary.

Annotation The notes and commentary that follow opinions printed in A.L.R., A.L.R.2d, etc.

Answer The pleading that responds to or answers the allegations of the complaint.

Antitrust Law The law governing unlawful restraints of trade, price fixing, and monopolies.

APA *See* Administrative Procedure Act.

Appeal as a Matter of Right The appeal of a case that an appellate court must hear; it has no discretion on whether to take the appeal.

Appearance Going to court to act on behalf of a party to the litigation. The first time this is done, the attorney files a *notice of appearance*.

Appellant The party bringing an appeal because of dissatisfaction with something the lower tribunal did.

Appellate Brief A document submitted to an appellate court containing arguments on whether a lower court made errors of law.

Appellate Jurisdiction The power of a court to hear an appeal of a case from a lower tribunal to determine whether it made any errors of law.

Appellee The party against whom an appeal is brought. Also called the *respondent*.

Appendixes Additions to a volume or document printed after the body of the text.

Apprentice A person in training for an occupation under the supervision of a full member of that occupation.

Approval The recognition that comes from accreditation, certification, licensure, or registration. The ABA uses *approval* as a substitute for the word *accreditation*.

Approval Commission A group of individuals who investigate whether a paralegal school meets the criteria for approval established by the ABA.

Arbitration In lieu of litigation, both sides agree to allow a neutral third party to resolve their dispute.

Arraignment A court proceeding in which the defendant is formally charged with a crime and enters a plea.

Arrest To take someone into custody in order to bring him or her before the proper authorities.

Assertive Confident, prepared, and tactfully demonstrative about one's accomplishments and needs.

Assigned Counsel An attorney appointed by the court and paid with government funds to represent an individual who cannot afford to hire an attorney.

Associate An attorney employee of a law firm who hopes eventually to become a partner.

Associated Pertaining to an attorney who is an associate in a law firm.

Associate Member A nonattorney who is allowed to become part of—but not a full member of—a bar association. Sometimes called *affiliate member*.

Attestation Clause A clause stating that a person saw a witness sign a document.

Attorney Attestation A signed statement by an attorney that a paralegal applying for membership in a paralegal association meets designated criteria of the association, e.g., is employed as a paralegal.

Attorney–Client Privilege A client and an attorney can refuse to disclose communications between them whose purpose was to facilitate the provision of legal services for the client.

Attorney General The chief attorney for the government. *See also* Opinion of the Attorney General.

Attorney of Record The attorney who has filed a notice of appearance. *See also* Appearance.

Attorney Work Product *See* Work-Product Rule.

Authentication Evidence that a writing or other physical item is genuine and is what it purports to be.

Authority Anything that a court could rely on in reaching its decision.

Authorized Practice of Law Services that constitute the practice of law which a nonattorney has authorization to provide. *See also* Practice of Law, Professional Judgment.

Automatic Pagination A feature that enables a word processor to number the pages of the printed page automatically.

Background Research Checking secondary sources to give you a general understanding of an area of law that is new to you.

Backup To copy information.

Bail Property or a sum of money deposited with the court to ensure that the defendant will reappear in court at designated times.

Bailiff A court employee who keeps order in the courtroom and renders general administrative assistance to the judge.

Bar Prevent or stop.

Bar Coding A series of lines of different widths that can be read by a scanner.

Barratry Stirring up quarrels or litigation; illegal solicitation of clients.

Barrister A lawyer in England who represents clients in the higher courts.

Bar Treaties Agreements between attorneys and other occupations on what law-related activities of these other occupations do and do not constitute the unauthorized practice of law.

Baud Rate A unit of measurement used to indicate the speed of transmission over a modem.

Below (1) The lower tribunal that heard the case before it was appealed. (2) Later in the document.

Best Evidence Rule To prove the contents of a private writing, the original writing should be produced unless it is unavailable.

Beyond a Reasonable Doubt There is no reasonable doubt that every one of the elements of the crime has been established.

Bias Unfairly leaning in favor of or against someone; the potential for unfairness because of prior knowledge or involvement, leading to possible preconceptions and a lack of open-mindedness.

Bicameral Having two houses in the legislature. If there is only one house, it is *unicameral.*

Bill A proposed statute.

Billable Tasks Those tasks requiring time that can be charged to a client.

Billing Memorandum A draft bill which states disbursements, time expended, and billing rates of those working on the matter.

Blended Hourly Rate A rate is set depending on the mix of partners and associates working on the case.

Blind Ad A want ad that does not print the name and address of the prospective employer. The contact is made through a third party, e.g., the newspaper.

Block A group of characters, e.g., a word, a sentence, a paragraph. Block movement is a feature of a word processor that allows the user to define a block of text and then do something with that block, e.g., move it, delete it.

Board of Appeals The unit within an administrative agency to which a party can appeal a decision of the agency.

Boilerplate Standard language that is commonly used in a certain kind of document.

Boldface Heavier or darker than normal type.

Bond A sum of money deposited in court to ensure compliance with a requirement.

Brief *See* Appellate Brief, Brief of a Case, Trial Brief.

Brief of a Case A set of notes on the essential parts of a court opinion, e.g., facts, issues, holding, reasoning.

"Bugs" Manufacturing or design errors that exist in products such as computer hardware or software.

Bulletin Board An inexpensive, relatively small, user-run version of a commercial information service.

Bundled/Unbundled An hourly rate is *bundled* if overhead is included in this rate. It is *unbundled* if the various charges are broken out separately.

Burden of Proof The responsibility of proving a fact at trial.

Business Entry An out-of-court statement found in business records made in the regular course of business by someone whose duty is to make such entries. (An exception to the hearsay rule.)

Byte The storage equivalent of one letter, one punctuation mark, or one blank space typed into the computer.

CALR Computer-Assisted Legal Research.

Capital Partner *See* Income Partner.

Capper *See* Ambulance Chasing.

Caption of Appellate Brief The front of an appellate brief that prints the name of the parties, the name of the court, the docket number, and the kind of appellate brief it is.

Caption of Complaint The top of a complaint that identifies the names of the parties, the court in which the action is brought, the number assigned by the court, etc.

Caption of Opinion The title of an opinion (usually consisting of the names of the parties), the name of the court that wrote it, the docket number, the date of decision—all printed just before the opinion begins.

Career Ladder A formal promotion structure within a company or office.

CARTWHEEL A technique designed to help you think of a large variety of words and phrases to check in the index and table of contents of a law book.

Case (1) A legal matter in dispute or potential dispute. (2) The written decision of a court. *See also* Opinion.

Casebook A law-school textbook containing numerous edited court opinions.

Case Clerk An assistant to a paralegal; an entry-level paralegal.

Case Manager   An experienced legal assistant who can coordinate or direct legal assistant activities on a major case or transaction.

Case Note   A summary of and commentary on a court opinion in a law review.

Cause of Action   A legally acceptable reason for suing.

CD-ROM   Computer disk read-only memory. An optical information-storage system.

Cell   A storage location within a spreadsheet, used to store a single piece of information that is relevant to the spreadsheet.

Censure   A formal disapproval or declaration of blame. *See also* Reprimand.

Certificated   Having met the qualifications for certification from a school or training program.

Certification   The process by which a nongovernmental organization grants recognition to an individual who has met qualifications specified by that organization. *See also* Specialty Certification.

Certified   Having complied with or met the qualifications for certification.

Certified Legal Assistant (CLA)   The title bestowed by the National Association of Legal Assistants on a paralegal who has passed the CLA exam and has met other criteria of NALA. *See also* Specialty Certification.

Certified PLS   A Certified Professional Legal Secretary. This status is achieved after passing an examination and meeting other requirements of NALS, the National Association of Legal Secretaries.

CFLA   Certified Florida Legal Assistant. To earn this title, a paralegal must first pass the CLA (Certified Legal Assistant) exam of NALA, and then pass a special exam on Florida law.

Challenge for Cause   A request to exclude someone from a jury for a specified reason.

Character   A letter, number, or symbol. Character enhancement includes underlining, boldfacing, subscripting, and superscripting.

Chargeable Hour Schedule   A report that summarizes hours invested by attorneys and paralegals, usually on a monthly basis.

Charge to Jury   Instructions to the jury on how to go about determining the facts and reaching its verdict.

Charter   The fundamental law of a municipality or other local unit of government authorizing it to perform designated governmental functions.

Chinese Wall   Steps taken to prevent a tainted employee (attorney, paralegal, or secretary) from having any contact with the case of a particular client in the office. The employee is tainted because he or she has a conflict of interest with that client. A Chinese wall is also called an *ethical wall*. A tainted employee is also called a *contaminated employee*. Once the Chinese wall is set up around the tainted employee, the latter is referred to as a *quarantined employee*.

Circumstantial Evidence   Evidence of one fact from which another fact can be inferred.

Citation   A reference to any written material. It is the "address" where the material can be found in the library. Also called a *cite*.

Citator   A book containing lists of citations that can help you assess the current validity of an item and can give you leads to additional laws.

Cite   (1) A citation. (2) To give the volume and page number, name of the book, etc. where written material can be found in a library.

Cite Checking   Reading every cite in a document to determine whether the format of the cite conforms to the citation rules being used (e.g., the Bluebook rules), whether the quotations in the cite are accurate, etc.

Cited Material   The case, statute, regulation, or other document that you are shepardizing.

Citing Material   The case, article, or annotation that mentions whatever you are shepardizing, i.e., that mentions the cited material.

Civil Dispute   One private party suing another, or a private party suing the government, or the government suing a private party for a matter other than the commission of a crime.

CLA   *See* Certified Legal Assistant.

Claims-Made Policy   Insurance that covers only claims actually filed (i.e., made) during the period in which the policy is in effect.

CLAS   Certified Legal Assistant Specialist (an advanced certification status of NALA).

CLE   Continuing Legal Education. Undertaken after an individual has received his or her primary education or training in a law-related occupation.

Clergy-Penitent Privilege   A member of the clergy and a penitent can refuse to disclose communications between them that relate to spiritual counseling or consultation.

Closed-Ended Question   A relatively narrow question (e.g., how old are you?) that discourages the interviewee from rambling. Also called a *directed question*.

Closing   The event during which steps are taken to finalize the transfer of an interest in property.

Code   A set of rules, organized by subject matter.

Codefendant   More than one defendant being sued in a civil case (or prosecuted in a criminal case) in the same litigation.

Code of Ethics and Professional Responsibility   A statement of the ethical guidelines of the National Association of Legal Assistants.

Codified Cite   The citation to a statute that has been printed in a code and, therefore, has been organized by subject matter. *See also* Session Law Cite.

Codify   To arrange material by subject matter.

Command   An instruction typed into a computer.

Commingling   Mixing general law firms funds with client funds in a single account.

Common Law   Judge-made law in the absence of controlling statutory law or other higher law. *See also* Enacted Law.

Common Representation   *See* Multiple Representation.

Communications   A program that allows computers to communicate with each other, usually through telephone lines. *See also* Modem.

Compatible   (1) Information generated on an IBM computer that can also be used by another computer. (2) A program designed for an IBM computer that can also be run by other computers.

Competence, Attorney   Having the knowledge and skill that is reasonably necessary to represent a particular client.

Competent (evidence)   Capable of giving testimony because the person understands the obligation to tell the truth, has the ability to communicate, and has knowledge of the topic of his or her testimony.

Complaint   The pleading filed by the plaintiff that tries to state a claim or cause of action against the defendant.

Concurrent Jurisdiction   The power of a court to hear a particular kind of case, along with other courts that could also hear it.

Concurring Opinion   An opinion written by less than a majority of the judges on the court that agrees with the *result* reached by the majority but not with all of its reasoning.

Conference Committee   A committee made up of members of both houses of the legislature which meets to try to resolve differences in the versions of a bill that each house passed.

Confidential   That which should not be revealed; pertaining to information that others do not have a right to receive.

Conflict of Interest   Divided loyalty that actually or potentially places one of the participants to whom undivided loyalty is owed at a disadvantage. *See also* Divided Loyalty.

Conflicts Check   A check of the client files of a law firm to help determine whether a conflict of interest might exist between a prospective client and current or past clients. The person performing this check is often called a *conflicts specialist.*

Conflicts of Law   An area of the law that determines what law applies when a choice must be made between the laws of different, coequal legal systems, e.g., two states.

Confrontation   The right to face your accuser.

Connectors   Characters, words, or symbols used to show the relationship between the words and phrases in a query.

Constitution   The fundamental law that creates the branches of government and that identifies basic rights and obligations.

Contaminated Paralegal   *See* Chinese Wall.

Contest   To challenge.

Contingent Fee   A fee that is dependent on the outcome of the case.

Contract Attorney   *See* Project Attorney.

Contract Paralegal   A self-employed paralegal who often works for several different attorneys on a freelance basis. *See also* Freelance Paralegal.

Control Character   A coded character that does not print but is part of the command sequence in a word processor.

Coordinates   In a spreadsheet program, the column letter and row number that define the location of a specific cell.

Corporate Counsel   The chief attorney of a corporation. Also called the *general counsel.*

Corporate Legal Department   The law office within a corporation containing salaried attorneys (in-house attorneys) who advise and represent the corporation.

Counterclaim   A claim or cause of action against the plaintiff stated in the defendant's answer.

Court of First Instance   A trial court; a court with original jurisdiction.

Credentialization   A form of official recognition based on one's training or employment status.

Credible   Believable.

Criminal Dispute   A suit brought by the government for the alleged commission of a crime.

Cross-claim   Usually, a claim by one codefendant against another.

Cross-examination   Questioning the witness called by the other side after direct examination.

Cumulative   That which repeats earlier material and consolidates it with new material. A cumulative supplement contains new supplemental material and repeats earlier supplemental material.

Cured   Corrected.

Cursor   The marker on the display screen indicating where the next character can be displayed.

Daisy Wheel Printer   A printer which uses a device resembling a flower that contains the alphabet and other characters on spokes.

Damages   An award of money paid by the wrongdoer to compensate the person who has been harmed.

Data   Information that can be used by a computer.

Database   A program used to store and organize information; a grouping of independent files into one integrated whole that can be accessed through one central point.

Data Manager   A data management software package that consolidates data files into an integrated whole, allowing access to more than one data file at a time.

Data Redundancy   The repetition of the same data in several different files.

Decision   *See* Administrative Decision, Opinion.

Declaration against Interest   An out-of-court statement made by a nonparty to the litigation that is against the interest of that nonparty. (An exception to the hearsay rule.)

Declaration of Bodily Feelings   An out-of-court statement or utterance made spontaneously about the person's present bodily condition. (An exception to the hearsay rule.)

Declaration of Mental State of Mind   An out-of-court statement made about the person's present state of mind. (An exception to the hearsay rule.)

Declaration of Present Sense Impression   An out-of-court statement that describes an event while it is being observed by the person making the statement. (An exception to the hearsay rule.)

Declaratory Judgment   A court decision establishing the rights and obligations of the parties but not ordering them to do or to refrain from doing anything.

Dedicated Word Processor   A system that can perform only word processing tasks.

Deep Pocket   Slang for the person or organization with enough money or other assets to be able to pay a judgment.

Default Judgment   A judgment for the plaintiff because the defendant failed to appear or to file an answer before the deadline.

Default Setting   A value used by the word processor when it is not instructed to use any other value.

Defense   An allegation of fact or the presentation of a legal theory that is offered to offset or defeat a claim or demand.

"Delegatitis"   An inordinate fear of delegating tasks to others.

Deletion   A feature of a word processor that allows you to remove a character, word, sentence, or larger block of text from the existing text.

Demurrer   Even if the plaintiff proved all the facts stated in the complaint, a cause of action would not be established.

Denturist   A nondentist who produces and dispenses removable dentures directly to the public.

Deponent   *See* Deposition.

Deposition   A pretrial discovery device consisting of a question-and-answer session involving a party or witness designed to assist the other party prepare for trial. The person who is questioned is called the *deponent*.

Depository Library   A library that receives free government publications to which it must admit the general public.

Depo Summarizer   An employee whose main job is digesting discovery documents.

Dictum   A statement made by a court that was not necessary to resolve the specific legal issues before the court. The plural of dictum is dicta.

Digest by Person   A summary of the information in a document pertaining to a certain individual.

Digest by Subject   A summary of the information in a document pertaining to a certain topic or subject.

Digesting   Summarizing discovery documents. *See also* Depo Summarizer.

Digests   (1) Volumes that contain summaries of court opinions. These summaries are sometimes called *abstracts* or *squibs*. (2) Volumes that contain summaries of annotations in A.L.R., A.L.R.2d, etc.

Directed Question   *See* Closed-Ended Question.

Directed Verdict   An order by the court that the jury reach a verdict for the party making the motion for a directed verdict.

Direct Evidence Evidence that tends to establish a fact (or to disprove a fact) without the need for an inference.

Direct Examination The first questioning of a witness you have called.

Disbarment The temporary or permanent termination of the right to practice law.

Disbursements Out-of-pocket expenses.

Disciplinary Rule (DR) *See* Model Code of Professional Responsibility.

Discount Adjustment A write down (decrease) in the bill.

Discoverable Obtainable through one of the devices of pretrial discovery, e.g., interrogatories.

Discovery Pretrial devices designed to assist a party prepare for trial. *See* Deposition, Interrogatories.

Disinterested Not working for one side or the other in a controversy or other legal matter; not deriving benefit if one of the sides prevails.

Disk Drive Hardware used to store and retrieve programs and information to and from diskettes.

Diskette A flat piece of plastic on which information can be placed or removed by the computer.

Dismissal without Prejudice A dismissal based on procedural, not substantive, grounds. The party can try to bring the case again.

Disqualification *See* Vicarious Disqualification.

Dissenting Opinion An opinion that disagrees with the result and the reasoning used by the majority.

District Court *See* United States District Court.

Diversity of Citizenship The parties to the litigation are from different states, and the amount in controversy exceeds the amount specified by federal statute.

Divided Loyalty The responsibility of protecting the interest of parties who are competitors or are otherwise at odds with each other. *See also* Conflict of Interest.

Docket Number The number assigned to a case by the court.

Doctor-Patient Privilege A doctor and a patient can refuse to disclose any confidential (private) communications between them that relate to medical care.

Document Clerk An individual whose main responsibility is to organize, file, code, or digest litigation or other client documents.

Documentation The manual on operating a computer; the accompanying documents.

Dot Matrix Printer A printer which uses tiny pins that press against or punch a ribbon to create a pattern of dots.

Double Density The disk drive can store information on the diskette in condensed mode.

Downtime The period during which the computer is unavailable because of technical difficulties.

DR Disciplinary Rule. *See* Model Code of Professional Responsibility.

Draft Write.

Draft Bill *See* Billing Memorandum.

Draw A partner's advance against profits.

Dual Sided The disk drive is capable of writing on both sides of the diskette.

DWI Descriptive Word Index, an index to the digests of West.

Dying Declaration An out-of-court statement concerning the causes or circumstances of death made by a person whose death is imminent. (An exception to the hearsay rule.)

EC Ethical Consideration. *See* Model Code of Professional Responsibility.

Editing In word processing, the act of changing or amending text.

EEOC Equal Employment Opportunity Commission, a federal agency that investigates job discrimination.

Element A portion of a rule which is a precondition of the applicability of the entire rule. The *element in contention* is the element of the rule about which the parties cannot agree. The disagreement may be over the meaning of the element or how it applies to a given set of facts.

Enacted Law Law written by the legislature (statutes), by the people (constitutions), and by an administrative agency (regulations). Law that is not the product of adjudication. *See* Adjudication.

En Banc By the entire court.

Enrolled Agent An individual authorized to represent taxpayers at all administrative proceedings within the Internal Revenue Service—this person does not have to be an attorney.

Enrollment *See* Registration.

Entry-Level Certification Certification of individuals who have just begun their careers.

Equity Partner A full owner of a law firm. *See also* Income Partner.

Estate All the property left by a decedent from which his or her debts can be paid.

Et al. And others.

Ethical Wall *See* Chinese Wall.

Ethical Consideration (EC) *See* Model Code of Professional Responsibility.

Ethics Rules embodying standards of behavior to which members of an organization are expected to conform.

Et Seq. And following.

Evidence That which is offered to help establish or disprove a factual position. A separate determination must be made on whether a particular item of evidence is relevant or irrelevant, admissible or inadmissible, etc.

Exclusive Jurisdiction The power of a court to hear a particular kind of case, to the exclusion of other courts.

Execution Carrying out or enforcing a judgment.

Executive Branch The branch of government that carries out, executes, or administers the law.

Executive Department Agency An administrative agency that exists within the executive branch of government, often at the cabinet level.

Executive Order A law passed by the chief executive pursuant to a specific statutory authority or to the executive's inherent authority.

Exempt Employee An employee who is not entitled to overtime compensation under the Fair Labor Standards Act because the employee is a professional, administrative, or executive employee. Paralegals are nonexempt, except for paralegal managers.

Exhausting Administrative Remedies Pursuing all available methods of resolving a dispute within the administrative agency before asking a court to review what the agency did.

Exhibit An item of physical or tangible evidence offered in court for inspection.

Ex Parte Hearing A hearing at which only one party is present. A court order issued at such a hearing is an *ex parte order*.

External/Adversary Memorandum of Law A memorandum written primarily for individuals outside of the office to convince them to take a certain course of action. *See also* Memorandum of Law.

Fact Particularization A technique designed to help you list numerous factual questions in order to obtain a comprehensive picture of all the facts that are relevant to a legal matter.

Fact Pleading A statement of every ultimate (i.e., essential) fact in the complaint.

Facts & Findings A periodical of the National Association of Legal Assistants.

Fair Labor Standards Act The federal statute that regulates conditions of employment such as when overtime compensation must be paid. *See also* Exempt Employee.

Federalism The coexistence of, and the interrelationships among, the state governments and the federal government, particularly with respect to the powers of each of these levels of government.

Federal Question A legal question that arises from the application of the United States Constitution, a statute of Congress, or a federal administrative regulation.

Fee-Generating Case The case of a client who can pay a fee out of the damages awarded or from his or her independent resources.

Fee Splitting A single client bill covering the fee of two or more attorneys who are not in the same firm.

Felony A crime punishable by a sentence of one year or more.

Field A subdivision of a record that holds a meaningful item of data, e.g., an employee number.

Field Search In WESTLAW, a search that is limited to a certain part of cases in its databases.

File A group of related data records, e.g., employee records.

Filed Formally presented to a court.

First Instance, Court of A trial court; a court with original jurisdiction.

Fixed Fee A flat fee for services. A set amount paid regardless of the outcome of the case or the amount of time needed to complete it.

Floppy Disk A disk drive that can use diskettes.

Format In word processing, the layout of the page, e.g., the number of lines and margin settings.

Formbook A manual that contains forms, checklists, practice techniques, etc. Also called a *practice manual* or *handbook*.

Formula A mathematical expression that is used in a spreadsheet.

Forum The court where the case is to be tried.

Forwarding Fee *See* Referral Fee.

FRCP Federal Rules of Civil Procedure.

Freedom of Information Act A statute that gives citizens access to certain information in the possession of the government.

Freelance Paralegal A self-employed paralegal who works for several different attorneys, or a self-employed paralegal who works directly for the public. Also referred to as an *independent paralegal.*

Friendly Divorce A divorce proceeding in which the parties have no significant disputes between them.

Full-Text Search A search through all of the information in a database.

Functional Resume A resume that clusters skills and talents together regardless of when they were developed.

General Counsel The chief attorney in a corporate law department.

General Jurisdiction The power of the court (within its geographic boundaries) to hear any kind of case, with certain exceptions.

General Practitioner An attorney who handles any kind of case.

General Schedule (GS) The pay-scale system used in the federal government.

Geographic Jurisdiction The area of the state or country over which a court has power to render decisions.

Global In word processing, an instruction that will be carried out throughout the document.

Go Bare To engage in an occupation or profession without malpractice insurance.

GOD The "Great Overtime Debate." *See* Exempt Employee.

Grand Jury A special jury whose duty is to hear evidence of felonies presented by the prosecutor to determine whether there is sufficient evidence to return an indictment against the defendant and cause him or her to stand trial on the charges.

Grounds Reasons.

Group Legal Services A form of legal insurance in which members of a group pay a set amount on a regular basis, for which they receive designated legal services. Also called *prepaid legal services.*

GS *See* General Schedule.

Guideline Suggested conduct that will help an applicant obtain accreditation, certification, licensure, registration, or approval.

HALT Help Abolish Legal Tyranny, an organization that seeks to reform the legal profession, primarily by eliminating the monopoly of attorneys over the practice of law.

Handbook *See* Formbook.

Harassment *See* Hostile Environment, Quid Pro Quo Harassment.

Hard Disk A disk drive that cannot be removed without taking the hardware apart.

Hardware The computer and its physical parts.

Header In word processing, a piece of text that is stored separately from the text and printed at the top of each page.

Heading The beginning of a memorandum that lists who the memo is for, who wrote it, what it is about, etc.

Headnote A small-paragraph summary of a portion of a court opinion, written by a private publisher.

Hearing Examiner One who presides over an administrative hearing.

Hearing Memorandum A memorandum of law submitted to a hearing officer.

Hearsay Testimony in court, or written evidence, of a statement made out of court when the statement is offered to show the truth of matters asserted therein, and thus resting for its value on the credibility of the out-of-court asserter.

Historical Note Information on the legislative history of a statute printed after the text of the statute.

Holding A court's answer to one of the legal issues in the case. Also called a *ruling.*

Hornbook A treatise that summarizes an area of the law.

Hostile Environment Harassment Pervasive unwelcome sexual conduct or sex-based ridicule which unreasonably interferes with an individual's job performance or creates an intimidating, hostile, or offensive working environment.

Hourly Plus Fixed Fee A specified hourly rate is used until the nature and scope of the problem are defined; a fixed fee is used thereafter.

Hypothetical Question A question in which the interviewee is asked to respond to a set of facts provided by the interviewer.

Id. Same citation as immediately above.

Impaired Attorney An attorney with a drug or alcohol problem.

Impaneled Selected, sworn in, and seated.

Impeach To challenge; to attack the credibility of.

Imputed Disqualification *See* Vicarious Disqualification.

Income Partner A special category of partner who does not own the firm in the sense of a full equity or capital partner. Also called a *permanent associate* and a *non-equity partner.*

Incremental Spacing   In word processing, a method by which the printer inserts spaces between words and letters to produce margins that are justified. Also called *microspacing.*

Independent Contractor   One who operates his or her own business and contracts to do work for others who do not control the details of how that work is performed.

Independent Paralegal   *See* Freelance Paralegal.

Independent Regulatory Agency   An administrative agency (often existing outside of the executive department) created to regulate an aspect of society.

Indexing   Identifying the page numbers on which certain topics appear in a document.

Indictment   A formal document issued by a grand jury accusing the defendant of a crime. *See also* Grand Jury.

Indigent   Poor, unable to pay for needed services.

Inferior Court   A lower court.

Information   A document accusing the defendant of a crime (used in states without a grand jury).

Informational Interview   An interview in which you find out about a particular kind of employment. It is *not* a job interview.

Information and Belief   To the best of my knowledge; good faith understanding.

Infra   Below, mentioned or referred to later in the document.

In-house Attorney   An attorney who is an employee of a business corporation. *See* Corporate Legal Department.

Initial Appearance   A court appearance during which the accused is told of the charges, a decision on bail is made, and arrangements for the next court proceeding are specified.

In Issue   In dispute or question.

Ink Jet Printer   A printer that uses a stream of ink sprayed on paper to produce the print.

In Personam Jurisdiction   *See* Personal Jurisdiction.

In Re   In the matter of.

Insertion   In word processing, a feature by which a character, word, sentence, or larger block of text is added to the existing text.

Instrument   A formal document that gives expression to a legal act or agreement, e.g., a mortgage.

Intake Memo   A memorandum that summarizes the facts given by a client upon becoming a client of the office.

Integrated Bar Association   A state bar association to which an attorney must belong in order to practice law in the state. Also called a *mandatory* or *unified bar association.*

Integrated Package   A software program that enables the user to use more than one kind of program simultaneously, e.g., word processing, database management, spreadsheet.

Intellectual Property Law   The law governing patents, copyrights, trademarks, and trade names.

Interim Suspension   A temporary suspension, pending the imposition of final discipline.

Interlocutory Appeal   An appeal of a trial court ruling before the trial court reaches its final judgment.

Intermediate Appellate Court   A court with appellate jurisdiction to which parties can appeal before they appeal to the highest court in the judicial system.

Internal/Interoffice Memorandum of Law   A memorandum written for members of one's own office. *See also* Memorandum of Law.

Interrogatories   A pretrial discovery device consisting of written questions sent by one party to another to assist the sender of the questions to prepare for trial.

Interstate Compact   An agreement between two or more states governing a problem of mutual concern.

Intra-agency Appeal   An appeal within an administrative agency, before the case is appealed to a court.

Jailhouse Lawyer   A paralegal in prison, usually self-taught, who has a limited right to practice law and to give legal advice to fellow inmates if the prison does not provide adequate alternatives for legal services. Also known as a *writ writer.*

Jargon   Technical language; language that does not have an everyday meaning.

Job Bank   A service that lists available jobs, usually available only to members of an organization.

Joint and Several Liability   Legally responsible together and individually.

Judgment   The decision of the court on the controversy before it.

Judgment Creditor   The party to whom damages must be paid.

Judgment Debtor   The party who must pay damages.

Judgment nov   A judgment of the court that is opposite or contrary to the verdict reached by the jury.

Judgment on the Merits   A decision on the substance of the claims raised.

Judicare   A system of paying private attorneys to provide legal services to the poor on a case-by-case basis.

Judicial Branch   The branch of government with primary responsibility for interpreting laws and resolving disputes that arise under them.

Jurisdiction   The power of a court. *See also* Geographic Jurisdiction, Subject-Matter Jurisdiction.

Justification   In word processing, a feature for making lines of text even at the margins.

K   A measure of capacity in a computer system.

Kardex   A file in which the library records the volume numbers and dates of incoming publications that are part of subscriptions.

Key Fact   A critical fact; a fact that was essential to the holding of the court.

Key-Word Search   A search through a list of specified words that function like an index to a database.

Label   Information used for describing some aspect of a spreadsheet.

LAMA   Legal Assistants Management Association.

Landmen   Paralegals who work in the area of oil and gas law. Also called *land technicians*.

Language   A program that allows a computer to understand commands and to carry them out.

Laptop   A portable computer, often powered by a rechargeable battery.

Laser Printer   A printer that uses a laser beam of light to reproduce images.

Lateral Hire   An attorney, paralegal, or secretary who has been hired from another law office.

Law Clerk   An employee of an attorney who is in law school studying to become an attorney or who has graduated from law school and is waiting to pass the bar examination. In Ontario, Canada, a law clerk is a trained professional doing independent legal work, which may include managerial duties, under the direction and guidance of a lawyer, and whose function is to relieve a lawyer of routine and administrative matters and to assist a lawyer in the more complex ones.

Law Directory   A list of attorneys.

Law Review   A legal periodical published by a law school. Sometimes called a *law journal*.

Lay Opinion Evidence   The opinion of someone who is not an expert.

Leading Question   A question that suggests an answer within the question.

Legal Administrator   An individual, usually a nonattorney, with broad management responsibility for a law office.

Legal Advice   *See* Professional Judgment.

Legal Analysis   The process of connecting a rule of law to a set of facts in order to determine how that rule might apply to a particular situation. The goal of the process is to solve a legal dispute or to prevent one from arising.

Legal Assistant   *See* Paralegal.

Legal Assistant Clerk   A person who assists a legal assistant in clerical tasks such as document numbering, alphabetizing, filing, and any other project that does not require substantive knowledge of litigation or of a particular transaction. *See also* Document Clerk.

Legal Assistant Division   A few state bar associations, e.g., Texas, have established special divisions which paralegals can join as associate members.

Legal Assistant Manager   A person responsible for recruiting, interviewing, and hiring legal assistants who spends little or no time working on client cases as a legal assistant. He or she may also be substantially involved in other matters pertaining to legal assistants, e.g., training, monitoring work assignments, designing budgets, and overseeing the billing of paralegal time. Also known as a *paralegal manager*.

Legal Bias   *See* Bias.

Legal Executive   A trained and certified employee of a solicitor in England; the equivalent of an American paralegal but with more training and credentials.

Legal Insurance   *See* Group Legal Services.

Legal Issue   A question of law; a question of what the law is, or what the law means, or how the law applies to a set of facts. If the dispute is over the truth or falsity of the facts, it is referred to as a *question of fact* or a *factual dispute*.

Legalman   A nonattorney in the Navy who assists attorneys in the practice of law.

Legal Technician   A self-employed paralegal who works for several different attorneys, or a self-employed paralegal who works directly for the public. Sometimes called an *independent paralegal* or a *freelance paralegal*.

Legislation   (1) The process of making statutory law. (2) A statute.

Legislative Branch   The branch of government with primary responsibility for making or enacting the law.

Legislative History   All of the events that occur in the legislature before a bill is enacted into a statute.

Letterhead   The top half of stationery which identifies the name and address of the office (often with the names of selected employees).

Leverage   The ability to make a profit from the income-generating work of others.

LEXIS   The legal research computer service of Mead Data Co.

Liable   Legally responsible.

Licensed Independent Paralegal   A paralegal who holds a limited license. *See* Limited Licensure.

Licensure   The process by which an agency of government grants permission to persons meeting specified qualifications to engage in an occupation and to use a particular title.

Limited Jurisdiction   The power of a court to hear only certain kinds of cases. Also called *special jurisdiction*.

Limited Licensure   The process by which an agency of government grants permission to persons meeting specified qualifications to engage in designated activities that are now customarily (although not always exclusively) performed by another license holder, i.e., that are part of someone else's monopoly.

Limited Practice Officer   A nonattorney in Washington state who has the authority to select and prepare designated legal documents pertaining to real estate closings.

Litigation   The formal process of resolving legal controversies through special tribunals established for this purpose. The major tribunal is a court.

Load   To move a program or information from a disk drive into the computer.

Lodestar   A mathematical formula based on a multiplier which relies on hourly rates and other factors.

Looseleaf Service   A three-ring (or post) binder containing pages that can be easily inserted or taken out. The service covers current information on a broad or narrow topic.

Magistrate   A judicial officer having some but not all the powers of a judge.

Majority Opinion   The opinion whose result and reasoning is supported by at least half plus one of the judges on the court.

Malpractice   Serious wrongful conduct committed by an individual, usually a member of a profession.

Mandate   The order of the court.

Mandatory Authority   Whatever a court must rely on in reaching its decision.

Mandatory Bar Association   *See* Integrated Bar Association.

Marital Communications   A husband and a wife can refuse to disclose communications between them during the marriage.

Maritime Law   *See* Admiralty Law.

Market Rate   The prevailing rate in the area.

Martindale–Hubbell   A national directory of attorneys.

Med-arb   In lieu of litigation, the parties to a dispute try arbitration after mediation is unsuccessful.

Mediation   In lieu of litigation, a neutral third party (the mediator) tries to encourage the parties to a dispute to reach a compromise.

Memorandum of Law   A memorandum is simply a note, a comment, or a report. A legal memorandum is a written explanation of what the law is and how it might apply to a fact situation.

Memorandum Opinion   A court opinion that does not name the judge who wrote the opinion.

Memory   The area inside the computer that contains programs and data which the programs help generate.

Menu   In word processing and other programs, a list of commands or prompts on the display screen.

Merge Printing   In word processing and other programs, a feature that allows a user to combine whole files and to place data from one file into specified locations in another.

Microcomputer   A computer small enough to fit on a desk.

Microfiche   *See* Microform.

Microform   Images or photographs that have been reduced in size. Microforms can be *microfilms* that store materials on film reels or cassettes, or *microfiche* and *ultrafiche* that store materials on single sheets of film..

Minimum-Fee Schedule   A published list of fees recommended by a bar association.

Misdemeanor   A crime punishable by a sentence of less than a year.

Model Code of Professional Responsibility   An earlier edition of the ethical rules governing attorneys recommended by the American Bar Association. The Model Code consisted of Ethical Considerations (ECs), which represented the objectives toward which each attorney should strive, and Disciplinary Rules (DRs), which were mandatory statements of the minimum conduct below which no attorney could fall without being subject to discipline.

Model Rules of Professional Conduct   The current set of ethical rules governing attorneys recommended by the American Bar Association. These rules revised the ABA's earlier rules found in the Model Code of Professional Responsibility.

Model Standards and Guidelines for Utilization of Legal Assistants A statement of ethical and related guidelines of the National Association of Legal Assistants.

Modem A device that allows one computer to send and receive information using regular telephone lines.

Monitor A display screen; a TV-like device used to display what is typed at the keyboard and the response of the computer.

Monitoring Legislation Finding out current information on the status of a proposed statute in the legislature.

Mouse A clicking device used as a partial substitute for typing commands into a computer.

Movant The party who formally requests a court to do something.

Multiple Representation Representing more than one side in a legal matter or controversy. Also called *common representation*.

Multitasking Having the capacity to run several large programs simultaneously.

NALA National Association of Legal Assistants.

NALS National Association of Legal Secretaries. *See also* Certified PLS.

National Paralegal Reporter A periodical of the National Federation of Paralegal Associations.

Neighborhood Legal Service Office A law office that serves the legal needs of the poor, often publicly funded.

Network Several computers connected together to share printers or hard disk drives.

Networking Establishing contacts with a relatively large number of people who might be helpful to you later. Similarly, you become such a contact for others.

NFPA National Federation of Paralegal Associations.

NJC Neighborhood Justice Center.

Nolle Prosequi A statement by the prosecutor that he or she is unwilling to prosecute the case.

Nominative Reporter A reporter volume that is identified by the name of the person responsible for compiling and printing the opinions in the volume.

Nonadversarial Proceeding Only one party appears in the proceeding, or both parties appear but they have no real controversy between them.

Nonbillable task A task for which an office cannot bill a client.

Nonequity Partner *See* Income Partner.

Nonexempt Employee *See* Exempt Employee.

Nonrebuttable Presumption *See* Presumption.

Notary Public A person who witnesses (i.e., attests to the authenticity of) signatures, administers oaths, and performs related tasks. In Europe, a notary often has more extensive authority.

Notes of Decisions Summaries of court opinions that have interpreted a statute. The notes are printed after the statute in annotated codes.

Notice Pleading A short and plain statement of the claim showing that the pleader is entitled to relief.

Notice of Appearance *See* Appearance.

Oath A sworn statement that what you say is true.

Occurrence Policy Malpractice insurance that covers all occurrences (e.g., a negligent error or omission) during the period the policy is in effect, even if the claim is not actually filed until after the policy expires.

Of Counsel An attorney with a special status in the firm, e.g., a semiretired partner.

Office Sharing Attorneys with their own independent practices who share the use and cost of administration such as rent, copy machine, etc.

Official Reporter A reporter that is published under the authority of the government, often printed by the government itself. An unofficial reporter is printed by a private or commercial publisher without specific authority from the government.

OJT On-the-job training.

On All Fours The facts are exactly the same, or almost the same.

Online Within the control of, or coming from, a central computer; in communication with a computer; through equipment under the control of a central processing unit.

On Point *See* Analogous.

Open-Ended Question A relatively broad question or request (e.g., "tell me about yourself") that forces the interviewee to organize his or her thoughts and to exert a relatively large measure of control over the kind and quantity of information provided.

Operating System A program that controls the overall operation of the computer, allowing it to do anything.

Opinion A court's written explanation of how and why it applied the law to the specific facts before it to reach its decision. Also called a *case*. Opinions are printed in volumes called *reporters*.

Opinion Letter A letter to a client explaining the application of the law and advising the client what to do.

Opinion of the Attorney General   Formal legal advice given by the attorney general to government officials.

Ordinance   A law passed by the local legislative branch of government (e.g., city council).

Original Jurisdiction   The power of a court to hear a particular kind of case initially. A trial court has original jurisdiction.

Outstanding   Still unresolved; still unpaid.

Overhead   The operating expenses of a business, e.g., cost of office space, furniture, equipment, insurance, clerical staff.

Padding   Adding something without justification.

Paralegal   A person with legal skills who works under the supervision of an attorney or who is otherwise authorized to use those skills; this person performs tasks that do not require all the skills of an attorney and that most secretaries are not trained to perform. Synonymous with *legal assistant*.

Paralegal Manager   *See* Legal Assistant Manager.

Paralegal Specialist   A job classification in the federal government.

Parallel Cite   An additional citation where you can find the same written material in the library.

Paraphrase   To rephrase something in your own words.

Parol Evidence Rule   Oral evidence cannot be introduced to alter or contradict the contents of a written document if the parties intended the written document to be a complete statement of the agreement.

Partner, Full   An attorney who contributes the capital to create the firm and to expand it, who shares the profits and losses of the firm, who controls the management of the firm, and who decides whether the firm will go out of existence.

Partnership   A group of individuals who practice law jointly and who share in the profits and losses of the venture.

People   The state or government.

Percentage Fee   The fee is a percentage of the amount involved in the transaction or award.

Per Curiam   By the court. A court opinion that does not name the particular judge who wrote the opinion.

Peremptory Challenge   A request that someone be excluded from a jury without any reasons stated for this request.

Personal Jurisdiction   The court's power over a particular person. Also called *in personam jurisdiction*.

Personal Liability   Being responsible because of what you wrongfully did or wrongfully failed to do. *See also* Vicarious Liability.

Personal Recognizance   The release of a defendant charged with a crime after a personal promise to return to court at a designated time. No bail is deposited.

Persuasive Authority   Whatever a court relies on in reaching its decision when it is not required to do so.

Petition   (1) A formal request or motion. (2) A complaint.

Physical Evidence   That which can be seen or touched. Also called *tangible evidence*.

Physician Assistant   An individual who is qualified by academic and clinical training to provide patient care services under the supervision and responsibility of a doctor of medicine or osteopathy.

PI Cases   Personal injury (tort) cases.

Plaintiff   The party initiating the lawsuit.

Plea Bargaining   An attempt to avoid a criminal trial by negotiating a plea, e.g., the defendant agrees to plead guilty to a lesser charge than initially brought.

Plead   To deliver a formal statement or response.

Pleading   A paper or document filed in court stating the position of one of the parties on the cause(s) of action or on the defense(s).

PL Number   Public Law number.

Plotter   A device that will hold a pen to a piece of paper and draw lines as instructed by commands you enter into the computer.

PLS   Professional Legal Secretary. *See also* Certified PLS.

Pocket Part   An insert that fits into a small pocket built into the inside back cover of a bound volume.

Point Heading   A party's conclusion to an argument it is making in an appellate brief.

Points and Authorities Memorandum   A memorandum of law submitted to a judge or hearing officer. Sometimes called a *trial memorandum*.

Poll   To question jurors individually in open court as to whether each agrees with the verdict announced by the foreman.

Popular Name   A statute that is identified by the name of a person, place, or topic rather than simply by a title and section number.

Practical Manual   *See* Formbook.

Practice Analysis Report   A report that analyzes where the firm is investing its time, where its income and profit are coming from, the amount of disbursements, etc.

Practice of Law   Engaging in any of the following activities on behalf of another: representation in court, representation in an agency proceeding, preparation of legal documents, or providing legal advice.

Praecipe   A formal request to the court (usually through the clerk) that something be done.

Prayer for Relief   The request for damages or other form of relief.

Pre-evaluation Memo   A memorandum sent to a supervisor before a formal evaluation in which the employee lists the following information (since the last formal evaluation): major projects, functions on those projects, names of co-workers on the projects, evidence of initiative, quotations on the quality of work, etc.

Preliminary Hearing   A hearing during which the state is required to produce sufficient evidence to establish that there is probable cause to believe the defendant committed the crimes charged.

Premium Adjustment   A write up (increase) of a bill.

Prepaid Legal Services   *See* Group Legal Services.

Preponderance of the Evidence   It is more likely than not that the fact is as alleged.

Presumption   An assumption that a certain fact is true. It is rebuttable if the court will consider evidence that it is false, and nonrebuttable if no such contrary evidence will be considered.

Pretrial Conference   A meeting between the judge (or magistrate) and the attorneys to prepare the case for trial, and perhaps to make one last effort to settle the case.

Prima Facie   On the face of it; that which would be legally sufficient, if believed, to support a verdict.

Primary Authority   Any *law* that a court could rely on in reaching its decision.

Print Formatting   The function of a word processor that communicates with the printer to tell it how to print the text on paper.

Print Review   In word processing, a feature that enables you to view a general representation on the screen of how the document will look when printed.

Private Law   *See* Statute.

Private Law Firm   A law firm that generates its income from the fees of individual clients.

Private Reprimand   *See* Admonition.

Private Sector   An office where the funds come from client fees or the corporate treasury.

Private Statute   *See* Statute.

Privilege   A special benefit, right, or protection. In the law of evidence, a privilege is the right to refuse to testify or to prevent someone else from testifying.

Privilege against Self-Incrimination   Persons cannot be compelled to testify in a criminal proceeding or to answer incriminating questions that directly or indirectly connect themselves to the commission of a crime.

Probable Cause   A reasonable basis to believe that the defendant is guilty of the crime(s) charged.

Probation   Supervised punishment in the community in lieu of incarceration. In the field of ethics, probation means: to allow an attorney to continue to practice, but under specified conditions, e.g., submit to periodic audits, make restitution to a client.

Pro Bono Work   Services that one volunteers to provide another at no charge.

Procedural Due Process   Procedural protections that are required before the government can take away or refuse to grant liberty or a public benefit.

Procedural Law   The rules that govern the mechanics of resolving a dispute in court or in an administrative agency, e.g., a rule on the time a party has to respond to a complaint.

Professional Corporation   The organization of a law practice as a corporation.

Professional Judgment   Relating or applying the general body and philosophy of law to a specific legal problem. When communicated to a client, the result is known as *legal advice.*

Project Attorney   An attorney who works either part-time or full time over a relatively short period. Also referred to as a *contract attorney.*

Prosecution   (1) Bringing a criminal case. (2) The attorney representing the government in a criminal case. (3) Going through the steps to litigate a civil case.

Prosecutor   The attorney representing the government in a criminal case.

Public Benefits   Government benefits.

Public Censure.   *See* Reprimand.

Public Defender   An attorney who is paid by the government to represent low-income people charged with crimes.

Public Domain   Available for use without permission or cost; not protected by copyright.

Public Law   *See* Statute.

Public Sector   An office where the funds come from charity or the government.

Public Statute   *See* Statute.

Quarantined Paralegal   *See* Chinese Wall.

Quasi-adjudication   An administrative decision of an administrative agency which has characteristics of court opinion.

Quasi-independent Agency   An administrative agency that has characteristics of an executive department agency and of an independent regulatory agency.

Quasi-judicial   Like or similar to a court.

Quasi-legislation   A regulation of an administrative agency that has characteristics of the legislation (statutes) of a legislature.

Query   A question that asks a computer to find something in its database.

Question of Law/Question of Fact   *See* Legal Issue.

Quid Pro Quo Harassment   Using submission to or rejection of unwelcome sexual conduct as the basis for making employment decisions affecting an individual.

Rainmaker   A person who brings fee-generating cases into the office.

RE   Concerning

Reasonable Fee   A fee that is not excessive in light of the amount of time and labor involved, the complexity of the case, the experience and reputation of the attorney, the customary fee charged in the locality for the same kind of case, etc.

Rebuttable Presumption   *See* Presumption.

Record   (1) The official collection of all the trial pleadings, exhibits, orders, and word-for-word testimony that took place during the trial. (2) A collection of data fields that constitute a single unit, e.g., employee record.

Redirect Examination   Questioning your own witness (i.e., one you called) after cross-examination by the other side of that witness.

Referral Fee   A fee received by an attorney from another attorney to whom the first attorney referred a client. Also called a *forwarding fee*.

Regional Digest   A digest that summarizes court opinions that are printed in full in its corresponding regional reporter.

Regional Reporter   A reporter that contains state-court opinions of states within a region of the country.

Registered Agent   An individual authorized to practice before the United States Patent Office. He or she does not have to be an attorney.

Registration   The process by which individuals or institutions list their names on a roster kept by an agency of government or by a nongovernmental organization. The agency or organization will often establish qualifications for the right to register, and determine whether applicants meet these qualifications. Also called *enrollment*.

Regulation   Any governmental or nongovernmental method of controlling conduct. *See also* Administrative Regulation.

Relevance   That which reasonably has a bearing on something; that which tends to help establish a fact as true or as false, as present or as missing. Evidence is relevant when it reasonably tends to make the existence of a fact more probable or less probable than it would be without that evidence.

Remand   Send the case back to a lower tribunal with instructions from the appellate court.

Reply Brief   An appellate brief of the appellant that responds to the appellate brief of the appellee.

Reporters   Volumes containing the full text of court opinions. *See also* Official Reporter.

Reprimand   A public declaration that an attorney's conduct was improper. This does not affect his or her right to practice. Also called a *censure* and a *public censure*.

Request for Admissions   A pretrial discovery device consisting of a series of written factual statements that a party is asked to affirm or deny.

Res Gestae Exceptions   Exceptions to the hearsay rule that consist of statements or utterances closely connected to or concurrent with an occurrence.

Res Judicata   A judgment on the merits will prevent the same parties from relitigating the same cause of action on the same facts.

Respondeat Superior   Let the superior answer. An employer is responsible for the wrongs committed by an employee within the scope of employment.

Respondent   *See* Appellee.

Restatements   A series of volumes that attempt to formulate existing law in a given area.

Retainer   (1) The contract of employment between attorney and client. (2) An amount of money paid by a client to make certain that an attorney will be available to work for him or her. (3) The amount of money or other assets paid by the client as a form of deposit or advance payment against future fees and costs.

Review   To examine in order to determine whether any errors of law were made. *See also* Appellate Jurisdiction.

Right Justified   In word processing, an even right side margin.

Root Expander (!)   The exclamation mark stands for one or more characters or letters added to the root of a word.

Rule   *See* Administrative Regulation, Rules of Court.

Rule-Making Function   Writing administrative regulations.

Rule of Three   Gross revenue generated through paralegal billing should equal three times a paralegal's salary.

Rules of Court   Rules of procedure that govern the conduct of litigation before a particular court.

Ruling   *See* Administrative Decision, Holding.

Run   To cause a program to (1) be loaded into the computer from a disk drive and (2) begin to perform its task.

Runner   *See* Ambulance Chasing.

Sanction   (1) A penalty or punishment imposed for unacceptable conduct. (2) To authorize or give approval.

Satisfy   To comply with a legal obligation.

Save   To cause a program or data that is in the computer memory to be moved or stored on a diskette or hard drive.

Scanner   A machine that allows a user to enter text and graphics without traditional typing.

Scope Note   The summary of coverage of a topic within a West digest.

Screen Formatting   In word processing and other programs, a feature that controls how the text will appear on the screen.

Scrolling   In word processing and other programs, moving a line of text onto or off the screen.

Search and Find   In word processing and other programs, a routine that searches for and places the cursor at a specified string of characters.

Search and Replace   In word processing and other programs, a routine that searches for a specified string of characters and replaces it with another string.

Search Criteria/Query   A computer research question; what you ask the computer in order to find something in a database.

Secondary Authority   Any *nonlaw* that a court could rely on in reaching its decision.

Second Chair   A seat at the counsel's table in the courtroom used by an assistant to the trial attorney during the trial.

Second-Tiered Attorney   *See* Staff Attorney.

Section (§)   A portion of a statute, regulation, or book.

Segment Search   In LEXIS, a search that is limited to a certain part of cases in its databases.

Self-Regulation   A process by which members of an occupation or profession establish and administer the rules on who can become a member and when members should be disciplined.

Senior Legal Assistant   An experienced legal assistant with the ability to supervise or train other legal assistants. He or she may have developed a specialty in a practice area.

Series   A set of books with its own internal volume-numbering system. When a new series in the set begins, the volume number starts again with 1.

Service Company   A business that sells particular services, usually to other businesses.

Service of Process   The delivery of a formal notice to a defendant ordering him or her to appear in court to answer the allegations of the plaintiff.

Session Law Cite   The citation to a statute that has not yet been printed in a code and therefore is organized chronologically. *See also* Codified Cite.

Settlement Work-up   A summary of the major facts in the case presented in a manner designed to encourage the other side (or its insurance company) to settle the case.

Sexual Harassment   *See* Hostile Environment, Quid Pro Quo Harassment.

Sheparizing   Using the volumes of *Shepards' Citations* in order to obtain the data available in these volumes, e.g., whether a case has been appealed, whether a statute has been repealed.

Slip Law   A single act passed by the legislature and printed separately, often in a small pamphlet. It is the first official publication of the act.

Slip Opinion   A single court opinion, which for many courts is the first printing of the case.

Software   Computer programs for performing tasks such as word processing and database management.

Sole Practice   A single attorney owns and manages the law firm.

Solicitor   (1) A lawyer in England who handles day-to-day legal problems of clients with only limited rights to represent clients in certain lower courts. *See also* Barrister. (2) In the United States, some high government attorneys are called solicitors, e.g., the Solicitor-General of the United States who argues cases before the United States Supreme Court for the federal government.

Special Edition State Reporter   A reporter that prints the court opinions of one state, which are also printed within the regional reporter that covers that state.

Special Interest Group   An organization that serves a particular group of people, e.g., a union.

Special Jurisdiction   *See* Limited Jurisdiction.

Specialty Certification   Official recognition of competency in a particular area of law. The National Association of Legal Assistants, for example, has a specialty certification program to recognize a person as a Certified Legal Assistant Specialist (CLAS). A paralegal must first become a Certified Legal Assistant (CLA), and then pass one of NALA's specialty exams. *See also* Certified Legal Assistant.

Spelling Checker   A computer software program that checks the spelling of words entered through a word processing program.

Spontaneous Declaration   An out-of-court statement or utterance made spontaneously during or immediately after an exciting event by an observer. (An exception to the hearsay rule.)

Spreadsheet   A ledger or table used for financial calculations and for the recording of transactions.

Squibs   *See* Digests.

Staff Attorney   A full-time attorney who has no expectation of becoming a full partner. Sometimes called a *second-tiered* attorney.

Staffing Agency   An employment agency providing part-time employees for businesses. Often the business pays the agency, which in turn pays the employee.

Standard Form   A preprinted form used frequently for various kinds of transactions or proceedings.

Standard of Proof   A statement of how convincing a version of a fact must be before the trier of facts can accept it as true.

Star-Paging   A notation (e.g., an asterisk or star) next to text within a page of an unofficial reporter which indicates where the same text is found in an official reporter. *See also* Official Reporter.

State Question   A legal question that arises from the application of the state constitution, a state statute, or a state administrative regulation.

Stating a Cause of Action   Including in the complaint those facts which, if proved at trial, would entitle the plaintiff to win.

Status Line   In word processing and other programs, a message line above or below the text area on a display screen that gives format and system information.

Statute   A law passed by the legislature declaring, commanding, or prohibiting something. The statute is contained in a document called an *act*. If the statute applies to the general public or to a segment of the public, it is called a *public law* or *public statute*. If the statute applies to specifically named individuals or to groups—and has little or no permanence or general interest—it is called a *private law* or *private statute*.

Statute in Derogation of the Common Law   A statute that changes the common law. *See* Common Law.

Statute of Limitations   The period within which the lawsuit must be commenced or it can never be brought.

Statutory Code   A collection of statutes organized by subject matter.

Stay   To delay the enforcement or the execution of a judgment.

Stipulated   Agreed to.

Subject-Matter Jurisdiction   The power of the court to resolve a particular category of dispute.

Subscript   In word processing and other programs, a character that prints below the usual text baseline.

Subscription   The signature of the attorney who prepared the complaint.

Substantive Law   The nonprocedural rules that govern rights and duties.

Summary   Quick, expedited, without going through a full adversarial hearing.

Summary Judgment, Motion for   A request by a party that a decision be reached on the basis of the pleadings alone, without going through an entire trial, because there is no dispute on any material facts.

Summons   A formal notice from the court ordering the defendant to appear.

Superior Court   Usually a trial court.

Superscript   In word processing and other programs, a character that prints above the usual text baseline.

Superseded   Outdated and replaced.

Supervising Legal Assistant   Someone who spends about fifty percent of his or her time supervising other legal assistants and about fifty percent on client cases as a legal assistant.

Supplemented   Added to.

Supra   Above, mentioned or referred to earlier in the document.

Supremacy Clause   The clause in the United States Constitution that gives the federal government supremacy over state and local governments in regulating designated areas.

Supreme Court   The highest court in a judicial system. (In New York, however, the supreme court is a trial court.)

Surrogate Courts   A special court with subject-matter jurisdiction over wills, probate, guardianships, etc.

Suspension   The removal of an attorney from the practice of law for a specified minimum period, after which the attorney can apply for reinstatement.

Sustain   To affirm the validity of.

"Swoose" Syndrome   Being recognized as part of the clerical staff in some respects and as part of the professional staff in others.

Syllabus   (1) A one-paragraph summary of an entire court opinion, usually written by a private publisher rather than by the court. (2) In *Shepard's Citations,* the syllabus refers to the headnotes of an opinion that summarize a portion of the opinion.

System An organized method of performing a recurring task.

Table of Authorities A list of the authorities a party is citing in a document, e.g., cases, statutes, law review articles.

Table of Cases A list of all the cases printed or referred to in the volume, and where they are found in the volume.

Table of Statutes A list of all the statutes printed or referred to in the volume, and where they are found in the volume.

Tainted Paralegal *See* Chinese Wall.

Tangible Evidence *See* Physical Evidence.

Template A set of formulas created to perform a designated task.

Testimonial Evidence That which someone says.

Text Buffer In word processing and other programs, an area set aside in memory to hold text temporarily.

Text Editing In word processing and other programs, the function that enables the user to enter and edit text.

Text File In word processing and other programs, a file that contains text, as opposed to a program.

Third-Party Complaint A complaint filed by the defendant against a third party.

Tickler A reminder system that helps office staff remember important deadlines.

Title Page A page at the beginning of a book that lists the name of the book, the author(s), publisher, etc. On this page, or on the next page, the latest copyright date of the book is printed.

Topic and Key Number The system used by West Publishing Company to organize the millions of small-paragraph summaries of court opinions in its digests.

Tort A private wrong or injury other than a breach of contract or the commission of a crime, although some breaches of contract and crimes can also constitute torts.

Transcribed Copied or written out word for word.

Transcript A word-for-word account.

Treatise, Legal A book written by a private individual (or by a public official writing as a private citizen) that provides an overview, summary, or commentary of a legal topic.

Treaty An international agreement between two or more countries.

Trial Book *See* Trial Brief.

Trial Brief An attorney's set of notes on how to conduct a trial, often placed in a *trial notebook*. Sometimes called a *trial manual* or *trial book*.

Trial de Novo A totally new fact-finding hearing.

Trial Manual *See* Trial Brief.

Trial Memorandum *See* Points and Authorities Memorandum.

Trial Notebook A collection of documents, arguments, and strategies that an attorney plans to use during a trial. Sometimes referred to as the *trial brief*. (It can mean the notebook in which the trial brief is placed.)

Ultrafiche *See* Microform.

Unauthorized Practice of Law Services that constitute the practice of law, which a nonattorney has no authorization to provide. *See also* Practice of Law, Professional Judgment.

Unbundled *See* Bundled.

Uncodified Organized chronologically rather than by subject matter.

Unicameral *See* Bicameral.

Unified Bar Association *See* Integrated Bar Association.

Uniform State Law A proposed statute presented to all the state legislatures by the National Conference of Commissioners on Uniform State Laws.

United States Court of Appeals The main federal appellate court just below the United States Supreme Court.

United States District Court The main federal trial court.

United States Supreme Court The highest court in the federal judicial system.

Universal Character (*) The asterisk stands for any character or letter in a query.

Unofficial Reporter *See* Official Reporter.

User Group Individuals using the same computer product who meet to discuss their experiences with it.

Validation Research Using citators and other sources to check the current validity of every authority you intend to rely on in your document.

Value A single piece of numeric information used in the calculations of a spreadsheet.

Value Billing The amount to be paid is based on the complexity of the legal problem, the expertise required of the attorney, and the number of hours devoted to the matter.

Valuing the Bill Determining whether there should be a write up or a write down of the bill.

Venue   The place of the trial.

Verdict   The final conclusion of the jury.

Verification   An affidavit stating that a party has read the complaint and swears that it is true to the best of his or her knowledge.

Veto   A rejection by the chief executive of a bill passed by the legislature.

Vicarious Disqualification   A law firm cannot continue to represent a client or cannot accept a new client because it has hired someone (attorney, paralegal, or secretary) who has a conflict of interest with that client.

Vicarious Liability   Being responsible because of what someone else has wrongfully done or wrongfully failed to do. *See also* Personal Liability.

Virtual Representation   In word processing and other programs, an approach to screen formatting that enables the user to see on the screen exactly how the printed output will look.

Voir Dire   The oral examination of prospective jurors for purposes of selecting a jury.

Wage and Hour Division   The unit within the U.S. Department of Labor that administers the Fair Labor Standards Act, which governs overtime compensation and related matters. *See also* Exempt Employee, Fair Labor Standards Act.

Waiver   The loss of a right or privilege because of an explicit rejection of it or because of a failure to claim it at the appropriate time.

Warrant   An order from a judicial officer authorizing an act, e.g., the arrest of an individual, the search of property.

WESTLAW   The legal research computer service of West Publishing Co.

Window   In a spreadsheet program, the portion of a worksheet that can be seen on the computer display screen.

Word Processor   A computerized system of entering, editing, storing, retrieving, etc. data.

Word Wrap   A word is automatically moved to the next line if it goes past the right margin.

Work-Product Rule   Notes, working papers, memoranda, or similar documents and tangible things prepared by the attorney in anticipation of litigation are not discoverable. *See also* Discoverable.

Write Down   Deduct an amount from the bill.

Write Up   Add an amount to the bill.

Writ of Certiorari   An order by an appellate court requiring a lower court to certify the record of a lower court proceeding and to send it up to the appellate court which has decided to accept the appeal.

Writ Writer   *See* Jailhouse Lawyer.

WYSIWYG   What You See (on the screen) Is What You Get (when the screen is printed).

■ Index

▪ N

▪ S

PRODUCTION CREDITS

Text Design: Roslyn Stendahl, Dapper Design
Copyediting: Sarah Entenmann
Composition: Parkwood Composition
Illustrations: Randy Miyake
Cover: Roslyn Stendahl, Dapper Design

PHOTO CREDITS

Paralegal Associations: Local

1. Determine how many paralegal associations exist in your state (or in any state where you hope to work). See Appendix B.

2. Photocopy the following form, fill out one form for each association you identify in step one, and mail the form to each association.

Date: _____

Dear Paralegal Association:

    I am a student at the following paralegal school:

_____

Would you be kind enough to answer the following questions:

    1. Can paralegal students be members of your association? If so, what are the dues for students?

    2. Does your association have a mentor program where an experienced paralegal member provides guidance or advice to new members?

    3. Do you have a student rate for subscriptions to your newsletter?

    4. Does your association have a job bank service? If so, can student members take advantage of this service?

    5. Would your association consider conducting a "Career Day" in which experienced paralegal members of your association describe work in different employment settings in the state?

Any other information you can send me about the association would be greatly appreciated.

    I hope to hear from you.

Sincerely,

_____

My Address: _____

_____

_____

Source: Statsky, *Introduction to Paralegalism* (West)

Paralegal Associations: National

Please send me information about the Federation.

My Name and Address:

Clip this form and mail to:

_____

_____

_____

Nat'l Federation of Paralegal
  Associations
P.O. Box 33108
Kansas City, MO 64114

Statsky, *Introduction to Paralegalism* (West)

Please send me information about NALA.

My Name and Address:

Clip this form and mail to:

_____

_____

_____

Nat'l Association of
  Legal Assistants
1601 South Main St., Suite 300
Tulsa, OK 74119

Statsky, *Introduction to Paralegalism* (West)

Please send me information about PLA

My Name and Address:

Clip this form and mail to:

_____

_____

_____

Professional Legal
  Assistants, Inc.
P.O. Box 31951
Raleigh, NC 27622

Statsky, *Introduction to Paralegalism* (West)

0–314–01061–0

90000

9 780314 010612